Having Fun
With
Baseball
Nicknames

Published by:

MLC Publications
7645 Currell Blvd.
Woodbury Mn. 55125
(612) 730-2520

Printed and bound in the United States of America

Library of Congress Cataloging in Publication Data

Blazovich, Phil, 1948-
  Having Fun With Baseball Nicknames: For baseball fans nine to ninety!
  Includes bibliography and two indices; one for the player's nicknames
  and one for the player's actual names.
  LCN# 97-93258   ISBN# 0-9657492-0-7

ACKNOWLEDGMENTS

Claudia Jara:	A friend of many years who "volunteered" to type
Marlene Dolney:	A second non-baseball gal who labored with the toughest typing job on earth, reading my writing and numbers
Suzy James:	The world's best speller and grammarian
Janell Blazovich:	She had so... many ideas
Kyle Blazovich:	He taught me that "booting one" had nothing to do with baseball
Ben Blazovich:	When the times were the darkest, he gave me the insight to see my way through. Thank you very much son
Linda Blazovich:	For your many suggestions and insights
Pete Edlund:	For giving me encouragement and support
Don Norrell:	A friend who read, critiqued and helped shape the direction the book should take. Your insights were always extremely helpful
Tony Rotondi:	A friend who has taken a personal interest since the beginning and been helpful because he believes and enjoys the project. You are one in a million
Paul Mielens:	There is always **ONE HERO**, the person who was absolutely irreplaceable!!! The magician who crafted the design, created the graphics, solved innumerable problems, and devoted a ridiculous amount of time simply because he wanted to help. Suffice to say, this book would not exist if it was not for you Paul!!!
Author's note:	In addition, my heartfelt thanks to my many friends, relatives and clients (especially Tony!) who have been 100% encouraging throughout and have forced me to finish my dream. Without this whole **BOOK TEAM'S** help, I would surely have struckout!

THANKS EVERYONE

phil b

HOW and WHY

How do you best read each team? Each "team" forms a book. The six page format for each book is as follows:

PAGE 1 INTRODUCTION: Information is presented in three paragraphs.
1.) Offers something educational about the topic or real group
2.) Introduces some of the "real" team
3.) Highlights a player of the team

PAGE 2 LINEUP: Fifteen featured players, boxed into three lines each. The text is career highlights. The lineup includes "starters" at eight positions, three pitchers and four reserves drawn from the roster on pages five and six.

PAGE 3 IT'SA FACT: Several facts about players on the roster. Focus is always on positive information. Sometimes the it'sa facts will include anecdotal stories or the origin of the player's nickname.

PAGE 4 TRIVIA: Twenty-five trivia questions, only emphasizing positives and including some nickname questions.

PAGE 5 AND 6 ROSTER: A columned, shaded, double fonted display, showing easily the players by position and in order of their lifetime performance.

PAGE 6 LINGO: Because the roster sizes vary, lingo related to the team theme is added to fill the page. In certain cases, additional trivia or it'sa facts are included to complete the page.

and

Why write this book? I hope to celebrate, educate, preserve and create with the text of this book. You must remember, it is a tremendous accomplishment to even reach the Majors. Imagine a player's family, acquaintances, neighborhood, church and even town as they celebrate his success! Sadly, only a few excellent Big Leaguers are placed on pedestals and revered nationally for their career achievements. This book attempts to recognize many many more players for their outstanding play. Through the strand of nicknames, the fun of topical lingo, the challenge of factual trivia and the information of it'sa fact, their deeds are resurrected. No, it is not a big "fall asleep" textbook, a "boring" biography or a "dirty laundry" tell all expose. Rather, the book is positive, upbeat and fun! The writing style is just me talkin' to you. So take five, relax, "bone up" on some facts, crack a smile and bring back some great memories. For you the Saturday afternoon fan, you have found the perfect "pick-up, put-down" escape that will be pleasantly revisited time and time again for years to come (sounds like a candidate for the toilet tank!). For you the serious baseball fan, you will additionally find this to be a ready reference and an essential addition to your library. Regardless of which you are, I promise you a book you will read and reread cover to cover!

DEDICATED TO:

Kauline Groskreutz, and her four boys: Cody, Ty,
BJ, and hubby Jon, who started me on this project

and

Linda, Janell, Ben and Kyle, who put up with me
during the three "short" years it took to complete

and

Larry Doby and Jackie Robinson
(I never found your nicknames)

Having Fun
With
Baseball
Nicknames

by
Phil Blazovich

Table of Teams

ANOTHER LEAGUE

1

Team

No woman has ever played Major League baseball. In 1931 seventeen year old Jackie Mitchell was signed to a minor league professional baseball contract. It was quickly disallowed by then Baseball Commissioner Kenesaw Mountain Landis. In 1952 Commissioner Ford Frick issued a ban against females playing professional baseball. This was certainly in part to thwart publicity stunts, such as the Eddie The Midget Gaedel situation. Since 1943 women had been playing in their own league, the All-American Girls Baseball League (AAGBL). The league featured all women teams and it would continue in existence for 11 summers. The movie "A League Of Their Own" has raised public awareness regarding this entertaining chapter of the national pastime.

The Another League Team is a sailor's dream. Outside the ballpark, the "shore leavers" would purchase a program and drool over the roster. The seamen would be fighting for the best box seats. The crew would be anxiously waiting for Bubbles, Toots, Gorgeous, Beauty, Honey, Darling and Baby Doll. No mate planned to overlook Blondy, Goldie, Topsy, Cuddles, Bunny, Bridgit and Liz. Bets would surely be made on who "was better", Roxy, Tilly, Dolly, Mandy, Polly , Molly and Daisy, or maybe Nellie, Bonnie, Katie, Connie, Sadie, Julie and Rosy. The deck hands could not wait to "check out" Sarah, Mary, Lena, Ellie, Fergie, Tami and Cuddles, or Flossie, Beverly, Lady, Sherry, Gracie, Junie and Dot. This squad is definitely another league! When the jocks trotted out, there would be a mutiny! The old seaman's hoax, bait and switch!

This team also has 30 Babes, but really, there is only one Babe. When his nickname is said, all minds think of George Herman Babe Ruth. He was baseball's greatest superstar and ambassador, in addition to its greatest pure power hitter. Remarkably, during his first five campaigns, he pitched exclusively. Babe was the American League's best left-handed pitcher, compiling an outstanding 80-41 record (1914-18). Subtracting The Bambino's 28 game final year, The Babe really had a 16 season batting career. The Sultan Of Swat hit for both average and power. His .342 lifetime batting average is only topped by eight players. The Babe batted over .350 eight summers, reaching a career high .393 in 1923. From 1920-32 the Bambino swatted 40+ homers 11 seasons (he failed in 1922 in 406 at bats and in 1925 with only 359 at bats). He is the only ballplayer to launch over 50 home runs in one season four times! The Sultan of Swat led the American League 13 times in slugging % (record), 12 times in home runs (record), 11 times in bases on balls (record), ten times in on base %, eight times in runs scored (record) and six times in RBI's! The Babe ranks second to Hammerin' Hank Aaron in career RBI's, trailing 2213 to 2297. Hank, it must be remembered, batted 12,364 times to Babe's 8399 at bats. The Bambino also ranks second in career home runs and runs scored (tie). His career home run % is 8.50, leading second place Ralph Kiner (7.09%) by nearly 21 percent! The Sultan Of Swat's career slugging % is .690, leading second place Ted The Kid Williams (.634) by nearly nine percent! The Babe had the three highest single season home run percentages (1920 - 11.79%, 1927 - 11.11% and 1921 - 10.93%)! He also had six of the top ten single season slugging percentages, including the top three ever achieved (1920 - .847, 1921 - .846, 1927 - .772)! The Babe is also first in career walks with 2056 and he holds the single season record of 170 free passes. He set the single season record for the most extra base hits (119) and the most total bases (457) in 1921 (85 singles, 44 doubles, 16 triples and 59 home runs). Incidentally, that year The Babe broke his own single season record of 29 home runs by 30 round trippers! The rest of the American League, collectively, blasted just 315 homers! When The Babe retired, he had a record 72 multi-homer games. George Herman Babe Ruth was a legend in his own time!

LINEUP

CA	Elston *Ellie* Howard

starred 14 summers. He was an outstanding leader, fielder and batter. Ellie, an AL All-Star nine times, two seasons was the Gold Glove winner. In 1958 he was voted the World Series MVP. His two out ninth inning three run HR to tie game #4 in the 1957 Fall Classic was awesome!

1B	*Gorgeous* George Sisler

shined for 15 seasons, then he traveled on to Cooperstown. A two time batting champ and .400 hitter (.407 in 1920 and .420 in 1922), Gorgeous George also led the Junior Circuit twice in hits and triples (one tie). His .340 career batting average is 14th all time!

2B	Nelson *Nellie* Fox

was known for his bottle bat. He poked 2161 singles in his 2663 career hits. This little lefty led the AL five summers in at bats and four seasons in hits. In his 19 summers Nellie fanned no more than 18 times in any one year. He was the third toughest Major Leaguer to K!

SS	Dave *Beauty* Bancroft

was a 16 year veteran who now is enshrined in the Hall of Fame. Beauty switch hit and stroked over 2000 safeties during his career. His great range and strong arm led Beauty to be even considered more valuable for his outstanding glove than his excellent bat.

3B	Paul *Molly* Molitor

,like fine wine, has gotten better with age. Molly has missed over 400 games in his career due to injuries, but he has always returned better than ever! A lifetime .300+ hitter and an excellent base runner (over 400 career steals), Molly continues to shine year after year!

OF	Dave *Winny* Winfield

came to the Majors directly from college, never playing a day in the minors! In his 21 seasons, and still active, Winny not only has accumulated 3000+ hits, 500+ doubles and 450+ home runs, but he also has accumulated 1800+ RBI's, 200+ stolen bases and seven Gold Gloves!

OF	George *Babe* Ruth

totally dominated baseball for 22 seasons. Babe had led Boston to two World Championships (1916 and 1918). After the Yankees purchased him in 1919, The Babe led them to seven Series. When Yankee Stadium was erected, it was known as "The House That Ruth Built".

OF	Sherwood *Sherry* Magee

was a great star in the early 1900's. For 16 summers he played in the NL. Sherry captured four RBI titles and two slugging crowns. 1910 was Sherry's best season. He led the Senior Circuit in batting, RBI's, slugging %, runs, total bases and on base %!

P	Ferguson *Fergie* Jenkins

was quietly dominant in an era (60's-70's) of several strong pitchers. Pitching in the "Friendly Confines", Fergie, from 1967-72, nevertheless won 20 or more games all six seasons! He won 24 contests and the Cy Young in 1971. Fergie retired ninth in K's and 24th (tie) in wins.

P	Charles *Babe* Adams

plied his skills over 19 seasons. Earlier a power pitcher, Babe hurt his arm after 113 wins. Losing most of three years in the minors, he returned as a control pitcher and won another 81 games! Babe won 20+ contests two seasons and painted 44 whitewashes during his career!

P	George *Babe* Ruth

won 94 games and lost only 46 contests for his career! In 1916 Babe recorded 23 victories (third), while leading the AL with nine shutouts and a 1.75 ERA. In 1917 Babe chalked up 24 V's (second). He went 3-0 in World Series play, allowing just three earned runs in 31 innings!

RES	John *Sadie* McMahon

was a late 19th century hurler. Four summers Sadie won 20+ games. 1890-91 were his top years. Sadie led the AA in wins (36), games (60), complete games (55) and innings (509) in 1890! The next season he again led in wins (35), complete games (53) and innings (503).

RES	Clarence *Ginger* Beaumont

was tabbed Ginger because of his red hair. He starred 12 seasons in the Senior Circuit around the turn of the century. Four times Ginger led the NL in hits, including three years consecutively (1902-04). His .357 batting average top all players in 1902!

RES	William *Baby Doll* Jacobson

,after two times up, stuck in 1919 at the age of 28. This started seven consecutive summers (1919-25) of his batting over .300. Baby Doll had his best summer in 1920. He hit .355 with 122 RBI's. In 1921 Baby Doll batted .352 with 211 hits, 16 triples and 102 RBI's!

RES	Ellsworth *Babe* Dahlgren

played for eight teams over 12 summers. His best season, 1944, Babe drove in 101 runs. In 1941 he powered 23 yard shots and knocked in 89 tallies. Babe is best remembered as the man who "took over" for Lou Gehrig at first base for the Yankees in 1939.

L to R: Nelson *Nellie* Fox, Elston *Ellie* Howard, George *Babe* Ruth, Paul *Molly* Molitor, Dave *Winny* Winfield

It'sa FACT

Charles **Babe** Adams: He was an excellent control pitcher. On July 17th, 1914 Babe pitched 21 innings without issuing a walk! For his career, he walked just 1.29 batters per nine innings, second best all time! During the 1920 season, in 263 innings, Babe issued only 18 bases on balls! His .62 walks per game, in 1920, is the best single season total this century!

William **Baby Doll** Jacobson and Clarence **Ginger** Beaumont: Baby Doll (September 9th, 1922) and Ginger (August 9th, 1899) both slashed three triples in one game.

Russell **Lena** Blackburne: After a short Major League career, he became famous for "his mud". In 1938 Lena started selling his mud to the AL for "rubbing up" baseballs to remove their gloss. The NL started purchasing it in the 50's. Lena's rubbing mud is now used exclusively by every Major League team.

Nelson **Nellie** Fox: He was a fabulous fielder. From 1950-63 Nellie anchored the keystone for the Southsiders. In that span he led all AL second sackers in putouts ten times, assists six times, fielding % six times and DP's five times! Let's vote Nellie into Cooperstown!

Max **Tilly** Bishop: Tilly was also known as Camera Eye. Although he was not a feared hitter, he was a prolific walker (20.42% of his at bats resulted in free passes). Only Ted The Kid Williams (20.76%) had a higher lifetime base on balls %.

Norman **Babe** Young: In 1940 and 1941 he starred for the New York Giants. During those two summers Babe poled 17 and 25 homers (second) and drove in 101 (fifth) and 104 (second) runs. After serving his country three years, Babe played parts of three more seasons, then he retired.

Gorgeous George Sisler: He was a remarkable player. In his first eight seasons George had a career .361 batting average. He missed all of 1923 due to illness , and when he did recover and return, Gorgeous George was not the same. George's 1922 season was his best. He was the AL MVP, leading the league in hits (246), runs (134), triples (18), stolen bases (51) and batting average (.420)! After he retired, Gorgeous George had the pleasure of seeing his two sons play in the Majors. Dave was a pitcher and Dick was an outfielder. In 1950 Dick, with the "Whiz Kids", played in the World Series his dad never reached during his Hall of Fame career.

Paul **Molly** Molitor and Dave **Winny** Winfield (the Minnesota Twins): Both grew up in the Midway section of St. Paul, Minnesota. Both starred for the University of Minnesota. Both have gone on to have great Major League careers. Both are known for giving to their fans and to their community. Both should be enshrined in Cooperstown!

Eddie **Babe** Klieman: He was a fireman. 1947 was his best year. That season Babe led the AL in both games (58) and saves (17, tie), plus he chalked up five wins.

Alfred **Roxie** Lawson: In 1937 he had a charmed year. Roxie went 18-7 to finish third in the AL in wins, but with a husky 5.26 ERA.

Tully **Topsy** Hartsel: During his playing days he often played over his head. Standing just 5'5", Topsy parlayed both his skill and size into a 14 year career. Five times he led the league in free passes. Twice Topsy led the AL in on base % and in 1902 he placed first in both runs (tie) and stolen bases.

Clarence **Tilly** Walker: He was a slugger whose career crossed over from the dead ball era into the lively ball era. Tilly was a contemporary of Babe Ruth. He and The Babe tied for the AL homer title in 1918! Babe finished first and Tilly tied for second in home runs in 1919. In 1920 and 1921 The Babe placed first and Tilly finished third and fourth in yard shots. Tilly's 37 long balls, in 1922, again ranked him second, but this time to Ken Williams.

Werner **Babe** Birrer: In his career he won only four times. Babe literally won his own game July 19th, 1955. Babe relieved and batted twice. He launched two three run homers!

Floyd **Babe** Herman: He played outfield 13 seasons. After batting .340 in 1928, Babe tore the National League apart, hitting .381 (second) in 1929. That summer he had 42 doubles, 21 homers and 113 RBI's. In 1930 Babe hit .393 (second)! His totals included 48 doubles, 35 homers and 130 RBI's! Babe also slashed 241 hits and scored 143 runs in 1930. His lifetime slugging % was .532, 24th all time!

Wilfred **Rosy** Ryan: A new concept in the 1920's was to utilize a pitcher as a reliever. Rosy led all NL hurlers in relief wins in 1922 and 1923. His three World Series relief wins, while hurling for John McGraw's Giants, are still the record.

John **Honey** Romano: He was the AL All-Star catcher in 1961-62. Honey blasted 21 and 25 homers, and he drove in 80 and 81 runs those two seasons.

Phil **Babe** Marchildon: He toiled for the basement dwelling Athletics. In 1942 Babe's record was 17-14, while the A's went a meager 55-99. He accounted for 31% of their wins that summer!

Paul **Molly** Molitor: In the 1993 World Series he was the deserving MVP.

TRIVIA*

1) Because he never smoked, swore or caroused, he earned his nickname.

2) He holds the record of three times hitting "for the cycle".

3) His 39 game hitting streak in 1987 is the seventh longest in Major League history.

4) He was the first black ballplayer to play for the Yankees and the first black ballplayer to win the AL MVP (1963)!

5) A native Canadian, he played junior hockey, but decided he wanted to play baseball more.

6) His final game behind the plate in his 22 year umpiring career was Don Larsen's gem.

7) A vocal player, he shouted out his future nickname whenever the pitcher threw a good pitch.

8) When Babe Ruth hit 60 home runs in 1927, whose record did he break?

9) Considered one of the greats of his age, he quit baseball to marry. His wife disapproved of ballplayers.

10) Although he never played college football, only basketball and baseball, he was drafted for all three sports!

11) His .367 batting average in 1936 is the highest season average for a catcher.

12) As a rookie pitcher, this left-hander twice defeated Walter Johnson. He later converted to the field.

13) He is the oldest baseball player to drive in 100 runs in one season (he is also the oldest to hit "for the cycle").

14) He was voted the 1959 AL MVP.

15) This speedy outfielder hit two triples in one inning July 22nd, 1926. (Hint: he was born in Beesville, Texas)

16) Ty Cobb, when a playing manager, removed himself for a pinch hitter, because he did not want to face this left-hander's wicked curve ball.

17) He held the AL record for the longest hitting streak (41 games) until Joltin' Joe broke his mark.

18) In 1971 he tagged six homers in 115 at bats. He also led the NL in wins, starts, complete games and innings pitched.

19) During his first full season (1909) he went 12-3 with an 1.11 ERA. In that year's World Series, he tossed three complete game victories and led Pittsburgh to the World Championship.

20) Shot down over Germany in WW II, he became a POW. This veteran came back to win 13 and 19 games in 1946 and 1947. He was elected to the Canadian Baseball Hall of Fame.

21) This slugger was also known as The Sultan Of The Swat and The Bambino.

22) He is the only player who has had five base hits in one World Series game (October 12th, 1982).

23) His 257 hits in one year (154 game season) has been the record since 1920.

24) He is the only player, at his age, to miss a full season due to injury (back surgery at age 37), then return to star again. He was, in 1990, voted the Comeback Player of the Year.

25) The Baby Ruth candy bar was named after this person (this makes up for #16).

* WICKED BEAUTIES answers found on page 235

ROSTER

CATCHERS:	Yr	Hits	AB's	Ave
Elston *Ellie* Howard	14	1471	5363	.274
Ron *Babe* Hassey	14	914	3440	.266
Eugene *Bubbles* Hargrave	12	786	2533	.310
John *Honey* Romano	10	706	2767	.255
Cornelius *Connie* Mack	11	659	2695	.245
Ernest *Babe* Phelps	11	657	2117	.310
Floyd *Babe* Baker	13	573	2280	.251
Eliseo *Ellie* Rodriguez	9	533	2173	.245
Elrod *Ellie* Hendricks	12	415	1888	.220
Tim *Bridgit* Donahue	8	354	1500	.236
Alfred *Roxy* Walters	11	317	1426	.222
Homer *Dixie* Howell	8	224	910	.246
Del *Babe* Wilber	8	174	720	.242
Amos *Darling* Booth	4	98	438	.224
Ed *Dixie* Parsons	3	52	295	.176
William *Lena* Styles	5	44	176	.250
Enoch *Ginger* Shinault	2	13	44	.295
Jay *Babe* Towne	1	10	36	.278
Jack *Roxy* Crouch	3	9	72	.125
Stan *Dolly* Gray	1	5	20	.250
Cornelius *Connie* Murphy	2	3	21	.143
Douglas *Dixie* Parker	1	1	5	.200
John *Honey* Barnes	1	0	0	.000

1ST BASEMEN:	Yr	Hits	AB's	Ave
Gorgeous George Sisler	15	2612	8267	.340
Ellsworth *Babe* Dahlgren	12	1056	4045	.261
Norman *Babe* Young	8	656	2403	.273
Gordon *Bubbles* Coleman	9	650	2384	.273
William *Babe* Borton	4	254	940	.270
Ed *Babe* Butka	2	11	50	.220
Stan *Dolly* Gray	1	5	20	.250
Harold *Babe* Danzig	1	2	13	.154
Bill *Mary* Calhoun	1	1	13	.077

2ND BASEMEN:	Yr	Hits	AB's	Ave
Nelson *Nellie* Fox	19	2663	9232	.288
Max *Tilly* Bishop	12	1216	4494	.271
Cornelius *Connie* Ryan	12	988	3982	.248
Herbert *Babe* Ellison	5	75	348	.216
Grayson *Gracie* Pierce	3	57	307	.186
Cornelius *Conny* Doyle	2	32	126	.254
Howard *Polly* McLarry	2	25	129	.194

SHORTSTOPS:	Yr	Hits	AB's	Ave
Dave *Beauty* Bancroft	16	2004	7182	.279
Sargent *Sadie* Houck	8	666	2659	.250
George *Maggie* Magoon	5	439	1834	.239
Russell *Lena* Blackburne	8	387	1807	.214
John *Blondy* Ryan	6	318	1330	.239
Wilbur *Roxey* Roach	4	151	608	.248
Mike *Mollie* Milosevich	2	92	381	.241
Monroe *Dolly* Stark	4	90	378	.238

SHORTSTOPS: (Cont.)	Yr	Hits	AB's	Ave
Charles *She* Donahue	1	47	215	.219
Maurice *Molly* Moore	1	20	88	.227
Hal *Blondie* Quick	1	10	41	.244
James *Dot* Fulghum	1	0	2	.000

3RD BASEMEN:	Yr	Hits	AB's	Ave
Paul *Molly* Molitor	17	2647	8610	.307
Ralph *Babe* Pinelli	8	723	2617	.276
Joseph *Goldie* Rapp	3	269	1064	.253
Arthur *Tillie* Shafer	4	212	776	.273
Julian *Julie* Wera	2	15	54	.278
Ernie *Junie* Andres	1	4	41	.098
Martin *Toots* Coyne	1	0	2	.000

OUTFIELDERS:	Yr	Hits	AB's	Ave
Dave *Winny* Winfield	21	3088	10888	.284
George *Babe* Ruth	22	2873	8399	.342
Sherwood *Sherry* Magee	16	2169	7441	.291
Fred *Dixie* Walker	18	2064	6740	.306
Floyd *Babe* Herman	13	1818	5603	.324
Clarence *Ginger* Beaumont	12	1759	5660	.311
William *Baby Doll* Jacobson	11	1714	5507	.311
Curt *Honey* Walker	12	1475	4858	.304
Clarence *Tilly* Walker	13	1423	5067	.281
Tully *Topsy* Hartsel	14	1336	4848	.276
William *Blondie* Purcell	12	1217	4563	.267
Bill *Little Eva* Lange	7	1055	3195	.330
Sherrard *Sherry* Robertson	10	346	1507	.230
Frank *Beauty* McGowan	5	316	1208	.262
Elias *Liz* Funk	4	261	976	.267
Bob *Molly* Molinaro	8	212	803	.264
Herbert *Babe* Barna	5	154	664	.232
Clarence *Babe* Twombly	2	109	358	.304
Paul *Molly* Meloan	2	109	431	.253
Jonathan *Mandy* Brooks	2	107	397	.270
Clint *Connie* Conatser	2	102	376	.271
Elliot *Babe* Bigelow	1	60	211	.284
Boris *Babe* Martin	6	44	206	.214
Jack *Bunny* Roser	1	27	113	.239
Foster *Babe* Ganzel	2	23	74	.311
Luther *Bonnie* Bonin	2	14	77	.182
Al *Bunny* Yates	1	13	47	.277
Dorsey *Dixie* Carroll	1	13	49	.265
Roy *Polly* Wolfe	2	6	29	.207
Verdo *Ellie* Elmore	1	3	17	.176
Walter *Rosy* Carlisle	1	1	10	.100
Ollie *Babe* Klee	1	0	1	.000

PINCH HITTERS:	Yr	Hits	AB's	Ave
Roy *Dixie* Upright	1	2	8	.250
Cornelius *Connie* Creeden	1	1	4	.250
Joe *Tilly* Green	1	0	1	.000
Wyatt *Roxy* Snipes	1	0	1	.000

ROSTER

PITCHERS:	Yr	Won	Lost	ERA
Ferguson *Fergie* Jenkins	19	284	226	3.34
Charles *Babe* Adams	19	194	140	2.76
John *Sadie* McMahon	9	173	127	3.51
Nelson *Nellie* Briles	14	129	112	3.44
Sherrod *Sherry* Smith	14	114	118	3.32
Mike *Buffy* LaCoss	14	98	103	4.02
George *Babe* Ruth	10	94	46	2.28
Nels *Nellie* Potter	12	92	97	3.99
Allen *Dixie* Sothoron	11	91	100	3.31
Frank *Dixie* Davis	10	75	71	3.97
Charles *Lady* Baldwin	6	73	41	2.85
Phil *Babe* Marchildon	9	68	75	3.93
Wilfred *Rosy* Ryan	10	52	47	4.14
Alfred *Roxie* Lawson	9	47	39	5.37
Clifford *Connie* Johnson	5	40	39	3.44
Bill *Beverly* Bayne	9	31	32	4.84
Gorham *Dixie* Leverett	5	29	34	4.51
Eddie *Babe* Klieman	8	26	28	3.49
Ewart *Dixie* Walker	4	25	31	3.52
Les *Toots* Tietje	6	22	41	5.11
Millard *Dixie* Howell	6	19	15	3.78
James *Dixie* Walker	6	17	27	3.99
John *Daisy* Davis	2	16	21	3.78
William *Dolly* Gray	3	15	51	3.52
Bunn *Bunny* Hearn	6	13	24	3.56

PITCHERS: (Cont.)	Yr	Won	Lost	ERA
Elmer *Bunny* Hearn	4	7	11	4.38
Clarence *Cuddles* Marshall	4	7	7	5.98
Frank *Flossie* Oberlin	4	5	24	3.77
Lowell *Lulu* Palmer	5	5	18	5.29
Werner *Babe* Birrer	3	4	3	4.36
John *Bonnie* Hollingsworth	4	4	9	4.91
Russ *Babe* Meers	3	3	3	3.98
Stan *Nellie* Rees	1	1	0	0.00
Elmer *Babe* Doty	1	1	0	1.00
Cornelius *Conny* McGeehan	1	1	0	4.50
Ralph *Tami* Mauriello	1	1	1	4.63
Harvey *Ginger* Clark	1	1	0	6.00
Wallace *Toots* Shultz	2	1	7	6.00
Walter *Sarah* Bernhardt	1	0	0	0.00
Oland *Dixie* McArthur	1	0	0	0.00
Woody *Babe* Davis	1	0	0	1.50
Maurice *Molly* Craft	4	0	4	3.57
Julius *Julie* Freeman	1	0	1	4.26
Mario *Babe* Picone	3	0	2	6.30
Foster *Babe* Blackburn	2	0	1	8.10

EXTRAS:
Albert *Dolly* Stark - Umpire
Francis *Fay* Vincent Jr.. - Baseball Commissioner 1989-92
The Fabulous Sports Babe - Great Sports Announcer

LINGO

Hugged the Line: Fielder plays close to the foul line to stop potential extra base hits

Hugged the Bag: Play close to the base (it is not hugging your ex mother-in-law)

Sewed It Up: Clinched the pennant

Hemmed Him In: Caught a player in a hot box

Peg: A throw

Sissy It Up: Throw softly

Punch and Judy Hitter: Swings soft, just tries to make contact

Ladies Day: Old tradition when women could come to the game for free or at reduced rates on certain days

Weak Sister: Easy team to beat

Screamer: (Shame on you!) hard hit ball

Shake Him Off: Pitcher wants the catcher to signal another pitch

Matinee: (This is a family book!) afternoon game

Put Him Down: Throw at a batter's head

Throw Him Out: Fielder relays ball to a basemen to force or tag out a runner

Sent Him to the Showers: Remove a pitcher from the game (also, what Linda does not do to me - thanks honey!)

Shut 'em Down: Don't allow any runs

Sent Him a Message: Throw at a batter's head

That's All She Wrote: It's too late now, the game is over

Fat Lady Sings: Game is cinched

He Fired a Beauty: A pitcher threw a good game

Diamond: A girl's best friend and a baseball infield

Gem: A no-hitter

Safe at Home: Where he better be

Slip Pitch: A change of pace

She's Going Going Gone: Words said as the baseball goes over the fence

Wasted a Pitch: Throw a pitch outside of the strike zone when ahead on the count

Handled a Good Pitch: Get a base rap off a hard to hit pitch

9

ATTITUDE

2

Team

Athletic success is not only physical, but also mental. A player must believe in himself. To envision success is the important step beyond conditioning and practice. Dizzy Dean was known for his boasting, but as Ol' Diz used to say, "It ain't braggin' if you back it up!" Coined phrases are not just phrases if you integrate them into your mental repertoire. Give it your all, never give up, roll up your sleeves, suck it up, never say die, dig in, never quit, step it up, reach back for more and rise to the occasion are ones that come to mind. Attitude is demonstrated in that extra effort. It is a catcher running as fast as he can down the first base line, just in case. It is the outfielder hustling as fast as he can to back up his fielding mate. It is the infielder extending and diving for any ball close, regardless of his chance of success. One play sticks in my memory. Pete Rose was playing first for the Phillies. A foul pop was hit between home plate and first. The catcher called for it. The ball bounced off of his glove and Pete (who always stood close by prepared and in a ready position "just in case") picked it off before it hit the ground. I am sure he "wasted" his back-up effort a thousand times, but the one time, when it was needed, Pete was there.

The Attitude Team covers the gamut of emotions a player may experience. On the up side, the team has members with the nicknames Sunny, Happy, Smiling and Grin, along with teammates whose monikers are Chipper, Cheerful, Chummy, Perky and Merry. Backing them up are Good Kid, Bubbles, Sweet, Laughing, A-1, Steady and Terrific. On the down side, the team has members with the nicknames Sad, Yip, Squawk, Crab and Cocky, along with teammates whose monikers are Grumpy, Brat, Bad News, Chippy and Gloomy. Do not despair, the team veterans Old Sport, Old Reliable, Old Hustler, Old True Blue and Old Faithful will lead the way by example. Remember, attitude is altitude!

One player charges by all others on the team. Pete Charlie Hustle Rose not only rewrote the record book with his stats, but it was his hustling attitude which set a new tone on effort and performance. Whitey Ford saw some rookie run to first after he received a base on balls (the baseball tradition is to "walk" to first). Whitey quipped, "who does he think he is, Charlie Hustle?" It stuck! Pete "looked" every pitch into the catcher's mitt. He "ran out" every play. He "came to play" every day. Pete "shook off" every injury. I coached my boys for ten summers and the one player I continually used as an example to emulate was Charlie Hustle. He always will be the epitome of what not only baseball, but also what life is all about. Play every day, play all out and play to win are the ingredients to success in any endeavor. Here is a quiz. It is the seventh game of the World Series. You are down by one run. There is one out in the bottom of the ninth inning and a runner is on third base. A shallow fly is hit. You send the runner on the tag up, but there is little chance he will score. Who would you want for your runner?... You got it!

LINEUP

| CA | Eugene *Bubbles* Hargrave | caught balls and strikes for 12 summers. Seven seasons, including six consecutive (1922-27), he hit over .300. Bubbles' .310 career batting average is tops for catchers. In 1926 he had his best year. Bubbles hit a lofty .353 for Cincinnati that summer! |

| 1B | Will *The Thrill* Clark | is the complete player. He is strong both in the field and at the plate. His smooth swing has generated four 20+ homer seasons, three 100+ RBI years and five .300 or higher batting averages! Just 30, The Thrill has many potential great seasons yet to come. Go Will! |

| 2B | *Sweet* Lou Whitaker | seems to get better with age. He hit .301 in 1994, his 18th year. Sweet Lou has over 1000 RBI's, 400 doubles, 200 homers and nearly 2300 hits. He has played his entire career in a Tiger uniform. Sweet Lou has combined with Tram at short to form a great keystone combination. |

| SS | James *Chippy* McGarr | played in three leagues for seven different teams during his ten years. He led all shortstops in fielding % in 1890. Chippy led the Cleveland Spiders in 1895 (hit .368) to the Temple Cup. Prior to the origination of the AL in 1901, the first and second place NL teams played for the Cup. |

| 3B | *Smiling* Stan Hack | was a Cubbie all his 16 seasons, plus he later managed them three summers. A four time All-Star, he was a model of consistency. From 1936-43, Smiling Stan averaged 177 base hits (twice led the league, one a tie), 85 walks, 101 runs, 31 doubles and .304 batting average! |

| OF | Pete *Charlie Hustle* Rose | was a 17 time All-Star in his sparkling 24 year career. He retired ranked first in hits, games, at bats and outs made. Pete also finished second in doubles and fourth in runs. He hit .300 for 15 seasons (won three Silver Bats) and led the league in hits seven times (two ties). |

| OF | Hardy *Old True Blue* Richardson | was a versatile player in the pre-1900 era. He played every position during his 14 year career. Old True Blue, in 1886, led the NL in hits and home runs (tie), while batting .351. In 1890 his 146 RBI's topped the Players League. Seven summers Old True Blue batted over .300. |

| OF | Ross *Pep* Youngs | was a star in his eight full seasons, but a kidney disease ended his career at 29 and his life at 30. His .322 career average places Pep 42nd. He finished fourth in batting in 1919 and third in both 1920 and 1924. The Veterans Committee elected Pep to the Hall of Fame in 1972! |

| P | Early *Gus* Wynn | was ambidextrous, but he settled on pitching right-handed. Five seasons he won 20 or more games. Gus, short for Gloomy Gus, won two strikeout crowns and one ERA title. He retired with 300 wins (tie 19th), 49 shutouts (tie 21st) and 2334 K's (28th). |

| P | *Sad* Sam Jones | threw balls and strikes for 22 campaigns, all in the AL. Twice he topped 20 victories. Sad Sam's 229 wins place him in a tie for 52nd and his 36 whitewashes were topped by only 59 hurlers. In 1923 Sad Sam had his best season, finishing 21-8 for the World Champion Yankees. |

| P | *Smiling* Al Orth | starred for 15 seasons at the turn of the century. From 1896 - 1907 he won in double digits. A submariner, Smiling Al, with the help of Happy Jack Chesbro, developed a spitter. With his "new pitch" he had his career year in 1906. Smiling Al won 27 times (first American League)! |

| MGR | Charlie *Jolly Cholly* Grimm | , after playing 16 seasons, became a playing mgr. for four plus summers. Taking the helm for the Cubs in 1932 with 55 games to go, they won 37, including 14 straight, and charged to the pennant! During his 19 managing campaigns, the easy going Jolly Cholly won over 1250 games. |

| RES | *Laughing* Larry Doyle | was an outstanding player for 14 years. During his career he not only finished tied for second, tied for third and fourth in HR's, but also Larry led the Senior Circuit in hits twice and once in doubles, triples and batting average. In 1912 he won the Chalmer Award (the then MVP). |

| RES | Tommy *Old Reliable* Henrich | , like many players, gave three years to his country (ages 30-32), but he came back to resume stardom. A five time All-Star, he topped the AL in three baggers twice and runs once. Old Reliable earned his nickname for his timely hitting, especially in World Series play. |

| RES | Gene *Old Faithful* Woodling | chased fly balls for 17 years, twice leading the Junior Circuit in fielding %. A solid hitter, he regularly rose to the occasion in World Series play. Old Faithful hit .400 in the 1949, .429 in the 1950, .348 in the 1952 and .300 in the 1953 Fall Classic! |

L to R: Will *The Thrill* Clark, Early *Gus* Wynn, Pete *Charlie Hustle* Rose, *Smiling* Stan Hack, *Sweet* Lou Whitaker

It'sa FACT

<u>Ed **Loose** Karger</u>: Toiling for the eighth place St. Louis Cards in 1907 (52-101), he won 15 games, including six by shutout!

Sunny Jim Bottomley: On September 16th, 1924 he had a unbelievable day. Sunny Jim singled in the first inning and drove in two runs. His double in the second inning scored one teammate. In the fourth Jim went deep with the sacks jammed. He went yard again, a two run shot, in the sixth inning. Sunny Jim lashed another two run single in the seventh. In the ninth Sunny Jim stroked his sixth safety, a single, to plate another run. That September day was sunny for Jim. He drove in 12 runs!

Archie **Happy** McKain: He was used exclusively in relief in 1940. Happy went 5-0 for the pennant winning Tigers.

Bob **Smiley** Keegan: In 1953 he reached the Majors, just 2½ months before his 33rd birthday. Smiley, in 1954, made the AL All-Star team and went 16-9 for the White Sox.

Sunny Jack Sutthoff: In 1903 he had a solid season for Cincinnati. Sunny Jack's log read 16-9 with three shutouts.

Joe **Gay Reliever** Page: He was the AL's premier stopper in the late 40's. Twice Joe led the Junior Circuit in both appearances and saves. In 1949 the Gay Reliever posted 13 victories and saved another 27! His stellar relief in game #7 of the 1947 World Series gave him the win and the Yankees the World Championship. Again in the 1949 Fall Classic Joe came to the rescue. He won game #3 and he saved the clinching game #5.

Sunny Jim Dygert: In 1907 he had his career year. Sunny Jim posted 21 victories with only eight defeats. He held opposing batters to a league leading measly .214 batting average.

Happy Jack Chesbro: His career of nine full and two part seasons was long enough for him to rack up 198 wins. From 1901-06 Happy Jack won 153 contests, an average of 25 victories per season! During that period he led the league in winning % three times and was first in both wins and shutouts (two ties) twice. In 1904 Jack pitched 454 innings, completed 48 games and posted a 1.82 ERA! His 454 frames is second highest since 1900 and his 48 route going performances is tops this century. Happy Jack is one of only two pitchers to win at least 12 consecutive games in both the NL and AL. He won 12 for the Pirates in 1902 and 14 for the Highlanders (Yankees) in 1904.

Sunny Jim Pastorius: Although Brooklyn finished 18 games below .500 in 1907, he won 16 and tossed four shutouts.

Pete **Charlie Hustle** Rose: Amazingly, his glove was as good as his bat! He came up as a second sacker, then played right, shifted to left, took over at the hot corner and ended up at first. Over the years Charlie Hustle was elected to the NL All-Star team at all five positions! In 1965, playing second, he led in putouts. In 1968, playing right field, he led in assists and in 1970 he was first in fielding %. In 1974, playing left field, he led in fielding %. In 1976, playing third base, he led in fielding %. In 1980, playing first base, he led in both assists and fielding %. Pete ranks tenth all time in fielding % for first basemen and he is third all time in fielding % for outfielders!

Early **Gus** Wynn: As a batter he switch hit. On September 15th, 1946 Gus blasted a pinch-hit grand slam, one of 17 tape jobs he hit during his career.

Charlie **Jolly Cholly** Grimm: He was known as the best left-handed banjo player in the Majors. For his career he recorded nearly 2300 hits (base hits). He combined with Buc teammates Walter Rabbit Maranville, George Possum Whitted and James Cotton Tierney to form a musical quartet.

George **Grin** Bradley: In 1876, the National League's first season, he was the pitching star. On July 15th, 1876 he posted baseball's first no-hitter! Grin finished the year with 45 wins, 16 whitewashes and a 1.23 ERA!

Cheerful Charlie Hickman: He was a slugger in the dead ball era. In 1902 Cheerful Charlie had his best season, finishing second in home runs and RBI's, and third in batting average and slugging %. Piano Legs also led the AL in both hits and total bases!

Happy Jack Stivetts: During the late 1800's he was as good as any player. As a 21 year old rookie in 1889, he led the American Association in ERA. From 1890-96 Happy Jack chalked up 180 victories, twice winning over 30 contests. With the lumber he was just as impressive. Happy Jack's career average was .297. In 1890 he poled seven homers (third) in just 226 at bats. He powdered eight yard shots and drove in 64 runs in just 68 games in 1894. Happy Jack could do it all!

Steady Eddie Lopat: Originally he was a first sacker. Moved to the mound, Steady Eddie won in double digits his first 11 seasons. He cooled off the ' 51 Giants in the World Series. Steady Eddie won games #2 and #5, allowing only one earned run in 18 frames.

Vernon **The Gay Castilion** Gomez: For his career he went 6-0 in World Series play. In consecutive Fall Classics (1936-37) Lefty's log read 2-0, winning the cinching game both years!

Al **Happy** Milnar: He finished third in the AL in wins and tied for the league lead in whitewashes in 1940.

Smiling Al Maul: His 1898 season certainly allowed him to live up to his nickname. Smiling Al's record was 20-7 with a 2.10 ERA.

TRIVIA*

1) Since 1900 only two pitchers have won 40 games in one season. His 41 wins in 1904 are the record.

2) He won the Gold Glove at his position in 1965, 1966 and 1969. In 1967 and 1968 George Boomer Scott won it.

3) His brother Pinky (William) was also a Major League catcher.

4) He succeeded Kenesaw Mountain Landis as the Commissioner of Baseball.

5) Also known as Farmer, he was easily recognized by his near ground touching arm swing in his wind up. (Hint: his nickname came from his hunting dog)

6) This fireballing right-hander led the NL in K's in 1955, 1956 and 1958.

7) Known for knocking down batters, it was suggested he was so mean he would even knock down his mother! He agreed, but added, his mom was a good hitter!

8) He was voted the 1963 National League Rookie of the Year. He also holds the Major League record of ten 200 hit seasons. (Hint: he was the Senior Circuit MVP in 1973)

9) In the five game 1981 NLCS he went 2-0, not allowing an earned run in 14 2/3 innings. He was shutout in game #2 of the World Series, but he came back to win game #6 and clinch the World Championship for the Dodgers.

10) He had two other nicknames. They were Goofy and Lefty.

11) On April 22nd, 1970 he was terrific. He fanned ten consecutive hitters and 19 for the game.

12) Not only did he toss a no-hitter September 4th, 1928, but amazingly, he also did not strikeout one batter! (Hint: he shares his nickname and his real name with another hurler on the roster)

13) On September 10th, 1985 he did what was thought for years to be impossible, he broke Ty Cobb's career hit record.

14) At the age of 39 he won the 1959 Cy Young award. He led the AL in wins and innings, plus he won game #1 of the World Series.

15) From 1934-37 he lived up to his nickname (for opposing pitchers). He averaged 173 hits, 90 runs, 40 doubles, 92 RBI's and batted .298.

16) Seven times he led all NL first sackers in fielding %. (Hint: his nickname rhymes)

17) This happy Hall of Famer set a Major League record by striking out the first nine batters in a ball game.

18) For nine consecutive seasons (1968-76) he struck out 200+ batters. His 3640 career ring ups place him fourth all time.

19) He holds the record of winning three All-Star games. (Hint: he was a southpaw)

20) Famous for his "knuckle curve," he was very happy on April 16th, 1972 when he threw a no-hitter.

21) He was voted Player of the Year in 1950. (Hint: his other nickname was Mugsy)

22) From 1935-40 this swift NL third sacker finished tied for fourth, tied for second, second, first, tied for first and second in stolen bases.

23) He had six hitting streaks of at least 20 games during his career. In 1978 he hit safely in 44 consecutive games, tying Wee Willie Keeler for the second longest consecutive game hitting streak.

24) He "won" the pitching Triple Crown (leading the league in wins, strikeouts and ERA). Only six American League twirlers have ever done it. He did it twice!

25) He earned his nickname with two game winning ninth inning pinch homers while playing for the 1962 Mets.

* POSITIVELY TOUGH answers found on page 235

ROSTER

CATCHERS:	Yr	Hits	AB's	Ave
Eugene *Bubbles* Hargrave	12	786	2533	.310
Frank *Yip* Owens	4	170	694	.245
Jack *Old Sport* Brennan	5	155	705	.220
Smiley John Bischoff	2	71	271	.262
George *Good Kid* Susce	8	61	268	.228
Paul *Pep* Florence	1	43	188	.229
Happy Jack Bellman	1	1	2	.500
Chester *Squawk* Crist	1	0	11	.000

1ST BASEMEN:	Yr	Hits	AB's	Ave
Sunny Jim Bottomley	16	2313	7471	.310
Charlie *Jolly Cholly* Grimm	20	2299	7917	.290
Will *The Thrill* Clark	9	1406	4658	.302
Joe *Pepi* Pepitone	12	1315	5097	.258
Cheerful Charlie Hickman	12	1176	3982	.295
Joe *Old Reliable* Start	11	1031	3433	.300
Marvelous Marv Throneberry	8	281	1186	.237
Chris *Crab* Lindsay	2	200	828	.242
Sunny Jim Hackett	2	86	372	.231

2ND BASEMEN:	Yr	Hits	AB's	Ave
Eddie *Cocky* Collins	25	3312	9949	.333
Sweet Lou Whitaker	18	2296	8321	.276
Laughing Larry Doyle	14	1887	6509	.290
Eddie *The Brat* Stanky	11	1154	4301	.268
Odell *Bad News* Hale	10	1071	3701	.289
Lemuel *Pep* Young	10	645	2466	.262
Hal *Grump* Irelan	1	39	165	.236
Joe *Old Hustler* Mathes	3	27	99	.273
James *Bad News* Galloway	1	10	54	.185
Al *A-1* Wright	1	1	1	1.000

SHORTSTOPS:	Yr	Hits	AB's	Ave
Bad Bill Dahlen	21	2457	9031	.272
Rowdy Richard Bartell	18	2165	7629	.284
James *Chippy* McGarr	10	872	3253	.268
Claire *Pep* Goodwin	2	142	603	.235
Harry *Happy* Buker	1	15	111	.135

3RD BASEMEN:	Yr	Hits	AB's	Ave
Smiling Stan Hack	16	2193	7278	.301
Scrappy Bill Joyce	8	970	3304	.294
Harry *Pep* Clark	1	20	65	.308
Bill *Pep* Conroy	1	8	60	.133
Eddie *Smiley* Turchin	1	3	13	.231
Larry *Chipper* Jones	1	2	3	.667
Henry *Pep* Peploski	1	2	10	.200
Bill *Happy* Hollahan	1	1	4	.250
William *Scrappy* Moore	1	1	8	.125
Happy Jack Kibble	1	0	8	.000

OUTFIELDERS:	Yr	Hits	AB's	Ave
Pete *Charlie Hustle* Rose	24	4256	14053	.303
Hardy *Old True Blue* Richardson	14	1688	5642	.299

OUTFIELDERS: (Cont.)	Yr	Hits	AB's	Ave
Gene *Old Faithful* Woodling	17	1585	5587	.284
Ross *Pep* Youngs	10	1491	4627	.322
Tommy *Old Reliable* Henrich	11	1297	4603	.282
Jackie *Flaky* Brandt	11	1020	3895	.262
Oscar *Happy* Felsch	6	825	2812	.293
John *Honest Eddie* Murphy	11	680	2373	.287
Ward *Grump* Miller	8	623	2244	.278
Sweet Lou Johnson	8	529	2049	.258
Estel *Crabby* Crabtree	8	396	1408	.281
August *Gloomy Gus* Williams	5	367	1398	.263
Lewis *Sport* McAllister	7	358	1450	.247
Otis *Grump* Clymer	6	355	1330	.267
Roaring Bill Hassamaer	3	305	1054	.289
William *Happy* Hogan	2	194	822	.236
John *Scrappy* Carroll	3	49	287	.171
William *Gentle Willie* Murphy	1	48	189	.254
Coaster Joe Connolly	4	45	168	.264
Hustling Dan O'Leary	5	44	181	.243
Sunny Jim Mallory	2	40	149	.268
Henry *Happy* Smith	1	18	76	.237
Happy Jack Cameron	1	11	61	.180
Alex *Spunk* Pitko	2	7	27	.259
Fredrick *Happy* Jack Lott	1	2	10	.200
Art *Merry* Merewether	1	0	1	.000

PITCHERS:	Yr	Won	Lost	ERA
Smiling Tim Keefe	14	342	225	2.62
Tom *Terrific* Seaver	20	311	205	2.86
Smiling Mickey Welch	13	307	210	2.71
Early *Gus* Wynn	23	300	244	3.54
Sad Sam Jones	22	229	217	3.84
Smiling Al Orth	15	204	189	3.37
Happy Jack Stivetts	11	203	132	3.74
Happy Jack Chesbro	11	198	132	2.68
Vernon *The Gay Castilion* Gomez	14	189	102	3.34
Steady Eddie Lopat	12	166	112	3.21
Burt *Happy* Hooton	15	151	136	3.38
George *Grin* Bradley	10	138	125	2.50
Sad Sam Gray	10	111	115	4.18
Sad Sam Jones	12	102	101	3.59
Smiling Al Maul	15	84	80	4.43
Ray *Old Blue* Moore	11	63	59	4.06
Sunny Jim Dygert	6	57	49	2.65
Joe *Gay Reliever* Page	8	57	49	3.53
Al *Happy* Milnar	8	57	58	4.22
Sheldon *Available* Jones	8	54	57	3.96
Ed *Loose* Karger	6	48	67	2.79
Sad Sam Zoldak	9	43	53	3.54
Bob *Smiley* Keegan	6	40	36	3.66
Happy Jack Townsend	6	35	82	3.59
Sunny Jim Pastorius	4	31	55	3.12
Sunny Jack Sutthoff	6	31	40	3.65
Hubert *Shucks* Pruett	7	29	48	4.63
Archie *Happy* McKain	6	26	21	4.26

ROSTER

PITCHERS: (Cont.)	Yr	Won	Lost	ERA
Joseph *Happy* Finneran	5	25	33	3.30
George *Smiler* Murray	6	20	26	5.38
Steady Pete Meegan	2	14	20	3.90
George *Charmer* Zettlein	1	4	20	3.88
George *Chummy* Gray	1	3	3	3.44
Smiling Pete Daniels	2	2	8	4.79
Smiling George Blackburn	1	2	2	6.82
Sunny Jim Hackett	2	1	6	4.69
George *Chippy* Gaw	1	1	1	4.85
Frank *Dreamy* Scanlan	1	0	0	1.64

PITCHERS: (Cont.)	Yr	Won	Lost	ERA
August *Happy* Foreman	2	0	0	3.18
John *Perky* Perkovich	1	0	0	7.20
Smiling Bock Baker	1	0	2	7.71
Elmer *Pep* Rambert	2	0	1	8.25
Otto *Pep* Deininger	1	0	0	9.75
Bill *Booster* Greason	1	0	1	13.50

EXTRAS:
Wrigley Field - *The Friendly Confines*
Albert *Happy* Chandler - Baseball Commissioner 1945-51

LINGO

Laugher: One sided game

Hustler: Player who goes all out on every play

Batter's Up: Player comes to the plate to bat

High: A pitch above the strike zone

It'sa FACT cont'd...

Sad Sam Gray: In 1928 and 1929 he was the St. Louis Brown's top hurler. Sad Sam went 20-12 and 18-15 those campaigns, leading the AL in innings and shutouts (tie) in 1929.

Scrappy Bill Joyce: He played eight seasons in the 1890's, the last three years he was a playing manager. Scrappy Bill is a forgotten slugger. In 1894 he hit 17 homers in 355 at bats. Scrappy Bill finished tied for second to Hugh Duffy (18 homers in 539 at bats). In 1895 he hit 17 homers in 474 at bats. Scrappy Bill finished second to Big Sam Thompson (18 homers in 538 at bats). Finally in 1896 Bill tied for the homer crown with Big Ed Delahanty (Scrappy: 13 tators in 475 plate appearances vs. Big Ed's 13 dingers in 499 official at bats). Scrappy Bill played only 908 games (need 1000), leaving him ineligible for "all time" lists. If he were qualified, Scrappy Bill would rank ninth in runs per game, place ninth in bases on balls % and finish sixth in on base %!

Eddie *The Brat* Stanky: He was an outstanding leadoff batter. From 1945-51 The Brat drove teams crazy. During those seven seasons, (the six he played everyday because one year he was injured) The Brat averaged 102 runs (once league leading), 128 free passes (led league three times) and 140 hits. His career .410 on base % places him in a tie for 25th!

Smiling Stan Hack: He was a solid player at the hot corner. During his career Smiling Stan led the league in putouts (four), assists (three), DP's (three) and fielding % (two).

Joe *Old Reliable* Start: From 1871-75 he played in the National Association (statistically unrecognized league before the National League started). In 1876, at age 33, Old Reliable began his official career. He played 11 summers. At age 35 Old Reliable led the NL in hits and finished fourth in batting average. At the young age of 41 he led all first basemen in fielding %, the fourth season Old Reliable had accomplished that.

Eddie *Cocky* Collins: What does it take to be a Hall of Famer? First, you should be a good fielder. He led AL second basemen in fielding % nine times, putouts seven times, DP's five times and assists four times! Second, you should have speed. He stole 744 bases, sixth all time. His 186 triples have been topped by only 11 players. Twice he swiped six bags in one game (September 9th, 1912 and September 22nd, 1912). Third, you should hit well. His 3312 career hits rank him eighth. His log is complete when his .333 career average is included! That is Eddie Cocky Collins' career. He was great!

Bad Bill Dahlen: On August 30th, 1900 he laced two triples in one inning! Bad Bill also legged out three triples in one game twice, on May 3rd, 1896 and June 6th, 1898.

Sad Sam Jones: On May 12th, 1955 he smiled when he fired a no-hitter!

BASEBALL NAMES

3

Team

The origin of baseball is a great story. As with anything historical, there are varying accounts. The accepted myth was that in 1839, on the shores of Lake Otsego, in the Village of Cooperstown, New York, Abner Doubleday "invented" the game. Actually, baseball had a long evolution. References to "baseball" go back to Revolutionary times. Also, several similar sport games contributed to portions of the emerging sport. Crickett and roundball shared some of today's baseball rules. In 1845 Alexander Cartwright formalized the "New York Game" of baseball (rules that their ball clubs abided by). Bases were set 90 feet apart and in a diamond shape. The three strike and three out rules were fixed. Runners could be thrown out at first base, rather than being hit by a thrown ball to be out. Within 20 years and the completion of the Civil War, baseball was proclaimed America's national pastime.

The Baseball Names Team fields an impressive crew. Four teammates are now in the Hall of Fame. They and their fellow players went to the plate to Hack, Rip and Swish at the baseball. Each mate hoped to Slug, Swat and Slam a Home Run, Four Sack or Round Tripper. Sometimes they had to settle for a Bloop, Topper or even a Bunt. In the field the team would Scoop, Shag and Snag a Line Drive or a Hotshot and hope not to Muff it or Boot it, because they had lost their Mitty or used a Strangeglove.

One player's accomplishments separate him from his teammates. Lewis Hack Wilson was a feared hitter. His 1930 season was record shattering. Hack drove in a Major League record 190 runs. His 56 round trippers are still the National League standard. Hack's .723 slugging % was the 15th best single season total and his 97 extra base hits rank in a tie for 14th! In addition, Hack batted a hefty .356! You may wonder, how did Lewis become known as Hack? There are three stories as to the origin of Wilson's nickname. First, a popular Chicago Cub who had just retired and whom Lewis physically resembled was Lawrence Hack Miller. A second theory says Wilson resembled a then popular wrestler, George Hackenschmidt. The third possibility deals with Lewis' build (5'6" and 190 pounds). Short and squat, he resembled a stack of bricks, commonly known as a "hack." Regardless, Lewis hacked his way to the Hall!

LINEUP

CA	George *Mitty* Mitterwald

wore the tools of ignorance for 11 campaigns. Three seasons, while calling pitches for the Minnesota Twins, he tagged 16, 15 and 13 home runs. In the 1970 American League Championship Series, Mitty batted .500 in a losing effort against the Orioles.

1B	Donnie *Baseball* Mattingly

is both an excellent fielder and hitter. He has led AL first sackers six times in fielding %. Donnie Baseball has topped the circuit in 2B's (three), hits (two) and RBI's (one). Five years he has driven in 100+ runs. Seven years he has hit over .300 and in 1984 he won the Silver Bat!

2B	Ed *Batty* Abbaticchio

was a middle infielder who started five seasons at the turn of century. Batty was a fast runner, a solid hitter and an outstanding gloveman. He averaged 26 stolen bases (1903-07), finished tied for second in RBI's in 1907 and twice led the NL in putouts and once in fielding %.

SS	Emory *Topper* Rigney

was a four year starter during his six seasons. He led AL shortstops twice in fielding % and once in assists. Two seasons Topper walked over 100 times. In 1924 he drove in 93 runs, had a .410 on base percentage and finished second to Babe Ruth in free passes.

3B	Eddie *The Walking Man* Yost

was an 18 year veteran who "walked" 1614 times (seventh most) or 18% of his at bats! The free passes helped him score 100+ runs five times. In the field The Walking Man led AL hot corner men eight times in putouts, two times in fielding % and once each in DP's and assists.

OF	Harry *Slug* Heilmann

is a Hall of Famer. His lifetime average places him tenth all time! During his career Harry pounded 542 doubles (13th), smashed 151 triples (tie 49th) and drove in 1539 runs (31st). Slug knocked in 100+ runs eight summers and four seasons he won the AL batting title.

OF	George *Rip* Van Haltren

was an outstanding player for 17 years (three primarily as a pitcher). He hit over .300 twelve years and scored 100+ runs 11 summers. For his career Rip stole 583 bags (18th), scored 1639 runs (27th), stretched 161 triples (38th), batted .316 (60th) and slugged 2532 hits (65th).

OF	Don *Groove* Baylor

had a fantastic 19 year career, reaching the ALCS with five different teams! Groove went 5/17 with ten RBI's in the Angels 1982 ALCS heartbreaking loss. In 1979 Groove led the AL in runs and RBI's, and was voted the American League MVP! His 338 dingers rank him 50th!

P	Truett *Rip* Sewell

twirled 12 years for the Bucs. Sticking his third try, in 1939, he already was nearly 32 years old. Rip started from 1940-44. He reeled off 89 wins, sharing the NL lead with 21 victories in 1943 and again winning 21 in 1944! His last campaign, at age 42, Rip went 6-1 as a short man.

P	Harry *Rip* Collins

fired bullets for 11 summers in the Junior Circuit. During his pitching career he had only two losing seasons. Six years Rip won in double digits. His 14-11 record in 1922 for the Beantowners was amazing, since the Bosox finished dead last in the American League.

P	Al *Boots* Hollingsworth

toiled for 11 years in the Majors. Eight seasons his teams played under .500 and three times his teams were cellar dwellers. Nevertheless, Boots had winning seasons in both 1942 (10-6) and 1945 (12-9) while chucking for the St. Louis Browns.

RES	Lewis *Hack* Wilson

had a too short 12 year career. From 1926-30 Hack was the most feared slugger in the National League. He finished first, tie for first, tie for first, third and first in HR's and placed second, second, third, first and first in RBI's. Hack also hit over .300 each year!

RES	Jack *The Ripper* Clark

was a premier player for 18 seasons. In the 12 summers he played 100 or more games, The Ripper swatted 20 or more yard shots 11 times and drove in at least 82 runs nine years. His 1987 campaign was his best. Jack mashed 35 tators and plated 106 tallies!

RES	Cletis *Clete* Boyer

was a slick fielding third sacker. He led all hot corner men three times in assists, twice in both DP's and fielding % and once in putouts. Clete's 1967 season yielded 26 dingers and 96 ribbies. After 16 summers Clete went to Japan and hit 71 more HR's in four seasons.

RES	James *Ripper* Collins

crushed the ball nine seasons in the NL. In 1934 he did it all! Ripper scored 116 runs (third), swatted 200 hits (third), slashed 40 2B's (tie fourth), belted 12 3B's (fourth), slugged 35 HR's (tie first), plated 128 runs (second) and batted .333 (fifth).

L to R: Donnie *Baseball* Mattingly, Don *Groove* Baylor, Lewis *Hack* Wilson, Jack *The Ripper* Clark, Harry *Slug* Heilmann

It'sa FACT

Frank **Home Run** Baker: From 1911-14 he won four consecutive home run crowns (one shared). Surprisingly, Home Run retired with more triples (103) than homers (96). He also led all Junior Circuit third sackers in putouts seven times, DP's three times and assists twice.

Eddie **Hotshot** Mayo: He was a four year starter. Hotshot led the AL in fielding % twice (In 1943 at third base and in 1945 at second base).

George **Mitty** Mitterwald: On April 17th, 1974 he had a career day, poling three homers and plating eight runs.

Eddie **The Walking Man** Yost: His 1956 season was amazing. He received 151 bases on balls (fifth highest ever), 32 more than his 119 base hits.

Larry **Hack** Miller: A son of a circus strongman, he was nicknamed after the wrestler George Hackenschmidt. Hack's 20 yard shots in 1923 placed him third in the Senior Circuit. He batted .352 in 1922, good for third in the league. Hack retired with a .323 batting average.

George **Boots** Grantham: He swatted the ball over .300 for eight consecutive seasons (1924-31). Boot's best year was 1930. He slugged 34 two baggers, 14 three baggers, 18 four baggers and batted .324.

James **Hack** Miller: His first official Major League at bat resulted in a home run (April 23rd, 1944).

Ray **Jockey** Kolp: Most of his career he toiled for losing teams. In one stretch Jockey's teams finished seventh, seventh, eighth, eighth, eighth and eighth (eight team league)! The summer his team finished second, Jockey went 14-4!

Ray **Rip** Radcliff: In September of 1934 he was a 28 year old rookie late season "call up". For the next seven summers he was a starter. Rip batted over .300 five years, ripping the ball at a .342 pace in 1940 (fourth in the AL). In 4074 career at bats, Rip went down on strikes only 141 times, retiring the 13th toughest batter to fan!

Two Game Johnny Beazley: His 1942 season was fantastic. He finished 21-6 with a 2.13 ERA, both second in the NL! Two Game won game #2 and the Series winning game #5 for the Cardinals.

Lynn **Line Drive** Nelson: This pitcher's unusual nickname came from his excellent hitting ability! Line Drive led the AL in pinch-hits and pinch at bats in 1937. In just 113 at bats that summer, he swatted four homers, drove in 29 runs and batted .354!

Charles **Home Run** Duffee: As a rookie in 1889 he finished third in tators. Two seasons later Home Run tied for fourth in round trippers. His career was cut short by his early death at the age of 28.

Hugh **Losing Pitcher** Mulcahy: He gained his nickname after leading the NL in loses in both 1938 and 1940. Hugh does not deserve his moniker. In 1938 he won ten of the "dead last" Phillie's 45 wins. Hugh posted three shutouts and 13 victories in 1940. The Phillies were again doormats, winning only 50 times in 1940.

Bill **Swish** Nicholson: From 1940-44 he averaged 26 dingers and 104 RBI's. Swish slugged four consecutive long balls on July 22nd (one) and July 23rd, 1944 (three).

Walker **Walk** Cooper: He had a dream game July 6th, 1949. Walk knocked in ten runs!

Jack **The Ripper** Clark: In 1987 he was awesome. The Ripper slugged 35 yard shots in just 419 at bats. He drove in 106 runs and led the NL in slugging %.

Bobby **Bloop** Fenwick: He was born in Naha, Okinawa.

Bibb **Jockey** Falk: When Shoeless Joe Jackson received his lifetime suspension, he replaced him. After his first two seasons, Bibb never fanned more than 25 times in any of his remaining nine summers.

William **Spike** Shannon: In 1907 Spike topped the Senior Circuit in both runs scored and at bats.

Donnie **Baseball** Mattingly: Most people think of his hitting, but he is also an outstanding fielder. From 1985-94 Donnie Baseball earned nine Gold Gloves. His 22 putouts in one game ties him for the Major League mark.

Eldon **Rip** Repulski: From 1953-57 he ripped the ball at a 17 homer and 68 RBI pace.

Jack **Slug** Burns: He was actually known for his defense. In the six seasons Slug started, he led AL first sackers three times in DP's and twice in assists.

TRIVIA*

1)   In 1987 he slugged six grand slams.

2)   He gained his nickname when he hit two consecutive game winning home runs during the 1911 World Series.

3)   He played against his brother Ken (the NL's MVP) in the 1964 Fall Classic. Both swatted homers in game #7.

4)   This Hall of Famer actually acquired his nickname for his slow foot speed.

5)   He and his older brother Mort were battery mates for six seasons (1940-45 Cards).

6)   This backstop went on to be both a manager and then a general manager.

7)   This tall (6'2"), lean (170 pounds) pitcher is nicknamed after a "thin piece of lumber".

8)   He threw a blooper ball. It was called an euphus pitch.

9)   This right-handed hurler gained his moniker for his rapier tongue.

10) He played in an all .400 outfield along with Big Ed Delahanty (.407) and Big Sam Thompson (.407)

11) He is one of three players to slug home runs in eight consecutive games (the other two are Ken Junior Griffey and Dale Long). He actually pounded ten yard shots during his streak.

12) He holds the AL career record for being hit by pitches with 190!

13) His 87 extra base hits in one season is the record for switch hitters. (Hint: he was a member of the Gas House Gang)

14) One season, while in the minors, he crushed 66 homers. In 1963 he led the AL in RBI's (118) and finished second in yard shots (42).

15) Although he batted less than .260 for his career, his on base average was .395, 53rd best!

16) At the "young" age of 35 he had his best season. In 1982 he led the NL in hits, doubles and RBI's (tie) and he earned the Silver Bat.

17) For his career he scored 1.06 runs per game. His 192 runs in 1894 are the single season record.

18) He won the AL batting title four times in the sequential odd years 1921, 1923, 1925 and 1927. He credited his teammate/manager Ty Cobb for his hitting success.

19) He won back to back HR and RBI titles in 1943-44. (Hint: a basketball player could have his nickname)

20) His 829 consecutive games is the eighth longest streak in Major League history.

21) He was the AL MVP in 1985. He hold the Major League record of ten consecutive games with an extra base hit.

22) He ripped consecutive pinch homers on August 22nd and August 24th, 1958.

23) On July 1st, 1925 he tagged two homers in one inning! That whole season he swatted only six dingers! But, it was a sign of things to come. This Hall of Famer led or shared the NL lead in cheap seaters four of the next five summers!

24) He ripped 340 career homers, placing him 47th all time on the strongboy list.

25) Eight seasons he received over 100 walks, six times leading the AL in free passes!

* HARD LINERS answers found on page 235

ROSTER

CATCHERS:	Yr	Hits	AB's	Ave
Walker *Walk* Cooper	18	1341	4702	.285
George *Mitty* Mitterwald	11	623	2645	.236
Carl *Swats* Sawatski	11	351	1449	.242
Paul *Slug* Richards	8	321	1417	.227
Alva *Rip* Williams	7	314	1186	.265
Sam *Slam* Agnew	7	314	1537	.204
Mackey *Hacker* Sasser	8	313	1163	.269
Bill *Hack* Warren	2	13	53	.245
Mike *Slugs* Ulisney	1	7	18	.389
Roy *Shag* Easterwood	1	7	33	.212
James *Hack* Miller	1	4	9	.444
Russ *Hack* Ennis	1	0	0	.000

1ST BASEMEN:	Yr	Hits	AB's	Ave
Donnie *Baseball* Mattingly	13	2021	6545	.309
James *Ripper* Collins	9	1121	3784	.296
Dick *Dr. Strangeglove* Stuart	10	1055	3997	.264
Jack *Slug* Burns	7	980	3506	.280
Glen *Rip* Russell	6	344	1402	.245
George *Scoops* Carey	4	313	1157	.271
Harry *Swats* Swacina	4	304	1189	.256
Charles *Slug* Tolson	5	78	275	.284

2ND BASEMEN:	Yr	Hits	AB's	Ave
George *Boots* Grantham	13	1508	4989	.302
Ed *Batty* Abbaticchio	9	772	3044	.254
Eddie *Hotshot* Mayo	9	759	3013	.252
Tom *Scoops* Carey	8	418	1521	.275
George *Hack* Simmons	4	234	951	.246
Harry *Spike* LaRoss	1	11	48	.229
Bobby *Bloop* Fenwick	2	10	56	.179
Richard *Rip* Conway	1	4	24	.167

SHORTSTOPS:	Yr	Hits	AB's	Ave
Emory *Topper* Rigney	6	669	2326	.288
Jimmy *Scoops* Cooney	7	413	1575	.262

3RD BASEMEN:	Yr	Hits	AB's	Ave
Eddie *The Walking Man* Yost	18	1863	7346	.254
Frank *Home Run* Baker	13	1838	5984	.307
Cletis *Clete* Boyer	16	1396	5780	.242
Art *Scoop* Scharein	3	189	776	.244

OUTFIELDERS:	Yr	Hits	AB's	Ave
Al *Mr. Scoops* Oliver	18	2743	9049	.303
Harry *Slug* Heilmann	17	2660	7787	.342
George *Rip* Van Haltren	17	2532	8021	.316
Sliding Billy Hamilton	14	2158	6268	.344
Don *Groove* Baylor	19	2135	8198	.260
Jack *The Ripper* Clark	18	1826	6847	.267
Bill *Swish* Nicholson	16	1484	5546	.268

OUTFIELDERS: (Cont.)	Yr	Hits	AB's	Ave
Bibb *Jockey* Falk	12	1463	4652	.314
Lewis *Hack* Wilson	12	1461	4760	.307
Raymond *Rip* Radcliff	10	1267	4074	.311
Mike *Hit Man* Easler	14	1078	3677	.293
Emmett *Snags* Heidrick	8	914	3047	.300
Eldon *Rip* Repulski	9	830	3088	.269
Clyde *Hack* Engle	8	748	2822	.265
William *Spike* Shannon	5	677	2613	.259
Charlie *Home Run* Duffee	5	518	1943	.267
Larry *Hack* Miller	6	387	1200	.323
Charles *Boots* Day	6	295	1151	.256
Bob *Bush* Borkowski	6	294	1170	.251
Erv *Four Sack* Dusak	9	251	1035	.243
Virgin *Rip* Cannell	2	221	913	.242
Joe *The Socker* Strauss	3	86	399	.216
Charlie *Bunt* Frisbee	2	52	165	.315
Home Run Joe Marshall	2	21	118	.178
Richard *Rip* Wade	1	16	69	.232
James *Shag* Thompson	3	16	79	.203
James *Swat* McCabe	2	15	46	.326
Mike *Mitty* Jordon	1	12	125	.096
Joe *Shags* Horan	1	9	31	.290
Francis *Shag* Shaughnessy	2	9	32	.281
Charlie *Home Run* Johnson	1	4	16	.250

PINCH HITTER:	Yr	Hits	AB's	Ave
Double Joe Dwyer	1	3	11	.273

PITCHERS:	Yr	Won	Lost	ERA
Truett *Rip* Sewell	13	143	97	3.48
Harry *Rip* Collins	11	108	82	3.99
Ray *Jockey* Kolp	12	79	95	4.08
Al *Boots* Hollingsworth	11	70	104	3.99
Joe *Fungo* Hesketh	11	60	47	3.78
Fred *Spitball* Anderson	7	53	57	2.86
Hugh *Losing Pitcher* Mulcahy	9	45	89	4.49
George *Rip* Van Haltren	9	40	31	4.05
Elmer *Spitball* Stricklett	4	35	51	2.84
Lynn *Line Drive* Nelson	7	33	42	5.25
Two Game Johnny Beazley	6	31	12	3.01
Bob *Round Tripper* Kipper	8	27	37	4.34
Zeriah *Rip* Hagerman	4	19	33	3.09
Leon *Shag* Chagnon	6	19	16	4.51
Billy *Muff* Muffett	6	16	23	4.33
Cletus *Boots* Poffenberger	3	16	12	4.75
Walter *Rip* Coleman	5	7	25	4.58
Floyd *Rip* Wheeler	4	4	8	4.18
John *Mitty* Gray	4	4	18	6.18
John *Rip* Vowinkel	1	3	3	4.17
John *Spike* Merena	1	1	2	2.92
Fred *Hack* Spencer	1	0	0	0.00

ROSTER

PITCHERS: (Cont.)	Yr	Won	Lost	ERA
Clay **Spike** Van Alstyne	2	0	0	3.00
Carl **Hack** Schumann	1	0	2	4.00
Arthur **Rip** Reagan	1	0	2	6.00
Raymond **Rip** Jordan	2	0	0	6.61
Tom **Spike** Borland	2	0	4	6.75
Reeve **Rip** McKay	1	0	0	9.00
Elmer **Herky Jerky** Horton	2	0	3	9.75
John **Rip** Egan	1	0	0	10.80

PITCHERS: (Cont.)	Yr	Won	Lost	ERA
Paul **Herky** Hinrichs	1	0	0	21.60
EXTRAS:				
Al **Extra Inning Umpire** Sudal - Umpire				
William **Spike** Eckert - Baseball Commissioner				
John **Rip** Egan - Umpire				
Henry **Shag** Crawford - Umpire				
Candlestick Park - "**The Stick**"				

LINGO

Walk: Four pitches outside of the strike zone allow a batter free passage to first base

Mitt: Baseball glove

Slump: A batter does not hit well for a long period of time

Slug: Hit a ball very hard

Slam: A home run. With the bases loaded, it is a grand slam

Shag: Run and catch a ball

Hack: Swing at a pitch

Fielder's Choice: Player can choose between getting a baserunner or the batter out

Hacker: A batter up at the plate swinging

Rip: Swing hard at a pitch. Also hit a ball hard

Bat Day: A team sponsors a giveaway (bats) to paying customers attending a specific game

Boot: Make an error (kick one)

Swat: Hit a ball hard

Baseline: Three feet either side of the foul lines (between home and first and between third and home). Three feet either side of the imaginary direct line between first and second and between second and third

Scoop: Field a grounder

Hotshot: Hard hit ball

Topper: A ball hit on the upper half, causing a slow roller

Groove One: Lay an easy to hit pitch in there for a batter to hit

Jockey: Player on the bench who calls out to disrupt the other team

Hitman: A good hitter

Snags: Catches a ball

Meet the Ball: Hit the ball while not swinging hard, just make contact

Bouncer: Ball hit that bounces on the ground

Muff: (Shame on you!) an error

Strikeout: Fail to hit the ball when batting. Other expressions are fanned, whiffed, K'd, rung up and sat down

Round Tripper: A home run

Four Sack: See above

Spitball: An illegal pitch thrown with moisture on part of the ball. It is hurled like a fastball. The "heavy" ball sinks unpredictably as it nears the plate. Sometimes Vaseline or slippery elm are used for the foreign substance rather than just saliva

Fungo: A long thin bat used in fielding practice

Herky Jerky: A pitcher's wind-up and delivery that is not smooth

Stick: Another name for a bat

Bat Around: The entire lineup goes to the plate in one inning

Line Drive: Ball hit hard and level

Real BIRDS

4

Team

The St. Louis Cardinals have a long, rich tradition in baseball history. First known as the Brown Stockings, they later became the Perfectos. In 1926 the now known Cardinals won their first pennant. Led by The Rajah, Rogers Hornsby, Chick Hafey and Sunny Jim Bottomley, they defeated the Yankees and were World Champs. As National League flag bearers in 1928, 1930 and finally World Series winners in 1931, these accomplishments only set the stage for their 1934 heroics. The "Gas House Gang" clawed their way to the pennant, edging Memphis Bill Terry's Giants. The Gang literally marched into Detroit playing "Hold Them Tigers" and mauled them in seven games. Newspapers ruled sports and daily highlighted each game, literally pitch by pitch. The 1934 Cards became household names and most players had nicknames. Tex (James Carleton), Ripper (James Collins), Spud (Virgil Davis), Dizzy (Jay Hanna Dean), Daffy (Paul Dean), The Lip (Leo Durocher), Fordham Flash (Frankie Frisch), Chick (Charles Fullis), Pop (Jesse Haines), Wild Bill (Bill Hallahan), Pepper (John Martin), Ducky (Joe Medwick), Dazzy (Clarence Vance) and Whitey (Burgess Whitehead) captured the nation's heart with their antics. In the 1940's, with stars like Stan The Man Musial, Enos Country Slaughter and Harry The Cat Brecheen, the Cards won four more flags and three World Championships. In 1953 August Busch Jr. purchased the Redbirds, saving them for St. Louis. In 1966 the team moved into their current home next to "The Arch", Busch Stadium. Their pennant drought had ended in 1964. Led by Bob Hoot Gibson, they again ruled the world. The Redbirds won three pennants (1964, 1967 and 1968) and two World Championships (1964 and 1967). With Whitey Herzog at the helm, the Birds were crowned World Champs in 1982, and also won flags in both 1985 and 1987.

The Real Birds are a high flying group. Four members are now perched in Cooperstown. A few members have had a hard time getting off the ground (Emu, Dodo and Penguin), but most teammates have soared. The squad (off the ground) is lead by ten Hawks and is backed by Eagles, Falcon, Quail, Thrush, Crow, Partridge, Sparrow, Pidge, Hummingbird and even a Vulture! Near to land are Duckies, Krane, Stork, Flamingo and Geese. As with all teams, there is an Ugly Duckling and a couple of Turkeys and Cuckoos, but, all in all, they are worth a Tweet and a Gander.

There are several outstanding Birds to choose from, but one player soars to mind, Andre The Hawk Dawson. He has been a marquee player who has toiled for years in obscurity. The Hawk has survived several knee operations and a horrible beaning. His consistency is what makes him a superstar. From 1977-1992, a 16 year stretch which includes the 1981 strike shortened season and his "beaning year," Andre has still averaged 27+ doubles, 24+ homers and 88+ RBI's! He has played in nearly 91% of his teams games. From 1977-83, before his "pins" went, The Hawk stole 21, 28, 35, 34, 26, 39 and 25 bases! Most baseball experts considered him the best defensive outfielder at his position. Let's give him the recognition he truly deserves!

LINEUP

CA	George *Birdie* Tebbetts

handled chores behind the plate for 14 seasons (gave three years to his country) in the American League. Four times he was voted to the All-Star squad. Birdie led all backstops in assists three consecutive summers (1939-41). He went on to manage 11 campaigns in the Majors.

1B	Jake *Eagle Eye* Beckley

is a Hall of Famer. During his 20 seasons he ripped 2930 hits, which rank him tied for 25th. Thirteen summers Eagle Eye hit over .300. His 244 career triples were only topped by three players! Fourteen campaigns Eagle Eye legged out ten or more three baggers.

2B	Sammy *Dixie Thrush* Strang

hailed from Chattanooga, Tennessee, contributing to his nickname. He starred ten years at the turn of the century. The Dixie Thrush was a versatile ballplayer. He played all infield positions, plus some outfield. In 1902 Sammy hit .295 and scored 108 tallies (third in AL).

SS	Ron *The Beak* Hansen

sparkled 15 years in the Junior Circuit. The AL's Rookie of the Year in 1960, Ron swatted 22 home runs for the Orioles and made the All-Star team. Four more seasons his homer total reached double figures, but The Beak never approached his first year numbers.

3B	Ron *The Penguin* Cey

helped form the Dodger infield (Cey, Russell, Lopes and Garvey) which held solid from 1973-81. The Penguin, a six time NL All-Star, walloped 20+ homers from 1975-85, only falling short (13) in the strike shortened 1981 season. He finished his career with 316 tators (59th).

OF	Tris *The Grey Eagle* Speaker

had a marvelous 22 year career on his way to the Hall. He was both an outstanding fielder and a superior batsman. The Grey Eagle's career marks of 3514 hits (fifth), 222 triples (sixth), .345 career batting average (seventh) and 1882 runs (eighth) tell his whole amazing story.

OF	Leon *Goose* Goslin

soared for 18 campaigns in the American League. From 1922-28 he hit .300 or more and he captured the batting crown in 1928 (.379). Eleven seasons Goose drove in 100+ runs. His 1609 career ribbies rank him 20th. Goose is a member of the Hall of Fame.

OF	Andre *The Hawk* Dawson

has already starred 19 seasons (through 1994). He is the complete player, hitting for both power and average, and playing great defensively! The Hawk has amassed 491 doubles and 428 dingers. With the aid of his rifle arm, Andre has won eight Gold Gloves in his great career!

P	Lon *Arkansas Hummingbird* Warneke

threw hummers for 15 summers. Only three times did he have a losing record. The Arkansas Hummingbird retired with a .615 winning % (52nd). From 1932-35 he won 22 18, 22 and 20 games. Lon's 22 wins, .786 winning %, 2.37 ERA and four shutouts (tie) all topped the NL in 1932!

P	Rich *Goose* Gossage

was a reliever extraordinaire over 22 seasons. The Goose marched in from the pen 900+ times, winning over 100 contests and saving more than 300 games! Rich, known for his heater, averaged 7.47 whiffs per nine innings during his entire career, 17th best!

P	Phil *The Vulture* Regan

was originally a starter for the Tigers. Traded to the Dodgers, The Vulture became their stopper. In 1966, his first season in Blue, he swooped into 65 games, went 14-1 and led the NL with 21 saves! From 1966-71 The Vulture averaged 61 games, nine wins and 14+ saves.

RES	*Turkey* Mike Donlin

was tabbed Turkey by his strut when he walked out to the diamond. He was an outstanding hitter. Turkey Mike finished third in batting in 1901 and 1903 and he placed second in 1901 and 1908! In 1908 Turkey Mike was voted, by the fans, baseball's most popular player!

RES	Ken *Hawk* Harrelson

played nine seasons in the Junior Circuit, but only five summers over 100 games. No matter, when Hawk "suited up," he was a force. In 1968 Ken poled 35 dingers (third) and drove in a league leading 109 runs! Hawk then belted 30 HR's and plated 92 runs in 1969.

RES	Clay *Hawk* Carroll

sparkled for 15 campaigns. A stopper his entire career, he flew in from the pen 703 times. From 1966-75 Hawk averaged 61+ games, twice leading the league. 1972 was his best campaign. Hawk made 65 appearances (first) and led the National League in saves with 37.

RES	Charlie *Cuckoo* Jamieson

also was known as The Hawk. He played 18 summers, all in the Junior Circuit. From 1919-31 Cuckoo hit over .300 ten times and never batted lower than .291! In 1924 he topped the American League in both at bats and hits, ranked second in runs and hit .345.

L to R: Ron *The Penguin* Cey, Leon *Goose* Goslin, Andre *The Hawk* Dawson, Rich *Goose* Gossage, Tris *The Grey Eagle* Speaker

It'sa FACT

Jake **Eagle Eye** Beckley: He had 23,709 putouts at first base, making Eagle Eye the all time leader.

Tris **The Grey Eagle** Speaker: His 792 doubles place The Grey Eagle first all time! The Grey Eagle also topped all outfielders in career assists! In addition, he was nearly impossible to fan. At the age of 39 Tris whiffed only eight times in 523 at bats!

Andre **The Hawk** Dawson: On July 30th, 1978 he slugged two homers in one inning! After 11 seasons with the Expos, The Hawk (in 1987) signed a blank contract (management to fill in what they wanted to pay him) to play for the Cubbies. He responded by leading the National League in homers and RBI's, and by winning the MVP!

William **Birdie** Cree: He was the Yankees left fielder eight summers. In 1911 Birdie hit .348 (fifth) with 22 triples (second) and swiped 48 bags (third).

Charlie **Eagle Eye** Hemphill: He was consistently among the league leaders in free passes, hence the nickname.

Ron **The Penguin** Cey: His nickname was easily coined. All you had to do was watch him run.

Joe **Duck** Lahoud: For his 11 year career he poled only 65 dingers, but on June 11th, 1969 Duck hit three HR's.

Joe **Ducky** Medwick: His 1937 season was unbelievable! Ducky led the National league in at bats (633), hits (237), doubles (56), homers (31-tie), runs (111), RBI's (154), total bases (406), slugging % (.641) and batting average (.374). Ducky was voted the MVP!

Mark **The Bird** Fidrych: With his long curly locks hanging out below the back of his cap, he was nicknamed after Big Bird on Sesame Street. In 1976, his inaugural season, The Bird was voted the AL Rookie of the Year, was the starting pitcher in the All-Star game and finished second for the Cy Young award! Mark went 19-9 with a league leading 2.34 ERA and he topped all hurlers with 24 complete games! A bum arm limited him to ten victories during the remainder of his career.

William **Pol** Perritt: From 1914-18 he won 81 games and recorded 23 shutouts! In 1917 Pol went 17-7, tossed five shutouts and posted an amazing 1.88 ERA!

Ralph **Hawk** Branca: In 1947 he dominated the Senior Circuit . Hawk's 36 starts (first), 148 K's (second), 280 innings (second), 21 wins (tie for second) and 2.67 ERA (third) carried the Dodgers to the Series.

Lon **Arkansas Hummingbird** Warneke: He went 2-0 in the 1935 Fall Classic, the Cubs only two wins. After throwing balls and strikes for 15 years, the Arkansas Hummingbird called them for seven more seasons.

Ken **Hawk** Harrelson: Along with his partner Wimpy (Tom Paciorek), he does the TV announcing for the Chicago White Sox. They do a fantastic job!

Leon **Goose** Goslin: His 173 career triples rank Goose 22nd in Major League history.

TRIVIA*

1) When he went into his windup, he paused for a long time on one leg. It led to his nickname.
2) He participated in more World Series (as either a player or a coach) than any other player.
3) He was the National League's last Triple Crown winner.
4) In back to back World Series this star hit three home runs in each Fall Classic.
5) He was considered, in his time, to be one of baseball's top players. "High Lonesome" married a famous vaudeville comedian and quit in mid career to act for two years, before resuming his ball playing career.
6) To help balance our trade deficit, this future Hall of Famer played in Japan one season.
7) Noted for playing a shallow center field, he completed four unassisted double plays!
8) He "rescued" Steve Garvey from third base when he came up with the Dodgers.
9) He was the first player to ever homer in his initial at bat in the Majors (April 16th, 1887).
10) His fifth relief stint during the 1975 World Series earned the victory for he and his Red's teammates in game #7. This Classic is considered, by many, the greatest World Series ever played!
11) Talking to himself and doing mound 'landscaping' were two of his quirks.
12) His promising career was ended at the young age of 26 from a hunting accident, which caused his leg to be amputated.
13) His 64 two baggers in 1936 are still the National League's standard.
14) This shortstop did the first unassisted triple play in 41 years and ninth all time (July 29th, 1968).
15) He saw them go from worst to best, playing his entire career for the New York Mets.

* BIRD BRAINERS answers found on page 235

ROSTER / LINGO

CATCHERS:	Yr	Hits	AB's	Ave
George *Birdie* Tebbetts	14	1000	3704	.270
Robert *Hawk* Taylor	11	158	724	.218
Danny *Beak* Kravitz	5	130	552	.236
Byrd *Birdie* Lynn	5	50	211	.237
Ken *Hawk* Silvestri	8	44	203	.217
George *Ducky* Hale	4	18	103	.175
Frank *Dodo* Bird	1	10	50	.200
Howard *Ducky* Holmes	1	5	27	.185
Charles *Sparrow* McCaffrey	1	1	1	1.000
George *Dodo* Armstrong	1	1	6	.167
William *Ducky* Pearce	2	0	4	.000

1ST BASEMEN:	Yr	Hits	AB's	Ave
Jake *Eagle Eye* Beckley	20	2930	9526	.308
Ed *Krane* Kranepool	18	1418	5436	.261
Ken *Hawk* Harrelson	9	703	2941	.239
Fred *Wingy* Whitfield	9	578	2284	.253
Prentice *Pidge* Browne	1	21	100	.210

2ND BASEMEN:	Yr	Hits	AB's	Ave
Frank *Bald Eagle* Isbell	10	1056	4219	.250
Sammy *Dixie Thrush* Strang	10	790	2933	.269
Marv *Ugly Duckling* Breeding	4	317	1268	.250
Harry *Bird Eye* Truby	2	73	260	.281

SHORTSTOPS:	Yr	Hits	AB's	Ave
Ron *The Beak* Hansen	15	1007	4311	.234
Dick *Ducky* Schofield	19	699	3083	.227
Ollie *Polish Falcon* Bejma	4	222	906	.245
Ewell *Turkey* Gross	1	3	32	.094
Joe *Tweet* Walsh	1	0	8	.000

3RD BASEMEN:	Yr	Hits	AB's	Ave
Ron *The Penguin* Cey	17	1868	7162	.261
Frank *Crow* Crosetti	17	1541	6277	.245
Bob *Ducky* Jones	9	791	2990	.265
Robert *Ducky* Detweiler	2	14	45	.311
James *Dodo* Lane	1	1	15	.067
Paul *Birdie* Speraw	1	0	2	.000

OUTFIELDERS:	Yr	Hits	AB's	Ave
Tris *The Grey Eagle* Speaker	22	3314	10196	.345
Leon *Goose* Goslin	18	2735	8656	.316
Andre *The Hawk* Dawson	19	2700	9643	.280
Joe *Ducky* Medwick	17	2471	7635	.324
Charlie *Cuckoo* Jamieson	18	1990	6560	.303

OUTFIELDERS: (Cont.)	Yr	Hits	AB's	Ave
Bill *Quail* Virdon	12	1596	5980	.267
Dave *Big Bird* Kingman	16	1575	6677	.236
Turkey Mike Donlin	12	1282	3854	.333
Charlie *Eagle Eye* Hemphill	11	1230	4541	.271
James *Ducky* Holmes	10	1014	3601	.282
William *Birdie* Cree	8	761	2603	.292
Joe *Duck* Lahoud	11	429	1925	.223
Walt *Cuckoo* Christensen	2	162	514	.315
George *Stork* Theodore	2	42	192	.219
William *Ducky* Hemp	2	25	117	.214
Aaron *Hawk* Pointer	3	21	101	.208
George *White Wings* Proeser	2	20	76	.263
Bill *Hawk* Mueller	2	14	94	.149
George *Partridge* Adams	1	3	13	.231
Charles *Ducky* Oertel	1	2	12	.167
John *Goose* Easton	2	0	3	.000

PINCH HITTER:	Yr	Hits	AB's	Ave
Cecil *Turkey* Tyson	1	0	0	.000

PITCHERS:	Yr	Won	Lost	ERA
Lon *Arkansas Hummingbird* Warneke	15	192	121	3.18
Rich *Goose* Gossage	22	124	107	3.01
Marty *Duck* Pattin	13	114	109	3.62
Clay *Hawk* Carroll	15	96	73	2.94
Phil *The Vulture* Regan	13	96	81	3.84
William *Pol* Perritt	10	92	78	2.89
Ralph *Hawk* Branca	12	88	68	3.79
Bill *Stork* Travers	9	65	71	4.10
Jim *Emu* Kern	13	53	57	3.32
Monte *Gander* Stratton	5	36	23	3.71
Mark *The Bird* Fidrych	5	29	19	3.10
James *Jay Bird* Hook	8	29	62	5.23
Frank *Crane* Reberger	5	14	15	4.52
Wynn *Hawk* Hawkins	3	12	13	4.17
Tom *Gray Flamingo* Brennan	5	9	10	4.40
Gene *Blue Goose* Moore	3	2	2	4.76
William *Crow* Spanswick	1	2	1	6.89
Johnny *Ducky* Tillman	1	1	0	0.90
Herbert *Ducky* Yount	1	1	1	4.14
Harry *Ducky* Swan	1	0	0	0.00
Bill *Bird Dog* Hopper	3	0	4	4.18
William *Sparrow* Morton	1	0	2	5.29
Garland *Duck* Shifflet	2	0	2	6.31
Tom *Little Hawk* Long	1	0	0	9.00

Ducks on the Pond: Runners in scoring position, waiting to be batted in

Hit a Dying Quail: Poorly hit ball that falls in front of the outfielder

Ruffles His Feathers: Upsets a player

Put up Goose Eggs: Allow no runs, zeroes up on the scoreboard

Flutterball: A knuckleball

Ball Hawk: A very fast outfielder who catches everything

Loosey Goosey: Calm and cool under pressure

Sitting in the Catbird Seat: Advantage (A "Red" Barber expression)

Shakes Him Off: Pitcher rejects his catcher's pitch choice

BODY PARTS

5

Team

It is no wonder that body parts form a nickname group. Everyone is aware of other peoples' appearance. If for some reason an individual has a physical flaw or oddity, it does not take kids very long to tab him. Many of the players in this group 'gained' their monikers naturally.

Although no body part is sacred from nicknames, some areas do command more attention than others. Head and feet stand out. Led by Zeke Banana Nose Bonura and Hall of Famer Ernie The Schnozz Lombardi, many Major Leaguers are known by their beaks, not to mention their eyes, dimples, jaw and chin. As for feet, one goes from Twinkletoes, Footsie and Footer, to Bigfoot, Slewfoot and Satchelfoot. I nearly forgot arms and legs. There are not only Rubber Arms, a Crooked Arm and a Glass Arm, but also Piano Legs, a Rubberleg and even Babe Ruth's Legs! Even though baseball at the Major League level is an all male group, there are some interesting 'female' body part nicknames. There are three Boobs, two Butts, The Lip, a Baby Face and Brains (Ladies, note I did include brains in <u>your</u> group!).

In reviewing this fun list that includes six members of the Hall of Fame and many well-known stars, one nickname, above all others, caught my fancy. I read it and smiled. I reread it and roared. Then I gave it the acid test. I had my wife Linda read it. She could not hold back a smile (trust me, she is tough). His name is Doug Eyechart Gwosdz. You gotta love nicknames!

LINEUP

| CA | Ernie *The Schnozz* Lombardi | starred 17 campaigns in his Hall of Fame career. Bocci was a seven time All-Star in the Senior Circuit. Offensively, in 1938, The Schnozz led the league in hitting and was voted the National League's MVP. Defensively, Ernie had a strong arm and was a great plate blocker. |

| 1B | Charles *Piano Legs* Hickman | was a versatile star, playing, during his career, every position. In 1900 Piano Legs finished second (tie) in triples and fourth in dingers. He led the AL in hits in 1902, finishing second (tie) in homers and batting. In 1903 Cheerful Charlie placed second in both dingers and RBI's. |

| 2B | Max *Camera Eye* Bishop | started nine (1925-33) of his 12 seasons. In those nine years, although no slugger, Tilly finished no lower than fourth in the AL in free passes, hence his nickname. Averaging 109 walks and hitting .274, Camera Eye's OBA was high. It helped him score 100+ runs four times. |

| SS | Leo *The Lip* Durocher | overlapped 17 playing seasons with 24 managing campaigns. The Lip brought home three pennants and seven seconds, winning 2000+ games during his skippering tenure. Known to argue with the "men in blue", Leo parlayed his feisty career to the shores of Lake Otsego. |

| 3B | Michael *Pinky* Higgins | was a three time American League All-Star at the hot corner. A model of consistency, for 12 seasons (1933-44) Pinky slugged 20+ doubles, slashed 130+ hits, drove in 73+ runs and never hit less than .267. During his career, five campaigns Pinky plated 90+ tallies. |

| OF | *Bucketfoot* Al Simmons | is a Hall of Famer. Al drove in over 100 runs in each of his first 11 seasons, three times plating over 150 runs! Six times he topped 200 hits, including five consecutive years (1929-33). A career .334 hitter, Bucketfoot Al led the league twice in hitting (1930 - .381 and 1931 - .390). |

| OF | Joe *Muscles* Medwick | was better known as Ducky, but his teammates tabbed him Muscles. This Hall of Famer hit .300+ eleven consecutive seasons! Six straight years Muscles drove in over 100 runs, peaking with 154 ribbies in 1937. His 540 career doubles place him 15th. |

| OF | George *Piano Legs* Gore | was a 19th century star, playing 14 summers. Eight times George hit over .300, leading the league with a lusty .360 in 1880. Three times Piano Legs topped the league in walks. His high on base % helped allow him to score 1.01 runs per game for his career, second all time. |

| P | Phil *Knucksie* Niekro | was an amazing competitor. His 318 career wins were bettered by only 13 twirlers. Phil, very quietly, led the league in innings (four), complete games (four), wins (two), ERA (one), and strikeouts (one) during his career. His 3342 K's rank Knucksie eighth overall. |

| P | Mordecai *Three Finger* Brown | was injured in a farm accident, losing his forefinger and permanently damaging his middle finger. From 1906-10 Three Finger was nearly unbeatable. He went 26-6, 20-6, 29-9, 27-9 and 25-14, with ERA's of 1.04, 1.39, 1.47, 1.31 and 1.86 and tossed 40 shutouts! |

| P | Eddie *Knuckles* Cicotte | was an outstanding pitcher for 14 years. His career ended in 1920 when he was banned from baseball due to the Black Sox scandal. Three campaigns Knuckles won over 20 games, twice leading the American League in wins, winning % and innings, and once leading in ERA. |

| RES | Ferris *Burrhead* Fain | came into his own his fifth season (1951), when he led all American League batters in hitting (.344). It was Ferris' first .300+ season. Not to be a fluke, Burrhead, in 1952, again led all hitters in batting average (.327), plus topped the league in doubles! |

| RES | Arthur *Pinky* Whitney | was a great third sacker. A starter in 11 of his 12 seasons, Pinky drove in over 100 runs four of his first five seasons, including 124 in 1932 (third in NL). His .342 average in 1930 was his best, but it was followed closely by .341 (1937) and .327 (1929). Pinky led in fielding % three years. |

| RES | Paul *Motormouth* Blair | played a great center field for 17 summers. Fleet footed, Paul played shallow. This combination allowed him to rob batters of many would-be hits and stuff opposing teams during their potential rallies! Motormouth won eight Gold Gloves for his defensive prowess! |

| COA | Johnny *Man of 1000 Curves* Sain | was not only both a great pitcher (139 wins) and excellent with the stick (hit .346 in 1947), but he also was an outstanding instructor. Johnny was the pitching coach for the Minnesota Twins from 1965 through 1966. That was one of six stops during his 17 year coaching career. |

L to R: Leo *The Lip* Durocher, Ernie *The Schnozz* Lombardi, *Bucketfoot* Al Simmons, Phil *Knucksie* Niekro, Mordecai *Three Finger* Brown

It'sa FACT

Mordecai **Three Finger** Brown: In 1906 he had a 1.04 ERA, the second best in baseball history. His 2.06 career ERA is the third best ever. Mordecai won five World Series games, including three by shutout. Little Napoleon, John McGraw, considered having his pitchers' forefingers amputated, so they, too, could get Three Finger's unusual spin on their pitches! (A good reason for a union.)

George **Piano Legs** Gore: On July 16th, 1888 he had five outfield assists in one game (record held by two players).

Johnny **Man of 1000 Curves** Sain: After serving for three years during WW II, he was back in the Majors at age 28 and strung together four 20+ win seasons during the next five summers. Johnny's 24 victories in 1948 topped the Senior Circuit. Boston's 1948 season slogan (due to a weak pitching staff) was "Spahn and Sain, then pray for rain."

Walt **No-Neck** Williams: He played full time one season, 1969. Walt responded, finishing sixth in batting (.304).

Roscoe **Rubberlegs** Miller: In 1901 he went 23-13, the third most wins by a Junior Circuit rookie. His 322 innings is the AL rookie record.

Glass Arm Eddie Brown: He played his first full year while turning 33. In that and the next three seasons, Eddie batted over .300. He led the NL in hits in 1926 with 201 safeties and finished third in batting (.326).

Henry **Banana Nose** Bonura: He crushed the ball for seven seasons. Playing concurrently with several of baseball's great first sackers (Hammerin' Hank Greenberg, Lou The Iron Horse Gehrig, Jimmie The Beast Foxx and Hal Trosky), Banana Nose was easily overlooked. For his career, Zeke averaged 33+ doubles, 17 homers and 100+ RBI's! He also led the league in fielding % for three summers!

Don **Footsie** Lenhardt: As a rookie in 1950 he pounded 22 homers.

Phil **Knucksie** Niekro: At age 30 he had amassed only 31 wins. By the 'old' age of 40, Phil had 197 wins and just kept going. Before retiring at the "young" age of 48, Knucksie had won another 121 games, finishing with 318 career wins!

Joe **Burrhead** Dobson: For 13+ seasons he consistently performed. From 1946-53 Joe never had a losing year. During the 1946-50 summers Burrhead tallied 76 victories, plus he won game #5 in the 1946 World Series.

Rollie **Bunions** Zeider: In his two most complete seasons, Bunions stole 49 and 47 sacks, ranking him third and fifth.

Willie **Puddin' Head** Jones: He was nicknamed after the song. A two time All-Star, Willie excelled both on the field and at the plate. From 1952-56 Puddin' Head led all third sackers in fielding % (tying the record of five consecutive seasons). Seven times he was tops in putouts. Over his career, Puddin' Head connected for 190 homers.

Michael **Pinky** Higgins: He had a Major League record 12 consecutive hits in 1938 (later tied by Walt Moose Dropo).

Max **Camera Eye** Bishop: He set the record for best fielding % ever for second basemen in 1926. Camera Eye broke his own record in 1932 (Bobby Grich now holds the record, set in 1985).

Merrill **Pinky** May: Although he played only five seasons, his son Milt caught in the Majors for 15 summers.

Eric **Boob** McNair: In 1932, playing in only 135 games, Boob (spell Boob backwards) led the AL with 47 doubles, plus had career highs in yard shots (18) and ribbies (95).

Arthur **Pinky** Whitney: He led NL third sackers in assists (four), putouts (three), double plays (three) and fielding % (three) during his career.

Ed **Satchelfoot** Wells: In 1926 he led the AL in shutouts.

George **Twinkletoes** Selkirk: He was an all-around player. A two time All-Star, George led all fly chasers in fielding % in 1939. Better remembered for his World Series play, Twinkletoes was a force in 1936. He went 8/24 with two homers, leading the Yanks over their cross-town rival, the Giants. In 1937 the two teams met again. Twinkletoes topped all Yanks with six RBI's in their five game win.

Phil **Knucksie** Niekro: On May 29th, 1976, he pitched against his brother Joe. Phil and Atlanta won the game 4-3. Knucksie did give up a solo shot, the only homer this player ever hit in his career. His brother Joe took him deep!

Blind Ryne Duren: He was a dominating relief pitcher in the early sixties. Blessed with a tremendous fast ball and questionable control (to keep batters loose), Ryne sat down hitters at over one per inning for his entire career! Blind Ryne whiffed 630 players in 589 innings, a rate of 9.63 per game. With more career innings, he would have ranked first all time!

Johnny **Footsie** Marcum: On September 7th, 1933 and September 11th, 1933 he fired consecutive shutouts. These were his first two Major League starts! Footsie won 17 games, plus batted a lofty .311 and pounded two homers in 1935.

TRIVIA*

1) His bases on balls % was 20.42, second only to Ted The Kid Williams. Five times in his career he had more free passes than hits in a season. It led to his nickname.

2) He and his brother (John Peter) combined for 3474 career hits.

3) He used the longest bat in baseball history, 38 inches. His batting style earned him his nickname.

4) Seven consecutive seasons he slashed 40 or more doubles! In 1936 he set the NL two bagger record with 64.

5) In late innings he replaced Babe Ruth in the outfield.

6) When the Babe was traded, he became the Yankee's new right fielder.

7) Along with his brother "Emery Board" Joe, these siblings won 539 games, the highest brother win total ever!

8) Born Peter Wyshner, he played the game as no other player ever did.

9) He shares the record of reaching base seven times in a nine inning game. Losing a fly ball in the sun, it bounced off his head, coining his nickname forever.

10) In 1978 he went 15-2. He was 12-2 in 49 relief appearances and 3-0 in three starts.

11) His two out successful suicide squeeze bunt scored the 12th inning run, helping the Orioles win the first ALCS game ever played.

12) In the 1982 ALCS (best of five that season), down 2-0 in games, he saved games #3 and #5. He fanned five of the ten batters he faced and he allowed no hits, runs or walks.

13) In the 1968 Fall Classic he slugged two triples in one game (Mark Lemke duplicated this in 1991). In 1966 he led the league in three baggers, the only NL catcher to do this.

14) This hurler ranks 14th all time in pitcher's batting average. He ranks first in triples (28) and seventh in hits (389). Later an umpire, he called the balls and strikes in the Toney/Vaughn "double no-hitter".

15) Fiery John McGraw gave him his nickname. He was the brave umpire who, on September 23rd, 1908, called Fred Merkle out for not touching second base, costing the Giants and McGraw the pennant.

16) His glasses were as thick as coke bottle bottoms and his hummer was clocked at 100 mph!

17) Born Aloys Szymanski, in Brewtown (Sudsville), he was also called the Duke of Milwaukee.

18) In 1933 the NL and AL Philadelphia teams each had a third baseman with the same nickname.

19) Known as slow footed, he nevertheless shares the Major League record of legging out four doubles in one game.

20) He was also known as Bye-Bye, because he bashed so many homers.

21) He made famous the quote "Good guys finish last!"

22) On July 29th, 1977, in inning #6, he fanned four batters.

23) It seems this slugger would never break a smile, hence his nickname.

24) He just talked and talked, so he was tabbed his nickname.

25) In 1935 he had an unbelievable season. Playing in only 138 games, he had 211 hits, scored 152 runs and drove in 165 runs! To top it off, he led all hitters, batting .381.

* EYEBROW WRINKLERS answers found on page 235

ROSTER

CATCHERS:	Yr	Hits	AB's	Ave
Ernie *The Schnozz* Lombardi	17	1792	5855	.306
Tim *Buckethead* McCarver	21	1501	5529	.271
William *Pinky* Hargrave	10	445	1601	.278
Fred *Bootnose* Hofmann	9	247	1000	.247
Ed *Dimples* Tate	6	179	822	.218
Danny *Beak* Kravitz	5	130	552	.236
Doug *Eyechart* Gwosdz	4	15	104	.144
Joe *Gummy* Wall	2	12	40	.300
Connie *Stone Face* Murphy	2	3	21	.143

1ST BASEMEN:	Yr	Hits	AB's	Ave
Jake *Eagle Eye* Beckley	20	2930	9526	.308
Charles *Piano Legs* Hickman	12	1176	3982	.295
Ferris *Burrhead* Fain	9	1139	3930	.290
Zeke *Banana Nose* Bonura	7	1099	3582	.307
Steve *Bones* Balboni	11	714	3120	.229
Hugh *Corns* Bradley	5	238	913	.261
Chris *Pinky* Lindsay	2	200	828	.242
Carroll *Footsie* Belardi	6	143	592	.242
Emanuel *Redleg* Snyder	2	41	257	.160
Fenton *Muscles* Mole	1	5	27	.185

2ND BASEMEN:	Yr	Hits	AB's	Ave
Max *Camera Eye* Bishop	12	1216	4494	.271
Dick *Brains* Padden	9	814	3157	.258
Rollie *Bunions* Zeider	9	769	3210	.240
Clarence *Footsie* Blair	3	243	890	.273
Tim *Good Eye* Shinnick	2	224	936	.239
Fred *Muscles* Vaughn	2	91	377	.241

SHORTSTOPS:	Yr	Hits	AB's	Ave
William *Bones* Ely	14	1331	5159	.258
Leo *The Lip* Durocher	17	1320	5350	.247
Eric *Boob* McNair	14	1240	4519	.274
Ron *The Beak* Hansen	15	1007	4311	.234
Clarke *Pinky* Pittinger	7	252	959	.263
Tom *Muscles* Upton	3	118	525	.225
Tom *The Arm* Hafey	2	67	270	.248
Joseph *Boob* Fowler	4	57	175	.326

3RD BASEMEN:	Yr	Hits	AB's	Ave
Michael *Pinky* Higgins	14	1941	6636	.292
Arthur *Pinky* Whitney	12	1701	5765	.295
Willie *Puddin' Head* Jones	15	1502	5826	.258
Merrill *Pinky* May	5	610	2215	.275
Albert *Butts* Wagner	1	59	261	.226

OUTFIELDERS:	Yr	Hits	AB's	Ave
Bucketfoot Al Simmons	20	2927	8759	.334
Joe *Muscles* Medwick	17	2471	7635	.324
George *Piano Legs* Gore	14	1612	5357	.301
Paul *Motormouth* Blair	17	1513	6042	.250
Jeff *Convict Face* Leonard	14	1342	5045	.266

OUTFIELDERS: (Cont.)	Yr	Hits	AB's	Ave
Charlie *Eagle Eye* Hemphill	11	1230	4541	.271
Cliff *Rubberhead* Heathcote	15	1222	4443	.275
Glass Arm Eddie Brown	7	878	2902	.303
George *Twinkletoes* Selkirk	9	810	2790	.290
Bris *Human Eyeball* Lord	8	707	2767	.256
Walt *No-Neck* Williams	10	640	2373	.270
Sammy *Babe Ruth's Legs* Byrd	8	465	1700	.274
Uriah *Bloody Jake* Evans	7	435	1831	.238
Don *Footsie* Lenhardt	5	401	1481	.271
Benny *Earache* Meyer	4	276	1041	.265
Joe *Muscles* Gallagher	2	133	487	.273
Nick *Tomato Face* Cullop	5	122	490	.249
Johnny *Patcheye* Gill	6	79	322	.245
One Armed Pete Gray	1	51	234	.218
Bill *Square Jaw* Ramsey	1	40	137	.292
Ed *Pinky* Swander	2	14	52	.269
Bob *Arch* Lennon	3	13	79	.165
Carl *Pinky* Jorgensen	1	4	14	.286
John *Skins* Jones	2	2	10	.200

PINCH HITTER:	Yr	Hits	AB's	Ave
Dick *Footer* Johnson	1	0	5	.000

PITCHERS:	Yr	Won	Lost	ERA
Phil *Knucksie* Niekro	24	318	274	3.35
Mordecai *Three Finger* Brown	14	239	130	2.06
Eddie *Knuckles* Cicotte	14	208	149	2.38
Al *Curveless Wonder* Orth	15	204	189	3.37
Emerson *Pink* Hawley	10	167	179	3.96
Johnny *Man of 1000 Curves* Sain	11	139	116	3.49
Joe *Burrhead* Dobson	14	137	103	3.62
Bob *Bigfoot* Stanley	13	115	97	3.64
Fred *Great Stoneface* Hutchinson	10	95	71	3.73
George *Old Wax Finger* Hemming	8	91	82	4.53
Hugh *One Arm* Daily	6	73	87	2.92
Allan *Rubberarm* Russell	11	71	76	3.52
Ed *Satchelfoot* Wells	11	68	69	4.65
Johnny *Footsie* Marcum	7	65	63	4.66
Barry *Shoulders* Latman	11	59	68	3.91
Bob *Foot* Locker	10	57	39	2.75
Claude *Jaws* Lockwood	12	57	97	3.55
Gene *Rubber Arm* Krapp	4	40	47	3.23
Roscoe *Rubberlegs* Miller	4	39	45	3.45
Blind Ryne Duren	10	27	44	3.83
Marv *Baby Face* Breuer	5	25	26	4.03
Willie *The Knuck* Ramsdell	5	24	39	3.83
Tom *Shoulder* Acker	4	19	13	4.12
Pete *Bigfoot* Ladd	6	17	23	4.14
Emmett *Pinky* O'Neill	4	15	26	4.76
Norm *Bones* Baker	3	14	15	3.42
Ralph *Bruz* Hamner	4	8	20	4.58
Frank *Limb* McKenry	2	6	6	3.10
Dick *Legs* Weik	5	6	22	5.90

ROSTER

PITCHERS: (Cont.)	Yr	Won	Lost	ERA
Archie *Lumbago* Stimmel	3	5	19	4.21
Cecil *Slewfoot* Butler	2	2	0	3.31
Chet *Chesty* Covington	1	1	1	4.66
Frank *Ribs* Raney	2	1	3	7.36
Floyd *Three-Finger* Newkirk	1	0	0	0.00
Walter *Footie* Ockey	1	0	0	3.38
Walter *Liver* Ancker	1	0	0	3.57
Walker *Foots* Cress	2	0	1	4.35
Bob *Crooked Arm* Cremins	1	0	0	5.06

PITCHERS: (Cont.)	Yr	Won	Lost	ERA
Robert *Bun* Troy	1	0	1	5.40
Jim *Bones* Blackburn	2	0	2	5.50
Ralph *Human Whipcord* Savidge	2	0	1	5.76

EXTRAS:
William *Little Joe Chest* McGowan - Umpire
Blind Bob Emslie - Umpire
Roy *Pinky* Bomgren - Great Guy
Don *The Eye* Riley - Great Sports Columnist

LINGO

Foot in the Bucket: Batter's front foot strides toward the corner base rather than the pitcher

Backstop: Catcher

Boner: A stupid play

Bonehead Play: See above stupid

A Skull: See two above definitions

Bottom: The lower half of the inning, when the home team bats

Throw a Curve: Fake a person out

No Hands: Terrible fielder

Double-header: Play two games in a row on one day

Brushback: A pitch meant to be high and inside

Split Finger: A pitch held between the fore and middle finger and when thrown, drops quickly as it reaches the plate. Its "father" is Roger Craig

Plant Foot: Batter's back foot

Knuckle Ball: A pitch, held by the knuckles or finger tips, which does not spin, causing it to dance or flutter

Palm Ball: A pitch held in the hand, losing wrist action. It has less speed, like a change up

Heads Up: Be alert

Leg Hitter: Batter who relies on his speed to get on base

Stick It in Your Ear: A high inside pitch

Meat Hand: The one with no glove on it

Rag Arm: Pitcher who can throw with little rest

Rubber Arm: Player who can easily pitch with little rest or warm-up

Ribbies: Runs batted in

Hard Nosed: Plays the game hard

Hit on the Nose: Hit the ball solidly

Ball Has Eyes: Batted ball somehow eludes the fielder

Seeing Eye Hit: Squint above

Keep Your Eye on the Ball: Ouch!

Skin: Dirt part of the infield

Side Out: One team has three outs

Given the Thumb: Thrown out of a game

Thumbed Out: See above

Toe Hold: Pitcher's foot (same as his pitching arm). He places his foot tip in the hole in front on the rubber, when starting his wind up (boy, this sounds complicated, unless you have pitched!)

Soft Touch: Pitcher that is easy to hit

Toe Plate: Leather piece on pitcher's "arm" foot toe allowing his shoe's tip to not wear out when he gets a toe hold (that wasn't so bad!)

Fisted One: A hit where the ball contacts the bat just above your grip

Back to the Wall: You can go nowhere. You must win this game or it is all over

Reaches Back for More: Pitcher needs a big pitch, so he sucks it up, goes to the well and gives him the dark one (how's that?)

Legged Out a Hit: Ran fast enough to reach first ahead of the ball

Heady Play: Opposite of a skull, a smart play

Muscled One: Swung hard and hit weakly, but by the strength of the swing, it had enough to fall in for a hit

Kicked It Around: Failed to field a ball

Head Hunting: Pitcher throws at the batter's head

Looks at a Pitch: Batter does not swing

Chin Music: Pitcher throws at the batter's head

Busting His Butt: Running and playing very hard

Face the Pitcher: Bat against him

Face the Batter: Pitch against him

Short Arm One: Throw without bringing your arm all the way back

Side Arm: Fire the ball across your body rather than "over the top"

One Handed Catch: When a player uses only his glove

Two Handed Catch: Player uses both his glove and his meat hand

Real BREWERS

6

Team

Milwaukee, also known as the Hops Capital of the World, had lost its Braves to Atlanta in 1965. The Seattle community received an expansion team in 1969, the Pilots. After one season, the struggling franchise headed to Wisconsin. It took a few seasons, but a triumvirate of players evolved to anchor the Brewers. Robin Yount (1974-93) came first. He won two MVPs, one in 1982 and a second in 1989. Jim Gumby Gantner and Paul Molly Molitor both joined the Crew in 1978 and stayed through 1992. For 15 seasons fans had three outstanding cornerstones on their club. Another long standing fixture is County Stadium. No, it is neither new nor does it have "high buck super boxes," but it is an intimate ballpark with its box seats right at field level. Of all the home parks I have been to, Milwaukee crowds are the best! No three piece suits here, just plaid shirts ordering beer and rooting for the home team.

The Real Brewers recognize the fact that Milwaukee is fondly known as Brewtown. Also answering to Sudsville, it is home to several beer making establishments. The "King of Beers" receives some free publicity from this squad. There are 39 Buds on the roster, plus 30 Buddies! The Real Brewers, though, are not just a two nickname group. Teammates also include Brewery, Suds and Maltzy; and Brandy, Sour Mash, Stinger and Highball. Definitely a heady team with a lot of spirit!

One player's nickname obviously labels him a premium. His name is mentioned in every bar and tavern across our land. His identity is constantly mentioned on television and radio commercials. Everybody wants him! This Real Brewer was born in 1891. His first name was Harry and his middle name was Budson. Folks called him Bud. His career totals read 74 at bats, 12 hits and a .162 batting average. That is the Major League log on Harry Bud Weiser.

LINEUP

CA	Warren *Buddy* Rosar

was a great defensive catcher. His fielding was perfect in 1946 (1.000). Only five other backstops have had errorless seasons! Buddy's 147 consecutive games without a miscue was topped by one game by the ML record holder Yogi Berra. Buddy led the AL in fielding % four times.

1B	John *Buddy* Hassett

was a hard hitting batter. During his rookie season for the Dodgers (1936), Buddy labeled 197 hits and swatted .310. In the next three summers, he topped .300 two more times. Buddy capped his seven year career with a World Championship his last season.

2B	Charles *Buddy* Myer

sparkled for 17 seasons in the Junior Circuit. Nine summers he hit at least .300 and when he retired, Buddy carried a career .303 average. In 1935 he won the AL batting crown and finished second in hits. Buddy's glove was excellent. He twice led the AL keystoners in fielding %.

SS	Derrel *Bud* Harrelson

was an outstanding glove man and a fiery team leader. Bud was the spirit of the 1969 "Miracle Mets." He was an All-Star selection twice and won the Gold Glove in 1971. Bud had 54 consecutive errorless games one season. After he retired, Bud returned to manage the Mets.

3B	David *Buddy* Bell

was a five time All-Star during his 18 seasons. He played for non-contending teams and subsequently stayed outside of the national spotlight. Buddy was a consistently strong hitter, pounding over 400 doubles, labeling over 200 homers and driving in over 1100 runs during his career.

OF	Harvey's *Wallbangers* Kuenn

was a career .300 hitter. Four years (one tie) he led the American League in base hits and three seasons finished first in doubles. Harvey batted over .300 eight times during his first nine summers. He was named to the All-Star team on eight occasions.

OF	Norm *Suds* Siebern

was a three time All-Star. He had his best campaign in 1962. Suds finished second in the American League in runs scored, bases on balls and RBI's, and placed fifth in batting. He was an everyday player for seven summers (1958-64) and Suds averaged 16 dingers and 75 ribbies.

OF	John *Buddy* Lewis

was a starter 8½ seasons, losing 3½ years to military service. He hit at a .300 clip four summers, retiring with a career .297 average. Three times Buddy stroked 190+ hits and four times he scored over 100 runs. Buddy chugged out a league leading 16 triples in 1939.

P	Harry *Bud* Black

is a 14 year veteran. The southpaw has hurled in both the American League and the National League. In 1984 Bud was the top man on the Royal's staff, leading them to the AL Championship Series with 17 regular season wins. Bud has won in double digits seven times.

P	*Brewery* Jack Taylor

twirled nine seasons in the Senior Circuit, the last seven as a starter. He topped 20 victories three campaigns and accumulated 120 wins during his short career. Brewery Jack was also a fine hitter. He batted .252 and poled five round trippers during his career.

P	Leavitt *Bud* Daley

was a reliever early in his career. In 1959 Harry Craft converted Bud to a starter. He responded with two consecutive All-Star seasons, winning 16 games in both 1959 and 1960. Buddy accomplished this even though his Athletics finished seventh and eighth those two years!

RES	John *Buddy* Kerr

played in the Big Show for nine seasons. Known more for his leather, he topped all National League shortstops in assists, putouts and DP's twice and led in fielding % once. Buddy had an amazing streak! He handled 383 chances in 68 games (July 1946 - May 1947) without a miscue!

RES	John *Bud* Clancy

played nine summers in the Majors. He was an excellent glove man, compiling a career .992% at first base. On April 27th, 1930 Bud accomplished what only two first sackers ever did, playing an entire game with no fielding chances. Three seasons Bud labeled the ball at .300+.

RES	Lee *Stinger* Stange

was a ten year veteran of the American League. He was both a spot starter and a short man during his pitching career. Stinger went 12-5 for Sam Mele's Twins in 1963. He made the record books on September 2nd, 1964 by fanning four batters in one inning!

COA	Gordon *Maltzy* Maltzberger

was used exclusively as a fireman, starring four seasons for the White Sox. He led (one tie) the American League in saves two consecutive summers (1943-44) and for his career, he compiled an outstanding 2.70 ERA. Maltzy was our Minnesota Twins' pitching coach from 1962-64.

L to R: Norm *Suds* Siebern, Harry *Bud* Black, Harvey's *Wallbangers* Kuenn, Derrel *Bud* Harrelson, Leavitt *Bud* Daley

It'sa FACT

Kiner's Korner: Prior to the 1947 season, Pittsburgh traded for Hammerin' Hank Greenberg. To accommodate his right-handed power, the left field wall was "brought in", with a temporary wall being erected and shortening the distance from 365' to 335'. This area (space between the two fences) was originally dubbed "Greenberg's Garden." Ralph Kiner, the 1946 National League homer champ with a paltry 23 dingers, labeled 51 four baggers in 1947, and went on to lead the Senior Circuit in home runs seven consecutive years (the Major League record)! The area was quickly re-nicknamed Kiner's Korner. When Ralph was traded in mid 1953, the temporary wall came down and 365' became the left field wall's distance again.

David ***Buddy*** Bell: Not only was he an outstanding hitter, but Buddy also was a great glove man. Three times he led the American League in fielding % and assists, and twice he topped all hot corner men in putouts and DP's. Buddy ranks fourth all time in games, assists and DP's for third sackers.

John ***Buddy*** Hassett: During his 3517 career at bats, he whiffed only 116 times! Due to World War II, Buddy's career was curtailed and he fell 71 games short of 1000 to qualify for "all time" ranking. His one strikeout per 30.32 at bats would have made him the tenth hardest player to fan. Buddy also shares the National League consecutive hit record of ten (1940).

John ***Buddy*** Lewis: He received his nickname from Charles ***Buddy*** Myer, who was his mentor and teammate.

John ***Buddy*** Kerr: In his first Major League at bat he launched one! In his next 3630 at bats, Buddy hit only 30 more homers.

Daniel ***Bud*** Hafey: His younger brother (by eleven months) was known as "The Arm." In 1939 both Bud and Tom played in the National League.

"Bernie Brewer": When a Brewer wallops a round tripper at home (County Stadium), Bernie slides into a huge beer mug to celebrate!

Roy ***Bud*** Parmelee: He was the number four starter for the Giants in the mid 1930's. From 1933-35 Bud went 13-8, 10-6 and 14-10 for Memphis Bill Terry's New Yorkers.

Brewery Jack Taylor: His playing days ended at age 26, due to his untimely death. During his short career, Brewery Jack was outstanding! He took a regular turn starting in 1894. Brewery Jack responded by winning 23, 26, 20, 16, and 15 games from 1894-98. His 1898 campaign was highlighted by Jack leading all NL hurlers in games, complete games and innings. P.S. His middle name was Budd.

Charles ***Buddy*** Schultz: He was a "shortman" most of his career. Buddy's best season was 1977. He went 4-1 as a reliever and 2-0 as a starter, finishing with an exceptional 2.32 ERA and an outstanding 2.75 to one strikeout to walk ratio.

Harvey ***'s Wallbangers*** Kuenn: In 656 at bats during the 1954 season he fanned only 13 times. That is only once every 50 plate appearances!

Wally ***The Beerman***: The world's greatest vendor!

TRIVIA*

1) He managed the Brew Crew to the 1982 World Series and his nickname is about the team.
2) He and his dad "Gus" (David) combined for 4337 career hits, the most of any father and son in baseball history.
3) Pete Rose's hard slide into him during the 1973 National League Championship Series led to their famous fight.
4) This shortstop turned outfielder was the 1959 American League batting champ.
5) His younger brother "Augie" (Gene) played twelve seasons, nine more than he did.
6) For the 1958 Yankees Sarge Bauer was in right, Mickey was in center, and he patrolled left. He won a Gold Glove for his defensive prowess that season.
7) He was Dizzy Dean's "Pawdner" when they did the Game of the Week during the 50's.
8) He tossed 6 2/3 shutout innings in relief to win the Series clinching game #5 in the 1961 Fall Classic.
9) He was the Junior Circuit's Rookie of the Year in 1953.
10) His middle name is his baseball playing dad's nickname.

* BUD WIZERS answers found on page 235

ROSTER/LINGO

CATCHERS:	Yr	Hits	AB's	Ave
Warren **Buddy** Rosar	13	836	3198	.261
Verne **Stinger** Clemons	7	364	1271	.286
Hollis **Bud** Sheely	3	44	210	.210
William **Buddy** Lewis	3	33	101	.327
Bernie **Bud** Hungling	2	33	137	.241
Richard **Buddy** Booker	2	6	33	.182
Cliff **Bud** Knox	1	4	18	.222
Joe **Jug** Kracher	1	1	5	.200

1ST BASEMEN:	Yr	Hits	AB's	Ave
John **Buddy** Hassett	7	1026	3517	.292
John **Bud** Clancy	9	504	1796	.281
Bayard **Bud** Sharpe	2	139	625	.222
Ray **Buddy** Barker	4	68	318	.214
Louis **Buddy** Gremp	3	65	291	.223
Frank **Buddy** Harris	1	25	95	.263

2ND BASEMEN:	Yr	Hits	AB's	Ave
Charles **Buddy** Myer	17	2131	7038	.303
Robert **Buddy** Blattner	5	176	713	.247
Newell **Bud** Morse	1	2	27	.074
Clyde **Bud** Bloomfield	2	1	7	.143

SHORTSTOPS:	Yr	Hits	AB's	Ave
Derrel **Bud** Harrelson	16	1120	4744	.236
John **Buddy** Kerr	9	903	3631	.249
Bobby **Wine-O** Wine	12	682	3172	.215
Roland **Buddy** Biancalana	6	113	550	.205
Mervin **Bud** Connolly	1	28	107	.262
Clarence **Buddy** Hicks	1	10	47	.213
Carl **Buddy** Peterson	2	9	38	.237
William **Bud** Hardin	1	1	7	.143
Harold **Buddy** Pritchard	1	1	11	.091

3RD BASEMEN:	Yr	Hits	AB's	Ave
David **Buddy** Bell	18	2514	8995	.279
Bill **Suds** Sudakis	8	362	1548	.234
Louis **Buddy** Blair	1	135	484	.279
George **Bud** Freeze	3	48	187	.257
Harold **Buddy** Hunter	3	5	17	.294

OUTFIELDERS:	Yr	Hits	AB's	Ave
Harvey's **Wallbangers** Kuenn	15	2092	6913	.303
John **Buddy** Lewis	11	1563	5261	.297
Norm **Suds** Siebern	12	1217	4481	.272
Charles **Buddy** Bradford	11	363	1605	.226
John **Buddy** Ryan	2	161	571	.282
Dan **Bud** Lally	2	131	498	.263

OUTFIELDERS: (Cont.)	Yr	Hits	AB's	Ave
Daniel **Bud** Hafey	3	78	366	.213
Sour Mash Jack Daniels	1	41	219	.187
Robert **Brandy** Davis	2	25	134	.187
Hubert **Bud** Bates	1	15	58	.259
Harry **Bud** Weiser	2	12	74	.162
Carl **Jug** Powis	1	8	41	.195
Drew **Buddy** Gilbert	1	3	20	.150
Arthur **Buddy** Crump	1	0	4	.000

PITCHERS:	Yr	Won	Lost	ERA
Brewery Jack Taylor	9	120	117	4.23
Harry **Bud** Black	14	117	114	3.77
Lee **Stinger** Stange	10	62	61	3.56
Leavitt **Bud** Daley	10	60	64	4.03
Roy **Bud** Parmelee	10	59	55	4.27
Eddie **Buddy** Solomon	10	36	42	4.00
Clarence **Bud** Podbielan	9	25	42	4.49
Luther **Bud** Thomas	7	25	34	4.96
Lyle **Bud** Tinning	4	22	15	3.19
Eldred **Bud** Byerly	11	22	22	3.70
Gordon **Maltzy** Maltzberger	4	20	13	2.70
Charles **Buddy** Schultz	5	15	9	3.68
Howard **Highball** Wilson	4	14	27	3.29
Arthur **Bud** Teachout	3	12	6	4.51
Jack **Buddy** Brewer	3	9	10	4.36
Everett **Bud** Lively	3	8	13	4.16
Harvey **Suds** Sutherland	1	6	2	4.97
Skelton **Buddy** Napier	4	5	6	3.92
George **Smooth** Lyons	2	5	3	4.72
Karl **Bud** Anderson	2	4	10	3.68
Bill **Bud** Black	3	2	3	4.22
Andrew **Bud** Messenger	1	2	0	4.32
Ray **Bud** Richmond	2	2	1	8.62
Gene **Suds** Fodge	1	1	1	4.76
Walter **Buddy** Harris	2	1	1	6.32
Bernard **Bud** Culloton	2	0	1	3.28
Jim **Buddy** Atkins	2	0	1	3.60
Chris **Bud** Haughey	1	0	1	3.86
John **Bud** Davis	1	0	2	4.05
Arnold **Jug** Thesenga	1	0	0	5.11
Gene **Jigger** Lansing	1	0	1	5.98
Sherwin **Bud** Swartz	1	0	0	6.75
Hal **Bud** Raether	2	0	0	6.75
Charlie **Bud** Bicknell	2	0	1	6.83

EXTRAS:
Allan **Bud** Selig - Brewer's Owner
Kiner's Korner - Temporarily found at Forbes Field

Nightcap: Second game of a double-header
Fly Chaser: An outfielder
Loaded One Up: Threw a spitball
Bottle Bat: Bat with a very thick handle
Label the Ball: Hit it hard

Chugged: Ran slow
Hops: What grounders do
A Double: A two base hit
A Triple: A big ice cream cone, Einstein
High and Tight : A pitch close to one's skull

CARTOON / CRAZY

7

Team

Each generation of little ones shares many of the same fantasies. Santa Claus, the Easter Bunny and the Tooth Fairy are all important people in their emerging lives. Combined with these "real people", the kids have their cartoon character friends. Over time, different popular characters have emerged, each capturing our imagination. My grandma and I would get up at 6:00 AM on Saturdays to watch her favorite, Krazy Kat. She used to roar at him! I grew up with Howdy Doody and The Mickey Mouse Club (Annette Funichello, AKA Dolly, will always be my favorite Mouseketeer). My kids were entertained by Big Bird, Peanuts and Road Runner. Today no one is bigger than Barney.

This team is crazy, especially when you have players referred to as Dizzy, Cuckoo, Sillie, Dorf, Mad, Dodo and Loco. If that is not enough, get a load of these characters. There is Chopper, Beany, Lil' Abner, Mortimer Snerd, Dino and Yogi. Add in Sluggo, Heathcliffe, Casper, Ziggy, Baby Huey, Gumby and Yosemite Sam. How about Peanuts, Scooter and Linus? On the roster are Mickey Mouse, Minnie, Goofy, Dumbo, Beauty, Monster, Sleepy, Thumper and The Beast. Don't overlook Popeye and Wimpy. There is Woody, Daffy, Bugs and Porky ..... badeep, badeep, badeep ..... that's not all folks!!

One player stands head and shoulders over the others. He was probably the greatest pitcher ever to "lace 'em up." His name was Walter Barney Johnson. He was nicknamed after the first Indy 500 winner (Barney Oldfield), because he was so fast. When a man plays for 21 seasons and he is a legend, he often acquires several nicknames. Barney was also called The Big Train, because he steam rolled over everyone. Earlier, Walter was known as the Weiser Wonder, because he starred for the Weiser Telephone Company. Barney won 417 games, the second highest total ever. In 11 of Walter's 21 seasons Washington played under .500, including seven seventh or eighth place finishes. Often "supported" by a weak hitting team, Barney suffered 65 shutout loses, including twenty-seven 1-0 defeats. In 1909, alone, he was shutout ten times! Nevertheless, Barney himself hurled a record 110 shutouts! During the stretch from 1910-19, Barney won over 20 games for ten consecutive years, twice winning over 30 contests. During those ten seasons, he not only won the strikeout crown nine times, but Barney also led the AL in shutouts six times (three times tied), complete games six times, wins five times, innings five times and ERA four times! In his era, batters fanned about 40% less often than today's hitters. Twelve seasons Barney led the AL in ring ups and for over 50 years his 3509 career K's were the benchmark. When he retired, Barney had struck out 20% more than Cy Young, 40% more than Christy Mathewson and 50% more than Rube Waddell, his three closest pursuers! If you were wondering, Barney could hit and hit for power! He had 547 career hits, 24 going the distance. In 1925, at the age of 38, Barney went 42/97 with six doubles, one triple, two homers, 20 RBI's and hit an unbelievable .433! For us trivia nuts, four seasons Walter personally hit more home runs than he gave up!!!!

LINEUP

CA | Lawrence _Yogi_ Berra is in the Hall of Fame. No player has won more than Yogi's three MVP awards (1951, 1954, and 1955). Fifteen seasons he was voted to the AL All-Star team. Just 5'8", Yogi, nevertheless, had 11 campaigns with 20 or more homers and five times drove in 100+ runs.

1B | Steve _Popeye_ Garvey stroked 2599 career hits. From 1974-80 Steve was a force. In that stretch, Popeye batted over .300 six times, had 200 or more hits six summers and drove in 100+ runs five campaigns. Steve, from 1974-80, also averaged 20+ homers and three seasons led the league in fielding %.

2B | Joe _Flash_ Gordon was a constant blaze. In his 11 seasons (gave two in service) Joe terrorized pitchers. Nine years Flash was the AL's All-Star second sacker. A rare power hitting keystoner, Joe three times placed in the top five in HR's and four summers drove in 100+ runs. Flash was the MVP in 1942.

SS | Phil _Scooter_ Rizzuto was only 5'6", but he stood tall in the field and is now at Cooperstown. Scooter gave three years to service, deferring his best seasons into his early 30's. After finishing second for the MVP in 1949, Scooter won it in 1950. Scooter earned the MVP with his bat, his glove and his spirit!

3B | Graig _Puff_ Nettles sparkled at third 2412 games (second all time). Puff ranks second all time in assists and DP's. His 1978 Fall Classic heroics in the field were spectacular. He led the AL in tators in 1976 and was tied for second in 1977. For his career Graig powered 390 homers, 28th all time.

OF | William _Dummy_ Hoy was tagged with his nickname, because he was deaf and dumb. At only 5'4" Dummy played over his head. Twice he led the league in walks. He stole 594 bases, which helped him score 1426 runs in just 14 seasons. Nine summers Dummy topped the century mark in runs scored.

OF | Charlie _Cuckoo_ Jamieson started 18 seasons in the Junior Circuit. From 1920-30 Charlie hit over .300 eight times, never batting less than .291 during that stretch. In 1923 Cuckoo hit .345 and led the league with 222 base hits. He batted a torrid .359 in 1924, his high water mark.

OF | Ralph _Road Runner_ Garr was very fast. Ralph played 13 summers, twice leading the NL (1974 and 1975) in triples. Three seasons Road Runner legged out 200 or more hits, topping the NL with 214 in 1974. Five times Ralph hit at least .300, finishing second in 1971 and 1972, and placing first in 1974!

P | Clarence _Dazzy_ Vance at the age of 31, won his first Major League game. This late bloomer holds the National League record for winning seven consecutive strikeout crowns! Dazzy led the Senior Circuit in shutouts four times (four ties), in ERA three summers and in wins two years.

P | Paul _Dizzy_ Trout spun pitches through the 40's and early 50's for the Tigers. In 1943 Dizzy tied for the AL lead in both wins and shutouts. Dizzy finished second to teammate Hal Newhouser for the MVP in 1944. That season he won 27 games (second) and led the league in innings, shutouts and ERA!

P | Vernon _Goofy_ Gomez won nearly 65% of his decisions, 15th best. Four times Goofy won more than 20 games! In 1934 and again in 1937 he won the pitching Triple Crown, first in wins, whiffs and ERA! Only three hurlers, Sandy Koufax, Barney Johnson and Old Pete Alexander, have won it more often.

RES | Jay Hanna _Dizzy_ Dean dominated NL hitters from 1932-36, before his 1937 mid season injury. During those five seasons Dizzy won 120 games. Four times he led the Senior Circuit in strikeouts and twice in wins. In 1934 Diz won 30 regular season games, two World Series tilts and the NL MVP!

RES | Saturnino _Minnie_ Minoso played 17 summers, having his best years in the 1950's. A six time All-Star, Minnie had speed, power and hit for average. Minnie led the AL in swipes three years and in triples three summers (one tie). He jolted 186 long balls, had four 100+ RBI seasons and hit .300+ nine times.

RES | Joe _Goofy_ Adcock was a power hitter in the 50's and 60's. His 5.09 home run % ranks Goofy 41st. Seven seasons he rocketed over 20 round trippers. In 1956 Goofy plastered 38 homers and chased across 103 runs! His 336 career dingers place him 51st on the strongboy list.

RES | George _Snuffy_ Stirnweiss had two fabulous seasons in his ten year career. In 1944 Snuffy led the AL in hits, triples (tie), runs and stolen bases. In 1945 he not only led the AL in hits, triples, runs and stolen bases, but Snuffy also led the Junior Circuit in slugging % and batting average!

L to R: Ralph _Road Runner_ Garr, Jay Hanna _Dizzy_ Dean, Walter _Barney_ Johnson, Phil _Scooter_ Rizzuto, Lawrence _Yogi_ Berra

It'sa FACT

Burt **Barney** Shotton: He was a selective hitter. Although he hit only nine home runs in 14 seasons, Barney, nevertheless, walked 12.61% of his at bats, twice leading the AL in free passes.

Cliff **Heathcliff** Johnson: In his 15 seasons he clubbed 196 homers. Heathcliff retired with a 4.97 home run %, ranking him 49th all time. Cliff was a designated hitter much of his career and also was an extraordinary pinch hitter. He went 68/277 with a Major League record 20 pinch-hit homers (7.22 home run %). On June 30th, 1977, Heathcliff hit two circuit shots in one inning.

Paul **Dizzy** Trout: Not only was he an excellent pitcher, but he also was a strong hitter. Dizzy hit grand slams on July 28th, 1949 and June 23rd, 1950. For his career Dizzy had 20 round trippers.

Lawrence **Yogi** Berra: In 1958 he went all season without committing an error and holds the record for consecutive errorless games for catchers. During World Series play Yogi had more at bats, hits and doubles than any Major Leaguer, and his 12 home runs and 39 RBI's each rank him second.

Steve **Popeye** Garvey: He ate his spinach during post season play. In the 1974 NLCS he hit .389 with two homers and five RBI's in four games. Steve walloped four homers and seven RBI's in four games in the 1978 NLCS! Again in 1981, Popeye powered two homers and five RBI's in the four game NL west playoff. He launched one homer with seven RBI's in the five game 1984 NLCS.

Graig **Puff** Nettles: He hit 20 or more homers in 11 seasons. Puff's career home run total ranks him 28th, one yard shot ahead of Johnny Bench and just behind Dale Murphy.

Clarence **Dazzy** Vance: In 1924 he won the pitching Triple Crown. Dazzy led the NL in wins with 28, strikeouts with 262 and ERA with 2.16. He was also voted the MVP that season!

Elwood **Woody** English: He starred for 12 seasons. In 1930 Woody hit .335 with 214 base hits, including 36 doubles, 17 triples, and 14 homers. Not bad power for a 155 pound shortstop!

Woodson **Woodie** Held: He was a hard hitting shortstop in the late 50's and early 60's. From 1957-65 Woodie blasted 170 home runs, averaging nearly one circuit blast every 21 at bats.

Jay Hanna **Dizzy** Dean: He was more than a player to baseball. In the age of newspapers describing all the action, Dizzy was the news. A bigger than life personality, Dizzy was always good for a quote. Radio was in its infancy when Diz retired. He became baseball's radio voice. Fans saw the game with his eyes. Years later, it was T.V.'s turn, trying to sprout nationally. Diz again became the nation's voice. I grew up spending Saturday afternoons with Diz and Buddy (Blatner), and later with his new sidekick Pee Wee (Reese). Spinning yarns in his folksy, English butchering way, Diz reminisced, told stories, and even sang for his audiences!

Claude **Wimpy** Osteen: For 18 summers he threw balls and strikes. He retired just four wins short of 200! Wimpy posted 40 shutouts, which places him in a tie for 42nd all time. From 1964-73 Claude won 12 or more games each season. Wimpy twice won 20 decisions in one year.

Don **Popeye** Zimmer: He earned his nickname, because of his strength. Popeye's career was nearly ended when he was beaned. He laid unconscious for several weeks, but fortunately he recovered and was able to resume his career.

Luther **Dummy** Taylor: He was an excellent pitcher for the Giants. During his nine season career, only twice did his ERA rise over 3.00. In 1904 Dummy won 21 games and tossed five shutouts.

William **Barney** McCosky: Seven days after his 22nd birthday he broke into the Big Leagues. Barney finished his rookie year hitting .311, with 190 hits (fourth), 14 triples (second) and scoring 120 runs (fourth). In 1940 Barney hit .340, leading the AL with 200 hits (tie) and 19 triples, and finishing third with 123 runs. Barney hit .324 and .293 in 1941 and 1942. He then gave three prime years to his country. Returning after the 1945 season, the next three years Barney hit .318, .328 and .326. His .312 career average is 71st all time.

Ken **Daffy** Sanders: Over ten summers he came in from the bullpen 407 times. In 1971 Daffy led the AL in appearances with 83 and saves with 31.

Minervino **Minnie** Rojas: He played just three seasons. Nevertheless, in 1967 Minnie went 12-7 for the Angels, leading the league in both relief wins and saves!

Harry **Peanuts** Lowrey: A solid player, during the later stages of his career he also became an excellent pinch hitter. Peanuts went 14/28 off the bench in 1952, the second highest single season pinch-hit batting average.

Joe **Goofy** Adcock: On May 26th, 1959 he hit Harvey The Kitten Haddix' first delivery to him in the bottom of the 13th over the fence. It was the only hit Harvey allowed that day. With teammates on second and first, you would think the final score would have been 3-0. No, Goofy passed Hammerin' Hank Aaron after rounding second base and only received credit for a double. The final score was 1-0!

TRIVIA*

1) These two Hall of Famers could be taken for a Disney film.

2) Although neither was noted as a pinch hitter, each had 12 pinch home runs in their 35 and 38 career pinch-hits.

3) A home state Wisconsin boy, he played his entire career for the Brew Crew. The way he walked coined his nickname.

4) He was so strong, it was said even his arm hairs had muscles. This rumor contributed to his nickname.

5) Some of his friends noted he looked like a Hindu practicing yoga. His nickname later formed a cartoon character from Jellystone Park.

6) After giving silly answers to a reporter's questions, this great pitcher was tabbed. Many people called this portsider Lefty.

7) He used to step off the back of the mound, face center field, talk to himself, slap his hand in his glove, turn and stomp back to the rubber. That's how he earned his nickname.

8) His hummer was so fast. He only had one pitch, a sidearm fast ball. The problem wasn't hitting it. The problem was seeing it.

9) In his infamous fight with teammate, Rich Goose Gossage, he broke the right-hander's thumb. The incident prompted this designated hitter to be traded to the Tribe.

10) His 18 total bases in one game, July 31st, 1954, is a Major League record. He did it with four home runs and one double.

11) This hurler is the only pitcher to win three All-Star games. He also drove in the first run ever scored in an All-Star tilt.

12) This Hall of Famer could only look up from his left field position when Maz hit the 1960 Series winning homer.

13) His Major League career spanned five decades!

14) In his first two seasons he won 38 games (including a no-hitter) and two World Series tilts. He hurt his arm and won only 12 more times during his career.

15) He was also nicknamed "Mountain Music", because he sang country songs. As a rookie in 1937, he won 20 games with a 2.61 ERA, both second best in the National League.

16) His first three career starts were shutouts. (Hint: this may fry your brain)

17) He played 18 seasons and hit over .300 four times. In 1981 he finished second in the AL batting race. (Hint: he broadcasts for the White Sox)

18) His son Dale had an 11 year career before retiring in 1987.

19) In 1934 everyone remembers the King, Carl Hubbell, fanning five future Hall of Famers consecutively in the All-Star game. This hurler was that game's winning pitcher. In four career All-Star appearances, he never allowed a run! (Hint: his other nickname was Chief)

20) The Polo Ground's center field fence stood 480 feet from home plate. The wall was 20 feet high. Only three home runs ever cleared that goofy fence. He hit one of them.

21) He appeared in 18 All-Star games and 25 World Series, all after his playing career ended! He was at these games with his comedy act.

22) Don Larsen's perfect gem overshadowed his three home runs and ten RBI's in the 1956 Fall Classic.

23) In 1974 he was the National League MVP. That year he was the All-Star game MVP. He also was the NLCS MVP.

24) He made a study of insects, inspiring his teammates to give him his nickname.

25) In the bottom of the 13th, he scored the winning and only run off Harvey Haddix, ending The Kitten's no-hitter and the game.

* CHARACTER ANALYZERS answers on page 235

ROSTER

CATCHERS:	Yr	Hits	AB's	Ave
Lawrence *Yogi* Berra	19	2150	7555	.285
Don *Sluggo* Slaught	13	1041	3688	.282
Cliff *Heathcliff* Johnson	15	1016	3945	.258
Eddie *Dorf* Ainsmith	15	707	3048	.232
Andrew *Barney* Gilligan	10	386	1865	.207
Ken *Ziggy* Sears	2	57	202	.282
Robert *Casper* Asbjornson	4	52	221	.235
Hank *Popeye* Erickson	1	23	88	.261
Eddie *Scooter* Tucker	1	6	50	.120
Ted *Porky* Pawelek	1	1	4	.250
George *Dodo* Armstrong	1	1	6	.167

1ST BASEMEN:	Yr	Hits	AB's	Ave
Jimmie *The Beast* Foxx	20	2646	8134	.325
Steve *Popeye* Garvey	19	2599	8835	.294
Joe *Goofy* Adcock	17	1832	6606	.277
Norm *Dumbo* Larker	6	538	1953	.275
Jim *Baby Huey* Maler	3	70	310	.226
Ed *Sleepy* Flanagan	2	42	168	.250
Robert *Ziggy* Hasbrook	2	1	9	.111

2ND BASEMEN:	Yr	Hits	AB's	Ave
Jim *Gumby* Gantner	17	1696	6189	.274
Felix *The Cat* Millan	12	1617	5791	.279
Phil *Yosemite Sam* Garner	16	1594	6136	.260
Joe *Flash* Gordon	11	1530	5707	.268
George *Snuffy* Stirnweiss	10	989	3695	.268
Felix *The Cat* Mantilla	11	707	2707	.261
Woodrow *Woody* Williams	4	314	1255	.250
Louis *Boze* Berger	6	270	1144	.236
Bob *Scooter* Malkmus	6	123	572	.215
Everett *Skeeter* Kell	1	47	213	.221
Barnett *Barney* Koch	1	21	96	.219
Matt *Dummy* Lynch	1	2	7	.286

SHORTSTOPS:	Yr	Hits	AB's	Ave
Dave *Beauty* Bancroft	16	2004	7182	.279
Phil *Scooter* Rizzuto	13	1588	5816	.273
Elwood *Woody* English	12	1356	4746	.286
Woodson *Woodie* Held	14	963	4019	.240
Lamar *Skeeter* Newsome	12	910	3716	.245
William *Woody* Woodward	9	517	2187	.236
James *Skeeter* Webb	12	498	2274	.219
Larvell *Sugar Bear* Blanks	9	446	1766	.253
James *Howdy* Caton	4	184	814	.226
Bernard *Barney* McLaughlin	3	169	696	.243
Clem *Scooter* Koshorek	2	84	323	.260
Herbert *Dummy* Murphy	1	4	26	.154
Charles *Snuffy* Oertel	1	2	12	.167

3RD BASEMEN:	Yr	Hits	AB's	Ave
Graig *Puff* Nettles	22	2225	8986	.248

3RD BASEMEN: (Cont.)	Yr	Hits	AB's	Ave
Gustaf *Barney* Friberg	14	1170	4169	.281
Don *Popeye* Zimmer	12	773	3283	.235
Floyd *Sugar Bear* Rayford	7	255	1044	.244
William *Skeeter* Barnes	9	159	614	.259
Roy *Linus* Staiger	4	104	457	.228
Jim *Woody* Woods	3	17	82	.207
Lee *Skeeter* Tate	2	14	85	.165
Cristobal *Minnie* Mendoza	1	3	16	.188
Elwood *Woodie* Wagenhorst	1	1	8	.125
James *Dodo* Lane	1	1	15	.067

OUTFIELDERS:	Yr	Hits	AB's	Ave
William *Dummy* Hoy	14	2044	7112	.287
Charlie *Cuckoo* Jamieson	18	1990	6560	.303
Saturnino *Minnie* Minoso	17	1963	6579	.298
Dave *Big Bird* Kingman	16	1575	6677	.236
Ralph *Road Runner* Garr	13	1562	5108	.306
Burt *Barney* Shotton	14	1338	4949	.270
William *Barney* McCosky	11	1301	4172	.312
Carson *Skeeter* Bigbee	11	1205	4192	.287
Harry *Peanuts* Lowrey	13	1177	4317	.273
Tom *Wimpy* Paciorek	18	1162	4121	.282
Forrest *Woody* Jensen	9	774	2720	.285
Gene *Road Runner* Clines	10	645	2328	.277
Paul *Peanuts* Lehner	7	455	1768	.257
Jerry *Popeye* Hairston	14	438	1699	.258
Dain *Ding-A-Ling* Clay	4	397	1540	.258
Lou *The Mad Russian* Novikoff	5	305	1081	.282
Bob *Scooter* Will	6	202	819	.247
Walt *Cuckoo* Christensen	2	162	514	.315
Roy *Dizzy* Carlyle	2	157	494	.318
Fred *Bugs* Kommers	2	120	441	.272
Roy *Woody* Wood	3	77	333	.231
Jose *Loco* Herrera	4	61	231	.264
Ed *Dummy* Dundon	2	27	179	.151
John *Thumper* DeMerit	5	23	132	.174
Bernard *Barney* Olsen	1	21	73	.288
Mark *Humpty Dumpty* Polhemus	1	18	75	.240
John *Daff* Gammons	1	18	93	.194
Elwood *Woody* Wheaton	2	17	89	.191
Art *Sillie* Thomason	1	12	70	.171
Everett *Dizzy* Nutter	1	11	52	.212
Rueben *Dummy* Stephenson	1	10	37	.270
Bernard *Barney* Reilly	1	5	25	.200
Roy *Deedle* Moran	1	2	13	.154
Andrew *Skeeter* Shelton	1	1	40	.025

PINCH HITTER:	Yr	Hits	AB's	Ave
Murray *Porky* Howell	1	2	7	.286

PITCHERS:	Yr	Won	Lost	ERA
Walter *Barney* Johnson	21	417	279	2.16

ROSTER

PITCHERS: (Cont.)	Yr	Won	Lost	ERA
Mel *Wimpy* Harder	20	223	186	3.80
Clarence *Dazzy* Vance	16	197	140	3.24
Claude *Wimpy* Osteen	18	196	195	3.30
Vernon *Goofy* Gomez	14	189	102	3.34
Paul *Dizzy* Trout	15	170	161	3.23
Jay Hanna *Dizzy* Dean	12	150	83	3.02
Woodrow *Woodie* Fryman	18	141	155	3.77
Luther *Dummy* Taylor	9	116	106	2.75
Clyde *Skeeter* Wright	10	100	111	3.50
Russ *The Mad Monk* Meyer	13	94	73	3.99
Cliff *Mickey Mouse* Melton	8	86	80	3.42
Tom *Bugs* Burgmeier	17	79	55	3.23
Roy *Popeye* Mahaffey	9	67	49	5.01
Al *The Mad Hungarian* Hrabosky	13	64	35	3.10
Dick *The Monster* Radatz	7	52	43	3.13
Paul *Daffy* Dean	9	50	34	3.75
Dick *Mortimer Snerd* Selma	10	42	54	3.62
Paul *Lil' Abner* Erickson	8	37	48	3.86
Ken *Daffy* Sanders	10	29	45	2.97
Bill *Bugs* Werle	6	29	39	4.69
Howie *Diz* Reed	10	26	29	3.72
Joe *Skeeter* Moeller	8	26	36	4.01
Doyle *Porky* Lade	5	25	29	4.39
Minervino *Minnie* Rojas	3	23	16	3.00
Albert *Beany* Jacobson	4	23	46	3.19
George *Barney* Schultz	7	20	20	3.63
Al *Clown Prince of Baseball* Schacht	3	14	10	4.48
Erv *Peanuts* Kantlehner	3	13	29	2.84
Al *Bozo* Cicotte	5	10	13	4.36
Frank *Porky* Biscan	3	7	9	5.28
Fred *Crazy* Schmit	5	7	36	5.45
Dave *Chopper* Campbell	2	4	10	3.82

PITCHERS: (Cont.)	Yr	Won	Lost	ERA
Bernard *Barney* McFadden	2	3	5	6.38
George *Barney* Barnicle	3	3	3	6.55
Virgil *Woody* Abernathy	2	1	1	3.64
Carl *Bugs* Moran	1	1	3	4.66
Les *Barney* Barnhart	2	1	1	6.75
Hardin *Lil' Abner* Cathey	1	1	1	7.42
Clyde *Mad* Hatter	2	1	0	8.44
Woodrow *Woody* Davis	1	0	0	1.50
Ed *Peanuts* Pinnance	1	0	0	2.57
Charlie *Bugs* Grover	1	0	0	3.38
Les *Wimpy* Willis	1	0	2	3.48
Steve *The Mad Russian* Rachunok	1	0	1	4.50
Vernon *Dazzy* Swartz	1	0	1	4.50
Harry *Bugs* Eccles	1	0	1	4.71
George *Dummy* Leitner	2	0	2	5.34
Byron *Barney* Slaughter	1	0	1	5.50
Bill *Beanie* Hall	1	0	0	5.79
Thomas *Woody* Crowson	1	0	0	6.00
Vern *Woody* Holtgrave	1	0	0	6.00
Bernard *Barney* Mussill	1	0	1	6.05
Jacob *Bugs* Reisigl	1	0	1	6.23
William *Dummy* Deegan	1	0	1	6.35
Wellington *Wimpy* Quinn	1	0	0	7.20
Jefferson *Woody* Upchurch	2	0	4	7.42
Barnes *Barney* Martin	1	0	0	9.00
William *Jack* Horner	1	0	1	9.00
Don *Dino* Williams	1	0	0	10.38
Howard *Dizzy* Sutherland	1	0	1	45.00

EXTRA:
John *Ziggy* Sears - Umpire

MORE TRIVIA*

A)   His large forearms and excellent hitting strength contributed to this first sacker's nickname.

B)   In 1960 Dick Groat edged him .325 to .323 for the NL batting title.

C)   Whenever there was trouble, he was "never around". His teammates gave him this nickname.

D)   He grew a large, droopy mustache while playing for the Athletics in the early '70's. It led to "Scrap Iron's" first nickname.

E)   He and his son, Rainbow, combined for 258 pitching victories, more than any other father and son.

F)   I grew up listening to him sing the Wabash Cannonball, quote "statics" and spin yarns to all us "pawdners".

G)   He didn't have a fast ball. He had a "fogger".

H)   He holds the National League "Ironman" record of 1207 consecutive games played.

I)   Quiet and shy, the press gave him his nickname anyway. It seemed logical, knowing his brother.

J)   For his career he had a 6-0 record in World Series competition. Two Fall Classics he went 2-0 and won the clinching World Championship game.

* CHARACTER ANALYZERS answers on page 235

CONDITION

8

Team

Baseball is now a 12 month occupation. The "off season" is really a time for Major Leaguers to play more ball (known as winter ball, it is played in Mexico, the Caribbean, Central America and South America) or "work" to maintain and/or improve their health. Three consecutive winters (1969-70 - 1971-72) Ralph Road Runner Garr was the batting leader in the winter Dominican League. In 1974 Road Runner won the NL Silver Bat. Other Major League batting champs who were also batting leaders in winter ball were Ricardo Rico Carty, Mateo Matty Alou and Dave The Cobra Parker. Rickey Man of Steal Henderson, during his first five seasons, hit only 35 home runs. He decided to build his strength and now has over 200 career dingers! Mark McGuire saw his average dip, so he committed to eye exercises, to better see and hit the ball, and he had great results! The dedication to exercise by Nolan The Express Ryan and Steve Lefty Carlton certainly contributed to these superstars' success. The conditioning they demanded of themselves both extended their careers in length and raised the level of their performances.

The Condition Team has a wide array of players, including three Hall of Famers. Some of the more fit players were known as Muscles, Road Runner, Jumping, Kip, Leaping, Jumping Jack, Jump Steady and Poosh "Em Up," while the less fit were Puff, Starvin' and Wimpy. The players in the more tapered section went by Slim, Skinny, Twig, Blade, Stick, Bones, String, Thin Man, Slats and Tiny, while in the broader category the team has not only Butterball, Pudge, Blimp, Fats, Tubby and Heavy, but also Roundman, Big Boy, Chub, Porky, Jumbo and Fatso.

One player lifts himself head and shoulders over all the others! Carlton Pudge Fisk is currently waiting his five years until they open the doors at the Hall for him. Pudge has fabulous career stats, but what really separates him from others is his determination. He lived to play baseball. To be a feared hitter and have your most productive home run and RBI season at age 37 is outstanding! To be an All-Star catcher at 43 is remarkable! To be a Major League catcher at age 45 is unbelievable! Pudge did all this. Just think, to play baseball's most physically demanding position for 24 campaigns! His big glove stats are amazing! When Carlton quit giving signs, he retired with the Major League record for most games caught and Pudge ranks second all time in putouts. His lumber stats are just as impressive. Carlton muscled 376 homers, jerked 421 doubles and pushed across 1330 runs. We all miss you!

LINEUP

| **CA** | Carlton *Pudge* Fisk | was an eleven time All-Star. This future Hall of Famer leads |

all catchers for their careers in games caught and career homers. Pudge slugged 20 or more round trippers eight seasons, batted .300 or more three years and knocked in 100 or more runs two times.

| **1B** | Ed *Jumbo* Cartwright | was a late bloomer. He became a starter in 1894 at 34! |

Jumbo hit over .300 twice in his five seasons. His .331 average in 1895 was his high water mark. He also led all first sackers in assists in 1895. Jumbo's 12 HR's in 1894 stood near the league lead as did his 17 triples in 1895.

| **2B** | *Poosh 'Em Up* Tony Lazzeri | was a team leader on the great Yankee teams of the 20's |

and 30's. During his 14 year career Poosh 'Em Up Tony drove in over 100 runs seven seasons. Five summers he hit over .300, with his .354 average in 1929 his best. Twice Tony finished third in the AL in round trippers.

| **SS** | Garry *Jump Steady* Templeton | starred 16 summers in the Senior Circuit. By age 21 he was |

the All-Star shortstop, led the National League in three baggers and hit .322. During the next two seasons (1977-78) Jump Steady twice led the league in triples and once topped all batsmen in base hits.

| **3B** | *Jumping* Joe Dugan | was the Yankees third sacker in the 20's. He "set the table" |

for Ruth and Gehrig. Jumping Joe was a consistent performer for 14 summers, but from 1922-24 he was exceptional. Jumping Joe averaged nearly 180 hits, slashed 30+ doubles and scored over 100 runs each year.

| **OF** | Bob *Fats* Fothergill | was an amazing hitter. His first eight seasons (1922-29) he |

hit over .300! In 1927 Fats had his best season. He finished fourth in batting average in the American League (.359) and he ranked fifth in RBI's (114). Fats' .325 career batting average places him a lofty 33rd all time.

| **OF** | Ron *The Roundman* Northey | was an outfielder for 12 summers. He played full time his |

first five years. In 1944 The Roundman finished third in both homers and RBI's in the Senior Circuit. From 1943-47 Ron averaged 16 homers and 70+ RBI's. His son Scott played briefly for the Royals in 1969.

| **OF** | Albert *Kip* Selbach | starred for 13 summers. He was very quick. Nine times Kip |

hit over ten triples, including a league leading 22 three baggers in 1895. He swiped 334 bags, which placed him in the top 100. Seven seasons Kip batted over .300, including five consecutive years (1894-98).

| **P** | *Fat* Freddie Fitzsimmons | twirled for 19 seasons, all in the National League. He |

chalked up 15 or more victories eight summers. In 1928 Fat Freddie won 20 games, his most wins. From 1926-34 Fat Freddie won in double figures. His 217 V's rank him tied for 66th all time.

| **P** | Harry *Slim* Sallee | was a tall, thin portsider. For 14 seasons he baffled |

batters with his side arm deliveries. From 1911-17 Slim posted 15, 16, 19, 18, 13, 14 and 18 victories. He had his best year in 1919. Slim went 21-7 and led Cincinnati to the World Championship.

| **P** | George *Jumbo* McGinnis | was born February 22nd, 1864 and was named George |

Washington McGinnis. He hurled just six summers, but George chalked up 102 wins. Jumbo won 25, 28 and 24 games his first three seasons. At the young age of 23 his Major League career was over!

| **RES** | Mark *The Blade* Belanger | was known more for his glove than his bat, and rightfully |

so. He was a fantastic fielder! The Blade won the Gold Glove at shortstop eight times from 1969-78. During his 17 seasons with the Baltimore Orioles they won four pennants and one World Series.

| **RES** | Jim *Jumbo* Nash | had a tremendous rookie year (1966). Jumbo went 12-1 |

with a 2:06 ERA his inaugural summer. He then won 12 and 13 games his next two seasons and again reached 13 victories in 1970. Jumbo stood 6'5" and tipped the scale at 230 pounds, hence his nickname.

| **RES** | Tom *Wimpy* Paciorek | starred for 18 seasons and now does announcing for the |

Chicago White Sox along with Ken Hawk Harrelson. From 1981-83, Wimpy had his three best years. He batted .326 (second in AL), .312 and .307 and was named to the 1981 All-Star team.

| **MGR** | Gene *Stick* Michael | is now a general manager. He was a field manager four |

seasons for the Yankees, leading them to the pennant in 1981. For ten seasons Stick played infield. Gene was a knowledgeable and slick glove man which compensated for his bat (note, I did not say stick!).

L to R: Garry *Jump Steady* Templeton, Mark *The Blade* Belanger, Carlton *Pudge* Fisk, Tom *Wimpy* Paciorek, *Fat* Freddie Fitzsimmons

It'sa FACT

Bob **Fats** Fothergill: During his career he often came off of the bench. Fats went 76/253 in his pinch hitting career and for a time was the all time pinch-hit leader. Fats' .300 pinch hitting batting average ranks him fifth all time. Bob hit both a home run and a triple in one inning September 26th, 1926 and July 28th, 1931. This feat has been accomplished just nine times and Fats is the only player to have done it more than once.

Sid **Pudge** Gautreaux: With Campy the Dodger's starting backstop, he was used primarily as a pinch hitter. In 1956 Pudge led the NL in both pinch-hit at bats and pinch-hits, going 16/53.

Poosh 'Em Up Tony Lazzeri: He was the first player to slam 60 home runs in one season. Poosh 'Em Up slugged them in 1925 while suiting up for Salt Lake City in the Pacific Coast League.

Fred **Pudge** Haney: During his seven year playing career (1922-29), he was a utility infielder. Pudge remained in baseball. Thirty-eight years later he piloted the 1957 Milwaukee Braves to the World Championship.

Sliding Billy Hamilton: Five times he led the NL in receiving free passes. Sliding Billy walked nearly 16% of his career at bats (18th best). His on base average topped the Senior Circuit five summers and his career OBA was fourth best. In 1894 Billy went 220/544 to hit an astronomical .404! Combined with his 126 bases on balls in 1894, Sliding Billy's .523 OBA was sixth best for one season!

James **Jumbo** Elliott: In 1931 Jumbo shared the league lead in wins with 19 and topped the NL in games with 52.

William **Slim** Harriss: He won 19 games for the Philadelphia A's in 1925. His full name was William Jennings Bryan Harriss, after the famous politician. At 6'6" 180 pounds, most people settled for calling him his nickname, Slim.

Fat Freddie Fitzsimmons: He threw a knuckle ball at three different speeds. It helped Fat Freddie through 19 campaigns, experiencing only four losing seasons. From 1926-34 he went 148-94 for the Giants, averaging a 16-10 record. In 1935 Fat Freddie tied for the league lead in shutouts with four, and his season record read 4-8!

Russell **Slats** Blackburne: At 5'11" and 160 pounds, he "qualified" for his second nickname. No one knew him as Russell, instead everyone called him Lena. Slats' mud, gathered from the Delaware River near his farm, has been the official rubbing mud used to prepare baseballs before games since 1938.

Ivan **Pudge** Rodriguez: He was "called up" at age 19. By age 20 Pudge had won the Gold Glove, and at 21 he was the American League's All-Star catcher! His rifle arm cuts down about 50% of all would-be base stealers!

Ernie **Tiny** Bonham: In 1942 he had a career season. Tiny went 21-5 (second in wins) and led the Junior Circuit in complete games (tie), shutouts and winning %. He hurled 226 frames and issued only 24 free passes in 1942!

Tom **Wimpy** Paciorek: John, his older brother, was up for a cup of coffee in 1963 and retired with a 1.000 batting average (3/3 with three RBI's). His little brother Jim, 13 ½ years his junior, played for the Brew Crew in 1987. Wimpy made his own mark, over 18 summers, from 1970-87.

Joe **Muscles** Medwick: The fans knew him as Ducky, but his teammates tabbed him Muscles. He flexed his biceps from 1934-39. He powered in over 100 runs each summer (106, 126, 138, 154, 122 and 117). He crushed 40 or more doubles each summer (40, 46, 64, 56, 47 and 48). He carried a .300 or over average each summer (.319, .353, .351, .374, .322 and .332). Muscles repetitiously sculpted a Hall of Fame career.

Ernest **Blimp** Phelps: No one called him Ernest, but he was often called Babe. Babe played parts of 11 seasons. In 1936 Blimp was given a chance to start and he rose to the occasion. He hit .367! Blimp fanned only 157 times in his 2117 career at bats.

Steve **Bones** Balboni: His nickname was more tongue-in-cheek. He sent over 180 balls bye-bye (his other moniker) during his career.

Edward **Slim** Love: During his six seasons, this 6'7" 195 pound hurler never had a losing record. P.S. Slim was born in Love, Mississippi!

Grover **Slim** Lowdermilk: His brother Lou and he were teammates with St. Louis in 1911.

Walter **Jumbo** Brown: At 6'4" 295 pounds, he lived up to his nickname. Jumbo led the NL in saves for both 1940 and 1941. Actually, in 1940, Jumbo tied for the lead in saves with Mace Brown, not to be confused with the later famous reliever Hal Skinny Brown (6'2" 182 pounds) or the pre-1900 reliever Richard Stub Brown (6'2" 220 pounds), but I suspect there is only a slim chance of that happening!

Tom **The Blade** Hall: He stood 6'0", but weighed only 155 pounds! Don't be fooled, The Blade fired the ball. From 1970-72 he pitched 155 1/3, 129 2/3 and 124 1/3 innings. He fanned 184, 137 and 134 batters, over one per inning! In the 1972 post season, The Blade went 1-0 in the NLCS, allowing only one run in 7 1/3 relief innings (fanning eight). He followed with four appearances in the World Series, allowing no runs in 8 1/3 innings (fanning seven).

TRIVIA*

1) He wore his hitting shoes on May 24th 1936. He jerked out two grand slams, a third dinger, a triple, and drove in 11 runs in one game!

2) He had four brothers who also played in the Majors (the record). His brother Big Ed is in the Hall of Fame.

3) He holds a share of the Major League record for pinch grand slams (three) with Rich Reese and Willie Stretch McCovey.

4) Most people called him by this nickname or by his other nickname, Babe, but his given name was Ernest.

5) He was a switch hitter. In 1979 he had pounded 100+ hits from each side of the plate!

6) As a rookie, this "gazelle" tied for the American League lead in three baggers with Joe Rudi.

7) This hurler played his entire career for the Cleveland Indians and was also nicknamed Chief.

8) His other handle was Octopus. He gathered the 1944 National League MVP.

9) His long ball power led to his other moniker, Bye-Bye.

10) I will never forget him sitting on the clubhouse floor crying tears of joy. Finally, at age 62, he had earned a World Series ring! He was the Minnesota Twins' first base coach in 1987 and one of the many unsung heroes of baseball who have given their all to the game they love.

11) After his playing days, he went on to become a great college coach and help many young men reach the Majors.

12) He originally wore #27 while playing for the Red Sox, but he turned it around and wore #72 while playing for the White Sox.

13) The Cardinals traded their hard hitting shortstop to the Padres for San Diego's slick fielding shortstop Ozzie The Wizard Of Oz Smith.

14) He jerked 12 of his career 24 yard shots in one season (he played 14 years). At 6'1" and only 155 pounds, it's easy to tell how this shortstop acquired his nickname.

15) It was the bottom of the 12th inning of game #6 in the 1975 World Series. He pumped out a homer, ending what many purists consider the greatest baseball game ever played!

16) This daring base runner earned his nickname for his head first slides.

17) In 1976 he won the American League home run crown. He retired ten long balls short of 400.

18) His 214 hits, 17 triples and .353 batting average were all National League leading in 1974.

19) He caught a record 312 consecutive games. (Hint: think Goodyear and "Gabby")

20) He set the Major League record when he scored 192 runs in a single season. Amazingly, he accomplished that in only 129 games!

21) He was the unanimous choice for the 1972 American League Rookie of the Year.

22) This Yankee finished third in the AL in home runs in 1927, trailing only George Babe Ruth (60) and Lou The Iron Horse Gehrig (47).

23) His career batting average places him seventh all time!

24) In 1940 he went 16-2, the fourth best winning % in baseball history.

25) This slim lefty issued, in one season, only 20 free passes in 227 2/3 innings.

* BRAIN CRUNCHERS answers found on page 236

ROSTER

CATCHERS:	Yr	Hits	AB's	Ave
Carlton *Pudge* Fisk	24	2356	8756	.269
Frankie *Blimp* Hayes	14	1164	4493	.259
Ernest *Blimp* Phelps	11	657	2117	.310
Ivan *Pudge* Rodriguez	4	420	1536	.273
Verne *Fats* Clemons	7	364	1271	.286
Ed *Tubby* Spencer	9	298	1326	.225
Walter *Heavy* Blair	7	272	1255	.217
Charles *Fatty* Briody	8	271	1186	.228
James *Tub* Welch	2	68	261	.261
John *Fats* Dantonio	2	33	135	.244
Frank *Tubby* Reiber	4	23	85	.271
Sid *Pudge* Gautreaux	2	20	81	.247
Joe *Stubby* Erautt	2	8	43	.186
Charlie *Slats* Dorman	1	1	2	.500
Lou *Jumbo* Harding	1	1	3	.333
Ted *Porky* Pawelek	1	1	4	.250
Tom *Slats* Wilson	1	0	1	.000

1ST BASEMEN:	Yr	Hits	AB's	Ave
Steve *Bones* Balboni	11	714	3120	.229
Ed *Jumbo* Cartwright	5	562	1902	.295
John *Chub* Sullivan	3	114	442	.258
Dawson *Tiny* Graham	1	14	61	.230
Fenton *Muscles* Mole	1	5	27	.185
Joe *Slim* Staton	2	4	19	.211
Clarence *Big Boy* Kraft	1	1	3	.333
Francis *Tubby* McGee	1	0	3	.000

2ND BASEMEN:	Yr	Hits	AB's	Ave
Poosh 'Em Up Tony Lazzeri	14	1840	6297	.292
Wayne *Twig* Terwilliger	9	501	2091	.240
Jerry *Slim* Kindall	9	439	2057	.213
Fred *Muscles* Vaughn	2	91	377	.241
Joe *Fats* Berger	2	71	371	.191
Ed *Husky* Walczak	1	12	57	.211
Al *Tiny* Tesch	1	2	7	.286

SHORTSTOPS:	Yr	Hits	AB's	Ave
Garry *Jump Steady* Templeton	16	2096	7721	.271
Marty *Slats* Marion	13	1448	5506	.263
William *Bones* Ely	14	1331	5159	.258
Mark *The Blade* Belanger	18	1316	5784	.228
Gene *Stick* Michael	10	642	2806	.229
Russell *Slats* Blackburne	8	387	1807	.214
Irv *Stubby* Ray	4	263	902	.292
Tom *Muscles* Upton	3	118	525	.225
Harvey *Chub* Aubrey	1	69	325	.212
Edmund *Stubby* Magner	1	7	33	.212
Ira *Slats* Davis	1	4	17	.235
James *Stub* Smith	1	1	10	.100

3RD BASEMEN:	Yr	Hits	AB's	Ave
Graig *Puff* Nettles	22	2225	8986	.248
Jumping Joe Dugan	14	1516	5410	.280
Al *Flip* Rosen	10	1063	3725	.285
Fred *Pudge* Haney	7	544	1977	.275
James *Jumbo* Davis	7	468	1723	.272
Bob *Jumbo* Barrett	5	169	650	.260

OUTFIELDERS:	Yr	Hits	AB's	Ave
Joe *Muscles* Medwick	17	2471	7635	.324
Sliding Billy Hamilton	14	2158	6268	.344
Albert *Kip* Selbach	13	1803	6158	.293
Ralph *Road Runner* Garr	13	1562	5108	.306
Tom *Wimpy* Paciorek	18	1162	4121	.282
Bob *Fats* Fothergill	12	1064	3269	.326
Ron *The Roundman* Northey	12	874	3172	.276
Leaping Mike Menosky	9	685	2465	.278
Gene *Road Runner* Clines	10	645	2328	.277
Frank *Pudgie* Delahanty	6	223	986	.226
Wally *Skinny* Shaner	4	175	629	.278
Joe *Muscles* Gallagher	2	133	487	.273
Howard *Slim Jim* Earl	2	127	513	.248
Steve *Flip* Filipowicz	3	40	179	.223
Frank *Jumbo* Whitney	1	33	139	.237
Bruce *Fatso* Sloan	1	28	104	.269
Jacob *Stump* Edington	1	16	53	.302
Arthur *Skinny* Graham	2	14	57	.246
Charlie *Skinny* Kalbfus	1	1	5	.200
Bob *String* Gandy	1	0	2	.000
Clarence *Slats* Jordan	2	0	7	.000
Frank *Fats* Kalin	2	0	7	.000

PINCH HITTERS:	Yr	Hits	AB's	Ave
Murray *Porky* Howell	1	2	7	.286
Carl *Skinny* McNabb	1	0	1	.000
Heavy George Wheeler	1	0	3	.000

PITCHERS:	Yr	Won	Lost	ERA
Mel *Wimpy* Harder	20	223	186	3.80
Fat Freddie Fitzsimmons	19	217	146	3.51
Claude *Wimpy* Osteen	18	196	195	3.30
Harry *Slim* Sallee	14	174	143	2.56
Ernie *Tiny* Bonham	10	103	72	3.06
George *Jumbo* McGinnis	6	102	79	2.95
George *Stump* Weidman	9	101	156	3.60
William *Slim* Harriss	9	95	135	4.25
Fat Jack Fisher	11	86	139	4.06
Hal *Skinny* Brown	14	85	92	3.81
Jim *Jumbo* Nash	7	68	64	3.58
James *Jumbo* Elliott	10	63	74	4.24
Frank *Stubby* Overmire	10	58	67	3.96

ROSTER

PITCHERS: (Cont.)	Yr	Won	Lost	ERA
Tom *The Blade* Hall	10	52	33	3.27
Frank *Thin Man* Allen	6	50	67	2.93
Nick *Jumbo* Strincevich	8	46	49	4.05
George *Slats* McConnell	6	41	51	2.60
Walter *Jumbo* Brown	12	33	31	4.07
Earnest *Tiny* Osborne	4	31	40	4.72
Alfred *Chubby* Dean	7	30	46	5.08
Ed *Slim* Love	6	28	21	3.04
Starvin' Marvin Freeman	8	25	12	3.77
Doyle *Porky* Lade	5	25	29	4.39
Grover *Slim* Lowdermilk	9	23	39	3.58
Chuck *Twiggy* Hartenstein	6	17	19	4.52
James *Tiny* Chaplin	4	15	24	4.25
Norm *Bones* Baker	3	14	15	3.42
Pat *Atlas* Perry	6	12	10	3.46
Daniel *Jumping Jack* Jones	1	11	7	3.14
Kyle *Skinny* Graham	4	11	22	5.02
Phil *Flip* Paine	6	10	1	3.36
Dick *Bones* Tomanek	5	10	10	4.95
Al *Pudgy* Gould	2	9	11	3.05
Walt *Tiny* Leverenz	3	7	31	3.15
Frank *Porky* Biscan	3	7	9	5.28
Mike *Skinny* Strahler	4	6	8	3.57
William *Slim* Emmerich	2	4	4	4.85
Richard *Stub* Brown	3	4	1	4.90

PITCHERS: (Cont.)	Yr	Won	Lost	ERA
Norm *Jumbo* Roy	1	4	3	5.13
Elmer *Tiny* Leonard	1	2	2	2.84
Bob *Butterball* Botz	1	2	1	3.43
Frank *Stubby* Mack	3	2	3	4.94
Edward *Slim* Foster	1	1	0	2.14
Ed *Jumbo* Barry	3	1	6	3.53
Oscar *Slim* Harrell	1	0	0	0.00
Lewis *Jumbo* Schoeneck	1	0	0	0.00
James *Kip* Dowd	1	0	0	0.00
Al *Stumpy* Verdel	1	0	0	0.00
Les *Wimpy* Willis	1	0	2	3.48
Charlie *Slim* Harding	1	0	0	4.50
Harry *Slim* Kinzy	1	0	1	4.98
Jim *Bones* Blackburn	2	0	2	5.50
Walt *Slim* McGrew	3	0	1	6.60
Carl *Stubby* Mathias	2	0	2	7.14
Wellington *Wimpy* Quinn	1	0	0	7.20
Oran *Skinny* O'Neal	2	0	0	9.24
Charles *Slim* Embry	1	0	0	10.13

EXTRAS:
Candlestick Park - *The Stick*
Charles *Chub* Feeney - President of the NL 1970-86
Phil *Fatso* Blazovich - baseball nickname book writer

LINGO

Muscle One: Due to the batter's strength, even though he "doesn't get all of it", he hit a homer

Kick One: Make an error

Skip a Rope: Jump up to avoid being hit on the foot by a pitch

Chase One Down: Run a long way to catch a fly ball

Fat One: An easy pitch to hit

Hopper: A ground ball

Skips Through: Ball bounces between fielders

Hops the Wall: Ball bounces and hits the fence

Short Hop: Ball hits the ground just in front of the fielder's glove

One Hopper: Ball bounces once then reaches the fielder

Two Hopper: See above - use your imagination

Three Hopper: You've got to be kidding!

Lift Him: Remove a player for a pinch hitter or remove a pitcher for a reliever

Jerk One: Hit a homer

Squeeze One: Catch a ball and not drop it

Cut Down: Throw a runner out who is attempting to advance a base

Fast: Don't eat, what do you think?

Out of Gas: Player tires out

Pumped Up: Motivated for a game

D. L.

9

Team

Currently if a player is injured, rather than "carrying" him on the roster when he is unable to "suit up", the team places him on the D.L. (disabled list). Now the ball club may replace the injured player with a healthy substitute, one usually brought up from their farm team. When a player is placed on the D.L., it is for a designated time, such as 15 or 30 days. For that period he is unable to perform for the parent club.

On this D.L. Team there are many players that need to mend, and even more who are menders. There are 71 Docs, many of them actual doctors. Doctor Bobby Brown, after retiring from baseball, was a practicing cardiologist for 25 years. In 1984 Doc came back to the game as the American League President. The D.L. Team's Docs will be kept busy. Whether it be a Pinch, Bash, Bruz, Bump, Stretch or Yank, several team members need attention. Others are Fidgety, Twitchy, Nervous, Jittery or have the Shakes. No wonder, they could have One Arm, Three Fingers, a Patcheye or No-Neck! That does not count two Crashes, a Whiplash or a Big Hurt.

One player, due to his nickname alone, stands out in this "unhealthy" group: Luke Old Aches and Pains Appling. The story has it, although a very durable player, he was a hypochondriac. Luke was always complaining about maladies and routinely was found on the trainer's table. Old Aches and Pains managed to be a starter through his 42nd year, playing 20 summers. At 40, when most ballplayers are coaches, Old Aches and Pains was the AL All-Star shortstop, played 139 games and hit .306! At age 41 Luke hit .314 in 139 games and at age 42 Luke hit .301 in 142 games! Since Luke led the league in errors five seasons, (he was very fast and got to many balls other players would not have reached) he was also dubbed Fumblefoot. We now only call him Mr. Hall of Fame!

LINEUP

| CA | Hal *Cura* Smith | hailed from Barling, Arkansas. In the three summers he |

played 100 or more games, Cura was twice named to the National League All-Star team. 1959 was his best season. While handling backstop duties for the Red Birds, Cura reached the bleachers 13 times.

| 1B | Willie *Stretch* McCovey | had a career which touched four decades (1959-80) and |

ended in Cooperstown. Rookie of the Year in 1959, Most Valuable Player in 1969 and Comeback Player of the Year in 1977 begin to tell Stretch's story. 521 homers (tie tenth) and 1555 RBI's (28th) say the rest.

| 2B | Elliott *Bump* Wills | is the son of Hall of Famer and base stealing great Maury |

Wills. Bump was an excellent bag swiper himself. He stole 196 sacks, finishing third in swipes in the AL in 1978 and fifth in 1979. Bump's 32+ steals and 75.1% success rate with Maury's 41+ steals and 73.8% success.

| SS | Luke *Old Aches and Pains* Appling | is the only American League shortstop to win two batting |

titles. In 16 of his 20 seasons he hit over .300. Known for fouling off pitches to get bases on balls, Luke ranks 25th in free passes and tied for 42nd in on base percentage for his career.

| 3B | James *Doc* Casey | played ten seasons. An eight year starter, he was the Cub's |

third baseman when a poem made famous "Tinker to Evers to Chance". In 1905, Doc, of the four infielders, was the only one to lead in fielding % at his position. He averaged over one hit per game for his career.

| OF | Roger *Doc* Cramer | was a 20 year star. Named five times to the American |

League All-Star team, he was a top fielder and an outstanding leadoff hitter. Eight times Doc batted .300 or more. His 2705 hits places him in the top 50 and nine seasons of 180+ hits helped him to that lofty total.

| OF | Harry *Doc* Gessler | was a left-handed batting right fielder. He played eight years |

just after the turn of the century. Doc's best summer was 1908. He finished third in batting, trailing only the Georgia Peach and Yahoo Sam Crawford. Doc also finished fourth in triples and third in slugging % in 1908.

| OF | Dick *Twitches* Porter | was trapped seven years in the minors because of a high |

price tag placed on him. Finally he reached the Majors in 1929 at age 27. Twitches' first four seasons he hit over .300. In 1930 he batted .350 in 119 games, scored 100 times and pounded 43 doubles.

| P | Milt *Gimpy* Pappas | hurled 17 seasons. He never had the "big year", yet from |

1958-72 Gimpy won in double figures 14 times. His 43 career shutouts (36th) and 1728 strikeouts (tie 64th) show his excellence. On September 2nd, 1972 Gimpy tossed a no-hitter, beating the Padres 8-0.

| P | *Fidgety* Lew Burdette | hailed from Nitro, West Virginia and was a dynamite pitcher. |

He won 20 or more games twice and tossed 33 career shutouts. A control specialist, Fidgety Lew's walks per nine innings were microscopic. In 1959 (1.18), 1960 (1.14) and 1961 (1.09) he was exceptional!

| P | Guy *Doc* White | was a tall, slim southpaw who twirled for 13 summers. |

In 1905 Doc went 18-6, topping the AL with a 1.52 ERA. The next season his 27 wins tied for the American League lead. Doc sutured 45 career shutouts (tie 28th) and his career 2.39 ERA ranks him 18th.

| RES | Dick *Dr. Strangeglove* Stuart | was a power hitter. In the seven seasons he played 100+ |

contests, Dick averaged 29 tators. In 1963 his 42 shots were the second most in the American League. Three seasons Dr. Strangeglove drove in over 100 runs, topping the Junior Circuit with 118 RBI's in 1963.

| RES | Frank *The Big Hurt* Thomas | can hurt you with his quick glove, his keen eye, his high |

batting average and his awesome power! From 1991-94 The Big Hurt has averaged 36+ doubles, 33+ homers, 106 runs, 120+ walks, .453 on base average, .596 slugging % and .326 batting average!

| RES | Dwight *Doc* Gooden | is an 11 year veteran, yet still young for a pitcher at age 30. |

A teenage phenomenon, Doc has already fanned nearly 2000 batters and his current 64.9 winning % would rank him 15th. Arm and drug troubles have slowed him. Let's pray he comes back just fine.

| RES | Bobby *Doc* Brown | was a utility player for the Yankees in the late 40's and |

early 50's. In 1619 regular season at bats Doc swatted only 14 three baggers, yet in 41 World Series at bats he spanked three triples. His three Fall Classic pinch-hits have never been topped.

L to R: Dwight *Doc* Gooden, Milt *Gimpy* Pappas, Luke *Old Aches and Pains* Appling, *Fidgety* Lew Burdette, Roger *Doc* Cramer

It'sa FACT

Willie **Stretch** McCovey: He scooped up his nickname from his first base play. Stretch was also an awesome and feared power hitter. I can still remember when a team put four players in the outfield to "defense" Stretch. He responded by smashing one off the wall! The word feared is not used loosely. After leading the NL in homers and RBI's in both 1968 and 1969, pitchers walked Stretch 137 times in 1970. Losing many RBI opportunities, Willie still knocked in 126 runs and hit 39 long balls in 1970.

Dick **Dr. Strangeglove** Stuart: He ranks 27th all time in home run percentage at 5.7%.

Dock Ellis: On June 12th, 1970 he fired a no-hitter. His real name is Dock, so he is not on the roster.

Roy **Doc** Miller: In 1911 he had a career year. Doc led the National League in hits and finished second in two baggers and batting average.

Yancy Wyatt **Doc** Ayers: In 1915 he had a fantastic year. Doc won 14 games and fashioned a 2.21 ERA. A control artist, he gave up only 38 free passes in 211 1/3 innings. In addition, Doc gave up only one home run all summer!

William **Doc** Scanlan: He had his best season in 1906, winning 18 of Brooklyn's 66 victories. Included in Doc's win total were six whitewashes.

Jittery Joe Berry: Except for two innings in 1942, he reached the Big Leagues in 1944 as a 39 year old reliever (see guys, we still have a chance!). In his first season Jittery Joe led (tie) the Junior Circuit in saves. He also topped all hurlers in appearances in 1945.

Sheldon **Available** Jones: He was just that, available! As a pitcher, regardless of when his last outing was, he was always ready. 1948 was Available's best season. He ranked second in the NL in appearances, starting 21 games and relieving in 34 contests. His 16-8 record placed him sixth in wins (tie) and second in winning %.

Harry **Doc** Tonkin: His short pitching career was all of 2 2/3 innings. Doc did come to the plate twice and went 2/2, retiring with a 1.000 batting average!

James **Doc** McJames: Born James McCutcheon James, he slightly changed his name. Except for a two game call up in 1895, Doc's real first season was in 1896 at age 22. He won 12 games for his ninth place team. In 1897 Doc led the NL in strikeouts and shutouts (tie), winning 15 for his sixth place club. Doc's 27 wins in 1898 was tied for third best and only one pitcher fanned more batters. His next summer Doc put up 19 more wins. Tragically, one month past his 28th birthday, he died.

Dwight **Doc** Gooden: His nickname was shortened from Doctor K (a K stands for a strikeout). Doc had an unbelievable season as a 20 year old in 1985. He went 24-4, winning 14 straight in one stretch. Doc's 24 wins, 16 complete games and 268 strikeouts all were league highs. His microscopic 1.53 ERA was the second lowest since 1919! Doc not only was the youngest pitcher ever awarded the Cy Young, but he also was selected unanimously!

Roger **Doc** Cramer: As a leadoff hitter, he led the AL in at bats seven times, the Major League record. Doc was the 16th most difficult player to strike out. He was rung up only once every 26.5 at bats. To put this in perspective, currently Tony Gwynn is baseball's most difficult strikeout. He fans about once every 20 at bats. Doc finished his fly chasing career eighth in putouts.

Why is Doc Cramer not in the Hall of Fame?

	YRS	AT BATS	RUNS	HITS	2B	3B	HR	RBI	AVE
Cramer	20	9140	1357	2705	396	109	37	842	.296
Appling	20	8856	1319	2749	440	102	45	1116	.310

Both were great fielders, both batted leadoff and both played in the same era.

	YRS	AT BATS	RUNS	HITS	2B	3B	HR	RBI	AVE
Rizzuto	13	5816	877	1588	239	62	38	563	.273

The Veterans Committee just elected Scooter to the Hall. He was a great leader and well deserving, but let's not forget Flit.

Henry **Doc** McMahon: On October 6th, 1908 he twirled his only game. Doc went the distance for the win, allowed three runs and walked no one. Doc also banged out two hits.

George **Pinch** McBride: He started nine of his 16 seasons. Pinch was known for his glove. In those nine years as a regular, he led all AL shortstops in DP's six times, fielding % five times and putouts three times.

Fidgety Lew Burdette: From 1953-62 he combined with Warren Spahn to create a righty-lefty combination which won 372 games! On August 18th, 1960 Fidgety Lew no-hit the Phillies 1-0. Not to be shown up, Spahny hurled the next two no-hitters in the Majors on September 16th, 1960 and April 28th, 1961!

TRIVIA*

1) A doctor in the off season, he went into the stands and saved a fan's life when the spectator was stricken by a heart attack (in 1978).

2) At age 19 he was the youngest player to be named Rookie of the Year.

3) I will never forget his 1958 Topps card. He posed left-handed using Spahny's glove.

4) Although his career batting average was a microscopic .123, he did hit 20 tators, including three in one game on August 27th, 1961.

5) He read medical books while Yogi, his roommate, was rumored to be reading comic books.

6) He hit 66 home runs in one season (in the minors).

7) He received 45 intentional walks in 1970.

8) He played football in college with Bo Jackson.

9) He and Sunny Jim Bottomley are the only players to twice have six hits in a nine inning game.

10) His .285 lifetime batting average places him fifth for pitchers.

11) In his first game in the Majors, July 30th, 1959, he had four hits, including two triples.

12) After his playing career, he went on to manage the Cleveland Indians from 1987-89.

13) His weak fielding and a Peter Seller's movie combined to form his nickname.

14) He hit 18 grand slams in his career, which places him second to Columbia Lou. His three pinch-hit grand slams tie him for the record.

15) He is big. He hits the ball so hard he hurts it. In 1993 and 1994 he was voted the AL MVP.

16) At age 27 he made the Majors. Already a practicing dentist in the off season, he drilled baseballs for five summers. He later drilled players three seasons as the manager for the Phillies. (Hint: his nickname is Doc and he shares his last name with an ex NFL "bridge playing" coach)

17) An outstanding center fielder, he was also called Flit (an insecticide), because he was death on 'fly' balls.

18) In 1927 he hit .316 with 179 hits, including four he yanked out. (Hint: another dentist, he shares the same last name as a reliever nicknamed Turk)

19) This hurler did not suffer his first losing season until his 12th year in the Majors. Amazingly, only one summer did his team finish above third place.

20) In Harvey The Kitten Haddix' 13 inning 1-0 loss, this hurler was the player who won the game tossing a 13 inning shutout.

21) He not only went 16-11 for the 1930 last place Phillies (52-102), but he also helped his own cause by batting .253 with three homers. (Hint: he shares his name with a famous rock singer)

22) Initially a Yankee, he came back to haunt them. He whooped them three times during the 1957 World Series, twice whitewashing them!

23) He was the Tiger's hitting hero in the 1945 Fall Classic. He had 11 hits, scored seven runs and batted .379, all team leading. He also stole a base, not bad for a 40 year old!

24) As a father-son combination they are eighth in hits, fifth in runs and currently first in stolen bases (through 1994). The son is on the roster.

25) He and his younger brother Jimmy combined to star for 24 seasons. They rank seventh in swipes as a brother combination. (Hint: take away a "T" from Jimmy and he could be an NFL coach)

* BRAIN SCANNERS answers found on page 236

ROSTER

CATCHERS:	Yr	Hits	AB's	Ave
Albert *Doc* Bushong	12	511	2392	.214
Hal *Cura* Smith	7	437	1697	.258
Verne *Stinger* Clemons	7	364	1271	.286
Chester *Pinch* Thomas	10	245	1035	.237
Howard *Doc* Edwards	5	216	906	.238
George *Doc* Yeager	6	168	705	.238
Michael *Doc* Kennedy	5	160	615	.260
William *Doc* Marshall	5	159	756	.210
Vic *Crash* Janowicz	2	42	196	.214
Harry *Doc* Sage	1	41	275	.149
Lou *Doc* Legett	4	25	124	.202
Leon *Doc* Martel	2	15	72	.208
Doug *Eyechart* Gwosdz	4	15	104	.144
Wally *Doc* Snell	1	3	8	.375
Ralph *Doc* Carroll	1	2	22	.091
Otto *Hickey* Hoffman	1	0	6	.000

1ST BASEMEN:	Yr	Hits	AB's	Ave
Willie *Stretch* McCovey	22	2211	8197	.270
Dick *Dr. Strangeglove* Stuart	10	1055	3997	.264
Wheeler *Doc* Johnston	11	992	3774	.263
Frank *The Big Hurt* Thomas	5	741	2271	.326
Howie *Stretch* Schultz	6	383	1588	.241
Jack *Stretch* Phillips	9	252	892	.283
Warren *Doc* Gill	1	17	76	.224
Willard *Doc* Hazleton	1	3	23	.130
William *Doc* Moskiman	1	1	9	.111

2ND BASEMEN:	Yr	Hits	AB's	Ave
William *Yank* Robinson	10	825	3248	.241
Elliott *Bump* Wills	6	807	3030	.266
Lawrence *Crash* Davis	3	102	444	.230
John *Doc* Kerr	2	28	111	.252

SHORTSTOPS:	Yr	Hits	AB's	Ave
Luke *Old Aches and Pains* Appling	20	2749	8856	.310
George *Pinch* McBride	16	1203	5526	.218
John *Doc* Lavan	12	954	3891	.245
Edward *Doc* Farrell	9	467	1799	.260
Edward *Doc* Marshall	4	170	658	.258
Bill *Bump* Akers	4	124	475	.261
Charles *Doc* Wood	1	1	3	.333
Fredrick *Doc* Wallace	1	1	4	.250
James *Stub* Smith	1	1	10	.100
Harry *Doc* Shanley	1	0	8	.000

3RD BASEMEN:	Yr	Hits	AB's	Ave
James *Doc* Casey	10	1122	4341	.258
Bobby *Doc* Brown	8	452	1619	.279
James *Doc* Prothro	5	191	600	.318

OUTFIELDERS:	Yr	Hits	AB's	Ave
Roger *Doc* Cramer	20	2705	9140	.296
Harry *Doc* Gessler	8	831	2969	.280

OUTFIELDERS: (Cont.)	Yr	Hits	AB's	Ave
Dick *Twitches* Porter	6	774	2515	.308
Homer *Doc* Smoot	5	763	2635	.290
Walt *No-Neck* Williams	10	640	2373	.270
Steve *Psycho* Lyons	9	545	2162	.252
Joe *Doc* Evans	11	529	2043	.259
Roy *Doc* Miller	5	507	1717	.295
Uriah *Bloody Jake* Evans	7	435	1831	.238
Pat *Doc* Carney	4	308	1248	.247
Marv *Twitch* Rickert	6	284	1149	.247
Luther *Doc* Cook	4	282	1028	.274
Benny *Earache* Meyer	4	276	1041	.265
Lou *The Nervous Greek* Skizas	4	196	725	.270
Pete *Bash* Compton	6	186	773	.241
William *Doc* Nance	4	182	657	.277
Johnny *Patcheye* Gill	6	79	322	.245
One Armed Pete Gray	1	51	234	.218
George *Hickie* Wilson	1	19	82	.232
Jacob *Stump* Edington	1	16	53	.302
Samuel *Doc* Ralston	1	15	73	.205
Charlie *Doc* Hall	1	1	12	.083
Billy *Doc* Queen	1	0	2	.000

PINCH HITTERS:	Yr	Hits	AB's	Ave
William *Doc* Bass	1	1	1	1.000
Harold *Doc* Daugherty	1	0	1	.000

PITCHERS:	Yr	Won	Lost	ERA
Mordecai *Three Finger* Brown	14	239	129	2.06
Milt *Gimpy* Pappas	17	209	164	3.40
Fidgety Lew Burdette	18	203	144	3.66
Guy *Doc* White	13	189	156	2.39
Dwight *Doc* Gooden	11	157	85	3.10
George *Doc* Medich	11	124	105	3.78
James *Doc* Crandall	10	102	62	2.92
George *Stump* Weidman	9	101	156	3.60
Lloyd *Gimpy* Brown	12	91	105	4.20
Fidgety Phil Collins	8	80	85	4.66
James *Doc* McJames	6	79	80	3.43
Hugh *One Arm* Daily	6	73	87	2.92
Yancy Wyatt *Doc* Ayers	9	65	79	2.84
William *Doc* Scanlan	8	65	71	3.00
Lee *Stinger* Stange	10	62	61	3.56
Eustace *Doc* Newton	8	54	72	3.22
Sheldon *Available* Jones	8	54	57	3.96
Jim *Sting* Ray	9	43	30	3.61
Ed *Doc* Lafitte	5	37	36	3.34
Medicine Bill Mountjoy	3	31	24	3.25
Blind Ryne Duren	10	27	44	3.83
Charles *Doc* Watson	3	22	21	2.70
Jittery Joe Berry	4	21	22	2.45
William *Wheezer* Dell	4	19	23	2.55
Frank *Doc* Reisling	4	15	19	2.45
Stan *Yank* Yerkes	3	15	24	3.66
Samuel *Doc* Landis	1	12	28	3.32

ROSTER

PITCHERS: (Cont.)	Yr	Won	Lost	ERA
Homer *Doc* Hillebrand	3	8	4	2.51
Ralph *Bruz* Hamner	4	8	20	4.58
Walter *Shakes* Huntzinger	4	7	8	3.60
Julio *Whiplash* Navarro	6	7	9	3.65
Johnny *Doc* Rutherford	1	7	7	4.25
Archie *Lumbago* Stimmel	3	5	19	4.21
Harley *Doc* Parker	4	5	8	5.90
Tom *Doc* Knowlson	1	4	6	3.49
Pat *Doc* Carney	3	4	10	4.69
Morris *Doc* Amole	2	4	10	4.75
Richard *Stub* Brown	3	4	1	4.90
Stew *Doc* Bowers	2	2	1	4.60
George *Doc* Leitner	1	2	6	5.68
Henry *Doc* McMahon	1	1	0	3.00
Merle *Doc* Adkins	2	1	1	5.00
Hartman *Doc* Oberlander	1	1	2	5.26
Harold *Doc* Martin	3	1	2	5.48
Bob *Doc* Vail	1	1	2	6.00

PITCHERS: (Cont.)	Yr	Won	Lost	ERA
Charlie *Yank* Brown	1	1	2	7.77
Floyd *Three-Finger* Newkirk	1	0	0	0.00
Ron *Stretch* Tompkins	2	0	2	3.96
Horace *Doc* Ozmer	1	0	0	4.50
Walter *Doc* Whittaker	1	0	0	4.50
Bob *Crooked Arm* Cremins	1	0	0	5.06
Hardy *Stretch* Boyles	2	0	4	5.79
Al *Stretch* Grunwald	2	0	1	6.63
Harry *Doc* Tonkin	1	0	0	6.75
Albert *Doc* Waldbauer	1	0	0	7.20
Harry *Doc* Imlay	1	0	0	7.24
Howard *Doc* Twining	1	0	0	13.50
John *Doc* Stafford	1	0	1	14.14
Ed *Doc* Edelen	1	0	0	27.00
Theodore *Doc* Sechrist	1	0	0	∞

EXTRA:
Mike *Stretch* Gelfand - Great KQR Radio Personality

LINGO

7th Inning Stretch: Middle of the 7th, all customers stand and sing *Take Me Out To The Ball Game*

Cripple: A 3-0 pitch, down the middle and easy to hit

Doctored the Ball: "Load up" the pitch or alter the ball's surface

A Bleeder: Poorly hit ball which the batter beats out for a hit

Scratch Hit: See above

Break One Off: Throw a curve ball

Doctor No: Terrible fielder

Lay One Down: Bunt

A Shot: Hard hit ball

Pull Hitter: Batter who hits the ball to his side of second base

Pinch Hit: A double owie! Person bats for a teammate

Pinch Runner: Person runs for a teammate

Stretches One: Adds an extra base to a hit

Yanked: Player is removed from the game

Poked: Hit the ball

Knocked Out: Pitcher does poorly and is yanked

Took His Head Off: Player ducks under a liner

Pounded: Pitcher is hit hard

Dead Ball: When a batter is hit by a pitch or when a runner is hit by a batted ball

Jolted: Hit a ball very hard

Crushed: See above

Jammed: Ball pitched too close to the batter

Stroked One: Had a good hit

Carry a Player: Have a player on your roster

Split Finger: A sinker type pitch, held between the middle and forefinger when thrown

Player Is Cut: Player is dropped from the team

Heartbreaker: Lose a close game

Choke: Perform poorly in the clutch

Cough It Up: Drop a catchable ball

Broke His Wrists: Swung at the ball

Cutoff: Player catches a throw rather than letting it go through to a base

ELEMENTS

10

Team

Elements are always a factor in playing baseball. Precipitation can delay or even postpone a game. Rain, fog and even snow have made playing contests impossible. Temperature can extremely influence players' performances. Imagine pitchers freezing in 35° cold during April or sweltering in 110° heat during August. More subtle conditions are wind and sun. Candlestick Park is known for its swirling winds, making easy pop-ups very difficult to catch, and Wrigley Field's friendly southerly breezes help create slugfests. Yankee Stadium's left field is its sun field. Twilight at "The House That Ruth Built" allows the third deck shadow to be between the mound and home plate, heavily favoring the pitcher over the batter. Then add in "man made" elements. The ground crew slants the foul lines (ex: lean toward fair territory) to help bunts or they put sand a few feet off first base to slow down potential base stealers (ask Maury Wills). Artificial turf allows infielders to play deeper, makes grounders go faster and permits liners in the gap to reach the wall. By making adjustments to the various elements, the players are able to perform better.

The Elements Team literally covers every weather condition. It is a team for all seasons, not just baseball. Spring will be Stormin', but after the Lightning and Thunderbolt, it will become Sunny with Sunshine and a Rainbow. Oh, there may be some Muck or be Dirty, Muddy, Slippery and Slick, but when it's no longer Stormy, the sun will change to Sunset, Twilight, Moonlight and Still. Summer will have a Storm. It could be a Gale, Tornado, Hurricanes or Cyclones! Be careful, dry weather can lead to Fire and Smoke. Autumn air can often become Nippy and Chilly. Frequently it is Gloomy, Dusty, Breezy and Windy. Before you know it, winter arrives with it's Snow and Frosty Icicles.

One player literally overshadows all others on the team, he is Denton Cy Young. His nickname Cy became a nickname for aspiring young (pun intended) pitchers for years to come. There was even Irv Cy the Second Young and Harly Cy the Third Young! My hero, the nickname guru Chris Boomer Berman, would probably have dubbed him "Amazingly Young." Cy reached the National League in 1890 at the age of 23. For the next 22 summers he wrote baseball record books. From 1891-1904 Cy put 14 fabulous, consistent seasons together. Only his 19 wins in 1900 kept him from winning 20 or more games each year. Cy averaged 28+ wins, five times topping 30 victories in this span. Amazingly, Young holds the Major League record for wins at the age of 34 (33), 35 (32), 36 (28), 37 (26), 38 (18), 40 (21), 41 (21) and 42 (19)! His secret was exceptional control. For his career he averaged 1.49 bases on balls per game. Six summers Cy walked fewer than one batter per nine innings. In 1904, at age 37, he issued only 29 free passes in 380 innings! At the young age of 41 Cy went 21-11. In 299 frames Cy gave up just one home run! His 1.26 ERA is the 13th best for a season! That summer he tossed his third no-hitter, whipping the Yankees 8-0 on June 30th, 1908. Cy also was good with the lumber. He holds the record for hits for twirlers. Cy pounded out 623 safeties, going deep 18 times! During his career Cy won every possible pitching honor but one, the Cy Young award!

LINEUP

CA	Forrest *Smoky* Burgess

swung his mean bat for 18 summers. A six time All-Star during his career, Smoky batted over .300 five campaigns, including a lofty .368 in 1954! Three seasons he led all backstops in fielding %. In later years Smoky became baseball's premier pinch hitter.

1B	*Sunny* Jim Bottomley

acquired his moniker because he was so cheerful. During his 16 season career, Sunny Jim nine times batted over .300. From 1924-29 he drove in over 100 runs each year, averaging 126! In 1928 Sunny Jim led in triples, homers (tie) and RBI's and he was voted the NL's MVP!

2B	George *Firebrand* Stovall

was a 12 year veteran. He played every position but pitcher and catcher during his career. From 1908-11 he led all Junior Circuit first sackers in fielding %. Firebrand was a playing manager from 1911-15 and was the first player to jump to the upstart Federal League in 1914.

SS	Charles *Dusty* Miller

was originally a shortstop, but he converted to the outfield. His first full season was 1895. Dusty batted .325 and both drove in and scored over 100 runs! Three of his four "starting" summers he hit over .300. In 1896 Dusty swiped 76 sacks (fourth).

3B	*Dirty* Jack Doyle

was born in Killorglin, Ireland. Dirty Jack played every position, but pitcher, during his 17 year career. Seven seasons the fiery player batted over .300, including five campaigns in a row (1893-97). In 1894 Dirty Jack hit .367 and drove in 100 runs. His 516 steals rank him 28th!

OF	Fred *Cy* Williams

was a late bloomer, becoming a regular in 1915 at age 27. The NL strongboy played until age 42. Part of Cy's career was in the dead ball era. He led the NL in homers in 1916 (12, tie), 1920 (15) and when the ball became lively in 1923 (41) and in 1927 (30, tie).

OF	Frank *Wildfire* Schulte

was one of the top power hitters of the dead ball era. From 1910-15 he placed third, second, and twice first (one tie) in HR's. Wildfire's best season was 1911. He slugged an amazing 21 HR's and plated 107 runs! Wildfire, an excellent base thief, stole home 22 times in his career!

OF	Johnnie *Dusty* Baker

is currently the manager of the San Francisco Giants. As a player Dusty's career spanned 19 years. The two time National League All-Star swatted 242 home runs and drove in over 1000 runs. Six summers Dusty went deep 20 or more times.

P	Denton *Cy* Young

was phenomenal. For his career Cy won 511 games, 94 more than Big Train, who is in second place! Cy ranks first in complete games with 749 and in innings pitched with 7356. His 76 career shutouts are fourth all time. Fifteen times Cy won 20 or more games (the record).

P	Amos *Hoosier Thunderbolt* Rusie

hailed from Mooresville Indiana. He made his Major League debut (1889) three weeks before his 28th birthday. Amos went on to win 20 or more games the next eight summers. Four consecutive seasons (1891-94) he won over 30 times! Amos captured five strikeout titles.

P	Mel *Dusty* Parnell

pitched his entire ten year career for the Red Sox. From 1948-53 he was Boston's ace, twice chalking up 20+ victories. Dusty led all AL hurlers with 25 wins in 1949. The big left-hander was also a good man at the plate. Dusty helped his own cause in 1951 by batting .309.

RES	*Stormin'* Gorman Thomas

ranks 29th all time in home run %. Two seasons (one tie) he led the Junior Circuit in long balls. Five times Stormin' Gorman slugged over 30 dingers. Three years he knocked in over 100 runs. During his career, 47% of his hits went for extra bases!

RES	James *Cy* Seymour

made his debut in 1896 as a 23 year old left-handed pitcher. By age 25 (1898) he led the NL in strikeouts and won 25 games. Cy converted to the outfield in 1901 and went on to bat over .300 seven times, once (1905) leading the Junior Circuit in batting average.

RES	Fredrick *Cy* Falkenberg

was a 6'5" right-hander. He twirled 12 seasons, mostly for second division clubs. Late in his career Cy had his two best years. Cy won 23 games (second in AL) and tossed six shutouts (fourth) in 1913. Jumping to the Federal League in 1914, Cy posted 25 V's and nine shutouts (first).

RES	Mike *Human Rain Delay* Hargrove

starred 12 summers in the Junior Circuit. Six years he batted over .300. The Human Rain Delay was also very selective as a batter. 14.78% of his at bats (41st) were bases on balls. He received over 100 free passes four seasons, twice leading the AL in free tickets.

L to R: Johnnie *Dusty* Baker, Forrest *Smoky* Burgess, Denton *Cy* Young, *Sunny* Jim Bottomley, *Stormin'* Gorman Thomas

It'sa FACT

<u>Frank **Wildfire** Schulte</u>: The Chalmers Award was given from 1911-14 by Hugh Chalmers, the President of The Chalmer Motor Company. It was to be presented to the best player in each league. The prize was a Chalmers "30" automobile. The first year Ty Georgia Peach Cobb won in the AL and Wildfire won in the NL. He had a career year, leading the NL in homers, RBI's (tie) and slugging %, and finishing third in triples and fourth in hits and runs scored.

<u>Cyril **Cy** Slapnicka</u>: His career in the Majors was very short. His fame came when he was a scout. Cy discovered and signed Rapid Robert Feller, Mel Wimpy Harder, Earl Rock Averill and Hal Trosky.

<u>Ralph **Cy** Perkins</u>: He was a defensive specialist. Cy led AL catchers in assists three times and DP's and putouts once each during his six starting seasons. Then he helped tutor and back-up Hall of Famer Gordon Mickey Cochrane the remainder of his 17 summers.

<u>James **Dusty** Rhodes</u>: His career was unique. He appeared in 576 games (only 297 in the field) over seven seasons. Dusty was a powerful hitter. In 1954 he slugged 15 yard shots and drove in 50 runs in only 164 at bats (a 9.15 homer %)! Dusty poled ten round trippers and had 36 RBI's in 176 at bats in 1952 and in 1953 his 11 seat reachers and 30 tallies knocked in came from only 163 at bats.

<u>Amos **Hoosier Thunderbolt** Rusie</u>: He terrified batters. During his time, (1889-98) he was the fastest pitcher and one of the wildest. Rule makers changed the pitching distance from 50' to 60' 6" mainly because of the Hoosier Tunderbolt. From 1890-95 Amos not only led the NL in strikeouts five times, but he also walked over 200 batters five seasons.

<u>Harry **Cy** Morgan</u>: From 1908-11 he won 14, 18, 18 and 15 games and tossed 12 shutouts. Two seasons (1909-10) Cy had ERA's of 1.81 and 1.55!

<u>Roy **Stormy** Weatherly</u>: In his Major League debut he legged out two triples and a single. Later that season he had a 20 games hitting streak, the AL rookie record. Stormy was the first outfielder (1943) to have ten putouts in a game twice in one season.

<u>James **Cy** Seymour</u>: Playing for Cincinnati in 1905, he had an unbelievable season. Cy led the NL in hits, doubles, triples, RBI's and batting average! Cy was second in homers by one, causing him to just miss the Triple Crown!

<u>Clint **Hondo Hurricane** Hartung</u>: In 1949, while chalking up nine wins, he poled four homers in only 63 at bats!

<u>Fred **Cy** Williams</u>: During his career he won four home run titles. Only four other National Leaguers have captured more homer crowns. Mike Schmidt led the league eight times. Ralph Kiner won seven consecutive crowns (1946-52). Master Mel Ott topped the circuit six times, as did Gavvy Cactus Cravath. Cy tied in NL homer crowns with Hall of Famers Hammerin' Hank Aaron, Chuck Klein, Lewis Hack Wilson, Willie Mays and Johnny The Big Cat Mize.

<u>Fred **Fireball** Wenz</u>: During his three season career Fireball appeared in 31 games and was undefeated!

<u>**Twilight** Ed Killian</u>: From 1904-06, he hurled 794 2/3 innings. Twilight Ed won 47 games, posted 12 shutouts and ... never yielded a home run! In 1907 he finally gave up two round trippers, but still Twilight Ed won 25 games (tie third) and finished with a 1.78 ERA!

<u>**Frosty** Bill Duggleby</u>: From 1901-06 he won 86 contest for the Phillies. Frosty Bill's two best seasons were 1901 and 1905. He won 18 and 19 games and posted five whitewashes each campaign!

<u>**Tornado** Jake Weimer</u>: He reached the NL (1903) at the age of 29 and took it by storm. In his first two seasons he won 20 games back to back, finishing third and fourth in ERA and fifth and third in K's. His next two years Tornado Jake won 18 and 20 games! Since he retired with 1472 2/3 innings, he missed the 1500 mark to be eligible for "all time" lists. Tornado Jake's 2.23 lifetime ERA would have placed him eighth all time!

<u>**Smokey** Joe Wood</u>: During spring training for the 1913 season, a fluke injury broke his right thumb. Coming back from the injury, he hurt his shoulder. Smokey Joe was never the same, and tragically one of the games greatest never fully reached his potential. Smokey Joe was so named for his fastball. It was considered as fast as The Big Train's heater. After winning 23 games in 1911, Joe was unbelievable in 1912. The 26 year old right-hander went 34-5, leading the AL in wins, winning %, complete games and shutouts, and finishing second in both K's and ERA! In the 1912 Fall Classic, Smokey Joe chalked up three more victories! Joe's .671 career winning % and 2.03 career ERA are not recognized because he did not have 1500 innings (1436 1/3). Joe would have been fifth and third all time!

<u>**Sunny** Jim Dygert</u>: At the age of 21 he reached the Majors. Two seasons later (1907) Sunny Jim won 21 games, second on his team, the Athletics. The other three starters for Connie Mack were Gettysburg Eddie Plank (24), George Rube Waddell (19) and Charles Chief Bender (16), all future Hall of Famers.

<u>Steve **Smokey** Sundra</u>: He won his last four decisions in 1938 and his first 11 games in 1939!

<u>Irv **Cy the Second** Young</u>: He was a 27 year old rookie in 1905 for the Boston Beaneaters (later Braves). The crosstown rival, Boston Pilgrims (later Red Sox), had Denton Cy Young, hence Irv's nickname. Cy the Second won 20 games in 1905 and 16 of Boston's meager 49 wins in 1906. Irv also "out won" his namesake both seasons!

<u>Darrell **Cy** Blanton</u>: As a 26 year old rookie in 1935 he won 18 games. Cy, a lefty with excellent control, also led all Senior Circuit hurlers in ERA and tied for the lead in shutouts that season.

TRIVIA*

1) The best pitcher in both leagues is voted an award named after this Hall of Famer.

2) In 1977 four Dodgers slugged 30 or more home runs. Steve Popeye Garvey (33), Carl Reggie Smith (32), Ron The Penguin Cey (30) and _____ (30).

3) His full name is Alan Mitchell Edward George Patrick Henry _____, but he was known as ... (Hint: for his last name think of a comedian and watermelons)

4) His older brother Scout (Jesse) was a pitcher. He hit his first Major League home run off of him.

5) A premier pinch hitter, he had 145 pinch-hits in his career. His 27 doubles and 142 RBI's are pinch-hit records and his 16 circuit blasts are third best.

6) His 11 pinch homers were the Major League standard for 31 seasons.

7) This backstop acquired his nickname, because he guarded the plate so well.

8) He was the first umpire to use hand signals for balls and strikes (before they shouted them). He later became the first chief of umpires.

9) He threw so...fast, he was as fast as a cyclone!

10) He was the AL 1974 Rookie of the Year. (Hint: his extremely slow batting technique frustrated pitchers and led to his nickname)

11) For his career he swatted only 54 homers. On August 26th, 1953 and July 27th, 1954 he hit three circuit blasts in one game!

12) Mark Whiten recently tied this happy-go-lucky slugger's Major League record of 12 RBI's in one game.

13) In 1978 his record was 25-3 (third best winning % ever). He tossed a league leading nine shutouts (tying the AL single season shutout record by a lefty, held by Babe Ruth) and had a 1.74 ERA. He won the Cy Young award.

14) Amazingly, he fired two no-hitters in one season (1952), but he still finished only 5-19 for the year!

15) Also called Paw Paw, he was famous for hitting homers on Sunday.

16) He and his father Dizzy combined to win 258 games, a record for a father and son.

17) He pitched an unbelievable 23 consecutive hitless innings, which included a perfect game!

18) Walter Barney Johnson, Robert Lefty Grove, Lynwood Schoolboy Rowe and he all share the American League record of 16 consecutive wins during one season.

19) He was the 1954 World Series' unlikely hero. He hit a three run pinch homer in the tenth inning to win game #1. His pinch single in game #2 tied it. Staying in, he then blasted a homer two innings later. Game #3 his bases loaded pinch single iced the contest. Game #4 he rested!

20) From 1981-86 he played for four teams and had a 39-40 record. From 1987-90 he went 84-45, winning 20 or more games four consecutive years!

21) On June 17th, 1978 he fanned 18 batters.

22) He signed 23 consecutive one year contracts to manage the Dodgers. His 2040 victories places him sixth all time for skippers. He also led "The Bums" to seven World Series appearances and four World Championships!

23) In 1988 and 1989 his log read 16-7 and 19-7.

24) Down 1-0 in the 1977 NLCS, he led the Dodgers to three straight wins. His grand slam won game #2 and his two run tator in game #4 put them into the Series.

25) For his career he is 8-0 in the ALCS and by going 2-0 in the 1989 World Series, he was voted the Classic's MVP.

* MIND BLOWERS answers found on page 236

ROSTER

CATCHERS:	Yr	Hits	AB's	Ave
Forrest *Smoky* Burgess	18	1318	4471	.295
Herold *Muddy* Ruel	19	1242	4514	.275
Ralph *Cy* Perkins	17	933	3604	.259
Rough Bill Carrigan	10	506	1970	.257
Grover *Slick* Hartley	14	353	1319	.268
Danny *Dusty* Kravitz	5	130	552	.236
Orie *Cy* Kerlin	1	0	1	.000

1ST BASEMEN:	Yr	Hits	AB's	Ave
Sunny Jim Bottomley	16	2313	7471	.310
Mike *Human Rain Delay* Hargrove	12	1614	5564	.290
Vernal *Nippy* Jones	8	369	1381	.267
Sunny Jim Hackett	2	86	372	.231
Kenneth *Cy* Rheam	2	57	283	.201
Daniel *Cyclone* Ryan	2	7	33	.212
Walter *Smokey* Alston	1	0	1	.000

2ND BASEMEN:	Yr	Hits	AB's	Ave
George *Firebrand* Stovall	12	1382	5222	.265
Jose *Chile* Gomez	3	142	627	.226
John *Stuffy* Stewart	8	63	265	.238
George *Gale* Staley	1	11	26	.423
Dallas *Windy* Bradshaw	1	0	4	.000

SHORTSTOPS:	Yr	Hits	AB's	Ave
Charles *Dusty* Miller	7	769	2557	.301
Dick *Slick* Howser	8	617	2483	.248
Ed *Cy* Cihocki	2	14	98	.143
Roy *Slippery* Ellam	2	14	98	.143
Dirty Dave Murphy	1	2	11	.182

3RD BASEMEN:	Yr	Hits	AB's	Ave
Dirty Jack Doyle	17	1806	6039	.299
Curt *Dirty* Bevacqua	15	499	2117	.236
Sunset Jimmy Burke	7	475	1947	.244
Dirty Al Gallagher	4	333	1264	.263
Seymour *Cy* Block	2	16	53	.302

OUTFIELDERS:	Yr	Hits	AB's	Ave
Fred *Cy* Williams	19	1981	6780	.292
Johnnie *Dusty* Baker	19	1981	7117	.278
Charles *Chili* Davis	14	1799	6663	.270
Frank *Wildfire* Schulte	15	1766	6533	.270
James *Cy* Seymour	16	1723	5682	.303
Stormin' Gorman Thomas	13	1051	4677	.225
Charlie *Smokey* Maxwell	14	856	3245	.264
Fred *Snow* Snodgrass	9	852	3101	.275
Roy *Stormy* Weatherly	10	794	2781	.286
Ward *Windy* Miller	8	623	2244	.278
Smokey Joe Wood	6	553	1952	.283
Harry *Wildfire* Craft	6	553	2104	.253
Lou *Slick* Johnson	8	529	2049	.258
Allen *Dusty* Cooke	8	489	1745	.280
August *Gloomy Gus* Williams	5	367	1398	.263

OUTFIELDERS: (Cont.)	Yr	Hits	AB's	Ave
James *Dusty* Rhodes	7	296	1172	.253
Clint *Hondo Hurricane* Hartung	6	90	378	.238
Bob *Hurricane* Hazle	3	81	261	.310
Wes *Icicle* Fisler	1	80	278	.288
Dakin *Dusty* Miller	1	46	176	.246
Sunny Jim Mallory	2	40	149	.268
Ike *Windy* Benners	1	39	211	.185
James *Sun* Daly	1	12	48	.250
Frank *Stuffy* Butler	1	6	22	.273
Galeard *Gale* Wade	2	6	45	.133
James *Icicle* Reeder	1	4	26	.154
Archibald *Moonlight* Graham	1	0	0	.000
Flemon *Cy* Neighbors	1	0	0	.000
Jim *Sunshine* McLaughlin	1	0	2	.000

PINCH HITTER:	Yr	Hits	AB's	Ave
Walt *Lightning* Irwin	1	0	1	.000

PITCHERS:	Yr	Won	Lost	ERA
Denton *Cy* Young	22	511	316	2.63
Amos *Hoosier Thunderbolt* Rusie	10	245	174	3.07
Virgil *Fire* Trucks	17	177	135	3.39
Ron *Louisiana Lightning* Guidry	13	170	91	3.29
Dave *Smoke* Stewart	15	165	122	3.86
Elton *Icebox* Chamberlain	10	157	120	3.57
Fredrick *Cy* Falkenberg	12	130	123	2.68
Mel *Dusty* Parnell	10	123	75	3.50
Smokey Joe Wood	11	116	57	2.03
George *Storm* Davis	13	113	96	4.02
Twilight Ed Killian	8	102	78	2.38
Tornado Jake Weimer	7	98	69	2.23
Bob *Dusty* Rhoads	8	97	82	2.61
Frosty Bill Duggleby	8	92	102	3.18
Steve *Rainbow* Trout	12	88	92	4.18
Harry *Cy* Morgan	10	78	78	2.51
Darrell *Cy* Blanton	9	68	71	3.55
Irv *Cy the Second* Young	6	63	95	3.11
James *Cy* Seymour	6	61	56	3.76
Cyclone Jim Duryea	5	59	67	3.45
Sunny Jim Dygert	6	57	49	2.65
Steve *Smokey* Sundra	9	56	41	4.17
Enos *Cy* Barger	7	46	63	3.56
John *Dusty* Rhodes	8	43	74	4.85
Still Bill Hill	4	36	69	4.16
Clydell *Slick* Castleman	6	36	26	4.25
Sunny Jim Pastorius	4	31	55	3.12
Sunny Jack Sutthoff	6	31	40	3.65
Clint *Hondo Hurricane* Hartung	4	29	29	5.02
Smokey Joe Finneran	5	25	33	3.30
William *Cy* Moore	6	16	26	4.86
George *Slick* Coffman	4	15	12	5.60
Joe *Cyclone* Miller	2	14	11	3.04
Cecilio *Cy* Acosta	4	13	9	2.66
John *Cy* Swaim	2	13	22	4.36

ROSTER

PITCHERS: (Cont.)	Yr	Won	Lost	ERA
John **Windy** McCall	7	11	15	4.22
Elmer **Smoky** Singleton	8	11	17	4.83
Edwin **Cy** Pieh	3	9	9	3.78
Wallace **Cy** Warmoth	3	8	5	4.26
Cyril **Cy** Buker	1	7	2	3.30
Bill **Dusty** Rhodes	1	5	12	7.60
Italo **Chilly** Chelini	3	4	4	5.83
Henry **Cy** Vorhees	1	3	4	3.94
Fred **Fireball** Wenz	3	3	0	4.68
Carl **Sundown** Yowell	2	3	4	5.40
Vernon **Slicker** Parks	1	3	2	5.68
Charlie **Cy** Young	1	2	3	5.91
Cyril **Cy** Slapnicka	2	1	6	4.30
George **Breezy** Winn	3	1	2	4.69
Sunny Jim Hackett	2	1	7	4.69
James **Smoky** Fairbank	2	1	2	5.49
Edwin **Cy** Twombly	1	1	2	5.86
Frederick **Cy** Alberts	1	1	2	6.18
Howard **Muck** McGraner	1	1	0	7.11

PITCHERS: (Cont.)	Yr	Won	Lost	ERA
Cyril **Cy** Morgan	2	1	1	7.39
Harley **Cy the Third** Young	1	0	3	2.62
William **Cy** Hooker	2	0	1	3.48
Joe **Smokey** Lotz	1	0	3	4.27
Cyrus **Cy** Malis	1	0	0	4.91
Sutherland **Cy** Bowen	1	0	1	6.00
Joe **Smoke** Kiefer	3	0	5	6.16
Alfred **Cy** Ferry	2	0	1	7.20
Gene **Slick** Host	2	0	2	7.31
Walt **Smoke** Justis	1	0	0	8.10
Lee **Flame** Delhi	1	0	0	9.00
Bill **Smoke** Herring	1	0	0	15.00
Arthur **Cy** Fried	1	0	0	16.20
Joe **Fire** Cleary	1	0	0	189.0

EXTRAS:
Charles **Cy** Pfirman - Umpire
Charles **Cy** Rigler - Umpire
Lynton **Dusty** Boggess - Umpire

LINGO

Weathered the Storm: Pitcher survives an inning in which he is hard hit

Bailed Him Out: Reliever comes in to save the earlier pitcher

Barn Storming: A team plays from town to town, taking on local competition

Dugout: Area where the ballplayers sit

Warm Up: Pitcher throws to prepare to enter the game

Duster: Pitch meant to come close to the batter's head

Hot Corner: Third base

Heater: Fastball

Rainbow: Curve

Hit the Dirt: Go to the ground to avoid being hit by a pitch

Hot Shot: Hard hit ball

Hot Stove League: During the winter (off season) fans discuss baseball

Heat Up: See warm up

Throwing Heat: Throwing fastballs

Fire: Throw

Putout: Fielder tags a player or forces him at a base to record an out

Froze: Batter cannot swing

Hot Foot: What Bert Blyleven was a specialist at

Rain Out: Game is postponed due to precipitation

Smoke: Fire the ball hard

Nip Them: Just beat the other team

Bats Went Cold: Can't seem to get a base hit

Nipped the Corner: Pitch is over the edge of the plate

Cool Him Off: Get a batter out

Showers: Where the pitcher who is removed goes

Flurry: Teams scores a bunch of runs

Dig In: Get set for a pitch

In the Hole: Ball hit between two infielders

Skied One: Hit a very high pop up

Blew It By Him: Threw an unhittable fastball

Blow the Save: Relief pitcher fails to hold the lead

Blow the Lead: Relief pitcher loses the lead

Blow Out: One team badly beats the other team

Blow the Game: Lose a game you should have won

Open the Flood Gates: Allow a team to score often

Hot Hand: Player is hitting well

Hot Streak: Team which can't lose

Hot Box: Player caught off base between two fielders who have the ball

Hot Seat: Where the manager sits when he consistently loses

Hot Head: Player who easily angers

Shade a Hitter: Play him to hit more to one direction than another

Sun Field: Outfield where the sun faces the fielder

Down Wind: Outfielder plays the batter deeper

Wind Sprints: Pitchers do these for conditioning

FAMILY

11

Team

For most people, they are introduced to baseball by their family. Usually mom and/or dad start playing catch with junior or sissy at an early age. Then it's plastic bat time! Before you know it, you have a slugger! Mickey Mantle was tutored from a young age on the National Pastime by both his dad and uncle. As kids grow up, it is often their brothers and sisters who they play with as they continue to develop their skills. Whether it's playing "500" in the street or organizing an "opposite field out" game across four back yards, it usually includes siblings. The Waners, Big Poison and Little Poison, are the only brothers to both reach Cooperstown. They would break corncobs until they were 'baseball size', and using a stick, would practice hitting. Both claimed their sister could hit better than either of them! The Delahanty clan had five boys reach the Majors, including Big Ed, a Hall of Famer. Four brothers from the O'Neill family were Big Leaguers (the two oldest were born in Galway, Ireland). For a time, Felipe, Matty, and Jesus Alou played outfield together on the same team! Fourteen other families also had three boys lace 'em up in the Big Show. Eight families had not only dad, but also two sons reach the Big Leagues. Gorgeous George Sisler, a Hall of Famer, was followed by sons Dick and Dave. More recently Mel Jr. and Todd Stottlemyre followed their dad. Currently both Robbie and Sandy Alomar Jr.. are playing and making dad proud.

The Family Team is quite a gathering. Three generations are included on this baseball family tree. The team leads off with three Old Folks, two Grandpas, a Grandmother, a Grandma and Granny. The middle of the order includes 21 Pops, six Dads, six Uncles, three Big Daddies, two Papas, Pappy, Pa, Mother, Moms and a Nanny. The bottom third is led by 20 Kids, 13 Juniors, seven Sonnies, four Babies, two Laddies, two Runts and a Sis. With a bench including three Boys, two Good Kids, a Child, a Cousin and a Godfather, this is no ordinary squad. Currently nine members of the Family Team are in the Hall of Fame and several players are possible future Cooperstown inductees.

One family member has grown head and shoulders over his teammates. Ted The Kid Williams is arguably the greatest hitter in baseball history. His statistics have been documented again and again, but some bear repeating. Ted not only won seven batting titles and was baseballs last .400 hitter, but he also hit .388 at age 39 and won his last Silver Bat at age 40! The Kid not only soared for 17 seasons (plus six and 37 games in 1952 and 1953), but he also soared for five years serving his country. Ted was a heroic pilot who flew both during World War II and in the Korean Conflict. His age 25, 26, 27, and most of his age 33 and 34 seasons were sacrificed. If one just took The Kid's totals from ages 21-38, averaged them, and then added the averages in for the five seasons he gave, Ted would have rewritten the record books. The Kid's "possible" numbers would have been 3479 hits (sixth), 691 doubles (fifth), 678 homers (third), 6364 total bases (second), 2594 bases on balls (first), 2371 runs (first) and 2411 RBI's (first). Of The Kid's many outstanding accomplishments, one is absolutely amazing to me. Ted hit four consecutive home runs. The Kid hit dingers September 7th, 1957, September 20th, 1957, September 21st, 1957 and September 22nd, 1957!

LINEUP

CA	Gary *The Kid* Carter

was a ten time All-Star over his 19 seasons. For his career, he ranks first in putouts and third in games. The Kid won three Gold Gloves and twice led NL backstops in fielding %. Nine seasons he muscled over 20 homers and four campaigns The Kid drove in 100 or more runs.

1B	Wilver *Pops* Stargell

was a big, strong left-hand hitter. During his career he pounded 475 balls "downtown" (tie 17th best). Pops' home run % of 5.99 (19th best) and his slugging % of .529 (27th best) verify his power. Willie was an All-Star seven times and five seasons Pops drove in over 100 tallies.

2B	William *Kid* Gleason

had an amazing career. Initially he was an outstanding pitcher, but when the distance to pitch lengthened from 50' to 60'6", he became less effective. Kid then converted and played second base. He retired with both 1944 base hits and 138 pitching victories!

SS	Lou *Good Kid* Boudreau

became a playing manager at the young age of 24! An eight time All-Star, he led AL shortstops in fielding % eight times from 1940-48! Good Kid won the 1944 batting title. He led the Cleveland Indians to the World Championship in 1948, batting a career high .355 and winning the MVP.

3B	Joe *Godfather* Torre

swung a mean bat for 18 seasons. A nine time All-Star, he slugged 20 or more round trippers six summers and the Godfather drove in 100 or more runs five campaigns. In 1971 Joe led the National League in hits (230), RBI's (137), batting average (.363) and won the MVP!

OF	Ted *The Kid* Williams

starred 19 seasons for the Beantowners. He was an 18 time All-Star. The Kid captured two MVP's and led the league in on base % 12 times, slugging % nine times and bases on balls eight times. Ted also won seven batting crowns during his illustrious Hall of Fame career!

OF	Leon *Daddy Wags* Wagner

finally got his chance to start when he was taken by the expansion Los Angeles Angels in 1961. The next six summers (1961-66) Daddy Wags was a feared power hitter. Only four American Leaguers (Killebrew, Mantle, Cash and Colavito) out homered him in that stretch!

OF	John *Pop* Corkhill

starred for ten seasons prior to the turn of the century. He was known more for his leather than his timber. Pop led all outfielders four seasons in fielding % and once in assists. 1887 was his best year at the dish. Pop hit a solid .311 for Cincinnati.

P	Charles *Kid* Nichols

started as a 20 year old rookie and he never looked back. From 1890-99 Kid won 297 games. His closest competition was Cy Young (267 wins). Seven years Kid won 30 or more games. Three straight summers (one tie) he led the NL in wins. Four seasons he completed every start!

P	Jesse *Pop* Haines

career lasted through his 44th year. During his 19 NL years he only had four losing records. Pop won 20 or more games three years. In 1927 he went 24-10, finishing second in wins and first in shutouts. Pop was the Series hero (1926), winning games #3 (shutout) and #7.

P	Wilfred *Sonny* Siebert

was a hard throwing right-hander. In 1965 he logged a 16-8 record, fanning over one batter per inning! Sonny duplicated his 16-8 ledger in 1966. Eight consecutive summers (1965-72) Sonny won in double digits. His 6.32 strikeouts per game places Sonny 53rd!

RES	Vern *Junior* Stephens

was a power hitting shortstop, a rare commodity! He was an eight time All-Star. In 1945 Junior led the American League in circuit blasts and three seasons (twice shared) he won the RBI crown. His 39 homers and 159 RBI's in 1949 were Junior's career highs!

RES	Granville *Granny* Hamner

starred 17 seasons, 16 with the Phillies. In 1954 he finished second in triples and tied for second in doubles. Three summers Granny was named to the NL All-Star team. He led the league in at bats in 1949. Granny's 21 homers and 92 RBI's in 1953 were his best marks.

RES	Ellis *Old Folks* Kinder

reached the Majors in 1946 as a 31 year old rookie. Old Folks had his best season in 1949. He had 23 V's (second in the AL) and tossed a league leading six shutouts (tie). After four summers as a starter, Ellis shifted to the bullpen. In 1951 he saved 14 (first) and went 11-2!

RES	Johnny *Grandma* Murphy

was the premier fireman from 1937-43. He led the American League four seasons in saves. Grandma was at his best in World Series competition. His record reads six World Series, eight games, four saves, two wins and no losses. His win in the 1939 Fall Classic was the clincher.

L to R: Gary *The Kid* Carter, Wilver *Pops* Stargell, Ted *The Kid* Williams, Wilfred *Sonny* Siebert, Leon *Daddy Wags* Wagner

It'sa FACT

Jim **Moms** McAndrew: While hurling for the Mets, he had the misfortune of being shutout four straight games in 1968.

Charley **Baby** Jones: He was the first Major Leaguer to bash two homers in one inning. Baby was an early baseball slugger. Charley led the NL in homers and RBI's (tie) in 1879.

Wilver **Pops** Stargell: On June 24th, 1965, May 22nd, 1968, April 10th, 1971 and April 21st, 1971, he launched three homers in one game. In 1971 Pops pounded a career high 48 home runs. His best summer was 1973. Pops led the NL in doubles with 43, home runs with 44 and RBI's with 119. On August 1st, 1970 Willie tagged three two baggers and jerked two out!

Arthur **Dad** Clarkson: His younger brother Walter and his Hall of Fame older brother John combined with Dad to win 385 games. This is the third highest brother win total, only trailing the Niekro and Perry boys.

Jimmy **Foxy Grandpa** Bannon: On August 6th, 1894 and August 7th, 1894 he slugged grand slams in two consecutive games. This occurred during the dead ball era and Foxy Grandpa had only 19 home runs for his career!

Ron **The Kid** Moeller: In 1956 he pitched in four games, including one start, for the Baltimore Orioles. The Kid was seventeen, and hence his nickname.

Gary **The Kid** Carter: Over a period of 157 games at catcher, The Kid had only one passed ball!

William **Kid** Gleason: His career had many unusual twists. In 1890 Kid won 38 games, finishing second in wins and shutouts (tie) and third in innings, games and complete games. As a full-time second baseman in 1897, Kid batted .319 and drove in 106 runs. Five seasons Kid was a manager. His first summer he piloted the 1919 White Sox. He was not implicated in the scandal. John Little Napoleon McGraw considered Kid the "most spirited" ballplayer he knew, and that included Ty Cobb!

The Bash Brothers: Oakland's Jose Canseco and Mark McGuire.

Mal **Kid** Eason: At the age of 21 he reached the Majors, hence his nickname. On July 20th, 1906 Kid hurled a no-no. For seven seasons after he retired, he called balls and strikes in the NL.

Ray **Pop** Prim: From 1933 through 1944 he hurled 162 innings in four short visits to the Big Show. In 1945, at the age of 38, Pop stuck. He helped the Cubs to the pennant, winning 13 games and leading the league with a 2.40 ERA. Pop only walked 23 batters in 165 1/3 frames, an average of 1.25 per game!

Uncle Charlie Moran: His career shows only two cups of coffee and 17 career hits. He went on to ump 23 seasons (1917-39). Uncle Charlie earned his nickname because he was a well liked umpire (please reread). He also played Pro Football and coached College Football. Uncle Charlie led little Centre College (Kentucky) to the 1921 National Championship. Their shocking defeat of powerhouse Harvard that season was 30 years later voted by the A.P. the biggest football upset of the 20th century!

Wilbert **Uncle Robbie** Robinson: The Hall of Fame now claims him. He was a star player and team leader for 17 seasons. On June 10th, 1892 Robbie went 7/7 in a nine inning game and drove in 11 runs! Later (1914-31) he managed the Brooklyn Dodgers. During his tenure the team was called the Robins in his honor. They were also called the Daffiness Boys. Uncle Robbie was not known for his discipline. In an attempt to crack down, he instituted a fine system for "bonehead plays". He promptly met with the umps at home plate and presented his laundry list!

Billy **Boy Umpire** Evans: At the young age of 22 he was behind the plate. Billy was the youngest person to umpire in the Majors, hence his nickname. He went on to umpire 22 summers and developed a reputation as an outstanding "man in blue". He was the third arbitrator elected to the Hall of Fame.

Jesse **Pop** Haines: He ranks second in wins as a Cardinal. On July 17th, 1924 Pop tossed a no-hitter versus Boston. Casey Stengel's liner off his glove nearly broke it up, but Pop's throw nipped Casey at first.

Winfield **Kid** Camp: His older brother Lew and he both played for Chicago in 1894. Kid tragically died at the young age of 24 during the off season. His older brother Lew lived 53 years longer, but he never again played in the Majors.

Charles **Pop** Snyder: For three consecutive seasons he led all NL catchers in fielding %. Occasionally Pop took his turn in the outfield. One game he had four assists!

Eddie **Kid** Foster: He played the hot corner for the Senators. Kid led the AL in at bats in 1912, 1914, 1915 and 1918.

Jim **Junior** Gilliam: In 1953 he was the NL Rookie of the Year. Junior led the league with 17 three baggers, drew 100 walks (tie second) and scored 125 runs (fourth).

Charles **Kid** Nichols: During his career he starred both on the mound and at the plate. Kid was known for his fast ball. He was considered as fast as the feared Hoosier Thunderbolt, Amos Rusie. Kid was the youngest player to reach the 300 win plateau, age 30. He ranks sixth in wins. In 1901 in 55 games Kid pounded seven triples and yanked four homers. Had he played a full year and hit proportionally, he would have led the league in 3B's and been second in HR's.

Wilfred **Kid** Carsey: As a 20 year old rookie he was treated rudely. Kid lost 37 games. His next four seasons (1892-95) he responded with four consecutive winning years. Kid's log read 19-16, 20-15, 18-12 and 24-16.

John **Sonny** Dixon: He led the AL in games in 1954, winning six times and saving five more.

George **Kiddo** Davis: His rookie season (1932) was great. He hit .309, pounded 39 doubles, rapped 178 safeties and scored 100 runs.

TRIVIA*

1) He led the AL in RBI's in 1990-92, knocking in 132, 133 and 124 runs.

2) From 1948-50, this American Leaguer drove in 137, 159 and 144 runs. No one has approached this three year total since.

3) His older brother Paul and he were teammates five seasons (1975-79) on the Cubs. They combined to win 93 games those five summers for the Northsiders.

4) At the age of 39 (in 1979) he was the NLCS MVP, the World Series MVP and shared the NL MVP.

5) He was the oldest of three brothers who reached the Majors. (Hint: brother Ken was the 1964 NL MVP)

6) Five players have poled two homers in an All-Star tilt. Willie Stretch McCovey, Joseph Arky Vaughan and Al Flip Rosen are three members of this exclusive family. The other two kids are on the roster.

7) His older brother Frank was a first sacker for the Braves in the 1957 and 1958 World Series. He never played in a Fall Classic, but he did win the 1971 NL MVP.

8) At age 38, if he had picked up just five "leg hits" during the 1958 season, he would have hit .400, not .388.

9) His brother Garvin (called Wes) and he both appeared at shortstop for the Phillies during the same season (1945). (Hint: his first name is similar to his brother's first name)

10) This Hall of Famer won eight RBI crowns. (Hint: his other nickname was Cap)

11) Both brothers are on the Family Team, but their nicknames are deceiving since Jimmy is the younger of the two siblings.

12) He was the leader of "The Family" and their theme song was 'We Are Family' by Sister Sledge.

13) He did the undone. In 1988 he slugged 42 homers and stole 40 bases and became baseball's first 40/40 man.

14) His younger brother Harry played five years in the Junior Circuit, but never approached his big brother's outstanding career. (Hint: think of Ralph Kramdon on the 'Honeymooners')

15) In 1921 he had the greatest offensive season in baseball history. He had a single season record 119 extra base hits (44 doubles, 16 triples and 59 homers) and batted .378!

16) His older brother Lefty hurled eight years in the Majors. The highlight of his ten year "marvelous" pitching career was winning game #1 of the 1954 World Series, when Dusty Rhodes' pinch homer made him and the Giants a winner.

17) His 54 circuit blasts in 458 official at bats yielded a season record 11.79 home run %. The same summer, his .847 slugging % also established the Major League single season standard!

18) His kid George hurled five seasons during the 50's. Dad, a Major League catcher, was a good father and taught him everything he knew.

19) As a rookie he set the Major League record, for first year players, by launching 49 round trippers.

20) He was also known as The Thumper and The Splendid Splinter, but he really preferred this nickname.

21) He retired with a 4.77 homer %, 66th all time. From 1961-66 he parked 28, 37, 26, 31, 28 and 23 tape jobs. (Hint: he has something in common with "The Flying Dutchman")

22) His dad and he not only both played in the Majors, but they also were teammates in 1990 and 1991.

23) He combined with Maurice Wes Parker, Maury Mousey Wills and Jim Frenchy Lefebvre in 1965-66 to complete a switch hitting infield.

24) For his career he averaged 6.66 strikeouts per nine innings, 30th all time. (Hint: he stood 6'5")

25) In 1916 this big left-hander finished 23-12. He led the AL with nine shutouts and posted a 1.75 ERA..

* RELATIVELY DIFFICULT answers found on page 236

ROSTER

CATCHERS:	Yr	Hits	AB's	Ave
Gary *The Kid* Carter	19	2092	7971	.262
Wilbert *Uncle Robbie* Robinson	17	1388	5075	.273
Charles *Pop* Snyder	15	737	3122	.236
William *Pop* Schriver	14	720	2727	.264
Adalberto *Junior* Ortiz	13	484	1894	.256
Bill *Dad Gum* Atwood	5	220	961	.229
Ed *Pop* Tate	6	179	822	.218
Phil *Grandmother* Powers	7	103	570	.181
George *Good Kid* Susce	8	61	268	.228
Frank *Kid* Withrow	2	31	153	.203
William *Pop* Schwartz	2	26	110	.236
Uncle Charlie Moran	2	17	77	.221
Frank *Dad* Meek	2	6	18	.333

1ST BASEMEN:	Yr	Hits	AB's	Ave
Adrian *Pop* Anson	22	2995	9101	.329
Wilver *Pops* Stargell	21	2232	7927	.282
Cecil *Big Daddy* Fielder	9	853	3295	.259
Mark *Bash Brother* McGuire	9	834	3342	.250
Frank *Pop* Dillon	5	298	1181	.252
Aloysius *Pop* Joy	1	28	130	.215
Fred *Papa* Williams	1	4	19	.211
George *Sonny* Kopacz	2	3	25	.120
Clarence *Big Boy* Kraft	1	1	3	.333
Ray *Grandpa* Wolf	1	0	1	.000

2ND BASEMEN:	Yr	Hits	AB's	Ave
William *Kid* Gleason	13	1944	7452	.261
Lonny *Junior* Frey	14	1482	5517	.269
Charles *Pop* Smith	12	941	4238	.222
Billy *The Kid* Martin	11	877	3419	.257
Milciades *Junior* Noboa	8	118	493	.239
Ernest *Kid* Mohler	1	1	9	.111

SHORTSTOPS:	Yr	Hits	AB's	Ave
Vern *Junior* Stephens	15	1859	6497	.286
Lou *Good Kid* Boudreau	15	1779	6029	.295
Granville *Granny* Hamner	17	1529	5839	.262
Norman *Kid* Elberfeld	14	1235	4561	.271
Eddie *Kasko Kid* Kasko	10	935	3546	.264
Roland *Sonny* Jackson	12	767	3055	.251
Hal *Childe Harold* Janvrin	10	515	2221	.232
Billy *The Kid* DeMars	3	50	211	.237
Charlie *Swamp Baby* Wilson	4	40	186	.215
Clarence *Cleary Daddy* Cross	2	37	164	.226
Ernie *Kansas City Kid* Smith	1	19	79	.241
Frank *Runt* Cox	1	13	102	.127
George *Kid* Stutz	1	0	9	.000

3RD BASEMEN:	Yr	Hits	AB's	Ave
Joe *Godfather* Torre	18	2342	7874	.297

3RD BASEMEN: (Cont.)	Yr	Hits	AB's	Ave
Jim *Junior* Gilliam	14	1889	7119	.265
Eddie *Kid* Foster	13	1490	5652	.264
Jimmy *Runt* Walsh	6	447	1571	.285
Froilan *Nanny* Fernandez	4	336	1356	.248
Uncle Bill Alvord	5	270	1069	.253
Alvin *Junior* Moore	5	204	774	.264
Emanuel *Sonny* Senerchia	1	22	100	.220
Willis *Kid* Butler	1	13	59	.220
Bert *Sonny* Hogg	1	0	1	.000

OUTFIELDERS:	Yr	Hits	AB's	Ave
George *Bambino* Ruth	22	2873	8399	.342
Ted *The Kid* Williams	19	2654	7706	.344
Billy *The Kid* Southworth	13	1296	4359	.297
Leon *Daddy Wags* Wagner	12	1202	4426	.272
Jose *Bash Brother* Canseco	10	1154	4315	.267
John *Pop* Corkhill	10	1120	4404	.254
Charley *Baby* Jones	11	1101	3687	.299
Ken *Junior* Griffey	6	972	3180	.306
George *Kiddo* Davis	8	515	1824	.282
Jimmy *Foxy Grandpa* Bannon	4	459	1433	.320
Chet *Pop* Chadbourne	5	345	1353	.255
Clarence *Pop* Foster	4	260	924	.281
William *Kid* Nance	3	182	657	.277
Uncle Tom Bannon	2	44	166	.265
Frank *Kid* Butler	7	43	255	.169
Joe *Pop* Durham	3	38	202	.188
Ed *Dad* Lytle	1	8	59	.136
Poster Boy Hercules Burnett	2	7	21	.333
Jim *Kid* O'Hara	1	6	29	.207
John *Sis* Hopkins	1	6	44	.136
Angie *Junior* Dagres	1	4	15	.267
George *Papa Bear* Halas	1	2	22	.091
Frank *Kid* Willson	2	1	11	.091
William *Kid* Summers	1	0	1	.000
Jim *Kid* McLaughlin	1	0	2	.000
Charlie *Pop* Reising	1	0	8	.000

PITCHERS:	Yr	Won	Lost	ERA
Charles *Kid* Nichols	15	361	208	2.95
Rick *Big Daddy* Reuschel	19	214	191	3.37
Jesse *Pop* Haines	19	210	158	3.64
Wilfred *Sonny* Siebert	12	140	114	3.21
William *Kid* Gleason	8	138	131	3.79
Wilfred *Kid* Carsey	10	116	138	4.95
Stan *Big Daddy* Williams	14	109	94	3.48
Ellis *Old Folks* Kinder	12	102	71	3.43
George *Bambino* Ruth	10	94	46	2.28
Johnny *Grandma* Murphy	13	93	53	3.50
Michael *Kid* Madden	5	54	50	3.92
John *Pa* Harkins	5	51	83	4.09

ROSTER

PITCHERS: (Cont.)	Yr	Won	Lost	ERA
Lew *Million Dollar Kid* Moren	6	48	57	2.96
Eugene *Junior* Thompson	6	47	35	3.26
Uncle Marv Grissom	10	47	45	3.41
William *Dad* Clarke	7	44	51	4.17
Arthur *Dad* Clarkson	6	39	39	4.90
Jim *Moms* McAndrew	7	37	53	3.65
Mal *Kid* Eason	6	36	72	3.39
Herman *Old Folks* Pillette	4	34	32	3.45
Bob *Junior* Kline	5	30	28	5.05
Ray *Pop* Prim	6	22	21	3.56
Cloyd *Junior* Boyer	5	20	23	4.73
Ray *Baby* Semproch	4	19	21	4.42
Walt *Pop* Williams	3	16	25	3.20
John *Sonny* Dixon	4	11	18	4.17
Paul *Pop* Gregory	2	9	14	4.72
Ron *The Kid* Moeller	4	6	9	5.78
Fred *Laddie* Link	1	5	7	3.30
George *Kid* Speer	1	4	4	2.83
Orie *Old Folks* Arntzen	1	4	13	4.22
James *Junior* Walsh	5	4	10	5.88

PITCHERS: (Cont.)	Yr	Won	Lost	ERA
Roy *Pop* Joiner	3	3	3	5.28
Jack *Pappy* Bruner	2	2	4	4.91
Cayt *Pop* Fauver	1	1	0	0.00
Berlyn *Sonny* Horne	1	1	1	5.09
Johnnie *Durango Kid* Seale	2	1	0	5.54
Ray *Dad* Hale	1	1	5	5.90
Harry *Kid* Keenan	1	0	1	0.00
Blaine *Kid* Durbin	1	0	1	5.40
Walter *Mother* Watson	1	0	1	5.79
Oliverio *Baby* Ortiz	1	0	2	6.23
Winfield *Kid* Camp	2	0	2	6.40
Clarence *Kid* Baldwin	1	0	0	9.00
Earl *Junior* Wooten	1	0	0	9.00
Cohen *Laddie* Renfroe	1	0	1	13.50
EXTRAS:				
Billy *Boy Umpire* Evans - Umpire				
Charles *Pop* Snyder - Umpire				
Cousin Ed Barrow - Manager				

LINGO

Parent Club: The Major League team for a minor league affiliate

Uncle Charley: Curve ball

Single: A one base hit

Double Up: Catch a ball then get a runner before he returns to his base

Foul Pop: Short fly in foul territory

Father: Player who does something first

Weak Sister: "Out" man in the lineup

Spoiler: A team with no chance to win a pennant, but can foil the chances of a contender

Old Folks: Oldster on the team

Gift: A run you do not deserve

Old-Timers Game: When me and the guys lace 'em up!

Split: Play two games, each team winning one

Cousin: Player hits a certain pitcher very well

Break Up: Slide hard into base to thwart a potential double play

Save: Pitcher relieves starter and preserves the victory

Open Day: Day on schedule with no game

Bonus Baby: Player gets cash to sign a pro contract

Pop in His Bat: Able to hit the ball hard

Pop in His Glove: Hard thrown ball makes a loud sound when it hits the glove

Spanked: Hit the ball hard

Punished Him: Team hit a pitcher hard

Pop Fly: Easily lofted ball hit into air

Pop Up: Ball hit in the air, but it does not carry beyond the infield

Held Him: Kept him close to the base

Squeeze Him: Runner from third advances on a bunt

FARM

12

Team

When a ballplayer turns pro, he seldom starts immediately playing in the Major Leagues. Depending on his skill level, the signee is placed on a minor league team best suited for his present abilities. As the individual demonstrates improvement, he is "promoted" to a higher level. The system of developing players and helping them "grow" became fondly known as the farm system. A Major League team forms working agreements with several minor league affiliates, to each create their own "step-up" network. Every Saturday (during baseball season) a special pre-game program on the Twins' radio broadcast is called "Down On The Farm". This segment recognizes ten players, within the Twins' farm system, who have performed well during the past week.

This Farm Team has a bumper crop of stars, including seven members of the Hall of Fame. Leon Goose Goslin, Joe Ducky Medwick, Walter Barney Johnson, Johnny The Big Cat Mize, Charles Chick Hafey, Charles Old Hoss Radbourn and Walter Rabbit Maranville have each reaped their reward in Cooperstown. The roster has Horses, Goats, Roosters, Chicks and Rabbits. It includes teammates called Ducky, Bunny, Bronco, Mule and Pig. Add in Bulls, Dogs, Cats, Farmers and a Plowboy and the team formed is a group Old McDonald would be proud of!

One member of the Farm Team, Jim Kitty Kaat, definitely was outstanding in his field (pun intended!). I can still hear Herb Carneal (the World's greatest announcer) say, "and pitching today for the Twins is Kitty". That said it all! Jim meets all the criteria (excellent pitcher, fielder and hitter; plus durable) for Hall consideration. As a pitcher, from 1962-1976, Kitty won in double figures 15 consecutive seasons. His 283 career wins rank him 26th. His strikeout to walk ratio was nearly 2½ to 1. Kitty retired with 2461 strikeouts, only headed by 21 hurlers. For his career he averaged just 2.15 bases on balls per game. As a fielder, from 1962-1975, Kitty won the AL Gold Glove each year. After the 1975 season he was traded to the Phillies (NL). Jim proceeded to win the NL Gold Glove 1976-77. In total, for 16 consecutive summers Kitty was awarded the Gold Glove! Only Brooks Robinson has equaled Jim's Gold Glove total. As a hitter, Kitty often helped "his own cause" with a timely hit. During his career he slashed 232 safeties, including 16 yard shots. Frequently Kitty also was used as either a pinch hitter or a pinch runner. Durability was Kitty's middle name. His log shows 25 seasons in the Majors. Fourteen campaigns he tossed over 200 innings. Jim's 4530 1/3 frames is 23rd all time. Jim Kitty Kaat was the complete player!

LINEUP

| CA | Harry *Farmer* Vaughn | played 13 seasons (1886-99) during baseball's early years. He played in the American Association, then the Players League, and his last eight summers in the NL. Three campaigns Farmer hit over .300 in the NL, and once he led all backstops in fielding %. |

| 1B | Fred *Crime Dog* McGriff | originally played for the Blue Jays. He became a starter in 1987. Since then Fred has averaged 34+ homers and 95+ RBI's, first for Toronto, then San Diego and now Atlanta. Crime Dog has a seven year streak (1988-94) of 30 or more homers in each season! |

| 2B | Tony *Chick* Cuccinello | was a starter 11 of his 15 seasons. In 1933 Chick was the NL's inaugural All-Star second baseman. Three times he led all keystone men in DP's and assists, and once in putouts. Five summers Chick hit over .300 and seven times he drove in over 70 runs. |

| SS | Maury *Mousey* Wills | reached the Majors at age 26 and stayed for 14 years. From 1960-65 he led the NL in steals. For his career Mousey stole 586 sacks, finishing 17th all time. In 1962 he had his best year. Maury collected 208 hits (second), scored 130 runs (second) and won the MVP! |

| 3B | Bill *Mad Dog* Madlock | starred 15 summers. He hit for both average and power during his career. Nine seasons Mad Dog hit over .300. In total he slammed 348 doubles and 163 home runs. Mad Dog's 9/24 effort in the 1979 World Series helped carry Pittsburgh to the World Championship. |

| OF | Greg *The Bull* Luzinski | was a power hitter. Size and strength led to his nickname. The Bull poled 307 homers in his playing days (tie 62nd). Four seasons he drove in over 100 runs and Bull led the National League in RBI's in 1975. For his career The Bull averaged .62 RBI's per game! |

| OF | Riggs *Old Hoss* Stephenson | sparkled 14 seasons. Twelve of his 14 years he batted over .300, including three times over .350! Old Hoss' career was limited by injuries or he, most likely, would have even more awesome lifetime totals. Old Hoss retired with the 19th highest career batting average. |

| OF | Jimmy *Pony* Ryan | was a huge star from the mid 1880's through the turn of the century. He played in the era when seasons had fewer games, but regardless, Pony amassed big career totals. He ranks 26th in runs, tied for 45th in triples, 53rd in stolen bases, tied for 57th in doubles and 69th in hits! |

| P | Charles *Old Hoss* Radbourn | toiled 11 seasons. He won 20 or more contests in nine of those campaigns. Old Hoss' 309 wins have been exceeded by only 16 hurlers. He was also very versatile, at times playing not only outfield but also playing third base, shortstop, second base and first base! |

| P | Orel *Bulldog* Hershiser | is awesome. He led the NL in innings pitched three straight seasons (1987-89). Bulldog's 1988 season was unbelievable. He went 23-8, leading the NL in victories, games and shutouts. That season he also won the NLCS MVP, the World Series MVP and the Cy Young! |

| P | George *Bull* Uhle | threw balls and strikes 17 summers. His two best seasons were 1923 and 1926. Bull went 26-16 in 1923, leading the league in wins, complete games and innings. He went one more, going 27-11 in 1926. Again Bull topped all AL hurlers in wins, complete games and innings! |

| RES | Harry *The Cat* Brecheen | played 12 summers in St. Louis (11 as a Cardinal and one as a Brown). He had only two losing seasons. 1948 was The Cat's best year. He clawed out 20 victories (second in NL), while leading the league in winning % (.741), shutouts (seven), strikeouts (149) and ERA (2.24)! |

| RES | Bob *Bull* Watson | charged through 19 seasons. He hit for both average and power. Seven summers Bull batted over .300 and retired at .295. Twice he drove in 100+ runs and consistently he hit the long ball, even in the cavernous Astrodome. Currently Bull is in baseball at the executive level. |

| RES | Leon *Bull* Durham | starred in the 1980's for the Cubs. Five seasons Bull bashed 20 or more long balls, plus he slugged two dingers in the 1984 NLCS (lost to the Padres). Personal problems led to his early Major League exit. Recently Bull has re-emerged, playing for St. Paul in the Northern League. |

| RES | Harvey *The Kitten* Haddix | starred 14 seasons in the Majors. He suffered only three losing seasons during his career. In 1953 The Kitten won 20 games and posted a National League leading six whitewashes! For his career Harvey averaged 6.34 K's per nine innings (52nd). |

L to R: Maury *Mousey* Wills, George *Bull* Uhle, Jim *Kitty* Kaat, Greg *The Bull* Luzinski, Harvey *The Kitten* Haddix

It'sa FACT

Johnny **Mutt** Riddle: Even though he was nine years older than his brother, Elmer, he did get to catch him for three seasons when they both played for Cincinnati.

Harry **The Cat** Brecheen: He was the hero of the 1946 World Series. In game #2 The Cat tossed a four hit shutout. He then twirled a seven hit, one run effort in game #6. The Cat fired two innings of relief to win game #7. His record was 3-0! The Cat pitched 20 innings and allowed only one earned run!

Thomas **Toad** Ramsey: This left-hander starred two seasons (1886-87), winning 38 and 37 games. Toad led the American Association in complete games (tie), innings and K's once each during that span.

George **Bull** Uhle: His .289 lifetime batting average ranks him second for pitchers! In 1923 Bull hit .361 (52/144). He led the AL in pinch-hits in 1924 with 11. For his career Bull had 90 extra base hits and nearly 200 RBI's.

Charles **Chick** Hafey: He suffered from sinus problems which led to four surgeries. Chick also had impaired vision from beanings. Nevertheless, in 1931, Chick won the NL batting crown, a first for a player wearing glasses. Chick shares the NL record of ten consecutive hits (1929) and he also holds the distinction of slashing the first hit in the All-Star game, a single off of Lefty Gomez.

Clarence **Chick** Galloway: In 1922 he had his best season, batting .324 for the Philadelphia Athletics. Chick finished tied for eighth that year in the MVP voting. His promising career ended at the age of 31 when he was beaned during batting practice and broke his skull.

Maury **Mousey** Wills: He managed just 20 homers in 14 seasons. Only six times did Mousey hit two or more homers in one year. On May 30th, 1962 Maury, a switch hitter, blasted a homer from each side of the plate!

Greg **The Bull** Luzinski: From 1975-78 he was a terror on NL pitchers. During that stretch, The Bull was a four time All-Star who hit over .300, smashed over 30 homers and drove in over 100 runs three times each.

Riggs **Old Hoss** Stephenson: He combined in 1929 with Lewis Hack Wilson and Hazen Kiki Cuyler to set a NL record. All three Cub outfielders drove in over 100 runs that season!

Jimmy **Pony** Ryan: He was a premier slugger in the "dead ball" era. He led the NL in dingers in 1888 and Pony finished third and tied for third in home runs in the 1889 and 1892 seasons.

Charles **Chick** Stahl: For ten years he graced the Majors. Chick was both a great defensive outfielder and an exceptional hitter. His lifetime batting average was .305. He tragically committed suicide at the age of 34.

William **Chicken** Wolfe: In 1890 he had a career year. Chicken won the batting crown in the American Association (.363) and also led the league in base hits (197).

Charles **Old Hoss** Radbourn: Pitching for Providence in the NL in 1884, he was a workhorse. Old Hoss started and completed 73 games! He notched 11 shutouts, hurled 678 2/3 innings and had a 1.38 ERA! Old Hoss is now "resting" in Cooperstown.

Mark **Fido** Baldwin: The Players League existed one season, 1890. He was the league's dominant pitcher. Fido won 34 times (first), completed 54 games (first), tossed 501 frames (first) and rang up 211 batters (first).

Rich **Goose** Gossage: Ten seasons he saved 20 or more games. Goose, a nine time All-Star, led the AL three summers in saves.

Bill **Bullfrog** Dietrich: This 16 year AL veteran's career probably best capsulizes baseball! Bullfrog toiled for .500 clubs throughout his career. He had only three winning seasons and he never led the league in any category. Bullfrog neither made an All-Star squad nor appeared in a Fall Classic. But, Bill won 108 games! On June 1st, 1937, he hurled a no-hitter! He gave his best years to the game, the fans and his team. What defines greatness?

Frank **Mule** Lary: He carried the load for the Tigers and earned his moniker. From 1955-61 Mule averaged 257+ innings (first three times), 16+ complete games (first three times, once tied) and 16+ wins (first once).

Tony **Chick** Cuccinello: On July 5th, 1935, he and his little brother Al, on opposing teams, each homered. This was a Major League first.

Bob **Horse** Lee: In 1964 and 1965 Horse won six and nine games, saved 19 and 23 contests and had ERA's of 1.51 and 1.92.

Gene **Blue Goose** Moore: His son "Rowdy" (Gene Jr.) played 14 seasons in the Majors as an outfielder.

Jim **Bulldog** Bouton: In the 1964 World Series he won games #3 and #6. Bulldog allowed only three earned runs in 17 1/3 innings.

Bruce **Bull** Edwards: He was the NL All-Star catcher in 1947 at the young age of 23. It was to be his only full season for the Dodgers. Roy Campy Campanella debuted in 1948 and changed Bull's career.

Rick **The Rooster** Burleson: His fielding gave him something to crow about. The Rooster led AL shortstops in putouts (three), assists (two), DP's (two) and fielding % (one) during his career.

TRIVIA*

1) He wrote *Ball Four*, the first "show and tell" athlete book.

2) He looked like his older teammate Harry The Cat Brecheen, so he was tabbed with his nickname.

3) Fourteen times he was the opening day pitcher, going 9-5 with seven shutouts.

4) In 1975 he scored baseball's one millionth run.

5) He holds the NL record for home runs in one season by a left-handed batter.

6) He ranks fourth all time in saves.

7) He and his younger brother, "Dordy" (George), combined to win 310 games in their careers.

8) In 1983 he swiped 41 sacks. In 1985 he pilfered 35 bags. His speed led to his nickname.

9) He acquired his nickname in 1882 when he played for Troy, a then member of the NL.

10) He was on the receiving end of Charlie Hustle's extra inning "slide" in the 1970 All-Star game.

11) In game #7 of the 1960 World Series, Maz hit the winning home run in the bottom of the ninth inning. It made this Pirate pitcher the winner.

12) He has led both the AL (1989) and the NL (1992) in home runs. Only John Buck Freeman and Wahoo Sam Crawford had ever done this before.

13) His son Bump (Elliott) played six seasons and, like his dad, he was an excellent base stealer.

14) His 104 stolen bases in 1962 set the then Major League record.

15) He won four batting crowns (1975 - .354, 1976 - .339, 1981 - .341 and 1983 - .323). Only Ty Georgia Peach Cobb, Honus Flying Dutchman Wagner, Rogers The Rajah Hornsby, Sir Rodney Carew, Big Dan Brouthers, Stan The Man Musial, Ted The Kid Williams, Tony Gwynn and Wade Boggs have won more batting titles!

16) He holds the single season pitching record of 59 wins!

17) This flame thrower, in five different seasons, averaged over one strikeout per inning!

18) This Twins reliever's other nickname was "Old Blue", after his hunting dog.

19) After being gone for eight seasons, this author, in 1978, made a comeback as a knuckle baller.

20) His other nickname was Yankee Killer, because he whipped them so often.

21) He hit for the cycle twice, once in each league (June 24th, 1977 and September 15th, 1979).

22) He won the AL strikeout crown 9 seasons. (Hint: his other nickname is The Big Train)

23) This Hall of Famer, from 1927-1931, hit .329, .337, .338, .336 and .349 while averaging 23+ tators and 100 ribbies.

24) His original nickname was Stumpy (he stood only 5'5"). He had an ability to wiggle his ears, and sure enough, he acquired a new nickname.

25) He set the record for pitching consecutive scoreless innings at 59 in 1988.

* MIND THRASHERS answers found on page 236

ROSTER

CATCHERS:	Yr	Hits	AB's	Ave
George **Doggie** Miller	13	1380	5167	.267
Doug **The Red Rooster** Rader	11	1302	5186	.251
Harry **Farmer** Vaughn	13	946	3454	.274
William **Farmer** Weaver	7	856	3082	.278
Harry **Horse** Danning	8	847	2971	.285
Ray **Mule** Fosse	12	758	2957	.256
Frank **Pig** House	10	494	1994	.248
Dick **Mule** Dietz	8	478	1829	.261
Bruce **Bull** Edwards	10	429	1675	.256
John **Bull** Henry	9	397	1920	.207
Andrew **Barney** Gilligan	10	386	1865	.207
Lew **Old Dog** Ritter	7	315	1437	.219
John **Horse** Orsino	7	252	1014	.249
Ken **Piggy** Suarez	7	150	661	.227
Martin **Chick** Autry	6	68	277	.245
Arthur **Old Hoss** Twineham	2	55	175	.314
Johnny **Mutt** Riddle	7	51	214	.238
Tom **Bunny** Madden	3	41	143	.287
Morris **Farmer** Steelman	4	31	142	.218
Steve **Hoss** Korcheck	4	23	145	.159
Herb **Workhorse** Crompton	2	20	102	.196
George **Ducky** Hale	4	18	103	.175

1ST BASEMEN:	Yr	Hits	AB's	Ave
Tony **Doggie** Perez	23	2732	9778	.279
Orlando **Baby Bull** Cepeda	17	2351	7927	.297
Johnny **The Big Cat** Mize	15	2011	6443	.312
Bob **Bull** Watson	19	1826	6185	.295
William **Kitty** Bransfield	12	1351	4999	.270
Andres **Big Cat** Galarraga	10	1216	4294	.283
Arnold **Chick** Gandil	9	1176	4245	.277
Fred **Crime Dog** McGriff	9	1136	3984	.285
Leon **Bull** Durham	10	992	3587	.277
Mo **The Hit Dog** Vaughn	4	422	1507	.280
Nelson **Chicken** Hawks	2	124	393	.316
Roy **Kitty** Brashear	2	124	463	.268
Charles **Chick** Tolson	5	78	275	.284
William **Chick** Autry	2	50	257	.195
Ernest **Mule** Shirley	2	21	100	.210

2ND BASEMEN:	Yr	Hits	AB's	Ave
Tony **Chick** Cuccinello	15	1729	6184	.280
Felix **The Cat** Millan	12	1617	5791	.279
Pete **Pecky** Suder	13	1268	5085	.249
Horace **Hoss** Clarke	10	1230	4813	.256
Felix **The Cat** Mantilla	11	707	2707	.261
Wilson **Chick** Fewster	11	506	1963	.258
Rex **Wonder Dog** Hudler	9	276	1079	.256
Art **Hoss** Hoelskoetter	4	225	952	.236
Robert **Rabbit** Saverine	6	206	861	.239
George **Rabbit** Nill	5	204	963	.212
Joe **Old Hoss** Ardner	2	88	415	.212
Joe **Horse Belly** Sargent	1	45	178	.253
Otis **Rabbit** Lawry	2	34	178	.191

SHORTSTOPS:	Yr	Hits	AB's	Ave
Walter **Rabbit** Maranville	23	2605	10078	.258
Maury **Mousey** Wills	14	2134	7588	.281
Rick **The Rooster** Burleson	13	1401	5139	.273
Clarence **Chick** Galloway	10	946	3583	.264
Harold **Rabbit** Warstler	11	935	4088	.229
Dick **Ducky** Schofield	19	699	3083	.227
Jackie **Rabbit** Tavener	6	543	2131	.255
Charles **Chick** Fulmer	6	365	1422	.257
Fred **Chicken** Stanley	14	356	1650	.216
Al **Bronk** Brancato	4	199	930	.214
Bernard **Barney** McLaughlin	3	169	696	.243

3RD BASEMEN:	Yr	Hits	AB's	Ave
Bill **Mad Dog** Madlock	15	2008	6594	.305
Gustaf **Barney** Friberg	14	1170	4169	.281
Billy **Horse** Cox	11	974	3712	.262
Billy **Bull** Johnson	9	882	3253	.271
Bob **Ducky** Jones	9	791	2990	.265
Wayne **Chick** Krenchicki	8	283	1063	.266
Billy **Bulldog** Grabarkewitz	7	274	1161	.236
Tommy **Rabbit** Glaviano	5	259	1008	.257
Ellis **Cat** Clary	4	171	650	.263
Clyde **Rabbit** Robinson	3	156	700	.233
Charles **Chick** Lathers	2	29	127	.228

OUTFIELDERS:	Yr	Hits	AB's	Ave
Leon **Goose** Goslin	18	2735	8656	.316
Jimmy **Pony** Ryan	18	2502	8164	.306
Joe **Ducky** Medwick	17	2471	7635	.324
Greg **The Bull** Luzinski	15	1795	6505	.276
Charles **Chick** Stahl	10	1546	5069	.305
Riggs **Old Hoss** Stephenson	14	1515	4508	.336
Charles **Chick** Hafey	13	1466	4625	.317
William **Chicken** Wolf	11	1440	4968	.290
Jimmy **Rabbit** Slagle	10	1340	4996	.268
Burt **Barney** Shotton	14	1338	4949	.270
William **Barney** McCosky	11	1301	4172	.312
Johnny **Hippity** Hopp	14	1262	4260	.296
George **Mule** Haas	12	1257	4303	.292
John **Wild Horse of the Osage** Martin	13	1227	4117	.298
Bob **Dog** Skinner	12	1198	4318	.277
James **Ducky** Holmes	10	1014	3601	.282
Ray **Rabbit** Powell	9	890	3324	.268
Clyde **Pooch** Barnhart	9	788	2673	.295
Eddie **Greyhound** Milner	9	607	2395	.253
Charles **Chick** Fullis	8	548	1855	.295
Bobby **Doggie** Del Greco	9	454	1982	.229
Joe **Duck** Lahoud	11	429	1925	.223
Dorrel **White Rat** Herzog	8	414	1614	.257
Charles **Chick** Shorten	8	370	1345	.275
Al **Bull** Ferrara	8	358	1382	.259
Walter **Piggy** French	6	297	981	.303
Frank **Piggy** Ward	6	223	780	.286
George **Pooch** Puccinelli	4	172	607	.283

ROSTER

OUTFIELDERS: (Cont.)	Yr	Hits	AB's	Ave
Walter *Chick* Mattick	3	115	506	.227
Ed *Mouse* Glenn	3	106	525	.202
Chet *Chick* Morgan	2	91	329	.277
Edward *Goat* Anderson	1	85	413	.206
Dino *Dingo* Restelli	2	65	270	.241
Joe *Poodles* Hutcheson	1	43	184	.234
Joe *Rabbit* Caffie	2	37	127	.291
Jack *Bunny* Roser	1	27	113	.239
William *Ducky* Hemp	2	25	117	.214
John *Jackrabbit* Gilbert	2	23	96	.240
Jim *Troy Terrier* Egan	1	23	115	.200
Bernard *Barney* Olsen	1	21	73	.288
Charles *Chick* King	5	18	76	.237

PITCHERS:	Yr	Won	Lost	ERA
Walter *Barney* Johnson	21	417	279	2.17
Charles *Old Hoss* Radbourn	11	309	195	2.67
Jim *Kitty* Kaat	25	283	237	3.45
George *Bull* Uhle	17	200	166	3.99
Charles *Chick* Fraser	14	175	212	3.68
Mark *Fido* Baldwin	7	156	165	3.36
Harvey *The Kitten* Haddix	14	136	113	3.63
Orel *Bulldog* Hershiser	12	134	102	3.00
Harry *The Cat* Brecheen	12	132	92	2.92
Frank *Mule* Lary	12	128	116	3.49
Rich *Goose* Gossage	22	124	107	3.01
Thomas *Toad* Ramsey	6	114	124	3.29
Dick *Bulldog* Pattin	13	114	109	3.62
Bill *Bullfrog* Dietrich	16	108	128	4.48
Bill *Chick* Hoffer	6	92	46	3.75
Brooks *Bull* Lawrence	7	69	62	4.25
Tom *Plowboy* Morgan	12	67	47	3.61
Atley *Swampy* Donald	8	65	33	3.52
Steve *Cat* McCatty	9	63	63	3.99
Ray *Farmer* Moore	11	63	59	4.06
Jim *Bulldog* Bouton	10	62	63	3.57
John *Mule* Watson	7	50	53	4.03
George *Farmer* Bell	5	43	79	2.85
Cliff *Mule* Fannin	8	34	51	4.85
Hank *Bulldog* Fischer	6	30	39	4.23

PITCHERS: (Cont.)	Yr	Won	Lost	ERA
Marino *Chick* Pieretti	6	30	38	4.53
Ed *Bull* Durham	5	29	44	4.45
Bob *Horse* Lee	5	25	23	2.70
Albert *Bronco* Jones	4	25	34	3.63
Jamie *Rat* Easterly	13	23	33	4.62
Bill *Barney* Wolfe	4	21	37	2.96
Milt *Mule* Watson	4	21	30	3.57
George *Barney* Schultz	7	20	20	3.63
Tom *Chick* Early	6	18	24	3.78
John *Chicken Hearted* Kirby	5	18	50	4.09
Dale *Horse* Mohorcic	5	16	21	3.49
Bob *Chick* Chakales	7	15	25	4.54
Bunn *Bunny* Hearn	6	13	24	3.56
Joseph *Chick* Robitaille	2	12	8	2.56
Carl *Collie* Druhot	2	8	10	3.08
Elmer *Bunny* Hearn	4	7	11	4.38
Al *Bull* Schroll	4	6	9	5.34
Lloyd *Chick* Davies	4	4	6	4.48
William *Bull* Wagner	2	4	3	5.64
John *Ox* Miller	4	4	6	6.38
Chester *Chick* Brandom	3	3	1	2.08
George *Kitten* Prentiss	2	3	3	5.31
Bernard *Barney* McFadden	2	3	5	6.38
George *Barney* Barnicle	3	3	3	6.55
Gene *Blue Goose* Moore	3	2	2	4.76
Louis *Bull* Durham	4	2	0	5.28
Don *Bull* Durham	2	2	11	5.83
Johnny *Ducky* Tillman	1	1	0	0.90
Sherman *Katsy* Keifer	1	1	0	2.00
William *Mutt* Wilson	1	1	1	3.46
Ed *Peck* Monroe	2	1	0	3.52
Art *Hoss* Hoelskoetter	3	1	5	4.54
Harry *Mule Trader* Kimberlin	4	1	4	4.70
David *Mutt* Williams	2	1	0	4.91
Les *Barney* Barnhart	2	1	1	6.75
Harry *Collie* Colliflower	1	1	11	8.17

EXTRAS:
William *Kitty* Bransfield - Umpire
Fred *Bull* Perrine - Umpire

LINGO

Horsehide: Baseball

Bullpen: Where pitchers warm-up before coming into the game

Catcall: A yell from the stands

Rabbit Ball: A lively ball, easy to hit far

Goat: Person who lost the game

Hog a Ball: Try to catch a ball another fielder has a better chance at catching

Putting Him Out to Pasture: Retiring a player

Workhorse: Pitcher who hurls more than others

Center/Left/Right Field: Areas beyond infield but before the fences

Infield: Area including all four bases

Middle Fielder: Second baseman or shortstop

Cut 'Em Down: Throw a runner out

Ducks on the Pond: Runners in scoring position

Dogging It: Not trying hard

Beefing Up Their Lineup: Adding stronger batters

FOREST ANIMALS

13

Team

Lurking in every jungle or forest are all kinds of animals. As a youth, hiking and camping were big summer activities. You never knew who was watching you. If you heard a noise, you didn't move, you froze and watched to see what it was. At night it was even scarier! Hang your food pack up high so the bears don't get it! Close the tent tight so no snakes come in. Keep a knife and flashlight by your sleeping bag, just in case. Then pray you don't become prey.

The Forest Animal team players would certainly put fear into the hearts of opposing competition. This team is home to 27 Moose, 16 Rabbits and five Snakes. Beware, there are six Bears, two Sugar Bears, a Big Bear, a Boogie Bear and three Bear Tracks. Do not overlook two Silver Foxes, two Squirrels and two Possums, or the Weasel, a Muskrat and a Wolfie! The jungle is home to five Tigers, two Lizards and two Cobras. Be careful, there is also a Gator, an Antelope, a Hippo and a Gorilla on the loose!

One team member who stands out in this group is Ryne Ryno Sandberg. Since 1982 he had been the Cub's second baseman, until recently calling it quits in 1994. His all-around play has allowed him to be considered one of the best keystone men to ever 'suit up'. Ryno is also my wife's favorite player. She has his jersey and even his Topps rookie card! Linda's maiden name is Sandberg. According to a Sports Illustrated article, Ryne's relatives are from Minnesota, just as Linda's are. She hopes they may be related!

LINEUP

CA	*Reindeer* Bill Killefer

was a 13 year player in the Senior Circuit. Reindeer was a rock behind the plate. Three times Bill led all backstops in fielding %. Three seasons he was first in putouts and in assists and twice Reindeer led all catchers in DP's. Bill also managed for ten campaigns.

1B	Bill *Moose* Skowron

starred 14 campaigns, launching 211 round trippers. Five summers Bill hit over .300. From 1956-62 Moose averaged 20+ homers and 81+ RBI's for the Bronx Bombers. Moose played in eight Fall Classics, hitting eight home runs (seventh) and driving in 29 runs (sixth).

2B	Ryne *Ryno* Sandberg

was the best second baseman of his time. In the field, Ryno won nine consecutive Gold Gloves (1983-91) and set records for consecutive errorless games (123) and total errorless chances (582). On the bases, he had over 300 steals. At the plate, he was the NL MVP in 1984.

SS	Walter *Rabbit* Maranville

started 17 of his 23 seasons, collecting over 2600 hits. His 177 triples ranks him 19th (tie). Rabbit dominated games at his position, often winning contests with his leather. His best offensive year was 1922. Rabbit had 198 hits and batted .295 for the Pittsburgh Pirates.

3B	Don *Tiger* Hoak

was a hard nosed ballplayer. Tiger played 11 seasons at the hot corner. Twice Don led the National League in fielding %, putouts and assists, and once topped third sackers in DP's. His 39 doubles with the Cincinnati Redlegs in 1957 were tops for the Senior Circuit.

OF	Jim *The Gray Fox* Northrup

added left-handed homer punch to the Tigers lineup from the mid 60's to the mid 70's. Playing regularly for nine seasons, Jim reached double digits for homers eight times. From 1968-70 The Gray Fox hit 21, 25 and 24 dingers and drove in 90, 66 and 80 runs.

OF	Clyde *Deerfoot* Milan

was a speedy outfielder. He ranks ninth all time in assists. During his 16 campaigns, Clyde hit over .300 four times. Best known for his speed on the base paths, Deerfoot stole over 40 sacks five different seasons and finished with 495 career pilfers (tie 32nd).

OF	Roy *Squirrel* Sievers

was the 1949 AL Rookie of the Year. Due to injuries, Roy's next four years were weak. Traded before the 1954 season to the Senators, he responded. In the next six summers Roy pounded 180 HR's and topped 100 RBI's four times! Squirrel led the AL in HR's and RBI's in 1957.

P	Clark *The Old Fox* Griffith

adjusted well to the 60'6" pitching distance (changed in 1893 from 50 feet). Clark won 20+ games seven times from 1894-1901. His best season was 1898. The Old Fox won 24 games and led the NL with a 1.88 ERA. Later, he became a manager and Major League team owner.

P	Jim *The Lizard* Bunning

deserves the Hall of Fame. Eight times Jim won 17 games or more, sharing the AL lead with 20 victories in 1957. Thirteen times he logged 200+ innings. Six times he "rang up" over 200 batters. Lizard finished 11th in strikeouts, tied for 42nd in shutouts and tied for 56th in wins.

P	James *Hippo* Vaughn

hurled 13 summers, mainly during the teens. He was the National League's premier lefty. From 1914-20, Hippo won 17+ games each year, ranking no lower than fifth in K's. In 1918 he led the NL in wins, ERA, shutouts, K's and innings. His lifetime ERA was 2.49 (tie for 27th).

RES	Ron *Gator* Guidry

starred 14 years for the Yankees. Ron led the league in both wins and ERA twice. Three times Gator had 20+ wins. An excellent fielder, he won five consecutive Gold Gloves (1982-86). His .651 career winning % is 14th best and Ron's lifetime strikeout ratio is 25th best.

RES	Walt *Moose* Dropo

stormed the AL in 1950, winning the Rookie of the Year. Moose racked up the numbers, pounding 34 homers and driving in a league leading (tie) 144 runs. Over the next dozen summers Moose never approached his initial stats, but in 1952 and 1953 Walt drove in 97 and 96 runs.

RES	Albert *Joey* Belle

was possibly the best player in baseball in 1994. He finished second in batting average, doubles and slugging %, third in HR's, RBI's and hits, and first in total bases! In the last four seasons Joey has had 28, 34, 38 and 36 homers, and 95, 112, 139 and 101 RBI's. He is awesome!

RES	Kevin *Boogie Bear* Mitchell

is a great player on the edge of superstar status. A good hitter with solid power, 1989 was Kevin's year. He tagged 47 homers, drove in 125 runs (both league leading) and was voted NL MVP. Rotator surgery cutoff a big '93 start and the strike in '94 cut short another big year.

L to R: James *Hippo* Vaughn, Jim *The Lizard* Bunning, Ryne *Ryno* Sandberg, Bill *Moose* Skowron, Walter *Rabbit* Maranville

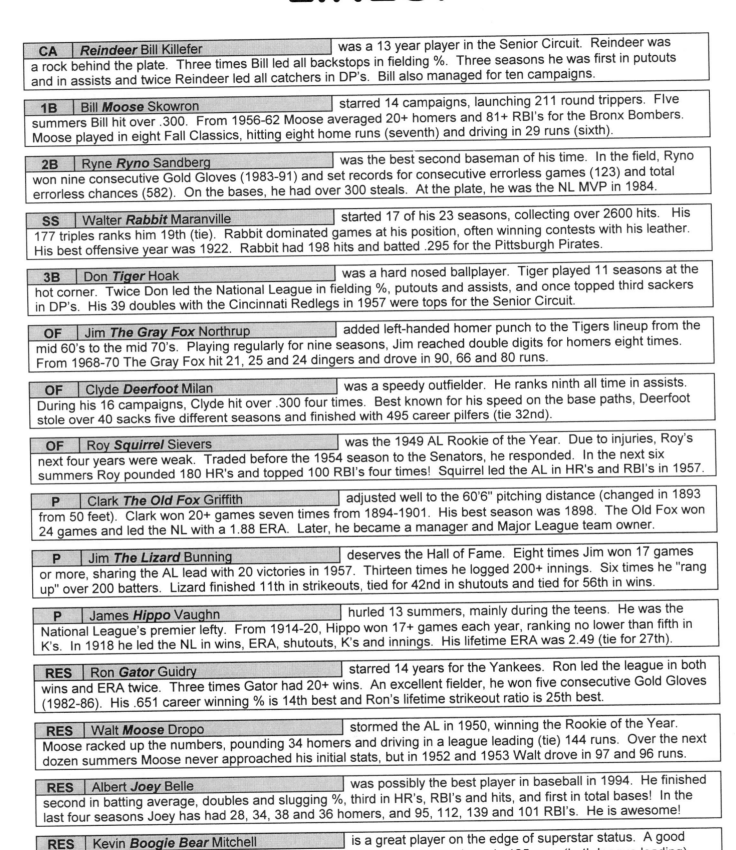

It'sa FACT

Bill **Moose** Skowron: He saved many of his big hits for the World Series. His grand slam in game #7 in 1956 sealed victory. In 1958's game #7, Moose's three run job again carried the Yanks to victory. In the 1960 Fall Classic, Bill pounded a then record tying 12 hits. Of his two home runs, one was again in game #7, but this time it was not enough. After Moose was traded to the Dodgers, he faced his ex-mates in 1963, leading a LA sweep. He launched one of the three Dodger round trippers.

Walter **Rabbit** Maranville: He played 23 seasons. As a shortstop Rabbit ranks first all time in putouts and third all time in assists. Six times he led NL shortstops in putouts, four times in DP's, and three times in both assists and fielding %. Rabbit also played second base three seasons. He led in fielding % twice, and led in putouts, assists and DP's once each. Rabbit won his last fielding % crown at age 41!

Dale **Moose** Alexander: He took the American League by storm! As a rookie in 1929, Moose had 215 hits (first), 137 RBI's (third) and 25 homers (fifth). His first four seasons, Dale hit .343, .326, .325 and .367. Fading to .281 in his fifth season, he went to the minors and never returned. He was considered a liability as a fielder. With DHing today, he could have prospered.

Al **Beartracks** Javery: During the early 40's he toiled for the Boston Braves. From 1940-45, the Braves only won from 59 to 68 games, never finishing higher than sixth place. In 1942 Al won 12 times, five by shutout. He amazingly won 17 times in 1943, posting five more whitewashes.

Danny **Bear** Frisella: He appeared in over 350 games, all but 17 as a fireman. Bear averaged nearly seven K's per nine innings and held opponents to a career .235 batting average. He tragically died in a dune buggy accident January 1st, 1977, at the age of 30.

Johnny **Bear Tracks** Schmitz: In 1941 he broke into the Majors. Missing 3 1/2 years for WW II, Bear Tracks came back to be a two time All-Star, while toiling for the hapless Cubs. He led the league in K's in 1946. In 1948, pitching for the 54 win, last place Cubs, Bear Tracks won 18!

Frank **Monkey** Foreman: He was a hurler at the turn of the century. His best season was 1889. Monkey won 23 games. An outstanding hitter, four times he topped .300. In 1891 Frank parked four home runs in only 157 at bats. In the dead ball era, that was unbelievable! His homer % exceeded all active players that season!

Earl **Moose** Wilson: He was a power pitcher and a power hitter. Moose averaged over six K's per nine innings for his career. He fired a no-hitter June 26th, 1962. Earl's 22 wins led (tie) the American league in 1967. With the stick, Moose had 35 career home runs. Two seasons he propelled seven for the distance!

Julius **Moose** Solters: At 28 he reached the Majors. His next three seasons, 1935-37, were awesome. Moose batted .319, .291 and .323; drove in 112, 134 and 109 runs; slashed 45, 45 and 42 doubles and socked 18, 17 and 20 homers. Never again a regular, he played part-time five more seasons.

George **Moose** Earnshaw: He earned his nickname because he was so strong. In the 1930 Fall Classic, Moose won game #2 going the route, allowing six hits and one run. In game #5 he allowed two hits and no runs, leaving after seven innings at 0-0. With just one day rest, Moose came back and fired a five hit and one run complete game effort, clinching the World Championship.

Harry **Moose** McCormick: After the turn of the century, he was frequently used by John Little Napoleon McGraw as a pinch hitter, a then seldom employed innovation.

Ray **Rabbit** Powell: A quick center fielder (hence the nickname), he four times reached double figures in triples. 1921 was Rabbit's best year. Ray had 191 hits, scored 114 runs and tied for the league lead with 18 three baggers.

Duke **The Silver Fox** Snider: He was a tremendous hitter. The St. Paul Saints were the Dodger's top farm team. As was the custom, the parent team would play an exhibition game with its minor league affiliate once during the season. I attended one just to see Duke. His hair was silver! During his career, The Silver Fox went five consecutive seasons (1953-57) hitting 40 or more homers. In 1954 Duke had his best season. He hit .341 (third), scored 120 runs (tie first) and pounded out 199 hits (second). The Silver Fox also had 40 tape jobs (fifth) and knocked in 130 runs (tie second) in 1954.

Sam **Bear Tracks** Mele: After his playing career, he managed the Minnesota Twins seven seasons. His real first name was Sabbath. As kids, though, we called him "Oat".

Ryne **Ryno** Sandberg: He was the complete ballplayer. Ryno, a "sure bet" future Hall of Famer, had both excellent power and speed. Five times Ryno hit over 20 home runs. He led the NL with 40 long balls in 1990. Seven seasons Ryno scored over 100 times. He led (one tie) the NL with 114, 104 and 116 runs scored in 1984, 1989 and 1990. Nine times Ryno swiped over 20 bags and his 19 triples in 1984 tied him for first.

TRIVIA*

1) In the six game 1959 World Series he was the hitting star. He stroked ten hits, including two doubles and two homers, and he drove in six runs.

2) He threw a perfect game, 27 up and 27 down, June 21st, 1964. He threw a perfect inning, nine pitches and three K's, August 2nd, 1959.

3) He was traded (as a throw-in) with Larry Bowa for Ivan DeJesus.

4) He formed a keystone combination with Charlie The Mechanical Man Gehringer. At only 5'5" he played big, hitting 15 triples in 1928.

5) Hailing from St. Paul Minnesota (his nephew John Hasselman has coached both my boys), he had three powerful seasons (1956-58), hitting 23, 19 and 26 round trippers.

6) He shares, with Pinky Higgins, the record of 12 consecutive hits.

7) His granddad tabbed him Mussolini, leading to his nickname.

8) Unbelievable, he was born in Moosup Connecticut! He was the 1950 AL Rookie of the Year, finishing ahead of Ed Whitey Ford and Alfonso Chico Carrasquel.

9) An avid hunter, he acquired his nickname from his favorite prey.

10) Sharing his name with a famous boxer (Hint: nicknamed Smokin'), he led the NL in pinch at bats and pinch-hits in 1954, going 20/62.

11) He was the manager of the Minnesota Twins during the 1965 Fall Classic. As a player he led (tie) the Junior Circuit in doubles in 1951.

12) They formed a quartet and sang for beer. Jim Cotton Tierney and Jolly Cholly Grimm were two members. The other two singing Pirates are on the roster.

13) Down three games to one in the 1968 World Series, the Tigers roared back. In game #6 he tagged a grand slam and in game #7 his two run triple, off "unhittable" Bob Gibson, led to the Series win.

14) In his first 69 wins, this pitcher whipped the Dodgers 18 times! So, they traded for him in 1951.

15) On June 17th, 1978 he whiffed 18 batters, an American League lefty record.

16) He is the only player to win the Rookie of the Year, the MVP and the Cy Young award during his career.

17) He and Fred Toney hooked up in a memorable game May 2nd, 1917. Both hurlers threw nine inning gems! He gave up two hits and a run in the tenth inning. Toney finished with a ten inning no-hitter.

18) He won over 100 games in both the NL and the AL. He also pitched a no-hitter in both leagues.

19) In 1960 he finished second in the National League MVP voting, losing to teammate Dick Groat.

20) His .990 career fielding % is the standard for all second sackers.

21) His older brother Red played seven seasons, four of which they played against each other.

22) In two of his five full seasons he led the league in triples. In 1893 he legged out 29 triples, fourth highest single season total ever. (Hint: he also pitched one season)

23) He was fleet of foot. He played eight seasons, starting four years. In those "starting" seasons (1902-05), he twice led AL outfielders in fielding % and twice (one tie) topped all players in stolen bases.

24) His brother Bing starred for 16 seasons, but he was in the Majors for only a cup of coffee.

25) He hurled the longest relief effort in a nine inning World Series game, seven innings. For that performance, he was the winning pitcher in game #2 of the 1956 Fall Classic.

* FOREST STUMP(ERS) prey on these answers found on page 236

ROSTER

CATCHERS:	Yr	Hits	AB's	Ave
Reindeer Bill Killefer	13	751	3150	.238
Tom *Deerfoot* Needham	11	311	1491	.209
Al *Moose* Lakeman	9	131	646	.203
Don *Moose* Leppert	4	122	532	.229
Bill *Moose* Drescher	3	37	139	.266
Gordon *Moose* Massa	2	7	17	.412

1ST BASEMEN:	Yr	Hits	AB's	Ave
Bill *Moose* Skowron	14	1566	5547	.282
Walt *Moose* Dropo	13	1113	4124	.270
Dale *Moose* Alexander	5	881	2450	.331
Perry *Moose* Werden	7	773	2740	.282
Frank *Turkeyfoot* Brower	5	371	1297	.286
Myron *Moose* Grimshaw	3	229	894	.256
John *Snake* Deal	1	48	231	.208
Don *Bear* Gile	4	18	120	.150
Fred *Snake* Henry	2	14	75	.187

2ND BASEMEN:	Yr	Hits	AB's	Ave
Ryne *Ryno* Sandberg	13	2080	7161	.290
John *Cub* Stricker	11	1107	4635	.239
Jack *Moose* Farrell	11	877	3613	.243
Charlie *Snake* Neal	8	858	3316	.259
Emil *Antelope* Verban	7	793	2911	.272
Robert *Rabbit* Saverine	6	206	861	.239
George *Rabbit* Nill	5	204	963	.212
Larry *Possum* Burright	3	73	356	.205
Otis *Rabbit* Lawry	2	34	178	.191
Frank *Rabbit* Fuller	3	11	63	.175
Don *Tiger* Leppert	1	8	70	.114
Stan *Rabbit* Benton	1	4	19	.211
Gene *Mousey* Markland	1	1	8	.125
Dallas *Rabbit* Bradshaw	1	0	4	.000

SHORTSTOPS:	Yr	Hits	AB's	Ave
Walter *Rabbit* Maranville	23	2605	10078	.258
Maury *Mousey* Wills	14	2134	7588	.281
Harold *Rabbit* Warstler	11	935	4088	.229
Jackie *Rabbit* Tavener	6	543	2131	.255
Larvell *Sugar Bear* Blanks	9	446	1766	.253
Ed *Lizard* Jurak	6	80	302	.265
Danny *Squirrel* Reynolds	1	12	72	.167

3RD BASEMEN:	Yr	Hits	AB's	Ave
Don *Tiger* Hoak	11	1144	4322	.265
George *Possum* Whitted	11	978	3630	.269
Mike *Cubbie* Cubbage	8	503	1951	.258
Tommy *Rabbit* Glaviano	5	259	1008	.257
Floyd *Sugar Bear* Rayford	7	255	1044	.244
Clyde *Rabbit* Robinson	3	156	700	.223
Muskrat Bill Shipke	4	110	552	.199

OUTFIELDERS:	Yr	Hits	AB's	Ave
Dave *The Cobra* Parker	19	2712	9358	.290
Duke *The Silver Fox* Snider	18	2116	7161	.295
Clyde *Deerfoot* Milan	16	2100	7359	.285
Roy *Squirrel* Sievers	17	1703	6387	.267
Jimmy *Rabbit* Slagle	10	1340	4996	.268
Jim *The Gray Fox* Northrup	12	1254	4692	.267
Kevin *Boogie Bear* Mitchell	10	1070	3742	.286
Davy *Kangaroo* Jones	14	1020	3772	.270
Julius *Moose* Solters	9	990	3421	.289
Pete *Monkey* Hotaling	9	931	3492	.267
Sam *Bear Tracks* Mele	10	916	3437	.267
Ray *Rabbit* Powell	9	890	3324	.268
Jim *Wolfie* Wohlford	15	793	3049	.260
Harry *Deerfoot* Bay	8	722	2640	.273
Walt *Moose* Moryn	8	667	2506	.266
Albert *Joey* Belle	6	654	2293	.285
Whitey *White Rat* Herzog	8	414	1614	.257
George *Deerfoot* Barclay	4	382	1538	.248
Harry *Moose* McCormick	5	356	1247	.285
Cliff *Tiger* Mapes	5	289	1193	.242
Eddie *Mongoose* Lukon	4	143	606	.236
Al *Deerfoot* Kaiser	3	104	481	.216
Joe *Moose* Taylor	4	74	297	.249
Cobra Joe Frazier	4	68	282	.241
Joe *Rabbit* Caffie	2	37	127	.291
John *Jackrabbit* Gilbert	2	23	96	.240
Don *Moose* Brown	2	11	44	.250
Bob *Rabbit* McHale	1	6	33	.182
George *Papa Bear* Halas	1	2	22	.111
John *Moose* Clabaugh	1	1	14	.071

PINCH HITTERS:	Yr	Hits	AB's	Ave
Virgil *Rabbit* Garriott	1	0	5	.000
Larry *Moose* Stubing	1	0	5	.000

PITCHERS:	Yr	Won	Lost	ERA
Clark *The Old Fox* Griffith	20	237	146	3.31
Jim *The Lizard* Bunning	17	224	184	3.27
James *Hippo* Vaughn	13	178	136	2.49
Ron *Gator* Guidry	14	170	91	3.29
Don *Tiger* Newcombe	10	149	90	3.56
Mike *Big Bear* Garcia	14	142	97	3.27
George *Moose* Earnshaw	9	127	93	4.38
Earl *Moose* Wilson	11	121	109	3.69
Bryan *Moose* Haas	12	100	83	4.01
Frank *Monkey* Foreman	11	96	93	3.97
Fred *Bear* Hutchinson	11	95	71	3.73
Johnny *Bear Tracks* Schmitz	13	93	114	3.55
Jesse *The Silver Fox* Petty	7	67	78	3.68
Tom *Snake* Sturdivant	10	59	51	3.74
Ron *Bear* Bryant	8	57	56	4.02

ROSTER

PITCHERS: (Cont.)	Yr	Won	Lost	ERA
Al *Beartracks* Javery	7	53	74	3.80
Jim *Bear* Owens	12	42	68	4.31
Don *Moose* Lee	9	40	44	3.61
Buffalo Bill Hogg	4	37	50	3.06
Danny *Bear* Frisella	10	34	40	3.32
Lewis *Snake* Wiltse	3	29	31	4.59
Eli *Moose* Grba	5	28	33	4.48
Bob *Moose* Lee	5	25	33	2.70
Don *The Weasel* Bessent	4	14	7	3.33
Perry *Moose* Werden	1	12	1	1.97
Roy *Rhino* Hitt	1	6	10	3.40

PITCHERS: (Cont.)	Yr	Won	Lost	ERA
Don *Tiger* Kaiser	3	6	15	4.15
Brad *The Animal* Lesley	4	1	3	3.86
George *Moose* Korince	2	1	0	4.24
Ralph *Moose* Miller	1	0	0	0.00
Art *Moose* Doll	2	0	1	3.00
Grant *Moose* Bowler	2	0	1	6.91
Paul *Gorilla* Gilliford	1	0	0	12.00
Arlas *Foxy* Taylor	1	0	1	22.50
EXTRA:				
Tiger Stadium - Detroit's Home Park				

LINGO

Man in the Monkey Suit: The umpire

Batting Cage: Net surrounding the space where you practice hitting, but don't chase the ball

Snake: Curve ball

Gopher Ball: Pitch hit for a home run

South Paws: On the back legs of a deer looking north

Rabid Fan: An extremely enthusiastic fan

Bear Down: Try harder to perform

In the Cage: Take batting practice in a netted cage

Rabbit Ball: One that is very lively

MORE TRIVIA*

A) His 318 yard shots rank him 56th all time. Amazingly, the Browns traded him even up for a player who he out homered 293 to three!

B) He held the post 1900 stolen base single season record with 88 pilfers until Ty Cobb stole 96 in 1915. His speed led to his nickname.

C) June 18th, 1961 he homered in his first Major League at bat. He only hit 14 more home runs during his career.

D) On April 14th, 1955, May 30th, 1955 and September 19th, 1956, this slugging pitcher hit two HR's in each game.

E) He won his first game at age 21 in 1969. In 1972 he won 14 times, tossing four shutouts. Everything came together in 1973. He topped all NL hurlers with 24 wins.

F) In 1956-57 he had back to back 16 win seasons. His 16-6 record in 1957 tied for first in winning %. His 2.54 ERA was second and his 16 wins were third (tie) in the AL.

G) In 1983 he unofficially (not enough decisions) led All-American League pitchers in winning % going 13-3 with three shutouts.

H) In 1978 he went 25-3, the best winning % for a hurler who won at least 20 games. His nine shutouts, for an American League lefty, tied Babe Ruth's record from 1916!

I) He and Lefty Grove formed a near unbeatable righty/lefty combination for the Athletics. From 1929-31 the A's won three pennants, usurping the Yankees. He won 24, 22 and 21 games those three seasons.

J) He went to the US Congress representing Kentucky once he "hung up" his cleats.

K) This lefty was also known as Louisiana Lightning.

L) He was part of the "Big Four" for the Indians in 1954. That year he led the AL in ERA and shutouts (tie), while posting a 19-8 record.

M) This future slugger was an All-American football player while in college.

N) He won his first game in the Majors at age 30, then carved a solid career for the then doormat Dodgers. His nickname came from his age.

O) He won consecutive NL batting titles in 1977 and 1978.

* FOREST STUMP(ERS) prey on these answers found on page 236

Real GIANTS

14

Team

The Giants have a long storied history. Starting in the late 1800's, the team was called the Gothams. They actually became known (nicknamed) as the Giants, because the squad had so many large players. In 1902 John Little Napoleon McGraw took the helm. He generaled the Giants 31 seasons, finishing first or second 21 times! In 1951 the boys from Coogan's Bluff came from 13 games back in August to win the flag. Three years later, led by Dusty Rhodes and Willie Mays, they ruled baseball. The team's move to San Francisco in 1958 began the opening of baseball to the whole country. In 1989 the Giants literally shook the sports world. On October 15th, prior to World Series game #3, an earthquake hit and swayed their fan packed stadium! Thank goodness no one was hurt! It brought new meaning to the word "wave".

The Real Giants include many true giants of the game. When a player is nicknamed Big, it often refers to how he played. Nine of the Major Leaguers on the roster are already Hall of Famers. Big Dan Brouthers, Big Ed Delahanty, Don Big D Drysdale, Walter The Big Train Johnson, Christy Big Six Mathewson, Johnny The Big Cat Mize, Big Sam Thompson, Big Ed Walsh and Paul Big Poison Waner are all members of that select group. Players with "Hall qualities" include Cecil Big Daddy Fielder, Andres Big Cat Galarraga, Randy The Big Unit Johnson and Frank The Big Hurt Thomas. The many others on the roster are Big just in the fact they were good enough to reach the Major Leagues, a very Giant accomplishment!

Christy Big Six Mathewson stands tall among the many Real Giants. His nickname qualifies him for this team. In his prolific career of 17 seasons, Matty actually played for the Giants all 17 summers and won 372 of his 373 victories while pitching for the New Yorkers. Big Six was both a great player and a great man. As a player, his yearly and career accomplishments were simply awesome! Christy won 20 or more games 13 years. Four summers he won 30 or more contests. He ranks tied for third in career wins, third in lifetime shutouts and fifth in overall ERA. Big Six was dominant. As a man, Matty became a national hero. In the day of rough and tumble, he was refined. In the day of little education, Christy had a college degree. In the day of tobacco chewing, hard drinking, and carousing, Big Six was clean cut and virtuous. He promised his mother that he would never pitch on Sunday. Christy kept his vow to his mother. Big Six was one of the "Five Immortals" originally enshrined at Cooperstown.

LINEUP

CA	Walker *Big Coop* Cooper

starred 18 seasons in the Senior Circuit. He was named to the All-Star team eight times. Big Coop also hit over .300 eight summers. His best season, by far, was 1947. Big Coop launched 35 home runs (fourth), drove in 122 runs (third) and batted .305 for the Giants.

1B	*Big* Ed Konetchy

started all of his 15 campaigns. An outstanding glove man, Big Ed led in fielding % eight times. His 181 career triples rank him 17th all time. Six seasons Big Ed stole 20 or more bases and four times he hit over .300. His ten consecutive hits in 1919 shares the NL record.

2B	*Big* George Crowe

was known more for his pinch hitting and his first base play. Big George's only full season was 1957. He responded with 31 homers and 92 RBI's! Fourteen of Big George's 81 career yard shots came as a pinch hitter. He held the career Major League record for three years.

SS	Daryl *Big Dee* Spencer

actually had two careers. For ten seasons he played in the National League and pounded 105 tators. Big Dee then played seven more summers in Japan. There shorter distances helped him stroke another 152 dingers. At 6'2", Big Dee was really big in Hankyu, Japan!

3B	*Big* Dan Brouthers

was the NL's first superstar. He starred from 1879-96 (also two games in 1904). In his 19 seasons Big Dan won seven slugging titles and five batting crowns. He led the National League in hits (three), doubles (three, one tie), runs (two), homers (two, one tie) and RBI's (two)!

OF	Paul *Big Poison* Waner

did it all in his 20 year Hall of Fame career. He was thought to be too small at 5'8", 150 pounds, but Big Poison played big. He slugged 605 two baggers (tenth), slashed 191 three baggers (tenth) and stroked 3152 hits (12th). Each of his first 12 summers he hit .300+!

OF	*Big* Ed Delahanty

was a prodigious hitter. He not only has the fourth highest career batting average, but he also was a power hitter! Three seasons Big Ed hit over .400! He led the league in 2B's (five, two ties), 3B's (one), HR's (two, one tie) and RBI's (three). From 1894-96 he hit .407, .404 and .397!

OF	*Big* Sam Thompson

sparkled for 15 summers, ten full time. He drove in over 100 runs eight times, including years of 165 and 166 RBI's! Big Sam led the NL in hits (three, one tie), doubles (two), triples (one), homers (two) and batting average (one). A bad back shortened his spectacular career.

P	*Big* Ed Walsh

is a Hall of Famer. For his career, he had a 1.82 ERA, the best ever! Big Ed, in 315 starts, had 57 shutouts (18.1% of his starts!). He led the AL in games (five, one tie), saves(five, two ties), innings (four), strikeouts (two) and ERA (two). In 1908 Big Ed posted 11 shutouts!

P	*Big* Ed Reulbach

fired pellets 13 seasons. Three consecutive years (1906-08) he led the NL in winning %, going 19-4, 17-4 and 24-7. For his career Big Ed ranks 21st in winning %. He also painted 40 whitewashes and retired with an excellent 2.28 ERA, sharing tenth place all time.

P	Rick *Big Daddy* Reuschel

toiled 19 summers, mostly for second division and often last place teams. Nevertheless, he had 11 years in which he won at least half his decisions and 13 campaigns with wins in double digits. His best summer, 1977, Rick went 20-10 for the 81-81 Cubs.

RES	Randy *The Big Unit* Johnson

has grown as a pitcher (not taller!). He has mastered his control at no loss in his strikeout productivity. The Big Unit has fanned over 200 batters per year from 1991-94, leading the AL the last three seasons in K's. He simultaneously has reduced his walks by 50%.

RES	Johnny *The Big Cat* Mize

gave three seasons (age 30-32) to his country. He starred 15 summers on his way to Cooperstown. During his career The Big Cat won four home run crowns (two shared), captured four slugging titles and earned three RBI crowns. His 359 yard shots rank him 41st.

RES	*Big* Bill Dinneen

stood tall 12 seasons. He won 20 or more games four campaigns. Big Bill was the hero of the first World Series in 1903. He led the AL Boston Pilgrims to win the best of nine series five games to three games. Big Bill fired two shutouts and won games #2, #6 and #8.

RES	*Big* Bill Lee

was known for his high leg kick and his blazing fast ball. He twirled 14 summers in the Senior Circuit. Four seasons Big Bill won 18 or more games. His best season was 1938. Big Bill led the National League in wins (22), shutouts (nine) and ERA (2.66).

L to R: Johnny *The Big Cat* Mize, Paul *Big Poison* Waner, Christy *Big Six* Mathewson, *Big* Ed Walsh, Randy *The Big Unit* Johnson

It'sa FACT

**Big** Tom Gorman: His career as a Major League ballplayer consisted of a late season call up in 1939, but Big Tom went on to umpire 26 years in the NL.

Johnny _**The Big Cat**_ Mize: The year he hit 51 homers (1947), The Big Cat fanned only 42 times. That is the only time a 50+ homer hitter struck out fewer times than his number of homers.

**Big** Dave Davenport: 1915 was his career year. Big Dave pitched in the short lived Federal League. That season he not only won 22 games (tied third), but he also led the league in games, complete games, innings, strikeouts and shutouts. Big Dave's younger brother, Claude, who was also 6'6", reached the Majors after Dave retired. Claude was also tabbed Big Dave!

Eldon _**Big Six**_ Auker: In 1935 Big Six (after Matty) went 18-7 and led the AL in winning %.

**Big** Bill Voiselle: The 1944 Giants record was 67-87. Nevertheless, Big Bill won 21 games (tie third) and led NL hurlers in both innings and strikeouts.

Walter _**Big Ed**_ Morris: His best season was 1928. Big Ed won 19 games while toiling for the last place Bosox (57-96). His career tragically ended when he was stabbed to death in a barroom scuffle.

**Big** Ed Reulbach: He pitched and won both games of a double-header. Both victories were shutouts! No one has ever duplicated that feat. Big Ed's 44 consecutive scoreless innings was the record nearly 30 years. On October 10th, 1906 Big Ed tossed a one hitter in the World Series.

**Big** Jack Sheridan: He umpired from 1885-1914. Big Jack invented the chest protector. It was out of necessity. He was the first umpire to crouch behind the catcher. Previously, they stood behind the pitcher.

**Big** Dan Brouthers: He was one of the premier sluggers of his era (1880-90's). For his career, Big Dan drove in .77 runs per game (12th), batted .342 (eighth), hit 205 triples (eighth) and scored .91 runs per game (seventh).

Paul _**Big Poison**_ Waner: Eight seasons he stroked over 200 hits. Big Poison captured three batting titles and his .333 lifetime batting average ranks him 23rd.

**Big** Ed Delahanty: He and his four brothers, Frank (Pudgie), Jim, Joe and Tom, all played in the Majors! Big Ed tragically and mysteriously fell to his death at Niagara Falls while still in the height of his career (age 35). His lifetime stats of 522 doubles (25th), 185 triples (13th), 1599 runs (35th) and 2597 hits (60th) could have ended much higher!

Cecil _**Big Daddy**_ Fielder: In 1990 he launched 51 HR's. Big Daddy became only the 11th player to reach 50.

**Big** Sam Thompson: He holds the career record of .92 RBI's per game.

**Big** Ed Walsh: A spitballer, he claimed to throw six varieties of spitters. After twirling five one-hitters, Big Ed hurled a no-hitter August 27th, 1911. His 464 innings in 1908 is the record for the 20th century.

**Big** Luke Easter: He "came up" late in 1949. Big Luke was a 34 year old rookie, held back because he was a Negro. From 1950-52 he slugged 28, 27 and 31 dingers and drove in 107, 103 and 97 runs. Big Luke could have had giant numbers if given a fair chance!

Jack _**The Giant Killer**_ Pfiester: In 1907 he had a 1.15 ERA, seventh best all time.

TRIVIA*

1) He and his little brother are the only siblings in the Hall of Fame.
2) In the 1905 World Series he won three games and all were shutouts!
3) He was the AL's 1993 and 1994 MVP.
4) He cut the sleeves off of his jersey to showoff his biceps. (Hint: he swatted 40, 49 and 47 homers in 1953-55)
5) He pitched for the Chicago White Sox (AKA The Hitless Wonders). In 1910 he lost 20 games, yet led the AL with a microscopic 1.27 ERA!
6) He combined in 1954 with Bob Lem Lemon, Early Gus Wynn and Rapid Robert Feller to lead the Indians to a record 111 wins.
7) In 1904 he started and completed, a post 1900 record, all 37 games he pitched. (Hint: he later became an umpire and called games for 29 years, also a record)
8) Sixteen consecutive seasons he batted at least .300. Six campaigns he swatted at .350 or better!
9) He hit three home runs in one game six times!
10) He led the AL in RBI's three consecutive years (1990-92) and led in HR's in both 1990 and 1991 (shared).
11) He was nicknamed after New York City's fastest horse drawn fire truck, because he was so fast. He also had exceptional control. In 1913 this hurler went 68 innings without issuing a free pass. Four seasons he walked less than one batter per nine innings.
12) In 1993 he flirted all year with .400, but he settled for a NL league leading .370 batting average.
13) His older brother Paul was a reliever and he was a starter. They played together for the Cubs in the 70's.
14) He smashed four homers in one game, all were inside the park.
15) These three Philadelphia outfielders all hit over .400 in one season (1894)! One was Sliding Billy Hamilton and the other two Hall of Famers are on the Real Giants.

* BIG THINKERS answers found on page 237

80

ROSTER

CATCHERS:	Yr	Hits	AB's	Ave
Walker *Big Coop* Cooper	18	1341	4702	.285
Willard *Big Bill* Brown	7	415	1589	.261
John *Big Pete* Peters	4	80	302	.265
Mark *Big Slick* Stewart	1	0	1	.000
Big Jim Sheehan	1	0	4	.000

1ST BASEMEN:	Yr	Hits	AB's	Ave
Big Ed Konetchy	15	2150	7649	.281
Johnny *The Big Cat* Mize	15	2011	6443	.312
Ted *Big Klu* Kluszewski	15	1766	5929	.298
Andres *Big Cat* Galarraga	10	1216	4294	.283
Dick *Big Stu* Stuart	10	1055	3997	.264
Cecil *Big Daddy* Fielder	9	853	3295	.259
Frank *The Big Hurt* Thomas	5	741	2271	.326
Big Luke Easter	6	472	1725	.274
Big Ed Stevens	6	308	1220	.252
Big Bill Abstein	3	150	619	.242
Big Bill Kelly	1	15	84	.179
Big Bill Hanlon	1	2	21	.095
Clarence *Big Boy* Kraft	1	1	3	.333

2ND BASEMEN:	Yr	Hits	AB's	Ave
Big George Crowe	9	467	1727	.270
Big Jim Clinton	6	393	1490	.264

SHORTSTOPS:	Yr	Hits	AB's	Ave
Daryl *Big Dee* Spencer	10	901	3689	.244

3RD BASEMEN:	Yr	Hits	AB's	Ave
Big Dan Brouthers	19	2296	6711	.342
Big Bill Massey	1	15	53	.283

OUTFIELDERS:	Yr	Hits	AB's	Ave
Paul *Big Poison* Waner	20	3152	9459	.333
Big Ed Delahanty	16	2597	7505	.346
Big Sam Thompson	15	1979	5984	.331
Dave *Big Bird* Kingman	16	1575	6677	.236
Kevin *Big Mac* McReynolds	12	1439	5423	.265
Big Al Libke	2	236	880	.268
Big Bill Renna	6	219	918	.239
Big Jim Fridley	3	105	424	.248
Big Bill Bagwell	2	42	143	.294
Jim *Big Train* Asbell	1	6	33	.182
Big Ed Clough	3	2	19	.105

PITCHERS:	Yr	Won	Lost	ERA
Walter *The Big Train* Johnson	21	417	279	2.17
Christy *Big Six* Mathewson	17	373	188	2.13
Rick *Big Daddy* Reuschel	19	214	191	3.37
Don *Big D* Drysdale	14	209	166	2.95
Big Ed Walsh	14	195	126	1.82
Big Ed Reulbach	13	182	106	2.28
Big Bill Dinneen	12	170	177	3.01

PITCHERS: (Cont.)	Yr	Won	Lost	ERA
Big Bill Lee	14	169	157	3.54
Earl *Big Ebbie* Moore	14	162	154	2.78
Mike *Big Bear* Garcia	14	142	97	3.27
Eldon *Big Six* Auker	10	130	101	4.42
Stan *Big Daddy* Williams	14	109	94	3.48
Harry *The Giant Killer* Coveleski	9	81	55	2.39
Randy *The Big Unit* Johnson	7	81	62	3.70
Big Bill Voiselle	9	74	84	3.83
Big Dave Davenport	6	73	83	2.93
Jack *The Giant Killer* Pfiester	8	71	44	2.02
Tall Paul Minner	10	69	84	3.94
Big Bill James	8	65	71	3.20
Big Mike Sullivan	11	54	66	5.11
Walter *Big Ed* Morris	5	42	45	4.19
George *Big Murph* Johnson	3	40	43	2.95
Big Bill Steele	5	37	43	4.02
Francis *Big Jeff* Pfeffer	6	31	39	3.30
Johnny *Big Serb* Miljus	7	29	26	3.92
Tall Paul Hartzell	6	27	39	3.90
Big Ed Klepfer	6	22	17	2.81
Carl *Big Train* Willis	8	22	16	4.09
Dallas *Big D* Green	8	20	22	4.26
Big Jack Katoll	4	17	22	3.32
Clarence *Big Gene* Wright	4	14	26	4.50
Big Jim Baskette	3	9	6	3.30
Frank *Big Pete* McKenry	2	6	6	3.10
Big Bill Schardt	2	5	16	3.67
Big Joe Willis	3	4	11	4.63
Les *Big Ed* Munns	3	4	13	4.76
Big Ben Shields	4	4	0	8.27
Big Jim Wiggs	3	3	4	3.81
Lou *Big Finn* Fiene	4	3	8	3.85
Big John Bogart	1	2	1	3.04
Big Dan Tripple	1	1	1	0.95
Big Joe Mulligan	1	1	0	3.63
Big Ed Hendricks	1	0	1	3.75
Claude *Big Dave* Davenport	1	0	0	4.50
Big Jim Murray	1	0	0	4.50
Armand *Big Ben* Cardoni	3	0	6	4.76
Big Bill Bolden	1	0	1	5.25
Big Dan Abbott	1	0	2	6.23
Gordon *Big Train* McNaughton	1	0	1	6.43
Big Jim Roberts	2	0	3	7.18
Big Tom Gorman	1	0	0	7.20
Big Sam Edmonston	2	0	1	9.00
George *Big Ed* Edmondson	3	0	0	9.64

EXTRAS:
Big Bill Dinneen - Umpire
Big Tom Gorman - Umpire
Big Jack Sheridan - Umpire
Olympic Stadium - *Big O*
Anaheim Stadium - *Big A*

GOURMET

15

Team

What could be more American than baseball and apple pie? I can still savor a brat on Yawkey Dr. (behind Fenway) or a frank with kraut on North Clark St. (in front of Wrigley.) As a teenager, I hawked food in Metropolitan Stadium (now the site of the famous Megamall) shouting 'peanuts' and 'popcorn.' Many an afternoon or evening has been spent watching in person or just listening to the game "out back", while having a burger and pop. Not surprisingly, in our culture many Gourmet nicknames become attached to our summer heroes. The Gourmet Team is a veritable feast, with eight Hall of Famers making the squad.

Leading off with appetizers, there are Peanuts, Chips, Crackers and Soups on the team. No meal is complete without vegetables, right Mom? The team has a Cuke, Spinach and a Tomato. Covering other food groups, fruits are in abundance, including Peaches, Grapefruit and a Banana. The main course has several choices on the menu. There are Ham and Beans, T-Bone and Spuds or try some Catfish and Noodles. To spice up your entrees, add condiments, be it Pepper, Sugar, Tabasco or just Sauce. No meal is complete without dessert. Do not count calories. Have some Pie, Cookies, Cake or Candy.

If there is one player who 'wedges' out from the group, it is Harold Pie Traynor. In his day, Pie was considered the best at the hot corner with a glove. A Hall of Famer, his bat alone would have gotten him to Cooperstown. As easy as his stats are to "look up", his nickname's origin is not. There are at least three stories. According to Harold's dad (a printer), he came home very dirty one day, as dirty as pied type (a grungy messy type). Mom said when she would send Harold for groceries, he always added pie to the list, because he loved it so much. If you doubt either, their parish priest, who was also his sandlot coach, claims he would ask the players what they wanted for a treat (after the game), and you guessed it, Harold always wanted pie!

LINEUP

CA	Jack *Peach Pie* O'Connor

had a 21 year career which started in 1887. Also known as Rowdy Jack, he caught pitches for six teams in three leagues during his time. Twice Peach Pie led the American Association in fielding %. His best season at the plate was 1890. Peach Pie feasted on pitching at a .324 clip.

1B	George *Candy* LaChance

was a turn of the century first sacker, starring 12 summers. 1895 was Candy's best year at the dish. He hit .312 with 108 RBI's, and his eight homers (in the dead ball era) were hefty. In 1903 George was a member of the inaugural World Series winning Boston Pilgrims.

2B	Bobby *Link* Lowe

was an excellent player, both offensively and defensively. In 1894 Link placed second in homers (tie) and batted at a .346 clip. Highlighting his season, on May 30th, 1894 Link slugged four homers and a single in one game! He is one of 13 players to ever hit four taters in one game!

SS	Norman *Tabasco Kid* Elberfeld

was known as a fiery player, hence the nickname. His large desire made up for his small size (5'7"). The Kid was a leader on the field, starring 14 seasons, including one summer as the playing manager. Three years the Tabasco Kid feasted at the plate at over .300.

3B	Harold *Pie* Traynor

was elected to the Hall of Fame. A dazzling fielder, he led the National League in putouts, assists, DP's and fielding % a total of 15 times. Playing in spacious Forbes Field, Pie sliced 164 career triples (30th all time). Ten seasons Pie hit over .300, including a lofty .366 in 1930!

OF	Roger "M&M Boys" Maris

was a complete ballplayer. He was solid defensively with a very strong arm. Not a one season fluke, twice Roger was the AL MVP. He ranks 39th in career home run %. From 1958-64 Roger averaged 32+ homers. In 1961, his glory year, he hit 62 HR's (one was canceled by rain).

OF	Ty *Georgia Peach* Cobb

won 12 batting titles, twice hitting over .400! The Peach also led the AL in hits (eight), slugging % (eight), runs (five), triples (four), doubles (three) and homers (one). For his career, Ty ranks first in batting average and runs, second in hits and triples, fourth in doubles and fifth in RBI's.

OF	Charles *Chili* Davis

hails from Kingston, Jamaica. Chili has starred 13 full seasons (plus eight AB in 1981), 12 times swatting 20 or more doubles and 13 times hitting in double figures for tators. Chili has quietly accumulated 250+ career homers, driven in over 1000 runs and is still going strong!

P	Jim *Catfish* Hunter

was voted into Cooperstown. From 1971-75 he terrorized American League batters. Catfish won 21, 21, 21, 25 and 23 games, tossed 25 shutouts and completed 96 games in that half decade! Jim won both the Cy Young award and the ERA crown in his 25 win 1974 season!

P	*Colby* Jack Coombs

was college educated, rare for ballplayers in the early 1900's. He starred 14 seasons. 1910 was an outstanding season for Jack. He won a league leading 31 games, 13 by shutouts (third best ever) and had a 1.30 ERA! Colby Jack then won three games in the 1910 World Series!

P	Jim *Cakes* Palmer

was a three time Cy Young award winner. His 268 wins place Jim 29th all time. From 1975-77 Cakes led the American League three consecutive years in wins. In 1975 he earned 23 wins, compiled a microscopic 2.09 ERA and painted ten whitewashes, all league leading.

RES	John *The Candy Man* Candelaria

has Sammy Davis Jr. to thank, because 'the Candy Man can'. At 6'7", he was an intimidating portsider. During his 18 seasons, The Candy Man won nearly 60% of his decisions. He accumulated 177 wins. In 1977 John went 20-5 and posted a NL league leading 2.34 ERA.

RES	Spurgeon *Spud* Chandler

won an incredible 71.7% of his games throughout his career. This would have ranked him number one all time, if he had pitched only 15 more career innings! In 1943 Spud led the AL in wins (20,tie), winning % (.833), ERA (1.84) and shutouts (five, tie). He was voted MVP that year.

RES	Ray *Cracker* Schalk

is a member of the Hall of Fame. Ray logged over 1700 games guarding the dish. At 5'9", 165 pounds, Cracker was small, but fast. He ranks first all time in DP's and second in assists. Ray innovated the backstop position. He was the first catcher to back up first and third base.

RES	Candido *Candy* Maldonado

was born in Humacao, Puerto Rico. Candy has played for seven teams in 14 years. When playing full-time, he clouted 20 or more dingers three times. His ten pinch-hit tators rank him 23rd. Candy clubbed two HR's in the 1992 ALCS and also went yard in the 1992 World Series.

L to R: Ty *Georgia Peach* Cobb, Jim *Catfish* Hunter, Harold *Pie* Traynor, Roger *"M&M Boys"* Maris, Charles *Chili* Davis

It'sa FACT

Ty **Georgia Peach** Cobb: During his career Ty stole home 35 times, placing him first all time. September 2nd, 1907, July 2nd, 1909, July 12th, 1911, July 4th, 1912, June 18th, 1917 and August 1st, 1924 were dates the Georgia Peach stole second, then third and finally home! Honus, the Flying Dutchman Wagner is the only player to even do this three times! Cobb had fourteen five+ hit games, the most all time. During his career he had hitting streaks of 21, 21, 25, 35 and 40 games. In one game the Georgia Peach had three homers, one double and two singles to tie for the AL total base record.

John **Beans** Reardon: He was the last of the cussin' umpires. Beans seldom threw players out. He would rather argue. He made an exception one time with Lewis Hack Wilson. He called Hack out on strikes. Hack flung his bat high in the air. Beans countered, "Hack, if the bat comes down, you're out of the game!".

Howie **Spud** Krist: A relief specialist, he went 10-0, 13-3 and 11-5 during the 1941-43 seasons.

Harry **Cookie** Lavagetto: Traded to the Dodgers in 1937 after three seasons in the Steel City, he anchored the hot corner and was the NL All-Star third baseman four of the next five years. Service cost Cookie 4½ seasons. He ended his career (and Bill Bevens) hitting a ninth inning two out pinch double in game #4 of the 1947 World Series to win the game and break up Beven's no-hitter!

Johnny **Pepper** Martin: Pepper also was known by his football nickname, The Wild Hoss of the Osage. He was part of the 1934 Gas House Gang. Three times Pepper led the NL in swipes. Pepper's .418 average in three World Series is the highest all time.

Bob **Bubble Up** Allison: He worked for a beverage company in the off season (when baseball salaries were not enough to get by on). He was the AL Rookie of the Year in 1959. Bob was the first Minnesota Twin to hit a home run (Sister Delphine, my seventh grade teacher, brought in a TV and I saw the 1961 Twins' inaugural opener). Bob hit it off Whitey Ford. He also hit the first Twins' grand slam (April 16th, 1961) and was the first Twin to tag three homers in one game (May 17th, 1963). His spectacular sliding catch saved game #2 of the 1965 World Series.

Johnny **Bananas** Mostil: A speedster, he once, while playing center field in an exhibition game, caught a foul ball! Two times Bananas led the AL in steals and once in runs. On defense, he twice led all fly chasers in putouts.

Camilo **Little Potato** Pascual: His overhand curve was considered as good as any in baseball. A slow worker, he "landscaped" a lot on the hill. A five time All-Star, Camilo led the AL in K's in 1961, 1962 and 1963. The Little Potato also led the Junior Circuit three times in both complete games and shutouts.

Harry **Peanuts** Lowrey: Near the end of his career Peanuts led the NL twice in pinch-hits.

Oscar **Spinach** Melillo: He was a smooth fielder. During his six full seasons Spinach topped the AL at the keystone four times in assists and DP's, three times in putouts and twice in fielding %.

Charles **Pretzels** Getzien: He starred in the 19th Century. A workhorse, he started 40 or more times for five seasons (1886-90). During that stretch, Pretzels completed 203 of his 215 starts, winning 119 times!

Bill **Soup** Campbell: During his career he appeared in 700 games, 691 in relief. In 1976 Soup went 17-5, leading the league in both winning % and in games. In 1977 his 31 saves topped the AL.

Luke **Hot Potato** Hamlin: He toiled nine summers, never winning more than 12 games except once. In 1939 Hot Potato was just that, going 20-13 for the third place Dodgers.

Taft **Taffy** Wright: WW II curtailed Taffy from being better known. As a 27 year old rookie in 1938, he hit .350. He followed by hitting .309, .337, .322 and .333 (part of 1942), but then he gave 3½ years to his country. At 34, Taffy resumed for three+ seasons. His lifetime .311 average is better than many Hall of Famers.

Robert **Ham** Hyatt: A part-time player for seven seasons, Ham was the first star pinch hitter. He holds the all time pinch-hit triple mark for both season and career (tied). During the dead ball era, he parked three pinch-hit homers in one season, a then record. Ham was the first player to reach the 50 pinch-hit level.

Baker Bowl: The stadium was named after Phillies owner William Baker. It was their home field from April 1904 until June 1938. The Bowl was also called The Hump. It measured only 280 ft. down the right field line (60 ft. wall) and 300 ft. in right center (47 ft. wall). Hall of Fame left-handed hitting slugger Chuck Klein, in five full seasons, won four homer titles, two RBI Crowns and the NL's second last Triple Crown (1933), while hitting at the Band Box.

TRIVIA*

1) He is the only player to ever "pull" this off. He drove in at least one run in 13 consecutive games in 1941.

2) On September 24th, 1906 he pitched a 24 inning complete game, winning 1-0.

3) This 21 game winner (1965) was the lead singer in his own band "_____ and the Kittens." (his nickname)

4) Known also as "The Boy Wonder," he is credited with inventing the curve ball.

5) From July 18th, 1936 to May 30th, 1937 he won a record 24 consecutive games!

6) He was "really cookin" when named the NL Rookie of the Year in 1974.

7) Because he was so adept at bunting to foul off two strike pitches, the rule was changed.

8) This Hall of Famer quit at the young age of 33. He wanted to spend time with his family and go fishing.

9) Nicknamed after a song during his childhood, he later had five consecutive years leading third basemen in fielding %, tying the NL record.

10) In the 1931 World Series St. Louis scored only 19 times. He drove in five runs, scored five runs, stole five bases and batted .500!

11) He played two seasons for the Lakers in the NBA.

12) Teammates dubbed him "Old Biscuit Pants." (Hint: he was also called "Columbia Lou" and he is not on the roster)

13) In 1951 he walked Eddie "The Midget" Gaedel (3'7") on four straight pitches. (Hint: think Hawaii)

14) He was the first AL pitcher to win back to back Cy Young awards (outright, not shared).

15) After attending Colby College (in Maine), he went on to have a career World Series pitching record of an amazing 5-0!

16) Hailing from Narrows, Ga, he was the first player elected to the Hall of Fame.

17) He tossed the first no-hitter of the 20th century July 12th, 1900. (Hint: use your "brains")

18) Although born in Leaksville, Mississippi, this NL pitcher and later US Congressman was nicknamed from where he called home in Alabama.

19) Detroit Tiger manager Ty Cobb did not want him. He threw that "fadeaway pitch" (screwball) which would surely hurt his arm.

20) Fighting Brights disease (an often fatal kidney inflammation), he was put on a diet of this, which gave him his nickname.

21) On June 27th, 1980 he pitched a no-hitter, missing a perfect game due to an error.

22) He won World Series games in three decades. In 1969, at age 20, he became the youngest pitcher to hurl a World Series shutout.

23) His career batting average is third highest ever for his position. He had seven consecutive .300+ seasons.

24) In 1922 at the young age of 27, this St. Louis Cardinal tragically died of typhoid fever.

25) His sore arm was hidden from the press. In game #7 of the 1962 World Series, with two outs in the bottom of the ninth and trailing 1-0, Felipe Alou was held at third on a base hit, for fear of his strong gun. Alou could have scored. Willie Stretch McCovey then lined out to Bobby Richardson and the Giants lost.

* MYSTERY STEWS answers found on page 237

ROSTER

CATCHERS:	Yr	Hits	AB's	Ave
Jack *Peach Pie* O'Connor	21	1417	5380	.263
Ray *Cracker* Schalk	18	1345	5306	.253
Virgil *Spud* Davis	16	1312	4255	.308
John *Honey* Romano	10	706	2767	.255
Dan *Link* Sullivan	5	183	788	.232
William *Pickles* Dillhoefer	5	134	600	.223
Clarence *Yam* Yaryan	2	45	173	.260
Jim *Cracker* Hamby	2	10	55	.182
George *Prunes* Moolic	1	8	56	.143
Siggie *Chops* Broskie	1	6	22	.273
Philip *Peaches* O'Neill	1	4	15	.267
Frank *Noodles* Zupo	3	3	18	.167
John *Pork Chop* Hoffman	2	3	21	.143
Jake *Tomatoes* Kafora	2	3	24	.125

1ST BASEMEN:	Yr	Hits	AB's	Ave
George *Candy* LaChance	12	1377	4919	.280
George *Juice* Latham	4	317	1277	.248
Robert *Ham* Hyatt	7	247	925	.267

2ND BASEMEN:	Yr	Hits	AB's	Ave
Bobby *Link* Lowe	18	1929	7074	.273
Octavio *Cookie* Rojas	16	1660	6309	.263
Oscar *Spinach* Melillo	12	1316	5063	.260
Al *Cod* Myers	8	788	3222	.245
John *Chewing Gum* O'Brien	6	486	1910	.254
Walter *Chip* Hale	6	107	373	.287
Rawmeat Bill Rodgers	2	65	268	.243
Tommy *T-Bone* Giordano	1	7	40	.175
Tom *Chip* Coulter	1	6	19	.316
Al *A-1* Wright	1	1	1	1.000
Lyle *Punch* Judy	1	0	11	.000

SHORTSTOPS:	Yr	Hits	AB's	Ave
Norman *Tabasco Kid* Elberfeld	14	1235	4561	.271
Joe *Oats* DeMaestri	11	813	3441	.236
John *Candy* Nelson	9	624	2457	.254
Mark *Peanut* Wagner	9	205	843	.243
Marty *Pepper* Berghammer	4	180	774	.233
Homer *Ham* Allen	1	15	59	.254
Francis *Salty* Parker	1	7	25	.280
Joe *Bananas* Benes	1	2	12	.167

3RD BASEMEN:	Yr	Hits	AB's	Ave
Harold *Pie* Traynor	17	2416	7559	.320
Willie *Puddin' Head* Jones	15	1502	5826	.258
Jimmy *Pepper* Austin	18	1328	5388	.246
Jim *Peanut* Davenport	13	1142	4427	.258
Harry *Cookie* Lavagetto	10	945	3509	.269
Chris *Spud* Sabo	7	846	3145	.269
Ed *Eggie* Lennox	6	379	1383	.274
Johnny *Peaches* Werhas	3	29	168	.173

3RD BASEMEN: (Cont.)	Yr	Hits	AB's	Ave
Tom *Ham* Connolly	1	26	141	.184
Andy *Pepper* Oyler	1	17	77	.221
Joseph *Pepper* Peploski	1	2	4	.500

OUTFIELDERS:	Yr	Hits	AB's	Ave
Ty *Georgia Peach* Cobb	24	4189	11424	.366
Jesse *Crab* Burkett	16	2850	8421	.338
Mickey *M&M Boys* Mantle	18	2415	8102	.298
Charles *Chili* Davis	14	1799	6663	.270
Buttermilk Tommy Dowd	10	1492	5511	.271
Curt *Honey* Walker	12	1475	4858	.304
Kevin *Big Mac* McReynolds	12	1439	5423	.265
Roger *M&M Boys* Maris	12	1325	5101	.260
Bob *Bubble Up* Allison	13	1281	5032	.255
Johnny *Pepper* Martin	13	1227	4117	.298
Harry *Peanuts* Lowrey	13	1177	4317	.273
Arnold *Bake* McBride	11	1153	3853	.299
Taft *Taffy* Wright	9	1115	3583	.311
Johnny *Bananas* Mostil	10	1054	3507	.301
Candido *Candy* Maldonado	14	974	3824	.255
George *Catfish* Metkovich	10	934	3585	.261
Doc *Brownie* Gessler	8	831	2969	.280
Johnny *Crabapple Comet* Rucker	6	711	2617	.272
Paul *Peanuts* Lehner	7	455	1768	.257
John *Spud* Johnson	3	400	1324	.302
Wade *Lollypop* Killefer	7	381	1537	.248
Charles *Curry* Foley	5	373	1305	.286
Jimmy *Little Stew* Stewart	10	336	1420	.237
Al *Cheese* Schweitzer	4	208	874	.238
Josh *Pepper* Clarke	5	193	809	.239
Frank *Squash* Wilson	4	120	488	.246
Clarence *Soup* Campbell	2	96	390	.246
Manuel *Potato* Cueto	4	86	379	.227
Charles *Punch* Knoll	1	52	244	.213
George *Pickles* Gerken	2	29	129	.225
Roland *Cuke* Barrows	4	19	99	.192
Eddie *Pepper* Morgan	2	14	66	.212
Roy *Pepper* Clark	1	11	76	.145
Jesse *Chip* Altenburg	2	9	31	.290
Frank *Sugar* Kane	2	2	11	.182
Frank *Jelly* Jelinich	1	1	8	.125

PINCH HITTER:	Yr	Hits	AB's	Ave
Alonzo *Candy* Harris	1	0	1	.000

PITCHERS:	Yr	Won	Lost	ERA
Jim *Cakes* Palmer	19	268	152	2.86
Carl *Mealticket* Hubbell	16	253	154	2.98
Jim *Catfish* Hunter	15	224	166	3.26
Jerry *Rolls* Reuss	22	220	191	3.64
Larry *Hot Potato* Jackson	14	194	183	3.40
John *The Candy Man* Candelaria	18	177	119	3.29

ROSTER

PITCHERS: (Cont.)	Yr	Won	Lost	ERA
Guy *Mississippi Mudcat* Bush	17	176	136	3.86
Camilo *Little Potato* Pascual	18	174	170	3.63
Colby Jack Coombs	14	158	110	2.78
Charles *Pretzels* Getzien	9	145	139	3.46
Jim *Mudcat* Grant	14	145	119	3.63
Frank *Noodles* Hahn	8	130	94	2.55
Strawberry Bill Bernhard	9	116	82	3.04
Tom *Candy* Candiotti	11	110	110	3.46
Spurgeon *Spud* Chandler	11	109	43	2.84
Wilmer *Vinegar Bend* Mizell	9	90	88	3.85
Bill *Soup* Campbell	15	83	68	3.54
Luke *Hot Potato* Hamlin	9	73	76	3.77
Doughnut Bill Carrick	5	63	89	4.14
Merritt *Sugar* Cain	7	53	60	4.83
Herb *Gallatin Squash* Perdue	5	51	64	3.85
Bob *Bluecheese* Bruce	9	49	71	3.85
Vinegar Tom Vickery	4	42	42	3.75
Steve *Hambone* Hamilton	12	40	31	3.05
Howie *Spud* Krist	6	37	11	3.32
Bob *Sugar* Cain	5	37	44	4.50
George *Filbert* Pearce	6	36	27	3.11
Leo *Sugar* Sweetland	5	33	58	6.10
George *Krum* Kahler	5	32	43	3.17
Charles *Curry* Foley	5	27	27	3.54
Ray *Peaches* Davis	4	27	33	3.87
Starvin' Marvin Freeman	8	26	12	3.77
Jim *Bluegill* Hughes	4	25	30	4.30
Albert *Beany* Jacobson	4	23	46	3.19
William *Candy* Cummings	2	21	22	2.78
Chauncey *Peach* Fisher	5	21	26	5.37
Taylor *T-Bone* Phillips	6	16	22	4.82
Kevin *Hot Sauce* Saucier	5	15	11	3.31
Jim *Catfish* Crawford	5	15	28	4.40
Erv *Peanuts* Kantlehner	3	13	29	2.84

PITCHERS: (Cont.)	Yr	Won	Lost	ERA
Jesse *T-Bone* Winters	5	13	24	5.04
George *Pea Soup* Dumont	5	10	23	2.85
Subway Sam Nahem	4	10	8	4.69
Oyster Tom Burns	4	8	5	4.09
Abe *Sweetbreads* Bailey	3	4	7	4.59
Tabasco Tom Tuckey	2	3	12	3.49
Arthur *Cookie* Cuccurullo	3	3	5	4.55
Harry *Beans* Keener	1	3	11	5.88
John *Pretzel* Pezzullo	2	3	5	6.36
Vinegar Bill Essick	2	2	4	2.95
Tom *Sugar Boy* Dougherty	1	1	0	0.00
Robert *Chip* Lang	2	1	3	4.36
Jim *Grapefruit* Yeargin	2	1	12	4.91
Phil *Hoagie* Haugstad	4	1	1	5.59
Frank *Ribs* Raney	2	1	3	7.36
Alonzo *Candy* Harris	1	0	1	0.00
Andy *Peaches* Nelson	1	0	0	2.00
Ed *Peanuts* Pinnance	1	0	0	2.57
Frank *Chip* Bennett	2	0	1	2.70
Dan *Cocoa* Woodman	2	0	0	2.94
Ken *Soup* Polivka	1	0	0	3.00
Clarence *Candy Ben* Beville	1	0	2	4.00
George *Peaches* Graham	1	0	1	5.40
Robert *Bun* Troy	1	0	1	5.40
Ulises *Candy* Sierra	1	0	1	5.53
Bill *Beanie* Hall	1	0	0	5.79
Hank *Pepper* Griffin	2	0	6	5.80
Bill *T-Bone* Koski	1	0	1	6.67
Andy *Apples* Lapihuska	2	0	2	7.04
Frank *Stewy* Stewart	1	0	1	9.00

EXTRAS:
John *Beans* Reardon - Umpire
Baker Bowl - Ball Park

LINGO

Cup of Coffee: A very short stay in the Majors

Can of Corn: An easy fly ball to catch

In a Pickle: Caught in a "hotbox" or "rundown", or at the movies with another woman

A Rhubarb: A fierce argument or fight

At the Plate: When a player is up to bat

The Dish: Another name for home plate

Guarding the Dish: What my dog does when we give her food, or when a catcher blocks the plate

Fling the Pea: Throw a pitch hard

Feasted on a Pitcher: A player gets base hit after base hit off of a certain pitcher

Serve One Up: Give up a HR on an "easy pitch"

Table Setter: Player who gets on base for others to hit home

Bean Ball: A pitch that hits a batter in the head

Hot Dog: A player who flaunts himself to the opposing team

Grapefruit League: Spring training in Florida

Player Jammed: (Sounds kinky) pitcher forces a batter to hit the ball off the lower part of his bat

Pill, Onion, Apple, Pea: Other names for a baseball

Fork Ball: A pitch held between the middle and forefinger that, when thrown hard, drops sharply at the plate

Lollipop: An easy pitch to hit

Pepper: A game where one player hits a softly pitched ball back to a group of players

Tator: A home run

Batter: A person who is attempting to hit

HAIRY

16

Team

Hair or lack of it has frequently led to nicknames. If there is one thing a person notices about a ballplayer, it is his locks. Oscar Gamble had a huge Afro. He was always trying to "set" his batting helmet on his head. How about Dan Gladden's hair flapping below his helmet as he rounded second following his grand slam in game #1 of the 1987 World Series. I can still picture Al Newman rubbing Kirby Puckett's shaved skull for luck or Mariner fans getting a "Buhner cut" to get into a game free. Matt Williams proves balding is beautiful.

The Hairy Team has several "cuts" of players. There are players known as Butch, Heinie, Buzz and Punk. Add in hair colors such as Whitey, Cotton and Blondy, and hair styles such as Fuzzy, Curly and Pigtail. Some hair care accessories are The Barber, Scissors, Razor and The Blade. Combined, these players definitely form a hair raising group!

After combing through the roster, one Major Leaguer sticks out from the others. Richie Whitey Ashburn is a player who has been overlooked by the Hall of Fame. He played in an era when center field meant Willie Mays, Mickey Mantle and Duke Snider. Whitey lacked the visible home run power and he toiled in obscurity (only two of his 15 seasons did his teams finish higher than fourth). As a fielder Richie "got to everything". Nine seasons he had 400+ putouts (tie for the record) and four times he exceeded 500 putouts (record). Whitey ranks second all time in both chances per game and putouts per game. As a batter Richie was the perfect "table setter". For his career, Whitey led the NL in on base % (four), walks (four, with one tie), hits (three) and batting average (two). As a base runner Richie was "quick quick". He often used his speed to bunt. Twice Whitey led the NL in triples. Twelve summers he finished in double figures for steals. In 1948 he won the NL Rookie of the Year and the base stealing title. Whitey's outstanding career should be punctuated on the shores of Lake Otsego!

LINEUP

CA	Harold *Butch* Wynegar	was a starter at the young age of 20. For seven of his 12 seasons he anchored the Twins at catcher. Butch's smiling face was used by then Twins' owner Calvin Griffith to promote his Minnesota baseball team. His catchy slogan was "Love that kid Butch".

1B	Carroll *Whitey* Lockman	played 15 summers and later managed for three seasons. From 1948-53 Whitey, while playing with the New York Giants, averaged 170+ hits, 90+ runs and .290+ batting average. His 383 career strikeouts in 5940 at bats helped make Whitey a "tough out".

2B	Don *Butch* Kolloway	played 12 years in the Junior Circuit. His best season was 1942, prior to his entering the service. Butch topped the American League in doubles with 40. Primarily used as a keystone man, Cab (his more famous nickname) finished his career playing first base.

SS	Terry *Cotton Top* Turner	had a career spanning 17 seasons. During those years he also played third, second and outfield. Two summers Cotton Top led the American League in fielding % at short and two other seasons he led in fielding % at the hot corner. In 1912 Cotton Top hit .308, his career high.

3B	Henry *Heinie* Groh	shined for 16 years. His "bottle bat" pounded out 1774 hits. In 1917 Heinie led the Senior Circuit in both hits and doubles. The next year he topped the league in runs and two baggers and finished second in hits. Five times Heinie led all third basemen in fielding %.

OF	Richie *Whitey* Ashburn	was an excellent player for 15 years. He was a fleet footed fielder, a quick intelligent base runner and a selective .300+ hitter. A five time All-Star, Whitey led the National League in many categories during his outstanding career. Currently he is a baseball announcer.

OF	Henry *Heinie* Manush	sparkled for 17 summers. He retired with a .330 batting average (28th), 491 two baggers (tie 35th) and 160 three baggers (tie 39th). Heinie twice led the AL in hits and doubles (both tied) and once paced the league in triples and batting average. Heinie is now in the Hall.

OF	Duke *The Silver Fox* Snider	had an 18 year career before being voted into Cooperstown. Seven seasons he batted over .300. From 1949-57 The Silver Fox drove in 92, 107, 101, 92, 126, 130, 136, 101 and 92 runs! His 11 career World Series yard shots rank Duke fourth all time for the Fall Classic.

P	Ed *Whitey* Ford	went 14 consecutive years without having a losing season. Only twice did he lose ten or more games in one summer. Three campaigns Whitey led all twirlers in winning % and wins (one tie), and two times he finished first in innings, ERA and shutouts (one tie).

P	Burleigh *Ol' Stubblebeard* Grimes	pitched 19 campaigns on his way to the Hall of Fame. A workhorse, he led the National League three times in innings. Five summers Ol' Stubblebeard won 20+ games, twice (1921 and 1928) tying for the league lead. His 270 career victories place him 28th all time.

P	Rollie *The Mustache* Fingers	came in from the pen for 17 summers. Four times he won in double figures and The Mustache's 107 career relief wins are fourth best. Rollie led in appearances and saves three times each. He retired the Major League save leader (341), but now he ranks third all time.

RES	Dick *Baldy* Rudolph	hurled for 13 seasons in the Senior Circuit. His best season, 1914, Baldy went 26-10 and posted six shutouts. He then led the "Miracle Braves" to a four game sweep of the favored Philadelphia Athletics. Baldy won games #1 and #4, yielding only one earned run.

RES	Clell *Butch* Hobson	for six of his eight seasons anchored the hot corner for the Red Sox. Butch's best season was 1977. He poled 30 dingers and tied for fourth in the Junior Circuit in RBI's with 112! From 1992-94 Butch returned to Beantown and managed the Bosox.

RES	Ken *Butch* Keltner	starred 13 years at third base, his first 12 summers with the Tribe. As a rookie, in 1938, Butch blasted 26 homers and drove in 113 runs! He clubbed a career high 31 tators and had 119 ribbies in 1948. Butch led in DP's five times, assists four times and fielding % three times.

MGR	Dorrel *Whitey* Herzog	played sparingly over eight seasons for four teams. He then went on to manage for 18 summers. During his managing career Whitey has piloted teams to six division titles, three pennants and in 1982 he led the St. Louis Cardinals to the World Championship!

L to R: Ed *Whitey* Ford, Henry *Heinie* Manush, Richie *Whitey* Ashburn, Burleigh *Ol' Stubblebeard* Grimes, Duke *The Silver Fox* Snider

It'sa FACT

Ed **Whitey** Ford: He fanned 18 batters in a 15 inning game October 2nd, 1965.

George **Whitey** Rohe: He had 868 career at bats and hit three triples. In the 1906 World Series Whitey slashed two triples in just 21 at bats.

Charles **Whitey** Alperman: In his only "full season", he shared the NL lead in triples with 16 (1907).

Henry **Heinie** Groh: He participated in five Fall Classics. Heinie went 9/19 and led the Giants past the Yankees in the 1922 World Series.

Burgess **Whitey** Whitehead: In his 3316 career at bats Whitey struck out only 138 times!

Carroll **Whitey** Lockman: He hit a home run in his first at bat, July 17th, 1945. Whitey had consecutive game leadoff homers, July 17th, 1953 and July 18th, 1953.

Henry **Heinie** Peitz: On July 2nd, 1895 he slash two triples in one inning.

Burleigh **Ol' Stubblebeard** Grimes: Two separate seasons he did the rare feat of both winning 20 games and hitting over .300. In 1928 Ol' Stubblebeard went 25-14 and hit .321. Eight years earlier he posted a 23-11 record and batted .306.

Russell **Buzz** Arlett: 1931 was his only season. Buzz batted .313 and finished tied for fourth in the NL in home runs!

Albert **Buz** Phillips: Although he never won a game as a pitcher, Buz did bat 6/13 with a home run.

Frank **Bald Eagle** Isbell: In the 1906 World Series game #5 he swatted a record four doubles.

George **Whitey** Kurowski: He played nine summers for the Cardinals. Whitey was a five year starter (1943-47) and each season was named to the All-Star team. In 1945 he had 21 homers, 102 RBI's and batted .323. Two years later Whitey slugged 27 yard shots, plated 104 runs and hit .310. Twice he led all hot corner men in fielding %.

Burleigh **Ol' Stubblebeard** Grimes: When he wound up, he kept the ball in his glove and brought his glove in front of his mouth. Ol' Stubblebeard, who chewed slippery elm, was the Major League's last legal spitballer. He used the threat of the pitch to help win 190 games in the 1920's, the most wins for any hurler in that decade.

Rollie **The Mustache** Fingers: The Oakland A's won three consecutive World Championships (1972-74). He was their closer. During the seven, seven and five game Fall Classics, The Mustache appeared in six, six and four of the contests. In 1972 and 1973 Rollie saved two games in each Series. In 1974 he not only saved two games in the Series, but he also won one game!

Dick **Slick** Howser: As the Kansas City Royal's manager, he had his best seasons in 1984 (AL Western Division title) and 1985 (World Championship). Slick tragically died from a brain tumor in 1987.

Sal **The Barber** Maglie: In 1951 he had his best season. Sal shared the NL lead in wins with 23. The Barber was also the winning pitcher in the 1951 All-Star tilt.

Henry **Heinie** Zimmerman: He had a career year in 1912. Heinie led the NL in hits (207), doubles (41), home runs (14) and batting average (.372). There is a controversy on whether his RBI total won him the Triple Crown. Regardless, it was an awesome year! In 1916 and 1917 Heinie did for sure lead the NL in RBI's!

Al **Fuzzy** Smith: He hit double digits for homers ten consecutive seasons (1954-63). Fuzzy was a two time All-Star and in 1961 he poled 28 long balls and drove in 93 runs (his career highs).

Al **Cotton** Brazle: He played ten summers, all for the Cardinals. Nine of the ten campaigns Cotton had a winning record!

Earl **Whitey** Sheely: He starred eight+ seasons. Whitey twice led the league in fielding % for first basemen (1926 and 1929). He averaged 30+ doubles and 90+ RBI's those eight years! Whitey retired with a .300 batting average.

Tom **Whitey** Hurd: As a 30 year old rookie, he went 2-0. Whitey's eight relief wins the next season (1955) led the AL. After one more season and three more wins, Whitey never returned to the Majors.

Clydell **Slick** Castleman: His .714 winning % (15-6) was second best in the NL in 1935.

Jesse **The Silver Fox** Petty: He won 17 games in 1926 for the sixth place Brooklyn Robins. The Silver Fox's 2.84 ERA was third best and he led the league in holding opponents to a .240 batting average.

James **Cotton** Tierney: He played six summers (1920-25). In 1922 Cotton hit .345 (fifth in NL) and in 1923 he had 187 hits and batted .312.

Chris **Style** Short: He starred 14 of his 15 years for the Phillies. Style, a tall lefty, four times won 17 or more games. Two seasons he fanned over 200 batters. Chris retired with a 6.31 K/nine inning ratio, ranking him 54th all time.

TRIVIA*

1) In 1976 this relief pitcher shared the NL Rookie of the Year award.

2) This left-hander holds the World Series record in wins (ten), strikeouts (94) and consecutive scoreless innings (32).

3) His two run tie breaking home run in the top of the ninth clinched the 1942 World Championship for the Cardinals.

4) His 33 game hitting streak is the tenth longest streak (tie) in the American League. During his great career he also had 19, 22, 26, 27 and 28 game hitting streaks.

5) The 1974 season was his year. He posted a 16-8 record, tossed five shutouts and led the NL in ERA.

6) His manager (Casey Stengel) made sure he never pitched in Fenway Park.

7) This first baseman stood 6'6". It helped him play in both the NBA and ABA.

8) On May 21st and May 22nd, 1926 this slugging first sacker hit six consecutive doubles and then a home run (a record seven consecutive extra base hits).

9) His game #7 World Series home run in 1965 won the game. During that Classic he went 8/27. He pounded two doubles, slugged two homers and drove in four runs.

10) This future manager pilfered 37 bases in 1961 (second in the AL).

11) Five consecutive seasons (1953-57) he hit 40 or more home runs.

12) This hurler was on the short end of Don Larsen's perfect gem.

13) He is ranked first on the all time list for winning % for pitchers.

14) He is ranked second on the all time list for winning % for pitchers.

15) In 1952 and 1953 he led the NL in saves. (Hint: think South America)

16) In 1981 he became the first reliever to win both the MVP and the Cy Young in one season.

17) In 1928 he had 241 hits (which included 47 doubles, 20 triples and 13 homers), 108 RBI's and batted .378! In 638 at bats he fanned only 14 times!

18) This Dodger won the homer crown in 1956 and the RBI crown in 1955. (Hint: AKA Duke of Flatbush)

19) Two other nicknames he acquired were "Slick" and "Chairman Of The Board".

20) He was awarded eight Gold Gloves while playing shortstop for the Orioles.

21) In 1961 he won the Cy Young award with a remarkable 25-4 record.

22) He slammed four tape jobs in the 1952 World Series, later topped by Mr. October's five homers in the 1977 Classic.

23) He was the pitching hero of the 1931 World Series, winning game #3 and game #7.

24) During his career he led both the NL (1977 and 1978) and the AL (1981) in saves.

25) In the 1960 World Series he tossed shutouts in games #3 and #6.

* HAIR RAISERS answers found on page 237

ROSTER

CATCHERS:	Yr	Hits	AB's	Ave
Harold **Butch** Wynegar	13	1102	4330	.255
Walter **Butch** Henline	11	611	2101	.291
Grover **Slick** Hartley	14	353	1319	.268
Ralph **Wig** Weigel	3	54	235	.230
Herb **Butch** Bremer	3	41	193	.212
Oscar **Cotton** Siemer	2	29	119	.244
Henry *Heinie* Beckendorf	2	25	137	.182
Alfred **Butch** Benton	4	16	99	.162
Bald Billy Barnie	2	11	61	.180
Manuel **Curly** Onis	1	1	1	1.000
Charles **Butch** Sutcliffe	1	1	4	.250
Willis **Butch** Rementer	1	0	2	.000
Harold **Whitey** Ock	1	0	3	.000

1ST BASEMEN:	Yr	Hits	AB's	Ave
Carroll **Whitey** Lockman	15	1658	5940	.279
Earl **Whitey** Sheely	9	1340	4471	.300
Dave *Scissors* Foutz	13	1253	4533	.276
Frank **Bald Eagle** Isbell	10	1056	4219	.250
Dan **Whitey** Meyer	12	944	3734	.253
Charles **Butch** Schmidt	4	292	1075	.272
Hughie **Cotton** Miller	3	112	496	.226
Anthony **Razor** Shines	4	15	81	.185
Fred **Fuzzy** Richards	1	8	27	.296
Charles **Cotton** Nash	3	3	16	.188

2ND BASEMEN:	Yr	Hits	AB's	Ave
Don **Butch** Kolloway	12	1081	3993	.271
Burgess **Whitey** Whitehead	9	883	3316	.266
Henry *Heinie* Reitz	7	800	2741	.292
James **Cotton** Tierney	6	681	2299	.296
William **Baldy** Louden	6	507	1942	.261
Charles **Whitey** Alperman	4	387	1632	.237
Emmett *Heinie* Mueller	4	324	1281	.253
George *Heinie* Smith	6	268	1126	.238
Walter **Punk** Gautreau	4	207	806	.257
Henry *Heinie* Scheer	2	73	345	.212
Alfred **Whitey** Federoff	2	56	235	.238
Henry **Baldy** Jones	1	28	127	.220

SHORTSTOPS:	Yr	Hits	AB's	Ave
Terry **Cotton Top** Turner	17	1499	5921	.253
Mark **The Blade** Belanger	18	1316	5784	.228
Charles *Heinie* Wagner	12	834	3333	.250
John *Heinie* Sand	6	781	3033	.258
Dick **Slick** Howser	8	617	2483	.248
William **Whitey** Wietelmann	9	409	1762	.232
John **Blondy** Ryan	6	318	1330	.239
Henry *Heinie* Schuble	7	235	935	.251
Henry *Heinie* Kappel	3	106	394	.269

SHORTSTOPS: (Cont.)	Yr	Hits	AB's	Ave
Clyde **Buzzy** Wares	2	55	250	.220
Henry **Cotton** Knaupp	2	18	98	.184
Roy **Whitey** Ellam	2	14	98	.143
Hal **Blondie** Quick	1	10	41	.244
James **Buzz** Clarkson	1	5	25	.200
Henry *Heinie* Smoyer	1	3	14	.214
George **Curly** Bullard	1	0	1	.000

3RD BASEMEN:	Yr	Hits	AB's	Ave
Henry *Heinie* Groh	16	1774	6074	.292
Ken **Butch** Keltner	13	1570	5683	.276
Henry *Heinie* Zimmerman	13	1566	5304	.295
George **Whitey** Kurowski	9	925	3229	.286
Clell **Butch** Hobson	8	634	2556	.248
Emil *Heinie* Batch	4	315	1253	.251
Joseph *Goldie* Rapp	3	269	1064	.253
George **Whitey** Rohe	4	197	868	.227
William *Heinie* Heltzel	2	17	108	.157
Eddie *Baldy* Palmer	1	11	52	.212
Harland *Hypie* Rowe	1	5	36	.139
Herman *Heinie* Odom	1	1	1	1.000

OUTFIELDERS:	Yr	Hits	AB's	Ave
Richie **Whitey** Ashburn	15	2574	8365	.308
Henry *Heinie* Manush	17	2524	7654	.330
Duke **The Silver Fox** Snider	18	2116	7161	.295
Al **Fuzzy** Smith	12	1458	5357	.272
Jim **The Gray Fox** Northrup	12	1254	4692	.267
William **Blondie** Purcell	12	1217	4563	.267
Lawton **Whitey** Witt	10	1195	4171	.287
Jackie **Flaky** Brandt	11	1020	3895	.262
Clarence *Heinie* Mueller	11	597	2118	.282
Lou **Slick** Johnson	8	529	2049	.258
Dorrel **Whitey** Herzog	8	414	1614	.257
Ralph **Buzz** Boyle	5	389	1343	.290
Elmer **Butch** Nieman	3	269	1050	.256
Mizell **Whitey** Platt	5	256	1002	.255
Bob **Butch** Will	6	202	819	.247
Russell **Buzz** Arlett	1	131	418	.313
Wallace **Butch** Davis	8	110	453	.243
Arthur **Butch** Weis	4	92	341	.270
William *Heinie* Heitmuller	2	87	321	.271
Robert **Buzz** Murphy	2	78	284	.275
Mel **Butch** Simons	2	52	194	.268
Dwight **Curlie** Dorman	2	28	77	.364
Pigtail Billy Riley	1	24	165	.145
Walter *Heinie* Jantzen	1	22	119	.185
Ed **Baldy** Silch	1	13	48	.271
Ed **Butch** Mierkowicz	4	11	63	.175
Francis **Butch** Alberts	1	5	18	.278

ROSTER

OUTFIELDERS: (Cont.)	Yr	Hits	AB's	Ave
Albert *Fuzz* White	2	3	15	.200
Harry *Whitey* Wolfe	1	2	10	.200
Howie *Cotton* Jones	1	0	2	.000

PINCH HITTER:	Yr	Hits	AB's	Ave
Henry *Heinie* Stafford	1	0	1	.000

PITCHERS:	Yr	Won	Lost	ERA
Burleigh *Ol' Stubblebeard* Grimes	19	270	212	3.53
Ed *Whitey* Ford	16	236	106	2.75
Dave *Scissors* Foutz	11	147	66	2.84
Chris *Style* Short	15	135	132	3.43
Dick *Baldy* Rudolph	13	121	108	2.66
Sal *The Barber* Maglie	10	119	62	3.15
Rollie *The Mustache* Fingers	17	114	118	2.90
Al *Cotton* Brazle	10	97	64	3.31
Cotton Ed Smith	10	73	113	3.82
Jesse *The Silver Fox* Petty	7	67	78	3.68
Henry *Heinie* Meine	7	66	50	3.95
Tom *The Blade* Hall	10	52	33	3.27
Charles *Whitey* Glazner	5	41	48	4.21
Doug *Buzz* McWeeny	8	37	57	4.17
Clydell *Slick* Castleman	6	36	26	4.25
Benn *Baldy* Karr	6	35	48	4.60
Charles *Heinie* Berger	4	32	29	2.60
Lee *Buzz* Capra	7	31	37	3.87
Lloyd *Whitey* Moore	7	30	29	3.75
Hal *Whitey* Wiltse	4	20	40	4.87
Clarence *Butch* Metzger	5	18	9	3.74
Warren *Curly* Ogden	5	18	19	3.79
George *Slick* Coffman	4	15	12	5.60
Tom *Whitey* Hurd	3	13	10	3.96

PITCHERS: (Cont.)	Yr	Won	Lost	ERA
Bob *Butch* Heffner	5	11	21	4.51
Vern *Whitey* Wilshere	3	10	12	5.28
Kirtley *Whitey* Baker	5	9	38	6.28
Roy *Butch* Sanders	2	7	10	2.75
Ed *Whitey* Appleton	2	5	12	3.25
Henry *Cotton* Pippen	3	5	16	6.38
Charles *Curly* Brown	4	3	8	4.20
Claude *Butch* Edge	1	3	4	5.23
Walter *Whitey* Hilcher	4	3	6	5.29
Alex *Whitey* Konikowski	3	2	3	6.93
Jim *Whitey* Hayes	1	2	4	8.36
Louis *Buzz* Stephen	1	1	1	4.76
Ted *Whitey* Guese	1	1	4	6.09
Ken *Curly* Jungels	5	1	0	6.80
Ernie *Curly* Ross	1	1	1	7.41
Ralph *Razor* Ledbetter	1	0	0	0.00
Blaine *Baldy* Thomas	1	0	0	0.00
Ken *Whitey* Miller	1	0	1	0.00
Francis *Whitey* Wistert	1	0	1	1.13
Edmund *Cotton* Minahan	1	0	2	1.29
Charlie *Buzz* Eckert	3	0	3	4.52
William *Buzz* Dozier	2	0	0	6.55
Charles *Butch* Schmidt	1	0	0	7.20
Henry *Heinie* Peitz	3	0	1	7.31
Gene *Slick* Host	2	0	2	7.31
Charles *Buzz* Wetzel	1	0	0	7.71
Albert *Buz* Phillips	1	0	0	8.04
Henry *Heinie* Elder	1	0	0	8.10

EXTRAS:
Roy *Cotton* Van Graflan - Umpire
Royal *Butch* Smith - Great Realtor

LINGO

Hairy Play: Scary play

Sent to the Showers: The pitcher is removed from the game early

Brushing Him Back: Pitch thrown inside to force the batter "off the plate"

Flake: Goofy player

Barber: Pitcher who gives "close shaves"

Buzzed Him: Pitch thrown close to a batter's head

Dusts His Whiskers: Pitch thrown close to a batter's head

By a Whisker: Very close play

Chin Music: Pitch thrown close to a hitter's face

HISPANIC

17 Team

The Hispanic players have had a huge impact on the sport of baseball. The first players came from Colombia and Cuba. Since then, Mexico, Venezuela, Puerto Rico, Panama, Dominican Republic, Virgin Islands, Nicaragua, Honduras, the Netherlands Antilles and Belize have all been homes to Major League players. Presented with a language barrier, cultural shock and a new country, these men have done the near impossible and maintained their focus, honed their skills and risen to achieve enormous success! Just examine the Texas Rangers roster of the last few years. Jose Canseco, Raphael Palmeiro, Juan Gonzalez, Julio Franco, Ruben Sierra, Ivan Rodriguez and Jose Guzman are names that quickly come to mind. Many of baseball's top players for several years now have had their roots from south of our border.

The way to qualify for the Hispanic Team is quite logical. Any Major Leaguer whose first name was altered or was given a nickname, and he is of Hispanic heritage, qualifies. A large number of ballplayers are in this exciting group! Additional roster space was needed to better accommodate and celebrate the immense contribution these players have and are making to the game.

The Hispanic Team has many exceptional members, but one man on the roster was both the complete player and the complete person. Roberto Bob Clemente (AKA Arriba) is in the Hall of Fame in Cooperstown and in the hearts of all Puerto Ricans. He gave his all to baseball for 18 years in the Major Leagues and gave his life to help earthquake victims in Nicaragua. (Bob had collected desperately needed supplies to help the suffering people in Managua. The mercy plane he was aboard crashed just after take off from San Juan. The 38 year old Roberto, still an active player, perished when the plane went down, stunning both all Puerto Ricans where he was a living national hero, and rocking the entire baseball world where he was an acclaimed superstar). The required five year wait for Hall of Fame consideration was waived and Arriba was inducted immediately. Roberto was an outstanding right fielder. He was blessed with a cannon for an arm. Five times he led the league in assists. From 1961-72 Bob won an amazing 12 consecutive Gold Gloves! Roberto was also an outstanding hitter. During his career Bob hit over .300 in 13 seasons. He placed fifth in batting once, finished fourth and second twice each, ranked third once and won the Silver Bat four times! Only nine Major Leaguers have won more batting titles than Arriba! That exclusive group includes Ty Georgia Peach Cobb, Honus Flying Dutchman Wagner, Sir Rodney Carew, Rogers The Rajah Hornsby, Ted The Kid Williams, Stan The Man Musial, Big Dan Brouthers and current superstars Wade Boggs and Tony Gwynn. When Roberto's career tragically ended, his then lifetime numbers became career totals. Bob had reached 3000 hits and his 166 triples were the second most in the last 50 years. His legacy included the 1966 National League MVP and the 1971 World Series MVP. In 1966 Bob had his best offensive season, reaching career season highs in both homers and RBI's. His 12/29 effort, which included two doubles, one triple and two homers, carried the Bucs to the 1971 World Championship. Viva Clemente!

LINEUP

CA	Antonio *Tony* Pena

has been an All-Star five times. He is not only a solid hitter, but Tony also is exceptional defensively. A rocket arm and an unique low to the ground receiving style are Tony's trademarks. He topped all National League backstops in fielding % in both 1988 and 1989.

1B	Atanasio *Tony* Perez

played 23 seasons and was fantastic. Seven seasons he knocked in over 100 runs and for his career Tony's 1652 RBI's rank him 18th! He also crushed 505 doubles (29th) and 379 homers (tie 33rd). In 1970 Tony had his most productive year smashing 40 HR's and plating 129!

2B	Antonio *Tony* Taylor

starred for 19 years. During his career he pounded out over 2000 hits and scored over 1000 runs. In 1963 Tony not only led all NL second sackers in fielding %, but he also stroked 180 base hits and touched home 102 times. Tony used his speed to steal 20 or more bags seven years.

SS	Octavio *Tony* Fernandez

is having a great career. He ranks first all time in fielding % for shortstops! Combine his fabulous glove with his strong bat and you have an exceptional player! With a few more seasons to add to his totals, Tony will surely rank very high among shortstops in career hits.

3B	Aurelio *Leo* Rodriguez

hails from Cananea, Mexico. He reached the Majors at just age 19 and went on to star for 17 summers in the Junior Circuit. His third base play allowed him to twice lead the American League in fielding %. Leo hit for double digits in round trippers five times during his career.

OF	Roberto *Bob* Clemente

starred for 18 years in the National League. A notorious bad ball hitter, he was hard to waste a pitch on! Bob was a line drive hitter who used all fields. His blazing speed helped him leg out ten or more triples nine times during his fabulous Hall of Fame career.

OF	Jose *Cheo* Cruz

has left an outstanding record. For 19 campaigns he laced 'em up. In 1983 Cheo banged out 189 hits to tie for the league lead. Eleven times Jose slashed 20+ doubles and seven seasons he hit over .300. He used his speed to swipe 20+ bases eight summers.

OF	Mateo *Matty* Alou

hails from Haina, D.R.. For 15 summers he chased fly balls in the NL. Matty batted over .300 eight seasons. From 1966-69 he never hit less than .331, winning one batting title and finishing fourth, third and second the other three years. Matty's 231 hits paced the NL in 1969.

P	Juan *Manito* Marichal

was inducted into the Hall in 1983. From 1963-69 he won over 20 games six seasons, twice (one tie) leading the NL in wins. Manito had ten shutouts in 1965 and won the ERA crown in 1969. The Dominican Dandy's control was near perfect, walking only 1.82 batters per game.

P	Luis *El Tiante* Tiant

twirled for 19 years in the Majors. Four summers he won at least 20 games and three years (one tie) he paced the AL in shutouts, finishing with 49 for his career (tie 21st). El Tiante's 2416 strikeouts are 24th all time. With Boston from 1973-76 El Tiante won 20, 22, 18 and 21 games.

P	Jose *Dennis* Martinez

is like a fine wine, he seems to get better with age. For 19 years (through 1994) he has been baffling batters. 1991 was his best season. Dennis topped the National League in shutouts, share the lead in complete games and won the ERA crown. Not bad for a 36 year old!

RES	Miguel *Mike* Cuellar

hurled for 15 campaigns. His career started slowly, posting only 42 victories his first six seasons. Traded to the Orioles in 1969, the next six years Mike won 125 games, including four "20 game" seasons. His 24 victories in 1970 shared the lead in the American League.

RES	Dolf *Pride of Havana* Luque

was a 20 year veteran who pitched into his 44th year. At 5'7", 160 pounds, he was not dominating in size, but in 1923 he towered over the National League. Dolf won 27 times (first), put up six shutouts (first) and won his first of two ERA crowns in his exceptional career.

RES	Ricardo *Rico* Carty

for eight of his 15 seasons, batted over .300. In 1964, as a NL rookie, he finished second in batting. Rico placed third in hitting in 1966. He won the Silver Bat in 1970 (.366) and also swatted 25 homers and drove in 101 runs! At 39, DHing, Rico poled 31 dingers and had 99 ribbies!

RES	Leonardo *Chico* Cardenas

sparkled at shortstop for 16 seasons in the Major Leagues. Leo was a five time All-Star and three seasons led the league in fielding %. Chico's best year was 1966. The Matanzas Cuba native reached the cheap seats for the Reds 20 times and drove in 81 runs.

L to R: Atanasio *Tony* Perez, Jose *Cheo* Cruz, Juan *Manito* Marichal, Luis *El Tiante* Tiant, Saturnino *Minnie* Minoso

It'sa FACT

Luis *Little Looie* Aparicio: In 1956 he was voted the AL Rookie of the Year.

Facundo *Cuno* Barragan: He launched a home run September 1st, 1961 in his first at bat. Dagoberto Bert Campaneris, on July 23rd, 1964, also launched one in his first at bat, but Campy did his on the first pitch!

Cesar *Coca* Gutierrez: His career lasted four seasons. During the Venezuelan's first, second and fourth years, Coca had three, seventeen and seven hits. On June 21st, 1970 he went 7/7, one of only five players to have seven hits in one game!

Renalso *Rennie* Stennett: On September 16th, 1975 this Panamanian copied Coca and went 7/7.

Manuel *Jungle Jim* Rivera: In his first seven seasons (1952-58) he played regularly. Jungle Jim ranked second, second, second, first, second, second and second in the AL in stolen bases!

Cesar *Pepito* Tovar: He had his best season in 1970. Pepito hit .300 and led the Junior Circuit in doubles (tie) and triples, plus finished second in runs and third in hits. In 1971 Cesar led the AL in hits, tied for second in runs and finished fourth in batting.

Pedro *Tony* Oliva: Poured from the same mold as Roberto Clemente, "Tony O" could flat out hit. In his totally dominating rookie year (1964), the Cuban led the AL in runs, hits, total bases, doubles and batting average! No one warned Tony about sophomore jinx, so he ignored it and finished third in total bases, doubles and RBI's, second in runs and first again in hits and batting average! Tony played regularly only 11 seasons (three as a limping DH) due to devastating knee injuries, but during that span he led the AL a total of five times in hits, four times in doubles (one tie) and captured three Silver Bats! In the field you never took liberties with his gun. His outfield play earned him a Gold Glove in 1966. There is a space in Cooperstown, let's vote in Tony!

Rogelio *Roger* Moret: A sometimes starter, sometimes reliever, he went 13-2 in 1973 and 14-3 in 1975. In the 1975 post season Roger won game #2 of the ALCS and made three appearances in the World Series, not allowing a run.

Felix *Tippy* Martinez: In 1979 he went 10-3 in 39 relief appearances. Tippy did not allow a home run all season!

Isidro *Sid* Monge: He hailed from Agua Preita Mexico and starred ten seasons, primarily as a reliever. In 1979 Sid won 12 games as a fireman and finished second in games and fifth in saves.

Oswaldo *Ozzie* Guillen: A starter since the age of 21 (except for a serious knee injury in 1992), this Venezuelan has held the White Sox shortstop position since 1985!

Alfonso *Chico* Carrasquel: He was an excellent fielding shortstop. Three times Chico led AL shortstops in fielding % and in one stretch he handled 297 chances without a miscue.

Osvaldo *Ozzie* Virgil Sr.: He was the first player from the Dominican Republic to reach the Majors (1956). Since then many players have followed, including his son Ozzie Jr.! A two time All-Star catcher, Ozzie Jr. pounded 18, 19, 15 and 27 homers from 1984-87.

Reyenaldo *Chito* Martinez: He was the first player from Belize to play in the Big Leagues.

Francis *Xavier* Hernandez: In 1992 he went 9-1 in 77 games and averaged nearly a whiff per inning.

Jorge *George* Bell: In 1987 he won the AL MVP. That year George led the league in RBI's with 134 and finished second in homers, smashing 47! From 1984-92 the Dominican Republic native averaged 27 tators and 101 ribbies!

Hensley *Bam-Bam* Meulens: He is the first player from the Netherlands Antilles (Curaco) to make the Big Show.

Jesus *Bombo* Rivera: In the Twin Cities he was a local hero. A song, "The Ballad of Bombo," was recorded about him. Bombo later starred two campaigns in Japan and stroked 37 homers.

Danilo *Danny* Tartabull: For the last nine seasons (1986-94) he has averaged nearly 25 homers per year. Four summers Danny has driven in over 100 runs. By contrast his dad, a nine year Major Leaguer, hit only two round trippers during his career.

Baldomero *Mel* Almada: In 1933 he was the first ballplayer from Mexico to play in the Major Leagues.

Roberto *Bobby* Bonilla: From 1987-94 he has averaged 31 doubles, 23 homers and 88 RBI's while playing for the Bucs and now the Mets.

Rafael *Mike* Almeida: He and a fellow Cuban (Armando Marsans) both debuted for Cincinnati July 4th, 1911. They were the Majors' first Cubans.

Manuel *Manny* Sanguillen: During his career he hit over .300 four seasons. In both 1970 and 1975 the Panamanian finished third in the NL in batting average.

Luis *Jud* Castro: He was the first ballplayer from Columbia to reach the Major Leagues.

Jesus *Manny* Trillo: His birth date was December 25, 1954. Manny was a four time All-Star with a great glove. He led all NL second sackers four times in assists, two times in putouts and once in both DP's and fielding %.

Alejandro *Alex* Carrasquel: He was the first Major Leaguer to come from Venezuela.

Juan *Senior Smoke* Berenguer: Born in Aguadulce, Panama, he was the unsung hero during the Minnesota Twins' 1987 World Championship year. A middle reliever, Senior Smoke averaged nearly one K per inning, while logging an 8-1 record. From 1988-90 he finished 8-4, 9-3 and 8-5. Demonstrative, Juan's clenched fist arm pump, after he whiffed an opponent, was a rousing fan pleaser.

Melquiades *Mel* Rojas: In 1992 his record was 7-1 with ten saves and a microscopic 1.43 ERA. He was just pleasing his uncle, manager Felipe Alou.

TRIVIA*

1) He was the 1990 AL Rookie of the Year. (Hint: his brother finished fifth in the 1988 NL Rookie of the Year voting)

2) 1984 was this Puerto Rican's year. He not only won the AL MVP, but he also won the Cy Young award! That season he led the league in appearances and finished third in saves.

3) His 1977 season was so fantastic (he batted .388 and won the AL MVP), team owner Calvin Griffith rewarded this Panamanian with a $100,000 bonus!

4) He was an AL All-Star at age 20. (Hint: he holds the Texas Ranger's consecutive hit record with eight safeties)

5) On July 28th, 1991 he hurled baseball's 13th perfect game.

6) He won 11 Gold Gloves during his career. (Hint: he played first base)

7) These three brothers from Puerto Rico all played in the NL. In 1973 they all played for the Cardinals.

8) In 1976 he was the first player from Nicaragua to make the Big Leagues; amazingly, he is still playing!

9) During his first nine seasons (1956-64) he led the AL in stolen bases each year. Three summers this Venezuelan speedster out swiped the second place finisher over two to one! He also led all AL shortstops in fielding % for eight consecutive years (1959-66)!

10) From 1980-84 he averaged 32+ homers and 100+ RBI's. This Venezuelan slugger won two homer crowns (shared) and one RBI title!

11) He finished second for the AL Rookie of the Year in 1951. When the Gold Glove award was introduced in 1957, he won three times in the first four years! At age 57 this extraordinary Cuban "laced 'em up" again, playing one more game for the White Sox!

12) In 1980 this Panamanian slugger led (tied with Mr. October) the AL with 41 round trippers and tied for second with 118 RBI's.

13) These three brothers from the Dominican Republic played on the same team, the San Francisco Giants, in 1963! (Hint: two are on the roster)

14) He was a fantastic outfielder. Three times he led the NL in fielding %. (Hint: this Cuban also was called Little Dynamite, because of the pop in his bat)

15) While a member of the 1968 Twins, this versatile Venezuelan played each position one inning and led them to victory! He is also credited with breaking up a record five no-hitters (ninth inning hits) during his career.

16) This heroic Puerto Rican was the second baseball player to be pictured on a stamp (the first was Jackie Robinson). He was also the first Hispanic player elected to the Hall of Fame.

17) He is less famous than his Major League twin brother, "The 40/40 Man."

18) For his career he is first in pinch-hits. The Dominican Republic native collected 150 hits in 505 at bats (.297).

19) In 1961 he appeared in 65 games for the Bronx Bombers. In those contests this Puerto Rican chalked up a league leading 29 saves and 15 relief wins!

20) In 1961, with the Giants, he led the NL in home runs and RBI's. With the Cardinals in 1967 he again not only won the NL RBI title, but this native of Ponce, Puerto Rico also was voted the MVP! (Hint: he was also known as the Baby Bull)

21) This Cuban was the first Hispanic player to win the MVP (AL 1965).

22) These two first sackers each crushed 379 long balls to tie for 33rd all time on the homer list.

23) In 1966 he led the NL in batting, edging his older brother Felipe.

24) He won seven Silver Bats, only Wagner and Cobb won more batting titles in their careers!

25) On July 19th, 1960, his first Big League start, this high kicking right-hander posted a one hitter, a pinch single by Clay Dalrymple. (Hint: his nickname means monkey)

* MUCHO TOUGHOS answers found on page 237

ROSTER

CATCHERS:	Yr	Hits	AB's	Ave
Antonio *Tony* Pena (D)	15	1569	5966	.263
Alfonso *Al* Lopez (A)	19	1547	5916	.261
Manuel *Manny* Sanguillen (P)	13	1500	5062	.296
Baudilio *Bo* Diaz (V)	13	834	3274	.255
Miguel *Mike* Gonzalez (C)	17	717	2829	.253
Jose *Joe* Azcue (C)	11	712	2828	.252
Paulino *Paul* Casanova (C)	10	627	2786	.225
John *Buck* Martinez (A)	17	618	2743	.225
Osvaldo *Ozzie* Virgil Jr.. (P)	11	549	2258	.243
Eliseo *Ellie* Rodriguez (P)	9	533	2173	.245
Adalberto *Junior* Ortiz (P)	13	484	1894	.256
Ivan *Pudge* Rodriguez (P)	4	420	1536	.273
Santos *Sandy* Alomar Jr.. (P)	7	390	1455	.268
Fermin *Mike* Guerra (C)	9	382	1581	.242
Javier *Javy* Lopez (P)	3	80	309	.259
Salvador *Chico* Hernandez (C)	2	61	244	.250
Rafael *Ray* Noble (C)	3	53	243	.218
Raul *Tony* Eusebio (D)	2	49	178	.275
Roberto *Bobby* Ramos (C)	6	44	232	.190
Facundo *Cuno* Barragan (A)	3	33	163	.202
Alberto *Al* Pardo (SP)	4	17	129	.132
Frederico *Freddie* Velazquez (D)	2	10	39	.256
Enrique *Hank* Izquierdo (C)	1	7	26	.269
Jesus *Chucho* Ramos (V)	1	5	10	.500
Manuel *Curly* Onis (A)	1	1	1	1.000
Francisco *Frank* Estrada (M)	1	1	2	.500
Rafael *Toby* Hernandez (V)	1	1	2	.500

1ST BASEMEN:	Yr	Hits	AB's	Ave
Rodney *Rod* Carew (CZ)	19	3053	9315	.328
Atanasio *Tony* Perez (C)	23	2732	9778	.279
Orlando *Cha Cha* Cepeda (P)	17	2351	7927	.297
Keith *Mex* Hernandez (A)	17	2182	7370	.296
Guillermo *Willie* Montanez (P)	14	1604	5843	.275
Constantino *Tino* Martinez (A)	5	350	1377	.254
Juan *Pancho* Herrera (C)	3	264	975	.271
Ramon *Ray* Webster (PA)	5	190	778	.244
Oswaldo *Ossie* Blanco (V)	2	20	102	.196
Hediberto *Eddie* Vargas (P)	2	10	39	.256
Regino *Reggie* Otero (C)	1	9	23	.391

2ND BASEMEN:	Yr	Hits	AB's	Ave
Antonio *Tony* Taylor (C)	19	2007	7680	.261
Octavio *Cookie* Rojas (C)	16	1660	6309	.263
Jorge *George* Orta (M)	16	1619	5829	.278
Jesus *Manny* Trillo (V)	17	1562	5950	.263
Rigoberto *Tito* Fuentes (C)	13	1491	5566	.268
Manuel *Julian* Javier (D)	13	1469	5722	.257
Roberto *Bobby/Beto* Avila (M)	11	1296	4620	.281
Renalso *Rennie* Stennett (PA)	11	1239	4521	.274
Roberto *Robbie* Alomar (P)	7	1174	3943	.298
Antonio *Tony* Bernazard (P)	10	970	3700	.262
Jose *Chico* Lind (P)	8	902	3537	.256
Manuel *Manny* Lee (D)	10	685	2692	.254

2ND BASEMEN: (Cont.)	Yr	Hits	AB's	Ave
Jose *Joey* Cora (P)	7	416	1601	.260
Ruthford *Chico* Salmon (PA)	9	415	1667	.249
Hiraldo *Chico* Ruiz (C)	8	276	1150	.240
Jose *Fernando* Gonzalez (P)	6	244	1038	.235
Jose *Chile* Gomez (M)	3	142	627	.226
Milciades *Junior* Noboa (D)	8	118	493	.239
Tomas *Gus* Gil (V)	4	87	468	.186
Ramon *Mike* Herrera (C)	2	76	276	.275
Angel *Luis* Alcaraz (P)	4	70	365	.192
Osvaldo *Ossie* Chavarria (PA)	2	52	250	.208
Angel *Remy* Hermoso (V)	4	47	223	.211
Luis *Jud* Castro (CO)	1	35	143	.245
Jose *El Hombre Goma* Rodriguez (C)	3	24	145	.166
Alejandro *Alex* Taveras (D)	3	11	53	.208
Vinicio *Chico* Garcia (M)	1	7	62	.113

SHORTSTOPS:	Yr	Hits	AB's	Ave
Luis *Little Looie* Aparicio (V)	18	2677	10230	.262
Dagoberto *Bert* Campaneris (C)	19	2249	8684	.259
Leonardo *Chico* Cardenas (C)	16	1725	6707	.257
Octavio *Tony* Fernandez (D)	13	1714	6024	.285
Oswaldo *Ozzie* Guillen (V)	10	1254	4563	.269
Zoilo *Zorro* Versalles (C)	12	1246	5141	.242
Alfonso *Chico* Carrasquel (V)	10	1199	4644	.258
Humberto *Chico* Fernandez (C)	8	666	2778	.240
Edgardo *Ed* Romero (P)	12	473	1912	.247
Roberto *Baby* Pena (D)	6	467	1907	.245
Eduardo *Eddie* Leon (A)	8	440	1862	.236
Guillermo *Willie* Miranda (C)	9	423	1914	.221
Teodoro *Ted* Martinez (D)	9	355	1480	.240
Alfonso *Kiko* Garcia (A)	10	351	1470	.239
Jesus *Pepe* Frias (D)	9	323	1346	.240
Don *Gil* Torres (C)	4	320	1271	.252
Jacinto *Jackie* Hernandez (C)	9	308	1480	.208
Wilfredo *Wil* Cordero (P)	3	278	1016	.274
Luis *Pimba* Alvarado (P)	9	248	1160	.214
Orlando *Marty* Martinez (C)	7	230	945	.243
Joaquin *Jackie* Gutierrez (CO)	6	227	957	.237
Argenis *Angel* Salazar (V)	5	188	886	.212
Alfredo *Freddie* Benavides (A)	4	135	534	.253
Vincio *Vinny* Castilla (M)	4	134	488	.275
Jose *Flaco* Arcia (C)	3	132	615	.215
Cesar *Coca* Gutierrez (V)	4	128	545	.235
Alejandro *Alex* Arias (A)	3	123	461	.267
Alfredo *Al* Pedrique (V)	3	111	449	.247
Gustavo *Gus* Polidor (V)	7	90	434	.207
Alfonso *Houston* Jimenez (M)	4	76	411	.185
Oswaldo *Ossie* Alvarez (C)	2	42	198	.212
Adalberto *Bert* Pena (P)	6	31	153	.203
Gabriel *Tony* Martinez (C)	4	30	175	.171
Antonio *Tony* Perezchica (M)	4	23	101	.228
Pompeyo *Yo-Yo* Davalillo (V)	1	17	58	.293
Cristobal *Chris* Colon (V)	1	6	36	.167
Rodolfo *Rudy* Hernandez (M)	1	4	21	.190

ROSTER

SHORTSTOPS: (Cont.)	Yr	Hits	AB's	Ave
Antonio **Mosquito** Ordenana (C)	1	2	4	.500
Eusebio **Papo** Gonzalez (C)	1	2	5	.400
Lorenzo **Chico** Fernandez (C)	1	2	18	.111
Francisco **Frankie** Libran (P)	1	1	10	.100
Alfredo **Al** Cabrera (CI)	1	0	2	.000

3RD BASEMEN:	Yr	Hits	AB's	Ave
Aurelio **Leo** Rodriguez (M)	17	1570	6611	.237
Leonardo **Leo** Gomez (P)	5	350	1427	.245
Froilan **Nanny** Fernandez (A)	4	336	1356	.248
Jose **Coco** Laboy (P)	5	291	1247	.233
Miguel **Mike** de la Hoz (C)	9	280	1114	.251
Napoleon **Nap** Reyes (C)	4	264	931	.284
Jacinto **Damion** Easley (A)	3	179	697	.257
Esteban **Manny** Castillo (D)	3	174	719	.242
Osvaldo **Ozzie** Virgil Sr.. (D)	9	174	753	.231
Ricardo **Rick** Joseph (D)	5	154	633	.243
Rafael **Mike** Almeida (C)	3	77	285	.270
Emanuel **Sonny** Senerchia (A)	1	22	100	.220
Manuel **Chico** Ruiz (P)	2	21	72	.292
Angel **Pete** Aragon Sr.. (C)	3	9	76	.118
Fermin **Alexis** Infante (V)	4	6	55	.109
Benny **Papelero** Valenzuela (M)	1	3	14	.214
Cristobal **Minnie** Mendoza (C)	1	3	16	.188

OUTFIELDERS:	Yr	Hits	AB's	Ave
Roberto **Bob** Clemente (P)	18	3000	9454	.317
Jose **Cheo** Cruz (P)	19	2251	7917	.284
Saturnino **Minnie** Minoso (C)	17	1963	6579	.298
Pedro **Tony** Oliva (C)	15	1917	6301	.304
Mateo **Matty** Alou (D)	15	1777	5789	.307
Jorge **George** Bell (D)	12	1702	6123	.278
Ricardo **Rico** Carty (D)	15	1677	5606	.299
Benjamin **Ben** Oglivie (PA)	16	1615	5913	.273
Cesar **Pepito** Tovar (V)	12	1546	5569	.278
Andres **Tony** Gonzalez (C)	12	1485	5195	.286
Antonio **Tony** Armas (V)	14	1302	5164	.252
Roberto **Bobby** Bonilla (A)	10	1290	4637	.278
Jesus **Jay** Alou (D)	15	1216	4345	.280
Danilo **Danny** Tartabull (P)	11	1180	4252	.278
Julio **Jerry** Morales (P)	15	1173	4528	.259
Manuel **Manny** Mota (D)	20	1149	3779	.304
Candido **Candy** Maldonado (P)	14	992	3916	.253
Manuel **Jungle Jim** Rivera (A)	10	911	3552	.256
Baldomero **Mel** Almada (M)	7	706	2483	.284
Domingo **Felix** Jose (D)	7	686	2431	.282
Roberto **Bobby** Estalella (C)	9	620	2196	.282
Otoniel **Otto** Velez (P)	11	452	1802	.251
Monte **Carmen** Castillo (D)	10	383	1519	.252
Hector **Heity** Cruz (P)	9	361	1607	.225
Pedro **Petey** Munoz (P)	5	323	1211	.267
Cleotha **Chico** Walker (A)	11	299	1217	.246
Rosendo **Rusty** Torres (P)	9	279	1314	.212
Manuel **Manny** Jimenez (D)	7	273	1003	.272

OUTFIELDERS: (Cont.)	Yr	Hits	AB's	Ave
Jose **Pepe** Mangual (P)	6	235	972	.242
Jesus **Bombo** Rivera (P)	6	220	831	.265
Benigno **Benny** Ayala (P)	10	217	865	.251
Hilario **Sandy** Valdespino (C)	7	176	765	.230
Gilberto **Gil** Flores (P)	3	121	464	.261
Reyenaldo **Chito** Martinez (B)	3	111	429	.259
Balmodero **Merito** Acosta (C)	5	111	436	.255
Hensley **Bam-Bam** Meulens (N)	5	101	457	.221
Manuel **Potato** Cueto (C)	4	86	379	.227
Jose **Loco** Herrera (V)	4	61	231	.264
Silvestre **Sil** Campusano (D)	3	53	262	.202
Angel **Jimmy** Rosario (P)	3	50	231	.216
Francisco **Frank** Campos (C)	3	41	147	.279
Luis **Canena** Marquez (P)	2	26	143	.182
Felipe **Monty** Montemayor (M)	2	26	150	.173
Jose **Papito** Vidal (D)	4	24	146	.164
Osvaldo **Ozzie** Canseco (C)	3	13	65	.200
Saturnino **Nino** Escalera (P)	1	11	69	.159
Carlos **Bobby** Trevino (M)	1	9	40	.225
Jacinto **Jack** Calvo (C)	2	9	56	.161
Jesus **Orlando** Alvarez (P)	4	8	51	.157
Arturo **Art** Lopez (P)	1	7	49	.143
Ignacio **Al** Javier (D)	1	5	24	.208
Angelo **Junior** Dagres (A)	1	4	15	.267
Rodolfo **Hector** Martinez (C)	2	4	15	.267
Luis **Puchy** Delgado (P)	1	4	22	.182
Tomas **Tom** Silverio (D)	3	3	30	.100
Felix **Elvio** Jimenez (D)	1	2	6	.333
Cirilo **Tommy** Cruz P)	2	0	2	.000

PINCH HITTERS:	Yr	Hits	AB's	Ave
Angel **Jack** Aragon (C)	1	0	0	.000
Rogelio **Roy** Valdez (C)	1	0	1	.000

PITCHERS:	Yr	Won	Lost	ERA
Juan **Manito** Marichal (D)	16	243	142	2.89
Luis **El Tiante** Tiant (C)	19	229	172	.330
Jose **Dennis** Martinez (NI)	19	219	171	3.63
Dolf **Pride of Havana** Luque (C)	20	194	179	3.24
Miguel **Mike** Cuellar (C)	15	185	130	3.14
Camilo **Little Potato** Pascual (C)	18	174	170	3.63
Edward Miguel **Mike** Garcia (A)	14	142	97	3.27
Pedro **Pete** Ramos (C)	15	117	160	4.08
Charles **Sid** Fernandez (A)	12	104	85	3.29
Teodoro **Teddy** Higuera (M)	9	94	64	3.61
Diego **Pablo** Segui (C)	15	92	111	3.81
Eduardo **Ed** Figueroa (P)	8	80	67	3.51
Guillermo **Willie** Hernandez (P)	13	70	63	3.38
Juan **Senior Smoke** Berenguer (PA)	15	67	62	3.90
Jose **Mike** Fornieles (C)	12	63	64	3.96
Aurelio **Senior Smoke** Lopez (M)	11	62	36	3.56
Felix **Tippy** Martinez (A)	14	55	42	3.45
Sandalio **Sandy** Consuegra (C)	8	51	32	3.37
Alejandro **Alex** Carrasquel (V)	8	50	39	3.73

ROSTER

PITCHERS: (Cont.)	Yr	Won	Lost	ERA
Isidro *Sid* Monge (M)	10	49	40	3.53
Rogelio *Roger* Moret (P)	9	47	27	3.66
Filomeno *Phil/Kemo* Ortega (A)	10	46	62	4.43
Arnulfo *Nino* Espinosa (D)	8	44	55	4.17
Luis *Yo-Yo* Arroyo (P)	8	40	32	3.93
Conrado *Connie* Marrero (C)	5	39	40	3.67
Ricardo *Ricky* Bones (P)	4	34	36	4.37
Manuel *Manny/Gyp* Salvo (A)	5	33	50	3.69
Vincente *Huevo* Romo (M)	8	32	33	3.36
Manuel *Manny* Sarmiento (V)	7	26	22	3.49
Minervino *Minnie* Rojas (C)	3	23	16	3.00
Bienvenido *Ben* Rivera (D)	3	23	17	4.52
Francis *Xavier* Hernandez (A)	6	22	16	3.57
Melquiades *Mel* Rojas (D)	5	21	15	2.79
Luis *Witto* Aloma (C)	4	18	3	3.44
Ramon *Ray* Monzant (V)	6	16	21	4.38
Edwin *Ed* Correa (P)	3	16	19	5.16
Maximino *Max* Leon (M)	6	14	18	3.71
Cecilio *Cy* Acosta (M)	4	13	9	2.66
Emilio *Tony* Fossas (C)	7	11	10	4.17
Jose *Acostica* Acosta (C)	3	10	10	4.51
Tomas *Tommy* de la Cruz (C)	1	9	9	3.25
Julio *Whiplash* Navarro (P)	6	7	9	3.65
Federico *Chi-Chi* Olivo (D)	4	7	6	3.96
Porfirio *Porfi* Altamirano (NI)	3	7	4	4.03
Alfredo *Fred* Martinez (A)	2	7	9	4.46
Eduardo *Ed* Acosta (PA)	3	6	9	4.05
Eduardo *Ed* Bauta (C)	5	6	6	4.35
Emilio *Pal* Palmero (C)	5	6	15	5.17
Rafael *Urbano* Lugo (V)	6	6	7	5.31
Nieves *Mardie* Corneja (A)	1	4	2	2.45
Rudolph *Rudy* Hernandez (D)	2	4	2	4.12
Jose *Pants* Santiago (P)	3	3	2	4.66

PITCHERS: (Cont.)	Yr	Won	Lost	ERA
Antonio *Tony* Menendez (C)	3	3	1	4.97
Carlos *Sandy* Ullrich (C)	2	3	3	5.04
Ricardo *Rich* Rodriguez (A)	4	3	4	5.73
Rodolfo *Rudy* Arias (C)	1	2	0	4.09
Manuel *Manny* Hernandez (D)	3	2	7	4.47
Ernesto *Chico* Escarrego (M)	1	1	3	3.67
Gregorio *Evelio* Hernandez (C)	2	1	1	4.45
Lazaro *Cholly* Naranjo (C)	1	1	2	4.46
Joselito *Jose* Cano (D)	1	1	1	5.09
Manuel *Manny* Seoane (A)	2	1	0	5.65
Dagoberto *Bert* Cueto (C)	1	1	3	7.17
Ramon *Johnny* Guzman (D)	2	1	0	10.13
Samuel *Sam* Mejias (D)	1	0	0	0.00
Manuel *Manny* Montejo (C)	1	0	0	3.86
Jorge *Pancho* Comellas (C)	1	0	2	4.50
Vibert *Webbo* Clarke (CZ)	1	0	0	4.64
Jose *Ramon* Lopez (C)	1	0	1	5.14
Ulises *Candy* Sierra (P)	1	0	1	5.53
Don *Gil* Torres (C)	2	0	0	5.59
Arnaldo *Nardi* Contreras (A)	1	0	0	5.93
Oliverio *Baby* Ortiz (C)	1	0	2	6.23
Patricio *Pat* Scantlebury (CZ)	1	0	1	6.63
Manuel *Manny* Muniz (P)	1	0	1	6.97
Fernando *Freddy* Rodriguez (C)	2	0	0	8.68
Silvio *Tony* Cheves (NI)	1	0	0	12.38
Ruperto *Rupe* Toppin (PA)	1	0	0	13.50
Esteban *Manny* Castillo (D)	1	0	0	23.63
Wenceslao *Vince* Gonzales (C)	1	0	0	27.00
Procopio *Tito* Herrera (M)	1	0	0	27.00
Guillermo *Memo* Luna (M)	1	0	1	27.00
Rogelio *Limonar* Martinez (C)	1	0	1	27.00
Jesus *Charlie* Cuellar (A)	1	0	0	33.75

Abbreviations: USA *(A)*   Belize *(B)*   Canal Zone *(CZ)*   Canary Islands *(CI)*   Columbia *(CO)*
Cuba *(CU)*   Dominican Republic *(D)*   Mexico *(M)*   Netherlands Antilles *(N)*
Nicaragua *(NI)*   Panama *(PA)*   Puerto Rico *(P)*   Venezuela *(V)*

It'sa FACT cont'd...

Luis *El Tiante* Tiant: He was one of the greatest pitchers ever, yet the Cuban never seemed to get his due acclaim. El Tiante was a strikeout artist. On July 3rd, 1968 he struck out 19 batters in ten innings. Twice, August 22nd, 1967 and September 9th, 1968, he fanned 16 hitters in nine innings. El Tiante's 1968 season was unbelievable! Luis went 21-9. In 258 1/3 innings he gave up only 152 hits! He held opposing batters to a .168 average, the lowest single season average in baseball history! El Tiante fanned 264 batters, over one per inning, and only walked 73! He posted nine shutouts and led the league with a 1.60 ERA. Denny McLain won 31 games that year and Luis was overlooked. In the 1975 post season Luis was fantastic. He won game #1 of the ALCS allowing just three safeties and one unearned run (his only start in the 3-0 sweep). El Tiante shutout the Big Red Machine in game #1 of the World Series. He then brought the Bosox even by winning game #4. Due to a rain day, and now down three games to two, Luis took the mound game #6 (the one Pudge Fisk won in the 12th), but left with no decision. Boston lost game #7 and the Series, causing El Tiante's great effort to again go unnoticed.

Jorge *George* Orta: In 1974 this left-hand hitting keystoner ranked second to Rod Carew in batting.

Roberto *Bobby* Avila: He was voted Mexico's outstanding athlete and later led the AL in batting (1954).

HOME

18

Team

Historically, teams perform better at home, than at their opponent's ballpark. Three reasons come easily to mind. One, the home team is literally at home. The players are not in a hotel living out of a suitcase. Nothing is better than your own easy chair, your own pillow and your friends and your family's support. Two, the home team has the true encouragement of their fans. The collective value of thousands of supporters is awesome. Think back to the 1987 World Series. White "homer hankies" were waving. The "fanometer" repeatedly was going "over the top" when the Twins did well (all seven games were won by the host team). Three, the home team knows the field quirks of their own park. For a left fielder to learn the caroms of The Green Monster takes years. In the 162nd game of the 1967 season, the Twins and Red Sox were in a dead heat for the flag. There were two outs in the top of the ninth, the Twins trailing 5-3 with a runner on first. Bob Allison hit one off The Monster, a "sure double". Yaz took the carom on one bounce, pivoted and gunned Allison out at second. The Red Sox won the pennant! That is the advantage of being the home team!

This Home Team refers to where the players hail from. Often the hometown heroes' nicknames had either their town, their area or their state in their moniker. Crisscrossing the nation, players come from Harlem to Honolulu, Bedford to Seattle, Paw Paw to Gulfport, Durango to Crabapple and even Climax to Coldwater! Not only is there a Death Valley and a Peaceful Valley, but also there are fourteen Dixies, five Rebels, two Rebs and three Yanks. Twenty-six players were dubbed Tex. Counting a Hoosier and a Buckeye, in all, eleven states are on the squad.

One player will always be in my memory. I "knew him" as Vinegar Ben Mizell. It was only when I started this book that I found out his name is really Wilmer Vinegar Bend Mizell!

LINEUP

CA	Roger *Duke of Tralee* Bresnahan

was originally a pitcher. He played all positions until John McGraw put him at catcher. The Duke was considered intelligent and innovative. He invented shin guards and improved catcher masks. The Duke of Tralee is a member of the Hall of Fame!

1B	Lee *Boomer from Birmingham* May

starred 18 seasons, with his career spanning three decades. For 11 consecutive summers (1968-78) the Boomer from Birmingham clouted 20 or more homers and drove in 80 or more runs! He led the AL in RBI's in 1976. Boomer's 354 long balls rank him 43rd all time!

2B	Don *Corinth Comet* Blasingame

was a 12 year Major League veteran. Hailing from Corinth, Mississippi, Don traveled across the Pacific to Japan and played three more seasons for the Nankai Hawks. After he ended his "second" playing career, Blazer stayed on in Japan and coached.

SS	Joseph *Arky* Vaughan

is a Hall of Famer. In Arky's 12 seasons prior to his service time, he was a nine time NL All-Star and batted over .300 eleven summers. Arky led the league three times in runs scored, bases on balls, on base % and triples. In 1935 he topped all NL hitters, batting .385.

3B	*Jersey* Joe Stripp

played the hot corner for 11 seasons. He was talented both as a hitter and as a fielder. Jersey Joe batted over .300 six of his nine full time years. He hit a career high .324 in 1931. Twice Jersey Joe led all National League third sackers in fielding %.

OF	*Wahoo* Sam Crawford

played 19 seasons on the road to Cooperstown. Eleven seasons Wahoo Sam hit over .300, capturing three RBI titles and two home run crowns. He also led the league in triples six times (once was a tie) and once each in doubles, runs scored and fielding %.

OF	Fred *Dixie* Walker

was an outstanding player for 18 seasons. A steady hitter, Dixie batted over .300 twelve times. He had back to back great seasons in 1944 and 1945, winning the National League batting title (.357) and following with the RBI crown (124) the next season.

OF	Gus *Ozark Ike* Zernial

was a power hitter at the half-century. From 1950-53 Ozark Ike led all American Leaguers in long balls with 133 and placed second in ribbies with 430. For his career Gus had a 5.74 homer %. His home run frequency ranks Ozark Ike 28th all time!

P	*Gettysburg* Eddie Plank

is in the Hall of Fame. Only two left-handers have more career wins. His 69 shutouts place Gettysburg Eddie fifth all time. During his 17 seasons Eddie won 14 or more games 16 summers and logged 20 or more V's eight campaigns. Eddie won nearly 63% of his decisions!

P	*Wabash* George Mullin

hurled for 14 summers. Five seasons he won 20 or more games and in 1909 Wabash George recorded 29 wins to lead the AL. From 1903-11 he won 17 or more games each year. In the 1908 Fall Classic George was 1-0 and in the 1909 World Series he won two contests.

P	Guy *Mississippi Mudcat* Bush

starred for 17 seasons. He was a versatile pitcher, used regularly as both a starter and as a reliever. Ten consecutive campaigns (1926-35) Mississippi Mudcat won in double digits. Guy also led or shared the National League lead in both relief wins and saves two times.

RES	*Tioga* George Burns

slashed over 2000 hits during his 16 year career. He led the AL in hits in both 1918 (178) and 1926 (216). Eight seasons Tioga George batted over .300. His 64 two baggers in 1926 set the then Major League record. He was voted the American League's MVP in 1926.

RES	*Death Valley* Jim Scott

was gone from the Majors before age 30. By age 29 he had won 107 games. Two seasons he reached the 20 victory circle. Death Valley Jim's best year was 1915. He won 24 times (tie second), had a 2.03 ERA (fourth) and recorded seven shutouts (tie first) for the White Sox.

RES	Cliff *Earl of Snohomish* Torgeson

had an exciting 15 year career. Torgie's two best seasons were 1950 and 1951. He belted 23 and 24 homers and drove in 87 and 92 runs respectively. The Earl of Snohomish also led the National League in runs scored in 1950 with 120 tallies.

MGR	*Memphis* Bill Terry

had an outstanding 14 year career. The first sacker retired with the 13th highest lifetime batting average (.341). Memphis Bill, during his last five "playing seasons" and the next five summers, was a manager. The Giants won three flags and one World Series under his leadership.

L to R: Lee *Boomer from Birmingham* May, Gus *Ozark Ike* Zernial, Wilmer *Vinegar Bend* Mizell, *Memphis* Bill Terry, *Wahoo* Sam Crawford

It'sa FACT

Tioga George Burns: On September 14th, 1923 he executed an unassisted triple play, one of only two completed by a first baseman.

Joseph **Arky** Vaughan: He hit left-handed. Arky's style was an awkward flat footed stance, but it did not stop him from making his way to Cooperstown.

Roger **Duke of Tralee** Bresnahan: He was the first backstop elected to the Hall of Fame.

Fred **Dixie** Walker: There have been over 300 brother combinations to play in the Majors. Dixie and his brother, Harry The Hat, were the only ones to both win batting titles!

Wahoo Sam Crawford: He has a record that will never be broken, 309 career triples. Wahoo hit ten or more three baggers 17 consecutive years. Another accomplishment Wahoo did (he is one of three players to do it) was to lead both the National League (1901) and the American League (1908) in home runs.

Gettysburg Eddie Plank: He played 17 seasons. During his career he never led the league in wins, ERA, or innings pitched. Nevertheless, for his career, Eddie notched 326 wins (11th), posted a 2.34 ERA (13th) and hurled 4495 2/3 innings (25th)!

Wabash George Mullin: He was one of the best pitchers with the stick. Wabash George hit over .250 ten of his 14 seasons. He retired with 401 hits and a .262 career batting average!

Lee **Boomer from Birmingham** May: His brother, Carlos, and he both played in the Majors. In the 1969 All-Star game they played against each other.

Tioga George Burns: In 1918 he had a great season. Tioga George led the AL in hits, finished second in both batting average and RBI's, and placed tied for third in home runs.

Gus **Ozark Ike** Zernial: He hit six homers in three games, a Major League record. In 1951 the White Sox traded Ozark Ike to the Philadelphia Athletics four games into the season. Gus went on to lead the AL in both circuit blasts and RBI's for the 1951 Phillies! As a bonus, he topped all outfielders in assists.

Fred **Dixie** Walker: His father Ewart also was a Major Leaguer. Even though their first names were different, both were known as Dixie.

Death Valley Jim Scott: On May 14th, 1914 Jim tossed a no-hitter. Unfortunately, his team was also held scoreless and Death Valley lost both the no-hitter and the game in ten innings, 1-0.

Salida Tom Hughes: He is one of the few hurlers to fire two no-hitters during his career. On August 30th, 1910 he lost a heart breaker in 11 innings, not giving up a hit until the tenth frame. June 16th, 1916 Salida Tom held the Bucs hitless, winning 2-0.

Clarence **Orient Express** Vance: He fired a no-hitter against the Phillies September 13th, 1925.

Wilmer **Vinegar Bend** Mizell: After his playing days were over, Vinegar Bend was elected to the U.S. Congress.

Amos **Hoosier Thunderbolt** Rusie: During his playing days, he was considered the fastest pitcher and nearly unhittable. Amos was directly responsible for the change from 50 foot pitching distance and throwing from a box area (prior to 1893) to the 60 foot 6 inch current distance and hurling off of a rubber. From 1889-1898 the Hoosier Thunderbolt won 245 games (including one season "lost" due to a hold out). At the young age of 27 he hurt his arm and never won another game!

Ewell **Reb** Russell: He came up in 1913 as a 24 year old rookie pitcher for the White Sox. Reb won 22 games (third), had a 1.90 ERA (fourth) and posted eight shutouts (second). After 59 more wins, arm problems ended Reb's pitching career. In 1922, as a 33 year old outfielder for the Bucs, Reb returned to the Majors. Playing 60 games, Ewell hit .368, pounded 12 homers and drove in 75 runs! After the 1923 season Reb left the Majors for good.

Ty **Georgia Peach** Cobb: By the young age of 34 Ty had laced his 3000th hit! No one has reached this milestone at a younger age.

TRIVIA*

1) In the five game 1970 Fall Classic he did his best. In a losing effort he slashed two doubles, slugged two homers and drove in eight runs for Cincinnati.

2) He is the last National Leaguer to hit over .400, cracking 254 hits (tie second highest total ever) that summer (1930).

3) In the teens two very successful players had the same name. Fortunately, one had a nickname. (Hint: an actor also shares their names)

4) He surrendered Babe Ruth's 713th and 714th career home runs.

5) He allowed, earlier in the game referred to above, Babe Ruth's 712th home run.

6) He was born in Leakesville, Mississippi, but he later acquired his nickname from this Alabama town.

7) Born on July 4th, this Indiana native hurled a no-hitter on his 32nd birthday.

8) Hailing from LeSeur, Minnesota, the Valley of the Jolly Green Giant, he was tabbed with his nickname.

9) He gained his moniker from this rhyming two syllable Michigan town.

10) He earned his nickname from this "chilly" town in Michigan. He was actually born in Wakashma, Michigan.

11) This famous NL slugger was born in Glasgow, Scotland.

12) Hailing from a small Iowa town, this was his first nickname. Later he was better known as Dazzy.

13) Reared in Oklahoma, he was, at one time, considered the fastest man from home to first.

14) He had a cannon for an arm, which helped him gain this hometown nickname.

15) The Old Professor gained his better known nickname from the town where he was born.

16) After he blew into the Majors as a pitcher, this Texan also played some outfield.

17) Born and raised in this Georgia town, he was the second Major Leaguer to hail from that town. The first was his uncle, who was better known to Brooklyn fans as Nap.

18) From his hometown one is able to look up at beautiful Mount Rainier in Washington state.

19) On the banks of this Nebraska river is the hometown (same name as the river) which gives this Hall of Famer his "wild" nickname.

20) Also known as Jo-Jo, his Texas hometown gives him his spooky nickname.

21) Two towns in Pennsylvania produced these two Hall of Famers. One town you may not recognize. (Hint: both were pitchers)

22) The banks of this beautiful river form the Minnesota/Wisconsin border. This young man from Studdard, Wisconsin went 20-16 as a Major League rookie.

23) Born in Coal Creek, Colorado, his nickname came from a nearby town.

24) His other nickname was the same as a TV situation comedy starring Jackie Cooper and featuring his talking dog Cleo (The Peoples' Choice).

25) He stroked the first base hit in Yankee Stadium, by George.

* HOMEWORK answers found on page 237

ROSTER

CATCHERS:	Yr	Hits	AB's	Ave
Roger *Duke of Tralee* Bresnahan	17	1252	4481	.279
Bedford Bill Rariden	12	682	2877	.237
Willard *California* Brown	7	415	1589	.261
Homer *Dixie* Howell	8	224	910	.246
Ross *Tex* Erwin	6	150	635	.236
Alfred *Queens* Jutze	6	141	656	.215
Ed *Dixie* Parsons	3	52	295	.176
Doyle *Tex* Aulds	1	1	4	.250
Douglas *Dixie* Parker	1	1	5	.200
Sid *Tex* Womack	1	0	3	.000

1ST BASEMEN:	Yr	Hits	AB's	Ave
Memphis Bill Terry	14	2193	6428	.341
Lee *Boomer from Birmingham* May	18	2031	7609	.267
Tioga George Burns	16	2018	6573	.307
Cliff *Earl of Snohomish* Torgeson	15	1318	4969	.265
William *Tex* Jones	1	6	31	.194

2ND BASEMEN:	Yr	Hits	AB's	Ave
Don *Corinth Comet* Blasingame	12	1366	5296	.258
William *Yank* Robinson	10	825	3428	.241
Carvel *Bama* Rowell	6	523	1901	.275
Charles *Tex* McDonald	4	304	1019	.298
Minooka Mike McNally	10	257	1078	.238

SHORTSTOPS:	Yr	Hits	AB's	Ave
Joseph *Arky* Vaughan	14	2103	6622	.318
Travis *Arkansas Traveler* Jackson	15	1768	6086	.291
Tommy *Rebel* McMillan	4	207	991	.209
Ernie *Kansas City Kid* Smith	1	19	79	.241

3RD BASEMEN:	Yr	Hits	AB's	Ave
Jersey Joe Stripp	11	1238	4211	.294
Scranton Bill Coughlin	9	972	3854	.252
Sammy *Dixie Thrush* Strang	10	790	2933	.269
Jersey Clyde Beck	6	354	1525	.232
George *Tex* Wisterzil	2	215	828	.260
Ed *Tex* Hoffman	1	2	13	.154

OUTFIELDERS:	Yr	Hits	AB's	Ave
Ty *Georgia Peach* Cobb	24	4189	11434	.366
Wahoo Sam Crawford	19	2961	9570	.309
Mickey *Commerce Comet* Mantle	18	2415	8102	.298
Fred *Dixie* Walker	18	2064	6740	.306
Carl *Reading Rifle* Furillo	15	1910	6378	.299
Earle *The Kentucky Colonel* Combs	12	1866	5746	.325
Bobby *Staten Island Scot* Thomson	15	1705	6305	.270
Joseph *Gause Ghost* Moore	12	1615	5427	.298
Charles *Casey* Stengel	14	1219	4288	.284
Gus *Ozark Ike* Zernial	11	1093	4131	.265
Ennis *Rebel* Oakes	7	1011	3619	.279
Charlie *Paw Paw* Maxwell	14	856	3245	.264
Johnny *Crabapple Comet* Rucker	6	711	2617	.272
Tom *Rebel* Oliver	4	534	1931	.277

OUTFIELDERS: (Cont.)	Yr	Hits	AB's	Ave
Ewell *Reb* Russell	9	262	976	.268
Clint *Hondo Hurricane* Hartung	6	90	378	.238
Ernest *Tex* Vache	1	79	252	.313
Bob *Tex* Nelson	3	25	122	.205
Jim *Troy Terrier* Egan	1	23	115	.200
Ernest *Tex* Jeanes	5	20	73	.274
Dorsey *Dixie* Carroll	1	13	49	.265
Allan *Panamanian Express* Lewis	6	6	29	.207
Frank *Tex* Carswell	1	4	15	.267
Peekskill Pete Cregan	2	2	21	.095

PINCH HITTER:	Yr	Hits	AB's	Ave
Roy *Dixie* Upright	1	2	8	.250

PITCHERS:	Yr	Won	Lost	ERA
Gettysburg Eddie Plank	17	326	194	2.35
Amos *Hoosier Thunderbolt* Rusie	10	245	174	3.07
Juan *Dominican Dandy* Marichal	16	243	142	2.89
Herb *Knight of Kennett Square* Pennock	22	240	162	3.60
Wabash George Mullin	14	228	196	2.82
Clarence *Orient Express* Vance	16	197	140	3.24
Sam *Goshen Schoolmaster* Leever	13	194	100	2.47
Dolf *Pride of Havana* Luque	20	194	179	3.24
Lon *Arkansas Hummingbird* Warneke	15	192	121	3.18
Guy *Mississippi Mudcat* Bush	17	176	136	3.86
Ron *Louisiana Lightning* Guidry	14	170	91	3.29
Charles *Nashville Narcissus* Lucas	15	157	135	3.72
Howie *Kentucky Rosebud* Camnitz	11	133	106	2.75
Vic *Springfield Rifle* Raschi	10	132	66	3.72
Death Valley Jim Scott	9	107	113	2.30
James *Tex* Carleton	8	100	76	3.91
Guy *Alabama Blossom* Morton	11	98	88	3.13
Cecil *Tex* Hughson	8	96	54	2.94
Allen *Dixie* Sothoron	11	91	100	3.31
Wilmer *Vinegar Bend* Mizell	9	90	88	3.85
Ewell *Reb* Russell	9	81	59	2.33
Roy *St. Croix Boy Wonder* Patterson	7	81	73	2.75
Ed *Jersey* Bakely	6	77	125	3.66
Frank *Dixie* Davis	10	75	71	3.97
Salida Tom Hughes	9	56	39	2.56
Ed *Wild Elk of the Wasatch* Heusser	9	56	67	3.69
Francis *The Naugatuck Nuggett* Shea	8	56	46	3.80
Herb *Gallatin Squash* Perdue	5	51	64	3.85
Dick *Nimrod Nifty* Stigman	7	46	54	4.03
Gene *Arkansas Traveler* Bearden	7	45	38	3.96
Seattle Bill James	4	37	21	2.28
Truman *Tex* Clevenger	8	36	37	4.18
Gorham *Dixie* Leverett	5	29	34	4.51
Coldwater Jim Hughey	7	29	80	4.87
Ewart *Dixie* Walker	4	25	31	3.52
Adam *Tex* Johnson	3	23	30	2.92
Millard *Dixie* Howell	6	19	15	3.78
Alvis *Tex* Shirley	5	19	30	4.25
James *Dixie* Walker	6	17	27	3.99

ROSTER

PITCHERS: (Cont.)	Yr	Won	Lost	ERA
John *Tex* Kraus	3	15	25	4.00
Murray *Tex* Wall	4	13	14	4.20
Jack *Gulfport* Ryan	3	5	5	2.88
Jack *Tex* Creel	1	5	4	4.14
Clyde *Pea Ridge* Day	4	5	7	5.30
John *Tex* Neuer	1	4	2	2.17
Charles *Tex* Pruiett	2	4	18	2.83
Jim *Troy Terrier* Egan	1	4	6	4.14
Roger *Peaceful Valley* Denzer	2	4	14	4.43
Frank *Texas Wonder* Hoffman	1	3	9	2.77
Spartanburg John McMakin	1	2	2	3.09
Ernie *Tex* Herbert	3	2	1	3.35
Bill *Rebel* McTigue	3	2	5	6.19
Karl *Rebel* Adams	2	1	9	5.01
Guy *Rebel* Cooper	2	1	0	5.33

PITCHERS: (Cont.)	Yr	Won	Lost	ERA
Johnnie *Durango Kid* Seale	2	1	0	5.54
Charlie *Yank* Brown	1	1	2	7.77
Don *Buckeye* Grate	2	1	1	9.37
Oland *Dixie* McArthur	1	0	0	0.00
Paul *Tex* Kardow	1	0	0	4.50
Harlem Joe Kiefer	3	0	5	6.16
Honolulu Johnnie Williams	1	0	2	6.35
Clarence *Climax* Blethen	2	0	0	7.32
Gomer *Tex* Wilson	1	0	0	14.73
Wedo *Southern* Martini	1	0	2	17.05
Roland *Tex* Hoyle	1	0	0	27.00

EXTRA:
Dixie Ewing - Awesome Realtor

LINGO

Texas Leaguer: A blooper that "falls in" between the infield and the outfield for a base hit

A Homer: A fan, who, no matter what, roots for his home team

Home Field Advantage: Home town fans root extra hard and the team knows the idiosyncrasies of their own baseball field

He's Going Home: Player running to cross home plate

Athletic Supporter: A jock strap

Hit in the Alley: Hit between two outfielders, also known as the gap

Forced Out: A player is called out for not reaching the next base ahead of the ball

Sent to the Showers: Pitcher is replaced during the game by another pitcher

Supporter: A fan

Fan: Short for fanatic, as in the Philadelphia . . .

MORE TRIVIA*

A) This "boy" won the first American League game, April 24th, 1901, beating the Cleveland Blues 8-2.

B) Born in Mill Creek, Utah, these mountains helped form his nickname.

C) His better known nickname was Spec. He also was named after his Connecticut hometown.

D) Yes, there is a town that formed his nickname.

E) Born in Edgewater, his hometown nickname is not close to Heaven or Hell, but it is close to Purgatory.

F) His hometown is the capital of our 50th state.

G) His nickname was after the county in Ireland where his family came from.

H) He was from Narrows, Georgia. He ranks second all time in hits and triples, fourth in doubles and stolen bases and first in runs scored.

I) This dazzling left-hander led the NL in strikeouts seven consecutive seasons (1922-28)!

J) This Oklahoman won the AL Triple Crown in 1956.

K) In 1910 he led the AL in RBI's with 120. He had 32% more ribbies than his Detroit teammate who finished second in the league (Ty Georgia Peach Cobb - 91)!

* HOMEWORK answers found on page 237

Real INDIANS

19

Team

   The Cleveland Indians, AKA the Tribe, have their roots in the National League. Starting in 1879, they were known as the Spiders. In 1899 the Spiders were the league doormat, going 20-134, finishing 84 games out of first (they were probably mathematically eliminated before summer!). The Cleveland team resurfaced in the new Junior Circuit, better known as the American League, in 1901. Now they were known as the Blues, for their uniform color. For a short time they were called the Bronchos, but when Nap Lajoie starred for them, the fans dubbed the team the Naps. After the 1914 season, Lajoe left. The fans, influenced by the memory of a past player, Chief Louis Sockalexis, voted to call their home team the Indians.

   The Real Indians have no Spiders, Blues, Bronchos, or Naps on their roster. They do have nine Hall of Famers and also many other star players. All the Indians cannot be Chiefs, but there are 27 Chiefs and one Superchief on the Real Indians. With the help of 38 Bucks, a Warrior, a Redskin, a Savage, and a Millionaire Indian, they are ready for victory. Add in nine Hawks and a Little Hawk, five Bo's and a Big Bow, include Cochise once and Crazy Horse twice, and a diverse Nation emerges. This group also counts two Crows, two Kickapoos and a Cherokee as members.

   There is one Real Indian who has never been remembered enough for his accomplishments. His name is Ralph Hawk Branca. Forgetting "the shot", a less than 300 foot fly ball, Hawk starred 12 seasons, with 1947 being his best campaign. That year he went 21-12, leading the Dodgers to the flag. The Hawk finished second in strikeouts and innings pitched, tied for second in wins and third in ERA. During his career Hawk was named to three All-Star squads.

LINEUP

| CA | William *Buck* Ewing | starred 17 seasons prior to the turn of the century. Buck was considered by many as the greatest player of his era. He played all positions, but primarily was a catcher. Buck's 178 career triples place him 18th. This Hall of Famer topped .300 eleven seasons. |

| 1B | Lou *The Iron Horse* Gehrig | was one of the rare players to hit for both power and average. From 1926-38 Lou drove in over 100 runs each season, seven times knocking in over 150! The Iron Horse rattled the bleachers 493 times, 15th all time! He retired with a .340 average, also ranking him 15th! |

| 2B | Chuck *Buck* Herzog | was a steady player for 13 seasons. He played over 400 games at second base, shortstop and third base. In 1911 he had his best season. Buck pounded 33 doubles (tie fourth), stole 48 bags (fifth) and hit .290. In the 1912 Fall Classic Buck led the Giants attack going 12/30. |

| SS | Tim *Crazy Horse* Foli | played for 16 seasons. Tim twice led the league in fielding %. A tough batter to fan, he whiffed only 399 times in over 6000 at bats. In 1979 Crazy Horse was rung up only 14 times in 532 at bats. Playing for 'The Family' in the 1979 post season, he went 10/30 in the Fall Classic. |

| 3B | Frankie *Crow* Crosetti | played 17 seasons, all with the Yankees. Twenty-two years (two overlapping his playing career) the Crow was a Yankee coach. Frankie led the AL in stolen bases in 1938. From 1936-39 he scored over 100 runs per year. His six RBI's in the 1938 Series led their sweep of Chicago. |

| OF | *Indian* Bob Johnson | , from his rookie debut at age 26, until he 'hung 'em up' 13 summers later, was one of the most feared batters in baseball. In each of his first nine seasons Indian Bob hit at least 21 homers and drove in a minimum of 92 runs! Seven consecutive seasons (1935-41) he had 100+ RBI's. |

| OF | Owen *Chief* Wilson | was an all-around player for nine seasons. With his glove, Chief led the NL in fielding % twice. With his bat, he shared the league lead in RBI's in 1911. In 1912 Chief placed first in triples and tied for third in homers. He finished tied for fourth in 3B's and fifth in HR's in 1913. |

| OF | Zack *Buck* Wheat | starred 19 seasons and now is honored in Cooperstown. Hitting over .300 fourteen times, including .375 twice, Buck pounded out 2884 hits (28th). Zack had 476 doubles and his 172 three baggers tie him for 23rd. In 1918 he won the National League batting crown. |

| P | Mel *Chief* Harder | played longer for the Tribe, 20 seasons, than any player. He went on to coach for the Indians 15 more years. For 11 consecutive summers (1930-40) Chief won in double digits, twice reaching 20! In 1935 his 22 wins were second best and in 1933 Chief won the ERA title. |

| P | Charles *Chief* Bender | was used judiciously over his career, because Connie Mack did not want to wear out his arm. The Chief seldom started more than 25 games in a season, nevertheless he won 15 or more contests nine times, twice posting over 20 wins. In 1910 Chief went 23-5 with a 1.58 ERA. |

| P | Allie *Superchief* Reynolds | won his first game in 1943 at the age of 28, and went on to pace the AL in K's that year. From 1943-54, he won at least 11 times each summer and only twice had a losing season. Superchief's best year was 1952, going 20-8 and leading the AL in both shutouts (tie) and ERA. |

| RES | Frank *Buck* McCormick | starred 13 seasons, batting over .300 seven times. From 1938-40 Buck was fantastic. In 1938 he was third in batting. He finished second in hitting in 1939. In 1940 Buck led all NL'ers in hits for the third consecutive year (one tie)! Four summers he had over 100+ RBI's. |

| RES | Vincent *Bo* Jackson | is probably the most dynamic athlete of his time. He excelled not only on the diamond, but Bo also displayed his talents on the cinders as a world class sprinter and on the gridiron, first as a collegiate halfback (Heisman Trophy winner), and later as a pro running back. |

| RES | Wally *Cochise* Post | poled over 200 homers while on the warpath during the mid 50's into the early 60's. In 1955 Cochise blasted 40 homers, drove in 109 runs, slugged 33 doubles, collected 186 hits and scored 116 runs. Five times he tomahawked 20 or more HR's, including 20 in only 282 at bats in '61! |

| RES | John *Buck* Freeman | was the premier power hitter at the turn of the century. In 1899 Buck launched 25 HR's, two short of the then season record and 13 more than the player who finished second to him. His 122 RBI's were second best in 1899. Buck finished second in both HR's and RBI's in 1901. |

L to R: *Indian* Bob Johnson, Mel *Chief* Harder, Ralph *Hawk* Branca, Vincent *Bo* Jackson, Charles *Chief* Bender

It'sa FACT

Charles *Chief* Bender: He was born in Crow Wing County, Minnesota (my boys and I go fishing in that county every summer). Albert (coach Mack called him by his middle name) won 62% of his decisions, 33rd all time. Connie Mack considered him his best pitcher, if he had one game to win. Chief's 2.46 career ERA places him 23rd. He also posted 40 shutouts, only 41 players have thrown more.

Fred *Buck* Schemanske: During his career he batted just three times. Buck walked once and singled twice, driving in two runs. He retired with a batting average and slugging % of 1.000!

Vincent *Bo* Jackson: What a bizarre game! Bo had smashed three consecutive homers and had driven in seven runs in the first five innings! Bo was then forced to leave the game (subsequently went on the DL) when he was injured diving for a line drive off Neon Deion Sanders bat, which Deion legged out for an inside the parker. Weeks later, when Bo returned to the lineup, he homered his first at bat!

Lou *The Iron Horse* Gehrig: Three times he went ten plus consecutive games driving in at least one run. No other player has done this more than once! Only two players had more 200 hit seasons than Lou. In 1931 The Iron Horse produced more runs than anyone ever has. He scored 163 runs and drove in 184 runs. Subtract one run for each home run (46) and you get a net 301 runs produced. Power hitter Lou also stole home 15 times, 13th all time!

Grant *Buck* Jackson: Used primarily as a middle man throughout his 18 season career, he only had five losing seasons. In 1973 Buck was perfect, going 8-0 with nine saves and a 1.90 ERA.

Charles *Chief* Zimmer: He was captain of his minor league team, the Poughkeepsie Indians. Since he was the captain, Chief acquired his nickname.

Jack *Chief* Warhop: You guessed it, his nickname came from his last name! In 1914 this submariner was hopping mad. He went a dismal 8-15, but with a sparkling 2.37 ERA. The Chief tied a single season Major League mark by losing five games 1-0! Chief is one of six pitchers to steal home twice (one pitcher did it three times).

Charles *Chief* Bender: On May 8th, 1907 he was a sixth inning sub for the right fielder. Chief made it look easy, hitting two home runs - both inside the park! That entire season, as a pitcher, he only gave up one home run! Now you may think Albert was a slugger, but in 16 seasons Chief only clubbed one more home run!

Elon *Chief* Hogsett: He was a reliever, sometimes starter, who twirled mostly in the 30's. Twice Chief led the AL in relief wins. In four World Series appearances he allowed only one tally in 8 1/3 innings.

Al *Beartracks* Javery: Starring for the lowly Boston Braves from 1940-46, he won in double figures four times (1941-44). Those four summers the Braves never finished higher than 6th. In 1942 Beartracks won 12, five by shutout. He won 17 games in 1943, five again by shutout. Beartracks also led the league in innings and placed third in strikeouts in 1943.

Clarence *Lance* Rautzhan: During his short career he was a reliever for the Dodgers. On October 7th, 1977 he faced and retired one batter in the eighth inning of game #3 in the NLCS. The Dodgers rallied for three runs in the top of the ninth and made Lance the winner.

Tom *Buck* O'Brien: He debuted September 9th, 1911, going 5-1 with five complete games. Buck tossed two shutouts and had an ERA of 0.38! In 1912 he went 20-13, proving that the previous September was no fluke.

Frank *Buck* McCormick: During his career, he was the complete player. With his glove, in his nine full seasons, Buck led all first sackers six times in putouts, four times in fielding %, three times in DP's and twice in assists. His career .995 fielding % places him sixth. In 1946 his .999 fielding % was the third best one season total. With his bat, Buck fanned just 189 times in 5723 at bats, the tenth hardest batter to strikeout! In 1940 Frank was voted the NL's MVP.

Johnny *Bear Tracks* Schmitz: He toiled for the hapless Cubbies for seven plus seasons. Remarkably, Bear Tracks won 18 games (tie for third) with an ERA of 2.64 (fifth) in 1948. That year the last place Northsiders won only 64 times!

John *Chief* Meyers: For nine seasons he caught. From 1911-13 he led the Giants to three consecutive World Series appearances. The Chief hit .332 (third), .358 (second) and .312 those three summers. Each year he led the NL backstops in putouts.

110

TRIVIA*

1) He holds the Major League record for RBI's in one inning, six!

2) His 36 triples in 1912 set a single season record.

3) He was the first Native American elected to the Hall of Fame.

4) He was the opening day pitcher and President Franklin Roosevelt was in attendance. In the third inning his own third sacker hit him on the side of the face when throwing to first. This hurler continued, winning 1-0. X-rays discovered his jaw had been broken in two places.

5) Twice he had 100 or more extra base hits in one season (one of two players ever, the other was Chuck Klein). In 1927 he finished with 52 doubles, 18 triples and 47 homers.

6) During his 13 year career he averaged 30+ doubles, 22+ homers and 98+ RBI's.

7) During his career he pitched 13 innings in All-Star games and never allowing a run.

8) Johnny Dutch Master Vander Meer, Jim Maloney, Virgil Fire Trucks, Nolan The Express Ryan and he all have tossed two no-hitters in one season.

9) Always coming up big in World Series play, his post season record was 7-2. He won the clinching game in both the 1952 and 1953 Fall Classics.

10) In the 1911 World Series he lost game #1, but he came back to win game #4 and the Series clinching game #6.

11) He has the second most wins by a AL rookie pitcher, going 24-12 in 1908. (Hint: think season)

12) This stopper was the 1966 AL Fireman of the Year. He went 8-4, recorded a league leading 32 saves and posted a 1.99 ERA.

13) Many players have had two outfield assists in one inning, but only he has done it twice. (Hint: he also had ten career pinch home runs)

14) Some players have had three triples on one game, but he did it twice. (September 26th, 1897 and August 19th, 1898)

15) After a hip replacement, he defied all odds and returned to the Majors again. His first at bat back, he launched a home run!

16) He was perfect in post season play, going 2-0 in League Championship play and 1-0 in World Series competition. He won game #7 of the 1979 Fall Classic, capping the Pirates three game comeback.

17) He was the first player selected in the 1968 amateur draft.

18) On May 5th, 1962 he was the first rookie left-hander to throw a no-hitter, beating the Orioles 2-0.

19) He and his older brother Roy combined (for brothers who played in the Majors) to finish sixth in doubles and RBI's, and eighth in homers and triples.

20) These two brothers are the only siblings to both be inducted into the Hall of Fame.

21) This hurler was credited as the first pitcher to throw a slider.

22) His 23 grand slams are the Major League record.

23) In his rookie season he hit .355 and stroked 198 singles.

24) Playing in spacious Forbes Field, he laced 191 career triples, tenth all time. Ten consecutive summers he reached double figures for three baggers.

25) In 1927, the year Babe Ruth walloped 60 home runs, he won the AL MVP.

* SCALP SCRATCHERS answers found on page 238

ROSTER

CATCHERS:	Yr	Hits	AB's	Ave
William *Buck* Ewing	18	1625	5363	.303
Charles *Chief* Zimmer	19	1224	4546	.269
John *Chief* Meyers	9	826	2834	.291
Robert *Buck* Rodgers	9	704	3033	.232
John *Buck* Martinez	17	618	2743	.225
Clyde *Buck* Crouse	8	342	1306	.262
Tom *Deerfoot* Needham	11	311	1491	.209
Robert *Hawk* Taylor	11	158	724	.218
Ken *Hawk* Silvestri	8	44	203	.217
Hi *Buck* Ebright	1	15	59	.254
George *Squanto* Wilson	2	3	16	.188
Lewis *Crazy Horse* Meyers	1	0	3	.000

1ST BASEMEN:	Yr	Hits	AB's	Ave
Jake *Eagle Eye* Beckley	20	2930	9526	.308
Lou *The Iron Horse* Gehrig	17	2721	8001	.340
Frank *Buck* McCormick	13	1711	5723	.299
Ken *Hawk* Harrelson	9	703	2941	.239
Frank *Turkeyfoot* Brower	5	371	1297	.286
Jerry *Buck* Freeman	2	142	579	.245
Clarence *Buck* Etchison	2	72	327	.220
Emanuel *Redleg* Snyder	2	41	257	.160

2ND BASEMEN:	Yr	Hits	AB's	Ave
Charles *Buck* Herzog	13	1370	5284	.259
Frank *Bald Eagle* Isbell	10	1056	4219	.250
Tim *Good Eye* Shinnick	2	224	936	.239
Les *Buck* Burke	4	131	506	.259
Harry *Bird Eye* Truby	2	73	260	.281
George *Buck* Redfern	2	67	307	.218

SHORTSTOPS:	Yr	Hits	AB's	Ave
Hughie *Ee-Yah* Jennings	17	1527	4904	.311
Tim *Crazy Horse* Foli	16	1515	6047	.251
George *Bo* Strickland	10	633	2824	.224
Henry *Buck* Danner	1	3	12	.250

3RD BASEMEN:	Yr	Hits	AB's	Ave
Frank *Crow* Crosetti	17	1541	6277	.245
George *Buck* Weaver	9	1308	4809	.272
Odell *Chief* Hale	10	1071	3701	.289
Al *Bo* Boucher	1	119	516	.231
John *Buck* Gladman	3	56	380	.147
Ike *Chief* Kahdot	1	0	2	.000

OUTFIELDERS:	Yr	Hits	AB's	Ave
Tris *The Grey Eagle* Speaker	22	3514	10195	.345
Paul *Big Poison* Waner	20	3152	9459	.333
Wahoo Sam Crawford	19	2961	9570	.309
Zack *Buck* Wheat	19	2884	9106	.317
Andre *The Hawk* Dawson	19	2700	9343	.280
Lloyd *Little Poison* Waner	18	2459	7772	.316
Clyde *Deerfoot* Milan	16	2100	7359	.285

OUTFIELDERS: (Cont.)	Yr	Hits	AB's	Ave
Indian Bob Johnson	13	2051	6920	.296
Owen *Chief* Wilson	9	1246	4624	.269
John *Buck* Freeman	11	1235	4208	.293
Charlie *Eagle Eye* Hemphill	11	1230	4541	.271
Wally *Cochise* Post	15	1064	4007	.266
Vincent *Bo* Jackson	8	598	2393	.250
Ernie *Chief* Koy	5	515	1846	.279
George *Deerfoot* Barclay	4	382	1538	.248
Louis *Chief* Sockalexis	3	115	367	.313
Johnny *Chief* Blatnik	3	113	447	.253
Al *Deerfoot* Kaiser	3	104	481	.216
John *Chief* Kelty	1	49	207	.237
Aaron *Hawk* Pointer	3	21	101	.208
Bill *Hawk* Mueller	2	14	94	.149
Orth *Buck* Collins	2	6	24	.250
John *Buck* Hopkins	1	6	44	.136
George *Buck* Stanton	1	3	15	.200
Ed *Kickapoo* Kippert	1	0	2	.000

PINCH HITTERS:	Yr	Hits	AB's	Ave
Fred *Buck* Schemanske	1	2	2	1.000
El *Big Bow* Bowman	1	0	1	.000

PITCHERS:	Yr	Won	Lost	ERA
Mel *Chief* Harder	20	223	186	3.80
Charles *Chief* Bender	16	212	127	2.46
Louis *Buck* Newson	20	211	222	3.98
Bob *Warrior* Friend	16	197	230	3.58
Allie *Superchief* Reynolds	13	182	107	3.30
Mike *Big Bear* Garcia	14	142	97	3.27
Clay *Hawk* Carroll	15	96	73	2.94
Johnny *Bear Tracks* Schmitz	13	93	114	3.55
Ralph *Hawk* Branca	12	88	68	3.79
Grant *Buck* Jackson	18	86	75	3.46
Jack *Chief* Warhop	8	69	93	3.12
Kickapoo Ed Summers	5	68	45	2.42
Elon *Chief* Hogsett	11	63	87	5.02
Lee *Buck* Ross	10	56	95	4.94
Al *Beartracks* Javery	7	53	74	3.80
Jack *Chief* Aker	11	47	45	3.28
George *Chief* Johnson	3	40	43	2.95
Tom *Buck* O'Brien	3	29	25	2.63
Robert *Bo* Belinsky	8	28	51	4.10
Virgil *Chief* Cheeves	6	26	27	4.73
John *Chief* Urrea	5	17	18	3.74
Raleigh *Redskin* Aitchison	3	12	12	3.01
Wynn *Hawk* Hawkins	3	12	13	4.17
Michael *Bo* McLaughlin	6	10	20	4.49
Alexander *Buck* Freeman	2	9	11	4.70
Euel *Chief* Moore	3	9	16	5.48
Austin *Millionaire Indian* Tincup	4	8	11	3.10
Jesse *Scout* Stovall	2	8	14	3.76
Moses *Chief* Yellowhorse	2	8	4	3.93

ROSTER

PITCHERS: (Cont.)	Yr	Won	Lost	ERA
Jim *Buck* Brillheart	4	8	9	4.19
Clarence *Lance* Rautzhan	3	6	4	3.90
Jim *Buck* Buchanan	1	5	9	3.50
Lynn *Buck* Brenton	4	5	12	3.97
William *Cherokee* Fisher	3	4	21	3.06
Vallie *Chief* Eaves	5	4	8	4.58
Louis *Chief* LeRoy	3	3	1	3.22
Savage Tom Thomas	2	3	3	3.31
Frank *Chief* Harter	3	3	5	3.67
Charlie *Buck* Becker	2	3	5	3.92
Charles *Buck* Marrow	3	3	8	5.06
James *Buck* Becannon	3	3	8	5.93
William *Crow* Spanswick	1	2	3	6.89
Harvey *Buck* Freeman	1	1	4	7.20

PITCHERS: (Cont.)	Yr	Won	Lost	ERA
William *Chief* Chouneau	1	0	1	3.38
Ralph *Buck* Buxton	2	0	2	4.25
Robert *Buck* Fausett	1	0	0	5.91
William *Buck* Washer	1	0	0	6.00
John *Buck* Stanley	1	0	0	6.35
Lucas *Chief* Turk	1	0	0	6.94
Orlin *Buck* Rogers	1	0	1	7.20
James *Chief* Roseman	3	0	1	7.88
Harvey *Buck* Green	1	0	0	9.00
Tom *Little Hawk* Long	1	0	0	9.00
Arthur *Chief* Youngblood	1	0	0	14.54
Sol *Buck* Carter	1	0	0	19.29
Emmett *Chief* Bowles	1	0	0	27.00

LINGO

Powwow at the Mound: Coach and players meet to discuss strategy

Surrounds the Ball: Player circles under a fly ball

Advance Scout: Man who studies a future opponent and reports back on how to beat them

Scout: Man who searches for talented players and tries to sign them to a contract

Massacre: Beat an opponent badly

Scalp a Ticket: A person illegally selling game tickets to customers

War Club: Bat

Brave: Someone from Boston, prior to 1953, from Milwaukee from 1953-65 and someone now living in Atlanta

Tomahawked: Hit

MORE TRIVIA*

A) He holds the Major League record with 792 doubles. Eight times (one tie) he led the league in two baggers, five times pounding 50 or more.

B) His 222 career triples place him sixth all time. Surprisingly, he never led the league in three baggers.

C) This outstanding golfer and White Sox announcer led the AL in RBI's in 1968.

D) Born on the banks of this Nebraska river, it was the source of his nickname. A Hall of Famer, his 309 triples rank him first all time.

E) His 88 stolen bases in 1912 were the then single season Major League record (post 1900). His speed generated his nickname.

F) He acquired his silly nickname because he always "yelled it" when he coached at third base.

G) On June 3rd, 1932 he slugged home runs his first four times up. His last at bat he crushed his hardest shot, but it traveled to dead center field at Shribe Park. The ball was caught at the fence, 468 feet from home plate!

H) Connie Mack considered him the most talented player he ever saw. John McGraw held the same high opinion.

I) On May 12th, 1910 he no-hit the Cleveland Naps. It would have been rather interesting had they then been called the Indians. Headlines might have read "Chief tames Tribe".

J) He is currently the manager of the Bronx Bombers (gone after 1995).

* SCALP SCRATCHERS answers found on page 238

INTERNATIONAL

20

Team

America has been known as the "melting pot," with immigrants from the four corners of the world coming to our friendly shores. Many new arrivals sailed past the Statue of Liberty as they cast off their earlier lives, checked through Ellis Island and sought their new futures in the land of opportunity. Here, not held back by political, religious and cultural "caste systems," each individual had the chance to choose their own road and the distance they were able to travel. Frequently immigrants settled near their fellow countrymen. Their past traditions, native language and ties to "the Old Country" were a first generation cement that held these foreigners together as their transition took place. One example would be "Little Italy." Most major cities have an Italian neighborhood. "The Hill" in St. Louis spawned two Major League catchers, Joe Garagiola and Yogi Berra, who were neighborhood friends!

The International Team has players nicknamed for many countries. The most frequent are Holland, Sweden, Ireland and France, followed closely by Germany, Scotland, Greece and Turkey. Add in Russia, Italy and Poland, plus include Finland, Yugoslavia and Hungary and the team broadens its worldwide base. To complete the roster, players from the near south are drawn from Cuba, Panama and the Dominican Republic.

One player soars above all others on this squad. Honus Flying Dutchman Wagner was the NL's premier player of his time. What makes The Flying Dutchman's numbers even more remarkable is his era. The "dead ball" era was simply this. Dark, loosely wound, scuffed, cut and "doctored" balls were used. Ten homers in one season was rare. Sometimes 90-100 RBI's were league leader totals. ERA's of 2.00 or less were commonplace for good pitchers. By comparison, when the "lively ball" came, all hitting numbers rose dramatically. In 1930 only one pitcher in the NL had an ERA below 3.00! Lewis Hack Wilson led in homers and RBI's with 56 and 190 respectively. Compare this to 1902. That summer Honus led the league with 91 ribbies and poled three dingers (league leader had six). Now, when you look at his career totals, they become even more unbelievable! From 1899-1913 he hit at least .300 each summer, eight times capturing the batting crown (NL record). Nine seasons in his career he drove in an unheard of 100 or more runs, five times topping the NL. His six slugging titles were near Ruthian. The Flying Dutchman retired seventh in hits. In his low scoring era, Honus still ranks 16th in both runs and RBI's! Honus' speed led to his nickname, The Flying Dutchman. He was fast. His 722 pilfers are topped by only eight base stealers and his 252 three baggers rank third all time. Honus legged out 640 two baggers, bettered by only seven men. In the field, The Flying Dutchman also was outstanding! From 1912-15 he led all NL shortstops in fielding % four consecutive seasons! In 1908 Honus had an unbelievable season! The Pennsylvania native finished second both in runs and homers. Other than those two categories, The Flying Dutchman was first in hits, doubles, triples, RBI's, batting average, total bases, on base percentage, slugging percentage and stolen bases! That is total dominance! In his honor an 18 foot statue was erected outside Forbes Field in 1955. When Three Rivers Stadium was opened in 1970, Honus' statue was transferred to the new site.

LINEUP

CA	Darren *Dutch* Daulton

has risen from a backup to the National League's All-Star catcher! From 1992-94 he has been Mr. Clutch. In both 1992 and 1993 Dutch drove in over 100 runs. In 1994 he had accumulated 56 ribbies in just 69 games, but a serious injury ended his promising season.

1B	Keith *Mex* Hernandez

was the complete player. A five time All-Star, he hit over .300 six seasons. Mex led the Cards in the 1982 Fall Classic. His eight RBI's paced their attack. Six campaigns Keith had 90+ RBI's. Mex was also known for his glove. He topped the National League in fielding % twice.

2B	Otto *Dutch* Knabe

played most of his career for Connie Mack. Dutch was a solid fielder, leading American League keystoners twice in assists and once in putouts. Offensively, 1911 was his best year. Dutch worked 94 bases on balls and scored a career high 99 tallies for Philadelphia.

SS	Herman *Germany* Long

was a versatile player. Germany proved his speed by swiping 534 bags during his career to rank 26th. Germany proved his strength by leading the NL in home runs in 1900. Germany proved his glove by leading the league in DP's three times and putouts and fielding % twice each.

3B	Fred *Dutch* Hartman

played the hot corner at the turn of the century. He was a regular four of his six seasons and batted over .300 three of those six campaigns. Dutch could really scoot. He stole as many as 31 bases in one year and twice finishing among the league leaders in triples.

OF	Bobby *Staten Island Scot* Thomson

was an outstanding player for 15 years. He poled 20 or more yard shots eight seasons, reaching the cheap seats on 264 occasions to rank 92nd all time. From 1949-53 The Royal Express averaged 26+ dingers and 101+ RBI's! He led all National Leaguers in triples in 1952.

OF	Emil *Irish* Meusel

was an 11 year star. During his nine summers as a starter Irish batted over .300 six times. Four consecutive seasons (1922-25) he drove in over 100 runs, leading the NL in RBI's in 1923. Irish finished fourth twice (one tie) and second once in homers. In 1922 he ranked second in 3B's.

OF	Stanley *Frenchy* Bordagaray

was a regular only four of his 11 seasons. He played twice for Brooklyn, in addition to "suiting up" for four other teams. Frenchy was renown as a pinch hitter. In 1938 he went 20/43 (.465) pinch hitting (fourth best). The eighth player to reach 50 career pinch-hits was Frenchy.

P	*Parisian* Bob Caruthers

was awesome! In his seven full seasons (1885-91) he won 209 games, twice reaching the 40 win level. Parisian Bob led the American Association in winning % three times, wins two times and ERA and shutouts once each. His .282 career batting average is seventh best for hurlers!

P	Walter *Dutch* Ruether

hurled balls and strikes for 11 seasons, including two short stints. During his nine full years Dutch won in double figures eight times. He went 21-12 in 1922 and 18-7 in 1925, but his best campaign was 1919. Dutch posted a 19-6 record and won game #1 of the World Series.

P	Hubert *Dutch* Leonard

was a talented lefty. He twirled 11 summers, eight as a regular. All eight years Dutch won in double figures, six times winning 14 games or more. His 33 career shutouts place him in a tie for 85th place. In 1914 Dutch had his best season, going 19-5 with seven shutouts!

RES	Al *The Mad Hungarian* Hrabosky

in the 1970's terrified batters when he ran out from the pen. In 1974 Al went 8-1 in 65 appearances. The Mad Hungarian was named Fireman of the Year in 1975. His record was 13-3, 1.66 ERA and 22 saves (shared league lead). Al ranks tied for 29th in relief wins.

RES	Harry *Golden Greek* Agganis

was a famous college football player who chose baseball instead as his pro sport. The Golden Greek had a solid rookie year, stroking eleven home runs. Hitting .313 during his second season, he became ill, then tragically died of an embolism at the young age of 26.

RES	Emil *Dutch* Leonard

was a great right-handed knuckleballer. He hurled for 20 seasons, his last four as a stopper. Before he hung 'em up at age 44, Dutch had 12 summers winning ten or more games. In 1939 he posted his best record, going 20-8 (tie for third in wins) for the sixth place Senators.

RES	Johnny *Dutch Master* Vander Meer

won ten consecutive games in 1938. From 1941-43 he won 16, 18 and 15 contests and earned three consecutive NL strikeout crowns. The hard throwing lefty posted 29 shutouts and five summers racked up 15 or more victories for the Cincinnati Redlegs.

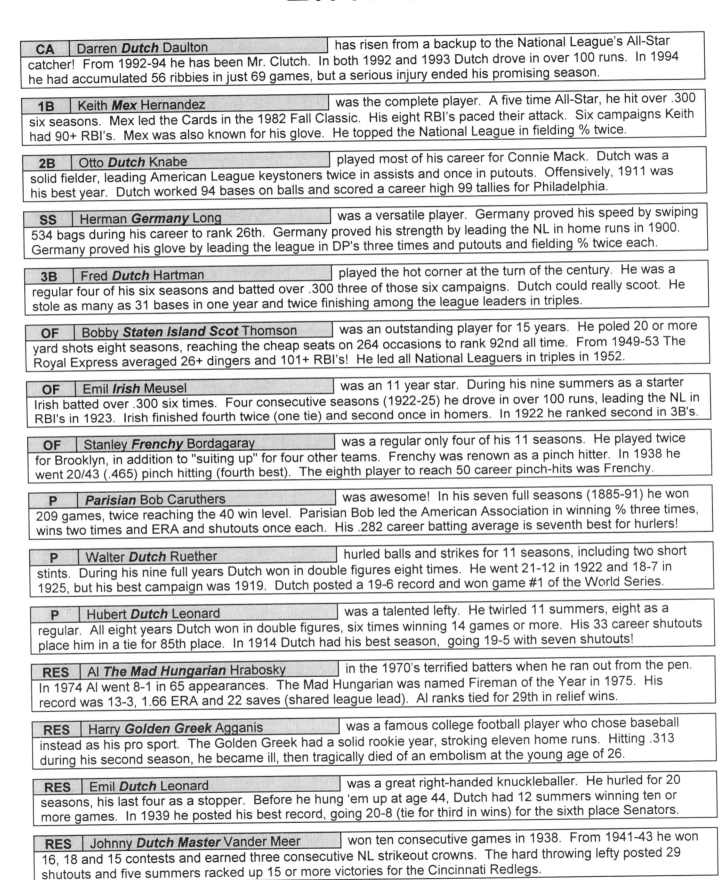

L to R: Bobby *Staten Island Scot* Thomson, Al *The Mad Hungarian* Hrabosky, Honus *Flying Dutchman* Wagner, Darren *Dutch* Daulton, Emil *Irish* Meusel

It'sa FACT

Stanley **Frenchy** Bordagaray: He played washboard for the Gas House Mudcat Band!

Joe **Germany** Schultz: Like father, like son! His son Dode, Joe Jr., went 43/160 as a pinch hitter. Dad, Germany, was 46/170 as a pinch hitter.

Bobby **Staten Island Scot** Thomson: He will always be remembered for his game #3 ninth inning playoff winning home run off hard luck Ralph Branca. His dinger has been called "The Shot Heard Around The World." In game #1 of the 1951 playoff Ralph Branca gave up a two run shot to lose it. The Staten Island Scot also hit that homer!!!

Charlie **Dutch** Bold: From his nickname one would never guess he was born in Kariskrona, Sweden.

Herman **Germany** Schaefer: In one of baseball's zanier events, after stealing second base and not drawing a throw to hopefully score a runner from third base, he returned (stole) to first base! The next pitch Germany re-stole second base, drew the throw and the runner on third made it home safely!

Clyde **Dutch the Clutch** Vollmer: On May 31st 1942 he hit the first Major League pitch thrown to him for a home run! Due to World War II and trips to the minors, he did not connect again in the Majors until 1947! Dutch the Clutch poled 22 yard shots in 1951, his best power season.

Omar **Turk** Lown: He served three years in the infantry during World War II. Turk was wounded in the Battle of the Bulge.

Claude **Frenchy** Raymond: During his career he was called in from the pen 442 times, saving 83 ball games. Twice, in 1966 (tie) and 1970, Frenchy finished fourth in saves.

Johnny **Big Serb** Miljus: His best season, 1927, he went 8-3 with a 1.90 ERA. As a spot starter Big Serb fired two shutouts in his six starts. He gave up no home runs the entire season (75 2/3 innings)!

Edward **Dutch** Zwilling: He played two summers in the short lived Federal League and was a hitting star. In the 1914 and 1915 seasons Dutch finished fourth and second in doubles, first and second in home runs, third (tie) and first in RBI's and second and fifth in total bases!

Hubert **Dutch** Leonard: He started two World Series games during his career. Dutch got the call Game #3 in 1915 and bested Old Pete Alexander 2-1 with a three hitter. In Game #4 of the 1916 Fall Classic Dutch tossed a five hit two run effort for the win.

Juan **Dominican Dandy** Marichal: His amazing control and unhittable stuff allowed him to walk only 1.82 hitters per nine innings (the third best in the last 35 years) and to fan nearly six batters per game. The Dominican Dandy painted 52 whitewashes, 18th all time. From 1963-69, except for his injury shortened 1967 season, Juan whiffed 248, 206, 240, 222, 218 and 205 players and walked only 61, 52, 46, 36, 46 and 54 hitters! The Dominican Dandy's six year composite strikeout to walk ratio was an outstanding 4.54 to one!

Parisian Bob Caruthers: In 1887 he played in 71% of his team's games. Parisian Bob finished fourth in homers, fifth in batting average, third in on base % and tied for second in slugging % that season! He was also 29-9 as a pitcher and led the American Association in winning %!

John **Swede** Hollison: Although his career was short lived, (just lasted one game), Swede lived a long time, going past his 99th birthday.

Walter **Dutch** Ruether: In the 1919 World Series he went 4/6 with a double, two triples and four RBI's. His only appearance in the 1925 World Series was as a pinch hitter! He ranks tied for 26th all time for pitchers' batting ave.

Emil **Irish** Meusel: For two consecutive World Series he was the hitting hero. In the 1921 Fall Classic Irish pounded ten hits and had a Series leading seven RBI's. The next fall Irish drove in seven of his Giants 18 runs in their five game win.

Dick **Turk** Farrell: His career was unusual in the path it took. Turk was originally a fireman, relieving 258 times and compiling a 37-30 record. Called on to start, he won in double figures four of the next five campaigns, three times being named to the NL All-Star team. His last four years Turk went back to the pen, answering 156 calls and going 17-16.

Charlie **Irish** Fox: Although his playing career was brief, Irish did manage for seven seasons in the Majors. He piloted the San Francisco Giants to the NL Western Division title in 1971.

Dolf **Pride of Havana** Luque: He was the first great Latin player in Major League baseball. During his 20 seasons the little right-hander (5'7") baffled batters, finally calling it a career at age 44. 1923 was his greatest summer. The Pride of Havana won 27 games to lead all NL hurlers. He also finished first in winning %, shutouts and ERA, and placed second in strikeouts, complete games and innings!

Emil **Dutch** Levsen: In 1926 he won 16 games for the Tribe. They amounted to 76% of Dutch's career wins.

116

TRIVIA*

1) He was the 1965 NL Rookie of the Year.

2) This spitballer threw two career no-hitters (August 30th, 1916 and June 3rd, 1918). In the second gem, a fellow southpaw hurler substituted for an injured outfielder and crushed a first inning homer (we now know this sub as Babe).

3) Hammerin' Hank Aaron is the first player in the baseball encyclopedia, he is the last.

4) His .688 winning % is the third highest all time.

5) In 1965 he posted ten shutouts. Only nine times since 1900 has a hurler painted more whitewashes.

6) As a 43 year old youngster, this Cuban pitched 4 1/3 innings of two hit shutout relief to win the clinching game of the 1933 World Series.

7) After five seasons as a part-time player for the Minnesota Twins, he came back to be their skipper for 3 1/2 summers.

8) He combined with Wes Parker, Mousey Wills and Junior Gilliam to form an all switch hitting infield for the Dodgers.

9) As a rookie, in 1944, he led the Cardinals during the Fall Classic in batting average, hits (tie) and RBI's (tie). (Hint: he was also known as The Antelope, because of his speed)

10) He was from Cairo, Illinois, which led to his nickname. (Hint: he is also on the Real Pirates for his other moniker, Long John, because he was tall and thin)

11) He was the stopper for the pennant winning 1959 "Go-Go" White Sox. He led all AL hurlers that season in saves.

12) He holds the record for the single season lowest ERA. In 224 2/3 frames he allowed only 24 earned runs (0.96 ERA)!

13) He pitched a no-hitter in the first night game ever played at Ebbets Field June 15th, 1938. (Hint: on June 11th, 1938 he no-hit the Boston Bees)

14) A designated runner, he scored 47 runs and stole 44 bags. You cannot tell it from his hits and at bats. (Hint: his nickname betrays his speed)

15) He and his brother Long Bob had statistically nearly identical outstanding careers. They met three consecutive seasons in the World Series. (Hint: his brother was a member of Murderers' Row)

16) In 1991 he was involved in a serious car accident along with teammate Lenny Nails Dykstra.

17) He co-won the 1979 NL MVP. He led the league in runs, doubles, batting average and on base %.

18) In his last game in the Majors (Game #6 1947 World Series), this "countryman" robbed Joltin' Joe DiMaggio and saved the game.

19) From 1963-69 he won over 20 games in six of the seasons!

20) He retired with the best fielding % of any pitcher. (Hint: think pyramids)

21) Three times during his career he stole consecutively second, third and home. Only Ty Cobb has done it more times.

22) This mad reliever was known for his fierce stare and Fu Manchu mustache.

23) He led the Senior Circuit in RBI's in 1992.

24) This announcer later became President of the United States.

25) From 1978-88 this slick fielder won 11 consecutive Gold Gloves.

* BORDERING INSANE answers found on page 238

ROSTER

CATCHERS:	Yr	Hits	AB's	Ave
Darren *Dutch* Daulton	11	700	2881	.243
Art *Dutch* Wilson	14	536	2056	.261
Charlie *Swede* Silvera	10	136	482	.282
Otto *Dutch* Denning	2	76	343	.222
Henry *Dutch* Dotterer	5	74	299	.247
Charles *Greek* George	5	53	299	.177
Charlie *Irish* Fox	1	3	7	.429
Bill *Dutch* Fehring	1	0	1	.000

1ST BASEMEN:	Yr	Hits	AB's	Ave
Keith *Mex* Hernandez	17	2182	7370	.296
Fredrick *Dutch* Schliebner	1	141	520	.271
Harry *Golden Greek* Agganis	2	135	517	.261
Heinz *Dutch* Becker	4	94	358	.263
Charlie *Dutch* Bold	1	0	1	.000

2ND BASEMEN:	Yr	Hits	AB's	Ave
Otto *Dutch* Knabe	11	1103	4469	.247
Herman *Germany* Schaefer	15	972	3784	.257
Emil *Dutch* Verban	7	793	2911	.272
Jim *Frenchy* Lefebvre	8	756	3014	.251
Lambert *Dutch* Meyer	6	262	994	.264
Ollie *Polish Falcon* Bejma	4	222	906	.245
Frank *Guido* Quilici	5	146	682	.214
Adolf *Dutch* Jordon	2	108	519	.208
Al *Dutch* Bergman	1	3	14	.214
George *Dutch* Distel	1	3	17	.176
Erling *Swede* Larsen	1	0	1	.000
Elbert *Scottie* Slayback	1	0	8	.000

SHORTSTOPS:	Yr	Hits	AB's	Ave
Honus *Flying Dutchman* Wagner	21	3415	10430	.327
Herman *Germany* Long	16	2127	7674	.277
Alex *Golden Greek* Grammas	10	512	2073	.247
Dave *Filipino* Altizer	6	433	1734	.250
Charles *Swede* Risberg	4	394	1619	.243
Roy *Irish* Corhan	2	90	426	.211
Herb *Dutch* Welch	1	11	38	.289
Elmer *Dutch* Weingartner	1	9	39	.231
Albin *Swede* Carlstrom	1	1	6	.167
Bertram *Dutch* Lerchen	1	0	15	.000

3RD BASEMEN:	Yr	Hits	AB's	Ave
Fred *Dutch* Hartman	6	622	2236	.278
William *Jap* Barbeau	4	160	712	.225
William *Scotty* Ingerton	1	130	521	.250
Harry *Dutchman* Fritz	3	96	423	.227
Herman *Dutch* Bronkie	7	87	360	.242
Art *Dutch* Kores	1	47	201	.234
William *Dutch* Ussat	2	3	17	.176

OUTFIELDERS:	Yr	Hits	AB's	Ave
Bobby *Staten Island Scot* Thomson	15	1705	6305	.270
Emil *Irish* Meusel	11	1521	4900	.310

OUTFIELDERS: (Cont.)	Yr	Hits	AB's	Ave
Stanley *Frenchy* Bordagaray	11	745	2632	.283
Joe *Germany* Schultz	11	558	1959	.285
Clyde *Dutch the Clutch* Vollmer	10	508	2021	.251
Edward *Dutch* Zwilling	4	364	1280	.284
Lou *The Mad Russian* Novikoff	5	305	1081	.282
Lou *The Nervous Greek* Skizas	4	196	725	.270
George *Turk* Alusik	5	167	652	.256
Al *The Little Italian* Gionfriddo	4	154	580	.266
Jim *Dutch* Bolger	7	140	612	.229
Olaf *Swede* Henriksen	7	131	487	.269
Frank *Frenchy* Genins	3	116	514	.226
Clarence *Dutch* Hoffman	1	87	337	.258
Arthur *Dutch* Meier	1	70	273	.256
Bernard *Frenchy* Uhalt	1	40	165	.242
Henry *Irish* McIlveen	3	38	177	.215
Franklin *Dutch* Wetzel	2	34	140	.243
Larry *Irish* Miggins	2	22	97	.227
Fredrick *Dutch* Scheeren	2	9	34	.265
Allan *Panamanian Express* Lewis	6	6	29	.207
Albert *Dutch* Mele	1	2	14	.143
John *Dutch* Rudolph	2	1	4	.250
Hal *Dutch* Bamberger	1	1	12	.083

PINCH HITTERS:	Yr	Hits	AB's	Ave
Ed *Irish* Conwell	1	0	1	.000
Harry *Dutch* Schirick .	1	0	0	.000

PITCHERS:	Yr	Won	Lost	ERA
Bert *Dutchman* Blyleven	22	287	250	3.31
Juan *Dominican Dandy* Marichal	16	243	142	2.89
Parisian Bob Caruthers	9	218	99	2.83
Dolf *Pride of Havana* Luque	20	193	179	3.24
Emil *Dutch* Leonard	20	191	181	3.25
Hubert *Dutch* Leonard	11	139	112	2.76
Walter *Dutch* Ruether	11	137	95	3.50
Johnny *Dutch Master* Vander Meer	13	119	121	3.44
Dick *Turk* Farrell	14	106	111	3.45
Don *The Sphinx* Mossi	12	101	80	3.43
John *Egyptian* Healy	8	76	136	3.84
Al *The Mad Hungarian* Hrabosky	13	64	35	3.10
Omar *Turk* Lown	11	55	61	4.12
Claude *Frenchy* Raymond	12	46	53	3.66
Russ *Dutch* Kemmerer	9	43	59	4.46
Eric *Swatting Swede* Erickson	7	34	57	3.85
Frank *Dutch* Hiller	7	30	32	4.42
Johnny *Big Serb* Miljus	7	29	26	3.92
Frank *Dutch* Henry	8	27	43	4.39
Andy *Swede* Hansen	9	23	30	4.22
Emil *Dutch* Levsen	6	21	26	4.17
Frank *Dutch* Ulrich	3	19	27	3.48
Lloyd *Dutch* Dietz	4	14	16	3.87
Art *Swede* Delaney	3	13	22	4.26
Earl *Irish* Harrist	5	12	28	4.34
Robert *Dutch* McCall	1	4	13	4.82

ROSTER

PITCHERS: (Cont.)	Yr	Won	Lost	ERA
Lou *Big Finn* Fiene	4	3	8	3.85
Johnny *Swede* Johnson	2	3	2	4.20
Thomas *Irish* Higgins	2	3	4	4.48
Sterling *Dutch* Stryker	2	3	8	6.57
Bert *Dutch* Brenner	1	1	0	2.77
Charles *Dutch* Lieber	2	1	2	4.01
Elmer *Swede* Burkart	4	1	1	4.93
Julius *Frenchy* Fournier	1	1	3	5.40
William *Dutch* Herriage	1	1	13	6.64
Allen *Dutch* Romberger	1	1	1	11.49
John *Swede* Hollison	1	0	0	2.25
William *Dutch* Hinrichs	1	0	1	2.57
Paul *Dutch* Gehrman	1	0	1	2.89
Leon *Swede* Carlson	1	0	0	3.65
Fred *Dutch* Lamline	2	0	0	4.29

PITCHERS: (Cont.)	Yr	Won	Lost	ERA
Steve *The Mad Russian* Rachunok	1	0	1	4.50
Vern *Turk* Curtis	3	0	1	5.70
Mort *Dutch* Flohr	1	0	2	5.87
Charles *Dutch* Schesler	1	0	0	7.28
Herman *Dutch* Kemner	1	0	0	7.63
George *Germany* Smith	1	0	0	9.00
Hugo *Dutch* Klaerner	1	0	2	10.90
Charles *Swedish Wonder* Hallstrom	1	0	1	11.00
Kurt *Dutch* Krieger	2	0	0	12.60

EXTRAS:
Ronald *Dutch* Reagan - Famous Baseball Announcer
Douglas W. *Scotty* Robb - Umpire
Lawrence *Dutch* Rennert - Umpire
DeWitt *Dutch* Bull - My Next Door Neighbor

TAG, YOU'RE IT!

Miss The Tag			Make			Go For The		
Duck The Tag			The Tag			Put	Tag	
Go			Tag	The		On		
For			Tag	Runner		The	Tag The	
The			The	Tag		Tag	Base	
Tag			Ball	Up		Apply The Tag		

YOU CAN ALSO **"AVOID THE TAG,"** BUT THAT WOULD BE NO FUN!

BASEBALL DOODLE SPOT:

LAS VEGAS

21

Team

When I think of Las Vegas, I not only think of gambling, but I also think of the glitter. It is a 24 hour a day town where national stars do extravagant shows, top singers perform their popular music and boxing champions defend their titles. Rolling craps, pulling handles or picking cards all become engrossing. Fortunes are literally won and lost before your very eyes.

The Las Vegas team has an interesting array of nicknames. Much like gambling, there is the 180 degree range from Hard Luck to Hotshot. Ballplayers stand in the spotlight of their performance, with their hits and misses, and wins and loses carefully tabulated. Going to the Nevada Mecca, you should bring plenty of Bucks, Stash and Jing. After converting your Skins to Chips, you are now ready. A true gambler should ignore the Neon Downtown, Boardwalk and Broadway, and get to the tables. Your game may be Blackjack. If you Flip good, you will have a Good Time and finish a Champ. If craps is your poison, warm those Bones, go for Little Joe and hope you are Lucky. If poker is your pleasure, try Stud. If you Bid well and finish Hi, you will have a Good Time. Forget the Bad News, its not a Jinx. Take a Tip, make a Pick, and walk away a Money Bags.

Although many players show Flash and Whoop-La, one twirler seemed to personify the squad. Shufflin' Phil Douglas (I love his first name) played nine seasons. Shuffled to five teams in his nine summers, Phil was down early, going 32-50 during his first four campaigns. Undaunted, he came back with five winning years. In 1921 Shufflin' Phil went 15-10, shared the NL lead in shutouts and was the pitching hero of the Fall Classic. After losing game #1 via a shutout, Phil came back to win both games #4 and #7. 1922 was Shufflin' Phil's last year. He went 11-4, and posted the league's lowest ERA! For his career, Phil broke even, going 94-93. If you go to Las Vegas and do that, you are a winner!

LINEUP

CA	Jimmie *Ace* Wilson

played 18 seasons, 14 summers as a regular. He also was a playing manager for the Phillies for five summers. Offensively, Ace batted over .300 five years. Defensively, he led all backstops in putouts (three), double plays (three) and assists (two) during his career.

1B	Billy *Bucks* Buckner

starred 22 seasons. He quietly put up Hall of Fame numbers. Eight times Billy Bucks hit over .300, leading the Senior Circuit in batting average in 1980. He had three 100+ RBI years, two 200+ hit years, and finished with 498 two baggers among his 2715 career hits.

2B	John *Bid* McPhee

belongs in Cooperstown. He starred 18 campaigns, 1882-99. Bid was fast, an exceptional fielder and a solid hitter. He stole 568 bags, 21st best. Bid led NL keystone players in DP's (ten), fielding % (eight), putouts (seven) and assists (six). Bid pounded 188 triples (11th all time).

SS	William *Bones* Ely

was Bid's contemporary, playing 14 summers. 1894 was Bones' best season at the plate. The 6'1" 155 lb. shortstop (source of his nickname) ate his Wheaties. He launched 12 homers, half his career total. In 1898 he led all National League shortstops in fielding %.

3B	Odell *Bad News* Hale

was a solid player, starting five seasons for the Tribe (1934-38). During that span, he hit over .300 three times and twice knocked in over 100 runs. Bad News laced 50 doubles, stretched 13 triples, scored 126 runs and hit .316 in 1936, his best campaign.

OF	*Neon* Deion Sanders

is an exceptional athlete. He has the potential for greatness Neon's speed on defense, strong arm and gas on the bases (second in swipes in 1994) all add to his hitting stroke. A two sport athlete, Neon has played in a World Series and he has also won a Super Bowl ring.

OF	James *Tip* O'Neill

was a pre-1900 star who played ten summers. Tip batted over .300 seven times, capturing consecutive batting crowns in 1887-88. He also finished second, third and fourth in batting three other summers. Tip's .326 career batting average is topped by only 31 players.

OF	Henry *Hy* Myers

was flanked by Otto Moonie Miller and by Hall of Famer Zack Buck Wheat. In 1919 Hy had his best summer, leading all National Leaguers in not only triples, but also in RBI's and slugging %. His 22 triples in 1920 again proved to be the mark to beat in the Senior Circuit.

P	*Black Jack* McDowell

is arguably the AL's best hurler in the 90's. Black Jack was runner-up for the Cy Young in 1992 and took the laurels in 1993. He has led the AL in complete games in 1991 and 1992 and in wins and shutouts in 1993. Black Jack won 20 games in 1992 and 22 games in 1993.

P	Charlie *Chinski* Root

won his first game at the age of 27. A starter for eight seasons, Chinski won 14+ games each year, with his 26 wins in 1927 leading the National League. His last eight campaigns Charlie both relieved and started. He retired at 42 with 201 wins, all as a Cubbie.

P	Ray *Wiz* Kremer

had a lifetime winning % that was 29th best. He played his entire ten year career for the Bucs. Wiz, a late bloomer, was a 30 year old rookie. Nevertheless, he reeled off seven straight winning seasons, averaging 18+ wins. Twice Wiz led the NL in both wins (shared) and ERA.

RES	Joe *Flash* Gordon

tore the Junior Circuit apart from 1938-50 (giving two plus of those years to his country). A nine time All-Star, Flash averaged 23 homers per year for his career. Four times he had 100+ RBI's and his 32 dingers is an American League second sacker record. Flash was the 1942 MVP.

RES	Al *Flip* Rosen

, after three cups of coffee, stuck in 1950. From 1950-55 he annihilated AL pitching. Flip led the American League twice in homers and RBI's and averaged 29+ long balls and 108 ribbies for those six summers. Injury forced him to prematurely hang 'em up after the 1956 season.

RES	Willis *Ace* Hudlin

hurled 15 of his 16 seasons for the Cleveland Indians. Nine campaigns Ace won in double figures, five times winning 15 or more games for the Tribe. Ace was also good with the stick. He slashing 180 career hits to help support "his cause".

RES	George *Win* Mercer

was an all-around player. He pitched nine seasons and often, between starts, played in the field. In 1897 Win won 20 games and hit .319. The following season he won 12 contests, played some at second , short and third, and batted .321. Win tragically died at age 28.

L to R: Al *Flip* Rosen, *Black Jack* McDowell, *Shufflin'* Phil Douglas, John *Bid* McPhee, Billy *Bucks* Buckner

It'sa FACT

Johnny **Whiz** Gee: This tall left-hander was really up there. Whiz stood 6'9"!

Carroll **Boardwalk** Brown: He combined his wins (17) with Gettysburg Eddie Plank (18 wins), Albert Chief Bender (21 wins) and Bullet Joe Bush (15 wins) to give the 1913 Philadelphia Athletics the World Championship.

Broadway Lyn Lary: His 107 RBI's in 1931 are still the record for a Yankee shortstop. Broadway led the AL once in swipes and twice finished second in pilfers. Only three players stole more bases in the 1930's than he did.

Black Jack Burdock: During his career he played four seasons in the National Association (1872-1875) and then 14 more summers in the National League. Playing in the 'bare handed era", Black Jack led all second sackers five times in fielding %.

Frankie **Fordham Flash** Frisch: He was the seventh hardest player to strike out, fanning only once every 33.7 at bats. He retired with the highest career batting average for a switch hitter (.316). His last five seasons Frankie was a playing manager, then he took the helm from the bench for 11 more campaigns.

Al **Flip** Rosen: In 1953 he was the AL MVP. Not only did Flip lead all third sackers in putouts and double plays, but he also led the league in homers, RBI's, runs and slugging %. His .336 batting average fell just one point shy of the batting title and a possible Triple Crown! Flip's four grand slams in 1951 tied the then Major League record.

James **Tip** O'Neill: In 1887 he was Mr. Everything in the American Association. Tip led the league in hits, runs, doubles, triples, homers, batting average, slugging and total bases! His .435 average is the second highest ever!

Neon Deion Sanders: He led the NL in triples in 1992 and Neon played in only 97 games!

John **Champ** Summers: On May 29th, 1979 this strong left-handed batter was traded to the Tigers. Champ responded to his new lair, and in 90 games he belted 20 homers, drove in 51 tallies and hit .313.

Ollie Lee **Downtown** Brown: In 1969 he swatted 20 dingers. Downtown went "downtown" 23 times in 1970. His little brother Oscar Lee Brown played five seasons for the Braves.

Good Time Bill Lamar: He played only 550 games in nine seasons. In 1925, his only full season, Good Time not only played in 138 games, but he also cracked 202 hits and batted .356!

John **Trick** McSorley: At 5'4" he, maybe, was the shortest Major Leaguer to ever play first base!

Art **The Great** Shires: He was a two sport performer. A "good hitter" in both his sports, The Great not only batted over .300 three of his four seasons, but he also boxed professionally one "off season"!

Stan **Stash** Lopata: In the mid 50's he emerged as the NL's premier catcher. A member of the All-Star team in both 1955 and 1956, Stash put up big numbers. He parked 22 in only 303 at bats in 1955 and he lost 32 balls and drove in 95 runs in 1956.

Joe **Flash** Gordon: He was a money player in the Fall Classic. As a rookie in the 1938 World Series, Flash led the Yankee's four game sweep. He hit .400, pounded two doubles, smashed one homer and drove in six tallies. In the 1941 World Series Joe reached base 14 times in 14 official at bats (seven hits and seven walks)! Flash led all batters in both average and hits, and he tied for the lead in homers, triples and RBI's! New York crushed Brooklyn four games to one.

John **Bid** McPhee: Ten seasons he scored over 100 runs. Nine years Bid legged out ten or more triples. He led the American Association in homers in 1886 and shared the lead for triples in 1887. Bid ranks first for keystone players in putouts and fourth in assists.

Ray **Wiz** Kremer: He was the pitching hero of the 1925 World Series. A 4-3 hard luck loser in game #3, Wiz rebounded with a six hitter to win game #6. Two days later, his four innings of clutch relief in game #7 earned him his second win and the Bucs the World Championship!

Joe **Old Hustler** Mathes: After his playing days he became a scout. Old Hustler did two remarkable things. One, he signed Albert Schoendienst after Red was overlooked at a tryout. Two, he recommended to Branch Rickey that Stan The Man Musial be converted from a pitcher to an outfielder.

Black Jack Burdock: He hit into one of baseball's most unusual plays. It was May 8th, 1878. The Boston Red Stockings (became the Braves) were playing the Providence Grays. Runners were on second and third and there were no outs. Black Jack hit a short fly to left and both runners took off. Paul Hines, the left fielder, charged in, caught the ball and proceeded to run and touch third base forcing one runner. He then fired to second to complete the triple play. Only after the game did the scorer realize that in fact Hines had made an unassisted triple play! Since runners must retrace their paths to their original bases and <u>neither</u> player had yet returned to third base, by touching third Paul had actually forced both runners and the throw to second was unnecessary!

Joe **Moon** Harris: He was a hard luck pitcher. On September 1st, 1906 Moon went 24 innings (to tie for the longest outing in AL history) and lost. He finished the season with a 2-21 record.

TRIVIA*

1) On April 30th, 1937 he pinch-hit his first Major League at bat and blackjacked a home run.

2) He won the NL ERA title three times. In 1971 he placed first with a microscopic 1.76 ERA.

3) This two sport performer won the MVP in the NFL.

4) Playing for the Braves in the 1992 World Series, he went 8/15, walked twice and swiped five bags.

5) When Donnie Baseball Mattingly drove in 145 runs in 1985, it tied his RBI total from 1953. No AL'er had driven in as many runs since 1953.

6) Handling the lumber in 1969, this pitcher walloped five homers in 79 at bats. (Hint: a guy like him only comes along ... very rarely)

7) He acquired his nickname, because he was so fast. (Hint: think what lightning does)

8) In a bizarre trade, he (a manager) was traded even up for Jimmy Dykes, another manager!

9) For players in the era from 1970 on, only Felix The Cat Millan and Glen Bruno Beckert went down on strikes less frequently. He failed to make contact only once every 20.7 at bats.

10) This "singer" is better known as the 1993 American League Cy Young winner.

11) He holds the Major League record of striking out ten consecutive batters.

12) He was the first Major Leaguer to wear glasses while playing. (Hint: he did not make a "big deal" about it)

13) He and his older brother Faye played part-time in the 50's and 60's. He gained his nickname for his two game winning pinch homers for the hapless 1962 Mets.

14) "Using his head", a line drive bounced off this third baseman's skull to his shortstop. The base runners were also stunned, and the shortstop turned a triple play (I guess you could say the batter bounced into a triple play)!

15) He was the NL MVP in 1931. He earned his nickname from his college football days.

16) On October 11th, 1992 he suited up for both a pro baseball and a pro football game.

17) Pressed into service when Ernie The Schnozz Lombardi was limited to three at bats in the 1940 Fall Classic, this 40 year old back-up caught six games, batted .353 and stole the Series' only base. (Hint: think golf)

18) Amazingly, he gave up only nine home runs in his 1598 1/3 inning career. In three consecutive seasons (1904-06), going nearly 800 innings, he never surrendered even one round tripper!

19) A converted outfielder, he played first base over 1500 games and set a Major League record of 184 assists in one season (1985). He ranks second in assists per game, placed in a tie for sixth overall in career assists and retired with a lofty .992 fielding %.

20) As a rookie (1950) he thumped 37 homers. That was the standard until 1987, when Mark McGuire found the seats 49 times.

21) This second sacker's home run in game #6 of the 1948 World Series led the Tribe to their last World Championship.

22) In the 1932 World Series Babe Ruth supposedly "called his shot" and hit the next pitch for a homer off this pitcher. (Hint: he has a "Polish" nickname)

23) Although they shared the same nickname, one went undefeated and the other never won, during their respective careers. (Hint: peek at the roster)

24) After spending 12 years with the Athletics, he came back to haunt them. He combined with Fransisco Barrios to no-hit his former mates July 28th, 1976. It was his last win!

25) Only three pitchers fanned more batters during their career. He whiffed over 200 batters nine consecutive seasons and during that span he won five strikeout crowns! Voted the NL Rookie of the Year in 1967, he also won the Cy Young award in 1969, 1973 and 1975. Now you know how he earned his nickname.

* DICEY PICKS answers found on page 238

ROSTER

CATCHERS:	Yr	Hits	AB's	Ave
Jimmie *Ace* Wilson	18	1358	4778	.284
Stan *Stash* Lopata	13	661	2601	.254
Broadway Aleck Smith	9	252	955	.264
Hiram *Hi* Ebright	1	15	59	.254
John *Stud* Bancker	1	11	72	.153
George *Miracle Man* Stallings	3	2	20	.100
John *Pick* Quinn	1	0	2	.000
Homer *Divvy* Davidson	1	0	4	.000

1ST BASEMEN:	Yr	Hits	AB's	Ave
Billy *Bucks* Buckner	22	2715	9397	.289
Steve *Bones* Balboni	11	714	3120	.229
William *Mox* McQuery	5	429	1581	.271
George *Juice* Latham	4	317	1277	.248
Art *The Great* Shires	4	287	986	.291
Marvelous Marv Throneberry	7	281	1186	.237
Allen *Ace* Elliott	2	44	182	.242
John *Trick* McSorley	3	23	94	.245
Leon *Biddy* Dolan	1	23	103	.223
Al *Broadway* Flair	1	6	30	.200
Hyland *Hy* Gunning	1	1	9	.111

2ND BASEMEN:	Yr	Hits	AB's	Ave
Frankie *Fordham Flash* Frisch	19	2880	9112	.316
John *Bid* McPhee	18	2250	8291	.271
Joe *Flash* Gordon	11	1530	5707	.268
Black Jack Burdock	14	944	3873	.244
Eddie *Hotshot* Mayo	9	759	3013	.252
George *Stud* Myatt	7	381	1345	.283
Johnny *Mr. Chips* Hudson	7	283	1169	.242
Walter *Chip* Hale	4	107	373	.287
Asa *Ace* Stewart	1	88	365	.241
George *Flash* Fallon	4	61	282	.216
Little Joe Wood	1	53	164	.323
Joe *Old Hustler* Mathes	3	27	99	.273
Jim *Bad News* Galloway	1	10	54	.185
Tom *Chip* Coulter	1	6	19	.316

SHORTSTOPS:	Yr	Hits	AB's	Ave
William *Bones* Ely	14	1331	5159	.258
Broadway Lyn Lary	12	1239	4603	.269
Henry *Lucky* Kessler	2	66	268	.246
Broadway Bill Schuster	5	61	261	.234
James *Champ* Osteen	4	60	304	.197
Clarence *Ace* Parker	2	37	207	.179
Emery *Moxie* Hengle	2	24	133	.180
Ray *Flash* Flaskamper	1	21	95	.221
Dino *Dynamo* Chiozza	1	0	0	.000

3RD BASEMEN:	Yr	Hits	AB's	Ave
Odell *Bad News* Hale	10	1071	3701	.289
Al *Flip* Rosen	10	1063	3725	.285
Fritz *Flash* Maisel	6	510	2111	.242
Little Joe Yeager	10	467	1853	.252

3RD BASEMEN: (Cont.)	Yr	Hits	AB's	Ave
Emil *Ace* Batch	4	315	1253	.251
Jack *Lucky* Lohrke	7	221	914	.242
Urbane *Pick* Pickering	2	205	798	.257
Derby Day Bill Clymer	1	0	11	.000

OUTFIELDERS:	Yr	Hits	AB's	Ave
Lloyd *Shaker* Moseby	12	1494	5815	.257
James *Tip* O'Neill	10	1386	4255	.326
Henry *Hy* Myers	14	1380	4910	.281
Ollie *Downtown* Brown	13	964	3642	.265
Good Time Bill Lamar	9	633	2040	.310
Wonderful Willie Smith	9	410	1654	.248
John *Champ* Summers	11	350	1371	.255
Neon Deion Sanders	6	326	1240	.263
Frank *Flash* Gilhooley	9	289	1068	.271
George *Bingo* Binks	5	277	1093	.253
Maurice *Flash* Archdeacon	3	128	384	.333
Lloyd *Low* Christenbury	4	113	414	.273
George *Lucky* Whiteman	3	70	258	.271
Steve *Flip* Filipowicz	3	40	179	.223
Fred *Penny* Bailey	3	23	124	.185
Charlie *Decker* Newman	1	14	73	.192
Fred *Tip* O'Neill	1	8	26	.308
John *Skins* Jones	2	2	10	.200
Arthur *Hi* Ladd	2	1	5	.200
Edward *Moxie* Divis	1	1	6	.167
Hiram *Hi* Church	1	1	9	.111
Frank *Flip* Lafferty	2	1	20	.050
Archibald *Moonlight* Graham	1	0	0	.000

PINCH HITTERS:	Yr	Hits	AB's	Ave
Stan *Stash* Goletz	1	3	5	.600
Merton *Moxie* Meixell	1	1	2	.500
Johnny *Tip* Tobin	1	0	1	.000

PITCHERS:	Yr	Won	Lost	ERA
Tom *Terrific* Seaver	20	311	205	2.86
Will *Whoop-La* White	10	229	166	2.28
Jerry *Rolls* Reuss	22	220	191	3.64
Charlie *Chinski* Root	17	201	160	3.59
Willis *Ace* Hudlin	16	158	156	4.41
Ray *Wiz* Kremer	10	143	85	3.76
George *Win* Mercer	9	131	164	3.99
Tricky Dick Donovan	15	122	99	3.67
Elroy *Sam Spade* Face	16	104	95	3.48
Twilight Ed Killian	8	102	78	2.38
Shufflin' Phil Douglas	9	94	93	2.80
Black Jack McDowell	7	91	59	3.50
Art *Hard Luck* Houtteman	12	87	91	4.14
Johnny *Blue Moon* Odom	13	84	85	3.70
Fidgety Phil Collins	8	80	85	4.66
Black Jack Wilson	9	68	72	4.59
Phenomenal John Smith	8	57	78	3.87
Fred *Lucky* Glade	6	52	68	2.62

ROSTER

PITCHERS: (Cont.)	Yr	Won	Lost	ERA
Bob *Mr. Chips* Chipman	12	51	46	3.72
Carroll *Boardwalk* Brown	5	38	40	3.47
Little Joe Yeager	6	33	49	3.74
Herman *Hi* Bell	8	32	34	3.69
Charlie *Broadway* Wagner	6	32	23	3.91
Jim *Little Joe* Edwards	6	26	37	4.37
Little Joe Presko	6	25	37	4.61
Russell *Jing* Johnson	5	24	37	3.35
Fred *Tricky* Nichols	5	24	44	3.37
Ed *The Only* Nolan	5	23	52	2.98
Winford *Win* Kellum	3	20	16	3.19
John *Stud* Stuart	4	20	18	4.76
Noble *Win* Ballou	4	19	20	5.11
Frank *Great Gabbo* Gabler	4	16	23	5.26
Norm *Bones* Baker	3	14	15	3.42
Fred *Moonlight Ace* Fussell	4	14	17	4.86
Winfield *Win* Noyes	3	11	15	3.76
Hal *Ace* Elliott	4	11	24	6.95
Phil *Flip* Paine	6	10	1	3.36
Henry *Hi* Jasper	4	10	12	3.48
Dick *Bones* Tomanek	5	10	10	4.95
Walter *Shakes* Huntzinger	4	7	8	3.60
Johnny *Whiz* Gee	6	7	12	4.41

PITCHERS: (Cont.)	Yr	Won	Lost	ERA
Charles *Spades* Wood	2	6	9	5.61
Walter *Lucky* Nagle	1	5	3	3.48
James *Hi* West	2	5	6	3.87
Robert *Riverboat* Smith	2	4	4	4.75
Joe *Moon* Harris	3	3	30	3.35
Mark *Moxie* Manuel	2	3	4	3.58
Wilhelmus *Win* Remmerswaal	2	3	1	5.50
Wonderful Willie Smith	3	2	4	3.10
Les *Lucky* Howe	2	2	0	3.38
Stan *Betz* Klopp	1	1	2	4.27
Robert *Chip* Lang	2	1	3	4.36
Joe *Win* Batchelder	3	1	0	5.66
Frank *Chip* Bennett	2	0	1	2.70
William *Lucky* Wright	1	0	4	3.21
Charlie *Victory* Faust	1	0	0	4.50
Jennings *Jinx* Poindexter	2	0	2	4.83
Ken *Broadway* Jones	2	0	1	5.40
Jim *Bones* Blackburn	2	0	2	5.50
Tom *Money Bags* Qualters	3	0	0	5.64
Jesse *Broadway* Jones	1	0	0	9.00
Joe *Ace* Stewart	1	0	0	9.64
Robert *Ace* Williams	2	0	0	16.00
Shady Bill Leith	1	0	0	18.00

LINGO

Blackjack One: Hit a homer

Chance: Opportunity to field the ball

Mr. Chips: Hits in the clutch

Money in the Bank: The team can count on him to come through in a big game

Nickel Curve: A slider

Deuce: Curve ball

Double: A two base hit

Decked: A batter goes to the dirt to avoid being hit by a pitch

Blue Dart: A hard hit ball

Money Player: One who performs his best when the game is on the line

Magic Number: The number of wins needed by a team to eliminate another club when fighting for the pennant

Under the Lights: Night game

Ace: The team's best pitcher

Payoff Pitch: The count is full and the next pitch will decide what happens

Foul Tip: What my brother-in-law gave me at the track

Free Pass: A walk

Quick Pitch: A pitcher fires the ball when the batter is not ready

Die on Third: A runner on third never scores as the third out is made

Die on Second: See above and think

Die on First: See page 649

Stud: Big strong hitter or pitcher

In the Hole: Down on the count (more strikes than balls) or a ball hit between two infielders

Bid for a Hit: Well hit ball, but it's caught for an out

Player Dealt: Player traded to another team

Stacked the Lineup: Start all players who could do good (example: all right-handed batters against a lefty)

Hit or Stay: Hit is any base hit. Stay is when a runner chooses not to advance

Cover: Guard a base

Bones: Thin guy

LAST NAME

22

Team

Last names are always a big source of nicknames. If you were born Blazovich, you would have first hand knowledge! At various times I have been called Blaz, Blazie, Blaze, Blazer and sometimes things not OK to say in mixed company! On my son Ben's ball team last summer, there was Kokes (Johnny Kokaisel), Harge (Mark Hargis), Swany (Jay Swansson) and Murph (Tom Murphy). So too in the Majors, many players acquire a last name nickname. Rather than introduce this obvious group, two rather than one player will be highlighted.

If you are from Minnesota, you love Kirby Puck Puckett. I can hear the stadium announcer say, "Krrrrrr…Beee… Puckett!!!," and the fans go crazy. He steps to the plate, sets his feet, pulls his sleeves up a little at the top of his shoulders, makes the sign of the cross, swings his bat quickly toward the pitcher twice and is ready to jump on the first delivery. A slap hitting, opposite fielding chopping, quick running and frequent bunting rookie came up in 1984. Of his 165 safeties, only 12 went for two bases and five went for three. His total included no homers, but did include 25 bunts (I hate bunts!). Tony Oliva, the Twins' great hitter and then hitting instructor, worked with Puck. To this day Kirby works extra hard and takes daily rips off of the tee to hone his swing. From the raw rookie emerged a powerful, free swinging, all fields slugger (who never bunts) that we know today. From 1985-94 Puck has averaged 197 hits, 92 runs, 36 doubles, 18 homers, 95 RBI's and a .320 batting average. Puck has led the AL in hits four times (one tie), including three consecutive years (1987-89). Kirby reached the 2000 hit plateau in just ten plus seasons! In the field he has won six Gold Gloves. Puck has the amazing ability to catch and release the ball in literally a heartbeat. His strong accurate arm has made toast of dozens of runners. But what makes Puck so good is he plays big when it counts.   He is the catalyst and the team both relies and rallies because of him. Whether it is Kirby going 9/21 with two doubles and one homer in the 1991 ALCS or Puck stroking a combined ten base knocks in two consecutive games (Major League record) against the Brew Crew in 1987, he does it with humility and his smile! Who could forget Kirby, somehow, while racing full speed, going up and over the wall to pluck a "sure homer" in inning #3 of game #6 of the 1991 World Series. Then eight innings later Puck "lost" a circle change to win the game in 11 innings and rescue the Series. Or it could be his quiet counciling (while in the outfield) of Petey Munoz and Shane Mack during a pitching change. Regardless, Puck is the heart, the soul and the spirit of the Twins!

How do you spell spectacular in only five letters? Try S.. P.. A.. H.. N..! From 1947-63 Spahny totally dominated the National League. Warren won ERA titles in three separate decades (1947, 1953 and 1961)! He is the winningest southpaw in Major League history with 363 wins (fifth all time). Spahny also ranks sixth in shutouts, eighth in innings and 15th in strikeouts. He was a workhorse. In the above 17 year span Warren won 20 or more games 13 seasons, and led or shared the league lead in victories eight times. Spahny ranks 19th in complete games, but the 18 players ahead of him all pitched in earlier times when one pitcher was expected to go "all the way." From 1947-63 Spahny only once ranked as low as fourth in complete games. He led the NL seven consecutive years (1957-63) (one tie) in route going performances! In 1963 Warren was 42! Spahny finished as low as third in innings pitched four times, otherwise he ranked either first or second every campaign from 1947-59! He also led all NL hurlers four straight seasons (1949-52) in strikeouts (one tie). Had Warren not lost three years to World War II, he may have finished second only to Cy Young in victories and certainly could have won over 400 games! In case you are wondering, did he hit like a pitcher? No! For 17 years in a row he reached the cheap seats at least once and at the age of 40 he went deep four times in just 94 at bats! He retired with 35 round trippers in his 363 (same as his wins trivia buffs!) career hits.

LINEUP

CA	Ted *Simba* Simmons

wore the tools of ignorance for 21 seasons, handling catching duties for 1771 games, eighth most all time. Simba was a powerful switch hitter who, when he hung 'em up, ranked in the top 50 in doubles and RBI's, and was just five tators short of the top 100.

1B	Carl *Yaz* Yastrzemski

arrived from Notre Dame an opposite field singles hitter and he became a pull hitting power hitter. After a weak 1981 season (age 41), Yaz worked hard and came back to have two more respectable years, a true example of his dedication. Yaz now has his plaque in Cooperstown.

2B	Bill *Maz* Mazeroski

played all his 17 seasons for the Pirates. Known mostly for his fielding and ability to "turn two" (Maz ranks first all time in keystone DP's), he became a national hero when he won the 1960 Fall Classic with a dramatic home run in the bottom of the ninth of game #7.

SS	Tommy *Corky* Corcoran

starred 18 summers straddling the turn of the century. Corky swiped 387 bags, ranking him 64th, and he legged out 155 triples, placing Corky 47th! His 2252 career hits nearly reaches the top 100. In the field Corky topped all shortstops in fielding % four times. How about the Hall?

3B	Fred *Lindy* Lindstrom

is in the Hall of Fame. During his 13 year career he batted over .300 seven times. In 1930 Lindy rocked pitchers at a .379 clip! His 231 hits in 1928 were league leading and his .358 average was third in the NL. Lindy was a contract hitter, fanning only once every 20 at bats.

OF	Frank *Robby* Robinson

was one of baseball's all time sluggers. His upright stance, left elbow over the plate batting style, was his trademark. Only three players hit more HR's in their career and Robby ranks sixth in extra base hits, tenth in runs, 14th in RBI's, 18th in slugging % and tied for 20th in doubles!

OF	Kirby *Puck* Puckett

is the complete ballplayer. He not only hits for power and average, but he is also an excellent fielder and runner. Puck is better yet as a team leader! He is an unselfish player and a tremendous community booster. Puck is the "franchise player" for the Minnesota Twins.

OF	Tom *Bruno* Brunansky

for eight consecutive seasons (1982-89) crushed 20 or more round trippers. Still active, Bruno already is in the top 100 in career home runs! His outstanding outfield play and strong accurate arm are just as valuable to his present team as is his booming bat.

P	Christy *Matty* Mathewson

was one of the "five immortals" inducted into the Hall of Fame. Starting in 1901, he won 20 or more games (over 30 four times) 13 of the next 14 seasons. Matty ranks, for his career, tied for third in wins, third in shutouts, fifth in ERA and seventh in winning %.

P	Warren *Spahny* Spahn

was possibly the greatest and certainly the most consistent lefty ever to lace 'em up. Reaching the Majors in 1942 (15 2/3 innings), he served in World War II and gave three years to his country. At the age of 25 (1946) Spahny chalked up his first victory, then added 362 more!

P	Jerry *Koos* Koosman

hails from Appleton Minnesota. He quietly amassed 222 wins (tie 60th) and whiffed 2556 batters (17th). Koos fashioned 33 whitewashes and two 20 win seasons during his career. In 1978 he posted a 3-15 record with the Mets, then went 20-13 in 1979 with the Twins!

RES	Don *Newk* Newcombe

was dominant. Debuting May 20th, 1949 at the age of 22, Newk still made the 1949 All-Star team, won 17 games and tied for the NL lead in shutouts! He followed with 19 and 20 wins, then he gave 2 1/2 years to his country. Back home, Newk won 20 and 27 games in 1955-56.

RES	Dan *Quiz* Quisenberry

came in when the game was on the line. 674 trips from the pen yielded 244 saves and 56 wins for this hard to hit submariner. From 1980-85 he topped all American League stoppers in saves five times (one tie) and led the Junior Circuit three times in appearances.

RES	Alan *Tram* Trammell

has played his entire career for the Tigers. He has combined for 18 seasons with his keystone mate Sweet Lou Whitaker to plug Detroit's middle. Tram put it all together in 1987. He batted .343 (third) with 205 hits (third) and finished runner-up for the American League MVP.

RES	Darryl *Straw Man* Strawberry

reached the Majors at the age of 21. His first nine summers he clouted 280 homers and averaged 92 RBI's per campaign. The Straw Man's high leg kick, left-handed stroke propels homers with apparent ease. Recently, troubles have come. Let's pray that Darryl overcomes them.

L to R: Frank *Robby* Robinson, Carl *Yaz* Yastrzemski, Warren *Spahny* Spahn, Kirby *Puck* Puckett, Don *Newk* Newcombe

It'sa FACT

Joe **Pepi** Pepitone: On May 23rd, 1962 he pounded two homers in one inning. Pepi also takes credit for being the first Major Leaguer to use a hand held hair dryer to maintain his locks.

Clyde **Mac** McCullough: He poled three tape jobs in one game in the 1942 season (that entire year he hit only five)

Emilio **Pal** Palmero: His career in the Majors started in 1915 and his last appearance was in 1928. Pal's career, during that stretch, exemplifies the determination and dedication of so many players,. In those 14 summers he had five short stays in the Big Show. Pal, in total, started 17 games, logging a 3-12 record. He relieved 24 times, posting a 3-3 result. Only two seasons did Pal even win a contest, yet he spent his life trying! We cannot forget him.

Kevin **Tap** Tapani: He never played high school baseball. His school had no team!

Carl **Oisk** Erskine: 1953 and 1954 were his two best seasons. In 1953 he was first in winning %, second in K's and tied for third in wins while going 20-6. The next summer Oisk placed third in K's and innings and tied for fourth in wins with 18 victories. In post season play he was awesome. In game #5 of the 1952 Fall Classic Oisk retired the last 19 batters he faced and won in 11 innings! After being knocked out of game #`1 of the 1953 World Series, Oisk came back to win game #4. He fanned 14 batters and set the then single game strikeout record.

Don **Newk** Newcombe: He is very active in baseball helping players fight alcoholism. Newk stands big! Great Job!

Mike **Pags** Pagliarulo: In 1986 and 1987 he launched 28 and 32 round trippers.

Ray **Jabbo** Jablonski: As a 26 year old rookie in 1953 he knocked in 112 runs. In 1954 Jabbo plated 104 tallies.

Johnny **Blanch** Blanchard: He could take the ball deep. In 1961 Blanch powdered 21 cheap seaters in just 243 at bats. For his career he had a 5.62 homer %.

Austin **Mac** McHenry: In 1920 he tied for fourth in home runs. The following season Mac placed fifth in doubles, fourth in homers, tied for third in RBI's and finished third in batting in the NL. The next year he was diagnosed with a brain tumor and Mac died at the young age of 27.

Frank **Robby** Robinson: In 1956 he was the unanimous choice for NL Rookie of the Year. On June 26th, 1970 Robby hit two grand slams in one game. He belted the only homer to go totally out of Memorial Stadium. It traveled an estimated 541 feet! In just 92 World Series at bats Robby slugged eight HR's, tying him for seventh. His fourth inning homer in game #4 of the 1966 Fall Classic won the contest 1-0 and gave the O's the World Championship!

Ted **Simba** Simmons: Eight seasons he swatted over .300, crushing 20+ homers six times and three summers driving in 100+ runs. In 1975 Simba batted .332 to finish runner-up for the NL Silver Bat.

Carl **Yaz** Yastrzemski: He was named to the All-Star team 18 times! Yaz' career was phenomenal! He ranks second in games played. Only two players batted more often than Yaz. His career hit total (3419) and double total (646) place him sixth and seventh among the immortals. Yaz is seventh in total bases, tenth in RBI's and 20th in homers. Throw in three Silver Bats and you have a record that pales most of "The Greats!"

Fred **Lindy** Lindstrom: At the age of 18 years, ten months and 13 days he became the youngest player to play in the World Series. In game #5 Lindy pounded four hits off The Big Train, Walter Johnson, and for the Series he went 10/30!

Dave **Rags** Righetti: Beginning his career as a starter, he had immediate success. Rags led the AL in ERA his first season and he tossed a no-no July 24, 1983 during his third summer. Since then Rags shifted to the pen and became an outstanding short man. For eight consecutive years (1984-91) Rags posted a minimum of 24 saves, including a league leading 46 saves in 1986.

Rick **Aggie** Aguilera: He is just a nice guy! I had the pleasure of fishing with him in the Don Shelby Bass Tournament-- it was fun Rick! But, he means business on the mound. From 1990-94 Aggie racked up 172 saves for TK and the Twins. Originally a starter with the Mets, Aggie will tell you he and Doc Goodin competed for dingers. Rick powdered three in just 138 at bats!

Kent **Teke** Tekulve: He was a tall, thin, bespectacled right-hander and I can still see him in the "old" black stove top Pirate hat with the yellow circle going around it. This unlikely appearing ballplayer was fantastic! He retired first all time in relief appearances, finished sixth in relief innings and placed tied for seventh in relief wins. From 1976-88, except for the strike shortened '81 season, Teke was called in over 60 times each summer. Four seasons he appeared in over one half of his teams games! At the young age of 40 Teke went 6-4 with 90 relief stints!

Dave **Winny** Winfield: Missing all of the 1989 season due to back surgery, he came back at age 39 to resume his great career. Winny topped 3000 hits and 500 doubles in 1993. His two run double in game #6 of the 1992 World Series brought Toronto the Championship. Winny's commitment outside of baseball through his foundation has benefited thousands of youngsters. His community dedication gives baseball its good name! Keep it up Dave!

Ed **Mack** McKean: He was a pre-1900 slugger who starred 13 summers. From 1893-96 he drove in over 100 runs each season. Mack's 158 career three baggers rank him 44th.

Bob **Lem** Lemon: From 1948-56 he was devastating. Lem won 186 games (20 or more seven times). He led the AL several times in complete games (five, three ties), innings (four) and wins (three, two ties) during that span. For his career Lem blasted 37 yard shots! Four seasons he launched five or more homers!

128

TRIVIA*

1) In 1967 he was the last Major Leaguer to win the Triple Crown.

2) When this all-around athlete graduated from college, he was drafted to play pro baseball, pro basketball and pro football!

3) During his career he led all NL second sackers nine times in assists, eight times in DP's, five times in putouts and three times in fielding %. He was so fast at "turning two," he was often called "No Touch".

4) The street beyond the left field fence at the old Metropolitan Stadium (now the site of the Mall of America) was named after this Minnesota Twins' Hall of Fame slugger. (Hint: this humble slugger was also known as The Bashful Basher of Power Alley)

5) In the 1905 World Series he tossed three consecutive shutouts in just six days! He fanned 18 and only walked one, while putting up 27 goose eggs!

6) He won the MVP in the NL (1961) and the AL (1966). He is the only player to win it in both leagues!

7) In game #5 of the 1920 World Series, he completed the third ever unassisted triple play! (Hint: he played second base for the Tribe)

8) From 1953-55 this NL strongboy and former All-American gridironer from the University of Indiana crushed 40, 49 (league leading) and 47 tape jobs.

9) He was the 1991 AL Rookie of the Year. His deke of Lonnie Smith in game #7 of the 1991 World Series allowed the Twins to win it all in ten innings.

10) He led the AL four consecutive years (1965-68) in thefts and six times during his career. His 649 lifetime steals rank him 14th all time!

11) This pitcher could really hit. In 1955 he went 42/117 (.359), stroking nine doubles, one triple, seven homers and driving in 23 runs. His batting average was 21 points higher than the league leader! (Hint: his other nickname was Tiger)

12) He was not known to throw lollipops, just heat. This 6'7" lefty in 1977 went 20-5 and won the NL ERA title.

13) These two players each reached 3000 hits, but neither star had a .300 career batting average.

14) In 1966 he won the second last Triple Crown.

15) Originally he came up as a second baseman. He was an All-Star at third base, left field and first base during his Hall of Fame career. (Hint: his number three matches his career home run % ranking, topped only by Babe Ruth and Ralph Kiner)

16) This scrappy, hard nosed, ala Pete Rose ballplayer in 1994 challenged Earl King of Doublin' Webb's Major League record 67 two baggers in one season. He had stretched 45 doubles, but lost his last 49 games and any chance for the record, due to the ill timed 1994 baseball strike.

17) This righty threw pellets for the Bosox in the late 50's through the 60's. On May 12th, 1961 he struck out 17 batters in one game and on August 1st, 1962 he no-hit the White Sox 1-0. (Hint: think of a dance)

18) His 40 home runs, as a catcher, in 1953, are the Major League record.

19) In his first World Series game (game #1, 1982) he had five base hits, a record in World Series play. In the 1993 Fall Classic he was voted the MVP. (Hint: his 39 game hitting streak in 1987 is the seventh longest of all time)

20) From July of 1993 to April of 1994 he won 15 straight ball games! He also was able to help his own cause. On May 2nd, 1994 he cracked two hits... in one inning!

21) He won six home run crowns (four outright) during his great career.

22) He painted two masterpieces in his career. On June 19th, 1952 he no-hit the Cubs and on May 12th, 1956 he no-hit the Giants.

23) I left no stone unturned to discover he has the fewest career wins for a post 1900 hurler who pitched two no-hitters.

24) He led the 1969 "Miracle Mets" to the World Championship by winning game #2 and the clinching game #5. For his career he was undefeated in post season play (3-0 in World Series and 1-0 in League Championship).

25) He was a one man wreaking crew in the five game 1987 ALCS. He went 7/17 with four doubles, two homers and nine RBI's.

* SIRY SURNAMES answers found on page 238

ROSTER

CATCHERS:	Yr	Hits	AB's	Ave
Ted *Simba* Simmons	21	2472	8680	.285
Wilbert *Uncle Robbie* Robinson	17	1388	5075	.273
Roy *Campy* Campanella	10	1161	4205	.276
Clyde *Mac* McCullough	15	785	3121	.252
George *Mitty* Mitterwald	11	623	2645	.236
Jim *Pag* Pagliaroni	11	622	2465	.252
Carl *Swats* Sawatski	11	351	1449	.242
Clyde *Sukey* Sukeforth	10	326	1237	.264
Johnny *Blanch* Blanchard	8	285	1193	.239
Jerry *Zimmy* Zimmerman	8	203	994	.204
John *Big Pete* Peters	4	80	302	.265
Ferrell *Andy* Anderson	2	61	234	.261
Ralph *Wig* Weigel	3	54	235	.230
Clarence *Yam* Yaryan	2	45	173	.260
Art *Watty* Watson	2	32	95	.337
Jim *Mack* McDonnell	3	20	95	.211
Jim *Cuddy* Cudworth	1	17	116	.147
Howard *Mape* Maple	1	10	44	.244
Al *Schelley* Schellhase	2	7	49	.143
Jack *Red* Redmond	1	6	34	.176

1ST BASEMEN:	Yr	Hits	AB's	Ave
Carl *Yaz* Yastrzemski	23	3419	11988	.285
Billy *Bucks* Buckner	22	2715	9397	.289
Ted *Big Klu* Kluszewski	15	1766	5929	.298
Kent *Herbie* Hrbek	14	1749	6192	.282
Charlie *Commy* Comiskey	13	1531	5796	.264
Ed *Krane* Kranepool	18	1418	5436	.261
Joe *Pepi* Pepitone	12	1315	5097	.258
Dick *Big Stu* Stuart	10	1055	3997	.264
Harry *Swats* Swacina	4	304	1189	.256
Charles *Luke* Lutenberg	1	48	250	.192
Guy *King Tut* Tutwiler	2	16	79	.203
Tom *Ham* Hamilton	2	13	66	.197
Karl *Koley* Kolseth	1	6	23	.261

2ND BASEMEN:	Yr	Hits	AB's	Ave
Bill *Maz* Mazeroski	17	2016	7755	.260
Tony *Cooch* Cuccinello	15	1729	6184	.280
Miller *Hug* Huggins	13	1474	5558	.265
Juan *Sammy* Samuel	12	1440	5543	.260
Bill *Wamby* Wambsganss	13	1359	5237	.259
Frank *Pot* LaPorte	11	1185	4212	.281
Burgess *Whitey* Whitehead	9	883	3316	.266
Tim *Tuff* Teufel	11	789	3112	.254
Ed *Batty* Abbaticchio	9	772	3044	.254
Fresco *Tommy* Thompson	9	762	2560	.298
John *Bernie* Berardino	11	755	3038	.249
Chuck *Knobby* Knoblauch	4	643	2212	.291
Wayne *Twig* Terwilliger	9	501	2091	.240
Frank *Parky* Parkinson	4	335	1311	.256

2ND BASEMEN: (Cont.)	Yr	Hits	AB's	Ave
Steve *Lombo* Lombardozzi	6	294	1264	.233
Claude *Davey* Davidson	2	18	88	.205

SHORTSTOPS:	Yr	Hits	AB's	Ave
Alan *Tram* Trammell	18	2260	7872	.287
Tommy *Corky* Corcoran	18	2252	8804	.256
Bert *Campy* Campaneris	19	2249	8684	.259
Ed *Mack* McKean	13	2083	6890	.302
Bobby *Wine-O* Wine	12	682	3172	.215
William *Woody* Woodward	9	517	2187	.236
George *Maggie* Magoon	5	439	1834	.239
Jimmy *Little Mac* Macullar	6	319	1541	.207
Harvey *Little Mac* McClellan	6	257	1162	.221
Orlando *Marty* Martinez	7	230	945	.243
Al *Bronk* Brancato	4	199	930	.214
Fred *Chappie* Chapman	3	36	187	.193
Ray *Flash* Flaskamper	1	21	95	.221
Walter *Tap* Tappan	1	8	39	.205
Walt *Tommy* Thomas	1	2	13	.154

3RD BASEMEN:	Yr	Hits	AB's	Ave
Paul *Molly* Molitor	17	2647	8610	.307
Harmon *The Killer* Killebrew	22	2086	8147	.256
Fred *Lindy* Lindstrom	13	1747	5611	.311
Steve *Boo* Buechele	10	1023	4136	.247
Mike *Pags* Pagliarulo	10	886	3660	.242
Ray *Jabbo* Jablonski	8	687	2562	.268
Mike *Cubbie* Cubbage	8	503	1951	.258
Pete *Casty* Castiglione	8	462	1670	.255
Bill *Suds* Sudakis	8	362	1548	.234
Billy *Gabby* Grabarkewitz	7	274	1161	.236
Urbane *Pick* Pickering	2	205	798	.257
Fred *Tommy* Thomas	3	193	859	.225
Leo *Tommy* Thomas	2	57	269	.212
Jim *Woody* Woods	3	17	82	.207
William *Pat* Patterson	1	14	35	.400

OUTFIELDERS:	Yr	Hits	AB's	Ave
Dave *Winny* Winfield	21	3088	10888	.284
Frank *Robby* Robinson	21	2943	10006	.294
Kirby *Puck* Puckett	11	2135	6706	.318
Tom *Bruno* Brunansky	14	1543	6289	.246
Kevin *Big Mac* McReynolds	12	1439	5423	.265
Darryl *Straw Man* Strawberry	12	1232	4756	.259
Leon *Daddy Wags* Wagner	12	1202	4426	.272
Ival *Goodie* Goodman	10	1104	3928	.281
Lee *Maz* Mazzilli	14	1068	4124	.259
Steve *Hendu* Henderson	12	976	3484	.280
Jim *Wolfie* Wohlford	15	793	3049	.260
Austin *Mac* McHenry	5	592	1959	.302
Sam *Jet* Jethroe	4	460	1763	.261

ROSTER

OUTFIELDERS: (Cont.)	Yr	Hits	AB's	Ave
Estel **Crabby** Crabtree	8	396	1408	.281
Rupert **Tommy** Thompson	6	294	1107	.266
George **Andy** Anderson	3	289	1007	.287
George **Bingo** Binks	5	277	1093	.253
Fred **Ossie** Osborn	3	228	907	.251
Bob **Molly** Molinaro	8	212	803	.264
Tommy **Obie** O'Brien	5	198	714	.277
Albert **Ty** Tyson	3	197	704	.280
Wid **Matty** Matthews	3	188	663	.284
George **Pooch** Puccinelli	4	172	607	.283
Karl **Ole** Olson	6	160	681	.235
Frank **Dole** Doljack	6	151	561	.269
Fred **Ike** Eichrodt	4	121	516	.234
Clint **Connie** Conatser	2	102	376	.271
Roy **Woody** Wood	3	77	333	.231
Harry **Army** Armbruster	1	63	265	.238
Steve **Flip** Filipowicz	3	40	179	.223
Bill **Gunner** McGunnigle	3	35	202	.173
Felipe **Monty** Montemayor	2	26	150	.173
Ralph **Matty** Mattis	1	21	85	.247
Johnnie **Ty Ty** Tyler	2	17	53	.321
Harry **Welch** Welchonce	1	14	66	.212
Luther **Bonnie** Bonin	2	14	77	.182
Mel **Primo** Preibisch	2	9	44	.205
Verdo **Ellie** Elmore	1	3	17	.176
Hal **Mac** McClure	1	2	6	.333
Lamar **Jake** Jacobs	2	2	10	.200
Frank **Jelly** Jelinich	1	1	8	.125

PITCHERS:	Yr	Won	Lost	ERA
Christy **Matty** Mathewson	17	373	188	2.13
Warren **Spahny** Spahn	21	363	245	3.09
Jerry **Koos** Koosman	19	222	209	3.36
Bob **Lem** Lemon	13	207	128	3.23
John **The Candy Man** Candelaria	19	177	122	3.33
Don **Newk** Newcombe	10	149	90	3.56
Harry **Gunboat** Gumbert	15	143	113	3.68
Bret **Sabes** Saberhagen	11	134	94	3.19
Rich **Goose** Gossage	22	124	107	3.01
Carl **Oisk** Erskine	12	122	78	4.00
Alphonse **Tommy** Thomas	12	117	128	4.11
Bill **Monbo** Monbouquette	11	114	112	3.68
Fred **Hutch** Hutchinson	10	95	71	3.73
Kent **Teke** Tekulve	16	94	90	2.85
Tom **Bugs** Burgmeier	17	79	55	3.23
Dave **Rags** Righetti	15	79	77	3.44
Mark **Porch** Portugal	10	73	57	3.78
Kevin **Tap** Tapani	7	69	52	3.94
Leon **Caddy** Cadore	10	68	72	3.14
Warren **Hack** Hacker	12	62	89	4.21
Dan **Quiz** Quisenberry	12	56	46	2.76

PITCHERS: (Cont.)	Yr	Won	Lost	ERA
Rick **Aggie** Aguilera	10	56	53	3.29
Bill **Stoney** Stoneman	8	54	85	4.08
Bob **Mr. Chips** Chipman	12	51	46	3.72
Bill **Goobe**r Zuber	11	43	42	4.28
Don **Stan the Man Unusual** Stanhouse	10	38	54	3.84
Claude **Weeping Willie** Willoughby	7	38	58	5.84
Norwood **Gibby** Gibson	4	34	32	2.93
Dan **Sac-Man** Plesac	9	33	41	3.48
Leo **Kiki** Kiely	7	26	27	3.37
Frank **Pap** Papish	6	26	29	3.58
Sig **Jack** Jakucki	3	25	22	3.79
Gordon **Maltzy** Maltzberger	4	20	13	2.70
Leon **Shag** Chagnon	6	19	16	4.51
Steve **Mingo** Mingori	10	18	33	3.03
Billy **Muff** Muffett	6	16	23	4.33
Frank **Great Gabbo** Gabler	4	16	23	5.26
Bob **Chick** Chakales	7	15	25	4.54
Kent **Pete** Peterson	8	13	38	4.95
Max **Ski** Fiske	1	12	12	3.14
Wynn **Hawk** Hawkins	3	12	13	4.17
Bill **Gunner** McGunnigle	2	11	8	2.81
Ralph **Commy** Comstock	3	11	14	3.72
Jose **Acostica** Acosta	3	10	10	4.51
Art **Chic** Ceccarelli	5	9	18	5.05
Eddie **Matty** Matteson	2	8	5	2.36
Ambrose **Putty** Puttmann	4	8	9	3.58
Clyde **Foots** Barfoot	3	8	10	4.10
Arthur **Ole** Olsen	2	8	7	4.95
John **Gabe** Gabler	3	7	12	4.39
Foster **Eddie** Edwards	5	6	9	4.76
Emilio **Pal** Palmero	5	6	15	5.17
Jon **Warbler** Warden	1	4	1	3.62
Marv **Rotty** Rotblatt	3	4	3	4.82
Italo **Chilly** Chelini	3	4	4	5.83
Emil **Hill Billy** Bildilli	5	4	8	5.84
Ralph **Brick** Brickner	1	3	1	2.18
Lou **Big Finn** Fiene	4	3	8	3.85
Danny **Ozzie** Osborn	1	3	0	4.50
George **Barney** Barnicle	3	3	3	6.55
Johnny **Grod** Grodzicki	3	2	2	4.43
Pete **Gabe** Gebrian	1	2	3	4.48
Al **Pie** Piechota	2	2	5	5.66
Bob **Greenie** Greenwood	2	1	2	3.92
Cy **Slap** Slapnicka	2	1	6	4.30
Art **Hoss** Hoelskoetter	3	1	5	4.54
Paul **Stu** Stuffel	3	1	0	5.73
Ray **Luke** Lucas	5	1	1	5.79
Wayne **Ossie** Osborne	2	1	1	5.91
Les **Barney** Barnhart	2	1	1	6.75
Ray **Gordy** Gordinier	2	1	0	6.94
Chet **Nick** Nichols	6	1	8	7.19

Real MARINERS

23

Team

In 1977 an expansion team, the Seattle Mariners, embarked on their maiden season, playing in the American League west. It would be safe to say their voyage has been wavy, finally finishing above .500 in 1991, their 15th try. Over the years the club has had some players doing yeoman's work and then some. Gaylord Perry, in May of 1992, won his 300th game (great trivia question). Alvin Davis slugged 27 homers and drove in 116 runs on his way to being voted the American League 1984 Rookie of the Year. Mark Langston handcuffed batters, winning strikeout crowns in 1984, 1985 and 1987. In 1992 Edgar Martinez captured the batting championship. All their home games are played at the Kingdome. The stadium's 23 foot right field wall is called Walla Walla (named after a Southern Washington town). The U.S.S. Mariner shoots off its cannon after every Mariner yard shot. On the bizarre, Kong Kingman strikes again (see Real Twins). On April 11th, 1985 Big Bird hit a ball off of a roof support wire, turning a sure homer into a flyout.

The Real Mariners are no motley crew, but rather a shipshape outfit. The fleet not only has six Tugs, four Steamboats and two Steamers, but also has a Battleship, a Gunboat and a Submarine. The crew is heavy on leaders. There are eight Caps, seven Skips and three Admirals in charge of three Sailors, three Popeyes, and an Ancient Mariner. Manning their stations, the crew will catch Shad, Crab and Octopus, and will harpoon a Sea Lion, a Penguin and a Whale.

Even though there are six Hall of Famers on the Real Mariners, one player sails to the forefront, Joe The Yankee Clipper DiMaggio. A fast, smooth center fielder, he seemed to glide to fly balls. A Yankee his entire career, Joe became The Yankee Clipper. Although his accomplishments were many, Joltin' Joe is best remembered for "his streak", hitting safely in 56 consecutive games. In game 57, The Yankee Clipper was robbed twice to sink his streak. Joe then resumed the next day to hit safely for another 16 straight games! His streak could have been 73 games! Only nine times have players even topped 35 games. Second place, a tie between Wee Willie Keeler (1897) and Pete Charlie Hustle Rose (1978) is 44 games. The Yankee Clipper's streak has stood since 1941 and it quite likely will remain the standard another 50+ years.

LINEUP

CA	George *Foghorn* Miller

played 13 seasons at the end of the 19th century. During his career Foghorn played every position but pitcher. In 1894 he hit a career high .339 and he blasted eight homers (dead ball era). In 481 at bats that year, Foghorn fanned only nine times, less than once every 50 at bats!

1B	Adrian *Cap* Anson

was probably the best known and most dominant player manager of the 19th century. Cap starred 22 summers, 20 as a playing manager. He was always among the league leaders in both batting and fielding. Cap's final port was the dock on Lake Otsego at Cooperstown.

2B	Gene *Skip* Mauch

was a utility player for his nine playing seasons. Gene went on to manage 26 summers, the fourth longest time for helmsmen. Skip was voted the National League Manager of the Year three times in his career. His 1900+ wins place Skip among the greatest skippers ever.

SS	Marty *The Octopus* Marion

was the premier shortstop of the '40s'. He covered the infield, leading the National League 11 times in various fielding categories. The Octopus was also a leader. His value is best illustrated in 1944. Batting in the #8 hole and hitting just .267, he was still voted the National League MVP!

3B	*Captain* Eddie Mathews

was a feared left-handed batter. His 512 career home runs were only topped by 11 players. The Captain captured four RBI titles and two home run crowns. In his first 14 seasons, he hit no fewer than 23 yard shots each year. The Captain's 6.00 homer % ranks him 17th all time.

OF	Jesse *Crab* Burkett

was an unbelievable hitter. He hit over .400 two consecutive seasons (1895-96)! Crab won three batting crowns, slashed 182 triples (tie 15th), pounded 2850 hits (32nd), scored 1720 runs (17th) and batted .338 (16th) during his career. Jesse is now in the Hall.

OF	Fred *Cap* Clarke

was the complete player. He was a fast runner, a great fielder and an excellent hitter. Cap stole 506 sacks (tie 31st) and legged out 220 triples (sixth). Twice he led all fly chasers in fielding %. With his stick, Cap hit over .300 in 11 seasons. Cap hangs his hat in Cooperstown.

OF	Joe *The Yankee Clipper* DiMaggio

starred in 13 brilliant seasons (he gave three to his country, ages 28-30). Joltin' Joe hit over .300 eleven summers. A 13 time All-Star, he won three American League MVPs! The Yankee Clipper drove in over 100 runs nine seasons and scored 100+ runs eight campaigns.

P	Carl *Sub* Mays

was a right-handed sidearmer (submariner - hence the nickname). He won over 62% of his contests, only 38 pitchers did better. Five seasons Sub won 20 or more games. 1921 was his best summer. Logging a 27-9 record, Carl led the AL in wins (tie), winning % and games.

P	Harry *Gunboat* Gumbert

twirled for 15 campaigns. He was primarily a starter his first ten seasons, winning in double figures eight times. Gunboat then became a reliever. In 1947 he led all short men in wins. In 1948 Gunboat not only led all firemen again in wins, but he also led in games and saves.

P	Eldon *Submarine* Auker

starred ten summers in the Junior Circuit, reaching 13 or more wins eight times. Submarine had only two losing seasons. In 1935 he had his best year. He posted an excellent 18-7 record and Submarine topped all American League hurlers that summer in winning %.

RES	Frank *Tug* McGraw

coined "You've gotta believe." Tug more than pulled his weight during his career. The premier stopper of his time, Tug ranks 11th in both relief games and relief wins for his career. Three seasons Tug logged an ERA of 1.70 or less. Now that is relief!

RES	Tommy *Foghorn* Tucker

starred for 13 summers, averaging 145 hits per year. Foghorn led the National League in both hits and batting average in 1899! Four times he hit over .300. Foghorn scored 100+ runs in a season five times and twice he lead all National League first sackers in fielding %.

RES	Dan *Cap* McGann

sparkled for 12 seasons in the Major Leagues. Cap was outstanding both in the field and at the plate. Six seasons he led all Senior Circuit first sackers in fielding %. Four summers Cap hit over .300. In Game #3 of the 1905 Fall Classic he drove in four runs for the Giants.

RES	Bob *Steamer* Stanley

was a Red Sox his entire 13 year career. Used mostly in relief, his 85 relief wins place Steamer 13th all time. In 1963 Bob won eight times and saved 33 more. During the 1986 Fall Classic Steamer made five appearances and pitched 6 1/3 innings of scoreless relief!

L to R: *Captain* Eddie Mathews, Marty *The Octopus* Marion, Joe *The Yankee Clipper* DiMaggio, Carl *Sub* Mays, Adrian *Cap* Anson

It'sa FACT

<u>Fred *Cap* Clarke</u>: On June 30th, 1894, his first game, Cap had five hits, four singles and a double.

<u>Frank *Tug* McGraw</u>: He was asked what he did with his large raise, Tug answered, "90% I'll spend on good times, women and Irish whisky. The other 10% I'll probably waste." Asked why he loved his '54 Buick, Tug responded, "Its radio played old music." Yes, he was a left-hander. A nearly unhittable one. During post season play he showed his best. In the 1969 NLCS Tug allowed no runs in three innings, gaining a save. In the 1973 NLCS, Tug yielded no runs in five innings, earning a save. Again in the 1977 NLCS, Tug gave up no runs in three innings, posting a save. In the 1981 NL east division playoffs Tug threw shutout ball for four innings, collecting a win. In World Series play Tug also continued to perform. During the 1973 Fall Classic, Tug appeared in five games, ringing up a win and a save and fanning 14 in 13 2/3 innings! Leading the Phillies in 1980, Tug won game #5 and saved the final game (#6). Tug already had also saved game #1.

<u>Jesse *Crab* Burkett</u>: He played during the dead ball era. Crab's best home run season was 1901 when he clouted ten dingers, third best in the NL. On May 22nd and May 23rd, 1901 Crab hit consecutive game leadoff homers.

<u>Carl *Sub* Mays</u>: The Boston Red Sox were led by him to their last World Championship (1918). Sub won game #3 and game #6 (final). He won both games 2-1, allowing only seven and three hits.

<u>Eldon *Submarine* Auker</u>: A fine hitting pitcher, Sub hit .308 in 1936 and he slugged three round trippers in 1937.

<u>George *Showboat* Fisher</u>: He made the Big Show in 1930 as a 31 year old rookie (after two cups of coffee). In 92 games Showboat hit .374, driving in 61 runs.

<u>Adrian *Cap* Anson</u>: He had a lifetime batting average of .329. Five seasons he played in the National Association (league before the National League whose statistics are not recognized). Cap batted .359 for those five years. The "official" 22 years he played, he batted over .300 an amazing 19 summers, finally retiring at age 45! Eight seasons Cap led the league in RBI's! He also captured three slugging crowns and two batting titles. Cap was awesome!

<u>*Sailor* Bill Posedel</u>: In 1938 he made the Majors at age 31. Toiling for the seventh place Boston Braves in 1939, Sailor Bill went 15-13 with five shutouts. His 12 wins were hard earned in 1940, as the Braves again finished seventh. After serving his country, Barnacle Bill returned as a 39 year old reliever and went 2-0 in 1946.

<u>Flint *Shad* Rhem</u>: For twelve seasons he pitched in the Senior Circuit. In Shad's best year (1926), he tied for the league lead in wins. His 20-7 log helped carry the Cardinals to the pennant that summer.

<u>Joe *The Yankee Clipper* DiMaggio</u>: His career .579 slugging % is sixth best. The Yankee Clipper also averaged .89 RBI's per game, fourth all time.

TRIVIA*

1) He was the first baseball player to appear on the cover of a *Sports Illustrated*.

2) He hit 361 career home runs, nearly matching his 369 career strikeouts.

3) He acquired his nickname from his initials.

4) After his playing career he managed for 26 seasons, but he never reached the World Series.

5) He, like Ty Cobb, split his hands apart when batting (to have more bat control). He, also, is in the Hall of Fame.

6) He got mad at his teammate Joe Tinker over a small item and they did not speak for 33 years! (Hint: his nickname tips it off)

7) His other nickname was Dr. Strangeglove.

8) His season batting average of .372 was the highest achieved by a switch hitter.

9) While playing in the minors (the Pacific Coast League), he set the minor league record when he hit in 61 consecutive games.

10) He hit over .300 in each of his first 15 seasons.

11) He was the first ballplayer to wear sunglasses when playing on the ballfield.

12) This zany portsider used to slap his glove on his thigh after he struck a batter out.

13) Tall and gangly in appearance, he still managed to catch every ball hit his way. His looks led to his nickname.

14) Off the field he was mild mannered. On the diamond, this Hall of Famer lived up to his nickname.

15) His playing a harmonica, while riding on the team bus, caused a big incident.

* DEEP SIXERS answers found on page 238

ROSTER / LINGO

CATCHERS:	Yr	Hits	AB's	Ave
George *Foghorn* Miller	13	1380	5167	.267
George *Admiral* Schlei	8	455	1918	.237
Jim *Little Nemo* Stephens	6	286	1262	.227
Claude *Admiral* Berry	5	165	753	.219
Alfred *Skip* Jutze	6	141	656	.215
John *Tug* Arundel	4	45	260	.173
Clarence *Skipper* Roberts	2	29	138	.210
Hank *Popeye* Erickson	1	23	88	.261
John *Cap* Clark	1	19	74	.257
Fred *Whale* Walters	1	16	93	.172

1ST BASEMEN:	Yr	Hits	AB's	Ave
Adrian *Cap* Anson	22	2995	9101	.329
Steve *Popeye* Garvey	19	2599	8835	.294
Tommy *Foghorn* Tucker	13	1882	6479	.290
Dan *Cap* McGann	12	1482	5222	.284
Dick *The Ancient Mariner* Stuart	10	1055	3997	.264
Chris *Crab* Lindsay	2	200	828	.242
Philip *Skip* James	2	6	36	.167

2ND BASEMEN:	Yr	Hits	AB's	Ave
Johnny *Crab* Evers	18	1659	6137	.270
Al *Cod* Myers	8	788	3222	.245
Foghorn George Myatt	7	381	1345	.283
Gene *Skip* Mauch	9	176	737	.239

SHORTSTOPS:	Yr	Hits	AB's	Ave
Marty *The Octopus* Marion	13	1448	5506	.263
Phil *Supersub* Linz	7	322	1372	.235
Francis *Salty* Parker	1	7	25	.280

3RD BASEMEN:	Yr	Hits	AB's	Ave
Captain Eddie Mathews	17	2315	8537	.271
Ron *The Penguin* Cey	17	1868	7162	.261
Don *Popeye* Zimmer	12	773	3283	.235
Ed *Battleship* Gremminger	4	356	1420	.251
Joseph *Skippy* Roberge	3	112	508	.220
Bill *Cap* Narleski	2	95	358	.265
Foghorn Dick Van Zant	1	8	31	.258
Howard *Cap* Fahey	1	0	8	.000

OUTFIELDERS:	Yr	Hits	AB's	Ave
Jesse *Crab* Burkett	16	2850	8421	.338
Fred *Cap* Clarke	21	2672	8568	.312
Joe *The Yankee Clipper* DiMaggio	13	2214	6821	.325
Carl *Skoonj* Furillo	15	1910	6378	.299

OUTFIELDERS:(Cont.)	Yr	Hits	AB's	Ave
Harry *Nemo* Leibold	13	1109	4167	.266
John *Shad* Barry	10	1073	4014	.267
Lee *Captain Midnight* Walls	10	670	2558	.262
Algernon *Algie* McBride	5	464	1589	.292
Charles *Cap* Peterson	8	269	1170	.230
Walt *Seacap* Christensen	2	162	514	.315
George *Showboat* Fisher	4	114	340	.335
John *Tug* Thompson	2	21	102	.206
James *Steamer* Flanagan	1	7	25	.280
Lou *Skippy* Schiappacasse	1	0	5	.000
Les *Tug* Wilson	1	0	7	.000

PITCHERS:	Yr	Won	Lost	ERA
Carl *Sub* Mays	15	207	126	2.92
Harry *Gunboat* Gumbert	15	143	113	3.68
Eldon *Submarine* Auker	10	130	101	4.42
Bob *Steamer* Stanley	13	115	97	3.64
Flint *Shad* Rhem	12	105	97	4.20
Frank *Tug* McGraw	19	96	92	3.14
Roy *Popeye* Mahaffey	9	67	49	5.01
Claude *Skip* Lockwood	12	57	97	3.55
Charley *Sea Lion* Hall	9	54	47	3.09
Sailor Bill Posedel	5	41	43	4.56
Ralph *Sailor* Stroud	3	20	20	2.94
Allyn *Fish Hook* Stout	6	20	20	4.54
George *Foghorn* Bradley	1	9	10	2.49
Fay *Scow* Thomas	4	9	20	4.95
Lee *Skip* Pitlock	3	8	8	4.53
Rees *Steamboat* Williams	2	6	8	4.42
Clem *Steamboat* Dreisewerd	4	6	8	4.54
Charles *Dory* Dean	1	4	26	3.73
Robert *Riverboat* Smith	2	4	4	4.75
Les *Nemo* Munns	3	4	13	4.76
Minot *Cap* Crowell	2	2	11	5.27
Ed *Skipper* Donalds	1	1	0	4.50
Steamboat Bill Otey	3	1	5	5.01
John Paul *Admiral* Jones	2	1	0	6.06
Willard *Nemo* Gaines	1	0	0	0.00
Clay *Shad* Roe	1	0	1	0.00
Larry *Tug* Milton	1	0	0	2.25
Bill *Skip* Crouch	1	0	0	3.38
Clarence *Steamboat* Struss	1	0	1	6.43
Grier *Skipper* Friday	1	0	1	6.90
Sailor Joel Newkirk	2	0	1	7.27
Marsh *Cap* Williams	1	0	6	7.89

Around the Horn: Infielders throw from base to base
On Board: Player is on a base
A Catch: Position player fields a ball
Decked: Batter hits the dirt to miss being hit by a pitch

Portsider: Player who throws with his left arm
Bails Him Out: Reliever comes in to save a starter
Anchored: Player holds his fielding position
On Deck: Waiting to bat next

OCCUPATION

24

Team

In this day and age, the "average" salary for Major League ballplayers is over one million dollars! The Big League minimum (1995) is currently $109,000. Counting the per/player revenue from baseball cards and products (ex. hats), most players today, if their careers last long enough, are able to financially set themselves for life. In the past years it was different. Baseball income was often not enough to support players and their families 'year around'. After their ball career, ex-players would surely have to find another occupation. In the Twin Cities, Bob Allison (1959 AL Rookie of the Year) worked for a beverage company and Zoilo Versalles (1965 AL MVP) later toiled for the Bloomington school system.

On the Occupation Team, many nicknames originate from the player's prior military service, the teammate's current leadership qualities and the squad member's past or present off season employment. The "military ranks" include three Majors, seven Sarges, three Soldiers and a Bomber. Long on leaders, there are five Generals, four Colonels, a Chairman of the Board, a Peerless Leader, and a Boss. A versatile squad, there are ten Sheriffs, seven Farmers, a Milkman, a Shoemaker, a Union Man and a Miner. Add in the name tags Fireman, Junkman, Spaceman, Lawman, Moonman, Hac-Man, Hit Man and G-Man, and man what a team!

One player is very special. He earned his nickname because of his fast ball. Smokey Joe Wood had an amazing career. At the age of 23 he was the most dominant pitcher in the American League (1912). A fluke injury the following spring effectively ended Smokey Joe's promising pitching career. After three years of comebacks and two seasons gone from the Majors, he returned to the Big Leagues as an outfielder! Smokey Joe played five more seasons and batted .298. His pitching career was dashed, but Joe overcame the odds and continued to play the game he loved! Smokey Joe is an inspiration!

LINEUP

CA	Connie *The Tall Tactician* Mack	played as a catcher for 11 seasons before the turn of the century. After his playing days, Connie managed for 53 years and, in time, became a team owner. The Tall Tactician's squads won 3731 games under his guidance, 968 more contests than any other manager!

1B	Frank *The Peerless Leader* Chance	started his career in 1898. The last ten seasons of Frank's 17 ball playing years he was a playing manager, hence his nickname. From 1906-10 The Peerless Leader led the Chicago Cubs to the World Series four times and to the World Championship twice!

2B	Arthur *Circus Solly* Hofman	played 14 summers. Very versatile, he played at all the infield positions and also at times in the outfield. Circus Solly had his best season in 1910, leading the Chicago Cubs to the Fall Classic. That summer he batted .325 (third) and smashed 16 triples (tied third).

SS	Ozzie *The Wizard of Oz* Smith	was originally considered "all-field and no-hit", gaining his nickname because he caught balls humanly impossible to reach! Seven times he led all NL shortstops in fielding %! His first six seasons Ozzie batted only .235, but since (last 11 summers), he has hit .278!

3B	Gary *The G-Man* Gaetti	is starring currently for the Royals, playing next to another G-Man, Greg Gagne! Gary has gained religion and lost his mustache. The G-Man is both a leader on the field and at the plate. He still has both his great glove and his "shoulder to shoulder" home run swing.

OF	Gary *Sarge* Matthews	starred 16 summers. In the 1981 NL division playoff, Sarge went 8/20. His three homers, eight RBI's and 6/14 effort topped all players in the 1983 NLCS. His 1984 NLCS record included two dingers and five RBI's. Sarge had 192 hits, including 27 of his 234 career HR's, in 1979.

OF	Garry *Secretary of Defense* Maddox	chased flies for 15 summers. A career National Leaguer, he was a well respected gloveman. Garry earned his nickname while winning eight consecutive Gold Gloves (1975-82) The Secretary of Defense's best year at the plate was 1976. He batted .330 and finished third in the NL.

OF	Earle *The Kentucky Colonel* Combs	scored 113 or more runs eight consecutive years (1925-32). In 1927 he led the American League in both hits (231) and triples (23). The Kentucky Colonel hit .300 or better ten of his 12 seasons! A skull fracture abruptly shortened his Hall of Fame career.

P	Hoyt *Sarge* Wilhelm	had a late start in the Majors at age 28, but he still played 21 summers! The most games for a pitcher (1070), most innings as a reliever (1871) and most relief wins (124) are his records. He is the only twirler to capture ERA crowns in both leagues (1952 - NL, 1959 - AL).

P	Alvin *General* Crowder	was a star. Between 1928 and 1933 the General won 21, 17, 18, 18, 26 and 24 games. The last two seasons (1932-33), his win totals were league leading totals (1933 shared). The General recorded 15 straight victories in 1932, one win short of the American League record.

P	*Smokey* Joe Wood	at the age of 23 he was All World. He went 34-5 in 1912, leading the AL in wins, in shutouts (ten) and in complete games (35). Smokey Joe also finished second in ERA (1.91) and whiffs (258) that year. Joe then won three contests in the 1912 Fall Classic!

RES	Ray *Wiz* Kremer	pitched his entire career for the Pirates. He led the NL twice in wins (both ties), twice in ERA and once in shutouts (tie). In the 1925 Fall Classic, the Bucs trailed three games to one. Wiz won game #6, going the route. He then tossed four innings of clutch relief to win game #7!

RES	Dom *The Little Professor* DiMaggio	was the youngest and the fastest of the three DiMaggio brothers. In ten full seasons (and one with three at bats) he was a seven time American League All-Star. Dom twice led the Junior Circuit in runs scored and once each in triples (tie) and in stolen bases.

RES	Sal *The Barber* Maglie	was lured to play in Mexico after WW II, missing the 1946-49 seasons. During his first full season in the Majors, The Barber turned 33. For the next eight years he terrorized batters, winning over 65% (ninth) of his decisions. On September 25th, 1956 he trimmed the Phillies with a no-no!

MGR	Ralph *Major* Houk	earned his nickname in the military. He rose from private to major through battlefield commissions as a Marine in WW II. During his 20 years as a manager, the Major led his squads to 1619 wins, three American League pennants and two World Championships.

L to R: Hoyt *Sarge* Wilhelm, Connie *The Tall Tactician* Mack, *Smokey* Joe Wood, Gary *The G-Man* Gaetti, Sal *The Barber* Maglie

It'sa FACT

Frank **Piano Mover** Smith: In 1907 he went 23-10. Frank was shutout in seven of his ten loses! Two years later Piano Mover won 25 times (second in AL), and led the league in games (51), complete games (37), innings (365) and K's (177)!

William **The Old Arbitrator** Klem: He is one of seven umpires in the Hall of Fame. The Old Arbitrator pioneered the inside chest protector.

Ray **Farmer** Moore: His career wound down in Minnesota. I can still see his pendulum arm swing windup. His hand and glove nearly touched the ground. Halsey Mr. Baseball Hall, the Twins' colorman, called him Old Blue, after his hunting dog.

Alvin **General** Crowder: He acquired his nickname from the head of the World War I draft department, General Enoch Crowder.

Jim **Sarge** Bagby: His career spanned nine years. During his six "full seasons" he averages 19+ wins per campaign. In 1920 Sarge had a fabulous campaign. He led the AL in wins (31), games (48), complete games (30) and innings (339 2/3). Sarge was the last Junior Circuit pitcher to win 30 games, before Denny McLain did it 48 years later! Sarge and his son Jim Jr. combined to win the second most games, for a father/son pitching combination, in Major League history (224 contests).

Jim **Professor** Brosnan: He was the Red's fireman in their 1961 pennant winning season. The Professor authored ten relief wins and 16 saves!

Bill **Wizard** Hoffer: He "came up" as a 24 year old rookie in 1895. That season he went 31-6, leading the National League in winning %. The Wizard proved he was no fluke, casting his spell again in 1896. He finished 25-7 and again topped all hurlers in winning %.

Monte **Prof** Weaver: In 1932 he had his best season, winning 22 contests. Prof combined with another "occupation" teammate, Alvin General Crowder, to win 48 games between them that summer.

Walter **Smokey** Alston: He had a very short Major League playing career. On September 27th, 1936 The Big Cat, Johnny Mize, was given the thumb. Smokey was sent in . He batted once and fanned. Smokey still made his lasting mark in the Majors. He is one of 11 outstanding managers who have been enshrined in Cooperstown!

Charles **Old Sarge** Street: In 1912 he ended, unofficially, his playing career. Gabby, as he was called in his playing days, started managing in the Majors in 1929. His management style led to his second nickname. In 1931 Old Sarge put on the tools of ignorance one more time. He played errorless, but Old Sarge drew the collar, going 0/1.

Harold **Little Colonel** Reese: He was not a one year phenomenon. The Little Colonel was selected to the NL All-Star team nine consecutive seasons (1946-54)! Pee Wee was the Dodger's team leader and that led to his second moniker.

Gary **The G-Man** Gaetti: On Tuesday August 19th, 1992 my family and I attended a baseball game at Fenway Park. The Red Sox hosted the Angels. During warm-ups The G-Man drifted back by the center field wall. Kyle (my handsome son and awesome ballplayer) and I yelled down to Gary and said "We in Minnesota missed him." Gary turned and said sarcastically, "Yeah, sure." Then my "birthday boy" remembered that The G-Man also has his birthday on August 19th (Kyle read his baseball cards looking for this fact years earlier and suddenly remembered it! See mom, cards educate!). So Kyle yelled down, "Happy Birthday!" Gary turned, smiled and came to the base of the wall. He was the nicest guy. Almost immediately he told us to wish Bruno (Tom Brunansky, his former Twins teammate and now Bosox right fielder) Happy Birthday too! Bruno's birthday was August 18th! It has to be lonely to be on the road on your birthday, yet The G-Man immediately thought of his friend. He is a class guy. And Gary, we really DO miss you in Minnesota!

Forrest **Smoky** Burgess: He was one of baseball's greatest pinch hitters. Smoky pinch-hit 145/507 during his career. His 27 doubles and 142 RBI's are tops and his 145 safeties are second best.

Smokey Joe Wood: He and Walter Barney Johnson both had winning streaks in 1912. The Big Train had already set the AL record with 16 consecutive wins. Smokey Joe had won 13 straight. They met head to head on September 1st. It lived up to its billing. The game ended 1-0. Smokey Joe won. He continued his streak also to 16 wins, but then he too suffered defeat. The AL record of 16 straight wins in one season, twice more tied, still stands!

Milkman Jim Turner: He, as a 33 year old rookie in 1937, took the NL by storm. Milkman Jim delivered 20 wins (tie second), 24 complete games (first), five shutouts (tie first) and a 2.38 ERA (first). Age shortened his Major League playing career, but he still brought home 69 wins. When his playing days ended, Milkman Jim coached for 24 seasons in the Majors.

Russ **Sheriff** Van Atta: On April 25th, 1933 he made his Big League debut. The Sheriff secured four hits. Not bad for a pitcher!

Leon **Caddy** Cadore: On May 1st, 1920 he pitched a 26 inning complete game. The contest ended 1-1. It was the longest pitching outing in baseball history!

Joe **Fireman** Beggs: He had his career year in 1940. Fireman logged a 12-3 record and led the NL in saves (tie). He held opponents to a 2.00 ERA and allowed only one home run all season!

Joe **Fireman** Page: For seven plus years he was Mr. Bullpen for the Yankees. In 1948 and 1949 he led the league in appearances and in 1947 (tie) and 1949 Fireman paced all stoppers in saves.

TRIVIA*

1) His birth name was Cornelius Alexander McGillicuddy. The name that we know him, in itself, is a nickname.

2) He was also known as "The Waiter". He was the leadoff man for "Murderers' Row" (1927 Yankees). His job was to get on base and wait.

3) He started two triple plays (both grounders taken "around the horn") in one game. His glove is in the Hall of Fame commemorating that July 17th, 1990 game.

4) This Hall of Famer hit a home run in his first at bat. He then hit a triple in his second at bat. Throughout the remainder of his career he never hit another homer or triple! (Hint: he was wounded in the Battle of the Bulge)

5) What identical middle names do Dom The Little Professor DiMaggo and his two brothers all have? (Hint: think Foytack and Assenmacher)

6) This zany pitcher was fined by the baseball commissioner for supposedly sprinkling marijuana on his pancakes!

7) He was the hard luck loser in the 1956 World Series game #5 against Don Larsen. He acquired his moniker because he threw close to batters' heads.

8) He went five consecutive seasons with an ERA below 2.00. During that stretch he won 127 games, 38 by shutout! (Hint: this was his second nickname, his pre-baseball occupation)

9) Casey The Old Professor Stengel gave him this nickname, because he would always "go with him" in the big games.

10) In the 1958 World Series, down three games to one, this ex-marine helped lead the Yankee's winning charge! He powdered four home runs during that Fall Classic!

11) All the members of this famous double play combination are in Cooperstown. It went Tinker to Evers to....

12) This current player is best known for his glove, but he has, for his career, stolen more bases than he has struck out (through 1994).

13) He appeared in only one game in the 1951 and 1952 Fall Classics. Both times he saved game #7!

14) He was the first pitcher to ever hit a home run during the World Series (October 10th, 1920).

15) On October 4th, 1969, this outfielder turned pitcher won the first ever ALCS game.

16) He drove in his older brother for the winning run in the 1949 All-Star game.

17) Known for his great speed, this Hall of Famer was called "The Mail Carrier" early in his career. This "Bluegrass Stater" went on to lead the AL three years in triples and on August 22nd, 1927, he legged out three triples in one game.

18) He was the first skipper to pilot his own son on the ball field.

19) He struck out only 3.3% of his at bats (18th lowest ever). His hits seemed to remarkably always get through, leading to his three word nickname.

20) This is awesome. He did not allow a home run in three consecutive seasons (1907-09) covering 653 innings! (Hint: his nickname might indicate he played in an orchestra)

21) For his first three years he wove his magic spell (78 wins), but after three more seasons, he disappeared.

22) This reliever appeared in six World Series. He went 2-0 with four saves and a 1.10 ERA!

23) He was a coal miner before he walked on diamonds.

24) His humorous, out of this world behavior, over his long career, led to his nickname.

25) Mickey Mantle, the Hall of Fame switch hitting outfielder, made only one exception when batting. The Mick batted right-handed against this near impossible to hit right-handed pitcher.

* OCCUPATIONAL HAZARDS answers found on page 239

ROSTER

CATCHERS:	Yr	Hits	AB's	Ave
Forrest *Smoky* Burgess	18	1318	4471	.295
Harry *Farmer* Vaughn	13	946	3454	.274
William *Boileryard* Clarke	13	858	3346	.256
William *Farmer* Weaver	7	856	3082	.278
Ray *Iron Man* Mueller	14	733	2911	.252
Connie *The Tall Tactician* Mack	11	659	2695	.245
George *Admiral* Schlei	8	455	1918	.237
Charles *Boss* Schmidt	6	360	1480	.243
Bob *Sarge* Kearney	8	316	1356	.233
Charles *Old Sarge* Street	8	312	1501	.208
Charles *Alderman* Briody	8	271	1186	.228
Claude *Admiral* Berry	5	165	753	.219
Ralph *Major* Houk	8	43	158	.272
Morris *Farmer* Steelman	4	31	142	.218

1ST BASEMEN:	Yr	Hits	AB's	Ave
Walter *Union Man* Holke	11	1278	4456	.287
Frank *The Peerless Leader* Chance	17	1273	4297	.296
Del *Sheriff* Gainer	10	438	1608	.272
Jim *Shamus* Kane	1	35	145	.241
Walter *Smokey* Alston	1	0	1	.000

2ND BASEMEN:	Yr	Hits	AB's	Ave
Arthur *Circus Solly* Hofman	14	1095	4072	.269
Ron *Little General* Theobald	2	193	779	.248
Joe *Little General* Wood	1	53	164	.323
Irv *Major* Hach	1	11	51	.216

SHORTSTOPS:	Yr	Hits	AB's	Ave
Ozzie *The Wizard of Oz* Smith	17	2365	9013	.262
Harold *Little Colonel* Reese	16	2170	8058	.269
Gil *Colonel* Hatfield	8	295	1190	.248
Tommy *Judge* Mee	1	3	19	.158

3RD BASEMEN:	Yr	Hits	AB's	Ave
Gary *The G-Man* Gaetti	14	1698	6689	.254
Mike *Moonman* Shannon	9	710	2780	.255
Art *Sheriff* Ewoldt	1	7	32	.219
John *Soldier Boy* Murphy	2	6	25	.240

OUTFIELDERS:	Yr	Hits	AB's	Ave
Gary *Sarge* Matthews	16	2011	7147	.281
Earle *The Kentucky Colonel* Combs	12	1866	5746	.325
Garry *Secretary of Defense* Maddox	15	1802	6331	.285
Dom *The Little Professor* DiMaggio	11	1680	5640	.298
Pete *The Gladiator* Browning	13	1646	4820	.341
Hank *Sarge* Bauer	14	1424	5145	.277
Jeff *Hac-Man* Leonard	14	1342	5045	.266
Les *Major* Mann	16	1332	4716	.282
Don *Mandrake the Magician* Mueller	12	1292	4364	.296
Jay *Moonman* Johnstone	20	1254	4703	.267
Casey *The Old Professor* Stengel	14	1219	4288	.284
Disco Danny Ford	11	1123	4163	.270
Mike *Hit Man* Easler	14	1078	3677	.293

OUTFIELDERS: (Cont.)	Yr	Hits	AB's	Ave
Charlie *Smokey* Maxwell	14	856	3245	.264
Hal *Sheriff* Lee	7	755	2750	.275
Rudy *Lawman* Law	7	656	2421	.271
James *General* Stafford	8	583	2128	.274
Smokey Joe Wood	14	553	1952	.283
Maurice *Bomber* Van Robays	6	493	1844	.267
Dave *Sheriff* Harris	7	406	1447	.281
Fred *Shoemaker* Nicholson	5	247	794	.311
Walter *Judge* McCredie	1	69	213	.324
Harry *Army* Armbruster	1	63	265	.238
Tom *Sleuth* Fleming	3	22	99	.222
Ralph *Sarge* Mitterling	1	6	39	.154
Coalyard Mike Handiboe	1	1	15	.067

PITCHERS:	Yr	Won	Lost	ERA
Iron Man Joe McGinnity	10	246	142	2.66
Mordecai *Miner* Brown	14	239	130	2.06
Ed *Chairman of the Board* Ford	16	236	106	2.75
Sam *Goshen Schoolmaster* Leever	13	194	100	2.47
William *Brickyard* Kennedy	12	187	159	3.96
Alvin *General* Crowder	11	167	115	4.12
Eddie *Junkman* Lopat	12	166	112	3.21
Hoyt *Sarge* Wilhelm	21	143	122	2.52
Ray *Wiz* Kremer	10	143	85	3.76
Frank *Piano Mover* Smith	11	139	111	2.59
Jim *Sarge* Bagby	9	127	88	3.11
Brewery Jack Taylor	9	120	117	4.23
Sal *The Barber* Maglie	10	119	62	3.15
Bill *Spaceman* Lee	14	119	90	3.62
Smokey Joe Wood	11	116	57	2.03
Billy *Digger* O'Dell	13	105	100	3.29
Ted *Pitching Professor* Lewis	6	94	64	3.53
Dick *Professor* Hall	16	93	75	3.32
Johnny *Fireman* Murphy	13	93	53	3.50
Bill *Wizard* Hoffer	6	92	46	3.75
John *Sheriff* Blake	10	87	102	4.13
Joe *Butcher Boy* Benz	9	76	75	2.43
Monte *Prof* Weaver	9	71	50	4.36
Frank *Fiddler* Corridon	6	70	67	2.80
Milkman Jim Turner	9	69	60	3.22
Leon *Caddy* Cadore	10	68	72	3.14
Tom *Plowboy* Morgan	12	67	47	3.61
Ray *Farmer* Moore	11	63	59	4.06
Joe *Fireman* Page	8	57	49	3.53
Steve *Smokey* Sundra	9	56	41	4.17
Jim *Professor* Brosnan	9	55	47	3.54
Bob *Sarge* Kuzava	10	49	44	4.05
George *Sarge* Connally	12	49	60	4.30
Joe *Fireman* Beggs	9	48	35	2.96
Fiddler Bill McGee	8	46	41	3.74
George *Farmer* Bell	5	43	79	2.85
Earl *Teach* Caldwell	8	33	43	4.69
Russ *Sheriff* Van Atta	7	33	41	5.60
Smokey Joe Finneran	5	25	33	3.30

ROSTER

PITCHERS: (Cont.)	Yr	Won	Lost	ERA
Ralph *Judge* Works	5	24	24	3.79
Marshall *Sheriff* Bridges	7	23	15	3.75
Joe *Professor* Ostrowski	5	23	25	4.54
Ralph *Sailor* Stroud	3	20	20	2.94
Alex *Colonel* Ferson	3	18	25	4.37
Grady *Butcher Boy* Adkins	2	12	27	4.34
Elmer *Smoky* Singleton	8	11	17	4.83
Jesse *Scout* Stovall	2	8	14	3.76
Walter *Judge* Nagle	1	5	3	3.48
Charlie *Sheriff* Gassaway	3	5	9	4.04
Emmett *Ramrod* Nelson	2	5	4	4.07
Jim *Sheriff* Constable	5	3	4	4.87
John *Sheriff* Gaddy	1	2	0	0.69
Clarence *Pop-Boy* Smith	3	1	4	4.21
Harry *Mule Trader* Kimberlin	4	1	4	4.70
Berlyn *Trader* Horne	1	1	1	5.09
George *Three Star* Hennessey	3	1	2	5.20

PITCHERS: (Cont.)	Yr	Won	Lost	ERA
Ed *The Pitching Poet* Kenna	1	1	1	5.29
Jim *Smoky* Fairbank	2	1	2	5.49
John *Sheriff* Singleton	1	1	10	5.90
John Paul *Admiral* Jones	2	1	0	6.06
Lester *General* Sherman	1	0	1	0.00
Harry *Farmer* Vaughn	1	0	0	3.86
Al *Soldier* Carson	1	0	0	4.05
Joe *Smokey* Lotz	1	0	3	4.27
Howard *Judge* Craghead	2	0	0	6.26
Sailor Joel Newkirk	2	0	1	7.27
George *Soldier Boy* Curry	1	0	3	7.47
James *Farmer* Burns	1	0	0	9.00
Dale *Mountain Man* Roberts	1	0	0	9.00

EXTRAS:
Veterans Stadium - *The Vet*
William *The Old Arbitrator* Klem - Umpire

LINGO

Clown: An umpire

Junkman: Pitcher who throws only slow curves and change-ups

Tailor Made: An easy grounder for a double play

Gashouse Gang: The 1934 Cardinals

Iron Mike: Pitching machine

Spies: Advance scouts

Scout: Person who searches for unsigned, talented players

Advance Scout: Person who studies upcoming opposition, looking for weaknesses

Free Agent: Player who is free to sign for any team

Robbed Him: Great defensive play to take away a hit

Thief: A base stealer

Journeyman: A player who is traded to several teams throughout his career

Grasscutter: A grounder that does not hop

Bouncer: A grounder that hops

Gloveman: A good fielder and Michael Jackson

Slider: A fast curve with a small break

Butcher: A bad fielder

Cleanup Hitter: Number four batter in the lineup

Mop-up Man: Reliever who comes in when the game has no chance of being won

Fly Chaser: Outfielder

Leadoff Man: First man in the batting order

Circus Catch: Near impossible catch

Clubhouse Lawyer: Player who hears fellow players gripes and is their mouthpiece to management

Bench Jockey: Player, riding the pine, who verbally harasses the other team

Iron Man: Player who seldom sits, always plays

Professor: Knowledgeable player or manager

Hit Man: Player known for his hitting

Bum: Pitcher who just "was bombed"

Fireman: A relief pitcher who comes in to stop a rally and "save" the game

Takes Him Downtown: A batter hits a homer off a pitcher

Goes to Work on Him: A pitcher trying to handle a batter, usually in a crucial situation

Sends Him to the Showers: A manager replaces a pitcher

Just Another Day at the Office: When a pitcher routinely wins another game

Speed Merchant: Very fast player

Bad Bouncer: Anyone who throws me out of the bar

Public Enemy Number One: Curve ball

Retired: Get a batter out

Button Pusher: A manager who has an excellent team and needs little ability to manage

Handy Man: Player who can play several positions

P. R.

25

Team

The success or failure of a baseball franchise is in the team's ability to generate revenue. A good public relations department becomes essential. Many teams hold free baseball clinics to benefit young area athletes. Ballplayers make themselves locally visible through numerous community and charitable functions. Friendly and open communication with the press and media usually lead to positive articles and reporting. To boost attendance, often "special days" are scheduled. On Bat Day, the first 15,000 kids ages 1-15 receive a free bat.. Other give away dates tried have been Ball Day, Mug Day, Cooler Day, Cushion Day and Cap Day. Knot Hole Days allow eight kids in free with a paying adult, while Ladies Day and Family Day offer ticket discounts. One event I vividly recall in Minnesota was Halter Top Day. I have been personally assured it lived up to its billing! Oh yes, and how about Cleveland's 10¢ Beer Night. It was such a smashing success, the rowdy crowd caused the game to be forfeited and all future beer nights banned!

The real PR team is headed by two Hall of Famers. Grover Cleveland Pete Alexander and George Rube Waddell were arguably the best right-handed and left-handed pitchers of all time. Their revered nicknames were subsequently copied by many future ballplayers. This group has thirty-nine Major Leaguers called Pete (P) and thirty-three players tabbed Rube (R). Although there is no certainty that any of the players were really nicknamed (one exception) after Pete or Rube, in each case their monikers were not derivatives of their first names, hence "qualifying" for the real PR team.

George Rube Waddell and Grover Cleveland Pete Alexander both had storied careers and tragic endings. Rube was a dominating southpaw who decimated batters. Playing in an era of contact hitters, Rube was often unhittable. From 1902-07 he led the Junior Circuit in strikeouts each season. In 1903 he fanned 71% more batters than the twirler who finished second in K's! In 1904, 1905 and 1902 Rube led the runners-up in whiffs by 46%, 37% and 31%. His 349 ring ups during the 1904 campaign were the post 1900 record for 61 years, until another flame throwing lefty, Sandford Sandy Koufax finally topped Rube. Besides Koo Foo, only Nolan The Express Ryan has ever topped Rube's single season total (1973 and 1974). George was very simple, actually childlike. Connie Mack brought out his abilities or no one may ever have experienced any of Rube's tremendous talent. He drank. He drank a lot. He was fascinated by fire trucks and circuses. He would wander off, follow them, hire on and/or join them. One day he would hurl a gem, then disappear to "go fishing" or "tend bar." Some seasons he just drifted. He caught on with town teams or anyone who would support his habit. By the young age of 33 Rube was gone forever from the Major Leagues. In his ten "full" seasons and parts of three others, Rube posted 50 shutouts in just 340 starts. Rube's strikeout to walk ratio was nearly three to one, unbelievable for a power pitcher. Rube's lifetime ERA was topped by only five pitchers. Sadly, destroyed by alcohol, Rube slid into home at age 37. (Please see Pete's bio under *It'sa FACT*).

LINEUP

CA	Albert *Rube* Walker

was a backup catcher for 11 seasons. He played behind Mickey Owen, Smoky Burgess and Campy Campanella. Rube went on to coach 21 seasons. He is credited, while pitching coach for the Mets, with developing the five day rotation. Now all teams in the Majors use it.

1B	Ray Bloom *Rube* Bressler

was a hurler for seven seasons, then he converted to a position player his last 12 summers. From 1924-26 Rube, the hitter, batted .347, .348 and .357 and he retired with a career .301 average. In 1914 Rube, the pitcher, went 10-4 with a 1.77 ERA.

2B	Louis Rogers *Pete* Browning

was a pre-1900 star. He compiled a career .341 batting average, 11th best. Pete captured three batting crowns and hit over .300 in 11 of his 13 campaigns. Used primarily as an outfielder, Pete played every position but catcher. In 1887 Pete hit a whopping .402!

SS	James Edward *Pete* Runnels

was a versatile player. He came up as a shortstop, but later played every infield position. Pete led the AL in fielding %, once each at second and first. He was a left-handed "slap hitter" who utilized Fenway Park's Green Monster. From 1958-62 Pete hit over .300 each summer.

3B	Harold Patrick *Pete* Reiser

played for ten seasons. When he came up, Pete was considered the fastest man in baseball. In his first full season (1941) he finished second for the NL MVP award. Unfortunately, a serious head injury and then three years in his country's service robbed Pete of his vast potential.

OF	Ervin *Pete* Fox

starred 13 summers in the Junior Circuit during the 30's and 40's. A career .298 hitter, 1937 was his best season. Pete batted a solid .331, collecting 208 safeties and scoring 116 tallies. Four other campaigns he also hit over .300, before "hanging 'em up".

OF	Rueben Henry *Rube* Oldring

was a fleet footed outfielder. Two consecutive years (1910-11) he led American League outfielders in fielding %. Rube's best all-around season was 1913. He stole 40 bases, scored 101 runs and drove in 71 tallies. Twice in his 13 summers Rube topped .300.

OF	Ira James *Pete* Flagstead

was a hard hitting right fielder for 13 seasons. Pete batted over .300 five summers and retired with a very respectable .290 batting average. Twice he topped all outfielders in fielding % and once Pete had an amazing 33 outfield assists in one season!

P	Grover Cleveland *Pete* Alexander

had a spectacular 20 year career. In his first nine full seasons he led or shared the league lead in innings seven times; strikeouts, complete games and wins six times; shutouts five times and ERA four times! Old Pete was simply awesome!

P	George Edward *Rube* Waddell

rests in Cooperstown. He won 20+ games four consecutive summers (1902-05), including a league leading 27 victories in 1905. That year Rube also led the Junior Circuit in strikeouts and ERA, completing the Pitcher's Triple Crown! Only six American League hurlers have done it.

P	Richard Wm. *Rube* Marquard

is a Hall of Famer. The left-hander won 20+ games three straight years (1911-13), leading the Giants to three World Series appearances. Rube's 26 victories in 1912 led the NL. Eleven seasons he won in double digits and Rube's 201 career wins place him tied for 90th.

RES	John Clebon *Rube* Benton

threw balls and strikes 15 summers in the Senior Circuit. The portsider won in double digits seven times. In 1912 Rube won 18 contests, finished fourth in K's and led the league in games. His 16 victories in 1914 were hard earned, because his Redlegs were cellar dwellers.

RES	George Elvin *Rube* Walberg

twirled for 15 campaigns. The American League southpaw put together an excellent stretch from 1927-32 while hurling for Connie Mack's Philadelphia Athletics. During those six seasons Rube chalked up an outstanding 101 victories, including 20 wins in 1931.

RES	Ray Benjamin *Rube* Caldwell

toiled for the perennial second division Yankees his first nine seasons. Rube posted his best numbers in 1920, winning 20 games for the first place Tribe. Rube's best year was 1914. He won 17 games and had a 1.94 ERA for the sixth place Yanks.

RES	George *Rube* Foster

had a short, exciting career. During two part and three full seasons he was dominating. Rube painted 15 whitewashes in just 103 starts, and he allowed only six home runs in 842+ innings. During Rube's last two campaigns (307 innings), he allowed no round trippers!

L to R: James Edward *Pete* Runnels, Harold *Pete* Reiser, Grover Cleveland *Pete* Alexander, George Edward *Rube* Waddell, Richard *Rube* Marquard

It'sa FACT

Ira James **Pete** Flagstead: He set an American League record by participating in three outfield DP's in one game.

Ray Benjamin **Rube** Caldwell: On August 25th, 1918 he was struck by lightning while standing on the mound! It was Rube's turn to strike September 10th, 1919. He no-hit the Yankees.

John Henry **Rube** Robinson: During his six seasons in the Majors he never had an ERA over 3.00!

Grover Cleveland **Pete** Alexander: His rookie year was 1911. Pete won a rookie record 28 games and fanned 227 batters (in 1984 Dwight Doc Goodin broke Pete's rookie strikeout record). Counting the following 19 summers, Pete won a total of 373 games, topped only by Denton Cy Young and Walter The Big Train Johnson. From 1915-17 he put together the three best pitching seasons in modern baseball history. First, Pete won 31, 33 and 30 games. Since then only four players (Bagby, Grove, Dean and McLain) have won 30 or more games once each. Second, Pete hurled 376 1/3, 389 and 388 innings. Since then, the two highest yearly innings totals have been 376 and 376 2/3 (Mickey Lolich and Wilbur Wood). Third, Pete had ERA's of 1.22, 1.55 and 1.83. Since then only one ERA has been lower than his 1.22 ERA (Gibson 1.12). Fourth, Pete posted 12, 16 and eight shutouts. Since then, two pitchers have had 11 shutouts in one season (Koufax and Chance). Fifth, Pete had 36, 38 and 34 complete games. Since 1917 only once has his 34 complete games been topped (Feller, 36 games). Pete was afflicted with epilepsy. Early in his career he suffered a serious beaning injury which caused him lifelong problems. World War I injuries also impeded him. His recourse was the bottle. Alcohol contributed to his deterioration of health and his misfortunes in later life. Pete enjoyed glory on the field, but he suffered sadness off the field.

George **Rube** Foster: On June 16th, 1916 he tossed a no-hitter as Boston topped the Yanks 2-0.

Richard Wm. **Rube** Marquard: During the 1912 Fall Classic he pitched two complete game victories, allowing only one earned run. On April 15th, 1915 Rube no-hit Brooklyn. Later that season the Giants traded him to the Robins.

George Elvin **Rube** Walberg: In game #5 of the 1929 World Series he hurled 5 1/3 shutout relief innings and won the championship clinching game.

Harry Porter **Rube** Vickers: In his only full season he won 18 times. Rube posted six shutouts (third) and led the AL with six relief wins. Rube hurled 317 frames that year (1908) and did not allow a home run! In 458 career innings he was taken deep only once!

Pedro **Pete** Ramos: His career was spent with second division teams. From 1956-62, Pete won in double digits each season. He helped his own cause by slugging two homers in one game twice, May 30th, 1962 and July 13th, 1963!

John Clebon **Rube** Benton: In the 1917 Fall Classic he won game #3, posting a five hit shutout. Rube was the hard luck game #6 loser, allowing no earned runs. His Giants fell in six to the White Sox.

TRIVIA*

1) He won the American League Silver Bat (batting title) in both 1960 and 1962.
2) Although he never tossed a no-hitter, he did fire a record 16 one hitters!
3) After giving up a two strike HR, his mgr. Cookie Lavagetto publicly chastised him saying he must always "waste an 0-2 pitch." The next game, up on the count 0-2 and no one on base, he fired his fastball into the backstop!
4) Involved in a bidding war, the Giants paid the then unheard of price of $11,000 for him. His early failures led to this nickname, "The $11,000 Lemon."
5) Blessed with amazing control, he owned "the corner." He was often called "Old Low and Away."
6) This Pine City Minnesota boy (fabulous fishing there) combined with Big George Earnshaw and Robert Lefty Grove to lead the Philadelphia A's to three consecutive World Series appearances in 1929-31.
7) Also known as "The Gladiator," he was additionally dubbed the original "Louisville Slugger."
8) On June 10th, 1915 and June 11th, 1915 (dead ball era, Robert Braggo Roth led the AL with seven homers in 1915), this <u>pitcher</u> hit consecutive pinch-hit home runs!
9) He shares the Major League record of 16 shutouts in one season.
10) He won his first 19 decisions in 1912 (this ties the Major League record for consecutive wins in one season also done in 1888 by Sir Timothy Keefe)!
11) In the 1935 World Series he led Detroit with ten hits and four RBI's (tie). Three of his hits were doubles. In the 1934 Fall Classic he set the Series mark slamming six two baggers. (Hint: think Redd and Michael)
12) This flame throwing lefty set the then Major League single game strikeout mark at 16.
13) In 1941, at the age of 22, he played his first full year. He led the NL in runs, doubles (tie), triples, total bases and slugging %. He also led the league in batting!
14) In the 1915 World Series he won game #2 and the clinching game #5. At the plate he went 4/8, driving in the winning run in game #2. (Hint: a ballplayer who shares his name hit 52 homers one season)
15) He was the hero of the 1926 World Series. At 39 he was considered washed up, but he fooled everyone by pitching complete game victories in games #2 and #6. The following day the Cards held a 3-2 lead, but the bases were loaded and two were out in the home half of the seventh when he got the call. He fanned Poosh 'Em Up Tony Lazzeri to end the threat, then closed out the last two innings for the championship.

* **P**RETTY **R**OUGH answers found on page 239

ROSTER

CATCHERS:	Yr	Hits	AB's	Ave
Albert *Rube* Walker	11	360	1585	.227
Clyde Jennings *Pete* Manion	13	250	1145	.218
John *Big Pete* Peters	4	80	302	.265
Joseph Andrews *Pete* Sommers	4	67	339	.198
Richard Fred *Pete* Varney	4	47	190	.247
George F. *Pete* Lohman	1	21	109	.193
Ralph *Rube* Novotney	1	18	67	.269
Palmer Marion *Pete* Hildebrand	1	9	55	.164
Pierre *Pete* Lamer	2	2	11	.182
Jesse Hall *Pete* Allen	1	0	4	.000

1ST BASEMEN:	Yr	Hits	AB's	Ave
Raymond Bloom *Rube* Bressler	19	1170	3881	.301
Ralph Pierre *Pete* LaCock	9	444	1729	.257
Morris Elmer *Pete* Lister	1	18	65	.277
Francis Leroy *Pete* Shields	1	15	72	.208
Ed Arthur *Rube* Degroff	2	14	60	.233

2ND BASEMEN:	Yr	Hits	AB's	Ave
Louis Rogers *Pete* Browning	13	1646	4820	.341
Glenn Justice *Pete* Chapman	1	26	93	.280
Angel *Pete* Aragon Sr..	3	9	76	.118

SHORTSTOPS:	Yr	Hits	AB's	Ave
James Edward *Pete* Runnels	14	1854	6373	.291
Eugene Joseph *Pete* Turgeon	1	1	6	.167

3RD BASEMEN:	Yr	Hits	AB's	Ave
Harold Patrick *Pete* Reiser	10	786	2662	.295
Walter John *Rube* Lutzke	5	468	1876	.249
William R. *Pete* Johns	2	37	189	.196

OUTFIELDERS:	Yr	Hits	AB's	Ave
Ervin *Pete* Fox	13	1678	5636	.298
Rueben Henry *Rube* Oldring	13	1268	4690	.270
Ira James *Pete* Flagstead	13	1202	4139	.290
George William *Rube* Ellis	4	517	1985	.260
Anna Sebastian *Pete* Compton	6	186	773	.241
Ernest Augustus *Rube* Vinson	3	47	207	.227
Louis Joseph *Pete* LePine	1	20	96	.208
William James *Pete* Milne	3	14	60	.233
Milo Henry *Pete* Allison	4	13	60	.217
John Andrews *Rube* Ward	1	9	31	.290

OUTFIELDERS: (Cont.)	Yr	Hits	AB's	Ave
Oliver *Rube* Sellers	1	5	32	.156

PITCHERS:	Yr	Won	Lost	ERA
Grover Cleveland *Pete* Alexander	20	373	208	2.56
Richard Wm. *Rube* Marquard	18	201	177	3.08
George Edward *Rube* Waddell	13	191	143	2.16
George Elvin *Rube* Walberg	15	155	141	4.16
John Clebon *Rube* Benton	15	150	144	3.09
Ray Benjamin *Rube* Caldwell	12	133	120	3.22
Pedro *Pete* Ramos	15	117	160	4.08
George *Rube* Foster	5	58	34	2.36
John Henry *Rube* Robinson	6	42	37	253
Raymond Bloom *Rube* Bressler	7	26	32	3.40
Berthold Juneau *Pete* Husting	3	24	21	4.16
Harry Porter *Rube* Vickers	5	22	27	2.93
Walter S. *Rube* Manning	4	22	32	3.14
Welton Claude *Rube* Ehrhardt	6	22	34	4.15
Jacob Bowman *Rube* Geyer	4	17	26	3.67
Floyd Myron *Rube* Kroh	6	14	9	2.29
Ernest Herman *Pete* Henning	2	14	25	3.83
Alexander John *Rube* Schauer	5	10	29	3.35
Charles Samuel *Rube* Kisinger	2	9	12	3.00
Roy DeVerne *Rube* Marshall	4	8	10	4.17
Oscar Casper *Rube* Peters	2	7	8	4.06
Marvin Earl *Pete* Center	4	7	7	4.10
Charles Fred *Petie* Behan	3	7	15	4.76
Frank Gordon *Big Pete* McKenry	2	6	6	3.10
Dan Leslie *Rube* Adams	2	4	11	3.74
Harry Richard *Rube* Suter	1	2	3	2.47
James Arthur *Rube* Parnham	2	2	2	4.04
Frank Rolland *Rube* Dessau	2	2	4	6.53
Ed William *Rube* Kinsella	2	1	4	3.49
Bryan Owen *Pete* Young	2	1	0	3.86
Clarence *Pete* Sims	1	1	0	4.32
Byron W. *Rube* Yarrison	2	1	4	7.86
Edgar *Rube* Taylor	1	0	0	0.00
Clarence Willie *Pete* Fahrer	1	0	0	1.13
Manuel *Pete* Montejo	1	0	0	3.86
Friedrich C. *Pete* Schmidt	1	0	0	4.50
Frank Lane *Pete* Charton	1	0	2	5.26
Ed John *Rube* Albosta	2	0	8	6.15
Vernon Charles *Pete* Taylor	1	0	0	13.50
Warren Dawson *Pete* Rambo	1	0	0	14.73
Ivan *Pete* Loos	1	0	1	27.00

Real PADRES

26

Team

In 1969 the expansion San Diego Padres franchise came into existence. They have played all their home games in San Diego Stadium, since renamed Jack Murphy Stadium in 1980 for the sports editor who was instrumental in getting baseball to this Southern California mecca. After several years of struggling (last place their first six seasons), the Padres finally had their first winning season in 1978. The booming bat of Dave Winny Winfield, the magic glove of Ozzie The Wizard of Oz Smith and the strong arms of veteran Cy Young winner Gaylord Perry and Rollie The Mustache Fingers formed the team's strong core. In 1984, led by the home run bats of Steve Popeye Garvey and Graig Puff Nettles and the cannon arm of the Goose, Rich Gossage, the Padres made it to their only Fall Classic.

In the old days of baseball, players were often hard drinking, tobacco chewing rowdies and not allowed in first class hotels. When a "clean living player" who did not swear, drink, or smoke came along, invariably he was tagged Deacon or Preacher. Many of the Real Padres fit that composite. Nevertheless, the group also has seven Monks, six Chappies, four Parsons and even one Rabbi! Looking hard, the group also found an Immortal and an Angel, not to mention a Miracle Man and a Miracle Worker!

One player not yet mentioned rises off the roster as the top Real Padre. San Diego could have used his left arm. This southpaw is enshrined in Cooperstown. He was known as Mose. This second nickname came from his middle name, Moses. He led the Philadelphia Athletics to the promised land, overcoming the vaunted "Murderers' Row" Yankees to win pennants three consecutive seasons (1929-31). Reaching the Majors in 1925, Mose took over for The Big Train and won seven consecutive strikeout crowns. Nine seasons he was the Junior Circuit's ERA leader, the Major League record. From 1927-33 Mose went 172-54, winning 20 or more games each summer. His 1931 season of 31-4 was near perfect. Mose led all hurlers in wins, complete games (tie), shutouts, strikeouts and ERA. Because of a 'tainted' 1-0 loss, Lefty won "only" 24 of 25 decisions in one stretch! Mose won the MVP that year. For his career Mose placed himself at a higher level. His lifetime winning % of .680 is fifth best. His 300 win total is topped by only 17 players. Mose probably could have separated the Red Sea if Connie Mack had asked him!

LINEUP

CA	James *Deacon* McGuire

started his 26 year playing career as an 18 year old backstop for Toledo in 1884. Deacon played regularly until 1906, six times hitting over .300. From 1894-97 he batted .306, .336, .321 and .343. Deacon also was a playing manager for six seasons of his career.

1B	Gil *Miracle Worker* Hodges

should be in Cooperstown! From 1949-59 Gil averaged 30+ home runs and 101 RBI's. An eight time All-Star, he drove in over 100 runs seven consecutive summers (1949-55). His 370 circuit blasts rank him 38th all time. He also managed for nine campaigns.

2B	Bill *Deacon* McKechnie

was primarily a utility player in his 11 playing seasons. In 1914 Deacon had his best season, batting .304, stealing 47 sacks and scoring 107 tallies. He went on to manage 25 years in the Majors and was known for his fairness and was considered a fatherly type.

SS	Everett *Deacon* Scott

was an amazing player. Deacon was the premier gloveman of his era. From 1916-23, Everett led all Junior Circuit shortstops in fielding % eight consecutive seasons! He also topped all shortstops in putouts, assists and double plays twice each during that stretch.

3B	James *Deacon* White

was one of the pioneer players of baseball. He literally played every position. An excellent hitter, he led the embryo National League in RBI's its first two summers and also topped it in batting, triples and slugging % it's sophomore season. Eight of his 15 campaigns he hit .300+.

OF	*Orator* Jim O'Rourke

was a powerful hitter in the dead ball era. Jim slugged nearly 600 extra base hits. Eleven seasons Orator hit over .300. His four years in the National Association are not in his totals and during his time the seasons were shorter, making this Hall of Famer's stats even more amazing!

OF	Lloyd *Shaker* Moseby

earned his nickname not from a religious group, but from basketball. A 12 year star, Lloyd had both speed and power. Seven consecutive summers (1983-89) he swiped 20+ bags. Eight straight years (1983-90) Shaker rocked ten or more long balls, twice blasting 20+ yard shots.

OF	Ival *Goodie* Goodman

was a hard hitting right fielder, reaching the Big Show in 1935. Goodie led the NL in triples his first two years and in 1938 he finished second in homers. A shoulder injury sustained in the 1939 All-Star game ended Goodie's power and unfortunately after the 1940 season he faded.

P	Charles *Deacon* Phillippe

made his Major League debut one month before he turned 27. Deacon won 20 or more games his first five summers. Charles never had a losing season, winning 63% of his decisions. In 1903 Deacon went 25-9 and walked only 29 batters in 289 1/3 innings, unbelievable!

P	Frank *Sweet Music* Viola

is a workhorse. He pitched over 200 innings per year from 1983-92, missing only four scheduled starts! From 1984-92 Sweet Music won at least 13 games each summer, twice winning 20 or more contests. Frankie went 24-7 and won the Cy Young award in 1988.

P	Vern *Deacon* Law

played his entire career for the Steel City Bucs. Nine of his 16 seasons Deacon won ten or more games. In 1960 he not only won the Cy Young award, going 20-9, but he also won two games in the World Series and picked up the win in the second All-Star tilt.

RES	*Deacon* Danny MacFayden

deserved a better fate. His first five seasons (1926-30), the Red Sox finished dead last. Deacon managed to lead the AL in shutouts (tie) in 1929. He won 16 of Boston's 62 wins in 1931. Deacon had his best season in 1936 when he won 17 games for the Braves.

RES	Elwin *Preacher* Roe

was a left-handed spitballer (after it was illegal) who proved hard to hit. Preacher led the NL in K's in 1945 while with the Pittsburgh Pirates. Traded to the Dodgers after the 1947 season, he had his best years from 1948-53, going 12-8, 15-6, 19-11, 22-3, 11-2 and 11-3.

RES	Harry *Goody* Simpson

toured the Major Leagues in the 50's. Twice he led the Junior Circuit in triples and once he tied for second in three baggers. In 1956 Goody was chosen to the American League All-Star team, slugged 21 home runs and pushed across 105 runs (tied for fourth).

RES	Mark *Amazing* Grace

has lived up to his nickname since his 1988 rookie season. An outstanding fielder, Amazing holds the National League record for first baseman assists and Mark won the Gold Glove in both 1992 and 1993. Five of his last six seasons he has hit over .300, amazing!

L to R: Gil *Miracle Worker* Hodges, Frank *Sweet Music* Viola, Lefty *Mose* Grove, Vern *Deacon* Law, Everett *Deacon* Scott

It'sa FACT

James **Deacon** McGuire: He held the longevity record for playing 26 seasons until 1993. That year, The Express, Nolan Ryan played his 27th season!

Bill **Deacon** McKechnie: During mid-season 1916 a five player trade occurred between the Giants and the Redlegs. Three future Hall of Famers, Deacon Bill McKechnie, Edd Roush and Christy Big Six Mathewson were traded for Charles Buck Herzog and Wade Red Killefer.

Michael **Deacon** Morrissey: At 5'4", he had to be one of the shortest pitchers of all time.

Goodwin **Goody** Rosen: He hailed from Toronto Canada. In 1938, his first full season, Goody played right field for the Dodgers. He led all outfielders in assists and fielding %. Goody had a huge year at the plate in 1945. He finished third in triples (tie), batting average and total bases, and second in both hits and runs.

Frank **Sweet Music** Viola: While with the Twins, the night before he would start, Sweet Music would always eat spaghetti.

Ted **Parson** Lewis: He was born in Machynlleth, Wales. In his first full year, 1897, he won 21 games. Parson then went 26-8 in 1898, leading the NL in winning %. Three years and 46 wins later he was gone from the Majors.

James **Deacon** White: He played during the infancy of baseball. Deacon played five years in the National Association, the league from 1871-75 that preceded the National League. Those stats are not counted on official career records. Deacon "unofficially" hit .322, .344, .390, .303 and .366! Deacon had the first bingo ever in the National Association. Playing for Cleveland, Deacon tagged a double against Fort Wayne.

Brian **Harp** Harper: When he autographs baseballs, he includes a scripture quote.

Charles **Deacon** Phillippe: In 1903 he pitched in the first Fall Classic. Cy Young's Boston Pilgrims topped Honus Wagner's Pittsburgh Pirates in the best of nine Series 5-3. Deacon pitched five complete games in 13 days! He won three and lost two for the Bucs.

George **Bingo** Binks: He played parts of five seasons. His only full campaign, 1945 with the Senators, Bingo finished fifth in RBI's and tied for second in two baggers.

Joe **The Immortal One** Azcue: Twice he led AL backstops in fielding %. His lifetime .992 fielding % ranks him fifth.

Gil **Miracle Worker** Hodges: He was a smooth fielder. Three times he led all NL first sackers in fielding %. When the Gold Glove award was introduced in 1957, Gil won it three consecutive years. Because umps watch a first baseman's foot on close calls, Gil's "quick foot" led to his other nickname, No Touch. His moniker Miracle Worker came because he managed the 1969 Miracle Mets to the World Championship.

TRIVIA*

1) Harry Carey says this expression frequently (Halsey Mr. Baseball Hall also said it).
2) This Red Sox/Yankee was famous for his consecutive game streak. It started in 1916 and the streak went 1307 contests. Lou Gehrig broke his consecutive game record.
3) He is the only manager to take three different teams (Bucs, Cards and Redlegs) to the World Series.
4) He gained his nickname when he was ordained a minister in the Mormon Church.
5) In 1951 he went 22-3. This is the third highest single season winning % (min. 20 wins).
6) After he won the seventh game of the 1987 World Series, he told the world he was going to Disneyworld.
7) He had remarkable control. He averaged a minuscule 1.25 bases on balls per nine innings for his career. The best mark since 1900.
8) When future Hall of Famer Addie Joss died suddenly two days past his 31st birthday, this preacher/former ballplayer presided at his funeral.
9) This was his first nickname, but after playing for six teams in eight years, he became known as Suitcase.
10) He taught his younger brother "Whoop-La" the curve ball. Whoop-La went on to win 229 games!
11) In game #7 of the 1955 Fall Classic the Dodgers beat the Yankees 2-0. He drove in both runs, one with a single and the other with a sacrifice fly.
12) In a smooth move, the Pirates had Bing Crosby call this prospect's mom. It helped the Bucs land this highly sought after pitching prospect.
13) He hit the New York Met's first home run.
14) His son Vance played 11 seasons in the Majors.
15) On August 31st, 1950 he went 5/6 and slugged four home runs!

* PRAY ON THESE answers found on page 239

ROSTER/LINGO

CATCHERS:	Yr	Hits	AB's	Ave
James *Deacon* McGuire	26	1749	6290	.278
Brian *Harp* Harper	15	931	3144	.296
Joe *The Immortal One* Azcue	11	712	2828	.252
Ray *Deacon* Murray	6	184	731	.252
Faithful Fred Abbott	3	107	513	.209
Louis *Chappie* Graff	1	2	5	.400
George *Miracle Man* Stallings	3	2	20	.100
Cloy *Monk* Mattox	1	1	6	.167

1ST BASEMEN:	Yr	Hits	AB's	Ave
Gil *Miracle Worker* Hodges	18	1921	7030	.273
Mark *Amazing* Grace	7	1153	3804	.303
Howie *Steeple* Schultz	6	383	1588	.241
John *Monk* Sherlock	1	97	299	.324
George *Chappy* Lane	2	87	429	.203
Grover *Deacon* Jones	3	14	49	.286
Bill *Mary* Calhoun	1	1	13	.077

2ND BASEMEN:	Yr	Hits	AB's	Ave
Bill *Deacon* McKechnie	11	713	2843	.251
Tom *Parson* Nicholson	3	169	646	.262

SHORTSTOPS:	Yr	Hits	AB's	Ave
Everett *Deacon* Scott	13	1455	5837	.249
Argenis *Angel* Salazar	5	188	886	.212
Ray *Chappy* Charles	3	186	851	.219
Fred *Chappie* Chapman	3	36	187	.193
James *Chappie* Geygan	3	26	103	.252

3RD BASEMEN:	Yr	Hits	AB's	Ave
James *Deacon* White	15	1619	5335	.303
Will *Deacon* Smalley	2	113	540	.209
Jack *Angel Sleeves* Jones	2	71	279	.254

OUTFIELDERS:	Yr	Hits	AB's	Ave
Orator Jim O'Rourke	19	2304	7435	.310
Lloyd *Shaker* Moseby	12	1494	5815	.257
Ival *Goodie* Goodman	10	1104	3928	.281
George *Orator* Shaffer	11	974	3442	.283
Harry *Goody* Simpson	8	752	2829	.266
Otto *Moonie* Miller	13	695	2836	.245

OUTFIELDERS: (Cont.)	Yr	Hits	AB's	Ave
Goodwin *Goody* Rosen	6	557	1916	.291
Billy *The Evangelist* Sunday	8	498	2007	.248
Eric *Blue Devil* Tipton	7	439	1626	.270
John *Holy* Moses	11	438	1723	.254
George *Bingo* Binks	5	277	1093	.253
John *Monk* Cline	5	247	946	.261
Warren *Deacon* Newson	4	107	410	.261
George *White Wings* Proeser	2	20	76	.263
Edward *Deacon* Van Buren	1	11	44	.250
Mose *Rabbi of the Swat* Solomen	1	3	8	.375
Amzie *Chappie* Snodgrass	1	1	10	.100

PITCHERS:	Yr	Won	Lost	ERA
Lefty *Mose* Grove	17	300	141	3.06
Charles *Deacon* Phillippe	13	189	109	2.59
Frank *Sweet Music* Viola	13	175	146	3.67
Vern *Deacon* Law	16	162	147	3.77
Deacon Danny MacFayden	17	132	159	3.96
Elwin *Preacher* Roe	12	127	84	3.43
Ted *Parson* Lewis	6	94	64	3.53
Russ *The Mad Monk* Meyer	13	94	73	3.99
Bruce *Amishman* Sutter	12	68	71	2.83
Walt *Monk* Dubiel	7	45	53	3.87
Jack *Monk* Meyer	7	24	34	3.92
Wally *Preacher* Hebert	4	21	36	4.63
Fred *Deacon* Johnson	4	5	10	5.26
Con *Monk* Murphy	2	4	13	5.07
George *White Wings* Proeser	1	3	4	3.81
Emmett *Parson* Perryman	1	2	4	3.93
Michael *Deacon* Morrissey	2	1	3	2.23
Willie *Parson* McGill	1	1	0	3.44
George *Deacon* Darby	1	1	1	7.76
Ralph *Holy* Good	1	0	0	2.00
William *Deacon* Wright	1	0	4	3.21
Bill *Ding Dong* Bell	2	0	1	4.32
John *Deacon* Donahue	2	0	2	6.75
Jack *Preacher* Faszholz	1	0	0	6.94
Cal *Preacher* Dorsett	3	0	1	11.85

EXTRA:
Dark Star - Great WCCO Sports Announcer

The Dark One: Pitch a player cannot hit
Wore the Collar: Player goes hitless
Charity Hop: Grounder takes a nice high hop
Sacrifice: Player bunts a base runner to the next base, giving up his chance to get a base hit
Sacrifice Fly: Fly ball which allows a base runner on third base to tag up and advance to score a run
Father: Player who does something first
Pray for Rain: When down bad early in a game, a team hopes for the game to be rained out!
Steeple: Someone very tall
Bingo: Get a hit
Baptism by Fire: First time a player plays
Rang His Bell: Hit a player in the head
Sent Down: Player must go to the minors

Give a Sign: Something the catcher does to tell a pitcher what to throw or what a coach tells players to do
Blessed with Speed: A fast runner
He's Going Down: Batter is to be pitched high inside
A Gift: An undeserved run
In the BigInning: First three words of Baseball Bible
Buried Them: Beat a team badly
Went the Other Way: Hit to the opposite field (ex. right hander hits to right field)
The Ledger: The summation of a pitcher's results
Bible on the Hitter: "Book" on how to pitch to batters
Gave Himself Up: Perform a sacrifice
Converted: Player learns and plays a new position
Got the Call: Pitcher comes in from the pen
Called Up: Player in minors goes up to the Majors

Real PIRATES

27

Team

The Pittsburgh Pirates started in 1882 as a member of the American Association. The team was called the Allegheny Baseball Club. After the 1890 season, the then Allegheny Innocents merged with the defunct Players League Pittsburgh team to form the Pittsburgh Athletic Company. When the club signed a player (or stole him, as his previous team claimed), the Athletic Company was nicknamed the Pirates, and it stuck!

The Real Pirates have carved a baseball legacy as rich as buried treasure and pieces of eight. The nickname Cannon Ball, which six members have, was a pre-1900 term for a very fast pitcher (no one knew about rockets then!). Twelve players were tabbed Long, a moniker for tall players. Other crew members not only have colorful nicknames such as Bloody Jake, Patcheye, Bones and Whip, but some mates also respond to Salty, Rough, Rowdy and Bad. The decks are manned by Old Iron Hands, two Eagle Eyes, a Sure Shot and a Toy Cannon. Other men on board are three Gunners, two Sailors, Goodeye and Captain Hook. The castoffs include Stump, Stumpy, Stub and One Arm. In total, this skull and cross Bones crew would 'shiver me timbers' if I were an opposing team.

One Real Pirate looms high on the horizon. That man is George Sparky Captain Hook Anderson. Only seven managers have piloted 2000 victories while at the helm. Connie Tall Tactician Mack, John Little Napoleon McGraw, Marse Joe McCarthy, Stanley Bucky Harris, Walter Smokey Alston and Leo The Lip Durocher are the other six. They each are members of the Hall Of Fame. Captain Hook first managed in the Majors in 1970. For nine summers he captained the Big Red Machine. They captured five division titles, four pennants and two World Championships. In an era of long hair and beards, Sparky's mates were closely cropped and clean shaven. He ran a tight ship. Since 1979 Sparky has had skipper duties for the Tigers. In 1984 he led Detroit to the World Championship. Sparky became known as Captain Hook because he was so quick to yank his starters. He is also known for his habit of never stepping on the third base chalk line when going to and from the mound. His next port of call is on the shores of Lake Otsego.

LINEUP

CA	*Rough* Bill Carrigan

was a solid defensive player. He twice led the American League in fielding %. Rough Bill was a playing manager during the last 3½ years of his playing career. He piloted the Red Sox to consecutive World Series Championships in 1915-16.

1B	Jake *Eagle Eye* Beckley

is in the Hall of Fame. He starred 20 seasons in the Major Leagues (1888-1907), nine times hitting .325 or more! Eagle Eye fell just 70 hits short of 3000 for his sparkling career. He ranks second in games played and first in putouts recorded for first sackers.

2B	Fred *Sure Shot* Dunlap

combined with Pebbly Jack Glasscock to form an early keystone combo. Sure Shot led second sackers three times in fielding % and assists, and two times in putouts and DP's. In 1884 he led the Union Assoc., hitting a lusty .412. Fred also placed first in HR's, hits and runs!

SS	*Bad* Bill Dahlen

should be in the Hall. He starred 21 seasons and ranks, for shortstops, seventh all time in games, third in assists and second in putouts. Bill led the NL in assists (four), DP's (three) and fielding % (one). Bad Bill ranks 76th in hits and 36th in runs. He led the league in RBI's in 1904.

3B	*Long* Levi Meyerle

was one of baseballs' pioneers. He starred in the National Association, the first recognized Major League. Long Levi led in homers (tie) and batting average in its inaugural season (1871). Again in 1874 he was the batting leader. Those five years (1871-75) are not in his stats.

OF	Joe *The Yankee Clipper* DiMaggio

was simply great! He was voted the AL MVP in 1939, 1941 and 1947. He gave three years to his country (ages 28-30). In his 12½ seasons, The Yankee Clipper drove in 114 or more tallies nine campaigns. He led the near unbeatable Yanks to nine World Championships!

OF	*Long* Bob Meusel

was a member of the Yankees' "Murderers' Row." During his 11 seasons he slashed over 40 doubles, legged out ten or more triples and drove in over 100 runs five times each. Long Bob hit .300+ seven summers. In 1925 he led the Junior Circuit in both long balls and RBI's.

OF	Charlie *Eagle Eye* Hemphill

played his last ten seasons in the new Junior Circuit (American League started in 1901). He was small and fast. Eagle Eye stretched ten plus triples four times and stole 20+ bases five summers. His 42 pilfers in 1908 placed Charlie second in the American League.

P	George *Hooks* Dauss

had two appearances at the end of the 1912 season. He became a fixture for the Tigers the next 14 summers. Hooks won ten or more games every year, three times winning over 20! In 1915 Hooks won 24 contests, tying him for second in victories in the American League.

P	Jesse *Powder* Tannehill

was an immediate star. In 1898, his first full season, Powder won 25 contests. He went on to win 20 or more games five of his next seven years (1899-1905)! He issued only 1.56 walks per game over his career (fifth best since 1900) and Powder authored 34 shutouts.

P	*Sailor* Bob Shawkey

starred 15 summers in the Junior Circuit. Four seasons he won 20 or more games. Sailor Bob's best year was 1916, winning 24 times (second) and leading the league in saves (tie). In 1920 he won the ERA title and logged 20 victories for the New York Yankees.

RES	Ed *Cannonball* Morris

dominated the Amer. Assoc. for three summers (1884-86). In 1884, as a 21 year old rookie, he won 34 games and fanned 302 hitters. The next season Cannonball won 39 contests (second) and led the league in K's and shutouts. In 1886 he was first with 41 wins and 12 shutouts!

RES	Ewell *Whip* Blackwell

had his career cut short due to injury. When healthy, he was nearly unhittable. In 1947 Whip dominated the National League. He led the league in wins, complete games and strikeouts! On June 18th, 1947 Whip no-hit the Braves. He finished second for the 1947 MVP award.

RES	George *Hooks* Wiltse

hurled for 12 summers. Hooks won 12 or more games each of his first eight seasons (1904-11). Twice he won 20 or more games. In 1908 Hooks logged 23 victories and tossed seven shutouts. He and Christy Big Six Mathewson formed the Giant's great lefty/righty combo.

RES	Hugh *One Arm* Daily

lost his left hand as a result of an accident during his youth. His pre-1900 total of 483 strikeouts in 1884 is third highest ever. That summer One Arm finished second in the Union Association in wins, games, complete games, shutouts (tie) and innings pitched!

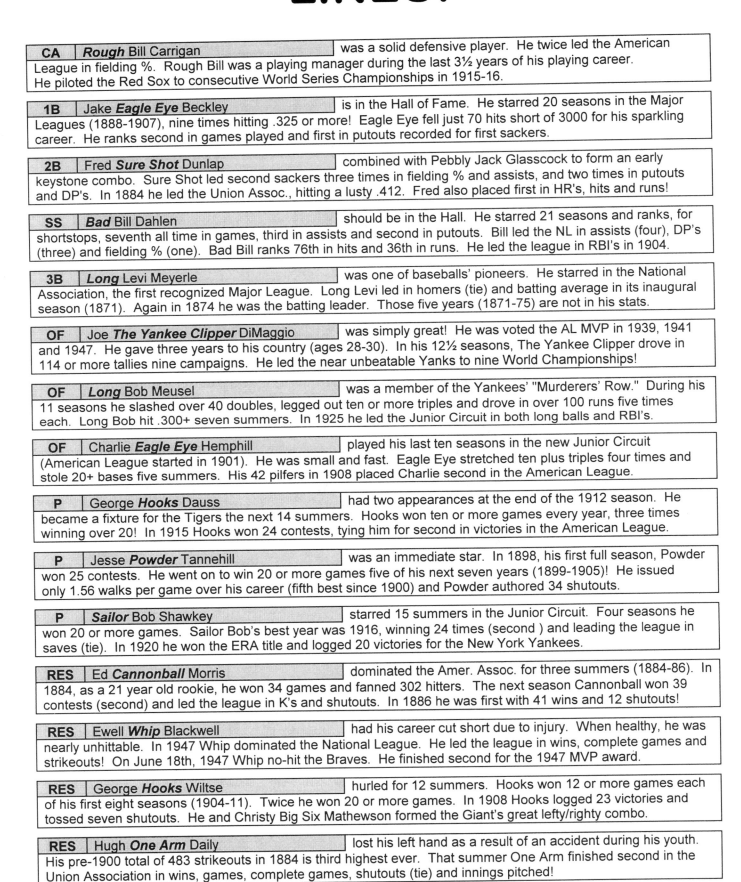

L to R: Ewell *Whip* Blackwell, *Bad* Bill Dahlen, George *Captain Hook* Anderson, Jimmy *The Toy Cannon* Wynn, *Long* Bob Meusel

151

It'sa FACT

Bill **Whip** Serena: During his career in the Majors he launched 48 homers in 1239 at bats. Whip holds the baseball record (in the minors) powdering 70 yard shots in one season!

George **Hooks** Dauss: This curve ball specialist won more games for Detroit (222) than any other Tiger pitcher.

Bad Bill Dahlen: He originally held the consecutive game hitting record of 42 games. His streak is now the fourth longest. After wearing the collar one game, Bad Bill then hit in 28 more consecutive games!

Rowdy Richard Bartell: A rough and tumble player, he earned his nickname. During his 18 year career, Rowdy Richard hit over .300 six times. In the field he led the league four times in assists and three times in DP's.

Long Tom Hughes: He starred with Denton Cy Young and Big Bill Dinheen in 1903 when each twirler won 20 or more games. Long Tom helped lead the Boston Pilgrims to the First World Series Championship. On August 30th, 1910 and June 16th, 1916, he hurled no-hitters.

Long John Healy: His second nickname was Egyptian. He was from Cairo, Illinois.

George **Hooks** Wiltse: While hurling for the Giants in 1904, he won 12 consecutive games. On July 4th, 1908 Hooks posted a ten inning no-hitter. He fanned four batters in inning #5, May 15th, 1906.

Long Jong John Reilly: On two separate occasions, June 14th, 1890 and October 13th, 1891, he smashed three triples in one game. Long John's 26 triples in 1890 are the ninth highest single season total (tie). In 1888 he just missed the Triple Crown. Long John led the Am. Assoc. in homers and RBI's, but he finished second in batting ave.

Joe **The Yankee Clipper** DiMaggio: Although he was a slugger, he seldom fanned. Seven of his 13 years Joe hit more homers than he whiffed. In 1941 (30 HR's) he K'ed only 13 times in 541 at bats.

Jake **Eagle Eye** Beckley: He slugged 243 triples (4th). Jake legged out 22, 19, 19, 19, 18 and 19 3B's from 1890-95.

Long Bob Meusel: He and his brother Irish combined to place (for brother combinations) 11th in hits, ninth in doubles, seventh in triples and fifth in RBI's.

Jesse **Powder** Tannehill: In 1900 he went 20-6 and hit .336! On August 17th, 1904 Powder fired a no-hitter against Chicago. His younger brother Lee was the Hitless Wonder's starting third sacker!

Long Charley Jones: He was Mr. Everything in 1879, leading the NL in runs, walks, homers and RBI's (tie).

Henry **Hooks** Wyse: His 1945 season was spectacular. Hooks' log read 22 wins (second), 278 innings (second) and 2.68 ERA (fifth). He and the Cubs made their last appearance in the World Series that fall.

Ledell **Cannonball** Titcomb: He had his day with destiny, Sept. 15th, 1890. Cannonball no-hit Syracuse 7-0.

Long Bob Ewing: During his eight "full" seasons he won in double digits each year. Long Bob won 20 games in 1905 and he posted a 1.73 ERA and 17 wins in 1907. His career 2.49 ERA ranks Long Bob tied for 27th all time!

Three Rivers Stadium: Often it is referred to as "The House That Clemente Built". The ballpark's name comes from the Monongahela, Allegheny and Ohio Rivers. Actually two rivers, the Monongahela and the Allegheny meet and form one river, the Ohio, but who's counting.

The Crow's Nest: It was the third deck (built in 1938) behind home plate at Forbes Field, home to the Pirates from 1909-70. Forbes Field was named after British General John Forbes. He captured Fort Duquesne in 1758, during the French and Indian War, and renamed it Fort Pitt. Today it is Pittsburgh.

TRIVIA*

1) On September 5th, 1921, July 3rd, 1922 and July 26th, 1928 he hit for the cycle. Only two players have done it three times. (Hint: his brother's nickname was Irish)
2) He was an excellent infielder with a strong accurate arm. It led to his nickname.
3) This Hall of Famer was often called Joltin' Joe.
4) He was not very big, but he sure could powder the ball.
5) In 1947 he won 16 consecutive games, all by going the route.
6) He and his brother, Snake (Lewis), combined to win a total of 168 games in their combined careers.
7) His 148 free passes in 1969 tied the NL single season record.
8) He and his two brothers, Vince and Dom (The Little Professor), combined to rank for brother combinations third in hits, second in homers and first in runs, doubles and RBI's.
9) From 1970-72 he averaged over one whiff per inning. He won 11 games in 1970, fanning 184 in 155 1/3 frames. In 1972 his log read 10-1, whiffing 134 in 124 1/3 innings.
10) He launched 22, 23 and 31 homers in 1969, 1966 and 1965. (Hint: think of a famous 1959 Bobby Darin song)
11) In 1941 he led the NL in runs, doubles (tie), triples, slugging % and batting ave. He placed second in the MVP.
12) He was a career National Leaguer. He batted over .300 thirteen times on his way to the Hall.
13) His very unorthodox delivery led to his nickname.
14) He signed the first six digit baseball contract. He was paid $100,000 for the 1949 season.
15) He was the winning pitcher in the inaugural game at Yankee Stadium.

* BURIED TREASURES answers found on page 239

ROSTER/LINGO

CATCHERS:	Yr	Hits	AB's	Ave
Rough Bill Carrigan	10	506	1970	.257
Harold *Rowdy* Elliott	5	97	402	.241
Thomas *Old Iron Hands* Sullivan	4	64	345	.186
Moses *Fleet* Walker	1	40	152	.263

1ST BASEMEN:	Yr	Hits	AB's	Ave
Jake *Eagle Eye* Beckley	20	2930	9526	.308
Long Jong John Reilly	10	1352	4684	.289
Phil *Hook* Todt	8	880	3415	.258
Bob *The Rope* Boyd	9	567	1936	.293
Bad Bill Eagan	3	90	382	.236
Harvey *Hooks* Cotter	2	82	311	.264

2ND BASEMEN:	Yr	Hits	AB's	Ave
Fred *Sure Shot* Dunlap	12	1159	3974	.292
Arnold *Stub* Hauser	5	349	1468	.238
Tim *Good Eye* Shinnick	2	224	936	.239
George *Captain Hook* Anderson	1	104	477	.218

SHORTSTOPS:	Yr	Hits	AB's	Ave
Bad Bill Dahlen	21	2457	9031	.272
Rowdy Richard Bartell	18	2165	7629	.284
William *Bones* Ely	14	1331	5159	.258
Mark *The Blade* Belanger	18	1316	5784	.228
Francis *Salty* Parker	1	7	25	.280
Frank *Hooker* Whitman	2	1	22	.045

3RD BASEMEN:	Yr	Hits	AB's	Ave
Bobby *Gunner* Reeves	6	402	1598	.252
Ed *Battleship* Gremminger	4	356	1420	.251
Bill *Whip* Serena	6	311	1239	.251
Long Levi Meyerle	3	123	374	.329
Hoke *Hooks* Warner	4	50	219	.228

OUTFIELDERS:	Yr	Hits	AB's	Ave
Joe *The Yankee Clipper* DiMaggio	13	2214	6821	.325
Long Bob Meusel	11	1693	5475	.309
Jimmy *The Toy Cannon* Wynn	15	1665	6653	.250
Charlie *Eagle Eye* Hemphill	11	1230	4541	.271
Long Charley Jones	11	1101	3687	.299
Gene *Rowdy* Moore	14	958	3543	.270
Pistol Pete Reiser	10	786	2662	.295
Mack *The Knife* Jones	10	778	3091	.252
Uriah *Bloody Jake* Evans	7	435	1831	.238
Long Tom Winsett	7	134	566	.237
Long Jim Holdsworth	4	132	522	.253
Clint *Hondo Hurricane* Hartung	6	90	378	.238
Bob *Hurricane* Hazle	3	81	261	.310

OUTFIELDERS: (Cont.)	Yr	Hits	AB's	Ave
Johnny *Patcheye* Gill	6	79	322	.245
One Armed Pete Gray	1	51	234	.218
Robert *Brandy* Davis	2	25	134	.187
Jacob *Stump* Edington	1	16	53	.302

PITCHERS:	Yr	Won	Lost	ERA
George *Hooks* Dauss	15	222	182	3.30
Jesse *Powder* Tannehill	15	197	116	2.79
Sailor Bob Shawkey	15	196	150	3.09
Ed *Cannonball* Morris	7	171	122	2.82
Harry *Gunboat* Gumbert	15	143	113	3.68
George *Hooks* Wiltse	12	139	90	2.47
Long Tom Hughes	13	131	175	3.09
Long Bob Ewing	11	124	118	2.49
Pistol Pete Ramos	15	117	160	4.08
George *Stump* Weidman	9	101	156	3.60
Ewell *Whip* Blackwell	10	82	78	3.30
Henry *Hooks* Wyse	8	79	70	3.52
Long John Healy	8	78	136	3.84
Hugh *One Arm* Daily	6	73	87	2.92
Edward *Cannon-Ball* Crane	9	72	96	3.99
Tom *The Blade* Hall	10	52	33	3.27
Sailor Bill Posedel	5	41	43	4.56
Ledell *Cannonball* Titcomb	5	30	29	3.47
Cannon Ball Bill Stemmeyer	4	29	29	3.67
Clint *Hondo Hurricane* Hartung	4	29	29	5.02
Ralph *Sailor* Stroud	3	20	20	2.94
Norm *Bones* Baker	3	14	15	3.42
Arnold *Hook* Carter	2	13	11	2.72
Ken *Hook* Johnson	6	12	14	4.58
Bill *Gunner* McGunnigle	2	11	8	2.81
Fred *Whip* Lasher	6	11	13	3.88
Dick *Bones* Tomanek	5	10	10	4.95
Al *Hook* Grabowski	2	9	6	4.07
Fay *Scow* Thomas	4	9	20	4.95
Julio *Whiplash* Navarro	6	7	9	3.65
John *Cannon Ball* Shaffer	2	7	14	4.57
Bill *Hooks* Miller	4	6	9	4.24
Long Herm Besse	5	5	15	6.79
Richard *Stub* Brown	3	4	1	4.90
Clarence *Hooks* Iott	2	3	9	7.05
Harry *Cannonball* Otis	1	2	2	1.37
Guy *Gunner* Cantrell	3	2	7	4.27
Long Tom Parsons	3	2	13	4.72
Earl *Hook* Henry	2	1	4	5.03
Al *Stumpy* Verdel	1	0	0	0.00
Jim *Bones* Blackburn	2	0	2	5.50
Long John Andre	1	0	1	5.80

Whip: A strong arm
Pitchers Duel: A close low scoring game
Hook: Curve ball
Castoff: Player let go from a team
Powdered One: Hit a home run
Slashed a Hit: Hit a ball very hard

Give Him the Hook: Remove the pitcher
Wave: Fans raise arms in succession
Long Ball: Home run
Long Man: Middle innings reliever
Skull: Very stupid play
Bones: Very thin person

PLAYED BIG

28

Team

One of the real advantages of baseball over some other sports is that a "special size" is not essential. An exceptional athlete of just normal proportions can easily excel. Even if you are below average in size, your chances are still reasonable in not only participating, but also in succeeding!

On the Played Big Team there are many big big stars. Eight players have already reached Cooperstown! Their nicknames are Little Steam Engine, Little Poison, Little Napoleon, Little Colonel, two Littles, Wee Willie and Mighty Mite. The roster also checks-in with nine Shorties, eight Bugs, seven Midgets and five Peewees. There are seven more Littles, five more Wee Willies, plus four Fleas, two Runts and a Half Pint! Add in a Little Dynamite, a Little Professor and two Little Generals, then include a Little Italian, Little Eva and a Little Stew. Maybe, just maybe, you will be a Little All Right!

One player stands head and shoulders above the group. He is referred to here by his second nickname, Little Colonel. Harold Pee Wee Little Colonel Reese was a leader. With the end of World War II, it was easy to assign a high rank to your team leader. Harold, as a youngster, was the Louisville, Kentucky marble champion. Pee Wee stuck more than in the marble ring! His stats are easy to quote, but the big one is this. For ten consecutive playing seasons (he gave three to his country in the middle) his fellow National Leaguers voted him on the NL All-Star team! That is Big!

LINEUP

CA | Jim *Little Nemo* Stephens , while with the St. Louis Browns, shared backstop duties his six seasons. At 5'6", Little Nemo was not large for a catcher, but he did pack some power. In 1909 Little Nemo tied for his team lead in yard shots and finished with the fourth highest home run % in the National League.

1B | James *Bug* Holliday starred for ten summers prior to the turn of the century. Barely 150 pounds, he played big. Bug led the American Association in home runs (shared) in 1889 and he led the NL in dingers in 1892! He swatted the ball at a .372 pace in 1894, one of six seasons Bug batted over .300!

2B | *Little* Joe Morgan was elected to the Hall of Fame his first year eligible. That says it all! Little Joe won back to back NL MVP's in 1975-76. He was the most prolific second baseman HR hitter. Nine years he stole 40 or more sacks. Little Joe was successful (for his career) 81% of his steals (13th).

SS | Luis *Little Looie* Aparicio was a starter all 18 seasons of his career. He led the Junior Circuit in assists his first six summers. Little Looie won nine Gold Gloves and led the league eight consecutive years (1959-66) in fielding %. His 2677 career hits place him in the top 50 all time.

3B | John *Little Napoleon* McGraw was not only a great player, but he was also an even greater manager! As a player, he was intense and combative. His .334 career batting average places him 21st. Little Napoleon is best remembered for managing 33 summers and winning 2763 games while at the helm.

OF | William *Wee Willie* Keeler had a Hall of Fame career which spanned 19 seasons. He "choked up" nearly half way up his bat. Wee Willie then poked, bunted and chopped 2932 hits at a .341 clip (12th best all time). For eight consecutive summers (1894-1901) he accumulated 200+ hits.

OF | Lloyd *Little Poison* Waner played 14 years along side his brother, Big Poison (Paul). He batted over .300 eleven of his 18 summers. Little Poison, barely 150 pounds, hit over .300 his first six seasons and led the National League once each in hits, runs (tie) and triples during his career.

OF | Jimmy *The Toy Cannon* Wynn was certainly one of the strongest hitters, ounce for ounce! He played during the 60's and 70's in the cavernous Astrodome, or his totals would be even greater. In 1967 The Toy Cannon finished second in the NL in dingers, and eight times in his 11 full seasons he hit 20 or more tators!

P | Jim *Little Steam Engine* Galvin was "the big guy" in his era. He toiled 14 seasons. Little Steam Engine could chug. His career marks are amazing. Jim had 360 wins (seventh), 639 complete games (second) and 5941 innings (second). In 1884 Gentle Jeems won 46 times and compiled a 1.99 ERA.

P | William *Wee Willie* Sherdel played his entire 15 years in the Senior Circuit. He was used both as a starter and in relief. Wee Willie led the NL three times in saves (twice out right) and six times in seven summers (1922-28) he won 15 or more games. In 1928 Wee Willie stood tall with 21 victories.

P | John *Wee Willie* Sudhoff hurled ten seasons at the turn of the century. Although he stood only 5'7", he was strong. Wee Willie completed 201 of his 240 starts (84%). He played for very weak teams throughout his career, limiting his record. In 1903 Wee Willie won 21 of his team's 65 victories!

RES | Freddie *The Flea* Patek was, in his era, the Major Leagues' shortest player at 5'4½", but he played big! The Flea was a three time All-Star and he finished in the top five in thefts six seasons. His 53 pilfers in 1977 topped the American League. Four times The Flea led in DP's at shortstop.

RES | Ernie *Tiny* Bonham "came up" as a 26 year old rookie in 1940. He went 9-3 with a 1.90 ERA his first summer. Tiny dominated in 1942. He finished 21-5, pacing the American League both in shutouts and winning %. Tiny tragically died at age 36 from complications after an appendectomy.

RES | Bibb *Jockey* Falk was the player who replaced Shoeless Joe Jackson after Joe was banished. He had big shoes to fill (well, maybe not!) and Jockey did just that. He terrorized AL hurlers for 12 seasons. Eight seasons Bibb hit over .300. His .352 average in 1924 placed Jockey third in the Junior Circuit.

MGR | Miller *Mighty Mite* Huggins stood only 5'6" and weighed 140 pounds, but he was a giant (or should I say Yankee) among managers. He faced down Babe Ruth and kept discipline on the mighty Yankee teams. Mighty Mite piloted 1413 victories and won six pennants and three World Championships.

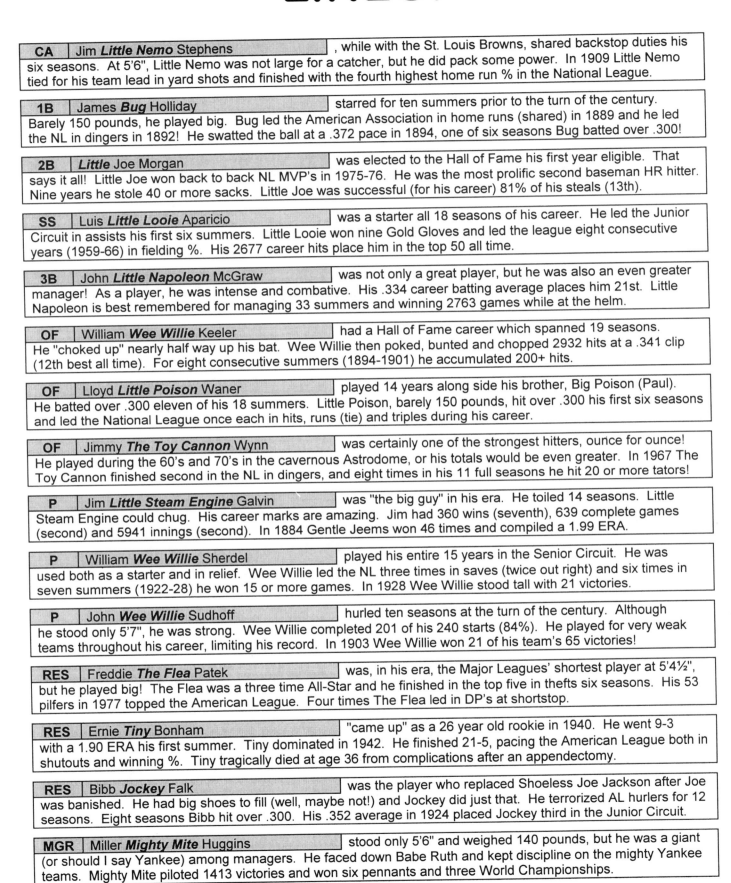

L to R: *Little* Joe Morgan, Luis *Little Looie* Aparicio, Harold *Little Colonel* Reese, William *Wee Willie* Keeler, Lloyd *Little Poison* Waner

155

It'sa FACT

Paul **Pee-Wee** Wanninger: Lou The Iron Horse Gehrig pinch-hit for him in the eighth inning and entered the game replacing Wally Pipp at first base. This was the start of Lou's 2130 consecutive game streak.

Don **Little** Liddle: He started and won the fourth and final game of the 1954 World Series.

Bill **Cricket** Rigney: He caught all infield pop-ups using the basket catch.

Little Joe Morgan: Ten times he was voted to the NL All-Star team. He scored over 100 runs in eight seasons. Little Joe, for his career, ended as the 25th highest run scorer.

Lloyd **Little Poison** Waner: Although Lloyd had only 27 career home runs, on September 4th, 1927, June 9th, 1929 and September 15th, 1938, both he and brother Paul went yard in the same game.

Jimmy **The Toy Cannon** Wynn: In 1969 Jimmy tied the NL mark when he received 148 free passes.

Jim **Little Steam Engine** Galvin: During his career he painted 57 whitewashes to tie for 11th all time. Little Steam Engine's 12 shutouts in one season (1884) has only been topped four times. Ten seasons he won 20 or more games. Twice he won 46 contests, but in no summer did Little Steam Engine lead the league in wins!

Miller **Mighty Mite** Huggins: He used his height to his advantage, leading the NL in walks four times (one tie).

Jimmy **Shorty** Slagle: He was the hero of the 1907 World Series. Shorty drove in one quarter of the Cub's runs and stole six bases.

Luis **Little Looie** Aparicio: The all time records for games played, DP's and assists at shortstop are his.

Tony **Little Dynamite** Gonzalez: The "pop" in his bat led to his nickname. He also was a superior gloveman. Three seasons Little Dynamite led NL outfielders in fielding %.

Tom **Bugs** Burgmeier: He ranks 16th in relief wins and tied for 15th in appearances. In 1982 Bugs went 7-0 in 40 appearances. He was 8-1 in 57 games in 1976. Bugs had only four losing seasons. Another St. Paul boy does great!

Claude **Little All Right** Ritchey: He basically played the same time as Hall of Famer Johnny Evers. Their stats are nearly identical!

	AB	RUNS	HITS	2B	3B	HR	RBI	AVE
Evers	6137	919	1659	216	70	12	538	.270
Ritchey	5919	708	1618	215	68	18	673	.273

Little All Right was also a slick fielder. He led the NL in fielding % five times, DP's three times and assists twice!

Bill **Shorty** Pleis: He was used primarily as a middle reliever. Many times I watched this smooth lefty make hitters look helpless.

Ernie **Tiny** Bonham: He tossed a four hitter in the clinching game #5 of the 1941 World Series.

Freddie **The Flea** Patek: In the 1976 and 1977 ALCS he played big! The Flea hit a hefty .389 in both series.

TRIVIA*

1) He holds the single season record of 202 singles. He also won two NL batting crowns. His best summer he batted an astronomical .424!

2) His big brother (also in the Hall of Fame) taught him how to hit, but he claimed their sister could hit better than both he and his brother!

3) He is second all time in games played at second base. He ranks third in assists, fourth in putouts and fifth in DP's. (Hint: he is currently an outstanding baseball announcer)

4) In a 1980 game he clubbed one double and three homers, leading the Royals to a 20-2 win over the Bosox.

5) He combined with Nellie Fox to form the "Go-Go White Sox" keystone combination.

6) This ballplayer stood 3'7" tall. He was inserted as a pinch hitter. Batting in a crouch, it was estimated he had a 1½" strike zone!

7) This umpire's other nickname was "Number One", because he was such a good umpire.

8) He broke Ty Cobb's single season stolen base record in 1962 when he swiped 104 sacks.

9) During his career he was issued 1865 free passes, third only to Babe Ruth and Ted The Kid Williams.

10) He was the 1956 AL Rookie of the Year. His first nine seasons he led the league in stolen bases.

11) For his career he fanned only once every 44+ at bats, second all time. In 1936, in 414 official at bats, he went down on strikes only five times!

12) An intense scrapper, he walked, was hit or got a hit, anything to get on base and score. His lifetime OBA is .466, third best all time.

13) He was the smallest and youngest of three ball playing brothers.

14) He averaged, for his career, fewer walks per nine innings (1.67) than any pitcher in the last 50 years.

15) His 689 career pilfers place this speedster 11th all time, yet he never led the league in steals!

* NOT SMALL THINKERS answers found on page 239

ROSTER/LINGO

CATCHERS:	Yr	Hits	AB's	Ave
Jim *Little Nemo* Stephens	6	276	1252	.220
Billy *Little Globetrotter* Earle	5	133	465	.286
Tony *Mighty Midget* Rego	2	26	91	.286

1ST BASEMEN:	Yr	Hits	AB's	Ave
James *Bug* Holliday	10	1134	3648	.311
William *Wee Willie* Clark	5	366	1273	.288
Dawson *Tiny* Graham	1	14	61	.230

2ND BASEMEN:	Yr	Hits	AB's	Ave
Little Joe Morgan	22	2517	9277	.271
Claude *Little All Right* Ritchey	13	1618	5919	.273
Miller *Mighty Mite* Huggins	13	1474	5558	.265
Bill *Cricket* Rigney	8	510	1966	.259
Frank *Human Flea* Bonner	6	244	949	.257
Nate *Peewee* Oliver	7	216	954	.226
Ron *Little General* Theobald	2	193	779	.248
Joe *Little General* Wood	1	53	164	.323
John *Shorty* Howe	2	14	69	.203
Ed *Mouse* Lyons	1	4	26	.154
Al *Tiny* Tesch	1	2	7	.286
Gene *Mousey* Markland	1	1	8	.125

SHORTSTOPS:	Yr	Hits	AB's	Ave
Luis *Little Looie* Aparicio	18	2677	10230	.262
Harold *Little Colonel* Reese	16	2170	8058	.269
Maury *Mousey* Wills	14	2134	7588	.281
Freddie *The Flea* Patek	14	1340	5530	.242
William *Shorty* Fuller	9	867	3679	.236
Davy *Tom Thumb* Force	10	623	2950	.211
Bob *Flea* Lillis	10	549	2328	.236
Arnold *Peewee* Hauser	5	349	1468	.238
Jimmy *Little Mac* Macullar	6	319	1541	.207
Harvey *Little Mac* McClellan	6	257	1162	.221
Paul *Pee-Wee* Wanninger	2	130	556	.234
William *Midget* Murphy	3	113	472	.239
Frank *Runt* Cox	1	13	102	.127
Maurice *Shorty* Dee	1	0	3	.000

3RD BASEMEN:	Yr	Hits	AB's	Ave
John *Little Napoleon* McGraw	16	1309	3924	.334
Little Joe Yeager	10	467	1853	.252
Jimmy *Runt* Walsh	6	447	1571	.285
Herman *Flea* Clifton	4	39	195	.200

OUTFIELDERS:	Yr	Hits	AB's	Ave
William *Wee Willie* Keeler	19	2932	8591	.341
Lloyd *Little Poison* Waner	18	2459	7772	.316
Dom *The Little Professor* DiMaggio	11	1680	5640	.298
Jimmy *The Toy Cannon* Wynn	15	1665	6653	.250
Tony *Little Dynamite* Gonzalez	12	1485	5195	.286
Bibb *Jockey* Falk	12	1463	4652	.314

OUTFIELDERS: (Cont.)	Yr	Hits	AB's	Ave
Jimmy *Shorty* Slagle	10	1340	4996	.268
Paul *Shorty* Radford	12	1206	4979	.242
Bill *Little Eva* Lange	7	1055	3195	.330
Mike *Tiny* Felder	10	564	2262	.249
Greg *Peewee* Briley	6	384	1518	.253
Jimmy *Little Stew* Stewart	10	336	1420	.237
Little Phil Geier	5	327	1315	.249
Al *Little Italian* Gionfriddo	4	154	580	.266
Fred *Bugs* Kommers	2	120	441	.272
Ed *Mouse* Glenn	3	106	525	.202
Glenn *Shorty* Crawford	2	89	306	.291
Ed *Midget* Mensor	3	54	244	.221
Alexander *Midget* Reilley	1	13	62	.210
Bill *Midget* Jones	2	12	53	.226
Bob *Shorty* Raudman	2	11	55	.200
Gene *Half-Pint* Rye	1	7	39	.179
Frank *Inch* Gleich	2	6	45	.133

PINCH HITTER:	Yr	Hits	AB's	Ave
Eddie *The Midget* Gaedel	1	0	0	.000

PITCHERS:	Yr	Won	Lost	ERA
Jim *Little Steam Engine* Galvin	14	360	308	2.87
William *Wee Willie* Sherdel	15	165	146	3.72
Ernie *Tiny* Bonham	10	103	72	3.06
John *Wee Willie* Sudhoff	10	103	135	3.56
Tom *Bugs* Burgmeier	17	79	55	3.23
Ray *Jockey* Kolp	12	79	95	4.08
Little Joe Yeager	6	33	49	3.74
Earnest *Tiny* Osborne	4	31	40	4.72
Little Bill Sowders	3	29	30	3.34
Bill *Bugs* Werle	6	29	39	4.69
Don *Little* Liddle	4	28	18	3.75
Jim *Little Joe* Edwards	6	26	37	4.37
Little Joe Presko	6	25	37	4.61
William *Wee Willie* Dammann	3	24	15	4.06
Bill *Shorty* Pleis	6	21	16	4.07
Don *Midget* Ferrarese	8	19	36	4.00
James *Tiny* Chaplin	4	15	23	4.25
Walt *Tiny* Leverenz	3	7	31	3.15
Elmer *Tiny* Leonard	1	2	2	2.84
Bruce *Little Pod* Ellingsen	1	1	1	3.21
Carl *Bugs* Moran	1	1	3	4.66
Charlie *Bugs* Grover	1	0	0	3.38
Harry *Bugs* Eccles	1	0	1	4.71
William *Wee Willie* Ludolph	1	0	0	4.76
Jacob *Bugs* Reisigl	1	0	1	6.23
George *Shorty* Wetzel	1	0	2	8.47
Tom *Little Hawk* Long	1	0	0	9.00

EXTRA:
William *Little Joe Chest* McGowan - Umpire

Short Lead: Runner stays close to the base
Short Hop: A ball bounces just before it is caught

Shorten Up: Batter slides his hands up the bat in preparation to bunt

Real REDS

29

Team

The Cincinnati Reds have evolved over the last 100+ years. Cincinnati was a charter member of the National League in 1876. Originally the team was called the Redstockings. Years later Cincinnati players were 'Redlegs'. Now they are simply 'the Reds'. In the 1970's the Reds were dubbed the 'Red Machine', because they reeled off win after win. The Redlegs played in Crosley field 58 summers. It was originally called Rotland field, but was renamed after Powel Crosley, a Cincinnati businessman who became the team's majority owner in the mid 30's. Currently the Reds play in Riverfront Stadium. The field has artificial turf and in left center it has a white circle. The circle was placed there to commemorate the September 10th, 1985, event, Charlie Hustle's 4192 career hit!

The 'Real Reds' are an awesome attack, particularly strong in pitching. 143 people are recognized, not only for their ability, but also, in most cases, for their red hair. There are some suspicious Reds, such as Art Red Herring and James Red Bird. Additionally, a Red Rooster, a Redleg and two Reds are included. To add confusion, there are five Red Smiths, two Red Barretts and two Red Padgetts!

One Redhead stands out above the others. His name is Albert Red Schoendienst. Red was involved in one of baseball's more bizarre happenings. It is the top of the eighth and the NL All-Stars are leading 9-7. There are two outs and Red is on third. Dean Stone is summoned from the bullpen. Before he hurls his first pitch, Red breaks for home and is gunned down. In the bottom of the eighth, Stone is pinch-hit for and the AL All-Stars score three runs to take the lead. Stone becomes the winning pitcher and he never threw a pitch! You read (no pun intended) it here first!

LINEUP

| CA | Charles *Red* Dooin | was an outstanding defensive catcher. During his 15 year |

Major League career, Red was a playing manager five seasons for the Philadelphia Phillies. Red tied for third in home runs in the National League's 1904 season, swatting 60% of his career total that summer.

| 1B | Don *Red* Padgett | was a versatile player. As a rookie outfielder in 1937, Red hit |

.314 with ten homers. Red switched to first base his sophomore year. In 1939 he hit a remarkable .399, but needed eight more at bats, so he did not qualify for the batting crown. Don lost four seasons to WW II.

| 2B | Albert *Red* Schoendienst | finally was elected to the Hall in 1989. A nine time All-Star, |

he posted seven .300+ seasons. Red batted .342 in 1953, ranking him second in the NL. Red accumulated 427 career two baggers, leading the NL in 1950 with 43. He six times led in fielding % at the keystone.

| SS | Ralph *Red* Kress | was an excellent all-around player for 14 seasons. Twice |

Red topped all American League shortstops in fielding %. At the plate, Red had a great stroke. From 1929-31 Red batted .305, .313 and .311 and drove in 107,112 and 114 runs for the St. Louis Browns.

| 3B | James *Red* Smith | was a seven year starter at the hot corner. During his nine |

season career, Red smashed nearly 1100 hits, including over 200 two baggers. In 1913, while playing for Brooklyn, Red led the National League with a career high 40 doubles, slashed 160 safeties and batted .298.

| OF | John *Red* Murray | was talented both at the plate and in the field. In 1909 Red |

led the Senior Circuit in home runs and ranked second in RBI's. He finished third in RBI's in 1910 and fifth in ribbies in 1912. Red led all National League right fielders in assists during the 1909 and 1910 seasons.

| OF | Al *Red* Wingo | was originally a pitcher, but he converted to the outfield, |

because of his good bat. In 1925 Red had his best season, hitting an awesome .370! Nevertheless, Red was the "piker" of the Tiger outfield. Harry Slug Heilman batted .393 and the Georgia Peach hit .378!

| OF | Wade *Red* Killefer | ,along with his younger brother William, both played in the |

early 1900's. Red's one full season was in 1915. That summer, playing for the Cincinnati Redlegs, Wade led the Senior Circuit in outfielder double plays and on offense legged out eleven three baggers.

| P | Charles *Red* Ruffing | hurled 22 campaigns during his Major League career and |

gave two more seasons to his country. Red's 273 wins place him 27th all time. From 1936-39 he won 20 or more games each season, going a combined 82-33 with 15 shutouts and 91 complete games.

| P | Leon *Red* Ames | was a 17 year National Leaguer who wore four teams |

uniforms before he "hung 'em up". In 1905 Red had his best year. He went 22-8, finishing third in wins and second in strikeouts. Twelve seasons Red won ten or more games and twice he led the league in saves.

| P | Jack *Red* Powell | fired balls and strikes for 16 summers. During Red's first 13 |

campaigns (1897-1909) he won in double digits each year! Four seasons he chalked up 20+ victories. For his career Red won 245 times (tie 42nd), tossed 46 shutouts (tie 26th) and completed 422 games (14th)!

| RES | Charles *Red* Lucas | toiled most of his career with second division clubs. |

Regardless, Red posted 157 victories, going 18-11 in 1927 and 19-12 in 1929. He led the Senior Circuit in complete games in 1929, 1931 and 1932. His four shutouts in 1928 tied Red for the National League lead.

| RES | Francis *Red* Donahue | started his career slowly, but he turned it around! After going |

0-1 his first two stays, Red went 7-24 and 10-35 his first two full summers. In his next nine seasons Red logged an outstanding 148-115 record, tossed 24 shutouts and won 20+ games three times!!

| RES | Urban *Red* Faber | played his entire 20 year Hall of Fame career with the White |

Sox. During his last 13 seasons the Sox never finished higher than fifth place (eight team league), but nevertheless, Red had four 20+ win seasons and captured two ERA crowns! Red is 35th all time in victories.

| MGR | Robert *Red* Rolfe | , after a great playing career, managed the Tigers for four |

seasons. Red's second place finish in 1950 earned him the American League Manager of the Year award. Unfortunately for Red, the Yankees, under the Old Professor, nipped his Tigers for the flag by three games.

L to R: Charles *Red* Ruffing, Charles *Red* Lucas, Albert *Red* Schoendienst, Robert *Red* Rolfe, Urban *Red* Faber

It'sa FACT

Ernie **Red** Padgett: In 1923 he was a late season call up. Red debuted October 3rd, 1923, and he played four games his first season. Playing shortstop October 6th, 1923, Red completed the fifth ever unassisted triple play! Walter Unionman Holke lined into the very rare play.

Robert **Red** Worthington: As a rookie fly catcher for the Braves in 1931, Red led all Senior Circuit outfielders in fielding %.

Charles **Red** Lucas: He was a complete player. As a pitcher, Red had excellent control. He walked only 1.61 batters per nine innings, seventh lowest since 1900! As a batter, Red hit over .300 six seasons. He compiled the eighth highest career batting average for a hurler. He finished his 15 year career with 404 hits.

John **Red** Murray: For eight seasons he played right field for the Giants. For years to come, right field in the Polo Grounds was known as "Murray's Hill" in memory of Red and his outstanding play.

Charles **Red** Ames: On April 15th, 1909 he pitched the game of his life. For nine innings Red was perfect, 27 up and 27 down. He fanned ten and did not allow one ball to be hit to the outfield! Unfortunately The Kaiser, Irvin Wilhelm, matched his goose eggs. Red finally gave up a hit in the tenth and ultimately lost the game in 13 innings.

Richard **Red** Smith: At Notre Dame he was a star halfback. Red went on to play in the NFL for five seasons, nearly five years longer than his short baseball career (one game).

Emmett **Red** Ormsby: During his baseball playing career, he only pitched in the minor leagues. Wounds sustained during World War I prematurely ended Red's career. Known as the "umpire with 12 kids", Red went on to support his clan by umping 19 seasons in the Major Leagues.

John **Red** Corriden: John Corriden Jr., his son, also reached the Majors, but John Jr. never shared his dad's nickname.

Urban **Red** Faber: He was one of the last "legal" spitballers. After Ray Chapman's death in 1920, (hit in the head by the hard to control spitter) the spitball was banned. The rules committee allowed 17 established pitchers to legally continue throwing it. Red pitched 13 more seasons using his spitter.

Walter **Red** Smith: He won a Pulitzer Prize. Red was considered, by many, to be the best baseball writer to ever pick up a pen.

George **Red** Munger: For nine of his ten seasons, he starred for the Redbirds. Red gave 2 1/2 years to his country. In his 'half season' in 1944 Red went 11-3 with a 1.34 ERA. Returning just before the 1946 Fall Classic, Red won game #4. He was twice named to the NL All-Star team. In 1947, his best summer, Red's record was 16-5 with six shutouts.

Philip **Red** Ehret: He was a hurler during the late 19th century. In 1890 Red had his best summer, winning 25 contests. Four more seasons he won 19, 18, 18, and 16 games. An excellent batter, Red had 274 career hits, including four home runs (in the dead ball era)!

Robert **Red** Rolfe: He played ten seasons for the Yankees, seven as a starter. During those seven summers, Red scored an average of 120 runs and batted over .300 four times. In 1939 Red led the AL in hits (213), doubles (46), runs (139) and batting (.329).

John **Red** Oldham: He pitched the ninth inning of the seventh game of the 1925 World Series. Down three games to one, the Bucs stormed back to win the final three contests (this was the first time in World Series play a team came back from that deficit). Red saved game #7, fanning two of the three Senators he faced.

Mike **Red** Hedlund: In 1971 he had his best season. Red went 15-8 for the expansion Royals, finishing with a 2.71 ERA (fourth).

Howie **Red** Camnitz: His brother Harry was four inches taller, but three years younger than him. In 1909 they both pitched for the Bucs. Red went on to out win Harry 133 to one. From 1908-12 Red sparkled. His log read 16-9 with a 1.56 ERA in 1908. The next season, Red's record was 25-6 with a 1.62 ERA. He also allowed only one home run in 260 innings (1909)! In 1911 and 1912 Red won 20 and 22 games.

Gene **Red** Desautels: He was outstanding defensively. Red led all AL catchers in fielding % in 1937 and for his career had a lofty .989 fielding average.

Charles **Red** Ruffing: Not only was he an outstanding pitcher, but he also was an excellent hitter. Red had a .269 career batting average. His 98 doubles, 207 runs and 273 RBI are all time marks for hurlers. Red's 521 hits place him third and his 36 home runs rank Red in a tie for third. On September 18th, 1930 and June 7th, 1936 Red went deep twice in one game! In the 1930 season Red finished 40/110, batting .364 with four homers and 22 RBI's!

Maurice Joseph **Red** Shannon: Both he and his twin brother Joseph Aloysius Shannon played for the Boston Braves in 1915.

TRIVIA*

1) This outfielder won the MVP and was elected to the Hall of Fame. (Hint: his MVP was in the NFL and he is enshrined in Canton, Ohio).

2) This Hall of Famer batted over .300 in eight of his 22 seasons. (Hint: this is a "rough one")

3) His brother, also a Major Leaguer, was nicknamed Reindeer Bill.

4) On July 6th, 1953 and July 11th, 1953 he twirled two shutouts in his first two starts. (Hint: a worthy beginning)

5) This pitcher hit a pinch grand slam July 15th, 1945. (Hint: think of what you do in the dining room)

6) At the age of 15 he lost several toes on his left foot. Because he could barely run, his dream of playing baseball had apparently ended. Instead of giving up, he switched to pitching and now stands in the Hall of Fame.

7) This pitcher was a great pinch hitter. He finished with a then record 114 career pinch-hits. Amazingly, not one pinch-hit was a home run. (Hint: his other nickname was Nashville Narcissus)

8) He caught a 60 yard touchdown pass in the 1928 Rose Bowl. The Quarterback, Grant Gillis, later was his teammate on the Senators.

9) This Nashville native holds the modern day record of completing 27 consecutive games.

10) On July 14th, 1915 this pitcher stole, in succession, second, third and then home! He stole home again on April 23rd, 1923 (the record for pitcher home steals is three).

11) After five long rough seasons toiling for the lowly Boston Red Sox, this future Hall of Famer had an unrespectable 39-93 record.

12) He hit in the #2 hole in front of Joe DiMaggio. That helps to explain why he scored over 100 runs seven consecutive seasons.

13) In the 1917 six game Fall Classic this fleet footed hurler won three contests, including games #5 and #6.

14) This Hall of Famer coined the phrase "they're tearin' up the pea patch".

15) He will always be remembered for his diving stop in the ninth inning of the final game of the 1921 World Series. While sitting down, he threw out Home Run Baker at first. (Hint: think about a glove maker)

16) Tuberculosis cost him the 1959 season and the redhead never played a full season after that.

17) Twice he led National League backstops in fielding %. Three times he poled 20+ homers while playing "at home" in the spacious Astrodome.

18) This Minnesota Twin third sacker had his first career hit off of Early Gus Wynn, a solid line drive to center.

19) An outstanding gloveman, he led all NL shortstops in fielding % in both 1950 and 1951.

20) His 14th inning homer July 11th, 1950 won the All-Star game.

21) The Braves traded him to the Cards, during the 1945 season, when his record was 2-3. He went on to finish 23-12, leading the NL in wins, complete games, and innings pitched. (Hint: Boston had to grin and bear it)

22) His World Series log reads 7-2, tying him for the second highest World Series win total.

23) He threw a no-hitter July 8th, 1898, beating Boston 5-0. (Hint: Marlo Thomas' lucky husband)

24) After his playing career, he managed 14 seasons. He guided the Cardinals to two pennants and the 1967 World Championship.

25) His older brother, Ivey, was a Big League catcher for 17 seasons. (Hint: if you don't know it, just wing it)

ROSTER

CATCHERS:	Yr	Hits	AB's	Ave
Doug *The Red Rooster* Rader	11	1302	5186	.251
Charles *Red* Dooin	15	961	4004	.240
Gene *Red* Desautels	13	469	2012	.233
Robert *Red* Wilson	10	455	1765	.258
John *Red* Kleinow	8	354	1665	.213
Raymond *Red* McKee	4	110	433	.254
Myron *Red* Hayworth	2	91	429	.212
Walt *Red* Kuhn	3	55	268	.205
James *Red* Steiner	1	15	79	.190
Jack *Red* Roche	3	14	49	.286
Willard *Red* Smith	2	7	45	.156
Jack *Red* Redmond	1	6	34	.176
Leo *Red* Murphy	1	4	41	.098
Clarence *Red* Munson	1	3	26	.115
Doc *Red* Carroll	1	2	22	.091
Louis *Red* Lutz	1	1	1	1.000
Frank *Red* Madden	1	1	2	.500
Richard *Red* Smith	1	0	0	.000

1ST BASEMEN:	Yr	Hits	AB's	Ave
Don *Red* Padgett	8	573	1991	.288
Emanuel *Redleg* Snyder	2	41	257	.160
James *Red* Holt	1	24	88	.273
Ken *Red* Landenberger	1	1	5	.200
Ernie *Red* Gust	1	0	12	.000

2ND BASEMEN:	Yr	Hits	AB's	Ave
Albert *Red* Schoendienst	19	2449	8479	.289
Johnny *Red* Rawlings	12	928	3719	.250
Maurice *Red* Shannon	7	277	1070	.259
Jerome *Red* Downs	3	179	790	.227
Owen *Red* Friend	5	136	598	.227
John *Red* Barkley	3	43	163	.264
Thomas *Red* Owens	2	37	189	.196
Edward *Red* Borom	2	36	144	.250
John *Red* Juelich	1	11	46	.239
Henry *Red* Bittman	1	4	14	.286
Jim *Reds* McGarr	1	0	4	.000

SHORTSTOPS:	Yr	Hits	AB's	Ave
Ralph *Red* Kress	14	1454	5087	.286
Virgil *Red* Stallcup	7	497	2059	.241
John *Red* Corriden	5	131	640	.205
Sam *Red* Crane	7	103	495	.208
Lindsay *Red* Brown	1	31	115	.270
Charles *Red* Roberts	1	6	23	.261
Marvin *Red* Smith	1	4	14	.286
Gene *Red* Sheridan	2	1	6	.167
Don *Red* Kellett	1	0	9	.000

3RD BASEMEN:	Yr	Hits	AB's	Ave
Robert *Red* Rolfe	10	1394	4827	.289

3RD BASEMEN: (Cont.)	Yr	Hits	AB's	Ave
James *Red* Smith	9	1087	3907	.278
Rich *Red* Rollins	10	887	3303	.269
Ernie *Red* Padgett	5	223	838	.266
James *Red* Woodhead	1	21	131	.160
John *Red* Calhoun	1	10	64	.156
John *Red* Hinton	1	1	13	.077

OUTFIELDERS:	Yr	Hits	AB's	Ave
John *Red* Murray	11	1170	4334	.270
Al *Red* Wingo	6	409	1326	.308
Wade *Red* Killefer	7	381	1537	.248
Robert *Red* Worthington	4	298	1037	.287
Emile *Red* Barnes	4	225	836	.269
Glenn *Red* McQuillen	5	176	643	.274
Thadford *Red* Treadway	2	105	394	.266
Morris *Red* Badgro	2	98	382	.257
Leo *Red* Nonnenkamp	4	69	263	.262
Roy *Red* Massey	1	59	203	.291
Luther *Red* Harvel	1	30	136	.221
Dwight *Red* Dorman	2	28	77	.364
Fred *Red* Bennett	2	27	97	.278
Paul *Red* Busby	2	15	56	.268
John *Red* Fisher	1	9	72	.125
Robert *Red* Thomas	1	8	30	.267
Albert *Red* Kelly	1	7	45	.156
Elmer *Red* Durrett	2	7	48	.146
Howard *Red* Camp	1	6	21	.286
Les *Red* Lanning	1	6	33	.182
John *Red* Marion	2	5	28	.179
Frank *Red* McDermott	1	4	15	.267
David *Red* Barron	1	4	21	.190
Bob *Red* Kinsella	2	3	12	.250
Stephen *Red* Tramback	1	1	4	.250
Maurice *Red* Jones	1	1	11	.091
James *Red* Bowser	1	0	2	.000
James *Red* Callahan	1	0	4	.000
John *Red* Connolly	1	0	7	.000

PINCH HITTERS:	Yr	Hits	AB's	Ave
Roy *Red* Ostergard	1	4	11	.364
Murray *Red* Howell	1	2	7	.286
Don *Red* Barbary	1	0	1	.000
Harvey *Red* Bluhm	1	0	1	.000

PINCH RUNNERS:	Yr	Hits	AB's	Ave
Bob *Red* Daughters	1	0	0	.000
Ben *Red* Mann	1	0	0	.000

PITCHERS:	Yr	Won	Lost	ERA
Charles *Red* Ruffing	22	273	225	3.80
Urban *Red* Faber	20	254	213	3.15
Jack *Red* Powell	16	245	254	2.97

ROSTER

PITCHERS: (Cont.)	Yr	Won	Lost	ERA
Leon **Red** Ames	17	183	167	2.63
Francis **Red** Donahue	13	165	175	3.61
Charles **Red** Lucas	15	157	135	3.72
Philip **Red** Ehret	11	139	167	4.02
Howie **Red** Camnitz	11	133	106	2.75
George **Red** Munger	10	77	56	3.83
Al **Red** Worthington	14	75	82	3.39
Charles **Red** Barrett	11	69	69	3.53
Cecil **Red** Causey	5	39	35	3.59
John **Red** Oldham	7	39	48	4.15
Art **Red** Herring	11	34	38	4.32
Charles **Red** Embree	8	31	48	3.72
Mike **Red** Hedlund	6	25	24	3.56
Meldon **Red** Wolfgang	5	15	14	2.18
Frank **Red** Barrett	5	15	17	3.51
George **Red** Witt	6	11	16	4.32
Japhet **Red** Lynn	3	10	8	3.95
Albert **Red** Nelson	4	10	12	4.54
Lloyd **Red** Hittle	2	7	11	4.43
Tom **Red** Fisher	1	6	16	4.25
Patrick **Red** Shea	3	5	5	3.80
Arnold **Red** Anderson	3	5	8	4.35
Alex **Red** McColl	2	4	4	3.70
Zeb **Red** Eaton	2	4	2	4.43
Clarence **Red** Phillips	2	4	4	6.42
Samuel **Red** Webb	2	3	2	3.72
Arthur **Red** Swanson	3	3	3	4.90
Scott **Red** Cary	1	3	1	5.93
Chester **Red** Hoff	4	2	4	2.49

PITCHERS: (Cont.)	Yr	Won	Lost	ERA
John **Red** Murff	2	2	2	4.65
Bob **Red** Mahoney	2	2	5	4.96
Allen **Red** Conkwright	1	2	1	6.98
Chester **Red** Torkelson	1	2	1	7.66
Russell **Red** Evans	2	1	11	6.21
Woodward **Red** Gunkel	1	0	0	0.00
John **Red** Waller	1	0	0	0.00
Nelson **Red** Long	1	0	0	1.13
Seabron **Red** Booles	1	0	1	1.99
Gerald **Red** Fahr	1	0	0	4.76
George **Red** Peery	2	0	1	5.00
James **Red** Bird	1	0	0	5.40
Plateau **Red** Cox	1	0	0	5.40
Francis **Red** Hardy	1	0	0	6.75
Clifford **Red** Hill	1	0	0	6.75
Elbert **Red** Schillings	1	0	0	6.75
Les **Red** Lanning	1	0	3	8.14
Charles **Red** Adams	1	0	1	8.25
Noah **Red** Proctor	1	0	0	13.50
Malton **Red** Bullock	1	0	2	14.04
Walt **Reds** Herrell	1	0	0	18.00
Leo **Red** Miller	1	0	0	32.40

EXTRAS:
Walter **Red** Smith - Writer
Walter **Red** Barber - Announcer
John **Red** Flaherty - Umpire
Emmett **Red** Ormsby - Umpire
Nicholas **Red** Jones - Umpire

I ALWAYS WONDERED WHY?

If a ball hits the foul pole, why it is actually fair?
If it is good to pull the ball, why it is not good to pull the pitcher?
If you throw an out pitch, why it is different from a pitch out?
If the field is level, why do you go down the line?

If you get the sign to steal, why it is different from the sign to take?
If you run over the bag, why it is different than over running the bag?
Out of all the ballplayers nicknamed Red, why have I never heard of many of them? (author's thought)

Bags can have so much more happen to them. You can ...

```
GUARD THE BAG              REACH              TOUCH THE BAG
TAKE AN EXTRA             THE BAG         STEAL SWEEP THE
HOOK        BAG          HIT    HUG        THE           BAG
THE          BAG         THE    THE        BAG
BAG STAY ON THE          BAG    BAG        TAG
CROSS BE ON THE          CLEAR THE BAG     UP        BAG IT
OVER        BAG          STRAY FROM THE BAG ON      LOAD THE
THE          BAG         JAM          TAG   THE          BAG
BAG LEAVE THE            THE          THE   BAG MISS THE BAG
COVER THE BAG            BAG          BAG   ROUND THE BAG
```

163

RINGER

30

Team

What is a ringer? No, he does not push a doorbell and run away. It is not an old style machine to wash clothes with (or get your "you know what" caught in it!). If you think it has to do with horseshoes, you are not even close. A ringer is a player, not on your team, that you illegally "add on" to make your squad stronger. His real name is buried and you call him by another roster person's name and hope no one gets wise.

There is one requirement to qualify for the Ringer Team. A player has to be known by a common name that has nothing to do with his real first or middle name. Believe it or not, I pared the group down to the top 150 "ringers," leaving nearly 200 more players in the locker room! Two "ringers" have their plaques enshrined in Cooperstown. They are Dennis Joseph Dan Brouthers and Edgar Charles Sam Rice.

One Real Ringer peals far above the crowd. Edgar Charles Sam Rice was a terrific player. A family tragedy caused him to temporarily give up baseball and wander. After three years Sam returned, but at the age of 27 he had only accumulated 62 base hits. He played the 1917 season, but Sam appeared in just seven games in 1918 due to the Great War. Now at age 29 he had only 247 career safeties. Sam went on to star 16 more summers. From 1919-30 he played in over 97% of his team's games, ten times batting over .300 and six times swatting 200+ hits. Sam led the American League twice in base knocks (one tie) and once each in three baggers (tie) and steals. His 2561 base hits after age 30 are only exceeded in number by Pete Charlie Hustle Rose. At the age of 40 Sam had an amazing season. He batted .349 and became the only 40 year old Major Leaguer to have over 200 hits in a season (207). That campaign Sam scored 121 runs, pounded out 35 doubles and slashed 13 triples. Sam was a line drive hitter who usually had to swing the bat only once. He struck out just nine times in 616 at bats in 1929! He fanned only ten times in 649 at bats in 1925! For his career he was the sixth toughest player to whiff, k'ing once every 33 official plate appearances (currently the hardest Major Leagues to strikeout is Tony Gwynn, once every 20 at bats). At the age of 45 Sam hung 'em up. He ranked in the top 100 in most offensive categories. The one that is phenomenal is his 14th place finish in triples. Sam hit 165 of his 184 three baggers after he turned 30!

LINEUP

CA	James Luther *Luke* Sewell	played 20 seasons as a catcher, the American League record

until Carlton Pudge Fisk passed him. Only one backstop has caught more than his three no-hitters. Luke was an excellent fielder, pacing the Junior Circuit four times in putouts and twice in assists.

1B	Henry John *Zeke* Bonura	starred for seven years. He batted over .300 four times and

also drove in over 100 runs four seasons. Zeke led all first sackers three years in fielding %. Banana Nose, his other nickname, averaged 33 doubles, 17 home runs and 100 runs batted in for his career!

2B	Ron Kenneth *Zeke* Hunt	played infield for 12 summers in the Senior Circuit. Zeke was

the NL's All-Star choice in 1964 and 1966 and two seasons he hit over .300. Between his ability to draw walks and his willingness "to take one for the team," Zeke retired with an outstanding .369 on base percentage.

SS	Owen Joseph *Donie* Bush	batted leadoff. At 5'6" and blessed with a great eye, Donie

led the AL five times in walks and scored over 100 tallies four seasons. He stole 404 bags (55th), including 35 or more for seven consecutive years (1909-15). Donie also led AL shortstops in assists (five) and putouts (three).

3B	Colbert Dale *Toby* Harrah	sparkled for 17 years in the AL. He poled 20 or more dingers

five times. Toby drove in over 70 tallies six seasons. Starting his career as a shortstop, Toby also handled chores at second, but he logged his most games at third. He fell just five homers short of 200 for his career.

OF	Edgar Charles *Sam* Rice	at 5'9" 150 pounds, was, ounce for ounce, as good as any

player to ever lace 'em up! During his 20 seasons Sam batted .300 or more 15 years and he never finished lower than .293. Of Sam's 34 career circuit blasts, 21 of his round trippers were inside the parkers.

OF	David Russell *Gus* Bell	was a complete player. During his 15 seasons, the four time

All-Star drove in over 100 tallies four times, including three straight years (1953-55). Not only blessed with power to launch 206 career homers, Gus also had the speed to lead the NL in triples (1951) and fielding (1958-59).

OF	Walter Scott *Steve* Brodie	sparkled for 12 summers at the turn of the century. He was

excellent in the field, leading all center fielders three times in fielding % and once in both putouts and assists. Five seasons Steve hit over .300, including .366 in 1894. His 134 ribbies in 1895 were topped by only one player.

P	William H. *Adonis* Terry	began his career slowly, absorbing 52 loses in his first two

seasons. During Adonis' next 12 years he turned it around. He won 20+ games three times, including 26 victories in 1890, and he retired with a winning record! Adonis' .249 career batting average ranks him 33rd for pitchers!

P	Leslie Ambrose *Joe* Bush	fired bullets for 17 years in the Majors. Nine seasons he won

15 or more contests, including five consecutive summers (1920-24). In 1922 Joe went 26-7 to finish second in wins and first in winning %. Bullet Joe, also an outstanding batter, hit over .300 in six campaigns!

P	Edward Joseph *Jeff* Pfeffer	threw balls and strikes in the teens and early 20's. In 1914,

his first season (other than 34 1/3 innings in two previous years), Jeff went 23-12, logging a 1.97 ERA. The next summer he posted 19 wins and a 2.10 ERA. Jeff's 1916 campaign yielded 25 more V's and a sizzling 1.92 ERA!

RES	Robert James *Rick* Monday	starred 19 seasons, six in the AL and 13 in the NL. Rick was

an exceptional fielder, twice leading the league in DP's and once in fielding %. His 241 career round trippers include a career high 32 in 1976. With just 13 more cheap seaters, Rick would have been in the top 100 all time!

RES	John Alexander *Andy* Messersmith	was an outstanding hurler during his 12 seasons. Andy

fanned 6.56 batters per game for his career, 36th best. His 2.86 career ERA ties Andy for 77th. 1974 was his best campaign. Andy shared the NL lead in wins with Phil Knucksie Niekro, both logged 20 victories!

RES	Howard Jonathan *Bob* Ehmke	twirled 15 seasons. From 1922-24 he won 17, 20 and 19

games. In game #1 of the 1929 World Series Bob (seven wins) was the surprise starter, selected by Mgr. Mack over Lefty Grove (20 wins) and Moose Earnshaw (24 wins). Bob won and fanned a then Series record 13 batters!

MGR	Alfred Manuel *Billy* Martin	managed for sixteen seasons and coached for four plus

summers. Billy always raised the level of his teams' play just by his presence. Intense, involved and baseball smart, The Kid won four seconds, five division titles, two pennants and one World Championship!

L to R: Alfred Manuel *Billy* Martin, David Russell *Gus* Bell, Edgar Charles *Sam* Rice, Robert James *Rick* Monday, Henry John *Zeke* Bonura

It'sa FACT

Leland Victor **Lou** Brissie: In World War II he sustained wounds which ultimately required 20 operations! Lou had to wear a steal brace and shin guard on his left leg to play. Nevertheless, he went 14-10 (1948) and 16-11 (1949) for the fourth and fifth place Athletics. Lou was named to the AL 1949 All-Star squad and tossed for three innings.

Dennis Joseph **Dan** Brouthers: He was a 19 year star in the 1880's and 1890's. Dan was the premier slugger of his era. He batted .300 or more 14 consecutive seasons (1881-94), capturing seven slugging titles and earning five batting crowns! His lifetime batting average of .342 is eighth all time!

Dennis Lawrence **Dan** McGann: His glove was sure. From 1899-1906 he led all first sackers in fielding % six years!

John Bernard **Hans** Lobert: In his prime he was considered the fastest man in the National League. As a publicity stunt, Hans raced against a horse around the bases… but he lost by a nose!

Edward Nagle **Ned** Williamson: He was a star third sacker in the 1880's. Ned led all hot corner men in assists seven seasons, DP's six seasons, fielding % five seasons and putouts two seasons!

John William **Jay** Johnstone: One of baseball's infamous practical jokers, he had to be a good player to last 20 years. Jay's 92 pinch-hits rank him 19th. In the 1981 World Series Jay went 2/3 as a pinch hitter. His two run shot in game #4 turned the tide and the Series. Trailing two games to one, the Dodgers went on to win the Series 4-2!

Edward **Danny** Green: He batted over .300 four of his eight seasons and swiped 28 or more bags five times. Danny led all NL center fielders in putouts in 1901 and topped all AL right fielders in DP's in 1903.

Louis Richard **Steve** Evans: In 1914 he tore up the new Federal League. Steve led in slugging % and triples (tie). He also finished second in doubles and batting average, and placed third in hits, homers (tie) and total bases (tie).

Darnell Glenn **Dan** Ford: The Twins traded him to the Angels prior to the 1979 season. Danny responded with 21 yard shots and 101 RBI's, his career highs.

Edgar Charles **Sam** Rice: In game #3 of the 1925 World Series, Earl Oil Smith smashed a long shot off of Fred Firpo Marberry. Sam went up over the wall and caught the ball as he fell out of sight behind the fence. A minute later Sam reappeared with the ball in his glove. The ump ruled Oil out and ultimately cost the Pirates the game! His "blind call" was the topic of controversy for years! When asked, Sam would never tell if, after his fall, he really had held the ball or not. Even after his entry into the Hall of Fame, Sam remained silent. He did reveal that he had written a letter, to be read only after his death, which would tell the truth. After Sam passed away, the truth, after 49 years, was revealed. Sam did catch and hold the ball!

Francis Xavier **Big Jeff** Pfeffer: His younger brother Edward Joseph was also known as Jeff. So there you have two brothers, neither named Jeff, both called Jeff! In case you were wondering, Big Jeff was two inches shorter and 25 pounds lighter than Jeff! This reminds me of the Little Big Horn. Which was it, little or big? Or how about jumbo shrimp or special ordinary life insurance? Come to think of it, this could create a flammable debate or an inflammable debate, your choice!!

Heber Hampton **Dick** Newsome: In 1941 he was a 31 year old rookie. Dick won 19 times, third best in the AL.

David Russell **Gus** Bell: He blasted three homers in one game twice, on July 21st, 1955 and May 29th, 1956.

John F. **Darby** O'Brien: He reach the Majors at the age of 21. By 24 Darby had chalked up 18 and 22 win seasons. He tragically died 35 days before he turned 25.

Frank S. **Terry** Larkin: He was a regular starter for three seasons and "put up" three nearly identical seasons.

Year	Win	Loss	Win%	Game	Start	C.G.	Inn	Hit	ERA
1877	29	25	.537	56	56	55	501	510	2.14
1878	29	26	.527	56	56	56	506	511	2.24
1879	31	23	.574	58	58	57	513	514	2.44

Leslie Ambrose **Joe** Bush: On August 25th, 1916 he was knocked out of the box after just three innings. Starting again August 26th, he walked Jack Graney to leadoff the game, then Joe retired the next 27 batters, fanning seven.

Matthew C. **Max** Surkont: He was up long enough to go 5-2 in nine games (1950). Max supplied his own best support. He went 10/23, a .435 pace, and slugged one round tripper.

Charles Monroe **Jeff** Tesreau: During his seven seasons he handcuffed batters with his spitball. Jeff tossed 27 shutouts in just 205 starts, 13%! His career ERA is tied for 20th all time and he held batters to just 7.24 hits per game, 11th best. From 1912-14 Jeff was cumulatively 65-30, including a no-hitter on September 6th, 1912.

William Van Winkle **Jimmy** Wolf: Of his 11 seasons, he put it all together in 1890. Jimmy led Louisville to the American Association flag. That summer he topped all players in both hits and batting average!

George Lemuel **Bob** Ewing: He toiled for teams that were primarily second division. Nevertheless, Bob won in double digits each of his eight full seasons, including a 20-11 log for the fifth place Cincinnati club in 1905. Bob's lifetime ERA ranks him tied for 27th all time.

TRIVIA*

1) On December 23rd, 1975 he and Dave McNally were declared baseball's first free agents.

2) After he quit playing baseball, he played the lead role in The Rifleman and Branded.

3) When managing in Oakland, his style of play became known as "Billy Ball."

4) A top athlete at Notre Dame, he was known for his physique. That shortened to form this first sacker's nickname.

5) An All-American quarterback at Ol' Miss, he opted instead to turn pro in baseball, foregoing the gridiron. (Hint: he handled backstop duties for the Yankees)

6) In 1971 he was hit by a pitch a record 50 times! He also holds the game record (three times) and the career record (243) for being plunked.

7) His son David Gus (Buddy) was christened (middle name) with his dad's nickname!

8) While chasing fly balls in Minnesota, we called him Disco Danny.

9) In 1953 the Senators finished 76-76. This big right-hander went 22-10 and topped all AL twirlers in wins, complete games and shutouts. He also helped his own cause by jerking three four baggers and batting .255. (Hint: his first two real names almost sound like an old president's name)

10) In 1974 and 1975 he won the NL Gold Glove for pitchers.

11) He held the single season home run record (27) for 36 years, until Babe Ruth broke it in 1920. The Bambino launched 29 round trippers. (Hint: he played third base)

12) In the 1976 NLCS his team was swept by the Big Red Machine 3-0, but this "practical joker" went 7/9 (.778) in an heroic losing effort.

13) He and his son hold the father/son record for hits (4337), doubles (736) and RBI's (2048).

14) In game #4 of the 1947 World Series he had a no-hitter going with two outs in the bottom of the ninth. His Yankees were leading 2-1, but the big right-hander had just issued his ninth and tenth walks. Harry Cookie Lavagetto pinch-hit and tagged a double, not only ending his date with destiny, but also hanging him with the heartbreaking loss. He never pitched again in a regular season game!

15) This scrappy Yankee infielder was the unlikely hero of the 1953 World Series. His final hit in game #6 drove in the Series winning run. His log for the Classic read 24 at bats, 12 hits, one double, two triples, two homers and eight RBI's.

16) In 1961, his last year as a player, he tagged out a baserunner off of second using "the hidden ball trick!" (Hint: he went on to be a fiery manager)

17) His two out ninth inning homer in game #5 of the 1981 NLCS put the Dodgers in the World Series. (Hint: the Mamas and Papas repeated his last name in one of their hit songs)

18) In 1949 he won the NL ERA title. (Hint: his last name at birth was Koslowski)

19) His career .212 opponents batting average is topped by only two hurlers, Nolan The Express Ryan and Sanford Sandy Koufax! (Hint: his teammate Mike Marshall edged him for the 1974 Cy Young award)

20) During his career he had hitting streaks of 27, 28 and 31 games. (Hint: he is not related to Boston's slugger of the 70's whose first name was Jim)

21) This pre-1900 star and Hall of Famer slugged 205 triples during his career, eighth all time.

22) This slugging third sacker accumulated 1153 bases on balls, tying for 42nd all time. His 13.48 walk % is 72nd highest. (Hint: his last name can be spelled backwards)

23) He topped the above player, finishing 41st all time in free passes. This shortstop's walk % is 13.84%, ranking him 62nd all time.

24) His coaching presence has been credited with raising Zoilo Zorro Versalles from a good player to the outstanding MVP player he became in 1965.

25) He managed the New York Yankees five different times. He and George Steinbrenner had an on and off love/hate relationship which led to his fires and rehires.

* MYSTERY GUESS(t)S answers found on page 239

ROSTER

CATCHERS:	Yr	Hits	AB's	Ave
James Luther **Luke** Sewell	20	1393	5383	.259
John Bannerman **Larry** McLean	13	694	2647	.262
John Herman **Hank** DeBerry	11	494	1850	.267
Myron Nathan **Joe** Ginsberg	13	414	1716	.241
Jerry Dean **Jake** Gibbs	10	382	1639	.233
Thomas H **Pat** Deasley	8	358	1466	.244
Tharon Leslie **Pat** Collins	10	306	1204	.254
Maurice Dailey **Toby** Atwell	5	290	1117	.260
Angelo John **Tony** Giuliani	7	157	674	.233
Conrad **Dell** Darling	6	151	628	.240
Edgar Fredrick **Ned** Yost	6	128	605	.212
Ambrose Francis **Bruce** Ogrodowski	2	119	516	.231
Artemus Ward **Nick** Allen	6	116	500	.232
John Augustus **Josh** Billings	11	106	488	.217
Andrew Daniel **Tony** Cusick	4	64	332	.193
Arthur Augustus **Ben** Egan	4	58	352	.165

1ST BASEMEN:	Yr	Hits	AB's	Ave
Dennis Joseph **Dan** Brouthers	19	2296	6711	.342
Dennis Lawrence **Dan** McGann	12	1482	5222	.284
Henry John **Zeke** Bonura	7	1099	3582	.307
Ulysses John **Tony** Lupien	6	632	2358	.268
Maurice Lennon **Dick** Burrus	6	513	1760	.291
James Murrell **Jake** Jones	5	181	790	.229
Frank Ellsworth **Jerry** Freeman	2	142	579	.245
Thomas William **Tim** Harkness	4	132	562	.235
Robert Troxell **Ray** Knode	4	55	207	.266
Fredrick Creighton **Newt** Hunter	1	53	209	.254
Kevin Joseph **Chuck** Connors	2	48	202	.238
Charles William **Luke** Lutenberg	1	48	250	.192

2ND BASEMEN:	Yr	Hits	AB's	Ave
Linus Reinhard **Lonny** Frey	14	1482	5517	.269
Ron Kenneth **Zeke** Hunt	12	1429	5235	.273
Minter Carney **Jackie** Hayes	14	1069	4040	.265
Alfred Manuel **Billy** Martin	11	877	3419	.257
D'Arcy Raymond **Jake** Flowers	10	433	1693	.256
Charles John **Paddy** Baumann	7	248	904	.274
Frank S. **Terry** Larkin	6	215	915	.235
Clifford Rankin **Pat** Crawford	4	182	651	.280
James Bugg **Jay** Partridge	2	167	645	.259
Romanus **Monty** Basgall	3	110	512	.215
Dimitrios Speros **Jim** Baxes	1	69	280	.246
Floyd Haskell **Jack** Farmer	2	47	175	.269
Frederick Winton **Tony** Daniels	1	46	230	.200

SHORTSTOPS:	Yr	Hits	AB's	Ave
Owen Joseph **Donie** Bush	16	1804	7210	.250
Arthur William **Otto** Krueger	7	427	1704	.251
George Watson **Zeke** Wrigley	4	222	861	.258
Warren H. **Bobby** Wheelock	3	201	854	.235
William Lewis **Chuck** Wortman	3	82	441	.186
Ryerson L. **Jack** Jones	2	71	279	.254
Wayne Allison **Chuck** Scrivener	3	59	310	.190

SHORTSTOPS: (Cont.)	Yr	Hits	AB's	Ave
James Earl **Ike** McAuley	5	44	179	.246

3RD BASEMEN:	Yr	Hits	AB's	Ave
Colbert Dale **Toby** Harrah	17	1954	7402	.264
John Bernard **Hans** Lobert	14	1252	4563	.274
Edward Nagle **Ned** Williamson	13	1159	4553	.255
Harry Harlan **Mike** Mowrey	13	1099	4291	.256
Norman Doxie **Tony** Boeckel	6	813	2880	.282
Otto Hamlin **Jack** Saltzgaver	6	199	764	.260
William John **Scotty** Ingerton	1	130	521	.250
Thomas Steven **Tucker** Ashford	7	111	510	.218
Meredith Hilliard **Marty** Hopkins	2	80	379	.211
Orville Francis **Sam** Woodruff	2	67	367	.183
Thaddeus Walter **Ted** Cieslak	1	54	220	.245
Leopold Theodore **Paul** Sentell	2	44	195	.226

OUTFIELDERS:	Yr	Hits	AB's	Ave
Edgar Charles **Sam** Rice	20	2987	9269	.322
David Russell **Gus** Bell	15	1823	6478	.281
Walter Scott **Steve** Brodie	12	1726	5699	.303
Robert James **Rick** Monday	19	1619	6136	.264
William Van Winkle **Jimmy** Wolf	11	1440	4968	.290
Edward Hugh **Ned** Hanlon	13	1317	5074	.260
John William **Jay** Johnstone	20	1254	4703	.267
Darnell Glenn **Dan** Ford	11	1123	4163	.270
Arthur Frederick **Solly** Hofman	14	1095	4072	.269
Edward **Danny** Green	8	1021	3484	.293
Allen Lee **Zeke** Zarilla	10	975	3535	.276
Louis Richard **Steve** Evans	8	963	3359	.287
Louis Baird **Pat** Duncan	7	827	2695	.307
William D. **Darby** O'Brien	6	805	2856	.282
Myron W. **Mike** McCormick	10	640	2325	.275
Herbert Clyde **Harry** Niles	5	561	2270	.247
George Elmer **Del** Howard	5	482	1833	.263
Judson Fabian **Jay** Kirke	7	346	1148	.301
Talbot Percy **Jack** Dalton	4	333	1163	.286
Andrew Jackson **Randy** Reese	4	321	1142	.281
Rogers Lee **Bobby** Brown	7	313	1277	.245
Elmer Joseph **Dick** Cox	2	261	832	.314
DeWitt Wiley **Bevo** LeBourveau	5	217	788	.275
Edgar Edward **Ned** Cuthbert	5	178	811	.219
Bartholomew J. **Bert** Griffith	3	174	581	.299
Bryshear Barnett **Brock** Davis	6	141	543	.260
Elton **Sam** Langford	3	136	495	.275
Eugene Reybold **Roy** Elsh	3	106	404	.262
Melvin Gray **Bob** Perry	2	103	387	.266
Scott Cook **Jack** McCandless	2	95	437	.217
Yale Yeastman **Tod** Sloan	3	94	402	.234
Evon Daniel **Denny** Williams	4	85	328	.259
Archibald W. **Al** Hall	2	80	314	.255
John F. **Denny** Driscoll	5	60	360	.167
Justin Howard **Mike** Fitzgerald	2	49	170	.288
Lloyd William **Gary** Gearhart	1	44	179	.246
Robert Lee **Pat** Dillard	1	42	183	.230

ROSTER

PITCHERS:	Yr	Won	Lost	ERA
William H. *Adonis* Terry	14	197	196	3.73
Leslie Ambrose *Joe* Bush	17	195	183	3.51
Howard Jonathan *Bob* Ehmke	15	166	166	3.75
Edward Joseph *Jeff* Pfeffer	13	158	112	2.77
Ellsworth E. *Bert* Cunningham	12	142	167	4.22
Perce Leigh *Pat* Malone	10	134	92	3.74
John Alex *Andy* Messersmith	12	130	99	2.86
George Lemuel *Bob* Ewing	11	124	118	2.49
Charles Monroe *Jeff* Tesreau	7	115	72	2.43
Edward Morgan *Ted* Lewis	6	94	64	3.53
George Bernard *Dave* Koslo	12	92	107	3.68
Frank S. *Terry* Larkin	5	89	80	2.43
Erwin Coolidge *Bob* Porterfield	12	87	97	3.79
Charles William *Jack* Harper	8	80	64	3.55
Frank Spruiell *Jakie* May	14	72	95	3.88
John Reid *Harry* McIntire	9	71	117	3.22
Melvin Allys *Bert* Gallia	9	66	68	3.14
Matthew C. *Max* Surkont	9	61	76	4.38
James Newton *Jesse* Duryea	5	59	67	3.45
John F. *Darby* O'Brien	4	59	65	3.68
Virgil Lee *Ned* Garvin	7	57	97	2.72
Norman Andrew *Nick* Cullop	6	57	55	2.73
Dominic Joseph *Mike* Ryba	10	52	34	3.66
Frank Ealton *Zeke* Wilson	5	52	44	4.03
Charles William *Carl* Fischer	7	46	50	4.63
Leland Victor *Lou* Brissie	7	44	48	4.07
Floyd Clifford *Bill* Bevens	4	40	36	3.08
John Perkins *Pat* Luby	4	39	41	3.91
John F. *Denny* Driscoll	4	38	39	3.08
Edward Oliver *Ted* Bowsfield	7	37	39	4.35

PITCHERS (Cont.)	Yr	Won	Lost	ERA
George Henry *Joe* Decker	9	36	44	4.17
Tracy Souter *Dick* Barrett	5	35	58	4.28
Heber Hampton *Dick* Newsome	3	35	33	4.50
Francis Xavier *Big Jeff* Pfeffer	6	31	39	3.30
Herbert Ehler *Hank* Thormahlen	6	29	30	3.33
Donald Dexter *Dan* Griner	6	28	55	3.49
John Bode *Bob* Osborn	6	27	17	4.32
Mario Cain *Milo* Candini	8	26	21	3.92
Clyde Elias *Chad* Kimsey	6	24	29	5.07
Miles Grant *Alex* Main	3	21	22	2.77
Darious Dutton *Dave* Hillman	8	21	37	3.87
Horace Guy *Dooley* Womack	5	19	18	2.95
Roman Anthony *Ray* Semproch	4	19	21	4.42
Elmer Nathan *Al* Corwin	5	18	10	3.98
Edward Parks *Davey* Dunkle	5	17	30	5.02
Leslie Fletchard *Bill* Fleming	6	16	21	3.79
Lawrence Donald *Bobby* Locke	9	16	15	4.02
Donald G. *Dan* Marion	2	15	11	3.42
Henry Levi *Johnny* Werts	4	15	21	4.29
Richard Frank *Rob* Gardner	8	14	18	4.35

EXTRAS:
Eugene F. *Bob* Hart - Umpire
Eugene *Ted* Hendry - Umpire
William J. *Barry* McCormick - Umpire
Julius *Chuck* Meriwether - Umpire
James M. *Jake* O'Donnell - Umpire
Leonardo T. *Paul* Sentelle - Umpire
Vito H. *Vic* Voltaggio - Umpire

It'sa FACT cont'd....

Maurice Lennon *Dick* Burrus: In 1925, his first of two consecutive "starting" seasons, he had 200 hits, batted .340, tied for fourth in doubles and led all first sackers in both fielding % and assists. Boston, after the 1926 season, traded for Jack Fournier, the 1924 NL home run champ, and Dick lost his starting position.

Harry Harlan *Mike* Mowrey: He was a solid gloveman at the hot corner. In the seven seasons Mike was a regular he led all third sackers three times in DP's and two times in both assists and fielding %.

Arthur Frederick *Solly* Hofman: He led the Cubs to the 1910 pennant. That summer Solly placed third in both batting and triples (tie), and finished fourth in RBI's.

Louis Baird *Pat* Duncan: From 1921-23 he batted .308, .328 and .327, and led NL outfielders in fielding % in 1923.

Ellsworth E. *Bert* Cunningham: He toiled for hapless Louisville from 1895-99 in the then 12 team NL. Louisville finished 12th, 12th, 11th, ninth and ninth in that stretch. Nevertheless, Bert went 77-75, including 28 wins (second) in 1898!

Perce Leigh *Pat* Malone: Both 1929 and 1930 were spectacular seasons for him. In 1929 Pat was the NL's only 20 game winner, posting 22 victories and also pacing the league in both shutouts and strikeouts! The following year Pat again led the Senior Circuit in wins with 20 (tie).

William H. *Adonis* Terry: He hurled two no-hitters during his career, July 24th, 1886 and May 27th, 1888.

Real ROCKIES

31

Team

Denver is the home for the "Orange Crush" and the Nuggets. For years, the Mile High City had a top farm club, but no Major League team. The faithful fans were rewarded when their city was awarded a new franchise in June of 1991. The National League, not having added any teams since 1969, added two. One became the Colorado Rockies. With the thin air at 5000 feet, the ball should carry, creating regular fireworks at their new Coors Park.

Colorado, for any non-resident and/or non-Colorado vacationer's information, is a beautiful state. Rocky Mountain National Park is simply breathtaking. The mining history of Leadville and the wonders of Colorado Springs are but two of many great locales in the Rocky Mountain State. All this helps to form the backdrop for the Real Rockies Team. Not only do they have Rocks and Stones, but also Coral, Jasper, Silver and even Diamonds! The Real Rockies have Salt Rock, Hardrock and Bedrock to be handled by Iron Hands and Miners. A strong team, there is a Tin Man, a Man of Steal and several Iron Men. If that is not enough, there is even an Iron Horse!

One player stands out in this group. Barely qualifying as a 'Rocky', Sandy Koufax comes up big as a man and a player. A credit to both his religious convictions and also to the pastime, Sandy chose not to pitch in game #1 of the 1965 Fall Classic, because that day was also Yom Kippur. Sandy came back to toss shutouts in game #5 and game #7 to give the Dodgers the World Championship. From 1961-66 Sandy was arguably the best pitcher in baseball. Five consecutive years he led the NL in ERA, three times it was under 2.00! Sandy won three strikeout crowns and also topped all hurlers three times in both wins and shutouts. In 1963 Sandy won both the MVP and the Cy Young, plus won the Cy Young again in 1965 and 1966 (at this time the award was given to only one pitcher, not one in each league). June 30th, 1962, May 11th, 1963, June 4th, 1964 and September 9th, 1965 were dates Sandy tossed no-hitters. His fourth was a perfect gem, 27 up, 27 down. For us trivia types, Sandy attended college on a basketball scholarship!

LINEUP

CA	Clint *Scrap Iron* Courtney

wore the tools of ignorance for 11 seasons. He was the first catcher to wear glasses when playing ball. Scrap Iron was second in the American League Rookie of the Year voting in 1952. That summer he paced all backstops in fielding %. Two campaigns Scrap Iron batted over .300.

1B	Harry *Jasper* Davis

starred for 15 seasons (and a few at bats in seven other seasons). An early 1900's power hitter, Jasper led the league in home runs four times, in doubles three summers and in RBI's two campaigns. His 28 three baggers in 1897 are the fifth highest single season total ever.

2B	Phil *Scrap Iron* Garner

sparkled for 16 seasons, primarily at the keystone. Phil was a three time All-Star during his career and now manages the Brew Crew. Fast, five seasons Scrap Iron stole over 20 bases. A solid hitter, Phil crushed 20+ doubles nine times and pulverized ten or more homers five times.

SS	*Iron Man* Cal Ripkin

is totally amazing. A cerebral player, Cal is outstanding in the field, both in fielding % and in field positioning. A smart runner, he knows when to take the extra base. An All-Star since 1983, Iron Man was voted American League Rookie of the Year (1982) and AL MVP (1983 and 1991).

3B	Everett *Rocky* Bridges

was much like Nellie Fox (in one way), because both played with "big chaws". Rocky was versatile and could hold down any infield position. In 1958, while with the Senators, Rocky was selected to the All-Star team. After retiring Rocky went on to coach for seven years.

OF	Tim *Rock* Raines

is awesome! Still active, Rock has over 2000 hits and 1000+ walks. Tim's 764 stolen bases place him fifth all time. Six consecutive seasons he had 70 or more swipes, four times leading the league. His stealing success rate is second all time! In 1986 Rock led the NL in batting.

OF	Earl *Rock* Averill

turned 27 during his rookie year. For the next ten summers he terrorized pitchers. Eight times Rock hit over .300, including .378 in 1936. Earl averaged 37 doubles, 12 triples, 22 homers and 107+ RBI's those ten outstanding years. His plaque is now found in Cooperstown.

OF	Rocco *Rocky* Colavito

was a slugger. Rocky hit 20+ tators 11 consecutive seasons (1956-66). Three years he topped 40 dingers, leading the AL with 42 in 1959. Six summers Rocky drove in over 100 runs, leading the AL with 108 in 1965. That same season Rocky also played errorless all 162 games!

P	*Iron Man* Joe McGinnity

was great. Reaching the Majors as a 28 year old rookie, Joe pitched ten seasons. He never had a losing campaign! In his first eight years Iron Man won 20+ games, twice topping 30 wins. Five times he led the league in wins. Iron Man is enshrined in the Hall of Fame.

P	Charles *Silver* King

played in baseball's early years. He was tabbed his nickname for his fair hair. Four seasons he won over 30 games. In 1888 Silver had his best season. He led the Amer. Assoc. in wins (45), games (66), complete games (64), shutouts (six, tie), innings (585) and ERA (1.64)!

P	Sanford *Sandy* Koufax

retired due to his arthritic left arm at the young age of 30. He dominated batters, fanning over one hitter per inning in his 2324 career frames. Sandy topped all National League hurlers in strikeouts four times. Three seasons, in his Hall of Fame career, he whiffed over 300 batters!

RES	Steve *Bedrock* Bedrosian

was a starter one year, then he became a feared stopper. Bedrock has averaged nearly seven K's per nine innings throughout his career. In 1987, in 65 relief appearances, he saved 40 games, won five contests and was voted the National League Cy Young award.

RES	*Diamond* Jim Gentile

(pronounced Genteal) was 64 games short of 1000, leaving him off many 'all time' lists. Diamond Jim's 6.13 home run % would place him 13th. He literally swung for the fences. Diamond Jim wore a pad on his right shoulder to protect himself from his own vicious swing.

RES	John *Rocky* Stone

starred in the Junior Circuit from 1928-38, starting eight summers. During those eight years, Rocky smashed 22+ doubles eight times, pounded 11+ triples seven times, batted over .300 six times and drove in 80+ runs four times. In 1936 Rocky hit .341, his best campaign.

RES	*Pebbly* Jack Glasscock

was the best fielder of his era, the late 1800's. Six seasons he topped all shortstops in fielding %. Jack always made sure no small rocks in "his area" would cause a bad bounce, hence his nickname. Twice Pebbly Jack led the National League in hits and once in batting average.

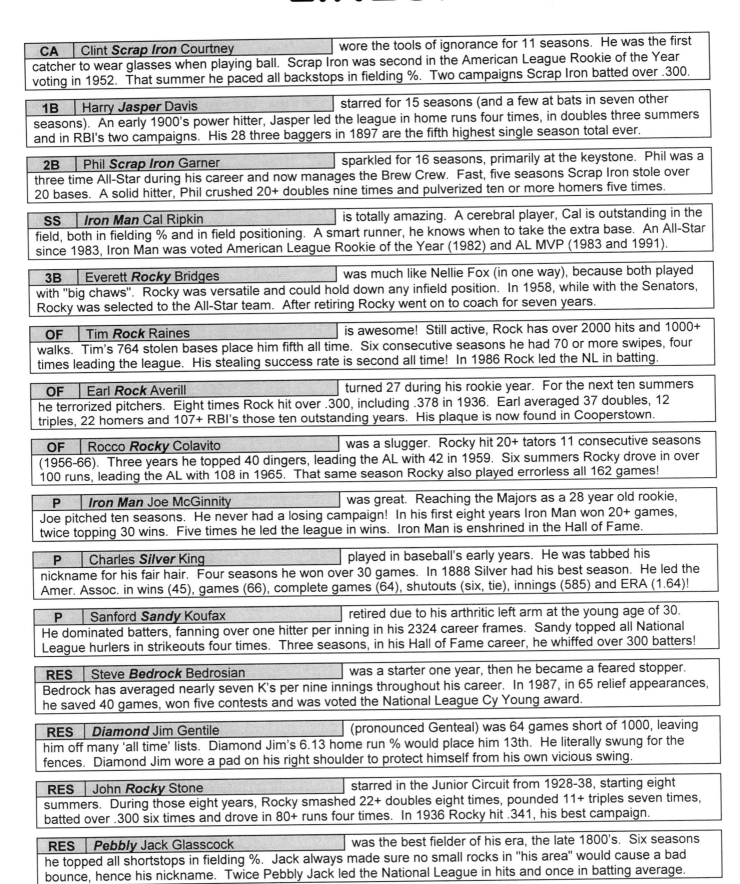

L to R: *Diamond* Jim Gentile, Harry *Jasper* Davis, Sanford *Sandy* Koufax, Rocco *Rocky* Colavito, Earl *Rock* Averill

It'sa FACT

Arthur **Sandy** Irwin: He injured his fielding hand so he used padding in his glove for 'protection'. It was the first fielding glove as we now know them.

Harry **Jasper** Davis: He was a nationally recognized trap shooter. Jasper, Albert Chief Bender and Gettysburg Eddie Plank traveled across the country to promote the sport.

Iron Man Joe McGinnity: In one month (August 1903) he pitched and won both games in three double-headers. He actually earned his nickname not from his 'Ironman' fete, but from his occupation.

Lou **The Iron Horse** Gehrig: Lou played in 2130 consecutive games. Never sitting down, he was dubbed his nickname.

Earl **Rock** Averill: In one inning, June 6th, 1937, he smashed a homer and a triple.

Iron Mike Caldwell: He did his best in the 1982 Fall Classic. Iron Mike fired a shutout in game #1. In game #5 he went eight innings to get the win. Unfortunately, Harvey's Wallbangers hit the floor in seven.

Rocco **Rocky** Colavito: He was a power hitter. One game Rocky smashed four tators. He hit dingers in the 1959, 1961 and 1962 All-Star tilts. His 1961 shot was the only AL run in an official 1-1 tie. His 5.75% homer percentage ranks Rocky 23rd and his 374 HR's place him 37th. On June 24th, 1962 Rocky pulverized seven hits in one game!

Clyde **Hardrock** Shoun: On May 15th, 1944 he no-hit Boston, missing a perfect game by issuing one walk.

Wiley **Iron Man** Piatt: He took the NL by storm in 1898. In his first two seasons Iron Man won 24 and 23 games. The left-hander faded and was gone in six years.

Francis **The Naugatuck Nuggett** Shea: As a 26 year old rookie in 1947, he went 14-5 with three shutouts. In that year's World Series he won games #1 and #5, as the Yankees downed the Dodgers in seven.

Phil **Scrap Iron** Garner: On Sept 14th, 1978, and Sept 15th, 1978 he hit grand slams in consecutive games.

Diamond Jim Gentile: In 1961 Jim crushed 46 homers (tied for third behind the M & M Boys) and drove in 141 runs (second).

TRIVIA*

1) He was the first NL player to hit a grand slam in the World Series.

2) During his career he fired two no-no's, April 17th, 1969 and October 2nd, 1972.

3) In 1978 he had his best season. His 22 wins ranked second in the AL. He also placed among the leaders in shutouts (tie second), ERA (third), innings (third) and complete games (first).

4) On August 23rd, 1968 he was the last position player (pressed into pitching) to hurl and win.

5) He was the youngest player enshrined in Cooperstown.

6) His 1955 seventh game catch "robbed" Yogi Berra and preserved the victory and World Championship for the Dodgers.

7) His teammate, Frank Home Run Baker, tied his then record, when he too led the league in homers four consecutive years (The current record holder is Ralph Kiner. He led the league seven straight seasons, 1946-52).

8) After going 5/12 in the three game 1979 NLCS sweep, he then went 12/24 and led the Buc's to the Series title.

9) On May 5th, 1961 he hit grand slams his first two at bats. His next time up, the sacks were again jammed. He hit a long sacrifice fly, barely missing his third slam!

10) Two of his sons have played in the All-Star game. He himself played in the 1970 mid-season Classic.

11) He and Hoyt Wilhelm are the only Hall of Famers to 'go yard' in their first Big League at bat.

12) His 14 game winning streak was halted when he was bested in 12 innings 1-0.

13) Three of his single season RBI totals ranked him second, fourth and sixth all time (184, 175 and 174!).

14) In 1959 he led the AL in homers and Harvey Kuehn led the AL in batting. After the season was completed, they were traded for each other, even up.

15) He and his brother Billy formed a keystone combination for the Orioles.

* UNPOLISHED GEMS answers found on page 240

ROSTER / LINGO

CATCHERS:	Yr	Hits	AB's	Ave
Clint *Scrap Iron* Courtney	11	750	2796	.268
Ray *Iron Man* Mueller	14	733	2911	.252
Frank *Silver* Flint	12	682	2852	.239
Santos *Sandy* Alomar Jr. .	7	390	1455	.268
Gary *Hardrock* Allenson	7	235	1061	.221
Thomas *Old Iron Hands* Sullivan	4	64	345	.186
Vincent *Sandy* Nava	5	61	345	.177
Ed *Scrap Iron* Kenna	1	35	118	.297
Diamond John Kelly	1	9	58	.155

1ST BASEMEN:	Yr	Hits	AB's	Ave
Lou *The Iron Horse* Gehrig	17	2721	8001	.340
Harry *Jasper* Davis	22	1841	6653	.277
Silver Bill Phillips	10	1130	4255	.266
Joe *Rocks* Start	11	1031	3433	.300
William *Klondike* Douglass	9	766	2797	.274
Diamond Jim Gentile	9	759	2922	.260
Glenn *Rocky* Nelson	9	347	1394	.249

2ND BASEMEN:	Yr	Hits	AB's	Ave
Phil *Scrap Iron* Garner	16	1594	6136	.260
Santos *Sandy* Alomar Sr. .	15	1168	4760	.245
Mike *Rocky* Tyson	10	714	2959	.241
Chuck *Iron Hands* Hiller	8	516	2121	.243
William *Iron Duke* Kenworthy	4	301	989	.304

SHORTSTOPS:	Yr	Hits	AB's	Ave
Iron Man Cal Ripkin	14	2227	8027	.277
Pebbly Jack Glasscock	17	2040	7030	.290
Arthur *Sandy* Irwin	13	934	3871	.241

3RD BASEMEN:	Yr	Hits	AB's	Ave
Everett *Rocky* Bridges	11	562	2272	.247
Chris *Tin Man* Brown	6	410	1523	.269
Ezra *Salt Rock* Midkiff	3	77	372	.207
Rocco *Rocky* Krsnich	3	59	275	.215
Bobby *Rocky* Rhawn	3	47	198	.237

OUTFIELDERS:	Yr	Hits	AB's	Ave
Rickey *Man of Steal* Henderson	16	2216	7656	.289
Tim *Rock* Raines	16	2152	7234	.298
Earl *Rock* Averill	13	2020	6358	.318
Rocco *Rocky* Colavito	14	1730	6503	.266
John *Rocky* Stone	11	1391	4494	.310
Iron Mike Kreevich	12	1321	4676	.283
Ron *Rocky* Swoboda	9	624	2581	.242
Edmundo *Sandy* Amoros	7	334	1311	.255

OUTFIELDERS: (Cont.)	Yr	Hits	AB's	Ave
Ford *Rocky* Garrison	4	180	687	.262
Hilario *Sandy* Valdespino	7	176	765	.230
Tobias *Sandy* Griffin	4	173	630	.275
Elmer *Silver* Zacher	1	28	132	.212
James *Sandy* Taylor	1	21	97	.216
George *Rocky* Schmees	1	21	125	.168
Diamond Joe Rickert	2	11	66	.167
Ed *Scrap Iron* Beecher	2	9	37	.243
Armstrong *Klondike* Smith	1	5	27	.185
Charles *Sandy* Piez	1	3	8	.375

PITCHERS:	Yr	Won	Lost	ERA
Iron Man Joe McGinnity	10	246	142	2.66
Mordecai *Miner* Brown	14	239	130	2.06
Charles *Silver* King	10	204	153	3.18
Sanford *Sandy* Koufax	12	165	87	2.76
Iron Mike Caldwell	14	137	130	3.81
Wiley *Iron Man* Piatt	6	86	79	3.61
Steve *Bedrock* Bedrosian	13	75	77	3.35
Clyde *Hardrock* Shoun	14	73	59	3.91
Harry *Rocks* McIntire	9	71	117	3.22
Francis *The Naugatuck Nugget* Shea	8	56	46	3.80
Bill *Stoney* Stoneman	8	54	85	4.08
Sandalio *Sandy* Consuegra	8	51	32	3.37
Iron Mike Prendergast	6	41	53	2.74
Ray *Iron Man* Starr	7	37	35	3.53
Ed *Rock* Rakow	7	36	47	4.33
Art *Sandy* Herring	11	34	38	4.32
Ulysses *Stoney* McGlynn	3	17	33	2.95
Ken *Coral* Gables	3	13	11	4.69
Gene *Sandy* Vance	2	9	8	3.83
George *Iron* Davis	4	7	10	4.48
Charles *Sandy* Burk	5	4	11	4.25
Carlos *Sandy* Ullrich	2	3	3	5.04
Rodney *Rocky* Childress	4	2	3	4.76
Hardy *Klondike* Kane	4	2	7	4.81
Archie *Iron Man* Campbell	3	2	6	5.86
Roy *Hardrock* Johnson	1	1	5	3.42
Alexander *Sandy* Wihtol	3	1	0	3.75
John *Sandy* McDougal	2	1	4	3.97
Floyd *Rock* Stromme	1	0	1	4.85
Glenn *Sandy* Liebhardt	3	0	1	8.96
Herb *Iron Duke* Hall	1	0	0	15.00
Diamond Jim Brady	1	0	0	28.42

EXTRA:
John *Rocky* Roe - Umpire

Iron Mike: Mechanical pitching machine

Iron Hands: A poor fielder

Diamond: The infield

Keystone: Second base

Steel City: Pittsburgh

Crushed, Smashed, Pulverized: What happens to a baseball when it is hit very hard

Rocked: Pitcher is hit very hard

Real ROYALS

32

Team

The Kansas City Royals were an expansion team. They were "born" in 1969 and were placed in the new American League Western Division. The Royals have, by far, been the most successful "startup" franchise. In just their third season, the K.C. crew won 85 games and finished over .500. In 1975 their 91 victories allowed them to finish a close second. Starting in 1976, the Royals won their first Western Division crown, unfortunately they were nipped in the fifth game of the ALCS by Chris Chambliss' ninth inning homer. Their 102 wins in 1977 were the highest total in the Majors, but they dropped the last two ALCS games at home to the Yankees. 1978 brought a third consecutive division title and a third consecutive ALCS loss. Finally, in 1980, the Royals won the league championship, but they fell to the Phillies in the Fall Classic. Between 1975-85 the Royals won six division titles and four times finished second! It all culminated in 1985. Coming back from three games to one game deficits in both the ALCS and the World Series, the Royals were crowned World Champions in the "Freeway Series."

The Real Royals are a gem studded crown of a team. Of the 41 squads assembled, the Real Royals have, by far, the most Hall of Fame members, seventeen! When a ballplayer receives a "regal nickname", it is often because of his spectacular career. The roster has not only Kings, Princes, Dukes, Lords, Barons, Counts and Sirs, but it also holds a Primo, a Kaiser, a Rajah, a Mahatma, an Earl, a Sultan, a Rex and a Queenie! Add in eight Mr's, two Governors, King Tut and a Clown Prince and the team should rule the world!

As hard as it is to pick between such an array of exceptional players, after just a few moments of thought, I knew there were two ballplayers I have always admired. These two stars had similar Hall of Fame careers. Ernie Mr. Cub Banks and Al Mr. Tiger Kaline were two jewels. Their paths had several similarities. Both were rookies in 1953. Both played for their team their entire career. Both were durable players who not only could hit for power, but they also were outstanding with the leather. Off the field, each was an ambassador for baseball within his community and each was the roll model many youngsters "looked up to." When you say their nicknames, earned over years of service, keep it heavy on the Mr.!

LINEUP

CA	Charles *Duke* Farrell

played for 18 seasons at the turn of the century. In 1891 Duke led the American Association in both home runs and RBI's (tie). In a game in 1897 Duke set a Major League record by cutting down eight runners trying to steal a base! Now that is simply awesome!

1B	*Sir* Rodney Carew

was the AL Rookie of the Year in 1967. He went on to hit over .300 fifteen consecutive season (1969-83)! Sir Rodney earned seven batting crowns in that span. In 1977 he tore up the AL. Rod led in hits (239), runs (128), triples (16) and batting average (.388) and won the MVP.

2B	Rogers *The Rajah* Hornsby

was baseball's greatest right-handed hitter. His .358 career batting average is second all time! Three seasons The Rajah hit over .400! He captured seven silver bats, including six straight (1920-25)! The Rajah led the NL in slugging % (nine), hits (four) and RBI's (four, one tie).

SS	Ernie *Mr. Cub* Banks

was a two time NL MVP (1958, 1959) and socked 512 HR's during his career (tied for 12th)! Three summers he led all shortstops in fielding %. In 1958 Mr. Cub did it all. He paced the NL in home runs, RBI's, total bases and slugging % and ranked second in runs and triples (tie).

3B	Bob *Mr. Team* Elliot

in his 15 seasons was named to the NL All-Star team on seven occasions. He cracked out over 2000 hits and six times drove in over 100 runs. In 1947 Mr. Team was voted the NL MVP. He led the Braves to the 1948 Fall Classic, pounding 23 homers and plating 100 runs.

OF	*Master* Melvin Ott

was the first NL player to hit 500 homers. At age 20 he hit .328 with 42 dingers and 151 RBI's! During his 22 seasons, Master Melvin topped the NL six times in HR's (three ties) and he knocked in 100+ runs nine years! Mel ranks 14th all time in yard shots and ninth in RBI's!

OF	Mike *King* Kelly

was called King because he was so popular with the fans! After a great career he tragically died of pneumonia, just one year following his retirement. An early baseball innovator, King is often credited with originating both catcher signals and the "hit and run" play.

OF	Reggie *Mr. October* Jackson

always swung hard, even with two strikes. He was paid to hit yard shots, and that is what he did. Mr. October tagged 563 HR's, the sixth best ever. A 14 time All-Star and the MVP in 1973, Mr. October blasted 18 post season homers and twice was voted the Fall Classic's MVP!

P	*Sir* Timothy Keefe

hurled 14 seasons and won 342 games (eighth). In the six year span from 1883-88, he won 222 contests, an average of 37 wins per year! Sir Timothy led the league in ERA (three), strikeouts (two), innings (two), games (two) and wins (two, one shared) during his Hall of Fame career.

P	Tony *Count* Mullane

was a dominating pitcher in the 19th century. The Count ruled from 1882-87 (missed 1885 due to a dispute). He went 30-24, 35-15, 36-26, 33-27 and 31-17 respectively. He recorded his 284 career victories in just 13 summers! The Count's 468 complete games are ninth best.

P	*King* Carl Hubbell

pitched his entire career for the Giants, dominating batters for 16 seasons. He won 62% of his career decisions. King Carl topped all NL pitchers in wins and ERA three times each. Five consecutive years (1933-37) Carl won 20+ games. He posted a remarkable ten shutouts in 1933!

RES	Paul *Duke* Derringer

"came up" as a rookie in 1931. He went 18-6 and led the NL in winning %. Traded in 1935 to the doormat Redlegs, Duke ultimately led them to two World Series appearances. In the 1940 Fall Classic he won games #4 and #7. Four seasons Duke logged 20 or more V's.

RES	*Prince* Hal Newhouser

recently was inducted into the Hall of Fame. Prince Hal lorded over batters from 1944-48. During those five campaigns he led all AL hurlers four times in wins (one tie) and two times in ERA, complete games and whiffs. Prince Hal won games #5 and #7 in the 1945 Fall Classic!

RES	John *The Count* Montefusco

gained his nickname from the movie The Count of Monte Cristo. He was the 1975 National League Rookie of the Year, going 15-9 and finishing second with 215 K's. The next season The Count topped the league with six whitewashes (tie) and won 16 decisions.

RES	Branch *The Mahatma* Rickey

was a part-time catcher during his playing days. He went on to manage for ten summers. Rising to the team operations level, The Mahatma is credited for developing the "farm system" and he probably is most remembered for his bringing Jackie Robinson to the Majors.

L to R: *King* Carl Hubbell, Ernie *Mr. Cub* Banks, Al *Mr. Tiger* Kaline, Rogers *The Rajah* Hornsby, *Master* Melvin Ott

It'sa FACT

Ernie **Mr. Cub** Banks: On three occasions (May 29th, 1962, June 9th, 1963 and September 14th, 1957) he hit three home runs in one game. He holds the National League record of five grand slams in one season (1955). On June 11th, 1966 Ernie legged out three triples in one game.

Master Melvin Ott: He was a feared hitter. Master Melvin led the National League in free passes six seasons. Four times (October 5th, 1929, September 1st, 1933, June 7th, 1943 and April 30th, 1944) Mel received five bases on balls in one game!

Leonard **King** Cole: As a rookie in 1910, he went 20-4 and led the National League in both winning % and ERA! That was the eighth highest win total by a first year pitcher.

Denny **Sky King** McLain: He won both the American League MVP and the Cy Young in 1968. People sometimes forget his great 1969 season included a league leading 24 wins, 325 innings, and nine shutouts!

Al **Mr. Tiger** Kaline: In his great career he had over 3000 hits. Mr. Tiger was also an outstanding right fielder. He won ten Gold Gloves!

King Carl Hubbell: He held the Buc's hitless on May 8th, 1929. King Carl, over two seasons (1936-37), won 24 consecutive games!

Elroy **The Baron** Face: The Pittsburgh forkballer won 22 consecutive contests over two seasons (1958-59)! The Baron won all 22 games in relief.

Sir David Stieb: He represented Toronto seven times in the All-Star game. Dave led the American League in shutouts in 1982 and ERA in 1985. On September 2nd, 1990 he hurled a no-hitter.

Reggie **Mr. October** Jackson: During his career he won four home run crowns (three shared) and three slugging titles. Six seasons Mr. October topped 100 RBI's and his 1702 career ribbies place him 17th all time.

Duane **Duke** Sims: He played for five teams over eleven years. Only three seasons Duke played 100+ games, but in 1970 Duke clouted 23 homers in just 345 at bats, a 6.67 home run %!

William **Iron Duke** Kenworthy: He played parts of four seasons, but his one full season (1914 in the Federal League) Iron Duke not only had fifteen homers (tie first), 40 doubles (second), 14 triples (third), 91 RBI's (fifth) and a .317 batting average (sixth), but he also led all second sackers in DP's and putouts!

Bob **Duke** Dillinger: After WW II, he "came up" in 1946 as a 27 year old rookie. His next three seasons (1947-49) Duke led the American League in stolen bases. In 1948 he also led the league in hits and batted .321. His .324 average in 1949 ranked him third. Duke finished his career with a .306 average.

Fred **Duke** Klobedanz: He had two big seasons (1897-98) with Boston (Beaneaters of the National League). The Duke combined with Kid Nichols to finish third and first in wins in 1897. That summer he went 26-7 and led the Senior Circuit in winning %. In 1898 Duke posted an excellent 19-10 record.

Al **Mr. Scoops** Oliver: During his career he smashed 2743 hits. A line drive hitter, he did lace most of his hits. Mr. Scoops stroked 529 doubles (19th) , including 20 or more two baggers 15 straight seasons (1970-84). In 1982, at the "young" age of 35, Mr. Scoops led the National League in hits, doubles, RBI's (tie) and won the batting title!

Roger **Duke of Tralee** Bresnahan: He was the first catcher elected to the Hall of Fame. His Irish family's roots were from the county of Tralee in Ireland, hence his nickname. Roger was highly regarded not only for his hitting and defense, but also for his leadership. The Duke was a playing manager at the age of 29.

Kent **Rex** Hrbek: A wrestling fan, he was tabbed after the wrestler, Adonis Rex.

Babe **Sultan of the Swat** Ruth: Without a doubt, he was, in his era, the dominant left-handed pitcher in the American League. During his three full seasons twirling, the Bambino went 18-8, 23-12 and 24-13. In 1916 Babe led the American League in ERA, games started and shutouts. He was at his best in the World Series. For his Fall Classic career, Babe went 3-0 and allowed only three earned runs in 31 innings!

Herb **Knight of Kennett Square** Pennock: He was the greatest lefty in the game at the time (according to the Mighty Mite, Miller Huggins). Not overpowering, Herb relied on control and hitter knowledge. It was said that only he and The Big Train were known to not throw at opposing batters. In 1948 the Knight of Kennett Square was elected to the Hall!

Al **Duke of Milwaukee** Simmons: His better known nickname came from his awkward batting style, because he always stepped in the bucket (Bucketfoot Al). Born Aloysius Szymanski in Brewtown, the Duke swung into Cooperstown in 1953.

TRIVIA*

1) His nickname was dubbed by teammate Thurman Munson when this slugger was benched in the fifth game of the 1977 ALCS. Later it became a huge positive! (See #22)

2) He is the only pitcher to win back to back MVP's.

3) This great shortstop Hall of Famer played more games (1239 to 1125) at first base.

4) He was intentionally walked five times in one game.

5) Although he pitched ten more seasons (including 169 more starts) after his no-hitter September 29th, 1976, that was his last shutout.

6) Ambidextrous, he hurled with both hands. In his era the players did not wear gloves. He would often "change arms" on a batter.

7) This slugger is the only player to hit four homers in two different Fall Classics.

8) He pitched and won the first night game in baseball history.

9) The oxymoron, a fast catcher, came true when he stole 36 bases in 1982.

10) From 1920-25 his composite batting average was .397!

11) In the 1934 All-Star game he fanned, consecutively, five future Hall of Famers, all with his "fadeaway."

12) He is the only player to ever twice score six runs in one game.

13) He holds the single season record of 67 doubles.

14) In 1910 he went 20-4 with a 1.80 ERA. In 1911 his record read 18-7. He contracted tuberculosis and died at age 29. (Hint: think of a nursery rhyme)

15) He hit more homers in one ballpark than any other player. He launched 323 yard shots at the Polo Grounds!

16) In 1934 he clouted six home runs in only 117 at bats. (Hint: a pitcher)

17) His third inning home run off Wild Bill Hallahan in the 1933 All-Star game was the first dinger ever hit in All-Star play.

18) I have his hitting book. He signed it and followed his signature with #3053.

19) He hit more homers (326) than any other Major Leaguer in the 1950's.

20) In 1913 he won a league leading eight games in relief for the World Champion Philadelphia A's. (Hint: his last name is nearly the same as the Yankee's skipper Ralph)

21) In 1922 he hit .401. He poked 42 homers, plated 152 runs, scored 141 runs, stretched 46 doubles, slammed 250 safeties, accumulated 450 total bases and slugged at a .722 pace (all league leading)!

22) In the 1977 Fall Classic he belted five homers. Three came in the final game on three consecutive swings!

23) His compact "wrist swing" whipped his 31 ounce bat to propel 512 round trippers.

24) He walked over 100 times in each of ten seasons. Only five players have received more free passes.

25) A was a shrewd base runner. He stole home a record tying seven times in 1961.

* KNIGHTLY CHALLENGERS answers found on page 240

ROSTER

CATCHERS:	Yr	Hits	AB's	Ave
Charles *Duke* Farrell	18	1563	5679	.275
Roger *Duke of Tralee* Bresnahan	17	1252	4481	.279
John *Duke* Wathan	10	656	2505	.262
Duane *Duke* Sims	11	580	2422	.239
Branch *The Mahatma* Rickey	4	82	343	.239
Gordon *Duke* Massa	2	7	17	.412
Albert *Duke* Kelleher	1	0	0	.000

1ST BASEMEN:	Yr	Hits	AB's	Ave
Sir Rodney Carew	19	3053	9315	.328
Al *Mr. Scoops* Oliver	18	2743	9049	.303
Prince Hal Chase	15	2158	7417	.291
Kent *Rex* Hrbek	14	1749	6192	.282
Cliff *Earl of Snohomish* Torgeson	15	1318	4969	.265
Guy *King Tut* Tutwiler	2	16	79	.203

2ND BASEMEN:	Yr	Hits	AB's	Ave
Rogers *The Rajah* Hornsby	23	2930	8173	.358
Jerry *Guv'nor* Browne	9	819	3006	.272
Jimmy *Lord* Jordon	4	327	1273	.257
William *Iron Duke* Kenworthy	4	301	989	.304
Tim *Silver King* Murnane	4	244	947	.258
Jack *King* Morrissey	2	33	128	.258

SHORTSTOPS:	Yr	Hits	AB's	Ave
Ernie *Mr. Cub* Banks	19	2583	9421	.274
Leo *Mr. Automatic* Cardenas	16	1725	6707	.257
Phil *Mr. Laffs* Linz	7	322	1372	.235
Johnny *Mr. Chips* Hudson	7	283	1169	.242

3RD BASEMEN:	Yr	Hits	AB's	Ave
Bob *Mr. Team* Elliot	15	2061	7141	.289
Bob *Duke* Dillinger	6	888	2904	.306
Frank *Governor* Ellerbe	6	389	1453	.268
Fred *King* Lear	4	39	166	.235
King John Karst	1	0	0	.000

OUTFIELDERS:	Yr	Hits	AB's	Ave
Al *Mr. Tiger* Kaline	22	3007	10116	.297
Al *Duke of Milwaukee* Simmons	20	2927	8759	.334
Master Melvin Ott	22	2876	9456	.304
Babe *Sultan of the Swat* Ruth	22	2873	8399	.342
Al *Mr. Scoops* Oliver	18	2743	9049	.303
Reggie *Mr. October* Jackson	21	2584	9864	.262
Edwin *Duke* Snider	18	2116	7161	.295
Michael *King* Kelly	16	1813	5894	.308
Duff *Sir Richard* Cooley	13	1576	5364	.294
Charlie *King Kong* Keller	13	1085	3790	.286
Earl *King of Doublin'* Webb	7	661	2161	.306
Eric *Dukie* Tipton	7	439	1626	.270
Dave *Mr. Clean* Nicholson	7	301	1419	.212

OUTFIELDERS: (Cont.)	Yr	Hits	AB's	Ave
George *Count* Puccinelli	4	172	607	.283
Charles *Count* Campau	3	153	572	.267
Tom *Tut* Jenkins	6	119	459	.259
Leon *Duke* Carmel	4	48	227	.211
James *Queenie* O'Rourke	1	25	108	.231
King Bill Kay	1	20	60	.333
Alexander *Duke* Reilley	1	13	62	.210
Mel *Primo* Preibisch	2	9	44	.205
Clarence *King* Lehr	1	4	27	.148

PITCHERS:	Yr	Won	Lost	ERA
Sir Timothy Keefe	14	342	225	2.62
Tony *Count* Mullane	13	284	220	3.05
King Carl Hubbell	16	253	154	2.98
Herb *Knight of Kennett Square* Pennock	22	240	162	3.60
Paul *Duke* Derringer	15	223	212	3.46
Prince Hal Newhouser	17	207	150	3.06
Sir David Stieb	15	175	135	3.41
Prince Hal Schumacher	13	158	121	3.36
Denny *Sky King* McLain	10	131	91	3.39
Elroy *The Baron* Face	16	104	95	3.48
Charles *Duke* Esper	9	101	100	4.39
Babe *Sultan of the Swat* Ruth	10	94	46	2.28
John *The Count* Montefusco	13	90	83	3.54
Elmer *Baron* Knetzer	8	69	69	3.15
Heinie *Count of Luxemburg* Meine	7	66	50	3.95
Leonard *King* Cole	6	56	27	3.12
Irvin *Kaiser* Wilhelm	9	56	105	3.44
Fred *Duke* Klobedanz	5	53	25	4.12
Bob *Mr. Chips* Chipman	12	51	46	3.72
Duane *Duke* Maas	7	45	44	4.19
Keith *The Count* Atherton	7	33	41	3.99
Byron *Duke* Houck	4	26	24	3.30
Xavier *Mr. X* Rescigno	3	19	22	4.13
Al *Clown Prince of Baseball* Schacht	3	14	10	4.48
Lew *King* Brockett	3	13	14	3.43
Charles *King* Lear	2	7	12	3.02
Lore *King* Bader	3	5	3	2.51
James *King* Brady	5	3	2	3.08
Prince Henry Oano	2	3	2	3.77
Norman *Duke* Plitt	2	3	6	4.77
Charles *King* Schmutz	2	1	3	3.52
Herb *Duke* Brett	2	1	1	3.97
Henry *Duke* Sedgwick	2	1	4	5.46
Leonard *King* Bailey	1	1	0	5.63
Harry *Duke* Markell	1	1	1	6.33
Thomas *Duke* Simpson	1	1	2	8.00
William *King* Brady	1	0	0	0.00
Norm *King* Lehr	1	0	0	3.07
Clair *Duke* Shirey	1	0	1	6.75
Al *Count* Doe	1	0	1	9.00

ROSTER

PITCHERS: (Cont.)	Yr	Won	Lost	ERA
Herb *Iron Duke* Hall	1	0	0	15.00
EXTRAS:				
Halsey *Mr. Baseball* Hall - Twins First "Colorman"				

EXTRAS: (Cont.)
Tom *King of Umpires* Lynch - Umpire
William *Lord* Byron - Umpire
Sir Sidney Hartman - Great Minneapolis Sports Newsman
Ban *Czar of Baseball* Johnson - AL President

LINGO

The Count: The number of balls and strikes

Duke It Out: A fight

The Count Is Full: When Bella has just drained another victim

MORE TRIVIA*

A) 1931 was his highlight season. He led the National League in wins (shared with 19), starts (35) and innings (284)! (Hint: he is also on the International Team)

B) He swooped into the Federal League in 1914-15. This hurler posted 19-11 and 18-15 season records.

C) He combined with King Carl Hubbell to form the third winningest lefty/righty combination in Major League history.

D) Cal Griffith rewarded him with a $100,000 bonus for his 1977 MVP season.

E) His 18-1 season (1959) was the best winning percentage of all time.

F) His 31 win season in 1968 was the first and last "30 win" campaign since Dizzy Dean in 1934.

G) He was the youngest player to win the American League batting title.

H) He led the American Association in homers in 1890. For his entire career he could count only one other homer!

I) In the 1948 World Series he led all Braves' batters in both home runs and RBI's.

J) He is one of only two players to ever win the Triple Crown twice!

K) He used to say, 'It's a great day for baseball, let's play two.'

L) One month after he turned 17, he was playing in the Big Leagues!

M) He was the first catcher to use shin guards.

N) Ralph Kiner and he are the only National League sluggers to hit 40 or more homers in five consecutive seasons.

O) He had more hits in one season (253) than any other right-handed batter.

* KNIGHTLY CHALLENGERS answers found on page 240

SCARY

33

Team

Our imaginations, often stimulated by the movies, help our senses feel emotions. I can vision The Terminator rising up from an unsurvivable fiery accident and relentlessly coming forward! I can see Rambo, invisible against a muddy tree trunk, opening his eyes so that we can see him. Just as we feel fear and terror, picture a pitcher in a critical situation having to face the "clean up" batter. How about a batter having to step into the box with the game on the line against the team's ace hurler. There is a reason certain players acquire their nicknames. I would personally rather pitch against Runt or bat against Shorty than pitch against The Beast or bat against The Monster!

The Scary Team has a roster whose nicknames would give your goose bumps goose bumps. No one terrifying moniker really dominates, rather it is a collection of frightening names. From the movies there are Psycho, Creeper, Rambo, Jaws, Road Warrior, Samson, Gladiator, King Kong, Cobra and The Terminator. You will believe in ghosts, because the squad has a Spook, Boo, The Phanton, two Shadows, Mysterious and The Gause Ghost. For true fear, there are The Killer, The Yankee Killer, The Giant Killer, The Dodger Killer, Hit Man, Savage, Capital Punisher, The Beast and Jack The Ripper! How about The Monster, The Wild Thing, The Mad Hungarian, Igor, Bruno, Boog, Mongo and Bubba for teammates? Add in Dirty, Rough, Bad, Rowdy and Tuffy and include Gorilla, Snake, Lizard, Rattlesnake and Spider and you definitely have the makings for another "Murderers' Row".

This is as formidable a roster and lineup as any nickname team. There are ten Hall of Famers and several other outstanding players. Harmon The Killer Killebrew was Minnesota's franchise player from 1961-74. He was not only a superior Major Leaguer who is now enshrined in Cooperstown, but he also was an excellent role model both on and off the field. The Killer was both versatile and unselfish. He always put his team first. Originally a second baseman, Harmon shifted to third base, later left field and ultimately first base. The Killer would never argue an umpires call or berate other players. Off the field he was regularly available within the community. He was a soft spoken, humble man (like a real hero should be!). In his honor, the street behind "The Old Met" was renamed Killebrew Drive!

LINEUP

CA	Ray *Iron Man* Mueller

was a backstop for 14 seasons. In 1944 he lived in his equipment, playing all 155 games as Cincinnati's catcher. Iron Man made the All-Star team that season and he recorded career highs in home runs, RBI's and batting average. That season launched his nickname Iron Man.

1B	Jimmie *The Beast* Foxx

was called The Beast by opposing pitchers! This strong farm boy hit for both power and average! Four seasons he had more RBI's than games played. Thirteen consecutive years (1929-41) The Beast drove in over 100 runs! Twelve straight summers (1929-40) he belted 30+ HR's.

2B	Charlie *The Mechanical Man* Gehringer

starred for 19 summers. Seven campaigns he led all AL keystoners in fielding %. Filling the #3 hole for the Tigers, The Mechanical Man seven seasons had 200+ hits, 40+ doubles and 100+ RBI's. In 1937 he won the batting crown (.371) and was voted the AL MVP!

SS	Johnny *Yatcha* Logan

anchored the Braves at shortstop for ten plus seasons of his 13 year career. A four time All-Star, he paced all NL shortstops in fielding % three times. 1956 was Yatcha's best summer at the dish. He led the NL with 37 two baggers, plus Johnny tagged 15 homers and plated 83 runs.

3B	Harmon *The Killer* Killebrew

was an Idaho strongboy and hit more dingers than every Major Leaguer but four! Eight times he slugged over 40 tators in one season, twice reaching the cheap seats 49 times! The Killer led the AL in homers six times (two ties), RBI's three times and won the AL MVP in 1969!

OF	Stan *The Man* Musial

sparkled for 22 seasons. When he retired, Stan The Man ranked 26th in batting average (.331), tied for 19th in triples (177), tied for 16th in home runs (475), fourth in both hits (3630) and RBI's (1951), third in doubles (725) and second in total bases (6134). What a man!

OF	Dave *The Cobra* Parker

was awesome. He was big, fast, crushed the ball and had a cannon for an arm! A two time batting champ (1977 and 1978), The Cobra won the NL MVP in 1978. He "hung 'em up" after 19 summers with 526 doubles (22nd), 339 homers (tie 48th) and 1493 RBI's (36th)!

OF	Rickey *Man of Steal* Henderson

currently holds the single season stolen base record of 130 (1982). His 1117 swipes (and counting) are the all time record. Eleven years the Man of Steal has topped the AL in pilfers, including seven straight summers (1980-1986)! His 63 leadoff dingers are also the all time record.

P	Bob *Warrior* Friend

toiled 16 campaigns, the first 15 summers for the Bucs. For eleven straight seasons (1955-65) he logged 200+ innings/year and led the NL in frames pitched in both 1956 and 1957. The Warrior, in 1958, posted 22 victories (tie first). Eight other years he won in double digits.

P	Dick *The Monster* Radatz

played just seven seasons in the Big Show, but his impact was significant. In his first three seasons The Monster dominated from the pen. He led the AL in relief wins three times and saves twice! The Monster (he stood 6' 6") averaged over one strikeout per inning for his career!

P	Mitch *The Wild Thing* Williams

is a hard throwing portsider. He has been a dominant force for nine seasons. As a 21 year old rookie he led the National League with 80 appearances. For his career (currently in limbo), The Wild Thing has already recorded 192 saves (19th) and 44 wins in his 592 games!

RES	Jeff *The Terminator* Reardon

ranks second all time in saves with 367! He reached 20+ saves eleven consecutive seasons (1982-92) and three times hit the 40 save mark! The Terminator is an unstoppable force who has come in from the bull pen 880 times during his 16 Major League campaigns!

RES	Dave *Kong* Kingman

ranks 21st in home runs for his career! He went deep 442 times during his 16 seasons. Known for "swinging for the fences," Kong retired with the fifth highest home run % (6.62)! His 48 dingers in 1979 topped the NL and Kong led the NL again in 1982 with 37 yard shots!

RES	Tom *The Terminator* Henke

for 13 seasons (through 1994) has been brought in with the game on the line 590 times. He posted 20 or more saves per year from 1986-93 and The Terminator led the American League in 1987 with 34 saves. He has fanned 9.95 batters per game for his entire career!

RES	Hughie *Ee-Yah* Jennings

is in the Hall of Fame. He played primarily at shortstop, leading the NL in fielding % from 1894-97. Ee-Yah had a .312 career batting average which included seasons of .386 (1895) and .398 (1896). For 14 years he managed the Tigers. Ee-Yah led them to three flags (1907-09).

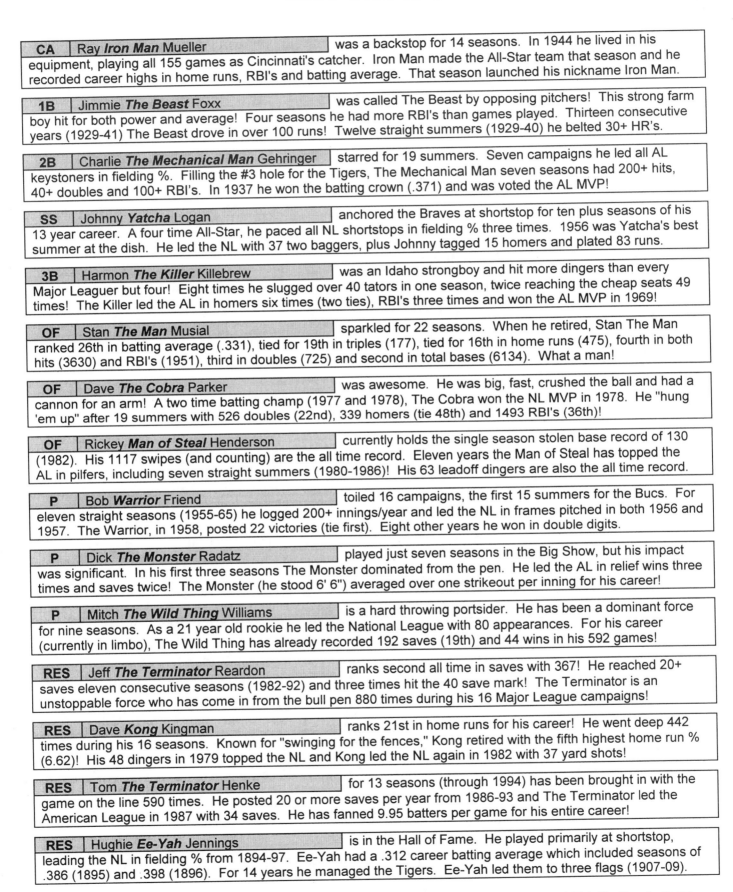

L to R: Jimmie *The Beast* Foxx, Dave *The Cobra* Parker, Harmon *The Killer* Killebrew, Stan *The Man* Musial, Dick *The Monster* Radatz

It'sa FACT

Stan **The Man** Musial: Stan had 1815 career hits at home and 1815 career hits on the road!

Both Stan **The Man** Musial and Jimmie **The Beast** Foxx: They both hit four consecutive homers during their careers!

| The Man | July 7th, 1962 (one) | and | July 8th, 1962 (three) |
| The Beast | June 7th, 1933 (one) | and | June 8th, 1933 (three) |

Dave **Kong** Kingman: During his career he walloped three home runs in one game four times; June 4th, 1976, May 14th, 1978, May 17th, 1979 and July 28th, 1979.

David **Boo** Ferriss: In his first two Big League starts, April 29th, 1945 and May 6th, 1945, he threw shutouts! In 1946 Boo went, during the regular season, 25-6 with six shutouts. Then October 9th, 1946 he twirled the 50th shutout in World Series history, whitewashing the Cardinals 4-0.

Stan **The Man** Musial: He originally was a pitcher. Stan The Man injured his throwing arm while in the minors, precipitating his conversion to the outfield. He became one of baseball's greatest hitters! During his fabulous career Stan The Man led the National League twice in RBI's, five times in both triples (two ties) and runs scored (three ties), six times in hits (one tie) and eight times in doubles! Stan combined the rare qualities of high batting average and power hitting. Six campaigns he posted 200 or more hits, ten summers he drove in over 100 runs and eleven times he crossed the plate 100+ times! Eighteen seasons Stan The Man hit over .300! He captured seven batting titles during his illustrious career (only Ty Cobb and Honus Wagner had more) and he won the NL MVP three seasons (1943, 1946 and 1948!). In addition, from 1949-58, he launched 20+ homers ten consecutive years. Stan The Man had his best season in 1948. He led the NL in runs (135), hits (230), doubles (46), triples (18), RBI's (131), total bases (429), slugging % (.702), OB % (.450) and batting average (.376). Stan also had 39 homers, one short of earning the Triple Crown!

Tom **Bruno** Brunansky: Bruno quietly has put up the numbers. From his rookie season (1982) through 1989, Bruno pounded at least 20 dingers per season! In the five game 1987 ALCS Bruno was a one man gang. He went 7/17 with four doubles, two homers and nine RBI's!

Charlie **King Kong** Keller: A force in the 40's, he finished second, third, second and third in homers in 1941, 1942, 1943 and 1946! King Kong ranked third, third and fifth in RBI's in 1941, 1942 and 1946! Charlie walked over 17% of his at bats, the 11th highest percentage all time!

Pete **The Gladiator** Browning: He captured three batting titles during his Hall of Fame career. The Gladiator's career batting average of .341 ranks him 11th all time!

Bad Bill Dahlen: Starring for 21 seasons, he did it well with both the glove and the bat. In the field Bad Bill ranks third all time in assists and second in putouts (for shortstops)! At the plate Bad Bill crushed out 2457 hits, scored 1589 tallies and drove in 1233 runs!

John **Boog** Powell: His first 14 seasons (played 17) he starred for the Orioles. Boog crushed 339 home runs, good for 48th all time. He also reached the seats six times in post season play. John finished third for the MVP in 1966, second for the MVP in 1969 and Boog was voted the AL's Most Valuable Player in 1970! Boog now runs Boog's Barbecue just beyond the right field fence at Camden Yards.

Jimmie **The Beast** Foxx: He was one of baseball's top sluggers. The Beast ranks ninth in home runs (534), eighth in home run % (6.57), sixth in both RBI's (1921) and RBI's per game (.83) and fourth in slugging % (.609). He was not only a power hitter, but he also hit for average. Double X won three batting titles and retired with a lifetime batting average of .325 (34th). The Beast was the AL MVP in 1932, 1933 and 1938 and he won the Triple Crown in 1933!

Rickey **Man of Steal** Henderson: He is remarkable. Rickey is baseball's greatest leadoff batter. In the last 50 years only one player, Joltin' Joe DiMaggio, has scored more frequently. The Man of Steal averages .79 runs per game. That is the measure! To accomplish this feat Rickey has walked over 16% (18th) of his at bats and has reached base at a .408 pace (tie 29th). Combining his ability to turn a base on balls or single "into a double" with a stolen base, the Man of Steal has ignited his teams to a higher level.

Kevin **Boogie Bear** Mitchell: In 1989 he put it all together. That season Boogie Bear belted 47 homers and drove in 125 runs (both league leading) and Kevin was named the NL MVP!

Fred **Firpo** Marberry: He was baseball's first recognized shortman. Firpo was used in two thirds of his games as a reliever. He became a specialist. In the early years of baseball, players relegated to bullpen duty were the less effective pitchers. Often the top starters came in as relievers when the game was "on the line." Firpo showed the way, regularly coming "out of the pen" with the game in doubt. From 1924-32 Firpo led the AL in saves five times!

TRIVIA*

1) He was baseball's first designated hitter.

2) If you were unfamiliar with his nickname, you would have thought the fans were always booing him.

3) He had six given names (Christian, Frederick, Albert, John, Henry and David), but he was known as _____.

4) He led the NL in shutouts (tie) in 1966 with five. He recorded all of them against the Dodgers!

5) He was tabbed his nickname for "swooping in" after another pitcher's "great start" and "picking up" an easy save.

6) His nickname originated because he "looked like" a boxer known as "The Bull of the Pampus."

7) He holds the round tripper record for a player's final season (35 in 1986).

8) His nickname meant John in Ukrainian-- still it sounds scary to me!

9) In August 1991 he went 8-1 with five saves, a record for relief wins in one month!

10) In 1958 he defeated the perennial pennant winning Yankees seven times in a row!

11) What do Leslie Floyd, John Phillips, Wycliffe Morton, Emory Church, Charlie Harris and Bill Clinton have in common?

12) He claimed his nickname (which he yelled from his third base coaching box) meant "watch out" in Hawaiian. Sorry, there are no Y's in the Hawaiian alphabet!

13) No one ever played "The Baggie" in right field at the Metrodome better than he did.

14) He homered in his last at bat. It was his 521st yard shot.

15) His new bat, made at a local woodshop, was coined after him, "The Louisville Slugger."

16) He is the only pitcher to lead the National League in ERA while twirling for a last placed team.

17) This often traded slugger played in all four divisions in one season (1977).

18) He opened the 1994 season with three homers in the first game. (Hint: Hillary tossed out the opening day ball)

19) Alex Karas created his nickname from the character he played in the movie "Blazing Saddles."

20) He was also known as the "Bashful Basher of Power Alley."

21) Willie "Pops" Stargell called him (his teammate) mobile, agile and hostile!

22) Up for two cups of coffee in the Majors, he finally hit pay dirt in Japan. In his ten seasons "across the ocean", he poled 277 dingers and won both the MVP and the Triple Crown in 1984.

23) His grounder eluded Bill Buckner and led the Mets to their game #6, 1986 World Series comeback win.

24) A Dodger fan supposedly dubbed this Hall of Famer's nickname when he shouted "here comes that man again."

25) With his little brother Stan, these brothers combined to win 296 games (fourth best).

* CRANIUM CRUSHERS answers found on page 240

ROSTER

CATCHERS:	Yr	Hits	AB's	Ave
Steve *Boomer* Yeager	15	816	3584	.228
Ray *Iron Man* Mueller	14	733	2911	.252
Rough Bill Carrigan	10	506	1970	.257
James *Bruno* Block	5	131	565	.232
Walt *Tarzan* Stephenson	3	17	61	.279

1ST BASEMEN:	Yr	Hits	AB's	Ave
Jimmie *The Beast* Foxx	20	2646	8134	.325
George *Boomer* Scott	14	1992	7433	.268
Dirty Jack Doyle	17	1806	6039	.299
John *Boog* Powell	17	1776	6681	.266
Ron *Boomer* Blomberg	8	391	1333	.293
Craig *Mongo* Kusick	5	291	1238	.235
Mike *Rambo* Diaz	4	169	683	.247
John *Snake* Deal	1	48	231	.208
Greg *Boomer* Wells	2	29	127	.228
Fred *Snake* Henry	2	14	75	.187

2ND BASEMEN:	Yr	Hits	AB's	Ave
Charlie *The Mechanical Man* Gehringer	19	2839	8860	.320
Johnny *The Trojan* Evers	18	1659	6137	.270
Glenn *Bruno* Beckert	11	1473	5208	.283
Julian *The Phantom* Javier	13	1469	5722	.257
Spider Bill Cissell	9	990	3707	.267
Charlie *Snake* Neal	8	858	3316	.259
Christian *Bruno* Betzel	5	333	1444	.231
Forrest *Spook* Jacobs	3	164	665	.247
Bad Bill Eagan	3	90	382	.236

SHORTSTOPS:	Yr	Hits	AB's	Ave
Bad Bill Dahlen	21	2457	9031	.272
Rowdy Richard Bartell	18	2165	7629	.284
Hughie *Ee-Yah* Jennings	17	1527	4904	.311
Johnny *Yatcha* Logan	13	1407	5244	.268
Wally *Spooks* Gerber	15	1309	5099	.257
Ed *Lizard* Jurak	6	80	302	.265
Leslie *Bubba* Floyd	1	4	9	.444
Charles *Spider* Wilhelm	1	2	7	.286

3RD BASEMEN:	Yr	Hits	AB's	Ave
Harmon *The Killer* Killebrew	22	2086	8147	.256
Steve *Boo* Buechele	10	1023	4136	.247
John *Bubba* Phillips	10	835	3278	.255
Fighting Harry Wolverton	9	833	3001	.278
Mike *Moonman* Shannon	9	710	2780	.255
John *Spider* Jorgensen	5	201	755	.266
Jim *Igor* Command	2	4	23	.174

OUTFIELDERS:	Yr	Hits	AB's	Ave
Stan *The Man* Musial	22	3630	10972	.331
Dave *The Cobra* Parker	19	2712	9358	.290
Ted *Thumper* Williams	19	2654	7706	.344
Rickey *Man of Steal* Henderson	16	2216	7656	.289
Joltin' Joe DiMaggio	13	2214	6821	.325

OUTFIELDERS: (Cont.)	Yr	Hits	AB's	Ave
Jack *The Ripper* Clark	18	1826	6847	.267
Frank *Capital Punisher* Howard	16	1774	6488	.273
Pete *The Gladiator* Browning	13	1646	4820	.341
Joseph *Gause Ghost* Moore	12	1615	5427	.298
Dave *Kong* Kingman	16	1575	6677	.236
Tom *Bruno* Brunansky	14	1543	6289	.245
Jay *Moonman* Johnstone	20	1254	4703	.267
Charlie *King Kong* Keller	13	1085	3790	.286
Mike *Hit Man* Easler	14	1078	3677	.293
Kevin *Boogie Bear* Mitchell	10	1070	3742	.286
Lee *Captain Midnight* Walls	10	670	2558	.262
Steve *Psycho* Lyons	9	545	2162	.252
Maurice *Bomber* Van Robays	6	493	1844	.267
Eric *Blue Devil* Tipton	7	439	1626	.270
Ed *Creeper* Stroud	6	320	1353	.237
Wycliffe *Bubba* Morton	7	248	928	.267
Harold *Tarzan* Wallis	5	216	886	.244
Pete *Bash* Compton	6	186	773	.241
Bob *Spook* Speake	4	170	761	.223
Bob *Road Warrior* Jones	9	133	603	.221
Harlin *Samson* Pool	2	129	426	.303
Karl *Tuffy* Rhodes	5	128	549	.233
Owen *Spider* Clark	2	106	405	.262
Cobra Joe Frazier	4	68	282	.241
John *Thumper* DeMerit	5	23	132	.174
Brian *Bam* McCall	2	3	15	.200
Charles *Tuffy* Stewart	2	1	9	.111
Joseph *Goobers* Bratcher	1	0	1	.000

PITCHERS:	Yr	Won	Lost	ERA
Iron Man Joe McGinnity	10	246	142	2.66
Jim *The Lizard* Bunning	17	224	184	3.27
Bob *Warrior* Friend	16	197	230	3.58
Ron *Gator* Guidry	14	170	91	3.29
Fred *Firpo* Marberry	14	148	88	3.63
Frank *The Yankee Killer* Lary	12	128	116	3.49
Ralph *Boog* Terry	12	107	99	3.62
Phil *The Vulture* Regan	13	96	81	3.84
Russ *The Mad Monk* Meyer	13	94	73	3.99
Harry *The Giant Killer* Coveleski	9	81	55	2.39
Jeff *The Terminator* Reardon	16	73	77	3.16
Jack *The Giant Killer* Pfiester	8	71	44	2.02
David *Boo* Ferriss	6	65	30	3.64
Al *The Mad Hungarian* Hrabosky	13	64	35	3.10
Tom *Snake* Sturdivant	10	59	51	3.74
Claude *Jaws* Lockwood	12	57	97	3.55
Dick *The Monster* Radatz	7	52	43	3.13
Mitch *The Wild Thing* Williams	9	44	55	3.53
Tom *The Terminator* Henke	13	40	41	2.73
Don *Stan The Man Unusual* Stanhouse	10	38	54	3.84
Dave *Tarzan* Lemanczyk	8	37	63	4.62
Emory *Bubba* Church	6	36	37	4.10
Larry *The Dodger Killer* Jaster	7	35	33	3.64
Roger *Spider* Nelson	9	29	32	3.06

ROSTER

PITCHERS: (Cont.)	Yr	Won	Lost	ERA
Lewis *Snake* Wiltse	3	29	31	4.59
Xavier *Mr. X* Rescigno	3	19	22	4.13
Frank *Shadow* Gilmore	3	12	33	4.26
Ralph *Bruz* Hamner	4	8	20	4.58
Elmer *Shook* Brown	5	7	11	3.48
Fredrick *Mysterious* Walker	5	7	23	4.00
Charlie *Bubba* Harris	3	6	3	4.84
Charles *Whammy* Douglas	1	3	3	3.26
Savage Tom Thomas	3	3	3	3.31
Tom *Rattlesnake* Baker	4	3	9	4.73
Brad *The Animal* Lesley	4	1	3	3.86

PITCHERS: (Cont.)	Yr	Won	Lost	ERA
Harry *Shadow* Pyle	2	1	4	4.54
Dick *Shadow* Carroll	1	0	0	3.60
Steve *The Mad Russian* Rachunok	1	0	1	4.50
Dale *Mountain Man* Roberts	1	0	0	9.00

EXTRAS:
Chris *Boomer* Berman - Great Announcer
Ben *Boomer* Blazovich - Awesome Son And Hitter
The Green Monster - Fenway's left field wall
Death Valley - Yankee Stadium's left-center field

LINGO

Butchered a Ball: Make an error

Fought off a Pitch: Foul off a hard pitch to hit

Go Down Swinging: Strikeout

Jolted One: Hit a ball very hard

Hit a Screamer: A very hard hit ball

Beat Out a Hit: Ran fast enough to reach first before the ball

Choke: Fail when it was your chance

Choke Up: Slide your hands up the bat to better control your swing

Squeeze: Bunt a player home from third base

Suicide Squeeze: What I faced when I had to say good-bye to Aunt Rose

Murderers' Row: Lineup of the 1927 Yankees known for killing pitchers

Wicked Hop: Ball that takes a bad bounce

Died on the Bases: Runners did not come home because three outs were made

Killed the Rally: Batter makes a critical out or fielder makes a key play

Shocker: An upset occurs

Cut Down: Player thrown out attempting to advance

Massacred: One sided win

Annihilated: See above

Slaughtered: What happens at the stock yards

It'sa FACT cont'd...

Jack *The Ripper* Clark: He ripped 20+ homers 11 seasons and his 340 career yard shots rank The Ripper 47th on the strongboy list!

George *Boomer* Scott: During his career he boomed out 271 long balls. In 1975 Boomer had his best season. He led the American League in both home runs (tie) and RBI's! Known more for his gold necklaces and his strong bat; one should not overlook George's excellent fielding ability. Boomer won eight Gold Gloves.

Julian *The Phantom* Javier: He played 13 seasons. His son Stan has now played ten years in the Majors. Not known for his bat, The Phantom materialized in the 1967 and 1968 Fall Classics, going 9/25 and 9/27 respectively!

Charlie *The Mechanical Man* Gehringer: He whiffed only 372 times in 8860 at bats. His three seasons with fewest strikeouts were 1930 (17 in 610 at bats), 1935 (16 in 610 at bats) and 1936 (13 in 641 at bats)!

Forrest *Spook* Jacobs: He slashed four hits in his first Major League game, April 13th, 1954.

SCHOOL

34

Team

Starting often in grade school, and certainly by junior high, kids compete to make their school teams. As part of the team, the players represent their school against other institutions in their district or conference. When students reach high school, they vie for positions on the B squad and ultimately the varsity. The same process continues each spring in college. During their school year classes, ballplayers learn and develop their educational skills to help them in their future. They also better learn and develop their diamond skills when competing at the collegiate level. Now, because of the competitive play in college, and the high percentage of future players prioritizing their education, college ball literally serves as the lower level minor leagues of years past. A few rare players can even "make the jump" from their college school team to the Majors. One example is Dave Winfield. Winny is from St. Paul, Minn. He played for Central High and then starred for the Gophers at the University of Minnesota. Drafted, Dave went directly to the San Diego Padres after his senior year.

The School team is an outstanding squad. Eight members are currently attending classes at Cooperstown! To qualify for admission to this team, the Major Leaguer's nickname has to do with the "educational" process. First, there is a dress code. Schoolmates should not be Sloppy, Tacky or Inky. Second, there is discipline. Whispering, Spittin', being Sillie, Grunting, Whistlin', Laughing, Hummers and being Noisy are not allowed! The Goshen Schoolmaster, a Prof, a Sub, two Professors and The Old Professor all expect the squad to Ad, Count, know Pi and no Guesses, or else they may get a C or a Big D! Third, there is a reward. Good Kids, Quiet and Silent, (not a Fibber, Cocky, a Braggo or any Fighting and Spitballs) will qualify for Columbia, Colby, Fordham, Harvard, Princeton and Yale.

One team member stands out from the others. Ken Junior Griffey is the near perfect student. At age 19, in 1989, Junior was a starting Major Leaguer. Through 1994, age 24, he has been TOTALLY AWESOME! Since his first season, Junior has hit over .300 every summer (1990-94). His power numbers have advanced each year, with the exception of the 1994 strike shortened campaign. Junior has taught opposing pitchers a lesson 22, 22, 27, 45 and 40 times and has sent home 80, 100, 103, 109 and 90 teammates from 1990-94. His 40 round trippers in just 111 games in 1994 led the American League! Combined with his fabulous batting skills, Junior is just as awesome defensively! He has been awarded the Gold Glove five consecutive summers (1990-94). As any teacher would say regarding an extraordinary pupil, "He has unlimited potential and the sky is the limit!"

LINEUP

CA	Charles *Gabby* Hartnett	was a 20 year player on his way to the Hall. An outstanding fielder, Gabby led all NL backstops six summers in fielding %. An excellent hitter, his three best seasons Gabby hit .339, .344 and .354! In 1930 he slugged 37 HR's and had 122 RBI's. Gabby won the NL's MVP in 1935.
1B	*Columbia* Lou Gehrig	starred at Columbia University. He went on to one of the greatest careers of all time. While playing 2130 consecutive games, Lou won two MVP's, captured a rare Triple Crown, slugged 200+ hits eight seasons, accumulated a .340 career batting average and poled 493 homers!
2B	Eddie *Cocky* Collins	was overshadowed by Ty Cobb. Eddie's stats are gigantic. Cocky was fast on the bases, great in the field and outstanding at the plate. He ranks sixth all time in stolen bases (744). Nine times Cocky led all AL keystoners in fielding %. His 3312 career hits are eighth best ever!
SS	Lonny *Junior* Frey	played 14 seasons, plus gave two years to his country. A dependable hitter, Junior was a three time All-Star. He led the Senior Circuit in stolen bases and scored over 100 runs in 1940. Twice Junior led all NL shortstops in fielding % and DP's, and once each in putouts and assists.
3B	Eddie *The Brat* Stanky	starred 11 seasons in the Senior Circuit. Three times he led the NL in free passes, and six times Eddie received more than 100 walks. Twice The Brat topped all National Leaguers in on base percentage. In 1950 New York writers voted Eddie the Player of the Year!
OF	Tony *"C"* Conigliaro	was a power hitter at an early age. He slugged a record 24 yard shots as a teenager! At age 20, he was the youngest player to lead the league in homers! Tony C had 104 career home runs by the age of 22! A tragic beaning in 1967 effectively short circuited his remarkable career.
OF	*Silent* George Hendrick	quietly starred for 18 seasons. Playing for six teams, he steadily put up the numbers. From 1973-83, Silent George blasted at least 16 home runs per summer and averaged over 80 RBI's per year, twice plating 100+ runs! His 267 yard shots place him in the top 100!
OF	*Silent* Mike Tiernan	starred 13 seasons (1887-99) for the New York Giants. In both 1890 and 1891 he shared the NL league lead in HR's! Twice Silent Mike banged out 21 triples and his 162 three baggers, in only 13 summers, rank him 38th! Seven years Silent Mike scored 100+ runs.
P	Don *Big D* Drysdale	had his 14 year career halted at age 33 by a rotorcuff injury. From 1962-65 Big D led the NL in starts. Three campaigns he won the strikeout crown. Big D twirled 49 shutouts, tying for 21st all time! His 25 wins in 1962 not only paced the league, but also helped Big D win the Cy Young!
P	*Fordham* Mort Cooper	was, from 1942-44, the top right-hander in the NL. He led the Cards to three straight World Series! In 1942 Fordham Mort led the league in wins (22), ERA (1.78) and shutouts (ten), and was voted MVP! He won 21 and 22 games and painted seven and six whitewashes in 1943 and 1944.
P	Waite *Schoolboy* Hoyt	hurled 21 seasons on his way to Cooperstown. He was the mainstay of the Yankees in the 20's, winning 155 games from 1921-29. In 1927 Schoolboy tied for the AL lead with 22 wins. 1928 was his best summer. Waite posted 23 of his 237 career V's for the Bronx Bombers!
RES	*Spittin'* Bill Doak	was a 16 year NL star. From 1914-24 he won in double digits nine summers, including 20 "big V's" in 1920. In 1914 Spittin' Bill went 19-6, leading the league in ERA at 1.72 and ranking second in whitewashes with seven. Bill again topped all Senior Circuit hurlers in ERA (2.59) in 1921.
RES	Adrian *Addie* Joss	tragically died two days after his 31st birthday. Addie logged 45 shutouts (28th best), tossed six one hitters, fired two no-hitters (perfect game October 2nd, 1908), won 20+ games four times and accumulated the second best career ERA, a microscopic 1.89! Addie rests in the Hall!
RES	Lynwood *Schoolboy* Rowe	anchored the pennant winning Tiger staff in 1934-35. He won 43 games and recorded nine shutouts those two summers. After winning 19 more contests in 1936, Schoolboy hurt his arm and never was the same. He did manage to fashion a 16-3 season, with limited action, in 1940.
MGR	Frankie *Fordham Flash* Frisch	had a Hall of Fame career as a second sacker, but then he went on to manage 16 seasons (first five as a playing manager). The Fordham Flash is best remembered for taking a rag tag group (Gashouse Gang) who had finished fifth in 1933 to the 1934 World Championship!

L to R: Don *Big D* Drysdale, Tony *"C"* Conigliaro, Ken *Junior* Griffey, Eddie *Cocky* Collins, Adrian *Addie* Joss

It'sa FACT

Harvard Eddie Grant: He died on October 5th, 1918 during WW I action in the Argonne Forest. A five foot high memorial, for Harvard Eddie, was placed at the base of the center field club house wall in the Polo Grounds.

Don *Big D* Drysdale: On April 17th, 1963 inning #2, he fanned four batters!

Columbia Lou Gehrig: 1927 was an outstanding year for him. Columbia Lou, nicknamed for his alma mater, was named the American League's MVP. That same year Babe Ruth hit 60 home runs! Lou, in 1927, led the AL in doubles with 52 and RBI's with 175. He also batted .373, swatted 47 homers, legged out 18 triples and posted a .765 slugging %! Babe earned $80,000 that campaign, while Columbia Lou was paid just $6,000.

Silent John Whitehead: As a rookie hurler for the Chicago White Sox in 1935, Silent John won the first eight games he started!

Addison **Ad** Gumbert: He was an outstanding hitter for a pitcher. In 1889, during the dead ball era, Ad walloped seven homers in just 153 at bats! His home run % far exceeded any other player that season!

Earl **Teach** Caldwell: 1946 was his best season! His 13 relief wins topped all AL relievers and Teach finished second in saves. He posted a 2.08 ERA, holding hitters to a minuscule .186 batting average.

Grunting Jim Shaw: He pitched in Walter The Big Train Johnson's shadow. Four seasons Grunting Jim won 15 or more games. In 1919 he led the AL in both games and innings (tie). That summer Grunting Jim also logged 17 wins for the seventh place Senators, who that season won only 56 times!

Hollis **Sloppy** Thurston: On August 22nd, 1923 inning #12, he had a perfect inning (nine pitches, three strikeouts)!

Don **Big D** Drysdale: In 1968 he pitched six consecutive shutouts, stringing 56 2/3 scoreless innings together. It was the Major League record until Orel Hershiser broke it in 1988. During the streak Big D hit a batter when the bases were loaded. In a rare call, the umpire ruled the batter did not avoid the pitch and disallowed the free base and the forced run. The Big D then retired him and kept his streak alive!

Monte **Prof** Weaver: In 1932 he went 22-10. Prof had the fifth highest win total for a rookie in the AL.

Waite **Schoolboy** Hoyt: In the 1921 World Series he pitched three complete games and gave up no earned runs! Nevertheless, Schoolboy was the hard luck game #8 loser (1-0 on an unearned run). Waite, who was also known as the Merry Mortician, "laid them away" in the 1928 Fall Classic. He pitched complete game victories in game #1 and Series clinching game #4. After his Hall of Fame career, Schoolboy was the Redlegs' announcer for several seasons.

Adrian **Addie** Joss: During his nine seasons he gave up a total of only 19 home runs. Two seasons Addie did not allow any home runs! The Hall of Fame voting committee waived the ten year minimum playing career rule for this great hurler, because of his early death at the height of his career.

Harry **Stinky** Davis: He was the Tiger's starting first sacker in 1932. Then a guy named Hammerin' Hank Greenberg came along, curtailing Stinky's promising career.

Dick **Hummer** Drott: In 1957, as a 20 year old rookie, he toiled for the last place Cubs. Hummer won 15 contests and ranked second (tie) in the NL in strikeouts, firing his "hummer".

Sam **Goshen Schoolmaster** Leever: He gained his nickname for his off season occupation. Sam's career winning % of .660 ranks him eighth all time. From 1899-1908 he won at least 14 games each season, four times reaching 20 or more victories! The Goshen Schoolmaster posted a 25-7 mark in 1903. That summer he led the NL in winning % (.781), shutouts (seven) and ERA (2.08)!

Carl **Sub** Mays: Combining with a young lefty, Babe Ruth, they each won two games in the 1918 Fall Classic. Sub's two victories (games #3 and #6) gave the Bosox their last World Championship.

Casey **The Old Professor** Stengel: On September 17th, 1912 he laced four hits in his first ball game!

Charles **Count** Campau: He played in only 75 of his team's 139 games in 1890. Amazingly, he led the American Assoc. with nine homers! His short career covered just three seasons and only 147 games. The Count hit only one other homer while in the Majors.

Robert **Braggo** Roth: On August 21st, 1915 he was traded with two players and cash for Shoeless Joe Jackson. Braggo completed the season, playing in only 109 games (154 game season). Nevertheless, he led the AL in homers and finished tied for third in triples!

Adrian **Addie** Joss: In 1908 he had a 1.16 ERA, the eighth lowest ever!

Tony **Count** Mullane: Hailing from Cork, Ireland, he won 30+ games five separate seasons during the early years of baseball! The Count was also called "Apollo of the Box" (before 1893 pitchers could wind up and throw from a pitching box rather than be stationary on a rubber). The Count (AKA Apollo - a Greek god) won 284 games during his career (tied for 24th). To add to his deception, he was ambidextrous. Pitching before players wore gloves, batters did not know which hand The Count would throw with!

William **Yale** Murphy: He stood just 5'3" and weighed 125 lbs., but Yale was "big enough" to be in the Big Leagues for three seasons!

Lynwood **Schoolboy** Rowe: For a hurler, he was an excellent hitter! During his career Schoolboy blasted 18 home runs, including grand slams July 22nd, 1939 and May 2nd, 1943!

TRIVIA*

1) His nickname came from this Maine College which he attended.

2) During his career he walked 1.43 batters per nine innings (370/2336), third best control ever.

3) In 1920 he was credited for developing the web in a baseball glove. Surprisingly, he was a pitcher. (Hint: now there was more glove for _____ into it)

4) Since his identically named dad played 19 seasons in the Big Leagues, it only seems natural for him to be called this.

5) Known by many nicknames, he was sometimes called "Old Biscuit Pants" and (same as the movie) "The Pride Of The Yankees".

6) He and Ted Williams tied for the RBI Crown with 159 ribbies in 1949. No one has driven in as many runs in one season since.

7) Well educated, he became an attorney and practiced law after he retired. His nickname is a good hint.

8) In 1949 he had a 34 game hitting streak, the sixth longest (tie) in the American League.

9) This "silent" rookie was dubbed his nickname by a reporter who rode next to him on a train.

10) His two younger brothers were both Major League third basemen. One, Ken, was the 1964 NL MVP.

11) This right-hander in 1924 won 20 games, including ten in a row, for the last place White Sox. An impeccable dresser (hint), he is probably best remembered for signing Ralph Kiner in his "scouting days".

12) His 22 wins in 1932 were ten more than in any of his eight other seasons. He had a masters in mathematics and taught in college.

13) In 1965 this slugging pitcher hit seven of his 29 career homers and batted .300.

14) He matched Dale Long and Don Mattingly's record of hitting a home run in eight consecutive games.

15) He and his brother Walker, in 1943, placed second and fifth in the NL MVP voting.

16) This stopper turned author wrote two books, "The Long Season" and "Pennant Run", while doing his pitching chores. His nickname is a tip-off.

17) This hurler was the 1975 NL Rookie of the Year. On September 29th, 1976 he no-hit Atlanta.

18) He debuted as an 18 year old hurler for the New York Giants. It led to his nickname.

19) On September 28th, 1938 the Cubs, led by their newly appointed playing manager, met the Pirates at Wrigley Field (trailed the Bucs by ½ game for the flag). Tied 5-5 after eight innings and darkness setting in, the umpires decided to play one more inning. With two outs, and two strikes, the playing manager hit the "homer in the gloamin'" and gave his Cubs the flag!

20) He gained his nickname from the college he attended on a football scholarship. His 23 career grand slams are the Major League record.

21) Also known as "The Beast", this Hall of Famer, for many years, held the career home run record for right-handed batters.

22) As a tough manager he was later known as "Old Sarge", but as a player he apparently communicated more easily.

23) He won 16 consecutive games in 1934, tying the AL record held also by Big Train Johnson, Smokey Joe Wood and Lefty Grove.

24) Famous for his side wheeling style, his pitching arm nearly dragged the ground when throwing. It led to his nickname.

25) He started the 1994 season by hitting three homers in the opener.

* MID SEASON EXAM answers found on page 240

ROSTER

CATCHERS:	Yr	Hits	AB's	Ave
Charles *Gabby* Hartnett	20	1912	6432	.297
Johnny *Gabby* Roseboro	14	1206	4847	.249
John *Noisy* Kling	13	1151	4241	.271
Adalberto *Junior* Ortiz	13	484	1894	.256
Charles *Gabby* Street	8	312	1501	.208
Joe *Gabby* Glenn	8	181	718	.252
Alfred *Skip* Jutze	6	141	656	.215
George *Good Kid* Susce	8	61	268	.228
Pius *Pi* Schwert	2	5	23	.217

1ST BASEMEN:	Yr	Hits	AB's	Ave
Columbia Lou Gehrig	17	2721	8001	.340
Jimmie *Double X* Foxx	20	2646	8134	.325
Jake *Guesses* Virtue	5	483	1764	.274
Harry *Stinky* Davis	3	320	1213	.264
William *Peek-A-Boo* Veach	3	76	353	.215
Bill *Blab* Schwartz	1	13	86	.151
Philip *Skip* James	2	6	36	.167
William *Ad* Yale	1	1	13	.077

2ND BASEMEN:	Yr	Hits	AB's	Ave
Eddie *Cocky* Collins	25	3312	9949	.333
Frankie *Fordham Flash* Frisch	19	2880	9112	.316
Laughing Larry Doyle	14	1887	6509	.290
Silent John Hummel	12	991	3906	.254
Tim *Tuff* Teufel	11	789	3112	.254
John *Chewing Gum* O'Brien	6	486	1910	.254
Walter *Punk* Gautreau	4	207	806	.257
Gene *Skip* Mauch	9	176	737	.239
Quiet Joe Knight	2	156	505	.309
Milciades *Junior* Noboa	8	118	493	.239
Jim *Imp* Begley	1	1	5	.200

SHORTSTOPS:	Yr	Hits	AB's	Ave
Vern *Junior* Stephens	15	1859	6497	.286
Lonny *Junior* Frey	14	1482	5517	.269
Daryl *Big Dee* Spencer	10	901	3689	.244
John *Schoolboy* Knight	8	636	2664	.239
Phil *Supersub* Linz	7	322	1372	.235
Alan *Inky* Strange	5	211	947	.223
Glen *Gabby* Stewart	3	158	742	.213
William *Yale* Murphy	3	113	472	.239

3RD BASEMEN:	Yr	Hits	AB's	Ave
Jim *Junior* Gilliam	14	1889	7119	.265
Eddie *The Brat* Stanky	11	1154	4301	.268
Harvard Eddie Grant	10	844	3385	.249
Fighting Harry Wolverton	9	833	3001	.278
Princeton Charlie Reilly	8	595	2380	.250
Billy *Gabby* Grabarkewitz	7	274	1161	.236
Alvin *Junior* Moore	5	204	774	.264
Grey *Noisy* Clarke	1	44	169	.260
Charles *Hummer* DeArmond	1	11	39	.282

OUTFIELDERS:	Yr	Hits	AB's	Ave
Silent George Hendrick	18	1980	7129	.278
Silent Mike Tiernan	13	1834	5906	.311
Dom *The Little Professor* DiMaggio	11	1680	5640	.298
Silent John Titus	11	1401	4960	.282
Casey *The Old Professor* Stengel	14	1219	4288	.284
Ken *Junior* Griffey	6	972	3180	.306
Tony *C* Conigliaro	8	849	3221	.264
Robert *Braggo* Roth	8	804	2831	.284
Whispering Bill Barrett	9	690	2395	.288
Glenn *Addie* Adams	8	452	1617	.280
Wilson *Dee* Miles	7	411	1467	.280
George *Count* Puccinelli	4	172	607	.283
Charles *Count* Campau	3	153	572	.267
Bill *Fibber* McGhee	2	146	537	.272
Karl *Tuffy* Rhodes	5	128	549	.233
Silent George Twombly	5	88	417	.211
Alta *Schoolboy* Cohen	3	13	67	.194
Art *Sillie* Thomason	1	12	70	.171
Lew *Noisy* Flick	2	7	40	.175
Angie *Junior* Dagres	1	4	15	.267
Charles *Tuffy* Stewart	2	1	9	.111

PITCHERS:	Yr	Won	Lost	ERA
Tony *Count* Mullane	13	284	220	3.05
Waite *Schoolboy* Hoyt	21	237	182	3.59
Don *Big D* Drysdale	14	209	166	2.95
Carl *Sub* Mays	15	207	126	2.92
Sam *Goshen Schoolmaster* Leever	13	194	100	2.47
Spittin' Bill Doak	16	169	157	2.98
Adrian *Addie* Joss	9	160	97	1.89
Colby Jack Coombs	14	158	110	2.78
Lynwood *Schoolboy* Rowe	15	158	101	3.87
Fordham Mort Cooper	11	128	75	2.97
Addison *Ad* Gumbert	9	123	101	4.27
Ted *Pitching Professor* Lewis	6	94	64	3.53
Dick *Professor* Hall	19	93	75	3.32
Fordham Johnny Murphy	13	93	53	3.50
John *The Count* Montefusco	13	90	83	3.54
Hollis *Sloppy* Thurston	9	89	86	4.24
Grunting Jim Shaw	9	84	98	3.07
Monte *Prof* Weaver	9	71	50	4.36
Claude *Skip* Lockwood	12	57	97	3.55
Dan *Quiz* Quisenberry	12	56	46	2.76
Jim *Professor* Brosnan	9	55	47	3.54
Fred *Spitball* Anderson	7	53	57	2.86
Silent John Whitehead	7	49	54	4.60
Eugene *Junior* Thompson	6	47	35	3.26
Columbia George Smith	8	41	81	3.89
Tacky Tom Parrott	4	39	48	5.33
Addison *Ad* Brennan	7	37	36	3.11
Elmer *Spitball* Stricklett	4	35	51	2.84
Keith *The Count* Atherton	7	33	41	3.99
Earl *Teach* Caldwell	8	33	43	4.69
Bob *Junior* Kline	5	30	28	5.05

ROSTER

PITCHERS: (Cont.)	Yr	Won	Lost	ERA
Dick *Hummer* Drott	7	27	46	4.78
Whistlin' Jake Wade	8	27	40	5.00
Joe *Professor* Ostrowski	5	23	25	4.54
Dallas *Big D* Green	8	20	22	4.26
Cloyd *Junior* Boyer	5	20	23	4.73
Adolph *Ad* Liska	5	17	18	3.87
Dave *Gabby* Jolly	5	16	14	3.77
Lee *Skip* Pitlock	3	8	8	4.53
Mumbles Bill Tremel	3	4	2	4.05
James *Junior* Walsh	5	4	10	5.88
Silent John Gillespie	1	3	3	4.52
Silent Jake Volz	3	2	4	6.10

PITCHERS: (Cont.)	Yr	Won	Lost	ERA
Slothful Bill Lattimore	1	1	2	4.50
Bill *Skip* Crouch	1	0	0	3.38
Bill *Ding Dong* Bell	2	0	1	4.32
Adam *Ad* Swigler	1	0	1	6.00
John *Ad* Brown	1	0	1	7.20
Earl *Junior* Wooten	1	0	0	9.00
Al *Count* Doe	1	0	1	9.00
Charles *Count* Weber	1	0	1	15.75
EXTRA:				
Anaheim Stadium - *Big A*				

LINGO

Professor: A knowledgeable baseball person

Spitball: A pitch (illegal) which the pitcher adds a "substance" to the ball to cause it to dramatically drop

Making the Grade: Doing well enough to be on the team

Doing His Homework: Learning about opposing pitchers and players

The Book: Tells opposing players strengths and weaknesses

Got His Attention: Throw a ball at a batter's head

Class Guy: Player who is a credit to the game

He Advanced: Runner goes to the next base

Read Him: Batter anticipates correctly what a pitcher will throw

Read His Move: Base runner anticipates correctly when to run to steal a base

Went to School on Him: Learn about a pitcher to hit him better

Sit Him Down: Get a batter out

MORE TRIVIA*

A) In the 1964 Fall Classic Bob Hoot Gibson went 2-1 and whiffed 31 Yankees (a Series record), but he gave up two homers to this player who hit only 11 career regular season dingers.

B) While handling catching chores for the Twins, his "imaginary brother" gave interviews to the press.

C) Jimmy The Toy Cannon Wynn in 1969 tied his NL record of 148 walks in one season.

D) He was the first catcher to hit 200 round trippers and drive in 1000 runs. He was also known as "Old Tomato Face", but his close friends called him by his middle name which was Leo.

E) A four sport athlete at Fordham College and a second team All-American halfback, he went on to the Big Show and ultimately to Cooperstown.

F) During the 1932 season he belted 58 official homers. He also "lost" two yard shots in canceled rainouts or he, too, would have hit 60 homers!

G) On September 14th, 1990 he and his dad hit back to back homers, the only time a father and son have done that!

H) In the 1923 World Series game #1 he hit a homer in the ninth to win it 5-4. In game #3 his seventh inning shot won it 1-0. (Hint: his other nickname tells where he was born)

I) His 15 stolen bases in 1950 were the lowest league leading total in baseball history.

J) He holds the AL outfielder record of handling 573 consecutive chances without committing an error.

* MID SEASON EXAM answers found on page 240

SWITCH

35

Team

The word switch is employed frequently in baseball. One use is in batting. If a player bats from either side of the plate, he is referred to as a switch hitter. The object of switch hitting is for the batter to hit from the opposite side of the plate as the pitcher's throwing arm. This should allow the hitter to see the ball better. Eddie Murray and Ozzie The Wizard of Oz Smith both bat from either side. A second use is in defense. When a player consistently hits the ball to a certain area, such as a pull hitter, the defense will switch over for him. Ted The Kid Williams and more recently Kent Herbie Hrbek would be defensed with three infielders between first base and second base, since both big lefties always yanked the ball. A third use is a manager strategy. It is done exclusively in the NL because pitchers still bat. It is called the double switch. When a pitcher is relieved, a position player is simultaneously replaced. The new pitcher is inserted into the batting order in the old fielder's slot (presumably the manager removes a player who is seven or eight batters away from coming up to bat). The double switch delays the need to quickly pinch-hit for the new hurler. Dorrel Whitey Herzog popularized this wise move.

To qualify for the Switch Team you must be known by your middle name and people presume it is your first name. Over 1000 players would qualify, but the roster is limited to only the more active Major Leaguers.

One player certainly is visible among this fantastic group. Lynn Nolan Ryan's accomplishments are unbelievable, yet he never was voted the Cy Young or the MVP! When you hear Nolan Ryan's name, you think first of strikeouts. You are right, but there is much more. Nolan not only struck out the most batters in baseball history, but he also was the most difficult pitcher to hit in the Majors. His dominating talent carried well into his 40's. Only 52 times have pitchers held batters to a .195 or lower batting average in one season. Of the 36 hurlers to reach this level, three have done it twice, two have done it three times, and one, Nolan Ryan, achieved it ten seasons! These stats coincide with the hits allowed per game numbers. The top 50 season performances in baseball history were done by 34 twirlers. Three pitchers have done it twice, two have done it three times, and one, Nolan Ryan, has achieved it ten seasons! Since 1900 only 23 times have pitchers fanned 300 or more batters in one season. Of the 12 moundsmen to reach that plateau, four have done it twice, one did it three times, and one, Nolan Ryan, achieved it six seasons, including the single season record of 383 K's! Fifty-three times hurlers have averaged, for one season, over nine K's per game (minimum of one inning per season game to qualify). Twenty-four different players have made this exclusive group. Only one, Nolan Ryan, has done it more than four times. The Express did it 14 seasons! Nolan's career strikeout number is hard to comprehend. He broke a 56 year old "untouchable" record in 1983. When The Express retired, he had surpassed Big Train by over 60%! That is comparable to breaking Hammerin' Hank Aaron's 755 homer mark by hitting 1225 homers or topping Pete Charlie Hustle Rose's 4256 hit record by stroking 6900 hits! He obliterated the lifetime strikeout record! Nolan has twice as many K's as the pitcher in 11th place! People casually mention, yeah Ryan tossed seven no-hitters, like so what is new? Only four pitchers have had three no-hitters and one had four no-hitters. No one is even close to Nolan! From 1987-91 Nolan was 40-44 years old. In 1987 he led the NL in K's, ERA, and OBA (opponent's batting average). He followed in 1988 to top all NL hurlers in K's. His 1989 season found The Express fanning 301 batters and holding batters to a league low .187 batting average. At 43, in 1990, for the fourth consecutive year, Nolan won the strikeout crown! He also led in OBA. Are you ready? At 44 Lynn whiffed 203 batters in just 173 frames, a rate of 10.56 per game. This is the eighth best in baseball history! Nolan also allowed only 5.31 base hits per game, the third best in baseball history! Hang on, he also held opposing batters to a .172 batting average, the third lowest in baseball history! For his career Nolan Ryan had 324 wins (tie 12th), 61 shutouts (tie seventh) 5386 innings (fifth), 9.55 K's per game (first), 6.56 hits per game (first), .204 OBA (first) and 5714 K's (first). Ryan rules!

LINEUP

CA	James *Tim* McCarver

starred 21 seasons in the NL. While with the Cardinals he was an All-Star two times and twice was the fielding % leader. Tim played his later years for the Phillies, always catching Lefty Carlton. Currently, Tim is doing an outstanding job announcing our national pastime.

1B	Carroll *Chris* Chambliss

played 17 summers in the Big Leagues. His leather helped Chris to a Gold Glove in 1978 and his bat powered 17 or more HR's six years. Chris was the hero of the 1976 ALCS. He went 11/21 with eight RBI's. His game #5 bottom of the ninth homer sent the Yanks to the Series.

2B	Edward *Chuck* Knoblauch

was the AL 1991 Rookie of the Year. He is a reincarnation of Pete Rose. Chuck even fires the ball hard when they go around the horn. He is a feisty, aggressive runner; a quick, sure handed fielder and a solid, determined batter, who maximizes his talents and keeps getting better.

SS	Lewis *Everett* Scott

was baseball's original ironman. Starting mid season 1916, until he was benched for poor play in 1925, Everett played 1307 consecutive games! During his streak, the third longest, he also led the American League in fielding % eight consecutive seasons from 1916 through 1923!

3B	William *Larry* Gardner

sparkled for 17 years in the AL. In 1920 Larry paced the Tribe with 118 RBI's and led them to the World Championship. That season he led all hot corner men in putouts, assists, DP's and fielding %. In 1921 he batted .321 with 120 RBI's. Six seasons Larry hit over .300.

OF	Herman *Tommy* Davis

had an outstanding 18 year career. He put together an awesome season in 1962 at the age of 23. Tommy led the National League in batting (.346), hits (230) and RBI's (153). In 1963 he again led the league in hitting! Six times, during his career, Tommy hit over .300.

OF	Samuel *Jimmy* Sheckard

starred 17 seasons, most after the turn of the century. He was fast and had power. Jimmy swiped 465 bags (38th) and led the NL twice in pilfers (one tie). His 19 three baggers in 1901 were tops. His 136 triples rank Jimmy tied for 69th. In 1903 Jimmy led the NL in homers.

OF	William *Ben* Chapman

was a 15 year star who broke-in in 1930. His stats would have been greater, but WW II interrupted his career. Ben was selected to the AL All-Star team the first three years (1933-35). He was fast, topping the league in pilfers (four) and 3B's (one). In 1938 Ben hit .340 (third).

P	Lynn *Nolan* Ryan

is a future Hall of Famer. He hurled a record 27 years, chalking up 20 seasons with at least ten victories! Nolan won a record 11 strikeout crowns and 12 seasons he led in opponents' batting average. Nolan is an ambassador to baseball as both a person and a player.

P	Rik *Bert* Blyleven

reached the Majors at 19 and for 22 seasons baffled batters with his curveball. His 287 wins place Bert 22nd. He also posted 60 shutouts, topped by only eight hurlers. Eight years Bert fanned at least 200 batters and his 3701 career K's trail only Lefty Carlton and Nolan Ryan!

P	Walter *Billy* Pierce

was a great pitcher. The little lefty's stats literally mirror Whitey Ford's, yet Billy has been overlooked. Billy was a seven time All-Star, posted 38 shutouts, won 14+ games ten times, and led the AL in wins (1957 shared), K's (1953) and ERA (1955). Why not the Hall?

RES	Wilmer *Dean* Chance

was gone from the Majors at the age of 30. Nevertheless, in a small interval Dean did big things. Seven straight years (1962-68) he won 12 or more games. In 1964 Dean led the AL in wins (20, tie) innings (278 1/3), ERA (1.65) and shutouts (11, fourth best since 1900)!

RES	William *Bob* Allison

was the AL's Rookie of the Year in 1959. That summer he jolted 30 homers and topped the AL in triples. Eight of his 13 seasons Bob cracked 20+ round trippers and his 256 circuit shots rank him in the top 100. Bob's friendliness made him a popular player in the Twin Cities.

RES	Arley *Wilbur* Cooper

tossed balls and strikes 13 of his 15 seasons for the Bucs in the teens and 20's. From 1917-24 Wilbur won 17, 19, 19, 24, 22 (shared league lead), 23, 17 and 20 games! He was a .239 career hitter. In 1922 Wilbur smashed four tators and in 1924 he batted a lusty .346!

RES	James *Bob* Shawkey

hurled brilliantly for 15 summers. Eight seasons he posted at least 16 victories and in 1916, 1919, 1920 and 1922 he entered the 20 victory circle. Sailor Bob led the American League in ERA in 1920. He fell just four wins short of 200 for his outstanding career!

L to R: Edward *Chuck* Knoblauch, Herman *Tommy* Davis, Lynn *Nolan* Ryan, Rik *Bert* Blyleven, George *Tom* Seaver

It'sa FACT

Billy **Mike** Smithson: At 6'8", he was the tallest player in baseball during his playing days. In 1984 and 1985 Mike led all AL hurlers in starts and he won 15 games each season for the middle of the pack Minnesota Twins.

James **Brad** Mills: Since he had only 43 hits, he was not included on the roster. Brad's fame came from helping Lynn Nolan Ryan break Walter Barney Johnson's career strikeout record. On April 27th, 1983 Brad became #3510!

Casimir **Jim** Konstanty: In 1950 there was no Cy Young award, but this reliever was voted the NL MVP. He set the then Major League record of 74 appearances. Jim's 22 saves and 16 relief wins paced The Whiz Kids to the pennant. Interestingly, Jim started game #1 of the World Series, his first start in four years! Doctor Bobby Brown (current AL president) doubled and came around on two sacrifice flies to beat Big Jim 1-0.

Urban **Johnny** Hodapp: Turning 25 at the end of the 1930 season, he had led the AL in hits and doubles, drove in 121 runs and finished sixth in batting. A serious knee injury forced his retirement and curtailed his very promising career. He does hold the record of twice in one game having two hits in one inning.

Umpire Crew: All these men "in blue" were known by their middle names. The crew is W. Ken Burkhart, J. Frank Dwyer, R. Dale Ford, H. Doug Harvey, G. Jim Honochick, E. Durwood Merrill, T. Steve Rippley and A. Hank Soar.

Allen **Ken** Berry: Only 25 times has an outfielder gone a whole season without committing an error. Ken is one of only four players to do it a record two times.

John **Owen** Wilson: This speedy fly chaser, nicknamed Chief, led all NL outfielders in fielding % in both 1914 and 1915. In 1911 Owen led the NL in RBI's (shared) and in 1912 Chief set a single season record for his 36 triples!

Loren **Dale** Mitchell: During his career he had five hitting streaks of over 20 games. In his first eight seasons Dale batted over .300 seven times. In 1948 and 1949 he topped AL outfielders in fielding %. At the dish, in 1948, Dale finished third in batting and second in hits, and, in 1949, Dale was fourth in batting and ranked first in both hits and triples. For us trivia buffs, Dale fanned to end Don Larsen's gem in 1956.

Joseph **Frank** Demaree: From 1935-40 he hit over .300 five of the six seasons. In 1936 Frank ranked fourth (NL) in batting and third in hits and in 1937 he finished fourth in hits, third in total bases and second in RBI's.

Harold **Pat** Kelly: His three run shot in the fourth and final game of the 1979 ALCS propelled the O's to the Series.

Howard **Earl** Averill: He reached the Majors just prior to his 27th birthday. For his first ten seasons Earl averaged 188 hits, 114 runs, 36 doubles, 12 triples, 22 homers, 107 RBI's and had a .323 batting average.

Samuel **Jimmy** Sheckard: In 1901, during the dead ball era, he slugged a grand slam in two consecutive games, September 23rd and September 24th. Jimmy's 147 walks in 1911 was the Major League record for nine seasons.

Herman **Tommy** Davis: He was an outstanding pinch hitter. In 1970 he went 13/28 (.464), the fifth best season mark. For players with 50 or more career pinch-hits, Tommy's .320 average (63/197) is tops!

Samuel **Paul** Derringer: He won 20 or more games four seasons, including three consecutive years (1938-40). Those summers he won 21, 25 and 20 contests! Duke won games #4 and #7 of the 1940 World Series.

Roy **Duane** Ward: He has averaged over one strikeout per inning for his career (1986-93). In 1991 Duane appeared in a league leading 81 games, saving 23 contests and fan8ning 132 batters in just 107 1/3 innings!

Jackson **Riggs** Stephenson: In his 14 year career he batted over .300 an amazing 12 times! During Old Hoss' three best seasons he hit .362, .367 and .371. Riggs' career batting average is .336, the 18th highest all time.

Jacob **Nellie** Fox: For his keystone career he ranked seventh in assists, third in putouts and second in DP's. Six campaigns he led all AL second sackers in fielding %.

George **Tom** Seaver: He was nearly unbeatable from 1969-73. Tom Terrific went 103-51 for that half decade and captured three ERA titles and three strikeout crowns! His 311 career wins were only bettered by 15 pitchers!

Henry **Lou** Gehrig: For his career, he ranked fifth in extra base hits and on base % and Lou finished third in RBI's and slugging %! He played every day for 14 years (2130 games) with no trainers, whirlpools or cortisone shots, and "managed" to hit a mere .340 and club 493 dingers! He was fantastic!

John **Frank** Dwyer: At 5'8" and 145 pounds he was slight for a pitcher. From 1891-98 Frank won 19, 21, 18, 19, 18, 24, 18 and 16 games. For his career he completed 270 of his 318 starts.

James **Hoyt** Wilhelm: He was extremely difficult to hit. His flutterball was so hard for his battery mate to catch, an enlarged glove was made so his catcher could at least block it! He held batters to a .216 batting average for his career, seventh lowest! His 7.01 hits per game places Sarge sixth all time! Hoyt's 2.52 ERA ranks him 30th. Of the 29 pitchers with lower ERA's, only one pitched more than one season outside of the dead ball era, when ERA's were much lower. Hoyt has the lowest career ERA of any player from 1920 and on!

Jonathan **Tom** Zachary: The tall left-hander hurled for 19 seasons. For eleven campaigns he won in double digits. Tom's best season was 1929, when he went 12-0 with a 2.48 ERA.

It'sa FACT

George **Ken** Griffey Jr. and Sr.: All father/son records could be rewritten before Ken Jr. calls it quits. Ken Sr. had a great 19 year career, cracking nearly 2150 hits, batting over .300 eight seasons and in 1976 finishing second in the batting race. Junior has emerged as not only a brilliant fielder, but also an excellent natural hitter. Playing in the Majors at just 19, Ken Jr. could have a long career and be one of the greatest. If smiles earn points, he is tops!

Darrah **Dean** Stone: Named to the 1954 AL All-Star team, he entered the Mid Year Classic with two outs in the top of the eighth inning. Albert Red Schoendienst was on third. Before throwing one pitch, Red broke for home and was gunned down. The American League rallied in the bottom of the eighth (pinch hitting for Dean) and took the lead. Virgil Fire Trucks pitched the ninth for the AL and preserved Dean's win, even though he never threw a pitch!

John **Wes** Covington: He played in about 60% of the Milwaukee Braves' games during their 1957 and 1958 pennant winning seasons. In 1957 Wes crushed 21 homers and drove in 65 runs in just 328 at bats. In 1958 Wes belted 24 yard shots and plated 74 tallies in just 294 plate appearances. He also batted a torrid .330!

Nathaniel **Milt** Gaston: On July 10th, 1928 he pitched a 14 hit shutout, the record.

John **Sherm** Lollar: In his career he was named to the AL All-Star team seven times. Sherm slugged 22 homers for the "Go-Go" White Sox in 1959. Five seasons he paced all backstops in fielding %. When Sherm retired after 18 campaigns, he ranked fourth in fielding % for catchers.

Steven **Rance** Mulliniks: From 1984-86 he led all AL third sackers in fielding %. At the dish Rance hit .324 in 1984.

James **Pat** Seerey: His 26 homers in 1946 ranked him fourth in the Junior Circuit. Pat was in good company, trailing only Hammerin' Hank Greenberg, Ted The Kid Williams and Charlie King Kong Keller.

Alphonse **Dante** Bichette: Getting a chance to play everyday for the expansion Colorado Rockies, he has responded by hitting over .300 in both 1993 and 1994. Dante's 95 RBI's in 1994 were third best in the National League.

Alvin **Jake** Powell: He led the Yankees to the 1936 Championship. Jake hit .455 (10/22), scored eight runs and drove in five tallies. His four bagger in game #6 helped clinch the Series.

Arthur **Bobby** Darwin: Starting for the Twins from 1972-74, Bobby slugged 22, 18 and 25 circuit blasts and knocked in 80, 90 and 94 runs.

Francis **Ray** Blades: His best season was 1925. Ray hit .342 for the Cardinals and scored 112 times. During his ten year career he batted over .300 five summers and retired with a .301 batting average.

Marcus **Wayne** Garland: In 1976 Wayne went 20-7 (third in AL in wins) and posted four shutouts.

Charles **Doug** Bair: Not reaching the Big Show until 27, he was a short and middle man still for 15 seasons! Doug's best year was 1978. He appeared in 70 games, won seven, saved 28 (third in NL) and had a fantastic 1.97 ERA!

Herbert **Scott** Perry: In the war shortened 1918 season, the woeful Philadelphia Athletics finished last with only 52 victories. Scott won 20 games (fourth in the AL) and led the Junior Circuit in complete games (tie) and innings pitched. His ERA was 1.98 and he served up only one gopher ball in 332 1/3 frames!

Rik **Bert** Blyleven: For his career he was 3-0 in League Championship games and 2-1 in World Series play.

Donald **Gene** Conley: In the 12th inning of the 1955 All-Star game he entered and fanned the three batters he faced. Stan The Man Musial homered in the bottom of the 12th to win it for Gene. It made up for his loss in 1954's All-Star game (see *It'sa FACT* on Darrah Dean Stone). Currently there has been much made of two sport stars. Gene, at 6'9", was also a star basketball player. In 1957 he was a member of the World Champion Milwaukee Braves and Gene won three consecutive World Championships (58-59 through 60-61) with the Boston Celtics!

Henry **Gene** Garber: Gene ranks fourth in relief appearances with 922 and was credited for 94 wins and 218 saves!

James **Doug** Bird: He appeared in 54 games during the 1979-80 seasons. Doug never lost, going 2-0 and 3-0!

William **Eddie** Robinson: His career was delayed by World War II. From 1948-53 Eddie played everyday. He was named to the AL All-Star squad four times. In those six summers Eddie averaged 21 homers and 95 RBI's. He reached his high water marks in 1951, when he finished third in both homers (29) and RBI's (117).

Maurice **Wes** Parker: He was a magician with his glove. Wes led all NL first sackers in fielding % five seasons. He was voted six consecutive Gold Gloves (1967-72). Wes' career .996 fielding % ranks him third!

Henry **Gene** Bearden: In his rookie season (1948) he went 20-7, led the AL in ERA and tied for second in both victories and shutouts. In the 1948 World Series Gene won game #3, firing a five hit shutout. He also saved the final game #6, posting 1 2/3 shutout innings.

Lloyd **Vern** Kennedy: On August 31st, 1935 he fired a no-hitter. In 1936 Vern had his best season, chalking up 21 victories (second in AL) for the Chisox.

John **Whitlow** Wyatt: During his first nine seasons he had only 52 starts. He went to Brooklyn in 1939 and by the following season, Whitlow was in the rotation. He responded with 70 wins from 1940-43. In 1941 Whitlow shared the league lead with 22 victories and topped all twirlers with seven whitewashes.

Carl **Reggie** Smith: A seven time All-Star, the switch hitter blasted 314 yard shots (60th)!

TRIVIA*

1) Snakebit, he allowed no hits in an eight inning loss (his team failed to score in the top of the 9th, so the <u>hitless</u> home team won) on July 1st, 1990!

2) In 1979 he became the third reliever to be voted the Cy Young award.

3) He won games #2 and #3 of the 1992 World Series. In four appearances over 3 1/3 frames he allowed no runs, one hit and fanned six Braves.

4) In 1993 this Philadelphia Phillie won his first eight games and finished the season with a 16-4 record.

5) He won the NL ERA crown in 1983. (Hint: he hurled for the Giants and only posted ten wins)

6) In 1982 and 1983 he led the AL in wins. His 24-10 record in 1983 helped him carry away that year's AL Cy Young award.

7) On September 20th, 1958 he baffled the Yankees, tossing a no-hitter. It was one of his 52 career starts.

8) He was the 1983 World Series MVP, going 5/13 with four doubles and a home run.

9) His Major League record of hitting a homer in eight consecutive games has now been tied by Donnie Baseball Mattingly and George Ken Griffey Jr..

10) His 23 career grand slams are the Major League standard.

11) In 1993 he hit for the cycle, the first Tiger to do that since Walter Hoot Evers hit for the cycle in 1950.

12) He was the third hardest batter to strikeout in baseball history, one whiff every 42.7 at bats. (Hint: he was famous for his chaw and bottle bat)

13) For his career he ranks 24th in homer % (5.77%). Once he hit four circuit clouts in one game! (Hint: he was the NL's 1978 Rookie of the Year, beating out Ozzie Smith)

14) He retired with 300 saves. From 1979-1984 he led the NL in saves five times.

15) His wife is the famous LPGA player Nancy Lopez.

16) In 1994 he led the AL in triples. It was the fourth straight year (one tie) he has led the league in three baggers!

17) He is a switch hitter who bats from a severe crouch, presenting a small target. In 1993 he topped the AL in free passes with 132.

18) He gained his nickname, Home Run, by hitting two timely four baggers which won consecutive games in the 1911 World Series.

19) In his first at bat he slugged a homer. His second at bat yielded at triple. He never hit another homer or triple in his career!

20) He won the AL Cy Young in 1986, 1987 and 1991.

21) Only one pitcher has won the ERA crown in both leagues (NL in 1952 and AL in 1959).

22) What do May 1st, 1991, May 15th, 1973, June 1st, 1975, June 11th, 1990, July 15th, 1973, September 26th, 1981 and September 28th, 1974 have in common? Now tell me who.

23) In 1992 he shared the AL league lead in wins, going 21-11 for the below .500 Rangers. (Hint: he was the winning pitcher in the 1992 All-Star game)

24) He won the 1993 AL ERA title. It helped that he tossed 33 consecutive scoreless innings.

25) This lefty, while toiling for the sixth place Indians in 1988, won 18 times. He fanned exactly four times the batters he walked (180 to 45), an amazing ratio for a power pitcher.

* SHIFTY STICK-LERS answers found on page 240

TRIVIA*

26) He was an outstanding catcher and the 1969 NL All-Star backstop while with the Cubs. He son Todd also became a Major League catcher, currently handling chores for the Mets.

27) He slugged a grand slam in game #1 of the 1987 World Series. He also scored the 1991 World Series game #7 winning and only run.

28) His brother Leroy was a great running back for the Cleveland Browns.

29) He and another player had a similar name. The difference was one silent letter at the end of his last name. (Hint: he was also known as The Boomer From Birmingham)

30) His son, whose first name was his middle name, was known by the same name. (Hint: his nickname was Rock and he is in the Hall of Fame)

31) Since 1949 he is the only Major Leaguer to drive in over 150 runs. (Hint: it is mentioned in the lineup)

32) From 1986-92 this right-hander fanned over 200 batters each summer.

33) In the 1957 Fall Classic this right-hander won games #2, #5 and #7, tossing two shutouts against the Yankees.

34) For his career he fired 60 shutouts to place ninth all time. (Hint: he was born in Zeist Holland)

35) Their fame came the hard way. One gave up Babe Ruth's 60th homer in 1927 and the other served up Roger Maris' 61st homer in 1961.

36) Four seasons he led the AL in base hits (one tie). In 1959 he was voted the MVP.

37) From 1968-76 he struck out over 200 batters nine consecutive seasons, capturing five strikeout crowns in that stretch.

38) His 184 RBI's in one season are the AL record.

39) He reached the Big Show at 28 and stayed for 21 seasons. He holds the record for game appearances with 1070. (Hint: he was known for his knuckler)

40) Here is a lollipop. He and his dad hit back to back homers while playing for the Mariners.

41) This deceptive portsider's style has allowed him to lead the NL in lowest opponents batting average three years and to strikeout more than a batter per inning three seasons. (Hint: he accomplished this in the 1980's while hurling for the Mets)

42) From 1990-92 he led the AL in both shutouts (one tie) and ERA for three consecutive seasons!

43) He tossed a 13 inning shutout, beating Harvey The Kitten Haddix May 26th, 1959. Harvey had a perfect game the first 12 innings!

44) In his first 15 years he never had a losing season. He was so terrific, he won at least 14 games in 13 of those summers.

45) What people don't usually know is, he ranks 13th all time with 15 steals of home. (Hint: he wore #4 because he batted fourth for the Yankees)

46) This dead ball era strongboy led the AL (one tie) in yard shots four consecutive seasons (1911-14).

47) In the 1928 World Series, a four game sweep, he went 6/11 (six walks) with a double, four home runs and nine RBI's. In the 1932 Fall Classic, a four game sweep, he went 9/17 (two walks) with a double, three home runs and eight RBI's.

48) He was known as The King of Doublin' for his record 67 two baggers in 1931.

49) In 1927, the year Babe Ruth hit 60 home runs, his teammate was voted the AL MVP. He later won the Triple Crown in 1934 and a second MVP in 1936.

50) Both these pitchers were members of the 1969 "Amazing Mets". They both retired with 61 career shutouts to tie for seventh all time! They also each fanned 19 batters in one game!

* SHIFTY STICK-LERS answers found on page 240

ROSTER

CATCHERS:	Yr	Hits	AB's	Ave
James *Tim* McCarver	21	1501	5529	.271
John *Sherm* Lollar	18	1415	5351	.264
William *Walker* Cooper	18	1341	4702	.285
John *Rick* Dempsey	24	1093	4692	.233
Leo *Ernie* Whitt	15	938	3774	.249
Lonas *Ed* Bailey	14	915	3581	.256
Cecil *Randy* Hundley	14	813	3442	.236
Lowell *Otto* Miller	13	695	2836	.245
James *Ken* O'Dea	12	560	2195	.255
John *Les* Moss	13	552	2234	.247
Edward *Patsy* Gharrity	10	513	1961	.262
Robert *Mike* Stanley	9	507	1873	.271
Henry *Frank* House	10	494	1994	.248
Robert *Earl* Grace	8	493	1877	.263
Nathan *Ed* Ott	8	465	1792	.259
Charles *Bruce* Edwards	10	429	1675	.256

1ST BASEMEN:	Yr	Hits	AB's	Ave
Henry *Louis* Gehrig	17	2721	8001	.340
Carroll *Chris* Chambliss	16	2109	7571	.279
Dudley *Mike* Hargrove	12	1614	5564	.290
William *Eddie* Robinson	13	1146	4282	.268
Maurice *Wes* Parker	9	1110	4157	.267
William *Frank* Isbell	10	1056	4219	.250
Frank *Don* Hurst	7	976	3275	.298
Dave *Dale* Alexander	5	811	2450	.331
Richard *Dale* Long	10	805	3020	.267
William *Hal* Morris	7	637	2035	.313
Oscar *Ray* Grimes	6	505	1537	.329
James *Mike* Hegan	12	504	2080	.242

2ND BASEMEN:	Yr	Hits	AB's	Ave
Jacob *Nellie* Fox	19	2663	9232	.288
Abram *Hardy* Richardson	14	1688	5642	.299
Nathaniel *Fred* Pfeffer	16	1671	6555	.255
Jesus *Manny* Trillo	17	1562	5950	.263
Manuel *Julian* Javier	13	1469	5722	.257
Frank *Otto* Knabe	11	1103	4469	.247
Arvel *Odell* Hale	10	1071	3707	.289
Kenneth *Jerry* Adair	13	1022	4019	.254
Chalmer *Bill* Cissell	9	990	3707	.267
Robert *Doug* Flynn	11	918	3853	.238
Urban *Johnny* Hodapp	9	880	2826	.311
John *Joe* Gerhardt	12	854	3770	.227
Robert *Denny* Doyle	8	823	3290	.250
James *Al* Myers	8	788	3222	.245
Graham *Eddie* Moore	10	706	2474	.285
Edward *Chuck* Knoblauch	4	643	2212	.291
James *Dalton* Jones	9	548	2329	.235
Elmer *Joe* Gedeon	7	515	2109	.244
John *Bert* Niehoff	6	489	2037	.240
Edwin *Dib* Williams	6	421	1574	.267
John *Joey* Amalfitano	10	418	1715	.244

SHORTSTOPS:	Yr	Hits	AB's	Ave
Lewis *Everett* Scott	13	1455	5837	.249
Donald *Eric* McNair	14	1240	4519	.274
Gordon *Craig* Reynolds	15	1142	4466	.256
Leonard *Gene* Alley	11	999	3927	.254
James *Wayne* Causey	11	819	3244	.252
Charles *Dal* Maxvill	14	748	3443	.217
David *Travis* Fryman	5	692	2519	.275
Kenneth *Andre* Rodgers	11	628	2521	.249

3RD BASEMEN:	Yr	Hits	AB's	Ave
William *Larry* Gardner	17	1931	6688	.289
John *Frank* Baker	13	1838	5984	.307
Walter *Arlie* Latham	17	1833	6822	.269
Charles *Ray* Knight	13	1311	4829	.271
Gustaf *Bernie* Friberg	14	1170	4169	.281
James *Bob* Horner	10	1047	3777	.277
Steven *Rance* Mulliniks	16	972	3569	.272
Roy *Max* Alvis	9	895	3629	.247
Ronald *Wayne* Garrett	10	786	3285	.239
Thomas *Mike* Shannon	9	710	2780	.255
Howard *Doug* Baird	6	492	2106	.234

OUTFIELDERS:	Yr	Hits	AB's	Ave
George *Ken* Griffey Sr..	19	2143	7229	.296
Herman *Tommy* Davis	18	2121	7223	.294
Samuel *Jimmy* Sheckard	17	2084	7605	.274
Carl *Reggie* Smith	17	2020	7033	.287
Howard *Earl* Averill ·	13	2019	6353	.318
William *Ben* Chapman	15	1958	6478	.302
Jackson *Riggs* Stephenson	14	1515	4508	.336
William *Curt* Walker	12	1475	4858	.304
Walter *Kevin* McReynolds	12	1439	5423	.265
Keith *Tony* Phillips	13	1420	5335	.268
William *Barney* McCosky	11	1301	4172	.312
William *Bob* Allison	13	1281	5032	.255
Bobby *Keith* Moreland	12	1279	4581	.279
John *Owen* Wilson	9	1246	4624	.269
Loren *Dale* Mitchell	11	1244	3984	.312
Joseph *Frank* Demaree	12	1241	4144	.299
Michael *Joe* Hornung	12	1230	4784	.257
Clinton *Dan* Gladden	11	1215	4501	.270
Harold *Pat* Kelly	15	1147	4338	.264
Arthur *Lee* Maye	13	1109	4048	.274
Allen *Ken* Berry	14	1053	4136	.255
James *Gorman* Thomas	13	1051	4677	.225
Samuel *Cliff* Carroll	11	995	3972	.251
George *Ken* Griffey Jr...	6	972	3180	.306
John *Emmett* Heidrick	8	914	3047	.300
Norman *Mike* Hershberger	11	900	3572	.252
Kenneth *Emmett* Seery	9	893	3547	.252
Kenneth *Lance* Johnson	8	845	3011	.281
Robert *Barry* Bonnell	10	833	3068	.272
John *Wes* Covington	11	832	2978	.279
George *Ed* Andrews	8	830	3233	.257

ROSTER

OUTFIELDERS: (Cont.)	Yr	Hits	AB's	Ave
Cyril *Roy* Weatherly	10	794	2781	.286
Donald *Chris* James	9	772	2958	.261
David *Beals* Becker	8	763	2764	.276
Robert *Randy* Bush	12	763	3045	.251
Arthur *Clyde* Engle	8	748	2822	.265
Francis *Ray* Blades	10	726	2415	.301
Alvin *Jake* Powell	11	689	2540	.271
Domingo *Felix* Jose	7	686	2431	.282
John *Eddie* Murphy	11	680	2373	.287
William *Earl* Webb	7	661	2161	.306
Alphonse *Dante* Bichette	7	661	2387	.277
Arthur *Vin* Campbell	6	642	2069	.310
George *Earl* McNeely	8	614	2254	.272
Arthur *Bobby* Darwin	9	559	2224	.251
John *Herbie* Moran	7	527	2177	.242
William *Ed* Hahn	6	484	2045	.237
Elmer *Ralph* Hodgin	6	481	1689	.285
Tyrus *Turner* Barber	9	442	1531	.289
Richard *Marty* Keough	11	434	1796	.242
Ralph *Dave* Engle	9	431	1643	.262
Charles *Ray* Demmitt	7	419	1631	.257
Edward *Wes* Schulmerich	4	417	1442	.289
George *Fred* Brickell	8	407	1448	.281
James *Pat* Seerey	7	406	1815	.224

PITCHERS:	Yr	Won	Lost	ERA
Lynn *Nolan* Ryan	27	324	292	3.19
George *Tom* Seaver	20	311	205	2.86
Rik *Bert* Blyleven	22	287	250	3.31
Samuel *Paul* Derringer	15	223	212	3.46
Jose *Dennis* Martinez	19	219	171	3.63
Arley *Wilbur* Cooper	15	216	178	2.89
Walter *Billy* Pierce	18	211	169	3.27
Selva *Lew* Burdette	18	203	144	3.66
James *Bob* Shawkey	15	196	150	3.09
Henry *Lee* Meadows	15	188	180	3.37
Jonathan *Tom* Zachary	19	186	191	3.73
John *Frank* Dwyer	12	176	152	3.85
William *Roger* Clemens	11	172	93	2.93
James *Hoyt* Wilhelm	21	143	122	2.52
Edward *Mike* Garcia	14	142	97	3.27
Ralph *Mike* Caldwell	14	137	130	3.81
Henry *Harry* Howell	13	131	146	2.74
Wilmer *Dean* Chance	11	128	115	2.92
Robert *Earl* Wilson	11	121	109	3.69
Walter *Kirby* Higbe	12	118	101	3.69
William *Watty* Clark	12	111	97	3.66
Charles *Walt* Terrell	11	111	124	4.22
Hubert *Max* Lanier	14	108	82	3.01
Bertram *Ray* Burris	15	108	134	4.17
John *Whitlow* Wyatt	16	106	95	3.79
Charles *Sid* Fernandez	12	104	85	3.29
Lloyd *Vern* Kennedy	12	104	132	4.67
John *Willie* Sudhoff	10	103	135	3.56

PITCHERS: (Cont.)	Yr	Won	Lost	ERA
Robert *Ed* Willet	10	102	99	3.08
John *Al* Benton	14	98	88	3.66
Dewey *La Marr* Hoyt	8	98	68	3.99
C. *Scott* Stratton	8	97	114	3.87
Nathaniel *Milt* Gaston	11	97	164	4.55
Henry *Gene* Garber	19	96	113	3.34
Albert *Max* Butcher	10	95	106	3.73
Forest *Greg* Swindell	9	92	85	3.74
Donald *Gene* Conley	11	91	96	3.82
Robert *Pat* Jarvis	8	85	73	3.58
Melton *Andy* Hawkins	10	84	91	4.22
Alexander *Ben* Sanders	5	80	70	3.24
Michael *Rick* Waits	12	79	92	4.25
James *Kevin* Brown	8	78	64	3.81
Don *Pat* Ragan	11	77	104	2.99
Billy *Mike* Smithson	8	76	86	4.58
J. *Lee* Richmond	6	75	100	3.06
James *Doug* Bird	11	73	60	3.99
James *Rick* Langford	11	73	106	4.01
Samuel *Dick* Coffman	15	72	95	4.65
Howard *Bruce* Sutter	12	68	71	2.83
Robert *Kevin* Appier	6	66	44	3.09
Casimir *Jim* Konstanty	11	66	48	3.46
Richard *Atley* Donald	8	65	33	3.52
Albert *Lee* Stange	10	62	61	3.56
William *Glenn* Abbott	11	62	83	4.39
James *Alex* Ferguson	10	61	85	4.93
Charlton *Atlee* Hammaker	10	59	67	3.61
Arnold *Barry* Latman	11	59	68	3.91
James *Greg* Hibbard	6	57	50	4.05
Michael *Scott* Bankhead	9	56	47	4.09
Charles *Doug* Bair	15	55	43	3.63
Larry *Ben* McDonald	6	55	47	3.86
Marcus *Wayne* Garland	9	55	66	3.89
John *Bruce* Dal Canton	11	51	49	3.67
William *Elmer* Jacobs	9	50	81	3.55
Edgar *Garland* Braxton	10	50	53	4.13
Charles *Bob* Hendley	7	48	52	3.97
James *Luke* Walker	9	45	47	3.65
Henry *Gene* Bearden	7	45	38	3.96
Clair *Bart* Johnson	8	43	51	3.94
Howard *Vic* Keen	8	42	44	4.11
Walter *Ed* Morris	5	42	45	4.19
Herbert *Scott* Perry	7	40	68	3.07
Ira *Tommy* Greene	6	38	19	3.86
Arthur *Lee* Guetterman	9	38	34	4.27
John *Fred* Sanford	7	37	55	4.45
Alton *Ray* Corbin	5	36	38	3.84
Robert *Chris* Knapp	6	36	32	4.99
Buford *Bill* Champion	8	34	50	4.69
Carl *Dave* Frost	6	33	37	4.10
Roy *Duane* Ward	8	32	36	3.19
Evan *Tracy* Stallard	7	30	57	4.17
Darrah *Dean* Stone	8	29	39	4.47

TRAVELING

36

Team

Any parent who has had kids competing in baseball knows about the "traveling team." Most communities, if large enough, have several "in house" teams. From this pool of players, some youngsters are selected to a tournament team. This group represents their community when playing other towns or suburbs. Often the tournaments are "away", requiring the parents to transport the players to the contest. In the Major Leagues, half of all games are played at the opponents' ballpark. For the away games, teams have to travel. Flight is common today, but for many years the train was the team's primary mode of transportation.

Eight members of the Traveling Team have steered their way to Cooperstown. To qualify for this superior squad, a player's nickname has to do with methods, speed or tools of travel. Teammates can not only leave home by Jeep, Truck or Van, but also by Blazer, Comet or Hot Rod to get to the ball game. If they are willing to pay, a player could not only take a Bus, Cab or Trolley Line, but also ride a Jet, Rocket or Glider. For shorter trips, a squad member could become a Walking Man or Hiker, going with Boots or Shoeless. He could arrive at his destination Rapid, Sudden, Quick or Slow. Regardless, he must be sure to bring his Suitcase or at least a Satchel.

One player soars to mind upon review of the team. Roger The Rocket Clemens is awesome. Jose Canseco, now his teammate, used to have his batting practice pitcher throw 'as fast as he could' from 46 feet to get ready to face The Rocket. Roger's "rocketlike" fastball has propelled him to great heights. Barring further arm trouble, The Rocket could finish with "out of this atmosphere" stats. From 1986-92, Roger won at least 18 games each summer and cumulatively tossed 32 shutouts!

LINEUP

CA	Frankie *Blimp* Hayes	played 14 seasons and was a five time All-Star. In 1944

Blimp set the season record (since tied) by catching 155 games. His 29 DP's in 1945 is the second highest total. While handling chores for the A's, Frankie poled 20 homers in 1939 his personal high for one campaign.

1B	Kent *Herbie* Hrbek	was a fixture for 14 seasons. Herbie dominated both as a

hitter and as a fielder. His bat and glove led the Twins to two World Championships. Herbie finished second in the 1982 Rookie of the Year voting and he also placed second in the 1984 Most Valuable Player balloting.

2B	Napoleon *Nap* Lajoie	,a Hall of Famer, starred 21 seasons. Nap ranks fifth all time

in doubles (657), tenth in hits (3242) and 17th in batting average (.338). During his career he led the league in doubles (five), batting average (four), hits (four) and RBI's (three). In 1901 Nap won the Triple Crown!

SS	Honus *Flying Dutchman* Wagner	is in the Hall of Fame. The Flying Dutchman was the best

offensive player in the NL during his era. He won eight batting crowns, six slugging titles and led the league in doubles (seven, one tie), RBI's (five), stolen bases (five), triples (three), runs (two, one tie) and hits (two).

3B	Earl *Sparky* Adams	, a 13 year veteran, was the consummate leadoff man. From

1925-27 Sparky led the National League in at bats. He scored 90+ runs six seasons. Playing 2B, SS and 3B during his career, Sparky led the league in fielding % three times. His 46 doubles in 1931 were league leading.

OF	Daniel *Rusty* Staub	played 23 seasons and was a six time All-Star. Rusty's

career marks are awesome. He pounded 499 doubles (30th), drove in 1466 runs (38th) and stroked 2716 safeties (42nd). Although not known as a power hitter, Rusty launched 292 round trippers during his career.

OF	*Shoeless* Joe Jackson	played 13 seasons (nine full ones) before being banned from

baseball. Joe's lifetime batting average of .356 is third all time! Shoeless Joe finished second in batting three times, third in batting three times and fourth in batting once. He also led all AL'ers in triples three times.

OF	Mickey *Mick the Quick* Rivers	starred 15 seasons and is probably best remembered for

hobbling like an old man to the plate, then exploding out of the batter's box. Mick the Quick led the AL in triples twice (one tie) and his 70 pilfers in 1975 topped the league. He finished fourth in batting in both 1977 and 1980.

P	*Rapid* Robert Feller	was a pitcher extraordinare! He totally dominated the AL.

Bob led or shared the league lead seven times in strikeouts, six times in wins, five times in innings and four times in shutouts. Rapid Robert fired three no-hitters and 12 one hitters during his fantastic Hall of Fame career!

P	*Sudden* Sam McDowell	was a tall, fast left-hander who dominated American League

hitters during his prime. From 1965-71 Sudden Sam was a six time All-Star and five times he was the Junior Circuit strikeout king. All this was accomplished while toiling for the perennial second division Indians.

P	Virgil *Fire* Trucks	played 17 seasons in the American League, twice winning

19 games and once chalking up 20 victories. In 1949 Fire led the league in both K's and shutouts (tie). If not for two prime seasons given to his country, Virgil quite likely would have topped 200 wins for his career.

RES	Albert *Sparky* Lyle	was a stopper for 16 years. He will always be remembered

for his chaw of tobacco! In 1977 Sparky appeared in 72 games (first), saved 26 wins (second) and won 13 tilts. For his career he ranks fifth in relief wins, seventh in games, seventh in relief innings and 11th in saves.

RES	Bill *Spaceman* Lee	twirled 14 years and acquired his nickname for his

'faroutness'. Regardless, Bill was dominating from 1973-75, winning 17 games each season and totaling 260+ innings per year. In 1973 Spaceman finished third in ERA and he was named to the AL All-Star team.

RES	Herman *Flying Dutchman* Long	was a starter the first 14 of his 16 seasons. He scored over

100 runs seven times, hit over .300 four times, drove in over 100 runs two times and led the National League in round trippers once! The Flying Dutchman stole 20 or more bases in each of his first 14 summers.

RES	Leroy *Satchel* Paige	earned the Hall primarily from his exploits before he reached

the Majors. Satchel starred in the Negro Leagues. In 1948, as a 42 year old "rookie", he still could fire that pill! Used mostly in relief, he led the AL with eight relief wins in 1952. In 26 career starts he tossed four shutouts!

L to R: Leroy *Satchel* Page, Albert *Sparky* Lyle, Roger *The Rocket* Clemens, *Rapid* Robert Feller, *Sudden* Sam McDowell

It'sa FACT

Leon **Caddy** Cadore: He pitched the Major's longest outing, going 26 innings on May 1st, 1920. It ended in a 1-1 tie.

Rapid Robert Feller: In 1946 he completed 36 games. Since 1916, this was the most games any pitcher had finished in one season. Like Ted Williams and many other Major Leaguers of his era, Bob lost a core portion of his career to the military. Enlisting on the day after Pearl Harbor, Rapid Robert missed 3¾ seasons (age 23-26), but he still won 266 games! Three wins were no-hitters. Rapid Robert posted them on April 16th, 1940 (opening day), April 30th, 1946 and July 1st, 1951.

Ed **Glider** Charles: On June 1st, 1968 and June 2nd, 1968 he stroked consecutive pinch homers.

George **Nap** Rucker: For his entire career (ten years) he toiled for hapless Brooklyn. Nap painted 38 shutouts (52nd all time) and had a career 2.24 ERA (19th all time). From 1907-13 Brooklyn's average record was 60-94. Nap averaged 16 of those wins each season, five plus coming by whitewash. His nephew, Johnny **Crabapple Comet** Rucker, (both hailed from Crabapple, Georgia) led all National Leaguers in 1941 in at bats, finishing third in doubles and fourth in both runs and hits.

Slow Joe Doyle: In his first two Major League starts, August 25th, 1906 and August 30th, 1906, he threw two shutouts.

Roger **The Rocket** Clemens: From 1986-92 he was the dominant American League pitcher. The Rocket struck out over 200 batters each season, leading or sharing the League lead five times in shutouts, four times in ERA and twice in both wins and complete games. The Rocket fanned a record 20 batters in one nine inning game April 29th, 1986.

Don **Blazer** Blasingame: He was the second hardest player to "double up" in Major League history, once every 123 at bats.

Eddie **The Walking Man** Yost: He was known for his good batting eye. Not a feared power hitter, Eddie nevertheless walked over 18% of his at bats, the eighth highest ever. His 1614 free passes are the seventh highest total. Six times The Walking Man led the American League in bases on balls. His 151 free passes in 1956 are the fifth highest single season figure. Eddie received 32 more walks than he had hits that year!

Virgil **Fire** Trucks: In 1952 he became one of only five pitchers to ever fire two no-hitters in one season. Amazingly, that season his record was a meager 5-19!

Mickey **Commerce Comet** Mantle: On October 8th, 1956 Mickey not only hit a homer, but he also made a spectacular catch to heavily contribute to Don Larsen's World Series 2-0 perfect gem.

Napoleon **Nap** Lajoie: He was an established star when he went to Cleveland. The fans were so happy about his arrival, they renamed their team The Naps in honor of him.

Lonnie **Skates** Smith: His nickname Skates originated because he sometimes slipped in the outfield. Lonnie did not slip with his bat. In 1991 he hit homers in three consecutive World Series games (National League record). He blasted a rare World Series grand slam in Game #5 of the 1992 Fall Classic!

Daniel **Rusty** Staub: In 1983 he had 24 pinch-hits (second highest season total) in 81 at bats (highest season total). Rusty is one of eleven players to reach the century mark in career pinch-hits.

Willie **Comet** Davis: He had a 31 game hitting streak in 1969, the tenth longest in the NL.

Albert **Sparky** Lyle: In the 1977 ALCS he was the hero. Sparky went 2-0, while appearing in four of the five contests. Down two games to one, Sparky pitched the last five innings to win game #4. Completing the comeback, he also won game #5.

Sudden Sam McDowell: He held opponents to a .215 batting average (fifth best) throughout his career! Sudden Sam averaged 8.86 whiffs per nine innings for his 15 years, third best all time! In 1965 he fanned 10.71 batters per regulation game, fourth highest K ratio in one season!

Bert **Campy** Campaneris: His 649 career stolen bases rank him 14th all time. Campy led the American League six times in thefts, topping the half century mark seven seasons!

Eddie **Sparky** Lake: He played eleven seasons, but only 1945-47 did he play full time. Not a high average hitter, Sparky made up for it with his excellent eye. He finished second, third and third in free passes during his "starting" years. In 1945 Sparky led all American Leaguers in on base percentage.   He was third in both stolen bases and runs in 1946 and in 1947 Sparky finished fifth in thefts and sixth in runs scored.

Rocket Ron Necciai: He won only one Major League game. His nickname originated before he reached the Big Leagues. On May 13th, 1952, while pitching for Bristol (Appalachian League), Rocket Ron threw a no-hitter and K'd 27 batters!

TRIVIA*

1) Going only 9-8 in 1965, this American League hurler nevertheless tied for the league lead in shutouts (five), topped the Junior Circuit in K's (225) and held opposing batters to a meager .185 batting average (twelfth lowest of all time). He acquired his nickname because of his fast ball.

2) Used for his speed, in 1973 he appeared in 35 games, scored 16 runs, stole seven bases, but he never officially batted! In the 1972 World Series, he appeared in six games, scored two runs, but he never officially batted! In his career he stole 44 bases, but he only had six career base hits. (Hint: think canal)

3) In 1946 this amazing fastballer struck out 346 batters, the fifth highest total since 1900.

4) In the 1919 World Series he led all Cincinnati batters in hits (ten) and average (.357). He also is a member of the College Football and Professional Football Halls of Fame.

5) His grand slam off left-hander Ken Daley in the sixth inning of game #6 in the 1987 World Series put the "noise meter" over the top.

6) During the summer before his senior year in high school, this 17 year old went 5-3. He also tied the then Major League record by whiffing 17 batters in one game. His fast ball led to his nickname.

7) In 1911 this rookie smashed the ball for a .408 pace, finishing second in batting average to Ty Cobb. He also ranked second that season in doubles, hits and runs (tie) and placed third in triples.

8) Originally a shortstop, he was converted to an outfielder and replaced the retired Joe DiMaggio.

9) He was the first American League reliever to capture the Cy Young award.

10) In college they called beer this name instead, forming the first half of his two word nickname.

11) While playing for the Expos, he was called 'Le Grande Orange'. His red hair tabbed his first nickname also.

12) Maligned for three errors in one World Series inning in 1966, people forget that this outfielder later won three consecutive Gold Gloves (1971-73). His nickname betrayed his speed.

13) Over 30% of his career wins were by shutout. (Hint: he is mentioned in *It'sa FACT*)

14) Once retired, he became a doctor. This left-hander's baseball claim to fame occurred in his rookie year, when he fanned Babe Ruth ten times in sixteen at bats! (Hint: think of a Heisman winner named Greg)

15) A highlight of his nine year career was winning game #5 of the 1953 Fall Classic. (Hint: think hamburger)

16) Even though he played in just 101 games, he still had the wheels to lead the NL in swipes in 1939.

17) At age 59 he pitched three scoreless innings, allowing only one hit, fanning one and walking no one.

18) He and his brother Hank combined for 293 career homers, 11th best brother combination.

19) He was not only a three time American League Cy Young winner (1986, 1987 and 1991), but he also was voted the AL's MVP in 1986. He was tagged his nickname because of his fast ball.

20) He was the 1950 NL Rookie of the Year. He topped the Senior Circuit in both 1950 and 1951 in stolen bases. His speed led to his obvious nickname.

21) He earned his second nickname, because he was traded so often. At first he was known as "Goodie".

22) In 1936 he hit a torrid .367 (second in the National League). This was the highest single season average for a backstop.

23) He was the first African-American to play in the Majors, debuting 2½ months ahead of his brother Welday.

24) After finishing his Major League career, he played three more seasons in Japan. He then went on to manage in Japan.

25) Babe Ruth copied his swing. Christy Mathewson said he was the greatest natural hitter. This batter fanned only 158 times in 4981 at bats during his career!

* MOVING TARGETS answers on page 241

ROSTER

CATCHERS:	Yr	Hits	AB's	Ave
Frankie *Blimp* Hayes	14	1164	4493	.259
Roy *Campy* Campanella	10	1161	4205	.276
Earl *Oil* Smith	12	686	2264	.303
Ernest *Blimp* Phelps	11	657	2117	.310
Grover *Slick* Hartley	14	353	1319	.268
Camilo *Cam* Carreon	8	260	986	.264
James *Truck* Hannah	3	173	736	.235
Billy *Little Globetrotter* Earle	5	133	465	.286
Clarence *Choo Choo* Coleman	4	91	462	.197
Thomas *Sleeper* Sullivan	4	64	345	.186
Vic *Crash* Janowicz	2	42	196	.214
Moses *Fleet* Walker	1	40	152	.263
James *Hub* Hart	3	27	127	.213
Eddie *Truck* Kearse	1	5	26	.192
Fletcher *Sled* Allen	1	3	23	.130
John *Nap* Shea	1	1	8	.125
Mark *Big Slick* Stewart	1	0	1	.000

1ST BASEMAN:	Yr	Hits	AB's	Ave
Kent *Herbie* Hrbek	14	1749	6192	.282
Fritz *Zip* Mollwitz	7	420	1740	.241
Sam *Skyrocket* Smith	1	49	206	.238
Joe *Speed* Walker	1	2	7	.286

2ND BASEMEN:	Yr	Hits	AB's	Ave
Napoleon *Nap* Lajoie	21	3242	9589	.338
George *Boots* Grantham	13	1508	4989	.302
Don *Blazer* Blasingame	12	1366	5296	.258
Don *Cab* Kolloway	12	1081	3993	.271
Hubert *Hub* Collins	7	790	2779	.284
Roy *Jeep* Hughes	9	705	2582	.273
Don *Jeep* Heffner	11	610	2526	.241
George *Mercury* Myatt	7	381	1345	.283
Russel *Rusty* Peters	10	289	1222	.236
Hot Rod Kanehl	3	192	796	.241
Marv *Sparky* Olson	3	110	457	.241
George *Sparky* Anderson	1	104	477	.218
Lawrence *Crash* Davis	3	102	444	.230
Charles *Truck* Eagan	1	4	30	.133

SHORTSTOPS:	Yr	Hits	AB's	Ave
Honus *Flying Dutchman* Wagner	21	3415	10430	.327
Alan *Tram* Trammell	18	2260	7872	.287
Bert *Campy* Campaneris	19	2249	8684	.259
Herman *Flying Dutchman* Long	16	2127	7674	.277
Travis *Arkansas Traveler* Jackson	15	1768	6086	.291
Roy *Radar* McMillan	16	1639	6752	.243
Johnny *Skids* Lipon	9	690	2661	.259
Dick *Slick* Howser	8	617	2483	.248
Eddie *Sparky* Lake	11	599	2595	.231
Johnny *Trolley Line* Butler	4	315	1251	.252
Otto *Squeaky* Bluege	2	62	291	.213

SHORTSTOPS:(Cont.)	Yr	Hits	AB's	Ave
Gene *Satchel* Verble	2	40	198	.202
Glenn *Sparky* Vaughan	1	5	30	.167

3RD BASEMEN:	Yr	Hits	AB's	Ave
Eddie *The Walking Man* Yost	18	1863	7346	.254
Earl *Sparky* Adams	13	1588	5557	.286
Ed *Glider* Charles	8	917	3482	.263
Lee *Jeep* Handley	10	902	3356	.269
Bob *Speed* Kelly	1	6	42	.143

OUTFIELDERS:	Yr	Hits	AB's	Ave
Daniel *Rusty* Staub	23	2716	9720	.279
Willie *Comet* Davis	18	2561	9174	.279
Mickey *Commerce Comet* Mantle	18	2415	8102	.298
Shoeless Joe Jackson	13	1772	4981	.356
Mickey *Mick the Quick* Rivers	15	1660	5629	.295
Lonnie *Skates* Smith	17	1476	5111	.289
Frank *Ping* Bodie	9	1011	3670	.275
James *Loafer* McAleer	13	1006	3977	.253
Harry *Suitcase* Simpson	8	752	2829	.266
Johnny *Crabapple Comet* Rucker	6	711	2617	.272
Alfred *Greasy* Neale	8	688	2661	.259
R.J. *Shoes* Reynolds	8	605	2270	.267
Suitcase Bob Seeds	9	537	1937	.277
Lou *Slick* Johnson	8	529	2049	.258
John *Herbie* Moran	7	527	2177	.242
Sam *Jet* Jethroe	4	460	1763	.261
Paul *Gulliver* Lehner	7	455	1768	.257
Buster *Bus* Mills	7	396	1379	.287
Fred *Squeaky* Valentine	7	360	1458	.247
Charles *Boots* Day	6	295	1151	.256
Lloyd *Citation* Merriman	5	291	1202	.242
Rosendo *Rusty* Torres	9	279	1314	.212
John *Zip* Collins	5	232	916	.253
John *Jet* Jeter	6	213	873	.244
Harvey *Hub* Walker	5	205	779	.263
Sleepy Bill Johnson	5	168	636	.264
Hubbard *Hub* Northen	3	159	584	.272
Maurice *Comet* Archdeacon	3	128	384	.333
Ed *Horn* Sauer	4	117	457	.256
Russell *Rusty* Kuntz	7	104	441	.236
Wes *Tripp* Sigman	2	42	129	.326
Art *Speedy* Ruble	2	30	145	.207
Kerry *Rusty* Tillman	3	13	56	.232
Elisha *Camp* Skinner	2	9	46	.196
James *Steamer* Flanagan	1	7	25	.280
Allan *Panamanian Express* Lewis	6	6	29	.207
Jim *Big Train* Asbell	1	6	33	.182
Frank *Wheels* Carswell	1	4	15	.267
John *Nap* Kloza	2	3	20	.150
Bruce *Squeaky* Barmes	1	1	5	.200
Eddie *Axel* Edmonson	1	0	5	.000

ROSTER

PINCH HITTERS:	Yr	Hits	AB's	Ave
Dick **Treads** Johnson	1	0	5	.000
Harry **Van** Vahrenhorst	1	0	1	.000

PITCHERS:	Yr	Won	Lost	ERA
Walter **The Big Train** Johnson	21	417	279	2.16
Jim **Little Steam Engine** Galvin	14	360	308	2.87
Nolan **The Express** Ryan	27	324	292	3.19
Rapid Robert Feller	18	266	162	3.25
Clarence **Orient Express** Vance	16	197	140	3.24
Virgil **Fire** Trucks	17	177	135	3.39
Roger **The Rocket** Clemens	11	172	73	2.93
Sudden Sam McDowell	15	141	134	3.17
George **Nap** Rucker	10	134	134	2.42
Bill **Spaceman** Lee	14	119	90	3.62
Bob **Steamer** Stanley	13	115	97	3.64
Albert **Sparky** Lyle	16	99	76	2.88
Dennis **Oil Can** Boyd	10	78	77	4.04
Al **Boots** Hollingsworth	11	70	104	3.99
Leon **Caddy** Cadore	10	68	72	3.14
Ed **Satchelfoot** Wells	11	68	69	4.65
Herb **Hub** Perdue	5	51	64	3.85
Gene **Arkansas Traveler** Bearden	7	45	38	3.96
Jim **Sting** Ray	9	43	30	3.61
Clydell **Slick** Castleman	6	36	26	4.25
Sleepy Bill Burns	5	30	52	2.72
Elwood **Speed** Martin	6	29	42	3.78
Hubert **Hub** Pruett	7	29	48	4.63
Leroy **Satchel** Paige	6	28	31	3.29
Dan **Rusty** Griner	6	28	55	3.49
Bob **Round Tripper** Kipper	8	27	37	4.34
Jim **Hot Rod** McDonald	9	24	27	4.27

PITCHERS: (Cont.)	Yr	Won	Lost	ERA
Slow Joe Doyle	5	22	21	2.85
Carl **Big Train** Willis	8	22	16	4.09
Russell **Rusty** Meacham	4	17	10	3.63
Cletus **Boots** Poffenberger	3	16	12	4.75
George **Slick** Coffman	4	15	12	5.60
Subway Sam Nahem	4	10	8	4.69
Julio **Whiplash** Navarro	6	7	9	3.65
Burt **Speed** Keeley	2	6	11	3.31
Henry **Hub** Pernoll	2	4	3	3.39
Dave **Chopper** Campbell	2	4	10	3.82
Robert **Riverboat** Smith	2	4	4	4.75
Bob **Speed** Geary	3	3	9	3.46
Sherman **Roadblock** Jones	3	2	6	4.73
Allen **Rusty** Gerhardt	1	2	1	7.07
Dan **Rusty** Tipple	1	1	1	0.95
Albert **Hiker** Moran	2	1	1	3.91
Fred **Speedy** Miller	1	1	1	4.71
Jim **Sparkplug** Keenan	2	1	2	6.37
Rocket Ron Necciai	1	1	6	7.08
Oscar **Hub** Knolls	1	0	0	4.05
Herbert **Hub** Andrews	2	0	0	4.63
Ted **Snooze** Goulait	1	0	0	6.43
Gordon **Big Train** McNaughton	1	0	1	6.43
Russell **Rusty** Richards	2	0	0	6.97
Gene **Slick** Host	2	0	2	7.31
Joe **Zip** Jaeger	1	0	0	12.00
Bill **Booster** Greason	1	0	1	13.50
Waldo **Rusty** Yarnall	1	0	1	18.00

EXTRA:
Atlanta Fulton County Stadium: *"The Launching Pad"*

LINGO

Out of Gas: A pitcher cannot go any further
Battery: Pitcher and catcher
New Battery: Bring in both a new pitcher and catcher
Carry: Player on a team roster
Riding the Bench: Not playing in the field
Riding the Umpire: Yelling at the umpire
Stranded: Left on base at the inning's end
Gave That Ball a Ride: Hit a lo..ooong home run
Hit the Cycle: In one game, hit a 1B, 2B, 3B and HR
Move Him Up: Advance the runner by a bunt or by a ball hit to the right side
Road Trip: Team travels to the opponents' ball parks
Clutch Player: Someone to count on when needed
Sparkplug: Player who inspires his teammates
Wheels: Can run *very* fast
Free Pass: Receive a base on balls
Walk: Receive a base on balls
Fire a Rocket: Throw a very fast pitch
Green Light: OK to hit a 3-0 pitch

Stop Sign: Base coach stops runner
Hit a Rocket: Hit a very hard line drive
Starter: Pitcher who starts the game
Drag Bunt: Bunt the ball as one starts to run to first
Fly Ball: Ball hit in the air to the outfield
Fly Out: A fly ball caught before it hits the ground
Round Tripper: A home run
Hit and Run: Batter is told to swing at the next pitch, while the base runner "goes" anticipating bat contact
Getaway Day: The last day of a series, before the visiting team leaves town
Route Going: Pitcher goes a full nine innings
Pilot: Another name for the manager
Pick 'Em Up: Add a player to your roster
Country Mile: Long distance - usually referring to a HR
Change of Scenery: Traded to another team
Run Over the Bag: Do this when a player runs to first
Caught in a Run Down: Same as in a hot box or pickle
Room Service: Pitcher serves up an easy to hit pitch

Real TWINS

37

Team

    In 1961 the Washington Senators moved to Minnesota. With St. Paul and Minneapolis' rivalry, sport teams, in the Twin Cities, never refer to just one town. Therefore, the Senators became the Minnesota (not Minneapolis) Twins. For 21 seasons all home games were played at Metropolitan Stadium (current site of the famous Mega Mall) in the city of Bloomington, but now the new home park is located in downtown Minneapolis and is referred to as The Dome or The Hump. The Homer Dome originally had turf which created "kangaroo bounces" and lots of ground rule doubles. Combine that with a gray white ceiling which causes visiting players to "'lose" routine fly balls and a right field wall that is a loose fitting canvas (AKA The Baggie) which allows baseballs to slide down it, not bounce off of it. The result is called a "home field advantage"! Greg Gagne, in one game, hit two near identical shallow high pop flys that were "lost." Landing and kangarooing, both "hits" went for inside the park home runs! In the Dome ceiling there are holes. Some "logical" engineering reason would be my guess. The ceiling is so high, it doesn't matter anyway. Enter strongboy, Dave Kong Kingman. He pulverizes one straight up. It goes up and up and yes, it never comes down! Ok, Abner Doubleday did not account for this. It was a "Dome Ruling," a ceiling double. Since becoming a Dome tenant, the Twinkies have twice become World Champions and brought great joy to our cities. In 1987 the Twins parlayed just 85 wins into an AL Western Division title. After upsetting the Tigers in five games for the pennant, the Minnesotans edged the Redbirds in seven for the World Championship. With Herbie, Puck, Bruno, Lombo, Sweet Music, The Terminator and The G-Man in the lineup, the team rose to the challenge. Three seasons later (1990) the Twins finished in the cellar. In 1991 they went from "the outhouse to the penthouse." The Twins edged the Braves in an exciting seven game World Series which was punctuated with five one run and three extra inning (including games #6 and #7) contests!

    As you might wonder, how do you get a team of Real Twins? Seven sets of Twins have actually reached the Majors, but that will not do. To qualify for the roster a player must be either an "identical twin" or a "fraternal twin." Identical twins on the Real Twins have nicknames which identically repeat themselves, such as Jo-Jo, Dodo, Put-Put, Boom-Boom, Bobo and Yo-Yo. Fraternal twins have monikers which are two parts and rhyme, such as Pee Wee, Hojo, Tito, Bow Wow, Loco and Rojo!

    One player, Kiki Cuyler, wet my curiosity. I have always wondered how do you get from his first name Hazen to his nickname Kiki. Cuyler played center field. Early in his career his teammates called him "Cuy." Often, when a ball was hit to short center, both the shortstop and the second baseman went back, as Hazen came in. Yielding to the forward moving center fielder, each infielder would call out "Cuy," often, coincidentally, in rapid order. It went "Cuy," "Cuy." It stuck and was phonetically spelled Kiki.

LINEUP

CA	Clarence *Choo Choo* Coleman

had a short four year career, playing his last three summers for the expansion New York Mets. In 1962, the Mets first season, Choo Choo shared receiving duties. He slugged six homers in 152 at bats. After another 112 games, Choo Choo chugged from the Majors.

1B	Orlando *Cha Cha* Cepeda

starred for 17 seasons. He was the NL Rookie of the Year in 1958 and the NL MVP in 1967. Cha Cha's 379 career dingers placed him tied for 33rd. Nine summers he batted over .300! In 1961, in addition to batting .311, Cha Cha paced the NL with 46 homers and 142 RBI's.

2B	Rigoberto *Tito* Fuentes

played in the Majors for 13 summers, 11 as a starter. Five seasons Tito stroked over 150 hits. In 1977 he pounded 190 safeties and batted a career high .309! Tito was also excellent with the leather! He led all National League keystoners in fielding % in 1973.

SS	Harold *Pee Wee* Reese

stands tall in the Hall of Fame. He was the NL All-Star shortstop ten times. Pee Wee gave three years to his country or his career stats would be even better! Not only did Pee Wee collect 2170 hits and score 1338 runs, but he also was the Dodger's team leader.

3B	Howard *Hojo* Johnson

is a versatile player, also playing shortstop and outfield. A switch hitter, Hojo powers the ball from both sides of the plate. In 1989 he finished second in long balls and fourth in RBI's. Hojo led the National League in both home runs (38) and RBI's (117) in the 1991 season!

OF	Hazen *Kiki* Cuyler

starred for 18 seasons on his way to the Hall. Ten years he batted over .300, four times topping .350! Kiki played a shallow center field and chased down everything. He was a swift runner. Kiki led the NL four times in SB's and his 26 triples in 1925 rank tied for second best since 1900.

OF	Joseph *Jo-Jo* Moore

played his entire 12 year career for the New York Giants. He was their leadoff hitter and left fielder. Jo-Jo was a six time National League All-Star and five seasons he hit over .300. Twice Jo-Jo stroked over 200 hits in one season and three summers he scored over 100 tallies.

OF	Willie *Boom Boom* Kirkland

was a hard hitting outfielder. He played nine summers in the Major Leagues. In Boom Boom's first six seasons he launched 20+ round trippers four summers. In 1961, while playing for the Tribe, he went deep 27 times and drove in 95 runs, Boom Boom's best season!

P	Louis *Bobo* Newson

had a career that spanned 20 seasons. Thirteen consecutive years (1934-46) he logged 200+ innings. Three summers Bobo won 20 or more games. In 1940 Bobo went 21-5 and led the Tigers to the Series. He won games #1 and #5 (three hit shutout), but Bobo lost game #7 (2-1).

P	Al *Giggi* Downing

was a flame throwing left-hander. In 1964 he went 13-8 and posted an American League leading 219 strikeouts! Giggi had his highest win total in 1971. He finished 20-9 and recorded five shutouts (tie for NL lead). For his career Giggi ranks 39th in K's per game at 6.50.

P	Jim *Abba Dabba* Tobin

was a knuckleballer and toiled nine seasons, mostly with second division teams. In 1944, with the sixth place Braves, Abba Dabba won 18 games, tossed five shutouts and led the NL in complete games. Jim was a solid hitter. He slugged 17 homers and batted .230 (career).

RES	Steve *Bye-Bye* Balboni

was a pure power hitter. In the seven summers he played over 100 games, five times he sent 20+ baseballs Bye-Bye. In 1985 Steve played full time and responded with his best season. Bye-Bye finished the campaign third in the American League in home runs with 36!

RES	Randy *Wojo* Myers

has been an outstanding reliever for a decade. Throwing heat from the portside, he has averaged an overpowering one strikeout per inning for his entire career! Wojo won games #1 and #3 for the New York Mets in the 1988 National League Championship Series.

RES	George *Jolting Jojo* Altman

played nine summers, seven for the Chicago Cubs. In the 1961 and 1962 seasons he was a terror. Named both campaigns to the NL All-Star squad, Jolting Jojo batted .303 and .318 and crushed 27 and 22 round trippers. In 1961 he also stroked a league leading 12 triples.

RES	Doug *Rojo* Rader

starred for 11 campaigns, then later returned to manage seven more seasons. In the field Rojo led all National League third sackers twice in putouts, assists, DP's and fielding %. Three seasons he crushed 20+ yard shots and four summers Rojo topped 80 RBI's.

L to R: Louis *Bobo* Newson, Steve *Bye-Bye* Balboni, Hazen *Kiki* Cuyler, Orlando *Cha Cha* Cepeda, Howard *Hojo* Johnson

It'sa FACT

Howard _Hojo_ Johnson: He is a 30/30 man (a player who in one season hits 30 or more homers and steals 30 or more bases). Only Bobby Bonds, Barry's dad, has done it more often (five times) than his three times. Hojo went 36 HR's/32 SB's in 1987, 36 HR's/41 SB's in 1989 and 38 HR's/30 SB's in 1991.

Louis _Bobo_ Newson: What do Wes Ferrell, Rick Ferrell, Mel Almada, Joe Vosmik, Vern Kennedy, Bob Harris, George Gill, Roxie Lawson, Chet Laabs, Mark Christman, Fritz Ostermueller, Archie McKain, and Roger Wolff have in common? They were all, at some time, traded for Bobo! In his 20 year career, he played for 16 teams! Amazingly, five different times Bobo "suited up" for the Senators!

Luis _Yo-Yo_ Arroyo: He was a journeyman pitcher. Used mostly as a reliever, he came to his fourth team, the Yankees, at the age of 33. His career log then had only 18 wins. In 1961 Whitey Ford went 25-4 and won the Cy. Young, but he only completed 11 of his 39 starts! Yo-Yo completed most of Whitey's games! In 1961 he relieved, in total, 65 times, saving a league leading 29 games and winning 15 more contests. Yo-Yo, with his "screwjy," was nearly unhittable when he "was on."

Alva _Bobo_ Holloman: In his 65 1/3 inning career he walked 50 batters. Primarily a reliever, Marty Slats Marion (his skipper) finally "gave in" and let Bobo have his first start May 6th, 1953. He pitched a no-hitter! It was Bobo's only shutout and only complete game in his career. Bobo won a mere three games in the Big Leagues.

Walter _Boom-Boom_ Beck: His nickname came from a sportswriter. In the early 30's the Phillies played in Baker Bowl. It was 280' down the right field, line, but with a 60' fence (The Green Monster is a mere 37')! In right center it was only 300' with a 47' fence! Brooklyn batters were pounding Beck. You first heard the crack of the bat, then the clank of the tin fence. The writer coined him Boom-Boom!

Aubrey _Yo-Yo_ Epps: On September 29th, 1935 he went 3/4, with a triple and three RBI's. It was Yo-Yo's only game in the Major Leagues!

Alfonso _Kiko_ Garcia: He starred in the 1979 Fall Classic. Kiko went 8/20 with three extra base hits and six RBI's. In game #3 he was a force. Kiko went 4/4 and drove in four tallies for the Orioles.

Al _Giggi_ Downing: In 1963 he held opposing batters to a meager .184 batting average, tenth lowest average ever!

TRIVIA*

1) Not too original, he called everybody this name. It ended up becoming his own nickname!
2) Hailing from Curaco, he is the first player to reach the Majors from the Netherlands Antilles.
3) On May 12th, 1942 he hit a pinch homer. The next day, May 13th, 1942, he pitched and won his game. He made it easy, because he parked three more homers!
4) Also known as The Little Colonel, he earned his better known nickname when he won the Louisville Kentucky marbles championship.
5) In 1930 he had a huge season in the NL. He pounded 50 doubles (second), laced 17 triples (tie third), scored 155 runs (second), slashed 228 hits (fifth) and drove in 134 runs (third)!
6) In 1959 he fell short on official at bats, or his .363 average would have won him the batting crown in the AL. (Hint: his son Terry played ten seasons in the Big Leagues)
7) His monster homer in the top of the tenth, during the fourth and final game of the 1983 ALCS, sent the Orioles on to the World Series.
8) Because he played too few ballgames (960 and 1000 are needed), he is not recognized on the all time home run % list. His 5.80% would rank him 24th.
9) On June 21st, 1970 he went 7/7. (Hint: think of a Florida beach)
10) A perfect inning is nine pitches yielding three strikeouts. This left-hander did it twice, on June 30th, 1962 inning #1 and on April 18th, 1964 inning #3.
11) On May 3rd, 1959 he hit four consecutive homers. The first dinger was powdered his last at bat of game one of a twin bill, then he launched three straight yard shots in game two.
12) During his career he led the NL in walks (four, one tie), on base % (four), hits (three), triples (two) and batting average (two).
13) With his big heart and bigger bat he led the Cards to the 1967 World Championship.
14) He was the first Florida Marlin to hit two HR's in a home game and also to hit two HR's in an away game.
15) He set the NL single season save record of 53 in 1993.

* CUCKOO LULUS answers found on page 241

ROSTER/LINGO

CATCHERS:	Yr	Hits	AB's	Ave
Clarence **Choo Choo** Coleman	4	91	462	.197
Stan **Polo** Andrews	4	32	149	.215
Frank **Dodo** Bird	1	10	50	.200
Jesus **Chucho** Ramos	1	5	10	.500
Aubrey **Yo-Yo** Epps	1	3	4	.750
George **Dodo** Armstrong	1	1	6	.167

1ST BASEMEN:	Yr	Hits	AB's	Ave
Orlando **Cha Cha** Cepeda	17	2351	7927	.297
Charlie **Jolly Cholly** Grimm	16	2313	7471	.310
Steve **Bye-Bye** Balboni	11	714	3120	.229
Hank **Bow Wow** Arft	5	229	906	.253
Lawrence **Bobo** Osborne	6	157	763	.206

2ND BASEMEN:	Yr	Hits	AB's	Ave
Rigoberto **Tito** Fuentes	13	1491	5566	.268
Nate **Peewee** Oliver	7	216	954	.226
Joseph **Jo-Jo** Morrissey	3	195	841	.232
Lee **Bee Bee** Richard	5	103	492	.209

SHORTSTOPS:	Yr	Hits	AB's	Ave
Harold **Pee Wee** Reese	16	2170	8058	.269
Alfonso **Kiko** Garcia	10	351	1470	.239
Arnold **Peewee** Hauser	5	349	1468	.238
Jesus **Pepe** Frias	9	323	1346	.240
Paul **Pee-Wee** Wanninger	2	130	556	.234
Cesar **Coca** Gutierrez	4	128	545	.235
Pompeyo **Yo-Yo** Davalillo	1	17	58	.293
Eusebio **Papo** Gonzalez	1	2	5	.400

3RD BASEMEN:	Yr	Hits	AB's	Ave
Doug **Rojo** Rader	11	1302	5186	.251
Howard **Hojo** Johnson	13	1196	4771	.251
Jose **Coco** Laboy	5	291	1247	.233
Gus **Gee-Gee** Getz	7	265	1114	.238
Loren **Bee-Bee** Babe	2	85	382	.223
James **Dodo** Lane	1	1	15	.067

OUTFIELDERS:	Yr	Hits	AB's	Ave
Richie **Put-Put** Ashburn	15	2574	8365	.308
Hazen **Kiki** Cuyler	18	2299	7161	.321
Charlie **Cuckoo** Jamieson	18	1990	6560	.303

OUTFIELDERS: (Cont.)	Yr	Hits	AB's	Ave
Joseph **Jo-Jo** Moore	12	1615	5427	.298
John **Tito** Francona	15	1395	5121	.272
Charlie **Paw Paw** Maxwell	14	856	3245	.264
Willie **Boom Boom** Kirkland	9	837	3494	.240
George **Jolting Jojo** Altman	9	832	3091	.269
Joyner **Jo-Jo** White	9	678	2652	.256
Nicholas **Dim Dom** Dallessandro	8	520	1945	.267
Greg **Peewee** Briley	6	384	1518	.253
Al **Humpty Dumpty** Nixon	9	372	1345	.277
Jim **Gee Gee** Gleeson	5	336	1277	.263
Terry **Tito** Landrum	9	248	995	.249
Doug **Poco** Taitt	4	217	824	.263
Walt **Cuckoo** Christensen	2	162	514	.315
Hensley **Bam-Bam** Meulens	5	101	457	.221
Jose **Loco** Herrera	4	61	231	.264
Johnnie **Ty Ty** Tyler	2	17	53	.321

PITCHERS:	Yr	Won	Lost	ERA
Louis **Bobo** Newson	20	211	222	3.98
Sandy **Koo Foo** Koufax	12	165	87	2.76
Al **Giggi** Downing	17	123	107	3.22
Jim **Abba Dabba** Tobin	9	105	112	3.44
Oscar **Flip Flap** Jones	3	44	54	3.20
Arnulfo **Nino** Espinosa	8	44	45	4.17
Luis **Yo-Yo** Arroyo	8	40	32	3.93
Bob **Bobo** Castillo	9	38	40	3.94
Walter **Boom-Boom** Beck	12	38	69	4.30
Randy **Wojo** Myers	10	33	47	3.11
Johnny **Jovo** Miljus	7	29	26	3.92
Leo **Kiki** Kiely	7	26	27	3.37
Bob **Bobo** Milliken	2	13	6	3.59
Federico **Chi-Chi** Olivo	4	7	6	3.96
Lowell **Lulu** Palmer	5	5	18	5.29
Con **Razzle Dazzle** Murphy	2	4	13	5.07
Alva **Bobo** Holloman	1	3	7	5.23
Dan **Cocoa** Woodman	2	0	0	2.94
Bill **Ding Dong** Bell	2	0	1	4.32
Michael **Ubbo Ubbo** Hornung	1	0	0	6.00
Elmer **Herky Jerky** Horton	2	0	3	9.75
Procopio **Tito** Herrera	1	0	0	27.00
Guillermo **Memo** Luna	1	0	1	27.00

Double Play: Two outs are gained from one at bat

Two Hopper: A two bouncer, usually easy to field

Double Up: Get two outs in one play. (Ex: fly ball out and a runner caught off base)

Go for Two: Try to stretch a single into a double

Turn Two: Execute a double play

The Deuce: Curveball

No-No: A no hit, no run game

Bye-Bye: Hit a home run

Double-Header: Two games played one after another

Two Bagger: A double

Twin Killing: See double play

Twin Bill: See double-header

Double Steal: Two base runners each steal a base on the same pitch

Double Clutch: What I would do with Farrah Fawcett and Jackie Smith

Lulu: See double clutch

UTILITY

38

Team

With the current team rosters limited to 25 players and most clubs carrying at least 11 arms (pitchers), it only leaves 14 slots for the position players. Since many teams keep three catchers, there remains at most four openings for the team's substitute or utility players. These ballplayers often back-up two, three or even four positions! As valuable cogs, they rest regulars, sub as defensive replacements, enter as pinch runners and frequently are called on to pinch-hit when the game is on the line. TK (Tom Kelly), the Twins' manager, often used Al Newman to rest his infielders. Although not a starter, Al logged a "full load" of playing time as one of the Twins' utility players.

The Utility Team is made up of players whose nicknames are utilized around the house. Outside, you will find a Stonewall, a Gate and an Icehouse. The garage holds Nails, Hammers, a Shovel, Picks and a Rope. You will find Jugs, a Kettle, a Pot and an Icebox in the kitchen. The laundry has a Sewing Machine, Scissors, Buttons and Snaps. The bathroom has a Tub, Suds, a Sponge and Razers. When you include a Duster, a Hoover, Handy Andy and Mr. Clean the team is set.

Hammerin' Hank Aaron is the player who "out shines" all other members on the team. Henry is the Major League career leader in home runs with 755 circuit blasts! More than "just" his homers, Hammerin' Hank had 2297 RBI's, 6856 total bases and 1477 extra base hits, all career leading! He also is tied for second in runs, third in hits, third in multi-homer games and ninth in doubles! Hankus Pankus had eleven 100+ RBI seasons, four times leading the league in runs driven in. He also topped the National League four seasons in home runs (one tie), doubles (one tie) and slugging %. Three summers Hammerin' Hank led in runs and two campaigns Henry finished first in both hits and batting average! After he retired as one of the all time greats, Hammerin' Hank moved upstairs as a baseball executive. For us trivia nuts, Hank hit "his number" in homers (44) four seasons!

LINEUP

| CA | James *Shanty* Hogan | starred for 13 seasons behind the plate. Twice he led all NL catchers in fielding % and once in putouts. Shanty batted .300 or more six times, including four years (1928-31) in a row. In 1930, he put it all together. Shanty hit .339, pounded 26 doubles, hit 13 homers and plated 75 runs. |

| 1B | *Hammerin'* Hank Greenberg | is one of baseball's greatest sluggers. He was the AL MVP in both 1935 and 1940. Hammerin' Hank hit over .300 his first eight seasons (1933-40), and during his service shortened career, he still managed to captured four home run titles (one tie) and four RBI crowns! |

| 2B | Frank *Pot* LaPorte | played for six teams over 11 summers. A regular by his second year, Pot also played some first base, third base and outfield. In 1911 he hit a career best .314, followed by a .311 season (1912). Pot, in 1914, led all batters in the Federal League in RBI's and again hit .311. |

| SS | Travis *Stonewall* Jackson | starred 15 seasons in the Senior Circuit on his way to Cooperstown. Knee injuries limited his career. With his glove, he led all shortstops in assists (four), fielding % (two) and DP's (two). Stonewall's best year with the lumber was 1929. He tagged 21 HR's and had 94 RBI's. |

| 3B | Brooks *Hoover* Robinson | played all his 23 seasons for the Orioles on his way to the Hall. Hoover sucked up 16 consecutive Gold Gloves (1960-75)! He led all AL hot corner men 11 times in fielding %, eight times in both putouts and assists and three times in DP's! His 2848 career hits rank him 33rd! |

| OF | *Hammerin'* Hank Aaron | quietly became one of the greatest stars of the game. Entering the Majors when it was very, very hard to be black, Hank carried and created respect. All his amazing records aside, Hammerin' Hank ranks first in the Baseball Encyclopedia for much more than his name. |

| OF | *Handy* Andy Pafko | starred 17 years in the 40's and 50's. He led the Cubbies to the 1945 pennant, finishing tied for third in RBI's and second in triples. From 1947-50 Andy was a four time All-Star, batting over .300 three summers. His 36 circuit clouts in 1950 were second most in the NL. |

| OF | Lenny *Nails* Dykstra | is a sparkplug player who hits, runs and fields with gusto! In 1990 Nails shared the National League lead in hits, but he saved his MVP type year for 1993. That summer Nails led the League in at bats, hits, runs and walks. His 143 runs were the most scored in the NL in 61 years! |

| P | Elton *Icebox* Chamberlain | reached the Majors at the tender age of 18. For the next seven summers Icebox won an average of 21 games per year! In 1889 he chalked up a career high 32 wins. Icebox also swung a mean bat. He collected 213 hits before his Major League career ended at the age of 28. |

| P | Dave *Scissors* Foutz | was both an outstanding pitcher and an excellent position player. Tall and thin (source of his nickname), he, in 1886, led the American Assoc. in wins (41) and ERA (2.11), plus tossed 11 shutouts! In 1887 Scissors posted a 25-12 record as a hurler and hit .357 with 151 safeties! |

| P | Matt *Matches* Kilroy | was hurling in the Majors at age 19. His first four summers (1886-89) he was phenomenal! In that span, Matches not only won 121 games, but he also led the American Association three years in complete games, two summers in games and once in wins (46 in 1887)! |

| RES | Bill Singer *Throwing Machine* | tossed pitches for 14 seasons. In 1969 he went 20-12 (Dodgers) and in 1973 his record was 20-14 (Angels). Three summers the Singer Throwing Machine put over 200 batters in stitches when he hemmed them (struck them out). On July 20th, 1970 Bill spun a no-no. |

| RES | *Toothpick* Sam Jones | fired the ball 12 seasons. Always chewing a toothpick, he was tabbed his nickname. In his first four full years (1955-58) batters must have felt their bats were toothpicks. Sam led the NL in K's three times! In 1959 Toothpick Sam paced the NL in both wins (21) and ERA (2.63)! |

| RES | Roy *The Sponge* McMillan | was also known as Radar and Phantom. All his monikers were for his excellent fielding ability. The Sponge, during his 16 Major League seasons, led all shortstops four years in both fielding % and assists and three campaigns in both putouts and DP's! |

| RES | Al *Mr. Scoops* Oliver | was almost unheralded in 18 seasons. A line drive hitter, he stroked 2743 hits (39th), 529 doubles (19th) and 825 extra base hits (50th)! Traded to the Expos at age 35, Mr. Scoops responded by leading the National League in hits, two baggers, RBI's and batting average in 1982! |

L to R: *Hammerin'* Hank Greenberg, *Toothpick* Sam Jones, *Hammerin'* Hank Aaron, Brooks *Hoover* Robinson, Al *Mr. Scoops* Oliver

It'sa FACT

John *The Hammer* Milner: He hammered 23 team leading homers when the Mets won the 1973 pennant. He was also a member of the Pittsburgh "family" in 1979, pounding 16 circuit blasts for the World Champion Bucs.

Allyn *Fish Hook* Stout: In 1931 he started his career perfect. During that season he went 6-0 in 30 appearances.

Elton *Icebox* Chamberlain: He was an ambidextrous pitcher.

Mack *The Knife* Jones: His nickname was from Bobby Darin's 1959 hit song. For his career, Mack's home run % was 4.3, placing him just short of the top 100 all time.

William *Gates* Brown: He was a powerful hitter. Used often as a pinch hitter, Gates twice (1968 and 1974) led the AL in pinch hits. Of his 107 pinch safeties, 16 were yard shots, ranking him tenth in hits and tied for third in dingers.

Handy Andy High: In Game #7 of the 1931 World Series he was the hero! Handy Andy delivered three of the Cards five team hits and scored twice. During his 13 seasons he fanned only 130 times in 4400 official at bats! Handy Andy was the fifth hardest ballplayer to whiff in baseball history!

Tom *The Blade* Hall: He was very thin, like a blade of grass. In 1970 he fanned 184 batters in 155 1/3 innings, allowing only 94 hits and going 11-6. The Blade, in 1972, was again awesome. In 124 1/3 innings he sat down 134 batters, allowing only 77 hits and going 10-1. For his career batters hit just .211 against him. Tom whiffed 8.41 batters per game. Had he pitched more innings, The Blade would rank fourth all time in both categories!

John *Duster* Mails: When Duster was "called up", he was a 25 year old late season addition with only 22 1/3 innings of Major League experience. Duster started eight games, completed six, tossed two shutouts, posted a 1.85 ERA and went 7-0! That fall, in the 1920 World Series, Duster relieved and logged 6 2/3 scoreless innings in Game #3. The next time out, Game #6, he tossed a three hit shutout and helped the Tribe to the World Championship!

Matt *Matches* Kilroy: He was a flame throwing left-hander who holds the pre-1900 record of 513 K's in a single season!

Clint *Scrap Iron* Courtney: As a rookie, in 1952, he led all AL backstops in fielding %. Scrap Iron finished a close second in the Rookie of the Year voting.

Earl *Oil* Smith: He had a well traveled 12 year career. Oil played in five World Series for three different teams. In the 1925 Fall Classic, he had a 7/20 effort for the Pirates.

Hammerin' Hank Greenberg: He gave 4½ years to his country or his career totals would be among the highest. Prior to WW II, from 1934-40, Big Henry terrorized the AL (except for 1936 due to injury). During that span he batted over .300 every summer and knocked in an average of 150 runs each season! Hammerin' Hank also averaged 39 homers and 45 doubles per year. His 63 two baggers in 1934 are the fourth highest season total. Hank's lifetime .92 RBI's per game is third best. Hammerin' Hank had the ninth best home run % (6.36%) and his career slugging % (.605) trails only George Babe Ruth, Ted The Kid Williams, Lou The Iron Horse Gehrig and Jimmy The Beast Foxx!

Mark *The Blade* Belanger: From 1971-80 The Blade won the AL Gold Glove at shortstop eight times!

Dennis *Oil Can* Boyd: Blood clots in his shoulder were discovered, limiting this slender right-hander. Oil Can had racked up 12, 15 and 16 wins from 1984-86.

Jimmy *Scoops* Cooney: He was from a baseball family. His younger brother Johnny was in the Majors 20 seasons and Scoops' dad, Jimmy, played three summers.

Ted *Cork* Wilks: He debuted for the Redbirds in 1944. As a 28 year old rookie starter, Cork went 17-4. He also led the league in winning %, tossed four shutouts and finished fourth in ERA. In 1946 Ted shifted to relief. Except for four starts that year, he appeared in 36 games as their stopper, going 8-0! Ted then went 4-0 in 1947, relieving in 37 contests. Cork, another name for stopper, went two consecutive seasons (1946-47) without a loss! In 1949 (10-3) and 1951 (3-5) Cork paced the NL in both games and saves!

Brooks *Hoover* Robinson: His career fielding % is the highest for third sackers! Hoover is also ranked first in games, putouts, assists and DP's for hot corner men!

Clarence *Brick* Owens: He received his nickname airmail. A "fan of his" plunked him on the skull with a brick! Brick is best remembered for tossing Babe Ruth after one batter, before Ernie Shore's perfect game (the Babe, then a pitcher, walked the first hitter. The Bambino argued Brick's "strike zone" and took an early shower! The walked batter was thrown out attempting to steal second base. Ernie proceeded to then retire the next 26 batters).

Francis *Silk* O'Loughlin: In true Irish Catholic tradition he claimed he never missed a call. Silk boasted "The Pope for religion, O'Loughlin for baseball, both infallible"! He was the first umpire to give Ty Cobb the thumb!

Al *Mr. Scoops* Oliver: Even though he was a 38 year old part-time player in the 1985 ALCS, Mr. Scoops drove in the winning run in Games #2 and #4, both times in the ninth inning!

Herbert *Buttons* Briggs: He won 19 games in 1904 for the second place Cubs. In 1905 Buttons fired five shutouts, pushing through eight wins.

TRIVIA*

1) When in college, he drank a little beer, AKA oil, hence his nickname.

2) He is best known for his glove. People sometimes forget in 1964 he was the AL MVP, slugged 28 homers and drove in a league leading 118 runs.

3) With Big Klu at first, Jabber at third, he and Johnny Temple anchored the keystone for the 1955-56 Redlegs.

4) On June 19th, 1963 he homered his first at bat (pinch-hit). On August 9th and August 11th, 1968 he hit consecutive pinch homers. (Hint: this premier pinch hitter "swung" for the Tigers)

5) On June 12th, 1962, July 12th, 1962 and August 14th, 1965 he and his younger brother Tommie homered in the same game.

6) He was the AL 1994 Rookie of the Year.

7) He hammered 58 homers in 1938.

8) My boy Ben played a game in Boyceville, Wisconsin, on a ball field named after this NL hometown hero.

9) He nailed four homers in the 1993 Fall Classic. Only Reggie's five yard shots in 1977 topped him.

10) In 1965 he reached the cheap seats 31 times for the Milwaukee Braves.

11) Because of his long droopy mustache, he acquired the nickname Yosemite Sam earlier in his career.

12) After he retired from Major League baseball, he went on to coach the Philadelphia Eagles to two consecutive NFL Championships and is enshrined in Canton!

13) Many baseball experts feel his performance in the 1970 Fall Classic, both with his glove and his bat, was the most dominating World Series any position player ever had!

14) A star shortstop with the Orioles, he and Brooks Hoover Robinson formed an impenetrable left side.

15) If you are wondering "Where is Waldo?", it is the town in Arkansas this Hall of Fame shortstop hails from! (Hint: think Civil War)

16) Along with Willie Pops Stargell and Roberto Bob Clemente, he was a member of Pittsburgh's Lumber Company.

17) In the 1972 NLCS he appeared twice, going 1-0. He allowed one run, three hits and whiffed eight in 7 1/3 frames. During the 1972 World Series he took the mound four times, tallying one save. He permitted no runs, six hits and fanned seven in 8 1/3 innings!

18) A teammate tossed him one (Hint: not a blonde), so he could fight his way out of trouble. This item became his nickname.

19) In 1973 he combined with Nolan The Express Ryan (383 K's) to fan 624 batters, the greatest two teammate, single season strikeout total ever!

20) He had the highest career winning % of any Major League twirler. (Hint: peak at the roster)

21) He brought attention to the ethical question should he, a Jew, play baseball on Yom Kippur. He heroically put his faith ahead of his passion!

22) His 183 RBI's in 1937 and 170 ribbies in 1935 are the third and eighth (tie) best season totals.

23) He hit many of these (his nickname) from 1956-60, batting over .300 four summers for the O's.

24) In his two seasons of full time play at first base, he lived up to his nickname by leading the league both seasons in fielding %.

25) He is still revered in Eau Claire, Wisconsin, where he was a star shortstop (minors).

* HEAD HAMMERERS answers found on page 241

ROSTER

CATCHERS:	Yr	Hits	AB's	Ave
James **Shanty** Hogan	13	939	3180	.295
Clint **Scrap Iron** Courtney	11	750	2796	.268
Earl **Oil** Smith	12	686	2264	.303
James **Tub** Welch	2	68	261	.261
Ed **Scrap Iron** Kenna	1	35	118	.297
Scooper Bill Schwartz	2	26	110	.236
Clifford **Tacks** Latimer	5	19	86	.221
Elwood **Kettle** Wirtz	4	14	86	.163
Medric **Bush** Boucher	1	5	17	.294
Howie **The Sponge** Storie	2	5	25	.200
Fletcher **Sled** Allen	1	3	23	.130
Joe **Jug** Kracher	1	1	5	.200
John **Pick** Quinn	1	0	2	.000

1ST BASEMEN:	Yr	Hits	AB's	Ave
Hammerin' Hank Greenberg	13	1628	5193	.313
Dave **Scissors** Foutz	13	1253	4533	.276
Norm **Suds** Siebern	12	1217	4481	.272
John **The Hammer** Milner	12	855	3436	.249
Bob **The Rope** Boyd	9	567	1936	.293
George **Scoops** Carey	4	313	1157	.271
Anthony **Razor** Shines	4	15	81	.185

2ND BASEMEN:	Yr	Hits	AB's	Ave
Phil **Scrap Iron** Garner	16	1594	6136	.260
Frank **Pot** LaPorte	11	1185	4212	.281
Tom **Scoops** Carey	8	418	1521	.275
Elijah **Pumpsie** Green	5	196	796	.246
Walter **Kit** Carson	2	10	40	.250

SHORTSTOPS:	Yr	Hits	AB's	Ave
Tommy **Corky** Corcoran	18	2252	8804	.256
Travis **Stonewall** Jackson	15	1768	6086	.291
Roy **The Sponge** McMillan	16	1639	6752	.243
Mark **The Blade** Belanger	18	1316	5784	.228
Jimmy **Scoops** Cooney	7	413	1575	.262
Cliff **Shanty** Daringer	1	42	160	.262
Marc **Hutch** Campbell	1	1	4	.250

3RD BASEMEN:	Yr	Hits	AB's	Ave
Brooks **Hoover** Robinson	23	2648	10654	.267
Handy Andy High	13	1250	4400	.284
Bill **Suds** Sudakis	8	362	1548	.234
Urbane **Pick** Pickering	2	205	798	.257
Art **Scoop** Scharein	3	189	776	.244

OUTFIELDERS:	Yr	Hits	AB's	Ave
Hammerin' Hank Aaron	23	3771	12364	.305
Al **Mr. Scoops** Oliver	18	2743	9049	.303
Handy Andy Pafko	17	1796	6292	.285
Lenny **Nails** Dykstra	10	1196	4171	.287
Mack **The Knife** Jones	10	778	3091	.252
Alfred **Greasy** Neale	8	688	2661	.259

OUTFIELDERS: (Cont.)	Yr	Hits	AB's	Ave
William **Gates** Brown	13	582	2262	.257
William **Bunk** Congalton	4	337	1163	.290
Dave **Mr. Clean** Nicholson	7	301	1419	.212
Tom **Brick** Mansell	3	199	767	.259
Bob **Magnet** Addy	2	108	387	.279
Bob **The Hammer** Hamelin	2	99	361	.274
Coaster Joe Connolly	4	45	168	.268
Cliff **Kit** Aberson	3	45	179	.251
George **Stopper** Staller	1	23	85	.271
Carl **Jug** Powis	1	8	41	.195
Grant **Snap** Dunlap	1	6	17	.353
Michael **Tack** Wilson	2	2	6	.333
Joe **Lumber** Price	1	0	1	.000
Bob **String** Gandy	1	0	2	.000
Sherman **Snapper** Kennedy	1	0	5	.000
Ray **Corky** Withrow	1	0	9	.000

PINCH HITTER:	Yr	Hits	AB's	Ave
George **Icehouse** Wilson	1	0	1	.000

PITCHERS:	Yr	Won	Lost	ERA
Elton **Icebox** Chamberlain	10	157	120	3.57
Dave **Scissors** Foutz	11	147	66	2.84
Matt **Matches** Kilroy	10	141	133	3.47
Bill Singer **Throwing Machine**	14	118	127	3.39
Billy **Bunker** Rhines	9	114	103	3.47
Jughandle Johnny Morrison	10	103	80	3.65
Toothpick Sam Jones	12	102	101	3.59
Fred **Hutch** Hutchinson	10	95	71	3.73
Dennis **Oil Can** Boyd	10	78	77	4.04
Ted **Cork** Wilks	10	59	30	3.26
Tom **The Blade** Hall	10	52	33	3.27
Herbert **Buttons** Briggs	5	44	47	3.41
John **Duster** Mails	7	32	25	4.10
Allyn **Fish Hook** Stout	6	20	20	4.54
Harold **Corky** Valentine	2	14	12	4.81
Clarence **Shovel** Hodge	3	14	15	5.17
Ambrose **Putty** Puttmann	4	8	9	3.58
Harvey **Suds** Sutherland	1	6	2	4.97
James **Kit** McKenna	2	4	9	5.31
Ellis **Cot** Deal	4	3	4	6.55
Gene **Suds** Fodge	1	1	1	4.76
Ralph **Razor** Ledbetter	1	0	0	0.00
Arnold **Jug** Thesenga	1	0	0	5.11
Gene **Jigger** Lansing	1	0	1	5.98
James **Rags** Faircloth	1	0	0	9.00

EXTRAS:
Clarence **Brick** Owens - Umpire
Francis **Silk** O'Loughlin - Umpire
Neil **The Hammer** Bjorkman - Awesome Ballplayer
Alan **Coop** Cooper - Great Radio Announcer
Jeff **Scoop** Cecil - Great Radio Announcer

LINGO

Handle Hit: Ball weakly hit, just above the hands, on the thin part of the bat

Roller: Ground ball

Gate: Number of paying customers for a game

Gate Crasher: Person who gets into the game for free

Screw Ball: A reverse curve ball, AKA "fadeaway"

Fence Busting: Hitting home runs

Spray Hitter: Batter hits to all fields

The Opener: First game of the season

Doormat: An easy team to beat

Whitewash: Shutout

On the Button: Hit a ball solidly

Mowed Down: Retire batters in order by strikeouts

Swing for the Fences: Try for a home run

Swing: Attempt to hit the ball with a bat

Sinker: A pitched ball that, when reaching the plate, drops

Nail Him: Throw a runner out, often an a tag play

Washed Up: Player has lost his ability

Shoestring Catch: Fielder catches the ball before it bounces, but just above the ground

Stick: Bat

Put the Wood to it: Hit the ball

Got Good Wood: Hit the ball hard

Scrub: A non starting player

Clean Hit: Base hit no one had a chance to catch

Hook: Curve ball

Given the Hook: Pitcher removed from the game

Lumber: Bat

Duster: Ball pitched close to a batter's head

Dusted Him off: Pitcher fired a pitch high and tight

Brush Back Pitch: See above

Fan: Person attending the game (short for fanatic)

In the Bucket: Batter's front foot steps away from the plate during his stride

Half Swing: Started the bat at the ball, but stopped

Went Down Swinging: Swung and missed at the third strike

Clothes Line: Hard hit (not high but level)

A Rope: See above

Looper: Soft hit that falls over the infield

Peg: Throw

Run Out the String: Go to a three ball two strike count

Pull the String: Throw a slow pitch, when the batter is expecting a fast ball

In the Cellar: In last place, the bottom of the league

Cellar Dweller: Always in last place

Jug: Curve ball

Cork: A reliever

Stopper: See above

Rung Up: Called out on strikes

Scoop: Catch a ball bouncing just in front of your glove

Sponge: A person who catches everything

Clipper: Someone who runs smooth and fast

Magnet: Ball seems to find the player's glove

Went to the Well Once too Often: Player repeats a successful action which is ultimately figured out

Field the Ball Cleanly: Catch a ball with no error

Switch: Player is able to bat both left and right-handed

Box Score: Game summary

Bleachers: Seats beyond the outfield fences

Circuit Clout: Home run

Bench Warmer: Non starter

On the Bench: Not playing in the field; sitting

Grab Some Bench: When a batter strikes out, he must go back to the dugout and sit down

Yard Shot: Home run

Senior Circuit: National league

Junior Circuit: American league, 25 years younger than the National League

Hitch: Player drops and raises his hand and bat as he starts into his swing

Busher: Player in the minors or should be there

Spun: Throw pitches

Handy Man: Player who can play several positions

Game Washed Out: Canceled because of rain

Pitcher: Player who throws the ball to the batters

Heater: Fast ball

Rug/Carpet: Artificial turf

Hit the Wall: Reach your limit

Drop One off the Table: Camilo Pascual's curve ball

Button Pusher: A manager who has an excellent team and needs little ability to manage

All the Tools: Player with a lot of ability

Basket Catch: Hold glove face up at your waist when catching fly balls and pop ups

Hung One: Throw a curve the breaks "belt high" over the center of the plate

Hung Out to Dry: Pitcher is left in the game even though the other team is hitting him hard

Grasscutter: Hard hit ball that hugs the ground

WILD WEST

39

Team

For years Major League baseball was played exclusively in the northeastern portion of our country. "Far west" was St. Louis and "way south" was Washington D.C.. With pro ballplayers emerging from all 50 states, the country needed to experience first hand the "national" pastime. Teams first moved to the west coast. Franchises then found Texas, Georgia, Minnesota and Wisconsin. In 1969 the East and West Divisions were born. Now, when the division race in the West is hotly contested, it is referred to as the Wild West.

This Wild West Team has some real tough hombres. Oh, there are five Hicks, four Dudes, a Coot and a Hill Billy, but do not be fooled. "Strappin' 'em on" are Kit, Hopalong, Hoot, Hondo, Wild Bill, Buffalo Bill and Pistol Pete. Be careful, Billy the Kid, Kasko Kid, Durango Kid, Kansas City Kid and Jesse are all out gunning. They are armed with Shotguns, Rifles, Bullets, Buckshot and Powder and they are looking for Sheriffs and a Lawman. This is a Rowdy group of Cowboys that only Zorro could Whip.

One Wild West player stands tall in the noonday sun. Clifford Carlton "Gavvy" Cravath (AKA Cactus) is that hero. He was the greatest home run hitter in the "dead ball" era. Cactus played his first full season in 1912 at the age of 31. For the eight seasons he started (1912-19), Cactus won six NL home run titles (five outright). In 1915 Gavvy set the "unbreakable" post 1900 record of 24 homers in one year! That same season the AL home run crown was won with seven home runs. Cactus' best season was actually 1913. He led the NL not only in homers, but also in hits, RBI's, slugging % and total bases. Gavvy also finished second in batting and fourth in doubles and triples (tie) in 1913. The lively ball and Babe Ruth quickly buried Cactus' statistical accomplishments, but, relative to his peers, Gavvy will never be shot down!

LINEUP

CA	Roy *Campy* Campanella

is in the Hall of Fame. He was held up, playing first in the Negro Leagues, or Campy's stats would have been awesome. In ten Major League seasons he was voted three National League MVP's! He was dominating both defensively and offensively his entire career.

1B	George *Boots* Grantham

laced 'em up 13 seasons. After his first full summer in the Big Leagues, Boots batted over .300 for the next eight years (1924-31). His best season was 1930. Boots batted .324, slugged 34 two baggers, slashed 14 three baggers, crushed 18 dingers and drove in 99 runs.

2B	Fred *Sure Shot* Dunlap

combined with Pebbly Jack Glasscock to form an early keystone combo. Sure Shot led second sackers three times in fielding % and assists and two times in putouts and DP's. In 1884 he led the Union Assoc., hitting a lusty .412! Sure Shot also placed first in HR's and hits!

SS	*Rowdy* Richard Bartell

was a fiery, competitive leader. He has Hall of Fame numbers. Starring 18 summers, Rowdy Richard hit over .300 seven seasons. Thirteen consecutive years (1929-41) he slashed 20 or more doubles, three times blasting 40 or more two baggers.

3B	Warren *Hick* Carpenter

played in the early days of baseball. His career spanned 12 seasons. In 1882 Hick led the American Association in both hits and fielding %, and finished second in batting average. What separates Hick from other hot corner men is that Hick played left-handed!!!

OF	Enos *Country* Slaughter

played from 1938-59 (he gave three summers to service). He was a ten time All-Star and now is a member of the Hall of Fame. A hustling, hard nose, "suit 'em up" player, Country had, for his career, 400+ doubles and over 1300 RBI's. His 148 three baggers are 53rd best.

OF	Carl *Reading Rifle* Furillo

had a cannon for an arm. He led all NL fly chasers in assists in 1950-51. No one ran on Skoonj! Surrounded by a famous cast (Duke, Pee Wee, Newk, Jackie, Campy and Gil) he quietly starred. From 1949-55 Carl topped 90 RBI's six times. Two years (1949-50) he plated 100+ runs.

OF	Frank *Hondo* Howard

was a prodigious home run hitter. He blasted 382 shots (tie 31st) and had a 5.89 homer % (21st best). Hondo put together three superior seasons from 1968-70. He powered 48, 48 and 44 tape jobs and chased in 106, 111 and 126 runs in those awesome campaigns!

P	Bob *Hoot* Gibson

is a Hall of Famer who could do it all. As a fielder, he won nine consecutive Gold Gloves (1965-73). As a hitter, Hoot pounded 24 tators, twice tagging five in one season. On the hill, he dominated. Ten times he won 15 or more games. Nine seasons he fanned over 200 batters.

P	Vic *Springfield Rifle* Raschi

fired bullets when he reached the Majors (after WW II) at the age of 27. He went on to win 66.7% of his decisions, fifth all time. From 1948-51 Vic gunned down batters regularly. He won 19, 21, 21 and 21 games and he also won three World Series contests!

P	*Wild* Bill Donovan

flung pellets for 18 seasons. He won 17 or more games eight times. Twice Wild Bill posted 25 wins. In 1901 his 25 victories led the National League. The 1907 season was Wild Bill's best. His log read 25-4 with a 2.19 ERA. His 2.69 career ERA places him tied for 53rd.

RES	Earl *Crossfire* Moore

was a hard to hit, flame throwing sidearmer. Playing for weak teams, his record is even more remarkable. As a 21 year old rookie, Crossfire won 16 of Cleveland's 54 victories. Seven years he won 15 or more games. In 1910 Crossfire won 22 times and led the NL in K's.

RES	Curt *Coonskin* Davis

was a 30 year old rookie who won 19 games. His team, the Phillies, won only 56 that season! Coonskin then won 16 of the team's 64 wins the next year! He won in double figures 11 of his 12+ seasons. In 1939 Coonskin logged 22 wins (third) and batted .381 (40/105)!

RES	*Wild* Bill Hutchinson

was a star pitcher and workhorse for Chicago in the 1890's. His numbers (throwing from the 50' pitching box) would be unheard of today. Comparatively, he was "the" pitcher of his time. From 1890-92 Wild Bill led the Senior Circuit in wins with 42, 44 and 37 victories!

RES	Billy *The Kid* Southworth

was a very good player for 13 seasons. Six summers he hit over .300 and The Kid retired with a .297 average. As a manager, Billy was even better. He built winning teams (four flags and two World Championships in 13 campaigns) and won true respect from his players.

L to R: Frank *Hondo* Howard, Enos *Country* Slaughter, Gavvy *Cactus* Cravath, Roy *Campy* Campanella, Bob *Hoot* Gibson

It'sa FACT

Gavvy *Cactus* Cravath: He played 56 games in the field and pinch-hit in 27 other contests during the 1919 season. In total, he managed to have 214 official at bats. Cactus led the NL in home runs that year with 12!

Fred *Cactus* Johnson: After going 2-0 in 1923, he returned to the Majors 15 years later. At the age of 44, Cactus won three more games!

Pistol Pete Ramos: This Cuban could hit the long ball. Two times, May 30th, 1962 and July 31st, 1963, Pistol Pete powdered two dingers in one game.

Zoilo *Zorro* Versalles: He "came up" from Cuba. Zorro was shy. He fielded erratically. But under coach Billy Martin's tutelage, Zorro matured. In 1965 he led the AL in at bats, doubles (tie), runs and total bases. Zoilo finished second in hits and third in stolen bases. He took the Twins to the 1965 World Series and was voted the AL MVP!

Glenn *Shotgun* Wright: On May 7th, 1925, while playing for the Pirates, he completed the sixth ever (currently 11 have been executed) unassisted triple play. Sunny Jim Bottomley hit the liner. Jimmy Scoops Cooney and Rogers The Rajah Hornsby were the other two outs. Ironically, Jimmy Scoops Cooney got even. He turned the seventh ever unassisted triple play May 30th, 1927 against the Pirates!

Earl *Crossfire* Moore: On May 9th, 1901 he fired the first no-hitter in the AL. Sadly, he lost in ten innings.

Bob *Hoot* Gibson: He won 251 games (38th), fanned 3117 hitters (tenth), averaged 7.22 K per game (18th) and tossed 56 shutouts (13th). His 1968 season was so dominating, the pitchers mound was subsequently lowered to give the batters a better chance! In 1968 Hoot won the Cy Young award. Pitching 304 2/3 innings, he allowed only 38 earned runs. He started 34 games and completed 28. Thirteen times Hoot fired a shutout! Only once this century has a hurler exceeded that number of whitewashes in one season!

Hughie *Ee-Yah* Jennings: Amos Rusie, the bullet throwing Hoosier Thunderbolt, broke his skull with a pitch. One season Ee-Yah was hit by pitches a then record 49 times! Ron Hunt put an end to that dubious standard, taking the record from him 75 years later.

Wild Bill Donovan: What he started, he finished. In 1903 Wild Bill completed all 34 of his starts.

John *Sheriff* Singleton: His only win, in his career, was a shutout.

Wild Bill Hallahan: He led all NL hurlers in strikeouts in 1930-31 and Wild Bill also tied for the lead in wins in 1931. He saved his best heroics for the 1931 World Series. Wild Bill authored a three hit shutout in game # 2, then went the route in a one run effort in game #5. Not finished, he squelched the A's ninth inning, game #7 rally. Wild Bill saved the game and the World Championship for the Cards!

Hal *Sheriff* Lee: The 1932 Phillies had an all .300 hitting outfield. He played with George Kiddo Davis and future Hall of Famer Chuck Klein. That season the Sheriff rounded up 42 doubles, ten triples, 18 home runs and had 85 RBI's.

Charlie *Shooter* Walters: He is now an award winning sports writer for the St. Paul Pioneer Press.

Bob *Hoot* Gibson: He fanned four batters, in the fourth inning, on June 7th,1965. Hoot tossed a perfect inning (nine pitches, three strikeouts) on May 12th, 1969, inning #7. Bob smashed two grand slams in his career (September 29th, 1965 and July 26th, 1973). Hoot powdered two World Series' HR's (October 8th, 1967 and October 6th, 1968).

Walter *Hoot* Evers: He rode roughshod on AL pitchers from 1947-50. During that span Hoot batted .296, .314, .303 and .323. He also twice drove in over 100 runs, and two times was named to the AL All-Star team.

Monte *Hoot* Pearson: He was perfect in World Series play. He started four times, in four different Fall Classics and went 4-0! In his combined efforts, Hoot allowed only 19 hits in 35 2/3 innings. He whiffed 28, walked only seven and had an ERA of 1.01! His best effort was a two hit shutout of Cincy in game #2 of the 1939 World Series.

Wild Bill Everitt: His career was five full and two partial seasons. In his amazing rookie year, Wild Bill hit .358, with 197 safeties and 129 runs scored. After four more .300+ seasons, he faded. His .317 career average is testimony to his batting prowess.

Bill *Wagon Tongue* Keister: He, too, had a five full and two partial seasons career. Coincidentally, Wagon Tongue also hit over .300 his five full summers. His best year was 1901, legging out a league leading 21 triples (tie) and batting .328. At retirement his average was a lofty .312.

Billy *Shotgun* Gardner: Five of his ten seasons he was an everyday ballplayer. In 1957 he responded with his best year. Shotgun blasted 36 two baggers (tie first) and also led the league in at bats and fielding % (second base).

Whoa Bill Phillips: 1902 was his career year. Whoa Bill reined in 16 victories, plus hit a lusty .342 (39/114).

John *Sheriff* Blake: Six consecutive seasons (1925-30) he won in double digits. In 1928 Sheriff won 17 contests, tied for the NL shutout lead and finished second in ERA.

TRIVIA*

1) He has the nickname of TV's Wild Bill Hickok's sidekick.

2) His 1.12 ERA in 1968 is the fourth lowest of all time.

3) On April 24th, 1915 he pinch-hit for Babe Ruth. (Hint: try to pick the forest from the trees)

4) In 1965 he became the first (of two) player to play one inning at each position during one game.

5) In Spanish the letter L is not pronounced. His "close pronunciation" became his nickname.

6) In 1958 he won the Cy Young award. He led the AL in wins, winning % and complete games (tie), and he finished second in shutouts and third in strikeouts.

7) Jimmy Stewart starred in a movie that, coincidentally, was this hurler's nickname.

8) In the 1967 World Series he won game #1, game #4 and hurled his third complete game victory in game #7. He also slugged a dinger in the clinching game!

9) He had his career tragically end from a car accident, which left him paralyzed.

10) This infielder acquired his nickname, because of his accurate throwing arm.

11) It was the eighth inning, game #7 of the 1946 World Series. Harry The Hat Walker singled. He left first at the "crack of the bat" and kept right on running. He scored from first base on a single! It was the World Championship winning run.

12) In 1942 he led the NL in hits, triples and total bases. He also placed second in both runs and batting average and finished third in RBI's and slugging %.

13) This Dodger set his sights on the 1953 batting crown.

14) When he played for the Senators, he was also known as the Washington Monument. (Hint: he stood 6'7")

15) He holds the Major League record for the most home runs in one season by a catcher.

16) An excellent hitter, for a pitcher, he "blasted" six triples in 122 at bats one season.

17) After going ten frames to win game #5 in the 1964 World Series, he came back on just two days rest to win game #7.

18) Down three games to one in the 1958 World Series, this Yankee hurler won game #5, saved game #6 and won game #7.

19) From 1894-98 he hit .335, .386, .401, .355 and .328. His .401 average was the highest season average for a shortstop.

20) He created his own fireworks July 4th, 1939. He blasted four rockets in the twin bill. In one game he drove in 11 runs, with two of his three yard shots grand slams! (Hint: think of Rowdy Yates, Gil Favor and Wooster)

21) On August 27th, 1938 he no-hit his former teammates, walking two Indians to miss a perfect game. (Hint: the 1958 AL Rookie of the Year (Albie) shared his last name)

22) His 12th World Series hit drove in the Series winning run in the ninth inning of game #6. He led the 1953 Yankees with one double, two triples, two homers and eight RBI's.

23) He led the AL in "rustling bases" in 1965, 1966, 1967, 1968, 1970 and 1972.

24) Although his nickname suggests the opposite, he stole. In fact, he stole 77 sacks in 1983.

25) He "sat down" 17 Tigers in game #1 of the 1968 Fall Classic. That is the World Series record for strikeouts in one game.

* SHOTS IN THE DARK answers found on page 241

ROSTER

CATCHERS:	Yr	Hits	AB's	Ave
Roy *Campy* Campanella	10	1161	4205	.276
John *Dude* Stearns	11	696	2681	.260
Forrest *Hick* Cady	8	216	901	.240
Harold *Rowdy* Elliott	5	97	402	.241
John *Shotgun* Peters	4	80	302	.265
Adrian *Pat* Garrett	8	51	276	.185
Otto *Hickey* Hoffman	1	0	6	.000

1ST BASEMEN:	Yr	Hits	AB's	Ave
George *Boots* Grantham	13	1508	4989	.302
Wild Bill Everitt	7	902	2842	.317
Bob *The Rope* Boyd	9	567	1936	.293
Del *Sheriff* Gainer	10	438	1608	.272
Dan *Davey* Crockett	1	29	102	.284

2ND BASEMEN:	Yr	Hits	AB's	Ave
Fred *Sure Shot* Dunlap	12	1159	3974	.292
Billy *The Kid* Martin	11	877	3419	.257
Billy *Shotgun* Gardner	10	841	3544	.237
Bill *Wagon Tongue* Keister	7	758	2433	.312
Billy *The Kid* DeMars	3	50	211	.237
Carl *Huck* Sawyer	2	14	63	.222
Wild Bill Leard	1	0	3	.000

SHORTSTOPS:	Yr	Hits	AB's	Ave
Bert *Campy* Campaneris	19	2249	8684	.259
Rowdy Richard Bartell	18	2165	7629	.284
Hughie *Ee-Yah* Jennings	17	1527	4904	.311
Zoilo *Zorro* Versalles	12	1246	5141	.242
Glenn *Buckshot* Wright	11	1219	4153	.294
Eddie *Kasko Kid* Kasko	10	935	3546	.264
Wild Bill Hunnefield	6	452	1664	.272
Tommy *Buckshot* Brown	9	309	1280	.241
Orville *Coot* Veal	6	141	611	.231
Eugene *Huck* Geary	2	30	188	.160
Ernie *Kansas City Kid* Smith	1	19	79	.241
Les *Dude* Channell	2	7	20	.350

3RD BASEMEN:	Yr	Hits	AB's	Ave
Warren *Hick* Carpenter	12	1202	4637	.259
Jim *Rawhide* Tabor	9	1021	3788	.270
Thomas *Dude* Esterbrook	11	741	2837	.261
Ivoria *Hilly* Layne	3	75	284	.264
Harold *Gomer* Hodge	1	17	83	.205
Art *Sheriff* Ewoldt	1	7	32	.219

OUTFIELDERS:	Yr	Hits	AB's	Ave
Enos *Country* Slaughter	19	2383	7946	.300
Carl *Reading Rifle* Furillo	15	1910	6378	.299
Frank *Hondo* Howard	16	1774	6488	.273
Billy *The Kid* Southworth	13	1296	4359	.297

OUTFIELDERS: (Cont.)	Yr	Hits	AB's	Ave
Gavvy *Cactus* Cravath	11	1134	3951	.287
Walter *Hoot* Evers	12	1055	3801	.278
Gene *Rowdy* Moore	14	958	3543	.270
Pistol Pete Reiser	10	786	2662	.295
Hal *Sheriff* Lee	7	755	2750	.275
Rudy *Lawman* Law	7	656	2421	.271
Harry *Dude* Blake	6	473	1877	.252
Dave *Sheriff* Harris	7	406	1447	.281
Hal *Hoot* Rice	7	307	1183	.260
Charles *Boots* Day	6	295	1151	.256
Bullet Jack Thoney	6	216	912	.237
Mike *Shotgun* Chartak	4	186	765	.243
Bill *Hopalong* Howerton	4	178	650	.274
Mark *Country* Davidson	6	149	661	.225
Jim *Sheriff* Jones	3	79	344	.230
Stan *Hondo* Hollmig	3	67	265	.253
George *Hickie* Wilson	1	19	82	.232
Walter *Kit* Carson	2	10	40	.250
Elisha *Camp* Skinner	2	9	46	.196

PITCHERS:	Yr	Won	Lost	ERA
Bob *Hoot* Gibson	17	251	174	2.91
Jesse *Powder* Tannehill	15	197	116	2.79
Bullet Joe Bush	17	195	183	3.51
Wild Bill Donovan	18	186	139	2.69
Wild Bill Hutchinson	9	184	163	3.58
Earl *Crossfire* Moore	14	162	154	2.78
Curt *Coonskin* Davis	13	158	131	3.42
Vic *Springfield Rifle* Raschi	10	132	66	3.72
Pistol Pete Ramos	15	117	160	4.08
Wild Bill Hallahan	12	102	94	4.03
Bullet Bob Turley	12	101	85	3.64
Monte *Hoot* Pearson	10	100	61	4.00
Al *Old Boots and Saddles* Brazle	10	97	64	3.31
John *Sheriff* Blake	10	87	102	4.13
Ewell *Whip* Blackwell	10	82	78	3.30
Al *Boots* Hollingsworth	11	70	104	3.99
Whoa Bill Phillips	7	70	76	4.09
Walter *Huck* Betts	10	61	68	3.93
Frank *Bullet* Miller	7	52	66	3.01
Lew *Hicks* Moren	6	48	57	2.95
Buffalo Bill Hogg	4	37	50	3.70
Russ *Sheriff* Van Atta	7	33	41	5.60
Clint *Hondo Hurricane* Hartung	4	29	29	5.02
Wild Bill Piercy	6	27	43	4.26
Albert *Cowboy* Jones	4	25	34	3.63
Wild Bill Widner	5	22	36	4.36
Cletus *Boots* Poffenberger	3	16	12	4.75
Tom *Shotgun* Rogers	4	15	30	3.95
Bullet Bob Reynolds	6	14	16	3.15
Jim *Cowboy* Winford	6	14	18	4.56

ROSTER

PITCHERS: (Cont.)	Yr	Won	Lost	ERA
Bill *Gunner* McGunnigle	2	11	8	2.81
Fred *Whip* Lasher	6	11	13	3.88
Frank *Cactus* Keck	2	10	12	3.51
Ray *Cowboy* Harrell	6	9	20	5.70
John *Buckshot* Skopec	2	8	5	3.26
Jesse *Scout* Stovall	2	8	14	3.76
Rifle Jim Middleton	2	7	12	4.51
Jeff *Jesse* James	2	6	6	4.51
Wild Bill Connelly	4	6	2	6.92
Charlie *Sheriff* Gassaway	3	5	9	4.04
Emmett *Ramrod* Nelson	2	5	4	4.07
Fred *Cactus* Johnson	4	5	10	5.26
Emil *Hill Billy* Bildilli	5	4	8	5.84
Wild Bill Luhrsen	1	3	1	2.48
George *Cowboy* Milstead	3	3	7	4.16
Tom *Rattlesnake* Baker	4	3	9	4.73
Jim *Sheriff* Constable	5	3	4	4.87
John *Sheriff* Gaddy	1	2	0	0.69
Ed *Hick* Hovlik	2	2	1	3.21

PITCHERS: (Cont.)	Yr	Won	Lost	ERA
Guy *Gunner* Cantrell	3	2	7	4.27
Johnnie *Durango Kid* Seale	2	1	0	5.54
John *Sheriff* Singleton	1	1	10	5.90
Hal *Hoot* Trosky Jr..	1	1	0	6.00
Glenn *Jingles* Cox	4	1	4	6.39
William *Buckshot* May	1	0	0	0.00
Harry *Huck* Wallace	1	0	0	0.00
Wild Bill Pierson	3	0	1	3.38
Bobby *Gunner* Reeves	1	0	0	3.68
John *Country* Davis	1	0	2	4.05
Mel *Country* Held	1	0	0	5.14
Charlie *Shooter* Walters	1	0	0	5.40
Wild Bill Pierro	1	0	2	10.55
Allen *Bullet Ben* Benson	1	0	1	12.10
Wild Bill Miller	1	0	1	13.50
EXTRAS:				
Cowboy Joe West - Umpire				
Bob *Gunner* Prince - Awesome Baseball Announcer				

LINGO

Advance Scout: Man who views the next opponent and helps prepare his team for them

Loaded Pitch: A spitball

Hit a Shot: Blast a home run

Handcuffed: Fooled by a pitch, the batter can't even manage a swing

Automatic: A strike thrown on a 3-0 count

Powder One: Hit a ball very hard, blast it

Scatter Gun: An erratic throwing arm

Shotgun: See above

Wild: Pitcher who cannot throw strikes

Have a Gun: Player with a strong arm

Have a Rifle: Peek above

Put the Gun on Him: Measure a pitcher's speed

Gun: A machine which measures a ball's velocity

Boot One: Make an error in the field (not a computer)

Shelled: A pitcher is hit hard

Hit a Rope: Hit a hard line drive

Gun Him Down: Throw a runner out when he attempts to advance

Crossfire: A sidearm thrower

Whip: A sidearm thrower

Wagon Tongue: Bat

Bases Loaded: All three bags are occupied by runners

Cactus League: Spring training in Arizona

Bullet, Pellet: Ball

Fire a Bullet: Throw a very fast pitch

Cocked His Arm: Arm goes to a throwing position

Pull the Trigger: Let the ball go - throw

Baseball Scout: Man who "looks" for talented players not yet signed by other teams

WILLIE / MICKEY

40

Team

Growing up in the 50's, the big debate was who was better, Mantle or Mays? These were often heated discussions fortified by both statistics and emotions. Living in the Twin Cities I had the pleasure of seeing Mickey at "The Met" several times, but, sad to say, I never once saw Willie play! Because of separate leagues, their outstanding careers were forced to be played "in parallel." For the millions of fans who have access to only one league, Willie and Mickey's careers form a compelling argument for inter-league play.

For this chapter I have to throw away the mold! All bets are off and all ground rules have changed! You cannot have a nickname book without Willie Mays and Mickey Mantle! What I found out was this, those were their real first names! What do you do? You use "book rules." He who writes the book, makes the rules. Therefore, any ballplayer whose real or nickname is Willie or Mickey qualifies for the Willie and Mickey Team!

Mickey Mantle was my boyhood hero. I had a Rawlings "Mickey Mantle" glove. I taught myself to switch hit. I played center field. I wanted to be like Mick (sorry Michael Jordan). As I passed through adulthood, a new Mickey Mantle was presented to me. Frankly, I had a hard time accepting his humanness and frailties. As he struggled and recovered, I became ashamed of myself. A new breed of Phoenix rose from the ashes of his earlier life. His catharsis was sincere. His message was humble. His impact was enormous! In one breath I thanked God, but in the next breath I wished He had given him just a few more innings!

Willie Mays, ounce for ounce, could be baseball's greatest player. His accomplishments are easy to repeat, but his impact is not. A black man in a then white man's game, he helped people become color blind. At no time, as a kid in a argument over who was better, do I recall one person ever say "yeah, but he is black." Think now. This was before Martin Luther King. Willie rose above all colors to become colorful. He did everything with flair. He spun all-around if he swung and missed! He ran out from under his hat when he stretched a triple! He caught the deepest fly balls with his "basket catch." He could do it all and he did it better!

LINEUP

CA	Gordon *Mickey* Cochrane

was an outstanding hitter throughout his 13 year career. He batted .331 his first year and exceeded .300 eight more summers. Mickey led Connie Mack's A's to three consecutive flags (1929-31), batting .331, .357 and .349. His .320 lifetime average is first for backstops.

1B	James *Mickey* Vernon

toiled the bulk of his 20 year career for the hapless Senators (three upper division finishes in 15 years). He had two super years. In 1946 Mickey ranked second in hits, first in 2B's and won the batting title. Eight years later he duplicated '46, plus he finished second in 3B's and RBI's!

2B	Willie Randolph

was a five time All-Star who held down second base for the Yanks for 13 summers. A throw-in by Pittsburgh in a three for one trade to get Doc Medich, Willie kept fooling people. In 1991, his 17th season, the "washed up" 37 year old had his best BA, .327, to place third in the AL.

SS	Michael *Mickey* Doolan

starred for 13 summers. His first nine seasons he anchored the Phillie's infield. In 1906 his 395 putouts were the ninth most ever recorded. From 1906-14 Mickey led all National League shortstops in assists six times, putouts five times, DP's four times and fielding % twice.

3B	William *Willie* Kamm

sparkled with his glove at the hot corner for 13 campaigns. Eight seasons, including six consecutive years (1924-29), Willie placed first in fielding % in the American League. His 2151 career putouts ranks him eighth all time for Major League third sackers.

OF	Willie Mays

did it all for 22 magnificent seasons. Willie batted over .300 ten summers and earned the batting title in 1954. The Say Hey Kid retired fourth in extra base hits and third in both total bases and home runs. The Gold Glove award began in 1957. Willie won it the first 12 years!

OF	William *Willie* Davis

was a speed merchant who displayed his talent 18 years. Twelve seasons he swiped 20 or more bases and Willie's 398 career pilfers place him 58th. Twice Willie led the NL in 3B's (one tie) and four seasons he hit over .300. He retired 64th in hits and seventh in outfield putouts.

OF	Mickey Mantle

was a feared hitter. He walked 17.62% of his at bats (ninth) and he led the AL five years in free passes. Mickey's lifetime on base % of .423 ties him for 13th . He also slugged 536 homers (eighth) at a 6.62 home run % (sixth). Mickey won four homer and four slugging crowns!

P	Michael *Mickey* Welch

was an enormous star in the 50' pitching distance era. His 307 victories place him 18th all time. Mickey's best year was 1885. He logged a 44-11 record. Mickey started and completed all 55 games, posted seven shutouts and had a minuscule 1.66 ERA for 492 innings.

P	Michael *Mickey* Lolich

starred in the shadow of Denny McLain, but actually he far exceeded him, recording 217 career victories (tie 67th) and posting 2832 lifetime strikeouts (12th). Mickey won 14 or more games 11 straight years (1964-74), topped with 25 V's and 308 K's (both league leading) in 1971!

P	Guillermo *Willie* Hernandez

came in from the bullpen 733 times over 13 summers. George Sparky Anderson (AKA Captain Hook) kept him busy in 1984. Willie appeared in 80 games, recorded 32 saves and posted a 1.92 ERA. He was voted both the AL MVP and the Cy Young award that season!

RES	Willie Wilson

has starred for 19 seasons. Quietly he has had a great career. Five years he has led the AL in 3B's (two ties). In 1982 Willie won the Silver Bat, one of six times he has topped .300. His 668 stolen bases currently rank him 12th! Willie's best pilfer year was 1979 with 83!

RES	Willie McGee

is having a fantastic career. With 13 seasons (through 1994) under his belt, he has already had several high points. In 1985 Willie led the Birds to the flag and paced the NL in hits, 3B's and batting average. Willie won his second Silver Bat in 1990! He also has over 300 career steals.

RES	Willie Horton

flexed his muscles for 18 campaigns in the Junior Circuit. His 325 career tators ranks him 54th in Major League history. In 1965 Willie placed third in dingers and second in RBI's. The four time All-Star finished second in yard shots and tied for fourth in ribbies in 1968.

RES	William *Wee Willie* Sherdel

threw from the portside for 15 years in the Senior Circuit. From 1922-28 Wee Willie, who stood 5'10", won 15 or more games six seasons. 1928 was his best campaign. Wee Willie won 21 contests (fourth) and led the St. Louis Cardinals to the National League pennant.

L to R: Michael *Mickey* Lolich, William *Willie* Davis, Mickey Mantle, Willie Mays, Willie McCovey

It'sa FACT

Michael **Mickey** Rocco: In 1944 he led the AL in at bats and finished fifth in base hits.

Mitchell **Mickey** Stanley: For 15 seasons he chased fly balls. During his career Mickey twice played a full season errorless (1968 and 1970). His .991 lifetime fielding % places him sixth all time!

Willard **Willie** Marshall: In 1947 he smashed 36 round trippers (third in NL) and drove in 107 runs (fifth).

Mickey Mantle: He played in 12 World Series. Mickey parked 18 balls and drove in 40 runs, both World Series career records. In game #5 of the 1953 Classic Mick hit a grand slam. His homer in game #5 of the 1956 Series was all the margin Don Larsen needed for his perfecto. Ironically, Mickey's own two best Classics ended in seven game Series losses. The roller coaster 1960 meeting with the Bucs was Mick's best. He went 10/25 with one 2B, three HR's and 11 RBI's. In 1964, vs. the Cards, Mick again smashed three HR's, added two 2B's and drove in eight runs.

Miguel **Mickey** Fuentes: Following his rookie season, Mickey was shot to death in a bar room scuffle in Puerto Rico.

Michael **Mickey** Welch: On August 28th, 1884 he struck out the first nine batters in the game, a record over 100 years old! On August 10th, 1889 he was the first Major Leaguer to pinch-hit. Mickey went down on strikes.

William **Willie** Kuehne: In 1922 he was sold to the Chicago White Sox for a then record $100,000!

Wilver **Willie** Stargell: During his career he bashed 475 yard shots. His 1973 season was staggering. Willie had 43 doubles, 44 homers, 119 RBI's and a .646 slugging %. Pops also blasted 48 dingers and drove in 125 runs in 1971.

Gordon **Mickey** Cochrane: He was beaned in 1937 and for ten days Mickey laid unconscious. Thankfully, he survived, but Mickey's Hall of Fame catching career was short circuited at the young age of 34.

Willie Mays: People forget that coming off his 1951 Rookie of the Year season, Willie played only 34 games in 1952, giving the remainder of 1952 and all of 1953 to his country. If you were to average Willie's performance from 1954-66 and multiply it by only 1.5, the Say Hey Kid's career totals would have been even greater. He <u>would</u> have finished fourth in hits, third in RBI's and second in runs scored and HR's! In case you are wondering, Willie <u>did</u> finish ninth in hits, seventh in RBI's, fifth in runs scored and third in HR's. On April 30th, 1961 Willie blasted four HR's in one game.

William **Wee Willie** Keeler: He is the shortest man in the Hall of Fame, but he stood tall among his peers. Wee Willie had eight consecutive 200+ hit years (1894-1901)! His .341 career batting average is 12th all time!

Phil **Mickey** Weintraub: On April 30th, 1944 he walloped a double, a triple, a homer and had 11 RBI's!

Nicholas **Mickey** Witek: He had a great 1943 season for the Giants. Mickey hit .314 (fifth), had 195 base hits (second) and only fanned 23 times in 622 at bats!

Michael **Mickey** Hatcher: In the 1988 World Series this fun-loving prankster slugged two homers (he hit only one home run during the regular season)! Mickey hit first inning shots in both game #1 and game #5 (final game).

Newton **Mickey** Grasso: He was a POW during World War II.

Guillermo **Willie** Montanez: In 1971 he was second for the NL Rookie of the Year. Willie had 30 HR's and 99 RBI's.

TRIVIA*

1) He hit four homers in the 1980 World Series. His two two homer games were a World Series first.
2) When asked how come he hit so well, this Hall of Famer answered, "I hit 'em where they ain't."
3) He was the tenth Major Leaguer to execute an unassisted triple play. (Hint: in 1992)
4) His lifetime batting average was .110. He surprised everyone and pounded his only career homer in game #2 of the 1968 World Series. (Hint: he also won three games in the Classic and was voted the Series MVP)
5) He claimed his new found home run prowess came from his breakfast cereal, Fruit Loops!
6) Sixteen of his 66 pinch-hits went yard, including three grand slams! (Hint: his nickname was Stretch)
7) Mickey Mantle was named after this Hall of Famer.
8) He won the Triple Crown in 1956. He launched 52 homers, plated 130 runs and batted .353!
9) Pete Charlie Hustle Rose tied his NL consecutive game hitting record of 44 in 1978. (Hint: think 5'4 1/2")
10) He led the NL in stolen bases four consecutive years (1956-59).
11) He holds the Major League career record for putouts by an outfielder with 7095.
12) In 1980 he set the Major League record for at bats with 705. That season he stroked 230 hits!
13) He was voted NL Rookie of the Year in 1959 (played in only 52 games)! He was voted the NL MVP in 1969 (missed the Triple Crown only on batting average). He was voted Comeback Player of the Year in 1977.
14) Only five Major Leaguers have had two or more "50 home run" seasons. Babe Ruth, Jimmie The Beast Foxx and Ralph Kiner are the other three. (Hint: this is a lollipop)
15) He was walked intentionally 45 times in 1970, the Major League record.

* W&M BOGGLERS answers found on page 241

ROSTER

CATCHERS:	Yr	Hits	AB's	Ave
Gordon *Mickey* Cochrane	13	1652	5169	.320
Arnold *Mickey* Owen	13	929	3649	.255
Mickey Tettleton	11	905	3734	.242
George *Mickey* O'Neil	9	475	1995	.238
Thompson *Mickey* Livingston	10	354	1490	.238
Newton *Mickey* Grasso	7	216	957	.226
William *Mickey* Devine	3	12	53	.226
Frank *Mickey* O'Brien	1	7	21	.333
Willie Royster	1	0	4	.000

1ST BASEMEN:	Yr	Hits	AB's	Ave
James *Mickey* Vernon	20	2495	8731	.286
Willie McCovey	22	2211	8197	.270
Guillermo *Willie* Montanez	14	1604	5843	.275
Willie Upshaw	10	1103	4203	.262
Willie Mays Aikens	8	675	2492	.271
Michael *Mickey* Rocco	4	444	1721	.258
Phil *Mickey* Weintraub	7	407	1382	.295
William *Wee Willie* Clark	5	366	1273	.288
Minor *Mickey* Heath	2	34	160	.213
Maurice *Mickey* Keliher	1	0	7	.000

2ND BASEMEN:	Yr	Hits	AB's	Ave
Willie Randolph	18	2210	8018	.276
Nicholas *Mickey* Witek	7	595	2147	.277
Michael *Mickey* Morandini	5	397	1525	.260
Neal *Mickey* Finn	5	274	1044	.262
Michael *Mickey* Corcoran	1	10	46	.217

SHORTSTOPS:	Yr	Hits	AB's	Ave
Michael *Mickey* Doolan	13	1376	5977	.230
Guillermo *Willie* Miranda	9	423	1914	.221
Michael *Mickey* Haslin	6	265	974	.272
Michael *Mick* Kelleher	11	230	1081	.213
Robert *Mickey* Micelotta	2	0	7	.000

3RD BASEMEN:	Yr	Hits	AB's	Ave
William *Willie* Kamm	13	1643	5851	.281
Willie Jones	15	1502	5826	.258
William *Willie* Kuehne	10	996	4284	.232
Gene *Mickey* Klutts	8	129	536	.241
Willie Greene	3	41	180	.226
William *Willie* Lozado	1	29	107	.271
Milton *Mickey* Rutner	1	12	48	.250

OUTFIELDERS:	Yr	Hits	AB's	Ave
Willie Mays	22	3283	10881	.302
William *Wee Willie* Keeler	19	2932	8591	.341
William *Willie* Davis	18	2561	9174	.279
Mickey Mantle	18	2415	8102	.298

OUTFIELDERS: (Cont.)	Yr	Hits	AB's	Ave
Wilver *Willie* Stargell	21	2232	7927	.282
Willie Wilson	19	2207	7731	.285
Willie Horton	18	1993	7298	.273
Willie McGee	13	1876	6300	.298
John *Mickey* Rivers	16	1660	5629	.295
Mitchell *Mickey* Stanley	15	1243	5022	.248
Willard *Willie* Marshall	11	1160	4233	.274
Michael *Mickey* Hatcher	12	946	3377	.280
Willie Kirkland	9	837	3494	.240
Willie Tasby	6	467	1868	.250
Willie Smith	9	410	1654	.248
Michael *Mickey* Brantley	4	295	1138	.259
Willie Norwood	4	207	854	.242
Danny *Mickey* Walton	9	174	779	.223
William *Gentle Willie* Murphy	1	48	189	.254
Frank *Mickey* Cross	1	3	5	.600

PINCH HITTER:	Yr	Hits	AB's	Ave
William *Willy* Fetzer	1	0	1	.000

PITCHERS:	Yr	Won	Lost	ERA
Michael *Mickey* Welch	13	307	210	2.71
Michael *Mickey* Lolich	16	217	191	3.44
William *Wee Willie* Sherdel	15	165	146	3.72
John *Wee Willie* Sudhoff	10	103	135	3.56
Milton *Mickey* Haefner	8	78	91	3.50
William *Willie* McGill	7	72	74	4.59
Guillermo *Willie* Hernandez	13	70	63	3.38
Maurice *Mickey* McDermott	12	69	69	3.91
Maurice *Mickey* Harris	9	59	71	4.18
Daniel *Mickey* Daub	6	45	52	4.75
Claude *Weeping Willie* Willoughby	7	38	38	5.84
William *Willie* Fraser	7	36	39	4.42
James *Willie* Ramsdell	5	24	39	3.83
William *Wee Willie* Dammann	3	24	15	4.06
Willie Banks	4	24	29	4.88
William *Willie* Blair	5	16	30	4.86
Michael *Mickey* Mahler	8	14	32	4.68
Ralph *Mickey* Scott	5	8	7	3.72
William *Willie* Adams	5	8	16	4.37
Bret *Willy* Gaff	3	4	5	4.06
Willie Smith	3	2	4	3.10
Miguel *Mickey* Fuentes	1	1	3	5.19
Willie Underhill	2	1	4	5.70
Willard *Willie* Mueller	2	1	0	6.14
Michael *Mickey* Westin	5	1	2	7.15
William *Willie* Garoni	1	0	1	4.50
Tullis *Mickey* McGowan	1	0	0	7.36
Wilfred *Willie* Prall	1	0	2	8.59

LEFTIES / LEFTOVERS

41

Team

Every book has a final chapter. This is it. I started out to create a "Lefty" team (stupid me!). The squad was hurtin' for third sackers, shortstops, keystone men and of course, backstops! There was also a group of Major Leaguers whose nicknames really did not fit into any other team. They were my "leftovers." But as different as peanut butter and jelly, these two subsets went together and formed a delectable treat of outstanding players!*

Sandwiched together are over 40 Lefties (my peanut butter) and an array of Leftovers (my jellies). Just as you have grape, strawberry, blueberry, peach, raspberry, plum, boysenberry and dozens of other tasty choices, so the Leftovers treat us to Duffy, Smudge, Bubby, Wid, Bucky, Cupid, Mookie and dozens of other excellent players. The Hall of Fame claims six members on this team. Three are Lefties and the other trio are Bucky, Jeptha and Highpockets.

When someone says Lefty, it is usually this southpaw who comes to mind. Steve Lefty Carlton was simply awesome. Just eight hurlers have won more games during their careers than Steve and only one threw any pitches after 1930. He and Spahny (Warren Spahn) accumulated their victories throwing livelier balls, facing smaller strike zones and competing against better coached and conditioned players. To reach the 329 victory plateau today requires not only huge talent, but also enormous longevity and determination. Talent wise, a player first must be outstanding to reach the Majors at a young age and second he must be even more outstanding to be inserted into the starting rotation. Lefty debuted at the early age of 20 and in his 22nd year began taking a regular turn on the mound. Longevity in baseball is always a product of determination, not just talent alone. A player must continue to improve, adjust, prepare and fine tune both physically and mentally. As talent erodes and mental disposition cracks, only a few manage to somehow maintain their high level. Lefty stayed in great physical shape. His exercising and conditioning were rigorous. Mentally Lefty avoided sporting distractions and remained magnifying glass focused. Steve went 18 consecutive seasons (1967-84), winning in double figures. During that remarkable run, he posted 15 winning seasons and his average line per year read 16-11, 34 starts, 261 innings and 212 strikeouts! His average campaign would be a career year for most hurlers. Way to go Lefty!

*The numbers in this group were enormous, so the team was limited to pitchers with at least ten career wins and position players with at least 100 career hits

LINEUP

CA	Frank *Pancho* Snyder

was a 16 year NL veteran. He was excellent defensively. Pancho led all backstops three times in fielding %, two times in putouts and once in assists and DP's. Three seasons he batted over .300. In 1922 Pancho hit a lusty .343. As a pinch hitter he batted .372, going 32/86.

1B	George *Highpockets* Kelly

is in the Hall of Fame. He starred 16 summers. From 1920-26 Highpockets tore up the NL. For six seasons he hit over .300. Highpockets finished in the top four in long shots four times, winning the home run title in 1921. He also won two RBI crowns (1920 and 1924).

2B	Clarence *Cupid* Childs

was a starter 11 of his 13 seasons. His .306 career average missed by .001 of making the top 100. Cupid's 14.99% base on balls (35th all time) combined with his batting average to create the 19th best on base %. Seven seasons Cupid tallied over 100 runs, averaging .87 per game.

SS	Edward *Eppie* Miller

was a 14 year National Leaguer, starting from 1940-48. He was named seven times to the All-Star team! Eppie was known for his glove. He topped all shortstops five times in fielding % (including four consecutive years, 1940-43) four times in DP's and three times in putouts and assists!

3B	Arlie *Freshest Man on Earth* Latham

was a star prior to 1900. He stole 739 sacks, placing him seventh all time. It helped Arlie scored 1478 runs (52nd all time) in just 1627 games, an average of .91 runs per game (eighth best). Nine seasons he scored over 100 runs. Arlie's 163 tallies in 1887 tie for ninth highest.

OF	Dwight *Dewey* Evans

very quietly had a great career. He was an outstanding right fielder whose arm was a cannon. Dewey cranked out 20 or more homers 11 years. In 1981 he tied for the homer crown. Dewey slugged 385 dingers (30th), stroked 483 two baggers (tie 42nd) and plated 1384 runs (48th).

OF	Edmund *Bing* Miller

reached the Majors at the age of 26. He starred for 16 seasons in the AL. From 1922-30 Bing hit over .300 eight summers. In 1922, his most productive year, Bing finished fifth in batting and tied for fourth in homers. He was the Majors 77th most difficult man to strikeout.

OF	John *Shano* Collins

was a speedy outfielder who sparkled 16 summers, all in the American League. Seven seasons Shano legged out ten or more three baggers, and for his career he ranks 74th in triples. From 1910-17 Shano stole bases at a double digit rate, twice reaching the 30 bag mark.

P	Steve *Lefty* Carlton

fired fast balls and hard sliders all the way to Cooperstown. Over 24 campaigns Lefty put fear in batters. He struck out 4136 hitters, second all time. Lefty's 329 wins are exceeded by only one left-hander, Warren Spahn. Six summers, during his career, he posted 20 or more wins.

P	Robert *Lefty* Grove

was arguably the greatest southpaw pitcher. He was held contractually for five years in the minors (went 109-36), until Connie Mack ponied up $100,600 (a then unheard of sum) for Lefty. If Lefty would have had those "extra" years, he may have challenged the 400 win mark.

P	Eppa *Jeptha* Rixey

was spotted by umpire Charles Cy Rigler when Jeptha hurled for the University of Virginia. The 6'5" chemistry student soon traded formulas for fast balls. He had four 20 or more win seasons, including 1922, his best summer. That year he led all National League twirlers with 25 wins!

RES	Lee *Specs* Meadows

was a National Leaguer his entire 15 year career. For 12 summers Specs finished in double digits for wins and six seasons he won 15 or more games. 1926 was Specs' best year. He finished tied for first in wins with 20, just one more victory than he racked up in both 1925 and 1927!

RES	William *Bucky* Walters

played third base his first four seasons. In 1935 Bucky converted to pitching. From 1936-46 he won ten or more games each year. Three times he led the NL in wins, innings and complete games. In 1939 Bucky led all NL hurlers in wins, K's and ERA, the Triple Crown of pitching!

RES	Clarence *Cito* Gaston

is currently the manager of the Toronto Blue Jays and has led them to three division titles and one World Championship. In his playing days Cito was an excellent hitter. His best year was 1970. He clouted 29 round trippers and batted .318 for the San Diego Padres.

RES	Francis *Lefty* O'Doul

was up four times in nine years for short stays as a hurler. He finally stuck at age 31 as an outfielder. His next seven seasons were huge! Lefty hit over .300 six times and won two batting crowns. In 1929 he hit .398 (only topped twice since) and collected 254 hits (tie second best).

L to R: Francis *Lefty* O'Doul, William *Bucky* Walters, Steve *Lefty* Carlton, Russell *Bucky* Dent, William *Mookie* Wilson

It'sa FACT

<u>Mike **Spanky** Squires</u>: In 1983 he won a Gold Glove for his play at first base. Spanky appeared in 143 games, but only batted 153 times. He was often a late game replacement. The left-handed fielder also made history by playing third base in 1983, a first in 50 years!

<u>Sam **Sandow** Mertes</u>: He did a rare feat during the dead ball era. Sandow hit consecutive game leadoff home runs June 8th and June 9th, 1900. He was nicknamed after the famous "touring muscleman".

<u>Joe **Unser Choe** Hauser</u>: On August 2nd, 1924 he clouted three homers and a double, setting the then AL single game total base record (Ty Cobb broke it in 1925). Unser Choe was a great slugger. In 1923 he finished fourth in circuit clouts and the following season Joe finished second in round trippers to Babe Ruth. A shattered kneecap in 1925 effectively ended his budding career, appearing in only 223 more games (62 as a pinch hitter). Unser Choe went to the minors and there smashed 63 long balls in 1930 and an astounding 69 shots in 1933 for the Minneapolis Millers! He is the only player in organized ball to hit over 60 home runs twice.

<u>Sylvester **Blix** Donnelly</u>: My friend Bob Schultz grew up in Olivia, Minnesota hearing stories about this hometown hero. As a 30 year old rookie in 1944, Blix hurled two shutout innings in game #1 of the Fall Classic. The Cardinals' right-hander came out of the pen again in game #2 and posted four shutout frames, fanned six, and won the contest.

<u>Hersh **Buster** Freeman</u>: In 1956 he was used exclusively as a reliever and posted a 14-5 record, leading the National League in relief wins. Buster's 18 saves and 64 games ranked him second in both categories.

<u>Bill **Lefty** Kennedy</u>: He topped the American League with 47 appearances in 1952. Lefty recorded five saves and had a 2.80 ERA. In 1946 he set a modern baseball record by fanning 456 batters (in the minors).

<u>Cal **Buster** McLish</u>: From 1944 to 1956 he was called up to the Big Show seven times. He won a total of ten games while chucking for Brooklyn, Pittsburgh, Chicago (NL) and finally Cleveland. At age 32, in 1958, Buster went 16-8 for the Tribe. Buster logged 19 victories, second best in the AL, in 1959.

<u>Smead **Smudge** Jolley</u>: As a rookie in 1930, he drove in 114 runs, batted .313 and had 66 extra base hits. Smudge had a .366 career minor league batting average, third best ever. Because of his weak fielding, Smudge played only four seasons in the Majors.

<u>Elvin **Buster** Adams</u>: He finished second in total bases, third in HR's and fourth in RBI's in the 1945 NL season.

<u>Hugh **Lefty** High</u>: He was one of three High brothers to play in the Big Leagues. Lefty, also known as Bunny, his middle brother Handy Andy and his youngest brother Charlie were one of 16 families which had three or more sons make it to the Big Show.

<u>Albert **Lefty** Leifield</u>: In 1906 Lefty twirled eight shutouts in 31 starts, going 18-13 with a 1.87 ERA.

<u>Stanley **Bucky** Harris</u>: He was named playing manager at age 27. During his first two seasons at the helm, he led the Senators to the flag twice and won the World Championship once! His 2157 victories place Bucky third all time for managers, but Sparky Anderson is closing in on him. Bucky also holds the AL record, for second sackers, of leading the league five consecutive years in DP's.

<u>Joe **Moon** Harris</u>: He was the first player to ever homer his initial World Series at bat. In that 1925 Fall Classic Moon hit .440 (11/25), which included two doubles, three tators and six ribbies. He retired 30 games short of 1000, so Moon's .317 career average, which would have placed him 52nd all time, goes literally unnoticed.

<u>Joe **Lefty** Shaute</u>: Not a strikeout artist, this crafty portsider fanned only 512 batters in 1,818 innings. Twenty whiffs, though, were at the expense of the Babe. Lefty, while toiling for the sixth place Tribe (67-86) in 1924, won 20 games!

<u>Walter **Lefty** Stewart</u>: In 1930 he had his best season, going 20-12 and finishing third in the AL in ERA. That summer his weak Browns only won 64 times! The next two campaigns Lefty won 14 and 15 games while St. Louis finished 44 and 45 games out! Traded to the pennant bound Senators in 1933, Lefty's log was 15-6 for Washington.

<u>James **Nixey** Callahan</u>: He was a versatile player. A pitcher earlier in his career, Nixey twice won 20 or more games (1898-99). He shifted to the field his last five plus seasons, and when he finally hung 'em up, Nixey had collected 901 base hits and 99 wins.

<u>Francis **Lefty** O'Doul</u>: He played in 970 games, falling just 30 short of the 1000 contests needed to be eligible for all time lists. Lefty's .349 career batting average would place him fourth! In 1929 he fanned only 19 times in 638 at bats while pounding 32 four baggers. For five seasons he had as many or more homers than strikeouts! On September 9th, 1930 and September 13th, 1930 Lefty stroked consecutive pinch homers.

<u>George **Lefty** Tyler</u>: The one month early 1918 World Series (season shortened due to The Great War) was the last time the Boston Red Sox won the World Championship. Lefty, hurling for the Cubs, tossed a one run six hit effort, winning game #2 on September 6th. On two days rest, (September 9th game #4) Lefty went seven frames in a no decision. The two runs he surrendered were knocked in with a triple by the opposing pitcher, George Babe Ruth. On September 11th, game #6, Lefty again started   This time it was on one days rest! Two unearned runs cost Lefty and the Cubs the game 2-1 and the Series 4-2. Boston sold Babe Ruth to the Yankees that winter. The "curse of the Bambino" (Boston has not won a World Series since selling Ruth) has haunted the Bosox ever since!

TRIVIA*

1) On September 15th, 1969 he struck out 19 batters in one game.

2) This hardluck portsider went 18 frames and lost 1-0 (May 15th, 1918).

3) In his first Major League at bat he busted a circuit blast. (Hint: he was a right-handed pitcher)

4) Hurling for the Bucs in four National League Championship Series and for the Angels in one American League Championship Series, he compiled a spotless 4-0 record and a 1.21 ERA.

5) On August 1st, 1941 while posting a shutout, he walked a record 11 batters. (Hint: his other nickname was Mose, short for his middle name Moses)

6) A versatile ballplayer, he has played second, short, third and outfield. In 1992 his ten consecutive hits tied the National League record.

7) His three run shot over The Green Monster won the 1978 one game playoff for the Yankees and ended the Beantowner's season.

8) In the 1978 World Series he was voted the MVP for his 10/24 performance and seven RBI's.

9) This portsider won four Cy Young awards.

10) This pitcher's full name was Calvin Coolidge Julius Caesar Tuskahoma _____.

11) In 1937, while hurling for the cellar dwelling Redlegs (56-98), he won 12 games and tied for the league lead with five shutouts. (Hint: his brother, Uncle Marv, also pitched ten years in the Majors)

12) His older brother Bill, also a catcher, was elected to the Hall of Fame.

13) This slugging infielder's other nickname was Junior. (Hint: he played with "The Kid")

14) In 1972 he went 27-10 for the last place Phillies. He won 45% of his team's games that Cy Young winning season. He also posted eight shutouts, logged a 1.97 ERA and fanned 310 batters!

15) This Hall of Famer earned his nickname because he was so tall.

16) In game #7 of the 1946 World Series his eighth inning single scored Enos Country Slaughter from first base.

17) His tenth inning grounder in game #6 of the 1986 World Series eluded Boston's first sacker after it hit the bag and the Mets' winning run scored. Snatching victory from defeat, the New Yorkers then won game #7 and continued the "curse of the Bambino."

18) This career .147 hitter drove in the first All-Star game run on July 6th, 1933. (Hint: this goofy southpaw also won the game)

19) His bingo, a double, drove in Bucketfoot Al Simmons with the World Series winning run in 1929.

20) Traded by the Redbirds to the Phillies ten games into the 1947 season, he went on to lead the NL in triples and batting! (Hint: his brother Dixie (Fred) led the NL in batting in 1944)

21) In his first seven Major League seasons he led the AL in strikeouts each summer!

22) On February 25th, 1972 he was traded "even up" for Rick Wise. Rick went on to win 113 more games in his career. He, too, went on to win 113 games.... and an additional 139 more games!

23) He won a Major League record nine ERA crowns during his Hall of Fame career.

24) He retired with 33 shutouts in just 217 career starts, a 15.2% ratio. That ranks him fifth all time among the top 100 shutout hurlers! The top four are Big Ed Walsh, Mordecai Three Finger Brown, Walter Barney Johnson and Adrian Addie Joss. (Hint: check *It'sa FACT* for him)

25) He shares the AL record of 16 consecutive wins. He was upset 1-0 by the doormat St. Louis Browns to end his 16 game win streak. The only run scored on a misjudged fly ball. He then went on to win his next five starts after that bitter pill loss!

* TRICKY TIDBITS answers found on page 241

ROSTER

CATCHERS:	Yr	Hits	AB's	Ave
Frank *Pancho* Snyder	16	1122	4229	.265
George *Moon* Gibson	14	893	3776	.236
Don *Duffy* Dyer	14	441	1993	.221
Tom *Satch* Satriano	10	365	1623	.225
Alva *Buff* Williams	7	314	1186	.265
James *Wickey* McAvoy	6	134	674	.199
George *Skeets* Dickey	6	101	494	.204

1ST BASEMEN:	Yr	Hits	AB's	Ave
George *Highpockets* Kelly	16	1778	5993	.297
John *Dots* Miller	12	1526	5805	.263
Joe *Moon* Harris	10	963	3035	.317
Harvey *Gink* Hendrick	11	896	2910	.308
Joe *Unser Choe* Hauser	6	580	2044	.284
Mike *Spanky* Squires	10	411	1580	.260
Louis *Boze* Berger	6	270	1144	.236
Harley *Lefty* Boss	4	139	519	.268

2ND BASEMEN:	Yr	Hits	AB's	Ave
Clarence *Cupid* Childs	13	1720	5618	.306
Tom *Tido* Daly	16	1582	5684	.278
George *Clancy* Cutshaw	12	1487	5621	.265
Stanley *Bucky* Harris	12	1297	4736	.274
Albert *Hobe* Ferris	9	1146	4800	.239
John *Move Up Joe* Gerhardt	12	854	3770	.227
Leon *Bip* Roberts	8	825	2786	.296
Edwin *Dib* Williams	6	421	1574	.267
Ford *Moon* Mullen	1	124	464	.267

SHORTSTOPS:	Yr	Hits	AB's	Ave
Vern *Buster* Stephens	15	1859	6497	.286
Edward *Eppie* Miller	14	1270	5337	.238
Russell *Bucky* Dent	12	1144	4512	.247
George *Specs* Toporcer	8	437	1566	.279
Frank *Dingle* Croucher	4	235	935	.251
James *Buster* Caton	4	184	814	.226

3RD BASEMEN:	Yr	Hits	AB's	Ave
Arlie *Freshest Man on Earth* Latham	17	1833	6822	.269
William *Wid* Conroy	11	1257	5061	.248
Walter *Dinty* Barbare	8	462	1777	.260
Norm *Bub* McMillan	5	353	1356	.260
William *Buster* Hoover	3	151	525	.288
Charles *Buster* Chatham	2	118	448	.263

OUTFIELDERS:	Yr	Hits	AB's	Ave
Dwight *Dewey* Evans	20	2446	8996	.272
Edmund *Bing* Miller	16	1936	6212	.312
John *Shano* Collins	16	1687	6390	.264
George *Dode* Paskert	15	1613	6017	.268
George *Duffy* Lewis	11	1518	5351	.284
George *Dandy* Wood	13	1467	5371	.273
William *Mookie* Wilson	12	1397	5094	.274
Sam *Sandow* Mertes	10	1227	4405	.279

OUTFIELDERS: (Cont.)	Yr	Hits	AB's	Ave
Francis *Lefty* O'Doul	11	1140	3264	.349
Ralph *Socks* Seybold	9	1085	3685	.294
James *Nixey* Callahan	13	901	3295	.273
Ed *Spanky* Kirkpatrick	16	824	3467	.238
Clarence *Cito* Gaston	11	799	3120	.256
Harry *The Hat* Walker	11	786	2651	.296
Wilbur *Lefty* Good	11	609	2364	.258
George *Tuck* Stainback	13	585	2261	.259
Morrie *Snooker* Arnovich	7	577	2013	.287
Elvin *Buster* Adams	6	532	2003	.266
Smead *Smudge* Jolley	4	521	1710	.305
George *Tuck* Turner	6	478	1496	.320
Charles *Lefty* Marr	4	418	1445	.289
Johnny *Lefty* Watwood	6	403	1423	.283
Hugh *Lefty* High	6	386	1546	.250
Alphonzo *Lefty* Davis	4	338	1296	.261
William *Bunk* Congalton	4	337	1163	.290
George *Hickory* Jackson	3	158	554	.285
James *Buster* Maynard	4	136	616	.221
Paul *Lefty* O'Dea	2	107	394	.272

PITCHERS:	Yr	Won	Lost	ERA
Steve *Lefty* Carlton	24	329	244	3.22
Robert *Lefty* Grove	17	300	141	3.06
Eppa *Jeptha* Rixey	21	266	251	3.15
William *Bucky* Walters	19	198	160	3.30
Vernon *Lefty* Gomez	14	189	102	3.34
Lee *Specs* Meadows	15	188	180	3.37
George *Lefty* Tyler	12	127	116	2.95
Albert *Lefty* Leifield	12	124	97	2.47
Thomas *Tully* Sparks	12	121	136	2.79
Thornton *Lefty* Lee	16	117	124	3.56
Charles *Togie* Pittinger	8	115	113	3.10
Bruce *Buster* Kison	15	115	88	3.66
Billy *Bunker* Rhines	9	114	103	3.47
Hickory Bob Harmon	9	107	133	3.33
Walter *Lefty* Stewart	10	101	98	4.19
James *Nixey* Callahan	8	99	73	3.39
Joe *Lefty* Shaute	13	99	109	4.15
Cal *Buster* McLish	15	92	92	4.01
George *Sassafras* Winter	8	83	102	2.87
Fred *Dupee* Shaw	6	83	121	3.10
Claude *Lefty* Williams	7	82	48	3.13
Bill *Lefty* Wight	12	77	99	3.95
Joe *Blitzen* Benz	9	76	75	2.43
George *Lefty* Brunet	15	69	93	3.62
Paul *Lefty* Minner	10	69	84	3.94
Atley *Swampy* Donald	8	65	33	3.52
Bob *Lefty* Weiland	12	62	94	4.24
Fred *Lefty* Heimach	13	62	69	4.46
Terry *Trees* Forster	16	54	65	3.23
Ken *Lefty* Chase	8	53	84	4.27
Charles *Buster* Brown	9	51	103	3.21
Carmen *Bunker* Hill	10	49	33	3.44

ROSTER

PITCHERS: (Cont.)	Yr	Won	Lost	ERA
Harry *Socks* Seibold	8	48	86	4.43
Al *Lefty* Schulz	5	47	62	3.32
Marius *Lefty* Russo	6	45	34	3.13
Monte *Lefty* Kennedy	8	42	55	3.84
Earl *Lefty* Johnson	8	40	32	4.30
Fred *Bubby* Talbot	8	38	56	4.12
Bobby *Lefty* Burke	10	38	46	4.29
Ralph *Lefty* Birkofer	5	31	28	4.19
Hersh *Buster* Freeman	6	30	16	3.74
Hank *Lefty* Thormahlen	6	29	30	3.33
George *Dut* Chalmers	7	29	41	3.41
Lee *Lefty* Grissom	8	29	48	3.89
Sylvester *Blix* Donnelly	8	27	36	3.49
Walt *Hickory* Dickson	5	26	50	3.60
Al *Lefty* Gerheauser	5	25	50	4.13

PITCHERS: (Cont.)	Yr	Won	Lost	ERA
Al *Lefty* Aber	6	24	25	4.18
Paul *Lefty* LaPalme	7	24	45	4.42
Phillip *Lefty* Weinert	9	18	33	4.59
Bill *Lefty* Kennedy	8	15	28	4.73
Howard *Lefty* Mills	5	15	30	6.06
Leslie *Buster* Narum	5	14	27	4.45
Arnold *Lefty* Carter	2	13	11	2.72
Frederick *Spec* Harkness	2	12	9	3.37
Ewald *Lefty* Pyle	5	11	21	5.03
Jim *Lefty* Faulkner	3	10	8	3.75
Frank *Lefty* Hoerst	5	10	33	5.17
Les *Buster* McCrabb	5	10	15	5.96
EXTRA:				
William *Bick* Campbell - Umpire				

It'sa FACT cont'd...

Charles *Togie* Pittinger: It seems no one remembers who finishes in second place. In 1902 he finished with 27 wins, a tie for second behind Smiling Jack Chesbro. Togie was also second in games, complete games and innings that season. In 1904 Togie finished with 23 wins, second behind Christy Big Six Mathewson.

Frank *Lefty* Killen: A star in the 1890's, he successfully made the transition from 50' to 60'6", winning 29 games at 50' in 1892 and winning a league leading 36 games at 60'6" in 1893.

Ralph *Socks* Seybold: He was an early Junior Circuit slugger. In the AL's first three seasons (1901-03) Socks socked home runs! He ranked fourth in both 1901 and 1903, and in 1902 Socks paced the league!

William *Mookie* Wilson: His 327 career steals place him one steal short of 100th all time. Mookie was successful on 76.9% of his attempts, only topped by 34 players.

George *Duffy* Lewis: His two run shot in the fifth and final 1915 World Series game knotted the score after eight frames and the Red Sox went on to win. Duffy's eight hits and five RBI's (Sox scored only 12 tallies in the Classic) topped all Boston players.

Lee *Specs* Meadows: He must have left a cab with its meter running. Specs was on the short end of the fastest (timewise) nine inning game in baseball history, 51 minutes!

Hickory Bob Harmon: He won 23 games (fourth in NL) in 1911. Hickory also finished second in games and innings pitched and third in complete games.

Thornton *Lefty* Lee: He and his son Don (right-handed) combined to win 157 games, the fifth highest father/son win total. In 1941 Lefty won 22 games (second in AL) and captured the ERA crown.

Thomas *Tully* Sparks: In 1907 he won 22 times, the best in the National League.

Fred *Lefty* Heinrich: As a pinch hitter he went 20/52, a .385 clip. That's not bad hitting for a pitcher!

Carmen *Bunker* Hill: His other nickname was Specs. Bunker was a part-time player all but two seasons. When he took a regular turn, Bunker won 16 and 22 games. His 22 victories placed him third in the NL in 1927.

Marius *Lefty* Russo: In game #4 of the 1943 World Series he collected his second two bagger (two of the six Yankee hits) and scored the winning run. Lefty also posted a seven hitter for the victory.

Vern *Buster* Stephens: His 159 RBI's in 1949 (tied Ted The Kid Williams) are the highest season total since then.

George *Lefty* Tyler: In last place July 18th, 1914, the "Miracle Braves" captured first place August 25th and won the pennant by a 10½ game margin! The Braves then swept the highly favored Philadelphia Athletics in the Series. The unbelievable comeback was led by Seattle Bill James, Baldy Randolph and Lefty (16 wins, including five shutouts).

William *Bucky* Walters: During the 1940 World Series he won two games. Bucky fired a three hitter in game #2 and he tossed a five hit shutout in game #6.

Your **It'sa FACT** *Additions*

Your **LINGO** *Additions*

Your **ROSTER** Additions

TRIVIA ANSWERS

Chapter 1 - Another League:
(WICKED BEAUTIES)

1) Charles *Lady* Baldwin
2) Floyd *Babe* Herman
3) Paul *Molly* Molitor
4) Elston *Ellie* Howard
5) Ferguson *Fergie* Jenkins
6) Ralph *Babe* Pinelli
7) Dave *Beauty* Bancroft
8) George *Babe* Ruth (59 HRs in 1921)
9) Bill *Little Eva* Lange
10) Dave *Winny* Winfield
11) Ernest *Babe* Phelps
12) *Gorgeous* George Sisler
13) Dave *Winny* Winfield
14) Nelson *Nellie* Fox
15) Curt *Honey* Walker
16) Bill *Beverly* Bayne
17) *Gorgeous* George Sisler
18) Ferguson *Fergie* Jenkins
19) Charles *Babe* Adams
20) Phil *Babe* Marchildon
21) George *Babe* Ruth
22) Paul *Molly* Molitor
23) *Gorgeous* George Sisler
24) Dave *Winny* Winfield
25) Ruth Cleveland (baby daughter of then President Cleveland) Got ya!

Chapter 2 - Attitude:
(POSITIVELY TOUGH)

1) *Smiling* Jack Chesbro
2) Joe *Pepi* Pepitone
3) Eugene *Bubbles* Hargrave
4) Albert *Happy* Chandler
5) Ray *Old Blue* Moore
6) *Sad* Sam Jones
7) Early *Gus* Wynn
8) Pete *Charlie Hustle* Rose
9) Burt *Happy* Hooton
10) Vernon *The Gay Castilian* Gomez
11) Tom *Terrific* Seaver
12) *Sad* Sam Jones
13) Pete *Charlie Hustle* Rose
14) Early *Gus* Wynn
15) Arvel *Bad News* Galloway
16) Charlie *Jolly Cholly* Grimm
17) *Smiling* Mickey Welch
18) Tom *Terrific* Seaver
19) Vernon *The Gay Castilian* Gomez
20) Burt *Happy* Hooton
21) Eddie *The Brat* Stanky
22) *Smiling* Stan Hack
23) Pete *Charlie Hustle* Rose
24) Vernon *The Gay Castilian* Gomez
25) *Marvelous* Marv Throneberry

Chapter 3 - Baseball Names:
(HARD LINERS)

1) Donnie *Baseball* Mattingly
2) Frank *Home Run* Baker
3) Cletis *Clete* Boyer
4) Harry *Slug* Heilmann
5) Walker *Walk* Cooper
6) Paul *Slug* Richards
7) Joe *Fungo* Hesketh
8) Truett *Rip* Sewell
9) Ray *Jockey* Kolp
10) *Sliding* Billy Hamilton (.404)
11) Donnie *Baseball* Mattingly
12) Don *Groove* Baylor
13) James *Ripper* Collins
14) Dick *Dr. Strangeglove* Stuart
15) Eddie *The Walking Man* Yost
16) Al *Mr Scoops* Oliver
17) *Sliding* Billy Hamilton
18) Harry *Slug* Heilmann
19) Bill *Swish* Nicholson
20) Eddie *The Walking Man* Yost
21) Donnie *Baseball* Mattingly
22) Eldon *Rip* Repulski
23) Lewis *Hack* Wilson
24) Jack *The Ripper* Clark
25) Eddie *The Walking Man* Yost

Chapter 4 - Real Birds:
(BIRD BRAINERS)

1) Tom *Gray Flamingo* Brennan
2) Frank *Crow* Crosetti
3) Joe *Ducky* Medwick
4) Leon *Goose* Goslin
5) *Turkey* Mike Donlin
6) Rich *Goose* Gossage
7) Tris *The Grey Eagle* Speaker
8) Ron *The Penguin* Cey
9) George *White Wings* Tebeau
10) Clay *Hawk* Carroll
11) Mark *The Bird* Fidrych
12) Monty *Gander* Stratton
13) Joe *Ducky* Medwick
14) Ron *The Beak* Hansen
15) Ed *Krane* Kranepool

Chapter 5 - Body Parts:
(EYEBROW WRINKLERS)

1) Max *Camera Eye* Bishop
2) Albert *Butts* Wagner
3) *Bucketfoot* Al Simmons
4) Joe *Muscles* Medwick
5) Sammy *Babe Ruth's Legs* Byrd
6) George *Twinkletoes* Selkirk
7) Phil *Knucksie* Niekro
8) *One Armed* Pete Gray
9) Cliff *Rubberhead* Heathcote
10) Bob *Bigfoot* Stanley
11) Paul *Motormouth* Blair
12) Pete *Bigfoot* Ladd
13) Tim *Buckethead* McCarver
14) Al *Curveless Wonder* Orth
15) *Blind* Bob Emslie

16) *Blind* Ryne Duren
17) *Bucketfoot* Al Simmons
18) Arthur *Pinky* Whitney and Michael *Pinky* Higgins
19) Ernie *The Schnozz* Lombardi
20) Steve *Bones* Balboni
21) Leo *The Lip* Durocher
22) Phil *Knucksie* Niekro
23) Jeff *Convict Face* Leonard
24) Benny *Earache* Meyer
25) *Bucketfoot* Al Simmons

Chapter 6 - Real Brewers:
(BUD WIZERS)

1) Harvey*'(s) Wallbangers* Kuenn
2) David *Buddy* Bell
3) Derrel *Bud* Harrelson
4) Harvey*'(s) Wallbangers* Kuenn
5) George *Bud* Freeze
6) Norm *Suds* Siebern
7) Robert *Buddy* Blattner
8) Leavitt *Bud* Daley
9) Harvey*'(s) Wallbangers* Kuenn
10) David Gus *Buddy* Bell (Dad: David Russell *Gus* Bell)

Chapter 7 - Cartoon / Crazy:
(CHARACTER ANALYZERS)

1) Dave *Beauty* Bancroft and Jimmie *The Beast* Foxx
2) Joe *Goofy* Adcock and Graig *Puff* Nettles
3) Jim *Gumby* Gantner
4) Jimmie *The Beast* Foxx
5) Lawrence *Yogi* Berra
6) Vernon *Goofy* Gomez
7) Al *The Mad Hungarian* Hrabosky
8) Walter *Barney* Johnson
9) Cliff *Heathcliff* Johnson
10) Joe *Goofy* Adcock
11) Vernon *Goofy* Gomez
12) Lawrence *Yogi* Berra
13) Saturnino *Minnie* Minoso
14) Paul *Daffy* Dean
15) Cliff *Mickey Mouse* Melton
16) Woodrow *Woodie* Fryman
17) Tom *Wimpy* Paciorek
18) Lawrence *Yogi* Berra
19) Mel *Wimpy* Harder
20) Joe *Goofy* Adcock
21) Al *Clown Prince of Baseball* Schacht
22) Lawrence *Yogi* Berra
23) Steve *Popeye* Garvey
24) Bill *Bugs* Werle
25) Felix *The Cat* Mantilla
A) Steve *Popeye* Garvey
B) Norm *Dumbo* Larker
C) Graig *Puff* Nettles
D) Phil *Yosemite Sam* Garner
E) Paul *Dizzy* Trout
F) Jay Hanna *Dizzy* Dean
G) Jay Hanna *Dizzy* Dean
H) Steve *Popeye* Garvey
I) Paul *Daffy* Dean
J) Vernon *Goofy* Gomez

TRIVIA ANSWERS

Chapter 8 - Condition:
(BRAIN CRUNCHERS)

1) *Poosh 'Em Up* Tony Lazzeri
2) Frank *Pudgie* Delahanty
3) Ron *Roundman* Northey
4) Ernest *(Babe) Blimp* Phelps
5) Garry *Jump Steady* Templeton
6) Carlton *Pudge* Fisk
7) Mel *Wimpy* Harder
8) Marty *Slats* Marion
9) Steve *Bones* Balboni
10) Wayne *Twig* Terwilliger
11) Jerry *Slim* Kindall
12) Carlton *Pudge* Fisk
13) Garry *Jump Steady* Templeton
14) William *Bones* Ely
15) Carlton *Pudge* Fisk
16) *Sliding* Billy Hamilton
17) Graig *Puff* Nettles
18) Ralph *Road Runner* Garr
19) Frankie *Blimp* Hayes
20) *Sliding* Billy Hamilton
21) Carlton *Pudge* Fisk
22) *Poosh 'Em Up* Tony Lazzeri
23) *Sliding* Billy Hamilton
24) *Fat* Freddie Fitzsimmons
25) Harry *Slim* Sallee
26) Carlton *Pudge* Fisk

Chapter 9 - D.L.:
(BRAIN SCANNERS)

1) George *Doc* Medich
2) Dwight *Doc* Gooden
3) *Fidgety* Lew Burdette
4) Milt *Gimpy* Pappas
5) Bobby *Doc* Brown
6) Dick *Dr. Stangeglove* Stuart
7) Willie *Stretch* McCovey
8) Frank *The Big Hurt* Thomas
9) Roger *Doc* Cramer
10) James *Doc* Crandall
11) Willie *Stretch* McCovey
12) Howard *Doc* Edwards
13) Dick *Dr. Strangeglove* Stuart
14) Willie *Stretch* McCovey
15) Frank *The Big Hurt* Thomas
16) James *Doc* Prothro
17) Roger *Doc* Cramer
18) Edward *Doc* Farrell
19) Milt *Gimpy* Pappas
20) *Fidgety* Lew Burdette
21) *Fidgety* Phil Collins
22) *Fidgety* Lew Burdette
23) Roger *Doc* Cramer
24) Elliot *Bump* Wills
25) Wheeler *Doc* Johnston

Chapter 10 - Elements:
(MIND BLOWERS)

1) Denton *Cy* Young
2) Johnnie *Dusty* Baker
3) *Dirty* Al Gallagher
4) George *Firebrand* Stovall
5) Forrest *Smoky* Burgess
6) Fred *Cy* Williams
7) Bill *Rough* Carrigan
8) Charles *Cy* Rigler
9) Denton *Cy* Young
10) Mike *Human Rain Delay* Hargrove
11) James *Dusty* Rhodes
12) *Sunny* Jim Bottomley
13) Ron *Louisiana Lightning* Guidry
14) Virgil *Fire* Trucks
15) Charlie *Smokey* Maxwell
16) Steve *Rainbow* Trout
17) Denton *Cy* Young
18) *Smokey* Joe Wood
19) James *Dusty* Rhodes
20) Dave *Smoke* Stewart
21) Ron *Louisiana Lightning* Guidry
22) Walter *Smokey* Alston
23) George *Storm* Davis
24) Johnnie *Dusty* Baker
25) Dave *Smoke* Stewart

Chapter 11 - Family:
(RELATIVELY DIFFICULT)

1) Cecil *Big Daddy* Fielder
2) Vern *Junior* Stephens
3) Rick *Big Daddy* Reuschel
4) Wilver *Pops* Stargell
5) Cloyd *Junior* Boyer
6) Ted *The Kid* Williams and Gary *The Kid* Carter
7) Joe *Godfather* Torre
8) Ted *The Kid* Williams
9) Granville *Granny* Hamner
10) Adrian *Pop* Anson
11) Jimmy *Foxy Grandpa* Bannon and *Uncle* Tom Bannon
12) Wilver *Pops* Stargell
13) Jose *Bruise Brother* Canseco
14) William *Kid* Gleason
15) George *Bambino* Ruth
16) *Uncle* Marv Grissom
17) George *Bambino* Ruth
18) George *Good Kid* Susce
19) Mark *Bruise Brother* McGuire
20) Ted *The Kid* Williams
21) Leon *Daddy Wags* Wagner
22) Ken *Junior* Griffey
23) Jim *Junior* Gilliam
24) Stan *Big Daddy* Williams
25) George *Bambino* Ruth

Chapter 12 - Farm:
(MIND THRASHERS)

1) Jim *Bulldog* Bouton
2) Harvey *The Kitten* Haddix

3) Walter *Barney* Johnson
4) Bob *Bull* Watson
5) Johnny *The Big Cat* Mize
6) Rich *Goose* Gossage
7) Charles *Old Hoss* Radbourn
8) Eddie *Greyhound* Milner
9) Jim *Troy Terrier* Egan
10) Ray *Mule* Fosse
11) Harvey *The Kitten* Haddix
12) Fred *Crime Dog* McGriff
13) Maury *Mousey* Wills
14) Maury *Mousey* Wills
15) Bill *Mad Dog* Madlock
16) Charles *Old Hoss* Radbourn
17) Rich *Goose* Gossage
18) Ray *Farmer* Moore
19) Jim *Bulldog* Bouton
20) Frank *Mule* Lary
21) Bob *Bull* Watson
22) Walter *Barney* Johnson
23) Charles *Chick* Hafey
24) Walter *Rabbit* Maranville
25) Orel *Bulldog* Hershiser

Chapter 13 - Forest Animals:
(FOREST STUMP(ERS))

1) Charlie *Snake* Neal
2) Jim *Lizard* Bunning
3) Ryne *Ryno* Sandberg
4) Jackie *Rabbit* Tavener
5) Walt *Moose* Moryn
6) Walt *Moose* Dropo
7) Bill *Moose* Skowron
8) Walt *Moose* Dropo
9) George *Possum* Whitted
10) *Cobra* Joe Frazier
11) Sam *Bear Tracks* Mele
12) Walter *Rabbit* Maranville and George *Possum* Whitted
13) Jim *The Gray Fox* Northrup
14) Johnny *Bear Tracks* Schmitz
15) Ron *Gator* Guidry
16) Don *Tiger* Newcombe
17) James *Hippo* Vaughn
18) Jim *Lizard* Bunning
19) Don *Tiger* Hoak
20) Ryne *Ryno* Sandberg
21) *Reindeer* Bill Killefer
22) Perry *Moose* Werden
23) Harry *Deerfoot* Bay
24) Ralph *Moose* Miller
25) Don *The Weasel* Bessent
A) Roy *Squirrel* Sievers
B) Clyde *Deerfoot* Milan
C) Don *Tiger* Leppert
D) Don *Tiger* Newcombe
E) Ron *Bear* Bryant
F) Tom *Snake* Sturdivant
G) Bryan *Moose* Haas
H) Ron *Gator* Guidry
I) George *Moose* Earnshaw
J) Jim *Lizard* Bunning
K) Ron *Gator* Guidry
L) Mike *Big Bear* Garcia
M) Walt *Moose* Dropo
N) Jesse *The Silver Fox* Petty
O) Dave *The Cobra* Parker

TRIVIA ANSWERS

Chapter 14 - Real Giants:
(BIG THINKERS)

1) Paul *Big Poison* Waner
2) Christy *Big Six* Mathewson
3) Frank *The Big Hurt* Thomas
4) Ted *Big Klu* Kluszewski
5) *Big* Ed Walsh
6) Mike *Big Bear* Garcia
7) *Big* Bill Dinneen
8) *Big* Dan Brouthers
9) Johnny *The Big Cat* Mize
10) Cecil *Big Daddy* Fielder
11) Christy *Big Six* Mathewson
12) Andres *Big Cat* Gallaraga
13) Rick *Big Daddy* Reuschel
14) *Big* Ed Delahanty
15) *Big* Ed Delahanty and *Big* Sam Thompson

Chapter 15 - Gourmet:
(MYSTERY STEWS)

1) Taft *Taffy* Wright
2) *Colby* Jack Coombs
3) Jim *Mudcat* Grant
4) William *Candy* Cummings
5) Carl *Mealticket* Hubbell
6) Arnold *Bake* McBride
7) Jesse "The Burkett Rule " *Crab* Burkett
8) Jim *Catfish* Hunter
9) Willie *Puddin' Head* Jones
10) Johnny *Pepper* Martin
11) Steve *Hambone* Hamilton
12) Lou *The Iron Horse* Gehrig
13) Bob *Sugar* Cane
14) Jim *Cakes* Palmer
15) *Colby* Jack Combs
16) Ty *Georgia Peach* Cobb
17) Frank *Noodles* Hahn
18) Wilmer *Vinegar Bend* Mizell
19) Carl *Mealticket* Hubbell
20) Oscar *Spinach* Melillo
21) Jerry *Rolls* Reuss
22) Jim *Cakes* Palmer
23) Virgil *Spud* Davis
24) William *Pickles* Dillhoefer
25) Roger *M&M Boys* Maris

Chapter 16 - Hairy:
(HAIR RAISERS)

1) Clarence *Butch* Metzger
2) Ed *Whitey* Ford
3) George *Whitey* Kurowski
4) Henry *Heinie* Manush
5) Lee *Buzz* Capra
6) Ed *Whitey* Ford
7) Charles *Cotton* Nash
8) Earl *Whitey* Sheely
9) Lou *Slick* Johnson
10) Dick *Slick* Howser
11) Duke *The Silver Fox* Snider
12) Sal *The Barber* Maglie
13) Dave *Scissors* Foutz
14) Ed *Whitey* Ford
15) Al *Cotton* Brazle
16) Rollie *The Mustache* Fingers
17) Henry *Heinie* Manush
18) Duke *The Silver Fox* Snider
19) Ed *Whitey* Ford
20) Mark *The Blade* Belanger
21) Ed *Whitey* Ford
22) Duke *The Silver Fox* Snider
23) Burleigh *Ol' Stubblebeard* Grimes
24) Rollie *The Mustache* Fingers
25) Ed *Whitey* Ford

Chapter 17 - Hispanic:
(MUCHO TOUGHOS)

1) Santos *Sandy* Alomar Jr.
2) Guillermo *Willie* Hernandez
3) Rodney *Rod* Carew
4) Ivan *Pudge* Rodriguez
5) Jose *Dennis* Martinez
6) Keith *Mex* Hernandez
7) Jose *Cheo,* Hector *Heity* and Cirilo *Tommy* Cruz
8) Jose *Dennis* Martinez
9) Luis *Little Looie* Aparicio
10) Antonio *Tony* Armas
11) Saturnino *Minnie* Minoso
12) Benjamin *Ben* Oglivie
13) Filipe, Jesus *Jay* and Mateo *Matty* Alou
14) Andres *Tony* Gonzales
15) Cesar *Pepito* Tovar
16) Osvaldo *Ozzie* Canseco
17) Manuel *Manny* Mota
18) Luis *Yo-Yo* Arroyo
19) Orlando *Cha Cha* Cepeda
20) Zoilo *Zorro* Versalles
21) Orlando *Cha Cha* Cepeda and Atanasio *Tony* Perez
22) Roberto *Bob* Clemente
23) Mateo *Matty* Alou
24) Rodney *Rod* Carew
25) Juan *Manito* Marichal

Chapter 18 - Home:
(HOMEWORK)

1) Lee *Boomer from Birmingham* May
2) *Memphis* Bill Terry
3) *Tioga* George Burns
4) Guy *Mississippi Mudcat* Bush
5) Charles *Nashville Narcissus* Lucas
6) Wilmer *Vinegar Bend* Mizell
7) *Wabash* George Mullin
8) Roger *Peaceful Valley* Denzer
9) Charley *Paw Paw* Maxwell
10) *Coldwater* Jim Hughey
11) Bobby *Staten Island Scot* Thomson
12) Clarence *Orient Express* Vance
13) Mickey *Commerce Comet* Mantle
14) Carl *Reading Rifle* Furillo
15) Charles *Casey* Stengel
16) Clint *Hondo Hurricane* Hartung
17) Johnny *Crabapple Comet* Rucker
18) Cliff *Earl of Snowhomish* Torgeson
19) *Wahoo* Sam Crawford
20) Joe *Gause Ghost* Moore
21) *Gettysburg* Eddie Plank and Herb *Knight of Kennett Square* Pennock
22) Roy *St. Croix Boy Wonder* Patterson
23) *Salida* Tom Hughes
24) Fred *Dixie* Walker
25) *Tioga* George Burns
A) Roy *St. Croix Boy Wonder* Patterson
B) Ed *The Wild Elk of the Wasatch* Heusser
C) Francis *Naugatuck Nugget* Shea
D) Clarence *Climax* Blethen
E) Johnnie *Durango Kid* Seale
F) *Honolulu* Johnnie Williams
G) Roger *Duke of Tralee* Bresnahan
H) Ty *Georgia Peach* Cobb
I) Clarence *Orient Express* Vance
J) Mickey *Commerce Comet* Mantle
K) *Wahoo* Sam Crawford

TRIVIA ANSWERS

Chapter 19 - Real Indians:
(SCALP SCRATCHERS)

1) *Indian* Bob Johnson
2) John *Chief* Wilson
3) Charles *Chief* Bender
4) Louis *Buck* Newson
5) Lou *The Iron Horse* Gehrig
6) *Indian* Bob Johnson
7) Mel *Chief* Harder
8) Allie *Superchief* Reynolds
9) Allie *Superchief* Reynolds
10) Charles *Chief* Bender
11) *Kickapoo* Ed Summers
12) John *Chief* Aker
13) Wally *Cochise* Post
14) Jake *Eagle Eye* Beckley
15) Vincent *Bo* Jackson
16) Grant *Buck* Jackson
17) Tim *Crazy Horse* Foli
18) Robert *Bo* Belinski
19) *Indian* Bob Johnson
20) Paul *Big Poison* Waner and Lloyd *Little Poison* Waner
21) Charles *Chief* Bender
22) Lou *The Iron Horse* Gehrig
23) Lloyd *Little Poison* Waner
24) Paul *Big Poison* Waner
25) Lou *The Iron Horse* Gehrig
A) Tris *Grey Eagle* Speaker
B) Tris *Grey Eagle* Speaker
C) Ken *Hawk* Harrelson
D) *Wahoo* Sam Crawford
E) Clyde *Deerfoot* Milan
F) Hughie *Ee-Yah* Jennings
G) Lou *The Iron Horse* Gehrig
H) Louis *Chief* Sockalexis
I) Charles *Chief* Bender
J) William *Buck* Showalter

Chapter 20 - International:
(BORDERING INSANE)

1) Jim *Frenchy* Lefebvre
2) Hubert *Dutch* Leonard
3) Ed *Dutch* Zwilling
4) *Parisian* Bob Caruthers
5) Juan *Dominican Dandy* Marichal
6) Dolf *Pride of Havana* Luque
7) Frank *Guido* Quilici
8) Jim *Frenchy* Lefebvre
9) Emil *Dutch* Verban
10) John *Egyptian* Healy
11) Omar *Turk* Lown
12) Hubert *Dutch* Leonard
13) Johnny *The Dutch Master* Vander Meer
14) Allan *Panamanian Express* Lewis
15) Emil *Irish* Meusel
16) Darren *Dutch* Daulton
17) Kieth *Mex* Hernandez
18) Al *The Little Italian* Gionfriddo
19) Juan *Dominican Dandy* Marichal
20) Don *The Sphinx* Mossi
21) Honus *Flying Dutchman* Wagner
22) Al *The Mad Hungarian* Hrabosky
23) Darren *Dutch* Daulton
24) Ronald *Dutch* Reagan
25) Kieth *Mex* Hernandez

Chapter 21 - Las Vegas:
(DICEY PICKS)

1) Clarence *Ace* Parker
2) Tom *Terrific* Seaver
3) Clarence *Ace* Parker
4) *Neon* Deion Sanders
5) Al *Flip* Rosen
6) Johnny *Blue Moon* Odom
7) Fritz *Flash* Maisel
8) Joe *Flash* Gordon
9) Billy *Bucks* Buckner
10) *Black Jack* McDowell
11) Tom *Terrific* Seaver
12) Will *Whoop-La* White
13) *Marvelous* Marv Throneberry
14) Arvel *Bad News* Hale
15) Frankie *Fordham Flash* Frisch
16) *Neon* Deion Sanders
17) Jimmie *Ace* Wilson
18) *Twighlight* Ed Killian
19) Billy *Bucks* Buckner
20) Al *Flip* Rosen
21) Joe *Flash* Gordon
22) Charlie *Chinski* Root
23) Les *Lucky* Howe and William *Lucky* Wright
24) Johnny *Blue Moon* Odom
25) Tom *Terrific* Seaver

Chapter 22 - Last Name:
(SIRY SURNAMES)

1) Carl *Yaz* Yastrzemski
2) Dave *Winny* Winfield
3) Bill *Maz* Mazeroski
4) Harmon *The Killer* Killebrew (Killebrew Dr)
5) Christy *Matty* Mathewson
6) Frank *Robby* Robinson
7) Bill *Wamby* Wambsganss
8) Ted *Big Klu* Kluszewski
9) Chuck *Knobby* Knoblauch
10) Bert *Campy* Campaneris
11) Don *Newk* Newcombe
12) John *The Candy Man* Candelaria
13) Carl *Yaz* Yastrzemski and Dave *Winny* Winfield
14) Frank *Robby* Robinson
15) Harmon *The Killer* Killebrew
16) Chuck *Knobby* Knoblauch
17) Bill *Monbo* Monbouquette
18) Roy *Campy* Campanella
19) Paul *Molly* Molitor
20) Mark *Porch* Portugal
21) Harmon *The Killer* Killebrew
22) Carl *Oisk* Erskine
23) Bill *Stoney* Stoneman
24) Jerry *Koos* Koosman
25) Tom *Bruno* Brunansky

Chapter 23 - Real Mariners:
(DEEP SIXERS)

1) *Captain* Eddie Mathews
2) Joe *The Yankee Clipper* DiMaggio
3) Charles Andrew *Cap* Peterson
4) Gene *Skip* Mauch
5) Adrian *Cap* Anson
6) Johnny *Crab* Evers
7) Dick *The Ancient Mariner* Stuart
8) *Foghorn* Tommy Tucker
9) Joe *The Yankee Clipper* DiMaggio
10) Adrian *Cap* Anson
11) Fred *Cap* Clarke
12) Frank *Tug* McGraw
13) Marty *The Octopus* Marion
14) Jesse *Crab* Burkett
15) Phil *Superb* Linz

TRIVIA ANSWERS

Chapter 24 - Occupation:
(OCCUPATIONAL HAZARDS)

1) Connie *The Tall Tactician* Mack
2) Earle *The Kentucky Colonel* Combs
3) Gary *The G-Man* Gaetti
4) Hoyt *Sarge* Wilhelm
5) Dom *Paul* DiMaggio
6) Bill *Spaceman* Lee
7) Sal *The Barber* Maglie
8) Mordecai *Miner* Brown
9) Whitey *Chairman of the Board* Ford
10) Hank *Sarge* Bauer
11) Frank *The Peerless Leader* Chance
12) Ozzie *The Wizard of Oz* Smith
13) Bob *Sarge* Kuzava
14) Jim *Sarge* Bagby
15) Dick *Professor* Hall
16) Dom *The Little Professor* DiMaggio
17) Earle *The Kentucky Colonel* Combs
18) Connie *The Tall Tactician* Mack
19) Don *Mandrake the Magician* Mueller
20) Frank *Fiddler* Corridon
21) Bill *Wizard* Hoffer
22) Johnny *Fireman* Murphy
23) Mordecai *Miner* Brown
24) Jay *Moonman* Johnstone
25) Hoyt *Sarge* Wilhelm

Chapter 25 - P.R.:
(**P**RETTY **R**OUGH)

1) James *Pete* Runnels
2) Grover Cleveland *Pete* Alexander
3) Pedro *Pete* Ramos
4) Richard *Rube* Marquard
5) Grover Cleveland *Pete* Alexander
6) George *Rube* Walberg
7) Louis *Pete* Browning
8) Ray *Rube* Caldwell
9) Grover Cleveland *Pete* Alexander
10) Richard *Rube* Marquard
11) Ervin *Pete* Fox
12) George *Rube* Waddell
13) Harold *Pete* Reiser
14) George *Rube* Foster
15) Grover Cleveland *Pete* Alexander

Chapter 26 - Real Padres:
(PRAY ON THESE)

1) Holy Cow!
2) Everett *Deacon* Scott
3) *Deacon* Bill McKechnie
4) Vern *Deacon* Law
5) Elwin *Preacher* Roe
6) Frank *Sweet Music* Viola
7) Charles *Deacon* Phillippe
8) Billy *The Evangelist* Sunday
9) Harry *Goody* Simpson
10) James *Deacon* White
11) Gil *Miracle Worker* Hodges
12) Vern *Deacon* Law
13) Gil *Miracle Worker* Hodges
14) Vern *Deacon* Law
15) Gil *Miracle Worker* Hodges

Chapter 27 - Real Pirates:
(BURIED TREASURES)

1) *Long* Bob Meusel
2) Fred *Sure Shot* Dunlap
3) Joe *The Yankee Clipper* DiMaggio
4) Jimmy *Toy Cannon* Wynn
5) Ewell *Whip* Blackwell
6) George *Hooks* Wiltse
7) Jimmy *Toy Cannon* Wynn
8) Joe *The Yankee Clipper* DiMaggio
9) Tom *The Blade* Hall
10) Mack *The Knife* Jones
11) *Pistol* Pete Reiser
12) Jake *Eagle Eye* Beckley
13) Ewell *Whip* Blackwell
14) Joe *The Yankee Clipper* DiMaggio
15) *Sailor* Bob Shawkey

Chapter 28 - Played Big:
(NOT SMALL THINKERS)

1) William *Wee Willie* Keeler
2) Lloyd *Little Poison* Waner
3) *Little* Joe Morgan
4) Freddie *The Flea* Patek
5) Luis *Little Looie* Aparicio
6) Eddie *The Midget* Gaedel
7) William *Little Joe Chest* McGowan
8) Maury *Mousey* Wills
9) *Little* Joe Morgan
10) Luis *Little Looie* Aparicio
11) Lloyd *Little Poison* Waner
12) John *Little Napoleon* McGraw
13) Dom *The Little Professor* DiMaggio
14) Ernie *Tiny* Bonham
15) *Little* Joe Morgan

Chapter 29 - Real Reds:
(RED HERRINGS)

1) Morris *Red* Badgro
2) Charles *Red* Ruffing
3) Wade *Red* Killefer
4) Al *Red* Worthington
5) Zeb *Red* Eaton
6) Charles *Red* Ruffing
7) Charles *Red* Lucas
8) Emile *Red* Barnes
9) Charles *Red* Lucas
10) Urban *Red* Faber
11) Charles *Red* Ruffing
12) Robert *Red* Rolfe
13) Urban *Red* Faber
14) Walter *Red* Barber
15) Johnny *Red* Rawlings
16) Albert *Red* Schoendienst
17) Doug *The Red Rooster* Rader
18) Rich *Red* Rollins
19) Virgil *Red* Stallcup
20) Albert *Red* Schoendienst
21) Charles *Red* Barrett
22) Charles *Red* Ruffing
23) Francis *Red* Donahue
24) Albert *Red* Schoendienst
25) Al *Red* Wingo

Chapter 30 - Ringer:
(MYSTERY GUESS(t)S)

1) John Alexander *Andy* Messersmith
2) Kevin Joseph *Chuck* Connors
3) Alfred Manuel *Billy* Martin
4) John Henry *Zeke* Bonura
5) Jerry Dean *Jake* Gibbs
6) Ron Kenneth *Zeke* Hunt
7) David Russell *Gus* Bell
8) Darnell Glenn *Dan* Ford
9) Erwin Coolidge *Bob* Porterfield
10) John Alexander *Andy* Messersmith
11) Edward Nagle *Ned* Williamson
12) John William *Jay* Johnstone
13) David Russell *Gus* Bell
14) Floyd Clifford *Bill* Bevens
15) Alfred Manuel *Billy* Martin
16) Alfred Manuel *Billy* Martin
17) Robert James *Rick* Monday
18) George Bernard *Dave* Koslo
19) John Alexander *Andy* Messersmith
20) Edgar Charles *Sam* Rice
21) Dennis Joseph *Dan* Brouthers
22) Colbert Dale *Toby* Harrah
23) Owen Joseph *Donie* Bush
24) Alfred Manuel *Billy* Martin
25) Alfred Manuel *Billy* Martin

TRIVIA ANSWERS

Chapter 31 - Real Rockies:
(UNPOLISHED GEMS)

1) Chuck *Iron Hands* Hiller
2) Bill *Stoney* Stoneman
3) *Iron* Mike Caldwell
4) Rocco *Rocky* Colavito
5) Sanford *Sandy* Koufax
6) Edmundo *Sandy* Amoros
7) Harry *Jasper* Davis
8) Phil *Scrap Iron* Garner
9) *Diamond* Jim Gentile
10) Santos *Sandy* Alomar Sr.
11) Earl *Rock* Averill
12) *Iron Man* Joe McGinnity
13) Lou *The Iron Horse* Gehrig
14) Rocco *Rocky* Colavito
15) *Iron Man* Cal Ripkin

Chapter 32 - Real Royals:
(KNIGHTLY CHALLENGERS)

1) Reggie *Mr. October* Jackson
2) *Prince* Hal Newhouser
3) Ernie *Mr. Cub* Banks
4) *Master* Melvin Ott
5) John *The Count* Montefusco
6) Tony *Count* Mullane
7) Edwin *Duke* Snider
8) Paul *Duke* Derringer
9) John *Duke* Wathan
10) Rogers *The Rajah* Hornsby
11) *King* Carl Hubbell
12) *Master* Melvin Ott
13) Earl *King of Doublin'* Webb
14) Leonard *King* Cole
15) *Master* Melvin Ott
16) *Prince* Hal Schumacher
17) Babe *Sultan of the Swat* Ruth
18) *Sir* Rodney Carew
19) Edwin *Duke* Snider
20) Byron *Duke* Houck
21) Rogers *The Rajah* Hornsby
22) Reggie *Mr. October* Jackson
23) Ernie *Mr. Cub* Banks
24) *Master* Melvin Ott
25) *Sir* Rodney Carew
A) Heine *Count of Luxenberg* Meine
B) Elmer *Baron* Knetzer
C) *Prince* Hal Schumacher
D) *Sir* Rodney Carew
E) Elroy *The Baron* Face
F) Denny *Sky King* McLain
G) Al *Mr. Tiger* Kaline
H) Charles *Count* Campau
I) Bob *Mr. Team* Elliot
J) Rodgers *The Rajah* Hornsby
K) Ernie *Mr. Cub* Banks
L) *Master* Melvin Ott
M) Roger *Duke of Tralee* Bresnahan
N) Edwin *Duke* Snider
O) Al *Duke of Milwaukee* Simmons

Chapter 33 - Scary:
(CRANIUM CRUSHERS)

1) Ron *Boomer* Blomberg
2) John *Boog* Powell
3) *Bruno* Betzel
4) Larry *The Dodger Killer* Jaster
5) Phil *The Vulture* Regan
6) Fredrick *Firpo* Marberry
7) Dave *Kong* Kingman
8) Johnny *Yatcha* Logan
9) Mitch *The Wild Thing* Williams
10) Frank *The Yankee Killer* Lary
11) All are known as Bubba
12) Hughie *Ee-Yah* Jennings
13) Tom *Bruno* Brunansky
14) Ted *Thumper* Williams
15) Pete *The Gladiator* Browning
16) Bob *Warrior* Friend
17) Dave *Kong* Kingman
18) Karl *Tuffy* Rhodes
19) Craig *Mongo* Kusick
20) Harmon *The Killer* Killebrew
21) Dave *The Cobra* Parker
22) Greg *Boomer* Wells
23) William *Mookie* Wilson
24) Stan *The Man* Musial
25) Harry *The Giant Killer* Coveleski

Chapter 34 - School:
(MID SEASON EXAM)

1) *Colby* Jack Coombs
2) Adrian *Addie* Joss
3) *Spittin'* Bill Doak
4) Ken *Junior* Griffey
5) *Columbia* Lou Gehrig
6) Vern *Junior* Stephens
7) *Harvard* Eddie Grant
8) Don *The Little Professor* DiMaggio
9) Charles *Gabby* Hartnett
10) Cloyd *Junior* Boyer
11) Hollis *Sloppy* Thurston
12) Monte *Prof* Weaver
13) Don *Big D* Drysdale
14) Ken *Junior* Griffey
15) *Fordham* Mort Cooper
16) Jim *Professor* Brosnan
17) John *The Count* Montefusco
18) Waite *Schoolboy* Hoyt
19) Charles *Gabby* Hartnett
20) *Columbia* Lou Gehrig
21) Jimmie *Double X* Foxx
22) Charles *Gabby* Street
23) Lynwood *Schoolboy* Rowe
24) Carl *Sub* Mays
25) Karl *Tuffy* Rhodes
A) Phil *Supersub* Linz
B) Adalberto *Junior* Ortiz
C) Eddie *The Brat* Stanky
D) Charles *Gabby* Hartnett
E) Frankie *Fordham Flash* Frisch
F) Jimmie *Double X* Foxx
G) Ken *Junior* Griffey
H) Casey *The Old Professor* Stengel
I) Dom *The Little Professor* DiMaggio
J) Ken *Junior* Griffey

Chapter 35 - Switch:
(SHIFTY STICK-LERS)

1) Melton *Andy* Hawkins
2) Howard *Bruce* Sutter
3) Roy *Duane* Ward
4) Ira *Tommy* Greene
5) Charlton *Atlee* Hammaker
6) Dewey *La Marr* Hoyt
7) James *Hoyt* Wilhelm
8) John *Rick* Dempsey
9) Richard *Dale* Long
10) Henry *Louis* Gehrig
11) David *Travis* Fryman
12) Jacob *Nellie* Fox
13) James *Bob* Horner
14) Howard *Bruce* Sutter
15) Charles *Ray* Knight
16) Kenneth *Lance* Johnson
17) Keith *Tony* Phillips
18) John *Frank Home Run* Baker
19) James *Hoyt* Wilhelm
20) William *Roger* Clemens
21) James *Hoyt* Wilhelm
22) 7 No-No's   Lynn *Nolan* Ryan
23) James *Kevin* Brown
24) Robert *Kevin* Appier
25) Forest *Greg* Swindell
26) Cecil *Randy* Hundley
27) Clinton *Dan* Gladden
28) Harold *Pat* Kelly
29) Arthur *Lee* Maye
30) Howard *Earl* Averill
31) Herman *Tommy* Davis
32) William *Roger* Clemens
33) Selva *Lew* Burdette
34) Rik *Bert* Blyleven
35) Jonathan *Tom* Zachary and Evan *Tracy* Stallard
36) Jacob *Nellie* Fox
37) George *Tom* Seaver
38) Henry *Louis* Gehrig
39) James *Hoyt* Wilhelm
40) George *Ken* Griffey Jr.and Sr.
41) Charles *Sid* Fernandez
42) William *Roger* Clemens
43) Selva *Lew* Burdette
44) George *Tom* Seaver
45) Henry *Louis* Gehrig
46) John *Frank* Baker
47) Henry *Louis* Gehrig
48) William *Earl* Webb
49) Henry *Louis* Gehrig
50) George *Tom* Seaver and Lynn *Nolan* Ryan

TRIVIA ANSWERS

Chapter 36 - Traveling:
(MOVING TARGETS)

1) *Sudden* Sam McDowell
2) Allan *Panamanian Express* Lewis
3) *Rapid* Robert Feller
4) Earle *Greasy* Neale
5) Kent *Herbie* Hrbek
6) *Rapid* Bob Feller
7) *Shoeless* Joe Jackson
8) Mickey *Commerce Comet* Mantle
9) Albert *Sparky* Lyle
10) Dennis *Oil Can* Boyd
11) Daniel *Rusty* Staub
12) Willie *Comet* Davis
13) *Slow* Joe Doyle
14) Hubert *Hub* Pruett
15) Jim *Hot Rod* McDonald
16) Lee *Jeep* Handley
17) Leroy *Satchel* Paige
18) Ed *Horn* Sauer
19) Roger *The Rocket* Clemens
20) Sam *Jet* Jethroe
21) Harry *Suitcase* Simpson
22) Ernest *Blimp* Phelps
23) Moses *Fleet* Walker
24) Don *Blazer* Blasingame
25) *Shoeless* Joe Jackson

Chapter 37 - Real Twins:
(CUCKOO LULUS)

1) Lewis *Bobo* Newson
2) Hensley *Bam-Bam* Meulens
3) Jim *Abba Dabba* Tobin
4) Harold *Pee Wee* Reese
5) Hazen *Kiki* Cuyler
6) John *Tito* Francona
7) Terry *Tito* Landrum
8) Steve *Bye-Bye* Balboni
9) Cesar *Coca* Gutierrez
10) Sandy *Koo Foo* Koufax
11) Charlie *Paw Paw* Maxwell
12) Richie *Put-Put* Ashburn
13) Orlando *Cha Cha* Cepeda
14) Greg *Peewee* Briley
15) Randy *Wojo* Myers

Chapter 38 - Utility:
(HEAD HAMMERERS)

1) Dennis *Oil Can* Boyd
2) Brooks *Hoover* Robinson
3) Roy *The Sponge* McMillan
4) William *Gates* Brown
5) *Hammerin'* Hank Aaron
6) Bob *The Hammer* Hamelin
7) *Hammerin'* Hank Greenberg
8) *Handy* Andy Pafko
9) Lenny *Nails* Dykstra
10) Mack *The Knife* Jones
11) Phil *Scrap Iron* Garner
12) Alfred *Greasy* Neale
13) Brooks *Hoover* Robinson
14) Mark *The Blade* Belanger
15) Travis *Stonewall* Jackson
16) Al *Mr. Scoops* Oliver
17) Tom *The Blade* Hall
18) *Jughandle* Johnny Morrison
19) Bill Singer *Throwing Machine*
20) Dave *Scissors* Foutz
21) *Hammerin'* Hank Greenberg
22) *Hammerin'* Hank Greenberg
23) Bob *The Rope* Boyd
24) George *Scoops* Carey
25) *Hammerin'* Hank Aaron

Chapter 39 - Wild West:
(SHOTS IN THE DARK)

1) Glenn *Jingles* Cox
2) Bob *Hoot* Gibson
3) Forrest *Hick* Cady
4) Bert *Campy* Campaneris
5) Zoilo *Zorro* Versalles
6) *Bullet* Bob Turley
7) Vic *Springfield Rifle* Raschi
8) Bob *Hoot* Gibson
9) Roy *Campy* Campanella
10) Fred *Sure Shot* Dunlap
11) Enos *Country* Slaughter
12) Enos *Country* Slaughter
13) Carl *Reading Rifle* Furillo
14) Frank *Hondo* Howard
15) Roy *Campy* Campanella
16) Jesse *Powder* Tannehill
17) Bob *Hoot* Gibson
18) *Bullet* Bob Turley
19) Hughie *Ee-Yah* Jennings
20) Jim *Rawhide* Tabor
21) Monte *Hoot* Pearson
22) Bill *The Kid* Martin
23) Bert *Campy* Campaneris
24) Rudy *Lawman* Law
25) Bob *Hoot* Gibson

Chapter 40 - Willie / Mickey:
(W&M BOGGLERS)

1) Willie Mays Aikens
2) William *Wee Willie* Keeler
3) Michael *Mickey* Morandini
4) Michael *Mickey* Lolich
5) Mickey Tettleton
6) Willie McCovey
7) Gordon *Mickey* Cochrane
8) Mickey Mantle
9) William *Wee Willie* Keeler
10) Willie Mays
11) Willie Mays
12) Willie Wilson
13) Willie McCovey
14) Willie Mays and Mickey Mantle
15) Willie McCovey

Chapter 41 - Lefties / Leftovers:
(TRICKY TIDBITS)

1) Steve *Lefty* Carlton
2) Claude *Lefty* Williams
3) Leslie *Buster* Narum
4) Bruce *Buster* Kison
5) Robert *Lefty* Grove
6) Leon *Bip* Roberts
7) Russell *Bucky* Dent
8) Russell *Bucky* Dent
9) Steve *Lefty* Carlton
10) Cal *Buster* McLish
11) Lee *Lefty* Grissom
12) George *Skeets* Dickey
13) Vern *Buster* Stephens
14) Steve *Lefty* Carlton
15) George *Highpockets* Kelly
16) Harry *The Hat* Walker
17) William *Mookie* Wilson
18) Vernon *Lefty* Gomez
19) Edmund *Bing* Miller
20) Harry *The Hat* Walker
21) Robert *Lefty* Grove
22) Steve *Lefty* Carlton
23) Robert *Lefty* Grove
24) Albert *Lefty* Leifield
25) Robert *Lefty* Grove

INDEX
by LAST NAME

INDEX
by NICKNAME
(Some may be found under "T" for *The*)

BIO

A die hard baseball nut is an apt description. Blessed with two baseball playing sons, ten years of community coaching experience and a mathematically organized "goofy" brain all helped, but my wife's advice was the real inspiration. After the umpteenth time "forgetting" specific spousal instructions within five minutes of receiving them, yet being known to have retained "zillions" of baseball facts and with little prompting being able to "spew them out" on a seconds notice, my bride sarcastically suggested, "If you could only figure out a way to take all of that totally useless knowledge and write it down, you could create a book!" As usual, after twenty-eight years of bliss, she now has yet another chance to say she told me so!

BIBLIOGRAPHY

__BOOK__	__AUTHOR/EDITOR__
Baseball Is A Funny Game	*Joe Garagiola*
The Baseball Encyclopedia	*Joseph Reihley*
The Ballplayers	*Mike Shatzkin*
The Book Of Baseball Records	*Seymour Siwolf*
Total Baseball	*John Thorn/Pete Palmer*
My First Fifty Years In Baseball	*Connie Mack*

AUTHOR'S STATEMENT

Over the years I have acquired much of my knowledge and facts from a number of special sources. Radio and TV announcers often use nicknames. Sport columnists, team media guides, team yearbooks, baseball cards and sport magazine articles have all been constant suppliers of information. My earliest recollection was Dizzy Dean. He used to carry on about Ewell Blackwell and Burliegh Grimes. "Why Pee Wee" (his "pardner" Pee Wee Reese), he used to say, "No one could hit ol' Ewell when he was on". And oh how Diz hated "them bases on balls". My first radio announcers were The Blainer, Blaine Walsh, and his sidekick Earl Gillespie. They did the play by play for the Milwaukee Braves, the closest Major League team to the Twin Cities until 1961. I can still recall them pulling out the fishin' net when a foul ball came their way! Whether it was Spawny pitching or Hankus Pankus powdering one, they were my baseball eyes. I later grew up with Herb Carneal and Halsey Hall. They were the Twins' announcers (the best in the world). Reading the St. Paul Dispatch and Pioneer Press daily and subscribing forever to Sport Magazine were constant sources of information. Now regularly reading Sports Illustrated, Baseball Weekly, The Sporting News and Baseball America, I am literally overdosing on facts and stats! But, I love it! Thanks again for letting me share with you Having Fun With Baseball Nicknames!

REORDER PAGE

I hope you have been enjoying the book. It could be the **PERFECT GIFT** for that hard to buy for friend (you know who). Surprise them with a personalized copy from you! As a current bookowner, you earn a **MUCH DESERVED REPURCHASE DISCOUNT.** Just use the coupon below and save! THANKS,

Blazing Phil

-- --

COUPON

REORDER OFFER (SUGGESTED RETAIL $29.95)

	NUMBER	COST/BOOK	SHIP/HAND	TOTAL*
SINGLE:	ONE	$ 20.00	$ 3.00	$ 23.00
DOUBLE:	TWO	$ 19.00	FREE	$ 38.00
TRIPLE:	THREE	$ 17.00	FREE	$ 51.00
HOMER:	FOUR	$ 15.00	FREE	$ 60.00
CYCLE:	FIVE (or more)	$ 14.00	FREE	$ 70.00

*Must add 6.5% tax in Minnesota

Circle Method of Payment: Check   Visa   Master Card

Cicle Number of Books: Single   Double   Triple   Homer   Cycle _____

Card Number _____   **Exp. Date** _____

Name _____

Signature _____

Street Address _____

City, State and Zip Code _____

-- --

MAIL TO:

MLC Publications
Att. *Blazing* Phil
7645 Currell Blvd
Woodbury MN, 55125